CLASSIC MOVIE TRIVIA

TURNER CLASSIC MOVIES

CLASSIC
MOVIE TRIVIA

FEATURING MORE THAN 4,000 QUESTIONS
TO TEST YOUR CINEMA SMARTS

FOREWORD BY **ROBERT OSBORNE**

CHRONICLE BOOKS
SAN FRANCISCO

A concerted effort has been made to trace the ownership of all material included in this book. Any errors that may have occurred are inadvertent and will be corrected in subsequent editions, if any, provided sufficient notification is sent to the publisher in a timely manner.

Library of Congress Cataloging-in-Publication Data:

TCM classic movie trivia
/ foreword by Robert Osborne.
    p. cm.
  ISBN 978-1-4521-0152-1 (pbk.)
 1. Motion pictures—United States—Miscellanea. 2. Motion picture actors and actresses—United States—Miscellanea. I. Osborne, Robert A. II. Chronicle Books (Firm) III. Title.

  PN1993.85.C53 2011
  791.43—dc22

                    2011005322

Manufactured in China
Designed by McGuire Barber Design

10 9 8 7 6 5 4 3

Chronicle Books LLC
680 Second Street
San Francisco, CA 94107
www.chroniclebooks.com

Contents

FOREWORD

Trivia, according to Webster's dictionary, is defined as "insignificant or inessential . . . trifles . . . trivialities of little importance."

Whoa, cowboy.

"Inessential"? "Of little importance"? To the learned Mr. Webster—whom I've always pictured as a scholarly Lewis Stone type or, in more recent movie terms, someone Anthony Hopkins could play in a heartbeat. While I have no doubt his definition is accurate ("trivia" does obviously derive from that word "trivial"), I do think to be fair about it Webster should include some indication of how enjoyable "trivia" can be, and the many hours of pleasure it can give us while simultaneously dispensing mountains of fascinating information. That's the aim in this particular book—to pass on juicy servings of trivia and fun facts about the world of movies that very likely haven't come your way before.

Why focus on movies? Well, motion pictures are what TCM is all about; this is the seventh book about movies from Turner Classic Movies. And of course, there's no other industry more talked about, read about, and argued about (positively and negatively) than the movies. Nor is there any other industry that seems to be so spellbinding to so many people. Ultimately, any film, no matter its importance—be it *Avatar* (2009), *The Godfather* (1972), or *Maisie Goes to Reno* (1944)—has to stand on its own merits. That said, it's often the *trivia* about that film that ultimately makes it so mesmerizing to us.

Would *To Have and Have Not* (1944) fascinate us quite so much without the backstory of Bogart and Bacall? Or the 1963 *Cleopatra* without trivia about Taylor and Burton?

Another case in point: a film in the TCM library from 1947 titled *Desire Me* starring Greer Garson, Robert Mitchum, and Richard Hart, made by the mighty MGM. Garson was, at the time, the #1 box-office draw among all the female stars in Hollywood, yet the film came and went without causing a ripple—nobody, apparently, desiring to see *Desire Me.* Watching the film today, it seems no better or worse than the majority of the last fifty films you've witnessed. It has an interesting, if far-fetched, storyline, appropriately dramatic performances, and atmospheric settings. It's nothing earth-shattering but basically okay. It's the *trivia* surrounding the film that makes it so enjoyable now.

It is, for instance, the only film up to that time from a major studio to be released without a director credited. (George Cukor began directing it but quit midway through production, after which Mervyn LeRoy took over; both Cukor and LeRoy so disliked the finished film, neither would let MGM put his name on it.) More trivia: When filming on *Desire Me* began, Robert Montgomery was Garson's leading man but he bolted after three weeks, and was replaced by newcomer Hart. And there's more: It's a film that was so shunned by Greer Garson's once-loyal fans it ended her five-year reign as the top box-office attraction among all the leading ladies in Hollywood; it also toppled her off the throne as the queen of the MGM studios.

Hearing all the juicy trivia that swirled around *Desire Me*, I couldn't wait to see it—a production so troubled that its two directors not only took a powder but then steered clear of acknowledging any connection to it? A film that also caused its leading man to scram and seriously derailed the career of a queen whose crown was made of celluloid rather than gold? Alas, apart from these delicious facts, the experience of seeing it was . . . well, somewhat trivial.

There are a million and one tales like that in the Hollywood story—tons of trivia, much of it in the pages that follow.

Trivia, we at TCM feel, is the icing on the cake when it comes to the movie experience, and the more you know the "incidentals" connected to a particular movie, the more enjoyable that movie is to watch. That's why we felt *Classic Movie Trivia* deserves a book all its own. If you don't mind a bit of bragging, we think it's the most substantial and best-illustrated book of its kind that's been done to date, and we hope you'll enjoy every page of it. We also hope you'll want to borrow the sentiment that Spencer Tracy used in describing Katharine Hepburn in 1952's *Pat and Mike*, "What's here is *cherce*!"

Robert Osborne
Host, Turner Classic Movies

FILM
ERAS

The Thief of Bagdad, 1924

Chapter 1

EARLY
HOLLYWOOD

Hollywood was becoming a boomtown in the 1920s, but the movie moguls who ran the burgeoning industry weren't hoping to strike it rich in oil or gold. They were digging for stars and stories that would lure audiences into movie theaters to sit in the dark and share in a nation's dreams.

In just a few decades, an industry that had started with Thomas Edison producing short, plotless films in a cramped New Jersey studio, for individual viewing on kinetoscopes, had grown into an international craze. By the 1910s, moviemakers had settled in Hollywood and its environs, drawn by a climate that made outdoor shooting a year-round possibility. The studios built there by the likes of Paramount, Fox, MGM, and Warner Bros. were miniature kingdoms. Each had its own stable of stars, directors, writers, designers, and technicians—all

the talent needed to produce films on a regular basis—under sometimes benign, sometimes despotic dictators like Jesse Lasky and Louis B. Mayer. The most successful also handled their own distribution and ran theater chains that provided a ready market for their product.

Early on, pioneers like Edwin S. Porter and Alice Guy-Blaché had demonstrated the appeal of movies that told stories. Others, most notably D. W. Griffith, developed the language of film to tell ever-bigger stories in early features like *The Birth of a Nation* (1915) and *Intolerance* (1916). As the studios grew, they competed for stories, whether from great novels like George Eliot's *Romola* (1924), an early hit for Metro-Goldwyn Pictures Corp.; classic plays like *Camille* (1921), which helped make Rudolph Valentino a star; or original flights of fancy like Douglas Fairbanks's heroic fantasy *The Thief of Bagdad* (1924).

But the heart of the industry was its stars. Early on, filmmakers didn't bother crediting their actors, not thinking anybody cared who they were. When audiences started creating their own names for their favorites, dubbing Mary Pickford "The Girl with the Golden Curls" and Florence Lawrence "The Biograph Girl," studio owners caught on. Pickford and Lawrence were among the first stars to win name recognition, but they were soon joined by the likes of Lillian and Dorothy Gish, Ronald Colman, and Gloria Swanson.

The studios carefully built specific images for their stars and exploited them in hand-picked properties. Charles Chaplin became one of the world's most recognizable celebrities as "The Little Tramp." Clara Bow was the "It Girl," the embodiment of youthful sexual abandon. William Haines and Harold Lloyd were the perfect all-American boys.

In the silent era, language was no barrier to stardom. The British Colman could be the perfect exotic lover without his clipped diction getting in the way simply because he looked the part. Studio talent scouts pored through the best of international cinema searching for talent, importing Vilma Banky from Hungary and Pola Negri from Germany and spotting the potential in a former barbershop assistant from Sweden who became Greta Garbo, one of the screen's biggest stars and greatest actors.

With no lines to deliver, training was not always a prerequisite to success. Though some of the screen's biggest stars—like Pickford, Chaplin, and the Gishs—had come from the theater, others had barely trod a board before making the trek to Hollywood.

Fay Wray worked her way up from the ranks of film extra, while Bow and Mary Astor were beauty contest winners. And an agriculture student from Italy who had picked up a few moves on the dance floor became the greatest screen lover in history—Rudolph Valentino.

The lack of sound was no impediment to twenties filmmakers, who had developed an eloquent screen language that could communicate the most subtle emotional nuances. Late silents like William Wellman's *Wings*, Tod Browning's *The Unknown,* and Frank Borzage's *7th Heaven* (all 1927) demonstrated just how fluid and expressive the medium could be. But with advances in audio technology, studios like Warner Bros. and Fox were eager to explore the potential of sound film. At first, their rivals dismissed it as a fad. But when Al Jolson sang and delivered a few impromptu lines in *The Jazz Singer* (1927), audiences went wild.

Sound triggered major upheavals in Hollywood. Silent stars like Banky and Negri, who had never lost their foreign dialects, were out. Others, like Colman, built new images based on their newly discovered voices. And Garbo, who put off making talking films as long as possible, was finally heard in 1930's *Anna Christie* to reveal a deep throaty voice that complemented her romantic persona perfectly. Even if they survived the coming of sound, the once-silent stars would have to face an influx of stage-trained actors like Paul Muni, Bette Davis, and Kay Francis. A new age was dawning.

1. The Deanna Durbin film *Spring Parade* (1940) is a remake of what film?

   A. *Frühjahrsparade* (1934)
   B. *Parada Primavera* (1923)
   C. *Parade Printemps* (1933)
   D. *Spring Parade* (1919)

2. What is the only Elinor Glyn adaptation to star Rudolph Valentino?

   A. *Beyond the Rocks* (1922)
   B. *Mad Hour* (1928)
   C. *Red Hair* (1928)
   D. *The Prince of Things* (1930)

3. What was director Tod Browning's first film with Lon Chaney?

   A. *Jim Bludso* (1917)
   B. *The Unholy Three* (1925)
   C. *The Wicked Darling* (1919)
   D. *The Wise Kid* (1922)

4. Irving Berlin wrote the title song for all of the following films except for which one?

   A. *Alexander's Ragtime Band* (1931)
   B. *Coquette* (1929)
   C. *Follow the Fleet* (1936)
   D. *Reaching for the Moon* (1933)

5. What is the setting of the 1929 Kay Francis film *Dangerous Curves*?

   A. Circus
   B. Farm
   C. Hospital
   D. Ski lodge

6. In what country was Samuel Goldwyn born?

   A. England
   B. France
   C. Germany
   D. Poland

7. Which of director Richard Boleslawski's films was made in Poland?

   A. *Cud nad Wisla* (1921)

   B. *Die Gezeichneten* (1922)
   C. *Khleb* (1918)
   D. *The Last of the Lone Wolf* (1930)

8. Which Gloria Swanson film is an adaptation of the play *Rain*, based on a story by W. Somerset Maugham?

   A. *Sadie Thompson* (1928)
   B. *The Trespasser* (1929)
   C. *Wife or Country* (1918)
   D. *Zaza* (1923)

9. With whom is Kathleen Kirkham having an affair in *The Married Virgin* (1918)?

   A. Al Jolson
   B. Douglas Fairbanks
   C. George O'Brien
   D. Rudolph Valentino

Don Juan, 1926

10. After leaving Paramount, Mary Astor signed with which studio in 1925?

    A. MGM
    B. RKO
    C. Universal
    D. Warner Bros.

11. Where was silent film star William Haines born?

    A. Massachusetts
    B. New York
    C. North Carolina
    D. Virginia

12. In 1915, Hal Roach began producing short comedies with what famous friend?

    A. Buster Keaton
    B. Charles Chaplin
    C. Harold Lloyd
    D. Roscoe "Fatty" Arbuckle

13. What was Greta Garbo's professed favorite of all her films?

    A. *Camille* (1936)
    B. *Grand Hotel* (1932)
    C. *Romance* (1930)
    D. *The Temptress* (1926)

14. Which leading lady went her whole life without ever getting a haircut?

    A. Ingrid Bergman
    B. Lillian Gish
    C. Loretta Young
    D. Mary Pickford

15. Which song from *Rocky Horror Picture Show* mentions Fay Wray?

    A. "Dammit Janet"
    B. "Rose Tint My World"
    C. "Sweet Transvestite"
    D. "The Time Warp"

16. In what picture did William Haines make his film debut?

    A. *Brothers Under the Skin* (1922)
    B. *Little Annie Rooney* (1925)
    C. *Souls for Sale* (1923)
    D. *Three Wise Fools* (1923)

17. James Mason portrayed Tom Tulliver in which adaptation of a George Eliot novel?

    A. *Daniel Deronda* (1921)
    B. *Romola* (1924)
    C. *Silas Marner* (1922)
    D. *The Mill on the Floss* (1937)

18. What film earned Lewis Milestone his first Academy Award?

    A. *All Quiet on the Western Front* (1930)
    B. *Of Mice and Men* (1940)
    C. *Seven Sinners* (1925)
    D. *Two Arabian Knights* (1927)

19. Which of these films by director Richard Boleslawski was not filmed in the United States?

    A. *Hollywood Party* (1934)
    B. *Khleb* (1918)
    C. *The Last of Mrs. Cheyney* (1937)
    D. *The Last of the Lone Wolf* (1930)

20. What film starring Paul Muni takes place in a waxworks museum?

    A. *Dr. Ehrlich's Magic Bullet* (1940)
    B. *Dr. Socrates* (1935)
    C. *Fog Over Frisco* (1934)
    D. *Seven Faces* (1929)

21. What was Gloria Swanson's first talkie?

    A. *Father Takes a Wife* (1941)
    B. *Sadie Thompson* (1928)
    C. *Sunset Blvd.* (1950)
    D. *The Trespasser* (1929)

22. Ethel Barrymore was born on August 15, 1879, in what city?

    A. Chicago
    B. New York
    C. Philadelphia
    D. San Diego

answers found on page 540

23. Which of the following animals does Rudolph Valentino keep in his Harvard dorm room in *The Young Rajah* (1922)?

A. A bulldog
B. A cheetah
C. A salamander
D. A tarantula

24. Frank Capra once held each of the following jobs except for which one?

A. Ditch digger
B. Newspaper salesman
C. Orange tree pruner
D. Rodeo star

25. Who is Kay Francis's rival in the 1929 film *Dangerous Curves*?

A. Clara Bow
B. Fay Wray
C. Gloria Swanson
D. Mary Pickford

26. In what year was John Barrymore born?

A. 1882
B. 1886
C. 1898
D. 1901

27. What silent film actress was Rudolph Valentino's first wife?

A. Gloria Swanson
B. Jean Acker
C. Nita Naldi
D. Pola Negri

28. How many times was Fay Wray married?

A. 1
B. 2
C. 3
D. 4

29. Which leading lady was born with the surname Gustafsson?

A. Audrey Hepburn
B. Greta Garbo
C. Ingrid Bergman
D. Marlene Dietrich

30. Paul Muni received his first Oscar nomination for what film?

A. *Scarface* (1932)
B. *Seven Faces* (1929)
C. *The Valiant* (1929)
D. *The World Changes* (1933)

31. Who directed Anna May Wong in *The Thief of Bagdad* (1924)?

A. Josef von Sternberg
B. Raoul Walsh
C. Tod Browning
D. William Wellman

32. Who plays the title character in the 1927 Anna May Wong film *Mr. Wu*?

A. Bela Lugosi
B. Boris Karloff
C. Lon Chaney
D. Peter Lorre

33. Frank Borzage was the first-ever recipient of the Academy Award for Best Director for which of his films?

A. *A Farewell to Arms* (1932)
B. *History Is Made at Night* (1937)
C. *7th Heaven* (1927)
D. *Stage Door Canteen* (1943)

34. In the 1929 Carole Lombard film *High Voltage*, a group of passengers on a bus are stranded during a snowstorm and take refuge where?

A. In a cave
B. In a church
C. In a department store
D. In a log cabin

Spotlight on
MARION **DAVIES** (1897–1961)

Marion Davies was raised by her mother to delight audiences with her beauty and talent and catch the eye of a man who could give her the good life. Neither woman could have imagined, however, that William Randolph Hearst would catch her in the chorus of a 1918 stage musical and never let her go. Hearst decided that she should be a superstar and turned a Harlem casino into a movie studio for her. He loved to see Marion in costume dramas, but it was as a comedienne, in films like 1928's *Show People*, that she truly lit up the screen. Despite disappointing box office, Hearst had no trouble getting MGM to release her films. They were only too glad to benefit from favorable treatment in his papers. As protected as Marion was by Hearst, however, he couldn't always get her the top roles she wanted at MGM, prompting Hearst to move his production unit (Cosmopolitan) to Warner Bros. After a few flops there, Marion happily retired from the movies in 1937, at the age of forty. Though she lived in a lavish manner, Marion also used her extraordinary wealth, acquired largely through clever real estate investments, to help friends and acquaintances who were struggling financially.

Polly of the Circus, 1932

Show People, 1928

1. **Marion Davies was the captain of her school's championship team in what sport?**

    A. Basketball
    B. Fencing
    C. Golf
    D. Volleyball

2. **All of the following films starring Marion Davies are set in New York except for which one?**

    A. *Blondie of the Follies* (1932)
    B. *Five and Ten* (1931)
    C. *Lights of Old Broadway* (1925)
    D. *Show People* (1928)

3. **Marion Davies and Clark Gable are newlyweds in which film?**

    A. *Little Old New York* (1923)
    B. *Polly of the Circus* (1932)

C. *Show People* (1928)
D. *The Bachelor Father* (1931)

4. **Marion Davies played the title role in all of the following films except for which one?**

    A. *The Pilgrim* (1923)
    B. *Getting Mary Married* (1919)
    C. *Runaway, Romany* (1917)
    D. *Yolanda* (1924)

5. **Which character did Marion Davies portray in the 1922 film *When Knighthood Was in Flower*?**

    A. Mary Tudor
    B. Morgan Le Fey
    C. Queen Catherine
    D. Queen Guinevere

---

answers found on page 540

EARLY HOLLYWOOD   **17**

35. In 1926 Joan Blondell won the Miss Dallas beauty pageant using what name?

A. Blondie McFarland
B. Goldie Blondell
C. Joanie Blake
D. Rosebud Blondell

36. Which of the following was Gary Cooper's final silent film?

A. *Betrayal* (1929)
B. *The Last Outlaw* (1927)
C. *The Shopworn Angel* (1928)
D. *Wings* (1927)

37. In 1925, George Marshall was put in charge of the shorts output for which studio?

A. Columbia
B. Fox
C. MGM
D. Paramount

Freaks, 1932

38. Director Tod Browning's *Freaks* (1932) was banned in the United Kingdom until what year?

A. 1934
B. 1951
C. 1962
D. 1999

39. Throughout his career, Valentino was credited under all the following names except which?

A. M. De Valentina
B. R. Di Volentina
C. Rudolph Volantino
D. Rudolpho De Valentine

40. What was Mary Astor's first-feature length film?

A. *John Smith* (1922)
B. *The Rapids* (1922)
C. *Sentimental Tommy* (1921)
D. *The Man Who Played God* (1922)

41. Which of these actors was one of the original thirty-six founders of the Academy of Motion Picture Arts and Sciences?

A. Frank Sinatra
B. Harold Lloyd
C. Humphrey Bogart
D. Peter O'Toole

42. In 1927, Norman Z. McLeod served as an assistant director on what William Wellman film?

A. *Night Nurse*
B. *The Cat's Pajamas*
C. *The Public Enemy*
D. *Wings*

43. Jason Robards Sr., a well-known silent film actor, appeared in which of these early films?

A. *Making a Living* (1914)
B. *The Bank* (1915)
C. *The Gamblers* (1929)
D. *The Idle Class* (1921)

44. Edward Arnold appeared in all of the following silent films directed by Arthur Berthelet except which one?

A. *The Misleading Lady* (1916)
B. *The Havoc* (1916)
C. *The Return of Eve* (1916)
D. *The Vultures of Society* (1916)

answers found on page 540

45. What was William Haines's first all-talking picture?

A. *Free and Easy* (1930)
B. *Navy Blues* (1929)
C. *Show People* (1928)
D. *The Duke Steps Out* (1929)

46. George Stevens got his start in the film industry as a cameraman on comedic shorts with whom?

A. Buster Keaton
B. Charles Chaplin
C. Laurel and Hardy
D. Lon Chaney

47. What was director Tod Browning's feature film debut?

A. *By the Sun's Rays* (1914)
B. *Jim Bludso* (1917)
C. *Outside the Law* (1920)
D. *Puppets* (1916)

48. Richard Thorpe directed Mickey Rooney in what film adaptation of a Mark Twain classic?

A. *Pudd'nhead Wilson* (1916)
B. *The Adventures of Huckleberry Finn* (1939)
C. *The Adventures of Tom Sawyer* (1938)
D. *The Prince and the Pauper* (1937)

49. With what popular jazz band did Franz Waxman perform in Germany during the 1920s?

A. Manheim Steamroller
B. The Berlin Music Express
C. The Waxman Five
D. The Weintraub Syncopaters

50. During WWI, director Richard Boleslawski fought for what country?

A. England
B. Germany
C. Russian Empire
D. United States

51. Who was Gloria Swanson's first husband?

A. Henri de la Falaise
B. Joseph P. Kennedy
C. Michael Farmer
D. Wallace Beery

52. The "Glasses Character" from the films of which Hollywood legend was the inspiration for Superman's disguise as Clark Kent?

A. Buster Keaton
B. Cary Grant
C. Clark Gable
D. Harold Lloyd

53. Which actor/actress was nicknamed "The Fourth Warner Brother"?

A. Mary Pickford
B. Cary Grant
C. Humphrey Bogart
D. Bette Davis

54. What subject did Rudolph Valentino study at a school in Genoa?

A. Agriculture science
B. Art history
C. Modern dance
D. Physics

55. In what city was film director Anthony Asquith born?

A. Brussels, Belgium
B. London, England
C. Oslo, Norway
D. Paris, France

56. What American painter painted Fay Bainter in 1918?

A. Alan Thompson
B. Carl Gaertner
C. John W. Wardman
D. Robert Henri

answers found on page 540

57. Which of the following actresses was born the same year Ford manufactured its first Model T?

A. Bette Davis
B. Elizabeth Taylor
C. Lillian Gish
D. Marion Davies

58. John Gilbert named his yacht after which Greta Garbo film?

A. *Camille* (1936)
B. *Queen Christina* (1933)
C. *The Temptress* (1926)
D. *Torrent* (1926)

59. What was William Haines's first part-talking film?

A. *Alias Jimmy Valentine* (1928)
B. *Excess Baggage* (1928)
C. *Navy Blues* (1929)
D. *Show People* (1928)

60. How old was Mary Astor when she debuted in her first film with her new stage name?

A. 12
B. 13
C. 14
D. 15

61. The Rudolph Valentino film *The Eagle* (1925) is based on a story by what writer?

A. Alexander Pushkin
B. Boris Pasternak
C. Leon Trotsky
D. Vladimir Nabokov

62. In 1925, Anthony Asquith cofounded what organization with luminaries such as George Bernard Shaw and H. G. Wells?

A. Director's Guild of Great Britain
B. Dramatic Arts Society
C. London's Film Society
D. London's Music Society

63. Which of director Richard Boleslawski's films was made in Russia?

A. *Bohaterstwo Polskiego Skauta* (1920)
B. *Cud nad Wisla* (1921)
C. *Khleb* (1918)
D. *The Gay Diplomat* (1931)

64. When was Paul Muni born?

A. 1895
B. 1900
C. 1905
D. 1910

65. Who directed Rudolph Valentino in *The Son of the Sheik* (1926)?

A. Clifton Webb
B. Douglas Fairbanks
C. George Fitzmaurice
D. Joseph Henabery

66. How many times was Greta Garbo married?

A. 0
B. 2
C. 4
D. 6

67. Before becoming an actress, I was a barbershop assistant in Stockholm. Who am I?

A. Audrey Hepburn
B. Greer Garson
C. Greta Garbo
D. Louise Brooks

68. Lillian Gish plays an Italian aristocrat in what silent film costarring Ronald Colman and Charles Lane?

A. *Cameo Kirby* (1923)
B. *Little Miss Smiles* (1922)
C. *The Wallop* (1921)
D. *The White Sister* (1923)

answers found on page 540

69. Who was Fay Wray's leading man in the 1928 film *The First Kiss*?
   A. Charles Chaplin
   B. Douglas Fairbanks
   C. Gary Cooper
   D. Robert Taylor

70. In the late 1920s, Michael Powell worked at Elstree Studios with what director?
   A. Alfred Hitchcock
   B. Charles Chaplin
   C. David Lean
   D. Rex Ingram

71. Although he never won for Best Director, how many times was King Vidor nominated for an Oscar?
   A. 1
   B. 2
   C. 5
   D. 7

72. Who plays Lillian Gish's blind sister in the 1921 film *Orphans of the Storm*?
   A. Clara Bow
   B. Dorothy Gish
   C. Gloria Swanson
   D. Mary Pickford

73. Rudolph Valentino plays the Duke of Chartres in which adaptation of a Booth Tarkington story?
   A. *A Sainted Devil* (1924)
   B. *Cobra* (1925)
   C. *Monsieur Beaucaire* (1924)
   D. *The Eagle* (1925)

74. Who directed Warner Oland in *Chinatown Nights* (1929)?
   A. Cecil B. DeMille
   B. Michael Curtiz
   C. Orson Welles
   D. William Wellman

75. What was Rudolph Valentino's response to a 1926 *Chicago Tribune* article that blamed him for effeminizing the American male?
   A. He challenged the writer to a boxing match.
   B. He demanded that Columbia cast him in more action films.
   C. He had the *Chicago Tribune* banned from Los Angeles newsstands.
   D. He wrote a response article in the *New York Times*.

The Patsy, 1928

76. Who directed Marion Davies and Marie Dressler in the 1928 film *The Patsy*?
   A. Frank Capra
   B. King Vidor
   C. Robert Mamoulian
   D. Victor Fleming

77. Hal Roach went to which studio to release his films after he left Pathé in 1927?
   A. Fox
   B. MGM
   C. United Artists
   D. Warner Brothers

78. Which Tod Browning film was a remake of 1927's *London After Midnight*?
   A. *Dracula* (1931)
   B. *Mark of the Vampire* (1935)
   C. *The Unholy Three* (1925)
   D. *The Unknown* (1927)

answers found on page 541

Spotlight on
JOHN **BARRYMORE** (1882–1942)

Few stars blazed as brightly or fell as precipitously as John Barrymore. He, sister Ethel, and brother Lionel constituted "the Royal Family of Broadway," with John clearly the king. The three were born into the theater, the third generation of an acting clan presided over by Mrs. John Drew, the grandmother who raised them. In 1914, John started making films in New York, often shooting a picture by day while performing on Broadway at night. Most notably, he starred in a 1920 adaptation of *Dr. Jekyll and Mr. Hyde*, winning praise for playing the transformation scene without makeup or trick photography. In the early thirties, he commanded the box office with romantic roles in films like *Don Juan* (1926) and *Grand Hotel* (1932) and character parts like *Svengali* (1931). He even teamed with Lionel and Ethel for the only time in 1932's *Rasputin and the Empress*. As famous as his acting, however, was his reputation as a drinker and womanizer. When he played the alcoholic actor in MGM's *Dinner at Eight* (1933), Hollywood insiders quipped that he was simply playing himself. During a rehearsal in May 1942, he collapsed. All he could say was, "This is one time I miss my cue." Ten days later, he passed away.

Don Juan, 1926

Grand Hotel, 1932

1. **How many Oscars did John Barrymore win?**

   A. 0
   B. 1
   C. 2
   D. 3

2. **In what film does John Barrymore play a crippled puppeteer?**

   A. *Svengali* (1931)
   B. *The Lotus Eater* (1921)
   C. *The Mad Genius* (1931)
   D. *The Man from Blankley's* (1930)

3. **How many children did John Barrymore have?**

   A. 2
   B. 3
   C. 5
   D. 9

4. **Edward Arnold played Dr. Remezov in what film starring John, Ethel, and Lionel Barrymore?**

   A. *Grand Hotel* (1932)
   B. *Rasputin and the Empress* (1932)
   C. *Reunion in Vienna* (1933)
   D. *The Spiral Staircase* (1945)

5. **On loan to Warner Bros., Mary Astor first starred with John Barrymore in what film?**

   A. *Beau Brummel* (1924)
   B. *Don Juan* (1926)
   C. *The Wise Guy* (1926)
   D. *Two Arabian Knights* (1926)

---

answers found on page 541

79. Film director Anthony Asquith's father, Herbert Asquith, held what political office in the United Kingdom from 1908 to 1916?

A. Chancellor of the Exchequer
B. Foreign Secretary
C. Minister of State
D. Prime Minister

80. In 1929, Lucien Ballard got his first job in the film industry at which studio?

A. Columbia
B. Paramount
C. RKO
D. Warner Bros.

81. Fay Wray grew up in what religious culture?

A. Catholic
B. Jewish
C. Mormon
D. Puritan

82. Moorcroft, the mansion Mary Astor's parents bought in Hollywood with her earnings, had been previously rented by whom?

A. Buster Keaton
B. Charles Chaplin
C. John Barrymore
D. Mary Pickford

83. How many times was Carole Lombard married?

A. 1
B. 2
C. 3
D. 4

84. Which one of his own films was Harold Lloyd's professed favorite?

A. *A Sailor-Made Man* (1921)
B. *Girl Shy* (1924)
C. *Grandma's Boy* (1922)
D. *The Kid Brother* (1927)

85. The Barbers Association of America threatened to boycott this unfinished Rudolph Valentino film unless the actor shaved his beard.

A. *A Sainted Devil* (1924)
B. *Cobra* (1925)
C. *The Eagle* (1925)
D. *The Hooded Falcon* (1924)

86. Which studio signed Paul Muni in 1929?

A. Fox
B. MGM
C. Universal
D. Warner Bros.

87. For which studio did William Haines work when he moved to Hollywood?

A. Fox
B. MGM
C. United Artists
D. Warner Bros.

88. In 1927 Gene Krupa became the first drummer to make a recording using what?

A. A bass drum pedal
B. A cowbell
C. A wood block
D. The cymbals

89. James Wong Howe was working a low-level job at Lasky Studios when what director hired him as a clap boy?

A. Cecil B. DeMille
B. Fred Niblo
C. Henry Hathaway
D. Victor Fleming

90. What was the name of Rudolph Valentino's Great Dane?

A. Alla
B. Kabar
C. Natacha
D. Sheik

91. Who costarred with Lon Chaney in director Tod Browning's *The Unknown* (1927)?

A. Bette Davis
B. Helen Chandler
C. Joan Crawford
D. Mary Nolan

92. What MGM film saved director Tod Browning's career after a battle with depression?

A. *Revenge* (1918)
B. *The Dangerous Flirt* (1924)
C. *The Day of Faith* (1923)
D. *The Unholy Three* (1925)

93. Fay Wray was selected as one of the Wampas Baby Stars in what year?

A. 1920
B. 1922
C. 1926
D. 1930

94. Whose evil brother does Rudolph Valentino play in the 1920 film *Passion's Playground*?

A. Gary Cooper's
B. John Gilbert's
C. Norman Kerry's
D. Richard Barthelmess's

95. Ronald Colman plays the title character in all of the following films except for which one?

A. *Beau Geste* (1926)
B. *Raffles* (1930)
C. *The Prisoner of Zenda* (1937)
D. *Young Mr. Lincoln* (1939)

96. Director Tod Browning's *Freaks* (1932) is based on what short story?

A. "Forbidden Love"
B. "Freakshow"
C. "Nature's Mistakes"
D. "Spurs"

97. Fred Astaire was a professional stage performer by what age?

A. 8
B. 5
C. 1
D. 10

98. The 1922 comedy short *Fultah Fisher's Boarding House*, directed by Frank Capra, was based on a poem by what author?

A. Charles Dickens
B. Edith Wharton
C. Mark Twain
D. Rudyard Kipling

99. Which 1921 Alexandre Dumas film adaptation stars Alla Nazimova and Rudolph Valentino?

A. *Camille*
B. *The Black Tulip*
C. *The Clemenceau Case*
D. *The Natural Son*

100. In what year did director Richard Boleslawski pass away?

A. 1925
B. 1931
C. 1935
D. 1937

101. Paul Muni made his screen debut in what film, for which he received his first Oscar nomination?

A. *Me and My Gal* (1932)
B. *The Last Flight* (1931)
C. *The Valiant* (1929)
D. *What Price Glory* (1926)

102. Michael Powell was the still photographer on which Alfred Hitchcock film?

A. *Blackmail* (1929)
B. *Champagne* (1928)
C. *The Farmer's Wife* (1928)
D. *The Ring* (1927)

answers found on page 541

103. How old was Jean Harlow when she died?

    A. 25
    B. 26
    C. 27
    D. 28

104. When Janet Gaynor won the Academy Award for Best Actress in 1929, it was the only time the award was given for work in multiple roles. Gaynor was nominated for her performances in all of the following films except which one?

    A. *7th Heaven*
    B. *Street Angel*
    C. *Sunrise: A Song of Two Humans*
    D. *The Shamrock Handicap*

105. Who was Nancy Carroll's costar in the 1928 film *The Shopworn Angel*?

    A. Clark Gable
    B. Douglas Fairbanks
    C. Gary Cooper
    D. Richard Dix

106. Adrian helped Natacha Rambova create Rudolph Valentino's costumes for which 1924 romance directed by Joseph Henabery?

    A. *A Sainted Devil*
    B. *Camille*
    C. *Moran of the Lady Letty*
    D. *The Eagle*

107. After moving back to New York in 1917, which studio did Tod Browning direct for?

    A. MGM
    B. Metro Studios
    C. RKO
    D. Universal

108. After William Haines stopped making films, what was his profession?

    A. Acting instructor
    B. Fashion designer
    C. Interior designer
    D. Screenwriter

109. What director did not work with William Haines?

    A. Billy Wilder
    B. Edward Sedgwick
    C. George Hill
    D. King Vidor

110. What was the title of Rudolph Valentino's 1923 book of poetry?

    A. *A Fashionable Life*
    B. *Day Dreams*
    C. *New Man*
    D. *Silent Screen*

111. Which actor played the title character in the 1929 thriller *Bulldog Drummond*?

    A. Gary Cooper
    B. Lionel Barrymore
    C. Robert Taylor
    D. Ronald Colman

112. William Haines sets out with Mary Pickford to avenge her father's murder in what film?

    A. *Brown of Harvard* (1926)
    B. *Little Annie Rooney* (1925)
    C. *Show People* (1928)
    D. *Way Out West* (1930)

113. In 1928, after doing a sound test with Mary Astor to prepare for talkies and finding her voice too deep, which studio released her from her contract?

    A. Fox
    B. MGM
    C. Paramount
    D. Warner Bros.

114. Which of the following actresses costarred with Warner Oland in *Flower of Night* (1925)?

    A. Billie Dove
    B. Mary Pickford
    C. Pola Negri
    D. Theda Bara

answers found on page 541

The Unknown, 1927

115. Which actor (shown above) played the role of Malabar the Mighty opposite Joan Crawford in the 1927 film *The Unknown*?

A. Lon Chaney
B. Douglas Fairbanks
C. Charles Chaplin
D. Norman Kerry

116. When was Fay Bainter born?

A. 1880
B. 1890
C. 1893
D. 1897

117. What is the name of the character played by Rudolph Valentino in the 1921 film *Camille*?

A. Alexander
B. Armand
C. Cenci
D. The Count

118. In his first role on Broadway, what was a notable first for Paul Muni?

A. Acted in English
B. Played multiple characters
C. Used dialogue
D. Wore elaborate outfits

119. What was Lewis Milestone's first feature film as director?

A. *All Quiet on the Western Front* (1930)
B. *Of Mice and Men* (1940)
C. *Seven Sinners* (1925)
D. *The Front Page* (1931)

120. William Haines costars with Constance Bennett and Joan Crawford in what film about three showgirls?

A. *Brown of Harvard* (1926)
B. *Little Annie Rooney* (1925)
C. *Sally, Irene and Mary* (1925)
D. *Show People* (1928)

121. Lupe Velez starred opposite Gary Cooper in which film directed by Victor Fleming?

A. *Adventure* (1925)
B. *Reckless* (1935)
C. *The Awakening* (1928)
D. *The Wolf Song* (1929)

122. William Haines plays football for a military academy and costars with Joan Crawford in what film?

A. *Brown of Harvard* (1926)
B. *Little Annie Rooney* (1925)
C. *Show People* (1928)
D. *West Point* (1928)

123. What is the name of Charles Chaplin's dog in the 1918 film *A Dog's Life*?

A. Dudley
B. Scraps
C. Spiffy
D. Spot

124. What was Mary Astor's film debut with her new stage name?

A. *John Smith* (1922)
B. *The Rapids* (1922)
C. *Sentimental Tommy* (1921)
D. *The Man Who Played God* (1922)

125. How tall was Gloria Swanson?

   A. 4'11"
   B. 5'11"
   C. 5'3"
   D. 5'7"

126. What actor did not costar with William Haines?

   A. Buster Keaton
   B. Cary Grant
   C. Jack Pickford
   D. Lon Chaney

127. Who costars with Rudolph Valentino in *Beyond the Rocks* (1922)?

   A. Clara Bow
   B. Gloria Swanson
   C. Louise Brooks
   D. Pola Negri

128. At the beginning of George Marshall's *Monsieur Beaucaire* (1946), who does King Louis XV pick to marry the Princess of Spain?

   A. The Count of Point Place, Wisconsin
   B. The Duke de Chandre
   C. The Earl of Canterberries
   D. The Prince of Castellenetina

129. What is the name of Rudolph Valentino's second wife?

   A. Alla Nazimova
   B. Jean Acker
   C. Natacha Rambova
   D. Pola Negri

130. W. C. Fields's character experiences a personality transformation after hypnosis in what comedy?

   A. *Babes on Broadway* (1941)
   B. *Running Wild* (1927)
   C. *Shop Talk* (1935)
   D. *The Big Wheel* (1949)

131. With whom did Benny Goodman make his first recordings in 1926?

   A. The Ben Pollack Orchestra
   B. The Chris Christian Trio
   C. The Hayden Reed Five
   D. The Seth Tufts Orchestra

132. What was Rudolph Valentino's birth name?

   A. Giovanni Rodolfo Figli di Guglielmi Giovinazzi di Marchesa
   B. Guglielmi Rodolfo Valentina d'Antoguolla di Sicilia
   C. Rodolfo Alfonso Raffaello Piero Filiberto Guglielmi di Valentino d'Antoguolla
   D. Rudolf Gabriello Donno Franco di Castellaneta

133. In what year was George Marshall born?

   A. 1891
   B. 1900
   C. 1905
   D. 1910

134. Which of these actors was not an original founder of the Academy?

   A. Charles Chaplin
   B. Douglas Fairbanks
   C. Harold Lloyd
   D. Mary Pickford

135. Director Tod Browning was hired by Universal Pictures to direct what classic horror film?

   A. *Dracula* (1931)
   B. *Frankenstein* (1931)
   C. *Phantom of the Opera* (1943)
   D. *The Wolf Man* (1941)

136. At the age of thirteen, Lupe Velez was sent to live in a convent located in what U.S. state?

   A. Louisiana
   B. Texas
   C. Utah
   D. Wyoming

answers found on page 541

137. What was director Tod Browning's last film under his Universal contract?

A. *Freaks* (1932)
B. *Miracles for Sale* (1939)
C. *The Unknown* (1927)
D. *White Tiger* (1923)

138. Why was Rudolph Valentino rejected from an Italian military academy?

A. He was deaf in his left ear.
B. He was four inches too tall.
C. His chest circumference was one inch too small.
D. His feet were too big.

139. Frank Capra was once cast as an extra in what film directed by John Ford?

A. *A Fight for Love* (1919)
B. *Bare Fists* (1919)
C. *That Certain Thing* (1928)
D. *The Outcasts of Poker Flat* (1919)

140. Greta Garbo appears as herself in which 1929 film?

A. *A Man's Man*
B. *Hollywood Canteen*
C. *The Player*
D. *Variety Girl*

141. Who played Anna May Wong's husband in *Bits of Life* (1921)?

A. Douglas Fairbanks
B. Harold Lloyd
C. John Gilbert
D. Lon Chaney

142. Fay Bainter is the aunt of what famous actress?

A. Audrey Hepburn
B. Dorothy Bainter
C. Dorothy Burgess
D. Mimi Gibson

143. In 1925, which studio signed Lewis Milestone as director?

A. MGM
B. RKO
C. United Artists
D. Warner Bros.

144. Warner Oland played Al Jolson's father in the 1927 film *The Jazz Singer*. Who played the same role in the 1980 remake?

A. Charlton Heston
B. Dan O'Herlihy
C. Laurence Olivier
D. Peter O'Toole

145. Which of the following actresses costars with Anna May Wong in *The Crimson City* (1928)?

A. Gloria Swanson
B. Joan Crawford
C. Myrna Loy
D. Norma Shearer

146. Sir John Gielgud made his screen debut in what silent film?

A. *The Magnificent Flirt* (1928)
B. *The Sheik* (1921)
C. *Torrent* (1926)
D. *Who Is the Man?* (1924)

147. What brand of condoms featured Valentino's silhouette on the package?

A. Eagle
B. Sheik
C. Trojan
D. Valentino

148. In how many Laurel and Hardy shorts did Jean Harlow act?

A. 2
B. 3
C. 6
D. 8

149. In 1921, film director Richard Thorpe began his career in the motion picture industry in what capacity?

A. Actor
B. Editor
C. Musician
D. Writer

150. In what country was Bela Lugosi born?

A. Bulgaria
B. Hungary
C. Poland
D. Romania

151. The 1927 Anna May Wong film *The Devil Dancer* was nominated for one Academy Award in what category?

A. Best Art Direction
B. Best Cinematography
C. Best Editing
D. Best Picture

Torrent, 1926

152. The 1926 film *Torrent* marked the Hollywood debut of what actress?

A. Norma Shearer
B. Lillian Gish
C. Greta Garbo
D. Mary Astor

153. What was Greta Garbo's astrological sign?

A. Cancer
B. Capricorn
C. Leo
D. Virgo

154. Joan Bennett costars with George Arliss in his performance as a noted British statesman in what film?

A. *Disraeli* (1929)
B. *The Man in the Iron Mask* (1939)
C. *The Son of Monte Cristo* (1940)
D. *The Women* (1939)

155. What film star/s did Hal Roach not employ during the 1920s and 1930s?

A. Buster Keaton
B. Harold Lloyd
C. Laurel and Hardy
D. Our Gang kids

156. What actress did not work with William Haines?

A. Joan Crawford
B. Marion Davies
C. Mary Pickford
D. Rita Hayworth

157. W. C. Fields's character in what silent film adopts an abandoned orphan?

A. *A Family Affair* (1937)
B. *Monsieur Beaucaire* (1946)
C. *Sally of the Sawdust* (1925)
D. *The Potters* (1927)

158. What did Rudolph Valentino name his Irish wolfhound?

A. Centaur Pendragon
B. Desmond Ruel
C. Mia
D. The Black Pirate

answers found on page 541

159. The 1929 Fay Wray film *The Four Feathers* was remade in 2002. What contemporary actress played Fay Wray's part in it?

A. Angelina Jolie
B. Hillary Swank
C. Kate Hudson
D. Reese Witherspoon

160. What famous millionaire and political patriarch was Gloria Swanson's longtime lover?

A. George H. Bush
B. Joseph P. Kennedy
C. Philip Mountbatten
D. William Randolph Hearst

161. In what country was Warner Oland born?

A. England
B. Italy
C. Russia
D. Sweden

162. Which of the following actresses costarred with Warner Oland in *Dream of Love* (1928)?

A. Clara Bow
B. Greta Garbo
C. Joan Crawford
D. Theda Bara

163. Lillian Gish plays an abused girl in love with a Chinese aristocrat in what film?

A. *The Birth of a Nation* (1915)
B. *Broken Blossoms* (1919)
C. *The Wind* (1928)
D. *Way Down East* (1920)

164. Which of the following actors was charged with bigamy in 1922 by the Los Angeles district attorney?

A. Buster Keaton
B. Gloria Swanson
C. Marion Davies
D. Rudolph Valentino

165. What was director Tod Browning's salary for *The Unholy Three* (1925)?

A. $10,000
B. $12,000
C. $3,000
D. $6,500

166. The albino cannibal outfits worn by the chorus girls in Buster Keaton's *Free and Easy* (1930) are also used in what William Haines film?

A. *Brown of Harvard* (1926)
B. *Little Annie Rooney* (1925)
C. *Show People* (1928)
D. *Way Out West* (1930)

167. Lothar Mendes took over directing the 1928 Fay Wray film *Street of Sin* after original director Mauritz Stiller left the picture depressed over the news that which movie star was in love with someone else?

A. Clara Bow
B. Gloria Swanson
C. Greta Garbo
D. Mary Pickford

168. Fay Wray got some of her first motion picture work in shorts from what famous producer?

A. Buster Keaton
B. Charles Chaplin
C. David O. Selznick
D. Hal Roach

169. Paul Muni portrays multiple characters in what film?

A. *Dr. Ehrlich's Magic Bullet* (1940)
B. *Fog Over Frisco* (1934)
C. *Seven Faces* (1929)
D. *The Secret Bride* (1934)

answers found on page 541

Spotlight on
ANNA MAY **WONG** (1905–1961)

The first Asian actress to become an international star, Los Angeles native Anna May Wong arrived in Hollywood too early to enjoy the career her talents deserved. When she made her film debut in the silent era, Asian women were stereotyped as innocent "Butterfly" types or evil "Dragon Ladies." Wong started out as the former, even playing a version of Madame Butterfly in *The Toll of the Sea* (1922), the second Technicolor feature, then moved into the latter with *The Thief of Bagdad* (1924). With most Asian roles played by Westerners, however, MGM once dubbed Wong "too Chinese to play a Chinese," and disappointed her by not even considering her for the lead in *The Good Earth* (1937). She found better opportunities in Europe and, oddly enough, B movies, which gave her the chance for non-stereotyped roles as businesswomen, detectives, and doctors. Wong largely gave up the screen during World War II to devote herself to Chinese war relief.

The Thief of Bagdad, 1924

She was on the verge of a comeback with a promised role in *Flower Drum Song* (1961) when she died at the age of fifty-six. Her legacy as a pioneer in humanizing Asian images on screen was recognized when the Asian Arts Awards named their Award of Excellence for her.

The Toll of the Sea, 1922

1. Anna May Wong plays Tiger Lily in the 1924 adaptation of *Peter Pan* based on the stories by which author?

   A. E. L. Doctorow
   B. J. M. Barrie
   C. L. Frank Baum
   D. P. L. Travers

2. In 1924, James Wong Howe photographed Anna May Wong in *The Alaskan* and what other film?

   A. *Forty Winks*
   B. *Mr. Wu*
   C. *Peter Pan*
   D. *Shanghai Express*

3. What is the name of Anna May Wong's character in *Mr. Wu* (1927)?

   A. Annabelle Wu
   B. Loo Song
   C. Lotus Flower
   D. Rose Li

4. The 1926 Anna May Wong film *A Trip to Chinatown* was based on a long-running musical play that featured what famous song?

   A. "After the Ball"
   B. "Happy Talk"
   C. "I Enjoy Being a Girl"
   D. "I Stayed Too Long at the Fair"

5. What was the last silent film in which Anna May Wong appeared?

   A. *Island of Lost Men* (1939)
   B. *Piccadilly* (1929)
   C. *The Crimson City* (1928)
   D. *The Silk Bouquet* (1926)

answers found on page 541

170. What film directed by Frank Capra was the first Columbia Pictures release to use sound effects?

A. *It Happened One Night* (1934)
B. *Lightnin'* (1925)
C. *Napoleon's Barber* (1928)
D. *Submarine* (1928)

171. In what Lewis Milestone film does a newspaper editor trick his best reporter into covering one last story before he retires?

A. *Anything Goes* (1936)
B. *Of Mice and Men* (1940)
C. *The Front Page* (1931)
D. *Two Arabian Knights* (1927)

172. One of Rudolph Valentino's first professional gigs was as Bonnie Blass's dance partner, a position he obtained after Blass's original partner left for Hollywood. Who was he?

A. Clifton Webb
B. Don Ameche
C. Reginald Denny
D. Rod La Rocque

173. Nancy Carroll starred in the 1928 film *The Shopworn Angel*. Who played her part in the 1938 remake?

A. Bette Davis
B. Fay Wray
C. Jean Arthur
D. Margaret Sullavan

174. W. C. Fields made his screen debut in what film?

A. *Orchids and Ermine* (1927)
B. *Pool Sharks* (1915)
C. *Shop Talk* (1935)
D. *The Big Wheel* (1949)

175. Fay Wray made her acting debut in what film?

A. *Gasoline Love* (1923)
B. *The Coast Patrol* (1925)
C. *Un-friendly Enemies* (1925)
D. *Your Own Back Yard* (1925)

176. Rudolph Valentino plays a Russian Cossack who spurns Catherine the Great's advances in which 1925 adaptation of a Pushkin novel?

A. *Captain Blood*
B. *Cobra*
C. *La Tempesta*
D. *The Eagle*

177. Ronald Colman's character in which film becomes a member of the French Foreign Legion?

A. *Beau Geste* (1926)
B. *Friend Indeed* (1937)
C. *One Against the World* (1939)
D. *Upstream* (1927)

178. What was the name of Anna May Wong's character in *Shame* (1921)?

A. Lotus Blossom
B. Lotus Flower
C. Marilyn Fu
D. Rose Li

179. What was the nickname of Harold Lloyd's character in *The Freshman* (1925)?

A. "Clumsy"
B. "Doc"
C. "Sleepy"
D. "Speedy"

180. Who was Marie Dressler's costar in the 1914 film *Tillie's Punctured Romance*?

A. Buster Keaton
B. Charles Chaplin
C. Harold Lloyd
D. Oliver Hardy

181. In what state was Carole Lombard born?

A. Illinois
B. Indiana
C. Ohio
D. Wisconsin

answers found on page 541

182. What Lon Chaney film was director Tod Browning's first foray into vampire movies?

A. *London After Midnight* (1927)
B. *Mark of the Vampire* (1935)
C. *The Mystic* (1925)
D. *The Virgin of Stamboul* (1920)

183. Which of the following leading ladies was not a Leo?

A. Esther Williams
B. Gloria Swanson
C. Mae West
D. Norma Shearer

184. In 1926, Paul Muni and wife Bella performed in what stage production?

A. *Four Walls*
B. *Ondine*
C. *The Heiress*
D. *The Lark*

185. Who directed Rudolph Valentino in *Blood and Sand* (1922)?

A. Fred Niblo
B. George Melford
C. Joseph Maxwell
D. Rex Ingram

186. Director Tod Browning's first wife, Amy Louise Stevens, was whose aunt?

A. Chloe Sevigny
B. Fisher Stevens
C. George Stevens
D. William Collier Jr.

187. William Haines works as a railroad engineer who falls in love with Elaine Hammerstein in what film?

A. *Brown of Harvard* (1926)
B. *Show People* (1928)
C. *The Midnight Express* (1924)
D. *Way Out West* (1930)

188. Which of her own films does Gloria Swanson watch in *Sunset Blvd.* (1950)?

A. *Male and Female* (1919)
B. *Queen Kelly* (1929)
C. *Sadie Thompson* (1928)
D. *The Trespasser* (1929)

189. What was Greta Garbo's last silent film?

A. *Champagne* (1928)
B. *North Star* (1925)
C. *Riches and Rogues* (1913)
D. *The Kiss* (1929)

West of Zanzibar, 1928

190. What was the name of Lon Chaney's character in director Tod Browning's *West of Zanzibar* (1928)?

A. Doc
B. Mr. Crane
C. Phroso "Dead-Legs"
D. Tiny

191. When was director Tod Browning born?

A. 1880
B. 1899
C. 1901
D. 1905

192. In 1920, Glenn Ford made his stage debut in what production?

A. *A Hatful of Rain*
B. *Inherit the Wind*
C. *The Apple Cart*
D. *Tom Thumb's Wedding*

answers found on page 541

193. Which leading lady stars in *The Wind* (1928)?

    A. Lillian Gish
    B. Louise Brooks
    C. Mae West
    D. Marion Davies

194. In what film does Rudolph Valentino play Amos Judd, a young American who finds out he is actually a nobleman from the Far East?

    A. *Blood and Sand* (1922)
    B. *The Son of the Sheik* (1926)
    C. *The Wonderful Chance* (1920)
    D. *The Young Rajah* (1922)

195. Marion Davies plays the title role in which film featuring W. C. Fields?

    A. *Alice Adams* (1935)
    B. *Janice Meredith* (1924)
    C. *Morning Glory* (1933)
    D. *That Hamilton Woman* (1941)

196. Film director Frank Capra originally intended to study what subject in college?

    A. Astronomy
    B. Chemical/electrical engineering
    C. Drama
    D. Philosophy

197. Which of these films did not star William Haines?

    A. *Brown of Harvard* (1926)
    B. *Montana Moon* (1930)
    C. *Show People* (1928)
    D. *Tell It to the Marines* (1926)

198. During production, which screen legend forbade all visitors from the set, including sometimes the director?

    A. Bette Davis
    B. Greta Garbo
    C. Katharine Hepburn
    D. Vivien Leigh

199. What actress earned an Oscar nomination for a role advertised as depicting "The Life, the Sins of a Royal Bad Girl!"?

    A. Bette Davis for *Jezebel* (1938)
    B. Gloria Swanson for *Queen Kelly* (1929)
    C. Maureen O'Hara for *Lady Godiva of Coventry* (1955)
    D. Norma Shearer for *Marie Antoinette* (1938)

200. Which leading lady was called the "First Lady of the Silent Screen"?

    A. Gloria Swanson
    B. Lillian Gish
    C. Mary Pickford
    D. Myrna Loy

201. What film gave Fay Wray her first starring role?

    A. *Doctor X* (1932)
    B. *King Kong* (1933)
    C. *The Most Dangerous Game* (1932)
    D. *The Wedding March* (1928)

202. As a teenager, Bette Davis posed naked for a statue of spring. After a manic hunt in 1982, the statue was found in the basement of which museum?

    A. Guggenheim Museum in New York
    B. Museum of Fine Arts in Boston
    C. Museum of Modern Art in New York
    D. Museum of Television and Radio in Los Angeles

203. James Wong Howe was an early proponent of a type of versatile camera dolly with four wheels that roll in any direction and a movable arm to hold the camera. What is it called?

    A. The crab dolly
    B. The cricket dolly
    C. The floating well
    D. The steadicam

204. When did Paul Muni's family emigrate to the United States?

   A. 1899
   B. 1902
   C. 1907
   D. 1910

205. Who won the first Academy Award for Best Actress?

   A. Gloria Swanson for *Sadie Thompson* (1928)
   B. Irene Dunne for *Cimarron* (1931) and *My Favorite Wife* (1929)
   C. Janet Gaynor for *7th Heaven* (1927), *Sunrise* (1927), and *Street Angel* (1928)
   D. Louise Dresser for *A Ship Comes In* (1928)

206. In 1927, Rudolph Valentino showed his allegiance to the much-maligned Roscoe "Fatty" Arbuckle by appearing as himself in one of the actor's shorts. What was it called?

   A. *Character Studies*
   B. *Close Relations*
   C. *Sunrise*
   D. *Tomalio*

207. Ronald Colman plays Lord Darlington in what film adaptation of an Oscar Wilde play?

   A. *Friend Indeed* (1937)
   B. *Lady Windermere's Fan* (1925)
   C. *Napoleon's Barber* (1928)
   D. *Upstream* (1927)

208. Who was the first President of the Academy of Motion Picture Arts and Sciences?

   A. Douglas Fairbanks
   B. George W. Cohen
   C. Irving Thalberg
   D. William C. DeMille

209. What was director Tod Browning's first talkie?

   A. *Dracula* (1931)
   B. *The Blackbird* (1926)
   C. *The Show* (1927)
   D. *The Thirteenth Chair* (1929)

210. In what year did Rudolph Valentino apply for U.S. citizenship?

   A. 1908
   B. 1913
   C. 1925
   D. 1930

211. Which leading lady initially felt so threatened by Jean Harlow that she tried to have her kicked off the set of *The Saturday Night Kid* (1929)?

   A. Clara Bow
   B. Gloria Swanson
   C. Joan Crawford
   D. Mary Pickford

212. Ronald Colman and Vilma Banky share the screen in all of the following films except for which one?

   A. *The Magic Flame* (1927)
   B. *The Night of Love* (1927)
   C. *The Sporting Venus* (1925)
   D. *Two Lovers* (1928)

213. Ethel Barrymore made her first screen appearance in which film?

   A. *Camille* (1921)
   B. *The Kiss of Hate* (1916)
   C. *The Nightingale* (1914)
   D. *The Unknown* (1913)

214. The plot of the 1921 Warner Oland film *Hurricane Hutch* concerns a formula for making paper out of what material?

   A. Birdseed
   B. Marble
   C. Seaweed
   D. Water

215. James Wong Howe used realistic lighting to film Lon Chaney and Loretta Young in what silent drama?

A. *He Who Gets Slapped* (1924)
B. *Laugh, Clown, Laugh* (1928)
C. *London After Midnight* (1927)
D. *The Unknown* (1927)

216. Which Tod Browning film starring Lon Chaney was remade into Chaney's only talkie?

A. *The Day of Faith* (1923)
B. *The Unholy Three* (1925)
C. *The Wicked Darling* (1919)
D. *The Wise Kid* (1922)

217. Which of the following films was Gary Cooper's first talkie?

A. *Bright Leaf* (1950)
B. *Good Sam* (1948)
C. *High Noon* (1952)
D. *The Virginian* (1929)

218. Lillian Gish plays the title role in which film costarring William Powell and Ronald Colman?

A. *Jackie* (1921)
B. *Little Miss Smiles* (1922)
C. *Mary of Scotland* (1936)
D. *Romola* (1924)

219. Why is it rumored that Louis B. Mayer terminated William Haines's contract with MGM?

A. Haines became notorious for not showing up on the set.
B. He refused to act in the films chosen for him.
C. He refused to hide his homosexuality.
D. His films had become unpopular.

220. What was Rudolph Valentino's older brother's name?

A. Alberto
B. Danielo
C. Giovanni
D. Nicolas

221. When Hal Roach arrived in Hollywood, what work did he first do?

A. Directing short films
B. Playing an extra in silent films
C. Producing
D. Writing scripts

222. In what place did Joan Blondell finish in the 1926 Miss America pageant?

A. First
B. Fourth
C. Second
D. Third

223. In what year was the Academy of Motion Picture Arts and Sciences founded?

A. 1921
B. 1925
C. 1926
D. 1927

224. In 1923, director Richard Boleslawski founded what theater company that evolved into the Actors Studio?

A. Actor & Director Theater Group
B. American Laboratory Theatre
C. Methods
D. Polish American Film Institute

225. In what year did Rudolph Valentino arrive in the United States?

A. 1913
B. 1920
C. 1926
D. 1931

226. What is the name of Warner Oland's character in *The Faker* (1929)?

A. Hadrian
B. Hannibal
C. Marvel
D. Orloff

answers found on page 542

227. In what Lewis Milestone film does a missionary try to help a streetwalker on a Pacific island?

A. *All Quiet on the Western Front* (1930)

B. *Rain* (1932)

C. *The Front Page* (1931)

D. *The Racket* (1928)

Show People, 1928

228. Who was Marion Davies's costar (shown here) in *Show People*?

A. William Haines

B. Douglas Fairbanks

C. Lionel Barrymore

D. Errol Flynn

229. What is the only film to have all four Young sisters (Loretta, Sally, Polly Ann, and Georgiana)?

A. *Sirens of the Sea* (1917)

B. *The Sheik* (1921)

C. *The Story of Alexander Graham Bell* (1939)

D. *The White Parade* (1934)

230. Who plays the title character in the 1924 Anna May Wong film *The Thief of Bagdad*?

A. Douglas Fairbanks

B. John Barrymore

C. John Gilbert

D. Rudolph Valentino

Anna Christie, 1930

Chapter 2

THE 1930s

Hollywood continued to build its dominant position in the entertainment industry in the 1930s, a decade that produced some of the most fondly remembered films of all time. Our movie-made memories are far from an accurate representation of Hollywood in that era. The lilting grace of a musical like *Top Hat* (1935) conceals the sweat and heated arguments that sent feathers flying during filming. Some of the era's most enduring pictures—like the ultimate giant monster flick *King Kong* (1933)—never received a single Oscar nomination, while Best Picture winners like *Cavalcade* (1933) and *The Life of Emile Zola* (1937) now seem little more than charming blips on history's radar. And some of the period's greatest stars—Miriam Hopkins, who had top billing in the early Technicolor hit *Becky Sharp* (1935), and Luise Rainer, the first

actor to win back-to-back Oscars (1936's *The Great Ziegfeld* and 1937's *The Good Earth*)—had faded out by decade's end.

As the 1930s started, the movie capital was still struggling through the transition to talking pictures. Early talkies tended to be fairly stagnant because noisy cameras had to be confined to a soundproof box to keep from interfering with sound recording. It took the development of a soundproof camera casing called a "blimp" to make the movies move again. Directors Cecil B. DeMille, Tay Garnett, and William Wyler have all claimed credit for the innovation.

The new medium continued to impact actors' careers. When early recording equipment revealed John Gilbert's voice to be a light tenor, it ended his days as a romantic lead. But the contrast between Janet Gaynor's husky speaking voice and her girlish, innocent image, helped keep her a star through the decade. Hollywood cast its net for stage players from Broadway and London who didn't need to study diction or conquer speech problems. When Charles Laughton became the first foreign actor to win an Oscar, for 1933's *The Private Life of Henry VIII*, his move into American films was inevitable. And after Greta Garbo's triumphant talkie debut in *Anna Christie* (1930), Hollywood scoured the international cinema for the next exotically accented beauty, with Marlene Dietrich and Ingrid Bergman among the most successful.

The studios also had to find ways to profit during the Great Depression. Films like *Gold Diggers of 1933*, with Joan Blondell singing "Remember My Forgotten Man," or the gangster classic *Angels with Dirty Faces* (1938), mined current headlines for drama. But the studios also offered an escape from real life with lavish costume dramas like *The Prisoner of Zenda* (1937) and adaptations of timeless classics like *David Copperfield* (1935).

As early talkies like Mae West's bawdy comedies and Tod Browning's shocking *Freaks* (1932) pushed the boundaries of what could be presented on screen, pressure groups like the Catholic Church's Legion of Decency cried for a national boycott of "indecent" pictures. In 1934, Hollywood responded with its own brand of censorship, strict enforcement of the 1930 Production Code, to guarantee that films taught proper moral lessons. As a result, a cleaned-up West was supplanted at the box office by more innocent leading ladies, particularly two prodigiously talented young women, Shirley Temple and Deanna Durbin. Both were contenders for the leading role in

MGM's prestige musical for 1939, *The Wizard of Oz*. But the role would go to another youngster, Judy Garland, who would eventually eclipse their fame.

Through it all, the star system continued, with talented newcomers like Lana Turner and Ronald Reagan being groomed for stellar status while the studios bought properties to bolster the images of reigning stars like Bette Davis, Clark Gable, and Katharine Hepburn. Supporting them were a stock company of seasoned character actors who specialized in playing corrupt businessmen (Edward Arnold), understanding aunts and mothers (Fay Bainter), sassy maids (Hattie McDaniel), and kindhearted old men (Henry Stephenson).

Ironically, the apotheosis of 1930s filmmaking came from outside the major studios. Independent producer David O. Selznick staked his reputation on the film version of Margaret Mitchell's *Gone With the Wind* (1939), counting on a best-selling story and established stars like Gable and Leslie Howard to counteract the box-office curse on Civil War pictures and bolster rising stars Vivien Leigh and Olivia de Havilland. The result was one of the best movies of Hollywood's greatest year, the rare film that combined acclaim in its own time (a record eight Oscars) with enduring popularity. Along with such classics as *Mr. Smith Goes to Washington*, *Wuthering Heights,* and *The Wizard of Oz*, it allowed Hollywood to end the decade on an all-time high.

1. Who starred in Zoltan Korda's 1933 film *Cash*?
   A. Edmund Gwenn
   B. Lionel Barrymore
   C. Mickey Rooney
   D. Wallace Beery

2. The 1930 film *Street of Chance,* directed by John Cromwell, received its only Academy Award nomination in what category?
   A. Best Cinematography
   B. Best Editing
   C. Best Screenplay
   D. Best Supporting Actor

3. Jack Carson plays the photographer-assistant of a New York City reporter opposite Allan Lane in what film?
   A. *Society Doctor* (1935)
   B. *This Marriage Business* (1938)
   C. *Times Square Lady* (1935)
   D. *To Each His Own* (1946)

4. What Shirley Temple film was Dick Foran's first movie?
   A. *Change of Heart* (1934)
   B. *Little Miss Marker* (1934)
   C. *Pardon My Pups* (1934)
   D. *Stand Up and Cheer!* (1934)

5. In what film is Shirley Temple kidnapped by her wicked aunt while her grouchy grandfather searches for her?
   A. *Dimples* (1936)
   B. *Heidi* (1937)
   C. *Just Around the Corner* (1938)
   D. *The Little Princess* (1939)

6. Janet Gaynor starred in the original 1937 version of *A Star Is Born*. Who directed it?
   A. Leo McCarey
   B. Michael Curtiz
   C. Victor Fleming
   D. William Wellman

7. In what year did Shirley Temple receive the Juvenile Performer Academy Award?
   A. 1933
   B. 1935
   C. 1937
   D. 1940

8. In what category did the 1931 film *À Nous la Liberté* receive its only Academy Award nomination?
   A. Best Art Direction
   B. Best Editing
   C. Best Musical Score
   D. Best Picture

Gold Diggers of 1933, 1933

9. What song does Joan Blondell's character perform in *Gold Diggers of 1933* that became an anthem of the Great Depression?
   A. "Remember My Forgotten Man"
   B. "Speaking of the Weather"
   C. "We're in the Money"
   D. "With Plenty of Money and You"

10. Who costarred with Valerie Hobson in the 1939 film *The Silent Battle*?
    A. Alec Guinness
    B. Maurice Evans
    C. Ralph Richardson
    D. Rex Harrison

11. Fay Wray almost becomes a wax sculpture of Marie Antoinette in what film?

    A. *King Kong* (1933)
    B. *The Most Dangerous Game* (1932)
    C. *The Mystery of the Wax Museum* (1933)
    D. *The Wedding March* (1928)

12. What was the first color film to win the Academy Award for Best Picture?

    A. *Gone With the Wind* (1939)
    B. *The Man Who Knew Too Much* (1934)
    C. *The Wizard of Oz* (1939)
    D. *Becky Sharp* (1935)

13. Basil Rathbone and Flora Robson costar in what unfinished film?

    A. *One Precious Year* (1933)
    B. *Renegades* (1930)
    C. *Viennese Nights* (1930)
    D. *Wild Company* (1930)

14. Lionel Barrymore and Maureen O'Sullivan star in which film directed by Richard Thorpe about fox hunting in the hills of Missouri?

    A. *Ah, Wilderness!* (1935)
    B. *Green Eyes* (1934)
    C. *The Mysterious Island* (1961)
    D. *The Voice of Bugle Ann* (1936)

15. In what year was Groucho Marx awarded an honorary Academy Award for Lifetime Achievement?

    A. 1961
    B. 1966
    C. 1974
    D. 1976

16. All of the following actors appeared in Henry Hathaway's 1939 film *The Real Glory* except for whom?

    A. David Niven
    B. Gary Cooper
    C. Reginald Owen
    D. Tyrone Power

17. Which of the following actresses costars with Marie Dressler in the 1932 film *Emma*?

    A. Ann Miller
    B. Carole Lombard
    C. Irene Dunne
    D. Myrna Loy

18. The 1938 film *The Drum,* starring Valerie Hobson, is set in what country?

    A. England
    B. India
    C. Spain
    D. Turkey

19. Shirley Temple was the box-office champion for three straight years in the 1930s. Which was not one of the three?

    A. 1935
    B. 1936
    C. 1937
    D. 1938

20. After *Angels with Dirty Faces* (1939), James Cagney reunited with Humphrey Bogart in what film?

    A. *The Roaring Twenties* (1939)
    B. *The Wagons Roll at Night* (1941)
    C. *They Drive by Night* (1940)
    D. *You, John Jones!* (1943)

21. In the 1932 film *Tess of the Storm Country,* Janet Gaynor's father is a retired what?

    A. Factory worker
    B. Fireman
    C. Police officer
    D. Sea captain

22. In the 1938 film *Brother Rat,* Ronald Reagan costarred with all of the following actors except which one?

    A. Eddie Albert
    B. James Cagney
    C. Jane Wyman
    D. Priscilla Lane

answers found on page 542

23. Who played Charles Laughton's daughter in the 1934 film *The Barretts of Wimpole Street*?

A. Elizabeth Taylor
B. Loretta Young
C. Norma Shearer
D. Vivien Leigh

24. What was George Sanders's film debut?

A. *Confessions of a Nazi Spy*
B. *Find the Lady*
C. *Love Is News*
D. *The Outsider*

David Copperfield, 1935

25. Which two Dickens adaptations earned consecutive Academy Award nominations for Best Picture in 1936 and 1937?

A. *David Copperfield* and *A Tale of Two Cities*
B. *Great Expectations* and *Oliver Twist*
C. *Nicholas Nickleby* and *Bleak House*
D. *Oliver Twist* and *A Christmas Carol*

26. Ida Lupino was promoted as the "English Jean Harlow" for what film?

A. *Her First Affaire* (1932)
B. *High Finance* (1933)
C. *Prince of Arcadia* (1933)
D. *The Ghost Camera* (1933)

27. In what movie did Bonita Granville make her film debut?

A. *Cavalcade* (1933)
B. *Little Women* (1933)
C. *Silver Dollar* (1932)
D. *Westward Passage* (1932)

28. What actor starred in the 1938 film *Spawn of the North* directed by Henry Hathaway?

A. David Niven
B. George Raft
C. Reginald Owen
D. Robert Taylor

29. In which film does Bela Lugosi appear with Greta Garbo?

A. *Anna Christie* (1931)
B. *Camille* (1936)
C. *Mata Hari* (1931)
D. *Ninotchka* (1939)

30. Jack Carson was featured in which comedy opposite Leslie Howard and Humphrey Bogart?

A. *Four's a Crowd* (1938)
B. *No Time for Comedy* (1940)
C. *Perfect Understanding* (1933)
D. *Stand-In* (1937)

31. Fay Wray's husband becomes stranded in Antarctica in what film?

A. *Dirigible* (1931)
B. *The Clairvoyant* (1935)
C. *The Most Dangerous Game* (1932)
D. *The Mystery of the Wax Museum* (1933)

32. How many Oscar nominations did *Angels with Dirty Faces* (1938) receive?

A. 1
B. 2
C. 3
D. 4

33. Claude Rains costarred opposite Olivia de Havilland in all of the following films except for which one?

A. *Anthony Adverse* (1936)
B. *Gold Is Where You Find It* (1938)
C. *The Adventures of Robin Hood* (1938)
D. *The Prince and the Pauper* (1937)

34. In *Little Miss Marker* (1934) starring Shirley Temple, the character Regret was named after what?

   A. Shirley Temple's first dog
   B. The literal meaning of the word
   C. The prize-winning 1915 racehorse
   D. The studio boss's favorite pet

35. Fox signed Hattie McDaniel to a contract to appear in what film with Shirley Temple and Lionel Barrymore?

   A. *Alice Adams* (1935)
   B. *I'm No Angel* (1933)
   C. *Judge Priest* (1934)
   D. *The Little Colonel* (1935)

36. In which of the following Ronald Reagan films does Louis Armstrong appear?

   A. *An Angel from Texas* (1940)
   B. *Going Places* (1938)
   C. *Hell's Kitchen* (1939)
   D. *Swing Your Lady* (1938)

37. In which Shirley Temple film did Arthur Treacher appear as a kindly butler?

   A. *Bright Eyes* (1934)
   B. *Curly Top* (1935)
   C. *Our Little Girl* (1935)
   D. *The Little Colonel* (1935)

38. Merle Oberon's first prominent role in cinema was in what Charles Laughton film?

   A. *Men of Tomorrow* (1932)
   B. *The Private Life of Henry VIII* (1933)
   C. *The Scarlet Pimpernel* (1934)
   D. *The W Plan* (1931)

39. In the 1933 film *From Hell to Heaven,* the guests at a hotel anxiously await to hear the outcome of what?

   A. A baseball game
   B. A boxing match
   C. A horse race
   D. A poker game

40. The 1934 film *Unfinished Symphony,* directed by Anthony Asquith, was based on the life of what classical music composer?

   A. Franz Schubert
   B. Georges Bizet
   C. Ludwig van Beethoven
   D. Pyotr Ilyich Tchaikovsky

41. What is the name of Valerie Hobson's character in the 1936 film *Secret of Stamboul*?

   A. Elizabeth
   B. Lydia
   C. Pinky
   D. Tania

42. Miriam Hopkins portrays Lavinia Penniman in what film starring Olivia de Havilland?

   A. *Dancers in the Dark* (1932)
   B. *The Heiress* (1949)
   C. *The Old Maid* (1939)
   D. *Wise Girl* (1937)

43. Cedric Hardwicke and John Mills costar in what film directed by Robert Stevenson?

   A. *On Borrowed Time* (1939)
   B. *The Barkleys of Broadway* (1949)
   C. *The King of Paris* (1934)
   D. *Tudor Rose* (1936)

44. Chico Marx performs the song "I'm Daffy Over You" for the first time in what film?

   A. *Animal Crackers* (1930)
   B. *Hold That Kiss* (1938)
   C. *Manhattan Melodrama* (1934)
   D. *The Cat and the Canary* (1939)

45. Fay Wray's 1933 film *One Sunday Afternoon* was remade in 1941 with what new title?

   A. *Back Street*
   B. *Invisible Ghost*
   C. *The Great Lie*
   D. *The Strawberry Blonde*

answers found on page 542

San Francisco, 1936

46. The 1936 film *San Francisco* costarring Spencer Tracy covers the famous earthquake that happened in what year?

A. 1905
B. 1906
C. 1907
D. 1908

47. In the 1937 film *Hollywood Hotel,* Dick Powell plays a member of Benny Goodman's Orchestra. What instrument does his character play?

A. Clarinet
B. Saxophone
C. Trombone
D. Trumpet

48. What actress costarred with Warner Oland as Shanghai Lil in *Shanghai Express* (1932)?

A. Claudette Colbert
B. Marlene Dietrich
C. Merle Oberon
D. Rita Hayworth

49. After *Footlight Parade* (1933), James Cagney reunited with Ruby Keeler in which film?

A. *Calling All Girls* (1942)
B. *Dames* (1934)
C. *Ready, Willing and Able* (1937)
D. *Shipmates Forever* (1935)

50. In the Shirley Temple film *Little Miss Marker* (1934), what actor had difficulty with some of the lines in the script?

A. Adolphe Menjou
B. Charles Bickford
C. Sam Hardy
D. Warren Hymer

51. In *Three Smart Girls* (1936), the three Craig sisters visit New York to prevent their father from marrying a calculating socialite. Who played the socialite?

A. Alice Brady
B. Barbara Read
C. Nan Grey
D. Nella Walker

52. David Niven was featured in which film starring Miriam Hopkins?

A. *Men Are Not Gods* (1936)
B. *Old Acquaintance* (1943)
C. *Splendor* (1935)
D. *The Old Maid* (1939)

53. Film director Frank Capra became President of the Academy of Motion Picture Arts and Sciences in what year?

A. 1922
B. 1930
C. 1935
D. 1950

54. Luise Rainer became the first performer to win an Oscar two years in a row after her performance in what film?

A. *Gold Is Where You Find It* (1938)
B. *Swing Your Lady* (1938)
C. *The Bells of St. Mary's* (1945)
D. *The Good Earth* (1937)

Spotlight on
CARY **GRANT** (1904–1986)

Cary Grant was his own greatest performance, a creature invented on screen from aspects of other actors he admired, including Douglas Fairbanks and Noël Coward. With time, he assumed the role offscreen as well, rising from humble beginnings as a child of England's slums to become the epitome of class. In love with the theater and silent comedy from his early years, he ran away to join a troupe of comedians when he

Bringing Up Baby, 1938

was fourteen, developing acrobatic skills he would use throughout his career. When he toured the United States in the twenties, he decided to stay and try his luck on Broadway, where he became a musical theater star. He was one of the many stage actors brought to Hollywood with the coming of sound. With the success of two sophisticated 1937 comedies, *Topper* and *The Awful Truth*, he became a star. Grant was a favorite with two of the era's greatest directors— Alfred Hitchcock (appearing in four of his films, starting with *Suspicion* in 1941) and Howard Hawks (starring in five of Hawks's films, starting with *Bringing Up Baby* in 1938)—which helped cement his iconic status. Grant reigned as one of Hollywood's leading stars until 1966, then retired from filmmaking to devote himself to family, charity work, and being Cary Grant—a role he played to perfection.

Suspicion, 1941

1. **Cary Grant plays which character in the 1933 film *Alice in Wonderland*?**

   A. The Mad Hatter

   B. The Mock Turtle

   C. The White Knight

   D. Tweedledee

2. **In the 1932 film *Hot Saturday*, Nancy Carroll costars with Cary Grant and what other actor?**

   A. Gary Cooper

   B. John Barrymore

   C. Randolph Scott

   D. Spencer Tracy

3. **In what Hal Roach film do Cary Grant and Constance Bennett return from the dead to help a henpecked husband?**

   A. *Merrily We Live* (1938)

   B. *There Goes My Heart* (1938)

   C. *Tit for Tat* (1935)

   D. *Topper* (1937)

4. **Although he never won, how many times was Cary Grant nominated for an Oscar?**

   A. 0

   B. 1

   C. 2

   D. 3

5. **What film pairing Cary Grant and Rosalind Russell was based on the play *The Front Page*?**

   A. *Design for Scandal* (1941)

   B. *Four's a Crowd* (1938)

   C. *His Girl Friday* (1940)

   D. *No Time for Comedy* (1940)

---

answers found on page 542

55. Janet Gaynor starred in the 1932 film *Tess of the Storm Country*. What actress starred in the silent 1922 version?

A. Clara Bow
B. Joan Crawford
C. Louise Brooks
D. Mary Pickford

56. Robert Donat was nominated for an Academy Award as Best Actor for his performance in what 1938 film?

A. *Four Daughters*
B. *Jezebel*
C. *The Citadel*
D. *You Can't Take It with You*

57. Nancy Carroll costarred with what actor in the 1938 film *There Goes My Heart*?

A. Fredric March
B. Henry Fonda
C. James Stewart
D. Robert Donat

58. Lewis Milestone became head of which studio in 1932?

A. MGM
B. RKO
C. United Artists
D. Warner Bros.

59. What was Robert Newton's first film?

A. *Fire Over England* (1937)
B. *I, Claudius* (1937)
C. *Reunion* (1932)
D. *The Green Cockatoo* (1937)

60. Who does Fred MacMurray romance in the 1935 film *Alice Adams*?

A. Barbara Stanwyck
B. Jean Harlow
C. Katharine Hepburn
D. Olivia de Havilland

61. Claude Rains plays the Earl of Hertford opposite Errol Flynn in what adventure film?

A. *Edge of Darkness* (1943)
B. *The Adventures of Robin Hood* (1938)
C. *The Prince and the Pauper* (1937)
D. *The Private Lives of Elizabeth and Essex* (1939)

62. Flora Robson portrays Empress Elisabeth in what biopic?

A. *Mr. Peabody and the Mermaid* (1948)
B. *The Rise of Catherine the Great* (1934)
C. *The Sea Hawk* (1940)
D. *Viennese Nights* (1930)

63. Cecil Kellaway plays Earnshaw in what film adaptation directed by William Wyler?

A. *Golden Boy* (1939)
B. *The Chiltern Hundreds* (1949)
C. *The Story of Vernon and Irene Castle* (1939)
D. *Wuthering Heights* (1939)

64. Which of the following actors starred with Gene Krupa in the 1939 film *Rhythm Romance*?

A. Bing Crosby
B. Bob Hope
C. George Burns
D. Sid Caesar

65. The 1937 film *Lost Horizon* was nominated for seven Academy Awards. How many did it take home?

A. 1
B. 2
C. 3
D. 4

66. Jack Carson was featured in all of the following films opposite James Stewart except for which one?

A. *Destry Rides Again* (1939)
B. *It's a Wonderful World* (1939)
C. *Mr. Smith Goes to Washington* (1939)
D. *Vivacious Lady* (1938)

answers found on page 542

67. In 1938, what special award did Deanna Durbin receive along with Mickey Rooney?

A. Academy Juvenile Award
B. Junior Academy Achievement
C. Junior Golden Globe
D. Special Achievement Award

68. In the 1932 Laurel and Hardy short *County Hospital*, what malady lands Oliver Hardy in the hospital?

A. A broken arm
B. A broken leg
C. A fever
D. A head injury

69. Besides *Three Smart Girls* (1936), what other Deanna Durbin film is said to have saved Universal from bankruptcy?

A. *Every Sunday* (1936)
B. *First Love* (1939)
C. *Mad About Music* (1938)
D. *One Hundred Men and a Girl* (1937)

70. What film adaptation of a Charles Dickens classic features Elsa Lanchester and W. C. Fields?

A. *David Copperfield* (1935)
B. *It's a Gift* (1934)
C. *Oliver Twist* (1948)
D. *You Can't Cheat an Honest Man* (1939)

71. Claude Rains portrays Napoleon Bonaparte in which film starring Marion Davies?

A. *Enchantment* (1921)
B. *Ever Since Eve* (1937)
C. *Hearts Divided* (1936)
D. *Page Miss Glory* (1935)

72. What was the name of Marie Dressler's last film before her death in 1934?

A. *Christopher Bean* (1933)
B. *Min and Bill* (1930)
C. *Prosperity* (1932)
D. *Reducing* (1931)

73. In how many of the Academy Award categories for which it was nominated did the 1934 film *It Happened One Night* lose?

A. 0
B. 1
C. 2
D. 3

74. Which of the following actors costars with Warner Oland in *The Black Camel* (1931)?

A. Basil Rathbone
B. Bela Lugosi
C. Boris Karloff
D. Lon Chaney

Grand Hotel, 1932

75. How many Academy Award nominations did the 1932 film *Grand Hotel* receive in addition to Best Picture?

A. 0
B. 2
C. 4
D. 6

76. Who played Deanna Durbin's mother in *Three Smart Girls* (1936)?

A. Alice Brady
B. Barbara Read
C. Nan Grey
D. Nella Walker

answers found on page 542

77. What actress married Lew Ayres in 1934?

    A. Claudette Colbert
    B. Gene Tierney
    C. Ginger Rogers
    D. Irene Dunne

78. The theatrical release of which W. C. Fields film coincided with the 1932 Olympic Games in Los Angeles?

    A. *If I Had a Million* (1932)
    B. *International House* (1933)
    C. *Million Dollar Legs* (1932)
    D. *The Golf Specialist* (1930)

79. Jack Carson and Ginger Rogers share the screen in all of the following films except for which one?

    A. *Carefree* (1938)
    B. *Having Wonderful Time* (1938)
    C. *The Story of Vernon and Irene Castle* (1939)
    D. *Vivacious Lady* (1938)

80. The 1939 film *Wife, Husband and Friend* was based on a novel by James M. Cain. What actress starred in it?

    A. Elizabeth Taylor
    B. Ginger Rogers
    C. Katharine Hepburn
    D. Loretta Young

81. Red Skelton made his screen debut opposite Ginger Rogers in what film?

    A. *Having Wonderful Time* (1938)
    B. *Monsieur Beaucaire* (1946)
    C. *Rendezvous* (1935)
    D. *The Cat and the Canary* (1939)

82. In 1933, Ida Lupino traveled to the United States under contract to which studio, where she tested unsuccessfully for *Alice in Wonderland*?

    A. MGM
    B. Paramount
    C. United Artists
    D. Warner Bros.

83. Ned Sparks played a character named Happy in all of the following films except for which one?

    A. *Double Cross Roads* (1930)
    B. *Lady for a Day* (1933)
    C. *Love Comes Along* (1930)
    D. *Too Much Harmony* (1933)

84. In the 1930 film *Raffles*, Kay Francis's character is engaged to a man who likes to steal what?

    A. Identities
    B. Jewelry
    C. Paintings
    D. Purses

85. Who plays the British drifter who passes through Bette Davis's Arizona cafe in *The Petrified Forest* (1936)?

    A. Humphrey Bogart
    B. James Mason
    C. Leslie Howard
    D. William Powell

86. What actress played Roddy McDowall's sister in *Murder in the Family* (1938)?

    A. Elizabeth Taylor
    B. Jessica Tandy
    C. Judy Garland
    D. Maureen O'Hara

87. What was Ronald Reagan's first feature starring role?

    A. *Hollywood Hotel* (1937)
    B. *Love Is on the Air* (1937)
    C. *Submarine D-1* (1937)
    D. *The Cowboy from Brooklyn* (1938)

88. In what Hal Roach film does an heiress take a job as a department store clerk?

    A. *Merrily We Live* (1938)
    B. *There Goes My Heart* (1938)
    C. *Tit for Tat* (1935)
    D. *Topper* (1937)

89. Fay Wray finances a treasure hunt expedition in what film?
   A. *Below the Sea* (1933)
   B. *Bulldog Jack* (1935)
   C. *Dirigible* (1931)
   D. *The Most Dangerous Game* (1932)

90. Who initially refused, but eventually agreed, to star in the Shirley Temple film *Rebecca of Sunnybrook Farm* (1938)?
   A. Gloria Stuart
   B. Jack Haley
   C. Randolph Scott
   D. Shirley Temple

91. An ape falls in love with Fay Wray in what film?
   A. *King Kong* (1933)
   B. *The Most Dangerous Game* (1932)
   C. *The Mystery of the Wax Museum* (1933)
   D. *The Wedding March* (1928)

92. Which of the following actors costars with Warner Oland in *Charlie Chan Carries On* (1931)?
   A. Charles Boyer
   B. Gary Cooper
   C. Ray Milland
   D. William Holden

93. Joan Bennett was the younger sister of what actress who appeared in *After Office Hours* (1935)?
   A. Barbara Bennett
   B. Constance Bennett
   C. Elizabeth Bennett
   D. Jill Bennett

94. What young actress costarred in the 1934 film *Now and Forever*, directed by Henry Hathaway?
   A. Margaret O'Brien
   B. Natalie Wood
   C. Shirley Temple
   D. Virginia Weidler

95. In the 1933 film *Adorable*, Janet Gaynor plays a what?
   A. Clothing designer
   B. Dancer
   C. Model
   D. Princess

96. What actress costarred with Charles Laughton in the 1932 film *The Sign of the Cross*?
   A. Claudette Colbert
   B. Joan Crawford
   C. Katharine Hepburn
   D. Norma Shearer

97. Bonita Granville is featured in what Mickey Rooney film?
   A. *A Family Affair* (1937)
   B. *Andy Hardy's Blonde Trouble* (1944)
   C. *Half a Sinner* (1934)
   D. *The Healer* (1935)

98. Ayn Rand suggested which of the following leading ladies play the lead in *The Fountainhead* (1949)?
   A. Grace Kelly
   B. Greta Garbo
   C. Louise Brooks
   D. Susan Hayward

A Midsummer Night's Dream, 1935

99. In addition to Film Editing, what other Oscar did *A Midsummer Night's Dream* (1935) win?
   A. Best Adaptation
   B. Best Assistant Director
   C. Best Cinematography
   D. Best Picture

100. Gertrude McCoy portrayed Lady Hamilton in what film opposite Cedric Hardwicke?

A. *Flying Down to Rio* (1933)
B. *Nelson* (1926)
C. *Rose-Marie* (1936)
D. *Times Square Lady* (1935)

101. To whom did Leslie Howard lose the Academy Award for Best Actor in 1934?

A. Charles Laughton
B. John Barrymore
C. Mickey Rooney
D. Paul Muni

102. Ned Sparks played which character in *Alice in Wonderland* (1933)?

A. Caterpillar
B. King of Hearts
C. Mad Hatter
D. Tweedledee

103. How many Oscars did *Angels with Dirty Faces* (1938) win?

A. 0
B. 1
C. 2
D. 4

104. Hattie McDaniel performed a duet with Will Rogers in what John Ford film?

A. *Alice Adams* (1935)
B. *China Seas* (1935)
C. *Judge Priest* (1934)
D. *Show Boat* (1936)

105. Paul Lukas helps Katharine Hepburn's character with her writing in what film?

A. *Dodsworth* (1936)
B. *Little Women* (1933)
C. *The Lady Vanishes* (1938)
D. *Watch on the Rhine* (1943)

106. Ida Lupino made her first film appearance in what film?

A. *Her First Affaire* (1932)
B. *Prince of Arcadia* (1933)
C. *The Ghost Camera* (1933)
D. *The Love Race* (1931)

107. What was the title of Louis Armstrong's 1936 autobiography?

A. *Give Me a Kiss to Build a Dream On*
B. *My Life in Jazz*
C. *Swing That Music*
D. *What a Wonderful World*

108. Robert Montgomery was featured in all of the following films directed by Richard Thorpe except which one?

A. *The Crowd Roars* (1938)
B. *The Earl of Chicago* (1940)
C. *The First Hundred Years* (1938)
D. *Three Loves Has Nancy* (1938)

109. For what film did Val Lewton receive his first screen credit?

A. *A Star Is Born* (1937)
B. *A Tale of Two Cities* (1935)
C. *Cat People* (1942)
D. *Gone With the Wind* (1939)

110. What Hal Roach short won an Academy Award in 1936?

A. *Bored of Education*
B. *General Spanky*
C. *Spooky Hooky*
D. *The Bohemian Girl*

111. In 1936's *One in a Million*, Don Ameche plays a reporter for what publication?

A. *New York Times*
B. *Newsweek*
C. *Paris Herald*
D. *Wall Street Journal*

112. At the age of fourteen, Deanna Durbin tried out for the voice of Snow White in *Snow White and the Seven Dwarfs* (1937). Walt Disney himself rejected her for what reason?

    A. Because of her contact to Universal
    B. For sounding like Judy Garland
    C. For sounding too mature
    D. For sounding too young

113. Hattie McDaniel gave her first film performance in what movie?

    A. *Blonde Venus* (1932)
    B. *The Boiling Point* (1932)
    C. *The Impatient Maiden* (1932)
    D. *Washington Masquerade* (1932)

114. What was Merle Oberon's salary for appearing in *The Dark Angel* (1935)?

    A. $100,000
    B. $250,000
    C. $333,333
    D. $60,000

115. Walter Huston appeared with James Cagney in only one film. What was it?

    A. *Devil Dogs of the Air* (1935)
    B. *Lady Killer* (1933)
    C. *Of Human Hearts* (1938)
    D. *Yankee Doodle Dandy* (1942)

116. In 1934, the Kansas Restaurant Association publicly thanked which leading lady for "stemming the dieting craze stimulated by the sylph-like figures of Dietrich, Crawford and Harlow and for restoring well-rounded curves to healthy U.S. women"?

    A. Ingrid Bergman
    B. Loretta Young
    C. Mae West
    D. Rosalind Russell

117. Although director Tod Browning wanted to hire an unknown European actor, Universal insisted he cast whom for the legendary title role in *Dracula* (1931)?

    A. Bela Lugosi
    B. Boris Karloff
    C. Lon Chaney
    D. Lon Chaney Jr.

118. Charles Laughton and Flora Robson costar in what unfinished film?

    A. *I, Claudius* (1937)
    B. *Renegades* (1930)
    C. *Viennese Nights* (1930)
    D. *Wild Company* (1930)

119. In 1930 Gary Cooper costarred with Marlene Dietrich in her first American film. What was it?

    A. *A Foreign Affair*
    B. *Morocco*
    C. *Shanghai Express*
    D. *The Devil Is a Woman*

120. What was Merle Oberon's film debut?

    A. *The Three Passions* (1928)
    B. *Men of Tomorrow* (1932)
    C. *The Battle* (1934)
    D. *These Three* (1936)

121. In *The Dark Angel* (1935), the role of Alan Trent was originally intended for what actor (who was having an affair with Merle Oberon)?

    A. Fredric March
    B. Herbert Marshall
    C. John Halliday
    D. Leslie Howard

122. How many Academy Award nominations did the classic 1933 film *King Kong* receive?

    A. 0
    B. 1
    C. 2
    D. 3

answers found on page 543

Spotlight on CAROLE **LOMBARD** (1908–1942)

Always the tomboy, Carole Lombard made her film debut in *A Perfect Crime* (1921)—at the age of twelve—after director Allan Dwan spotted her playing baseball with a bunch of boys. Within three years, she had dropped out of school to pursue acting full-time. A contract with comedy genius Hal Roach, for whom she starred in short films, started her on the road to the top. At Paramount, she began landing meaty roles, opposite future husband Clark Gable in *No Man of Her Own* (1932) and George Raft in the musical *Bolero* (1934). When the studio loaned her to Columbia to star opposite John Barrymore in one of the first screwball comedies, *Twentieth Century* (1934), the film made her a star. Lombard turned down the chance to star in director Orson Welles's first film, *Citizen Kane* (1941), preferring to stick to comedy in Alfred Hitchcock's *Mr. and Mrs. Smith* (1941) and Ernst Lubitsch's *To Be or Not to Be* (1942). She had finished work on the latter when she set out on a wartime bond-selling tour. Eager to get home after her last stop, she decided to fly. The plane crashed into Table Rock Mountain in Nevada, killing all on board.

Mr. and Mrs. Smith, 1941

The Gay Bride, 1934

1. **Carole Lombard costarred with which of the following actors in the 1931 film *Ladies' Man*?**

   A. Cary Grant

   B. John Barrymore

   C. Ralph Bellamy

   D. William Powell

2. **What actor was Carole Lombard's first husband?**

   A. Clark Gable

   B. Edward G. Robinson

   C. Fred Astaire

   D. William Powell

3. **In the 1934 Carole Lombard film of the same name, what does "Twentieth Century" refer to?**

   A. A band

   B. A nightclub

   C. A play

   D. A train

4. **Carole Lombard costarred with Bing Crosby in what film?**

   A. *Fools for Scandal* (1938)

   B. *Love Before Breakfast* (1936)

   C. *My Man Godfrey* (1936)

   D. *We're Not Dressing* (1934)

5. **What was the only film Carole Lombard made with future-husband Clark Gable?**

   A. *Lady by Choice* (1934)

   B. *No Man of Her Own* (1932)

   C. *Nothing Sacred* (1937)

   D. *The Gay Bride* (1934)

---

answers found on page 543

123. Hattie McDaniel reprised her stage role of Queenie in what film?

A. *Alice Adams* (1935)
B. *Imitation of Life* (1934)
C. *Judge Priest* (1934)
D. *Showboat* (1936)

124. In 1938, Edward Arnold was an MC on what radio program starring Nelson Eddy, Edgar Bergen, and Charlie McCarthy?

A. *Arch Oboler's Plays*
B. *The Chase and Sanborn Hour*
C. *The Goodrich Zippers*
D. *The Mysterious Traveler*

Rasputin and the Empress, 1932

125. Ethel Barrymore's 1932 film *Rasputin and the Empress* received one Academy Award nomination. What was it for?

A. Best Costume Design
B. Best Musical Score
C. Best Original Screenplay
D. Best Supporting Actor

126. In the 1932 comedy *Million Dollar Legs*, W. C. Fields plays the president of what fictional country?

A. Frenzinople
B. Happenstanceland

C. Klopstokia
D. Whotopia

127. Charles Boyer portrayed Napoleon Bonaparte in what film opposite Greta Garbo?

A. *Conquest* (1937)
B. *Desire* (1936)
C. *Now and Forever* (1934)
D. *Today We Live* (1933)

128. Who costarred with Leslie Howard in the 1932 film *Smilin' Through*?

A. Bing Crosby
B. Fredric March
C. Melvyn Douglas
D. Spencer Tracy

129. Paul Lukas played Alfred Hitchcock's villain in what film?

A. *Dodsworth* (1936)
B. *Little Women* (1933)
C. *The Lady Vanishes* (1938)
D. *Watch on the Rhine* (1943)

130. Paul Lukas journeys to the mansion of an eccentric widow due to a mysterious unsigned letter in what film?

A. *Dodsworth* (1936)
B. *The Casino Murder Case* (1935)
C. *The Lady Vanishes* (1938)
D. *Watch on the Rhine* (1943)

131. Wallace Beery won the Academy Award for Best Actor for his performance in what 1931 film?

A. *Arrowsmith*
B. *Grand Hotel*
C. *Shanghai Express*
D. *The Champ*

answers found on page 543

132. In what film is Shirley Temple left by her father in an exclusive seminary for girls when he has to go to Africa with the army?

A. *Dimples* (1936)
B. *Heidi* (1937)
C. *Just Around the Corner* (1938)
D. *The Little Princess* (1939)

133. Cedric Hardwicke played Bishop Bienvenu in what film opposite Fredric March?

A. *Les Misérables* (1935)
B. *Nell Gwyn* (1934)
C. *On Borrowed Time* (1939)
D. *The King of Paris* (1934)

134. What was Fay Bainter's film debut?

A. *Jezebel* (1938)
B. *Quality Street* (1937)
C. *This Side of Heaven* (1934)
D. *White Banners* (1938)

135. What actress costarred with Leslie Howard in the 1932 film *The Animal Kingdom*?

A. Ann Sothern
B. Irene Dunne
C. Katharine Hepburn
D. Myrna Loy

136. How much did Gary Cooper make for a couple months' work on the Shirley Temple film *Now and Forever* (1934)?

A. $129,000
B. $1,500,000
C. $211,000
D. $253,000

137. In the 1938 film *Dramatic School*, Luise Rainer's character works at a factory that assembles what?

A. Dresses
B. Gas meters
C. Hats
D. Tires

138. Katharine Alexander and Billie Burke costar in which comedy written by Rachel Crothers?

A. *I Met Him in Paris* (1937)
B. *Midnight* (1939)
C. *Private Worlds* (1935)
D. *Splendor* (1935)

139. Edward Arnold plays a scheming publisher in what film opposite Gary Cooper and Barbara Stanwyck?

A. *City Streets* (1931)
B. *Golden Boy* (1939)
C. *Meet John Doe* (1941)
D. *The Spoilers* (1942)

140. Lupe Velez would film seven reprisals of what character she made famous in the 1939 film *The Girl from Mexico*?

A. Carmelita
B. Naturich
C. Rosetta
D. Vera

141. Janet Gaynor starred in the 1935 film *The Farmer Takes a Wife*. Who directed it?

A. Frank Capra
B. George Cukor
C. Raoul Walsh
D. Victor Fleming

142. During the filming of *Freaks* (1932), director Tod Browning had a recurring nightmare about which actor?

A. Harry Earles
B. Henry Victor
C. Johnny Eck
D. Josephine Joseph

143. What was Claire Trevor's film debut?

A. *Life in the Raw* (1933)
B. *King of Gamblers* (1937)
C. *Star for a Night* (1936)
D. *Wild Gold* (1934)

144. Fay Wray helps investigate a series of cannibal-istic murders at a medical college in what film?

A. *Doctor X* (1932)
B. *The Most Dangerous Game* (1932)
C. *The Mystery of the Wax Museum* (1933)
D. *The Wedding March* (1928)

145. Between 1934 and 1940, how many films did James Cagney and Pat O'Brien make together?

A. 10
B. 6
C. 7
D. 8

146. W. C. Fields plays which character in the 1933 film *Alice in Wonderland*?

A. Humpty Dumpty
B. The Gryphon
C. The Mad Hatter
D. Tweedledee

147. How much did it cost for Universal to acquire the rights for director Tod Browning's *Dracula* (1931)?

A. $35,000
B. $40,000
C. $50,000
D. $65,000

148. Which film starring W. C. Fields was based on the Booth Tarkington play *Magnolia*?

A. *A Family Affair* (1937)
B. *Mississippi* (1935)
C. *Monsieur Beaucaire* (1946)
D. *The Cat and the Canary* (1939)

149. In the 1936 film *Poppy*, who is "Poppy"?

A. Farnsworth's father
B. McGargle's daughter
C. McGargle's grandfather
D. McGargle's puppy

Kongo, 1932

150. 1932's *Kongo*, starring Lupe Velez and Walter Huston, was a remake of which Lon Chaney film?

A. *Shadows* (1922)
B. *The Blackbird* (1926)
C. *The Light in the Dark* (1922)
D. *West of Zanzibar* (1928)

151. Ronald Reagan signed a seven-year contract in 1937 with which studio?

A. MGM
B. RKO
C. Universal
D. Warner Bros.

152. Fay Wray left Paramount in 1932 to sign with which studio?

A. Columbia
B. MGM
C. RKO
D. Universal

153. In what year did Deanna Durbin sign her con-tract with MGM, even though she was released shortly thereafter?

A. 1928
B. 1932
C. 1935
D. 1938

answers found on page 543

154. Claude Rains costarred opposite Errol Flynn in all of the following films except for which one?

A. *Anthony Adverse* (1936)
B. *The Adventures of Robin Hood* (1938)
C. *The Prince and the Pauper* (1937)
D. *The Sea Hawk* (1940)

155. The 1939 film *Golden Boy* received its only Oscar nomination in what category?

A. Best Actor
B. Best Actress
C. Best Musical Score
D. Best Original Screenplay

156. What character did Adolphe Menjou play in *One Hundred Men and a Girl* (1937)?

A. Garage Owner
B. John Cardwell
C. John R. Frost
D. Leopold Stokowski

157. In *First Love* (1939), Deanna Durbin's character gives her birth date, which is the same as Durbin's actual birth date. What is it?

A. December 4
B. February 14
C. July 31
D. October 17

158. What was Deanna Durbin's 1936 singing debut?

A. *Eddie Cantor Radio Hour*
B. *The Jack Benny Show*
C. *Every Sunday*
D. *Three Smart Girls*

159. Freddie Bartholomew made his Hollywood debut in what film costarring Lionel Barrymore and W. C. Fields?

A. *A Family Affair* (1937)
B. *David Copperfield* (1935)
C. *The Barber Shop* (1933)
D. *The Cat and the Canary* (1939)

160. In what film did Shirley Temple first sing her trademark song "On the Good Ship Lollipop"?

A. *Bright Eyes* (1934)
B. *Just Around the Corner* (1938)
C. *The Little Colonel* (1935)
D. *Wee Willie Winkie* (1937)

161. In what film did Edward Arnold portray King Louis XII of France?

A. *Cardinal Richelieu* (1935)
B. *Secret of the Blue Room* (1933)
C. *The Glass Key* (1935)
D. *The Higher Destiny* (1916)

162. The 1941 classic *That Night in Rio,* starring Carmen Miranda, was a remake of what 1935 film that featured Maurice Chevalier?

A. *Folies Amoureux de Paris*
B. *Folies Bergère de Paris*
C. *Les Chansons de Montmartre*
D. *Une Soirée Mondaine*

163. *The Private Life of Henry VIII* (1933), featuring Merle Oberon, was the first non-U.S. film to receive what?

A. Best Director award
B. Best Picture award
C. Best Picture nomination
D. Best Sound award

164. In what year did the Best Picture category first appear at the Academy Awards?

A. 1929
B. 1930
C. 1931
D. 1933

165. Constance Bennett is unforgettable as Marion Kerby in Norman Z. McLeod's *Topper* (1937), but whom did producer Hal Roach originally want for the role?

A. Carole Lombard

B. Jean Harlow

C. Mary Astor

D. Myrna Loy

166. Flora Robson and Merle Oberon costar in what unfinished film?

A. *I, Claudius* (1937)

B. *Renegades* (1930)

C. *Viennese Nights* (1930)

D. *Wild Company* (1930)

167. Deanna Durbin was an option to star in what Judy Garland feature?

A. *Babes in Arms* (1939)

B. *Babes on Broadway* (1941)

C. *Everybody Sing* (1938)

D. *The Wizard of Oz* (1939)

168. Miriam Hopkins played the title role in what film opposite Cedric Hardwicke?

A. *Becky Sharp* (1935)

B. *Bella Donna* (1934)

C. *Nell Gwyn* (1934)

D. *Times Square Lady* (1935)

169. Katharine Alexander plays Mrs. Rose Arbuthnot in what film adaptation of an Elizabeth von Arnim novel?

A. *Enchanted April* (1935)

B. *Friends and Lovers* (1931)

C. *Perfect Understanding* (1933)

D. *The Painted Veil* (1934)

170. Which actor costarred with Valerie Hobson in the 1935 film *Mystery of Edwin Drood*?

A. Bela Lugosi

B. Boris Karloff

C. Claude Rains

D. Peter Lorre

171. What film features both Luise Rainer and Maureen O'Sullivan?

A. *Love Crazy* (1941)

B. *My Man Godfrey* (1936)

C. *The Emperor's Candlesticks* (1937)

D. *The Story of Vernon and Irene Castle* (1939)

172. Luise Rainer costars in what biopic based on the life of composer Johann Strauss II?

A. *Love Crazy* (1941)

B. *Shall We Dance* (1937)

C. *Star of Midnight* (1935)

D. *The Great Waltz* (1938)

173. Fay Wray had her first lead role in what Erich von Stroheim box-office failure?

A. *King Kong* (1933)

B. *The Most Dangerous Game* (1932)

C. *The Mystery of the Wax Museum* (1933)

D. *The Wedding March* (1928)

174. Katharine Alexander portrays Queen Anne in which film opposite Maureen O'Sullivan and Edward Arnold?

A. *Cardinal Richelieu* (1935)

B. *Midnight* (1939)

C. *Rose-Marie* (1936)

D. *The Spiral Staircase* (1945)

175. What film won the Academy Award for Best Picture of 1932?

A. *Grand Hotel*

B. *One Hour with You*

C. *Shanghai Express*

D. *The Champ*

176. Which of these actors did not star in Richard Boleslawski's *Les Misérables* (1935)?

A. Cedric Hardwicke

B. Charles Laughton

C. Fredric March

D. Lawrence Tibbett

The Hunchback of Notre Dame, 1939

177. Which actress portrayed Esmaralda in *The Hunchback of Notre Dame* (1939)?
   A. Ava Gardner
   B. Marlene Dietrich
   C. Maureen O'Hara
   D. Norma Shearer

178. Luise Rainer and Lana Turner costar in what film?
   A. *Dramatic School* (1938)
   B. *Fashions of 1934* (1934)
   C. *Rendezvous* (1935)
   D. *The Girl Who Had Everything* (1953)

179. Who turned down a role in *The Wizard of Oz* (1939) to star in the Shirley Temple film *The Blue Bird* (1940)?
   A. Eddie Collins
   B. Gale Sondergaard
   C. Nigel Bruce
   D. Spring Byington

180. The 1935 Warner Oland film *Charlie Chan in Egypt* featured what young actress before she became a star?
   A. Jennifer Jones
   B. Joan Crawford
   C. Loretta Young
   D. Rita Hayworth

181. In the 1933 Laurel and Hardy classic *Sons of the Desert,* Stan and Ollie deceive their wives in order to go to a what?
   A. Bar
   B. Convention
   C. Movie
   D. Poker game

182. What actor costarred with Valerie Hobson in the 1936 film *Secret of Stamboul*?
   A. Cary Grant
   B. Claude Rains
   C. Gary Cooper
   D. James Mason

183. In what film does Shirley Temple star with her pickpocket grandfather in nineteenth-century New York City?
   A. *Dimples* (1936)
   B. *Heidi* (1937)
   C. *Just Around the Corner* (1938)
   D. *The Little Princess* (1939)

184. The 1932 Charles Laughton film *Island of Lost Souls* was based on a novel by what author?
   A. H. G. Wells
   B. Isaac Asimov
   C. Jules Verne
   D. Victor Hugo

185. What is the stage name of Janet Gaynor's character in the 1937 film *A Star Is Born*?
   A. Cathy Selden
   B. Hannah Brown
   C. Janet Finch
   D. Vicki Lester

186. Fay Wray became a naturalized U.S. citizen in what year?
   A. 1925
   B. 1930
   C. 1935
   D. 1940

answers found on page 543

Spotlight on
LESLIE **HOWARD** (1893–1943)

Leslie Howard would likely be disappointed to be best remembered for playing Ashley Wilkes in *Gone With the Wind* (1939). Not only did he dislike the role, but he only took the part in return for a chance to coproduce David O. Selznick's *Intermezzo: A Love Story* (1939), in which he costarred with Ingrid Bergman. He started acting as therapy while suffering from shell shock during World War I service, and soon was performing on London and New York stages. He actually achieved stardom on Broadway, creating his image as "the perfect Englishman" in such hits as *Outward Bound* and *Berkeley Square*, both of which he would later film. A notable ladies' man (he once said "[I] didn't chase women but . . . couldn't always be bothered to run away"), he was rumored to have had affairs with Tallulah Bankhead, Merle Oberon, and Norma Shearer, among others. But he was also a dedicated friend who insisted that Humphrey Bogart repeat his stage role when *The Petrified Forest* (1936) was filmed,

Gone With the Wind, 1939

thereby establishing Bogart's career. During the war years, Howard worked tirelessly for the British government and may have done some intelligence work as well. He died returning from a goodwill mission in Spain when the Germans shot down his plane.

The Petrified Forest, 1936

1. Leslie Howard costarred with which of the following actresses in the 1931 film *A Free Soul*?

   A. Dorothy Lamour
   B. Joan Crawford
   C. Norma Shearer
   D. Paulette Goddard

2. In the 1932 film *The Animal Kingdom*, Leslie Howard plays a what?

   A. Banker
   B. Shop clerk
   C. Veterinarian
   D. Writer

3. Leslie Howard played the title role in which film costarring Merle Oberon?

   A. *I, Claudius* (1937)
   B. *The Lodger* (1944)
   C. *The Private Life of Don Juan* (1934)
   D. *The Scarlet Pimpernel* (1934)

4. In which film did Leslie Howard reprise the role he had played on Broadway?

   A. *British Agent* (1934)
   B. *Stand-In* (1937)
   C. *The Lady Is Willing* (1934)
   D. *The Petrified Forest* (1936)

5. In the 1939 film *Intermezzo: A Love Story,* Leslie Howard plays a what?

   A. Concert violinist
   B. Fisherman
   C. Surgeon
   D. Writer

answers found on page 543

187. Who starred in the title role of Alexander Korda's 1933 film *The Private Life of Henry VIII*?

A. Burl Ives
B. Charles Laughton
C. Orson Welles
D. Wallace Beery

188. What was the name of the film based on Lillian Hellman's *The Children's Hour* and featuring Bonita Granville?

A. *Call It a Day* (1937)
B. *Maid of Salem* (1937)
C. *Song of the Saddle* (1936)
D. *These Three* (1936)

189. Jack Carson is a football player in what comedy?

A. *Harris in the Spring* (1937)
B. *Mr. Doodle Kicks Off* (1938)
C. *Music for Madame* (1937)
D. *The Kid from Texas* (1939)

190. In *One Hundred Men and a Girl* (1937) starring Deanna Durbin, Leopold Stokowski played the principal conductor. In reality, who was the actual principal conductor of the featured Philadelphia Orchestra by 1937?

A. Adolphe Menjou
B. Eugene Ormandy
C. Eugene Pallette
D. Leopold Stokowski

191. What was Hal Roach's first full-length feature?

A. *Chickens Come Home* (1931)
B. *Choo Choo!* (1932)
C. *Pardon Us* (1931)
D. *Spanky* (1932)

192. What film won the Academy Award as Best Picture of 1938?

A. *Boys Town*
B. *Jezebel*
C. *The Adventures of Robin Hood*
D. *You Can't Take It with You*

193. From what university did José Ferrer graduate in 1933?

A. Brown
B. Harvard
C. Princeton
D. Stanford

194. Robert Donat won the Academy Award for Best Actor for his performance in what 1939 film?

A. *Dark Victory*
B. *Goodbye, Mr. Chips*
C. *Of Mice and Men*
D. *Wuthering Heights*

195. In what Hal Roach film does an exiled caveman find love?

A. *One Million B.C.* (1940)
B. *Sons of the Desert* (1933)
C. *Tit for Tat* (1935)
D. *Topper* (1937)

196. For what film did Fay Wray wear a blonde wig over her naturally dark hair?

A. *King Kong* (1933)
B. *The Most Dangerous Game* (1932)
C. *The Mystery of the Wax Museum* (1933)
D. *The Wedding March* (1928)

197. Who costarred with Leslie Howard in the 1937 film *Stand-In*?

A. Clark Gable
B. Humphrey Bogart
C. Robert Taylor
D. William Powell

198. How many Oscar nominations did *A Midsummer Night's Dream* (1935) receive?

A. 0
B. 1
C. 3
D. 4

answers found on page 543

Brother Rat, 1938

199. Ronald Reagan met his first wife while working on *Brother Rat* (1938). What was her name?

A. Geraldine Fitzgerald

B. Ann Sheridan

C. Jane Wyman

D. Nancy Davis

200. To whom did Janet Gaynor lose the Best Actress Academy Award in 1938?

A. Katharine Hepburn

B. Luise Rainer

C. Norma Shearer

D. Vivien Leigh

201. What was the last film to star both Shirley Temple and Bill Robinson?

A. *Curly Top* (1935)

B. *Just Around the Corner* (1938)

C. *Little Miss Broadway* (1938)

D. *Poor Little Rich Girl* (1936)

202. The 1937 Samuel Goldwyn film *The Hurricane* was directed by whom?

A. Fred Zinnemann

B. John Ford

C. Mervyn LeRoy

D. William Wyler

203. In what film does Fay Wray survive being shipwrecked on an island only to be hunted like prey by a madman?

A. *King Kong* (1933)

B. *The Most Dangerous Game* (1932)

C. *The Mystery of the Wax Museum* (1933)

D. *The Wedding March* (1928)

204. What film lead to the American Humane Association (AHA) overseeing the treatment of animals in filmmaking?

A. *Gone With the Wind* (1939)

B. *Gunga Din* (1939)

C. *Jesse James* (1939)

D. *Stagecoach* (1939)

205. Charles Laughton stars in the title role opposite Merle Oberon in what unfinished film?

A. *Farewell Again* (1937)

B. *I, Claudius* (1937)

C. *The Whispering Shadow* (1933)

D. *Viennese Nights* (1930)

206. Besides England, where was director Tod Browning's film *Freaks* (1932) originally banned?

A. Australia

B. Germany

C. Mexico

D. Russia

207. Flora Robson portrays Queen Elizabeth I of England in what film opposite Errol Flynn?

A. *Fire Over England* (1937)

B. *The Sea Hawk* (1940)

C. *The Whispering Shadow* (1933)

D. *Viennese Nights* (1930)

208. Which actress starred in the 1931 film *Scandal Sheet,* directed by John Cromwell?

A. Barbara Stanwyck

B. Fay Wray

C. Gene Tierney

D. Kay Francis

209. Who costarred with Nancy Carroll in the 1938 film *That Certain Age*?

    A. Deanna Durbin
    B. Jeanette MacDonald
    C. Judy Garland
    D. Kathryn Grayson

210. Fay Bainter's debut as a stock actress was in what film?

    A. *Quality Street* (1937)
    B. *The Arkansas Traveler* (1938)
    C. *The Jewess* (1897)
    D. *This Side of Heaven* (1934)

211. What film featured Zeppo Marx's last appearance in a Marx Brothers film?

    A. *A Day at the Races* (1937)
    B. *A Girl in Every Port* (1952)
    C. *At the Circus* (1939)
    D. *Duck Soup* (1933)

212. Who played Esmeralda to Charles Laughton's Quasimodo in the 1939 film *The Hunchback of Notre Dame*?

    A. Hedy Lamarr
    B. Jennifer Jones
    C. Maureen O'Hara
    D. Susan Hayward

213. Hal Roach sold the contracts of the "Our Gang" kids to which studio in 1938?

    A. 20th Century-Fox
    B. MGM
    C. United Artists
    D. Warner Bros.

214. To whom did Leslie Howard lose the Academy Award for Best Actor in 1939?

    A. Charles Boyer
    B. James Cagney
    C. Robert Donat
    D. Spencer Tracy

215. For what film did Joan Bennett first become a brunette?

    A. *Eleven Men and a Girl* (1930)
    B. *The Man in the Iron Mask* (1939)
    C. *The Son of Monte Cristo* (1940)
    D. *Trade Winds* (1938)

216. The 1930 film *Follow Thru*, starring Nancy Carroll, is set where?

    A. In a hospital
    B. On a cattle ranch
    C. On a golf course
    D. On an ocean liner

217. Valerie Hobson played Elizabeth Frankenstein in the 1935 sequel *Bride of Frankenstein*. What actress originated the role in the first *Frankenstein* (1931)?

    A. Elsa Lanchester
    B. Helen Chandler
    C. Mae Clark
    D. Zita Johann

218. What actor portrays King Louis XI in 1938's *If I Were King*?

    A. Basil Rathbone
    B. Gary Cooper
    C. Paul Lukas
    D. Ronald Colman

219. Following the release of *The Story of Alexander Graham Bell* (1939), the telephone was often referred to by what name?

    A. Ameche
    B. Bogart
    C. Davenport
    D. Graham

220. Which was Merle Oberon's first American film opposite Maurice Chevalier?

    A. *Folies Bergère de Paris* (1935)
    B. *The Battle* (1934)
    C. *The Private Life of Henry VIII* (1933)
    D. *Wuthering Heights* (1939)

answers found on page 543

221. In what Hal Roach film does a playboy on the run hook up with a sideshow's beautiful owner?
    A. *Merrily We Live* (1938)
    B. *Road Show* (1941)
    C. *Tit for Tat* (1935)
    D. *Topper* (1937)

222. The dog who played Terry in the 1934 Shirley Temple film *Bright Eyes* was in what other famous film?
    A. *Benji* (1974)
    B. *Lassie Come Home* (1943)
    C. *Old Yeller* (1957)
    D. *The Wizard of Oz* (1939)

223. Harry Davenport plays Dr. Meade in what Oscar-winning film directed by Victor Fleming?
    A. *Captains Courageous* (1937)
    B. *Gone With the Wind* (1939)
    C. *The Wizard of Oz* (1939)
    D. *Treasure Island* (1934)

224. Who starred in William Wyler's 1936 film *Dodsworth*?
    A. James Stewart
    B. Melvyn Douglas
    C. Robert Donat
    D. Walter Huston

Top Hat, 1935

225. Fred Astaire first met what lifelong friend on the set of *Top Hat* (1935)?
    A. Hermes Pan
    B. Douglas Fairbanks Jr.
    C. Dolores Del Rio
    D. Irving Berlin

226. Edward Arnold played villain to James Stewart's character in the 1939 film *Mr. Smith Goes to Washington* and which other Frank Capra film?
    A. *Mr. Deeds Goes to Town* (1936)
    B. *The Donovan Affair* (1929)
    C. *The Miracle Woman* (1931)
    D. *You Can't Take It with You* (1938)

227. Flora Robson portrays which character in the 1934 film *The Rise of Catherine the Great*?
    A. Countess Olga
    B. Countess Vorontzova
    C. Empress Elisabeth
    D. Princess Anhalt-Zerbst

228. Hermione Gingold made her film debut in what Anthony Asquith picture?
    A. *A Gentleman of Paris* (1931)
    B. *Dance Pretty Lady* (1932)
    C. *Farewell Again* (1937)
    D. *The Rise of Catherine the Great* (1934)

229. Red Skelton plays a social director at "Camp Carefree" in what comedy?
    A. *Escapade* (1935)
    B. *Fashions of 1934* (1934)
    C. *Having Wonderful Time* (1938)
    D. *Perfect Understanding* (1933)

230. Ned Sparks was featured in all of the following films opposite Bing Crosby except for which one?
    A. *Anything Goes* (1936)
    B. *Going Hollywood* (1933)
    C. *The Star Maker* (1939)
    D. *Too Much Harmony* (1933)

231. How many Oscars did the 1934 film *Imitation of Life* win?
    A. 0
    B. 1
    C. 3
    D. 4

Citizen Kane, 1941

Chapter 3
THE 1940s

For Hollywood, the forties consisted of two main periods, the war years and after. During World War II, the studios were at their best when providing audiences with a combination of inspiring war films and sheer escapism. Afterward, the film industry was forced to react creatively to attacks from a variety of sources: the encroachment of television, labor disputes, the House Un-American Activities Committee's investigations of alleged Communist infiltration, the Supreme Court decision ordering the studios to divest themselves of their theater chains, and the new popularity of films from overseas competing for a now dwindling market.

With a war raging overseas, film attendance soared to an all-time high. Between 1942 and 1946, more than sixty million people attended the movies each week. What they often saw was a slate of films created to support the war effort. Gone from big-budget pictures were trenchant views of American life like *The Little Foxes* and *Citizen Kane* (both 1941). In their place were stories of military valor and romance like *A Guy Named Joe* (1943), with downed flier Spencer Tracy helping Van Johnson win his wings and court Tracy's former love. The home front also figured on movie screens, with *Stage Door Canteen* (1943) bristling with the excitement of the New York social club for military men staffed by Broadway stars like Ray Bolger, Tallulah Bankhead, and the legendary Katharine Cornell (in her only film appearance). Even escapist entertainment reflected current events, with backstage musicals like *The Fleet's In* (1942) and *The Gang's All Here* (1943) all about putting on a show for GIs and sailors.

Likewise, Hollywood showed people what they were fighting for by extolling simple American virtues in home-front dramas like *The Human Comedy* (1943), with Mickey Rooney holding down the fort, and historical stories like *Meet Me in St. Louis* (1944), with Judy Garland exploring the joys to be found in her own backyard. Spirituality also played a major role in inspiring audiences. Bing Crosby and Barry Fitzgerald brought the faith to an impoverished inner-city parish in *Going My Way* (1944), while Jennifer Jones rose to stardom as a young girl touched by visions in *The Song of Bernadette* (1943).

But among these stories of heroes and high ideals, Hollywood also released many titles aimed at pure diversion. Patrons could forget about the headlines by losing themselves in the comic antics of Bob Hope and Bing Crosby as they took to the road with Dorothy Lamour, or by catching the latest musical acts like Gene Krupa, the Glenn Miller Orchestra, and Brazilian bombshell Carmen Miranda—all at the movies. For the more serious minded, Bette Davis rose to new heights with a series of star vehicles, including *Now, Voyager* (1942) and *Mr. Skeffington* (1944), about what it meant to be a "modern" woman.

With many of Hollywood's top leading men off fighting, new male stars like Alan Ladd, Van Johnson, and Gregory Peck rose to prominence. On the distaff side, June Allyson claimed a place as the quintessential girl next door while pinup beauties like Rita Hayworth, Paulette Goddard, and Betty Grable cornered the market on all-American sex appeal. And with former child stars like Judy Garland and Deanna Durbin graduating to adult roles, a new generation of adorable youngsters—including Elizabeth Taylor, Margaret O'Brien, Jane Powell, and Roddy McDowall—stepped into their Buster Brown shoes.

When peace arrived in 1945 it was welcomed throughout the nation, except at the box office. Eager to start new families, returning servicemen and their new wives stopped going to the movies so often, even before television became a serious competitor. The audience that remained was increasingly siphoned off by an influx of foreign films. Some, like French clown Jacques Tati's *Jour de Fête* (1949) and Michael Powell's ballet film *The Red Shoes* (1948), were direct competitors with Hollywood escapism. Others, particularly such Italian neorealist classics as *Open City* (1945) and *Shoe-Shine* (1946), had a grittiness lacking in most Hollywood product. Rather than turning off war-weary audiences, these films offered a vision of life as they had come to see it during the decade's first half.

In response, Hollywood created a new realism of its own. Lewis Milestone and William A. Wellman did surprisingly well at the box office with their grunt's-eye view of military action in *A Walk in the Sun* (1945) and *Battleground* (1949), respectively. William Wyler tackled the plight of returning veterans in *The Best Years of Our Lives* (1946). And the new noir films like Jules Dassin's *The Naked City* (1948) took a more cynical view of the institutions of modern life—though these pictures hardly put an end to escapism. There was still a market for Esther Williams's aquatic musicals and the hillbilly antics of Ma and Pa Kettle. But by decade's end, Hollywood was changing in a big way.

1. In *Can't Help Singing* (1944), who played Deanna Durbin's senator father?
   A. Akim Tamiroff
   B. David Bruce
   C. Ray Collins
   D. Robert Paige

2. Billy Wilder met his future spouse Audrey Young on the set of what film?
   A. *A Foreign Affair* (1948)
   B. *Sabrina* (1954)
   C. *The Emperor Waltz* (1948)
   D. *The Lost Weekend* (1945)

3. The 1940 Kay Francis film *Little Men* was based on a novel by what author?
   A. Edith Wharton
   B. Edna Ferber
   C. Jane Austen
   D. Louisa May Alcott

4. In 1942, I left Hollywood and married a ski instructor almost twenty years my junior. Who am I?
   A. Barbara Stanwyck
   B. Clara Bow
   C. Elizabeth Taylor
   D. Norma Shearer

5. The 1948 Roddy McDowall film *Kidnapped* was based on the novel by what famous author?
   A. Ernest Hemingway
   B. Jack London
   C. John Steinbeck
   D. Robert Louis Stevenson

6. Shirley Temple received her first on-screen kiss in what film?
   A. *Kiss and Tell* (1945)
   B. *Miss Annie Rooney* (1942)
   C. *The Little Princess* (1939)
   D. *Young People* (1940)

7. The 1949 film *All the King's Men* won Academy Awards in all of the following categories except which one?
   A. Best Actor
   B. Best Picture
   C. Best Supporting Actor
   D. Best Supporting Actress

8. Cornel Wilde was nominated for an Academy Award as Best Actor in the 1945 film *A Song to Remember* for his portrayal of what famous composer?
   A. Beethoven
   B. Chopin
   C. Handel
   D. Rachmaninoff

9. Marjorie Main portrayed what character in films such as 1947's *The Egg and I* and 1956's *The Kettles in the Ozarks*?
   A. Birdie Hicks
   B. Ma Kettle
   C. Miss Bedelia
   D. Nancy Kettle

10. Jennifer Jones plays the title role in what film directed by Vincente Minnelli?
    A. *Alice Adams* (1935)
    B. *Jane Eyre* (1944)
    C. *Madame Bovary* (1949)
    D. *Woman of the Year* (1942)

11. Leslie Brooks and Nina Foch costar in what mystery?
    A. *A Piece of Cake* (1948)
    B. *Love in Pawn* (1953)
    C. *Nine Girls* (1944)
    D. *Room to Let* (1950)

12. Ronald Reagan wakes up with both his legs amputated in what film?

    A. *Dark Victory* (1939)
    B. *Kings Row* (1942)
    C. *Knute Rockne, All-American* (1940)
    D. *Santa Fe Trail* (1940)

13. In 1944, Ricardo Montalban married Georgiana, the half sister of which Oscar-winning actress?

    A. Claudette Colbert
    B. Joan Fontaine
    C. Katharine Hepburn
    D. Loretta Young

14. In which of the following categories did the 1943 film *Princess O'Rourke* receive its only Academy Award nomination?

    A. Best Director
    B. Best Original Screenplay
    C. Best Picture
    D. Best Supporting Actor

15. In the 1941 film *Tom, Dick and Harry,* what was the name of Burgess Meredith's character?

    A. Butch
    B. Dick
    C. Harry
    D. Tom

16. In the 1947 film *Possessed,* what actress plays a woman obsessed with Van Heflin's character?

    A. Jean Simmons
    B. Joan Crawford
    C. Joan Fontaine
    D. Paulette Goddard

17. In the 1941 film *Ball of Fire*, what actress does Gene Krupa accompany on the song "Drum Boogie"?

    A. Barbara Stanwyck
    B. Joan Crawford
    C. Lauren Bacall
    D. Rita Hayworth

18. Ethel Waters, Ethel Barrymore, and Jeanne Craine all received Academy Award nominations for what film?

    A. *Broadway Melody of 1940* (1940)
    B. *Miss Grant Takes Richmond* (1949)
    C. *Pinky* (1949)
    D. *The Barkleys of Broadway* (1949)

19. In what film did Jean Simmons first share the screen with her future husband, Stewart Granger?

    A. *Caesar and Cleopatra* (1946)
    B. *Foot Steps in the Fog* (1955)
    C. *The Way to the Stars* (1945)
    D. *Young Bess* (1953)

20. Alexander Korda's 1945 film *Perfect Strangers* won an Academy Award in what category?

    A. Best Actress
    B. Best Cinematography
    C. Best Director
    D. Best Writing, Original Story

21. Ralph Bellamy plays a Midwestern rancher, opposite Humphrey Bogart, in what film?

    A. *Brother Orchid* (1940)
    B. *Crossroads* (1942)
    C. *No Time for Comedy* (1940)
    D. *The Conspirators* (1944)

22. In 1942, James Agee became the film critic for which publication?

    A. *Newsweek*
    B. *The New York Times*
    C. *Time*
    D. *Vanity Fair*

23. Leslie Howard starred in the 1932 film *Smilin' Through*. Who played his role in the 1941 remake?

    A. Brian Aherne
    B. Donald Crisp
    C. Fredric March
    D. Robert Montgomery

answers found on page 544

The Strawberry Blonde, 1941

24. Jack Carson and Olivia de Havilland share the screen in 1941's *The Strawberry Blonde* and what other film?

A. *Fighting Caravans* (1931)
B. *Let's Live a Little* (1948)
C. *Princess O'Rourke* (1943)
D. *The Wedding Night* (1935)

25. Raymond Massey and Peter Lorre costar in 1944's *Arsenic and Old Lace* and what other film?

A. *Hotel Berlin* (1945)
B. *Streets of Laredo* (1949)
C. *The Barretts of Wimpole Street* (1957)
D. *The Dark Past* (1948)

26. In 1949, James Wong Howe shot test footage for which actress's proposed comeback film, entitled *La Duchesse de Langeais*?

A. Clara Bow
B. Greta Garbo
C. Louise Brooks
D. Pola Negri

27. Ethel Barrymore's 1947 film *The Farmer's Daughter* features an Academy Award–winning performance by which actress?

A. Grace Kelly
B. Katharine Hepburn
C. Loretta Young
D. Rosalind Russell

28. Peter Lawford appeared with Frank Sinatra for the first time in what film?

A. *It Happened in Brooklyn* (1947)
B. *Little Women* (1949)
C. *Mrs. Miniver* (1942)
D. *The Picture of Dorian Gray* (1945)

29. Anthony Quinn starred opposite Bob Hope, Bing Crosby, and Dorothy Lamour in the 1944 film *Road to Morocco* and what other "road" movie?

A. *Road to Hollywood* (1947)
B. *Road to Rio* (1947)
C. *Road to Singapore* (1940)
D. *Road to Utopia* (1946)

30. Harry Davenport played the title role in what film directed by Gus Meins?

A. *A Guy Named Joe* (1943)
B. *Grandpa Goes to Town* (1940)
C. *Skylark* (1941)
D. *Test Pilot* (1938)

31. For what film did composer Miklos Rozsa receive his first Oscar win?

A. *A Double Life* (1947)
B. *Ben-Hur* (1959)
C. *Spellbound* (1945)
D. *The Thief of Bagdad* (1940)

32. In 1945, film director Anthony Asquith cofounded what organization with Terence Rattigan and Anatole de Grunwald?

A. International Screenplays
B. Motion Picture Association
C. Olympia Film Society
D. The Avalon Table

Spotlight on BARBARA **STANWYCK** (1907–1990)

Barbara Stanwyck lost her mother at age two and was orphaned at four when her father abandoned his children to go off to sea. She went on the stage, first as a dancer and then as an actress, to support herself and her siblings. Marriage at twenty to vaudeville star Frank Fay brought Stanwyck to a Hollywood that was slow to warm up to her. The turning point came after a screen test was brought to the attention of director Frank Capra. His *Ladies of Leisure* (1930) revealed to the world a new star, an actress who, as Capra himself said, "doesn't act a scene—she lives it." Stanwyck's star rose even higher when she played the ultimate in self-sacrificing motherhood, the title character in *Stella Dallas* (1937). Next she proved herself adept at comedy in a pair of 1941 films, director Preston Sturges's *The Lady Eve* and director Howard Hawks's *Ball of Fire*. On a dare from writer-director Billy Wilder, she created one of the most memorable femmes fatales, the seductive murderess in *Double Indemnity* (1944). Adding to her display of versatility, she rounded out her career with several successful film and television westerns.

East Side, West Side, 1949

Stella Dallas, 1937

1. According to legend, Barbara Stanwyck modeled her walk after what animal?

   A. Cheetah
   B. Panther
   C. Snake
   D. Swan

2. Real-life couple Robert Taylor and Barbara Stanwyck share the screen in all of the following films except for which one?

   A. *His Brother's Wife* (1936)
   B. *Magnificent Obsession* (1935)
   C. *The Night Walker* (1964)
   D. *This Is My Affair* (1937)

3. What is Barbara Stanwyck's second film with Gary Cooper?

   A. *Ball of Fire* (1941)
   B. *Love in the Afternoon* (1957)

   C. *Night Nurse* (1931)
   D. *The Lady Eve* (1941)

4. In what film directed by John Cromwell does Barbara Stanwyck star?

   A. *Algiers* (1938)
   B. *Banjo on My Knee* (1936)
   C. *Made for Each Other* (1939)
   D. *The Prisoner of Zenda* (1937)

5. Barbara Stanwyck plays a single mother whose vulgarity stands in the way of her daughter's acceptance into high society in what tearjerker?

   A. *Ball of Fire* (1941)
   B. *Double Indemnity* (1944)
   C. *Stella Dallas* (1937)
   D. *The Lady Eve* (1941)

33. The 1941 Gene Krupa film *Ball of Fire* received Academy Award nominations in all of the following categories except what?

A. Best Actress
B. Best Art Direction
C. Best Original Score
D. Best Original Screenplay

34. The 1949 Doris Day film *My Dream Is Yours* features a delightful segment with what famous cartoon character?

A. Bugs Bunny
B. Donald Duck
C. Mickey Mouse
D. Popeye

35. The 1945 film *Rhapsody in Blue* was nominated for two Academy Awards. One was for Best Original Score. What was the other for?

A. Best Art Direction
B. Best Original Song
C. Best Screenplay
D. Best Sound

36. The 1947 film *The Macomber Affair,* directed by Zoltan Korda, was based on a story by what author?

A. E. L. Doctorow
B. Ernest Hemingway
C. F. Scott Fitzgerald
D. John Steinbeck

37. In *The Red Danube* (1949), Ethel Barrymore plays a what?

A. Art gallery owner
B. Headmistress
C. Hotel manager
D. Mother superior

38. The 1947 Rosalind Russell film *Mourning Becomes Electra* was based on the play by what writer?

A. Arthur Miller
B. Eugene O'Neill

C. Garson Kanin
D. Noël Coward

39. Jules Dassin's 1948 film *The Naked City* won two Academy Awards. One was for Best Cinematography. What was the other for?

A. Best Costume Design
B. Best Editing
C. Best Original Screenplay
D. Best Supporting Actress

40. In 1940, Edward Arnold published his autobiography under what title?

A. *Arnold Goes to Hollywood*
B. *Edward Goes to Hollywood*
C. *Headed for the Hills*
D. *Lorenzo Goes to Hollywood*

41. In the 1949 film *Make Believe Ballroom*, Gene Krupa appeared as himself along with all the following musicians except whom?

A. Frank Sinatra
B. Frankie Laine
C. Jimmy Dorsey
D. Nat "King" Cole

42. The 1940 Rex Harrison film *Night Train to Munich* received its only Academy Award nomination in what category?

A. Best Cinematography
B. Best Editing
C. Best Original Score
D. Best Original Screenplay

43. Benny Goodman appeared in the 1944 film *Sweet and Low-Down*, which was nominated for an Academy Award for Best Original Song. What was the name of the song?

A. "Believe in Love"
B. "I Believe in Miracles"
C. "I'm Making Believe"
D. "We Could Make Believe"

answers found on page 544

44. In what film did Paulette Goddard sing "A Sweater, a Sarong, and a Peekaboo Bang"?

A. *An Ideal Husband* (1947)
B. *Kitty* (1945)
C. *On Our Merry Way* (1948)
D. *Star Spangled Rhythm* (1943)

45. The 1943 Benny Goodman film *Stage Door Canteen* received an Academy Award nomination for Best Original Song. What was the name of the song?

A. "Don't Worry Island"
B. "Rumba Rumba"
C. "The Girl I Love to Leave Behind"
D. "We Mustn't Say Goodbye"

The Hucksters, 1947

46. British star Deborah Kerr made her Hollywood debut in the 1947 film *The Hucksters* opposite what leading man?

A. Robert Mitchum
B. Clark Gable
C. Charles Boyer
D. William Powell

47. The 1940 George Sanders film *The House of the Seven Gables* was based on a novel by what author?

A. Charles Dickens
B. Ernest Hemingway
C. Nathaniel Hawthorne
D. Willa Cather

48. In what film do Basil Rathbone and Nigel Bruce share the screen as characters other than Sherlock Holmes and Dr. Watson?

A. *Frenchman's Creek* (1944)
B. *I Wanted Wings* (1941)
C. *Practically Yours* (1944)
D. *To Each His Own* (1946)

49. Dalton Trumbo wrote the screenplay for what film directed by Victor Fleming?

A. *A Guy Named Joe* (1943)
B. *My Brother Talks to Horses* (1947)
C. *My Darling Clementine* (1946)
D. *The Search* (1948)

50. Natalie Wood made her official Hollywood debut opposite Orson Welles and Claudette Colbert in what film?

A. *I Married an Angel* (1942)
B. *The Man from Laramie* (1955)
C. *The Stranger* (1946)
D. *Tomorrow Is Forever* (1946)

51. Jennifer Jones won an Academy Award as Best Actress in which film?

A. *Since You Went Away* (1944)
B. *Tender Is the Night* (1962)
C. *The Idol* (1966)
D. *The Song of Bernadette* (1943)

52. Joseph Cotten was best man to Orson Welles at his 1943 wedding to what actress?

A. Ava Gardner
B. Jane Wyman
C. Rita Hayworth
D. Virginia Mayo

53. The 1949 Mark Robson film *Champion* won an Academy Award in what category?

A. Best Actor
B. Best Editing
C. Best Screenplay
D. Best Sound

answers found on page 544

54. Who directed the 1943 film *Shadow of a Doubt*?

A. Alfred Hitchcock
B. Orson Welles
C. Preston Sturges
D. William Wyler

55. In the 1949 Jacques Tati film *The Big Day*, the mail is delivered to a small rural village via what?

A. Bicycle
B. Cow
C. Horse
D. Roller skates

56. In 1943, James Donald appeared in what Noël Coward play opposite the playwright himself?

A. *House of Flowers*
B. *Present Laughter*
C. *The Honeys*
D. *Wonderful Town*

57. John Ireland made his film debut in what feature?

A. *A Walk in the Sun* (1945)
B. *My Darling Clementine* (1946)
C. *Somewhere in the Night* (1946)
D. *Wake Up and Dream* (1946)

58. Farley Granger was featured opposite David Niven and Teresa Wright in what film?

A. *A Piece of Cake* (1948)
B. *Enchantment* (1948)
C. *Love in Pawn* (1953)
D. *Room to Let* (1950)

59. In 1940, Carmen Miranda shared the screen with Betty Grable in which 20th Century-Fox production?

A. *Copacabana*
B. *Doll Face*
C. *Down Argentine Way*
D. *Love Detectives*

60. In the 1943 film *This Land Is Mine*, Charles Laughton plays a what?

A. Farmer
B. Football player
C. Lawyer
D. Teacher

61. Paul Lukas played Hedy Lamarr's dangerous husband in what film?

A. *Dodsworth* (1936)
B. *Experiment Perilous* (1944)
C. *The Lady Vanishes* (1938)
D. *Watch on the Rhine* (1943)

62. The 1948 film *The Naked City* won an Academy Award in which of the following categories?

A. Best Director
B. Best Editing
C. Best Original Score
D. Best Sound

63. In what Lewis Milestone film does Gary Cooper play a drifter accused of horse stealing?

A. *Of Mice and Men* (1940)
B. *Red Pony* (1949)
C. *Lucky Partners* (1940)
D. *Two Arabian Knights* (1927)

64. In 1948, Montgomery Clift signed a contract with Paramount that stipulated that he would only act in films directed by Billy Wilder, George Stevens, or what other filmmaker?

A. Elia Kazan
B. Nicholas Ray
C. Norman Krasna
D. Richard Brooks

65. Irving Berlin won an Academy Award for which song that he wrote for the 1942 film *Holiday Inn*?

A. "Change Partners and Dance with Me"
B. "Count Your Blessings Instead of Sheep"
C. "I Poured My Heart into a Song"
D. "White Christmas"

answers found on page 544

66. Cinematographer Freddie Young shot the 1949 film *Conspirator*. What actress starred in it?

A. Ava Gardner
B. Elizabeth Taylor
C. Grace Kelly
D. Ingrid Bergman

67. In which of the following categories was Ethel Barrymore's 1944 film *None but the Lonely Heart* not nominated for an Academy Award?

A. Best Actor
B. Best Director
C. Best Editing
D. Best Original Score

68. In the 1949 film *Whirlpool*, José Ferrer plays a what?

A. Escape artist
B. Hypnotist
C. Sculptor
D. Undertaker

Sister Kenny, 1946

69. In *Sister Kenny* (1946), Rosalind Russell plays a nurse fighting for acceptance of her polio treatment methods. In what country does the film take place?

A. The United States
B. Canada
C. England
D. Australia

70. Peter Lorre costars with which of the following actors in the 1941 film *All Through the Night*?

A. Clark Gable
B. Humphrey Bogart
C. James Cagney
D. John Garfield

71. Stewart Granger starred in the 1946 biopic *The Magic Bow* based on the life of which violinist-composer?

A. Anton Stamitz
B. Antonio Vivaldi
C. Leopold Mozart
D. Niccolo Paganini

72. Jane Wyman was nominated for an Academy Award as Best Actress for her performance in what 1946 film?

A. *Brief Encounter*
B. *Duel in the Sun*
C. *The Yearling*
D. *To Each His Own*

73. Janet Blair costarred with Rosalind Russell in which of the following films?

A. *Auntie Mame* (1958)
B. *My Sister Eileen* (1942)
C. *Sister Kenny* (1946)
D. *The Trouble with Angels* (1966)

74. The 1942 film *The Talk of the Town*, starring Cary Grant, was nominated for seven Academy Awards. How many did it win?

A. 0
B. 1
C. 2
D. 3

75. Harry Davenport played Dr. Ashlon in what film?

A. *Adventure* (1945)
B. *Jane Eyre* (1944)
C. *Skylark* (1941)
D. *The Farmer Takes a Wife* (1935)

answers found on page 544

76. In the 1949 film *Make Believe Ballroom*, Gene Krupa plays drums on a rendition of what song?

A. "Don't Get Around Much Anymore"
B. "It Had to Be You"
C. "Joshua Fit the Battle of Jericho"
D. "The Battle Hymn of the Republic"

77. In which film did Marjorie Main portray a lady blacksmith opposite Wallace Beery?

A. *Honky Tonk* (1941)
B. *It's a Big Country* (1951)
C. *The Shepherd of the Hills* (1941)
D. *Wyoming* (1940)

78. The 1945 Edward G. Robinson film *Our Vines Have Tender Grapes* tells the story of a rural family living in what state?

A. Indiana
B. Oklahoma
C. Tennessee
D. Wisconsin

79. John Ford was replaced by what director on the 1949 Ethel Barrymore film *Pinky*?

A. Elia Kazan
B. Frank Capra
C. John Huston
D. Vincente Minnelli

80. Natalie Wood rescues a lost collie in what film?

A. *Driftwood* (1947)
B. *Magic Town* (1947)
C. *Pot O' Gold* (1941)
D. *The Shop Around the Corner* (1940)

81. All of the following actors except which one costarred in Henry Hathaway's 1947 film *Kiss of Death*?

A. James Cagney
B. Karl Malden
C. Richard Widmark
D. Victor Mature

82. In which film did Paulette Goddard costar with Charles Boyer and Olivia de Havilland?

A. *Hold Back the Dawn* (1941)
B. *Reap the Wild Wind* (1942)
C. *Second Chorus* (1940)
D. *The Great Dictator* (1940)

83. How many Spanish-language films did Ricardo Montalban make in Mexico prior to his Hollywood debut in 1947's *Fiesta*?

A. 13
B. 26
C. 35
D. 9

84. In the 1940s, Merle Oberon appeared in how many films?

A. 10
B. 12
C. 15
D. 5

85. In what 1942 film did Carmen Miranda reteam with Betty Grable and Cesar Romero, both of whom she had worked with before?

A. *Moon Over Miami*
B. *Orchestra Wives*
C. *Song of the Islands*
D. *Springtime in the Rockies*

86. Hedy Lamarr played the starring role of Princess Veronica in which film directed by Richard Thorpe?

A. *Her Highness and the Bellboy* (1945)
B. *My Favorite Spy* (1951)
C. *The Strange Woman* (1946)
D. *The Student Prince* (1954)

87. The 1945 film *San Antonio* received an Academy Award nomination for Best Original Song. What was the name of the song?

A. "Lovers' Lament"
B. "Make Me Rich"
C. "Ride the Range"
D. "Some Sunday Morning"

88. Flora Robson portrays Queen Elizabeth I in the 1940 film *The Sea Hawk* and what other film?

A. *Fire Over England* (1937)
B. *It's Always Fair Weather* (1955)
C. *The Private Lives of Elizabeth and Essex* (1939)
D. *Two Thousand Women* (1944)

89. Deanna Durbin's third and final husband directed which of her films?

A. *Lady on a Train* (1945)
B. *Nice Girl?* (1941)
C. *Something in the Wind* (1947)
D. *Up in Central Park* (1948)

90. James Mason moves into a haunted mansion in which film?

A. *A Place of One's Own* (1945)
B. *Candlelight in Algeria* (1944)
C. *Hatter's Castle* (1942)
D. *They Met in the Dark* (1943)

91. *A Song to Remember* (1945), starring Merle Oberon, is a biopic about what famous pianist?

A. Eric Schneider
B. Frederic Chopin
C. Graziella Concas
D. Jonathan Biss

92. The 1949 film *No Sad Songs for Me* was nominated for an Academy Award in what category?

A. Best Cinematography
B. Best Editing
C. Best Musical Score
D. Best Supporting Actor

Abe Lincoln in Illinois, 1940

93. John Cromwell directed the 1940 film *Abe Lincoln in Illinois.* Who played the title character?

A. Fredric March
B. Gary Cooper
C. Henry Fonda
D. Raymond Massey

94. In the 1940 film *Dr. Erlich's Magic Bullet,* who plays Edward G. Robinson's wife?

A. Ann Sothern
B. Bette Davis
C. Kay Francis
D. Ruth Gordon

95. Flora Robson was featured in what epic starring Claude Rains and Vivien Leigh?

A. *Caesar and Cleopatra* (1945)
B. *King's Rhapsody* (1955)
C. *Penny Serenade* (1941)
D. *The Sea Hawk* (1940)

96. At eight years old, Natalie Wood costarred opposite Maureen O'Hara in what film?

A. *Bell, Book and Candle* (1958)
B. *Magic Town* (1947)
C. *Miracle on 34th Street* (1947)
D. *On Our Merry Way* (1948)

97. In 1940, Ricardo Montalban appeared in which stage production starring Tallulah Bankhead?

A. *Her Cardboard Lover*
B. *The Cocktail Party*
C. *The Dancers*
D. *The Potting Shed*

98. In 1949, Paulette Goddard and John Steinbeck formed what production company?

A. Actors Studio
B. Goddard Pictures
C. Monterey Pictures
D. United Artists

99. Elizabeth Taylor's first on-screen kiss was in what film?

A. *All the Brothers Were Valiant* (1953)
B. *Conspirator* (1949)
C. *Quo Vadis* (1951)
D. *Undercurrent* (1946)

100. James Cagney won the Academy Award for Best Actor for his portrayal of what famous person in the 1942 film *Yankee Doodle Dandy*?

A. Benjamin Franklin
B. Cole Porter
C. George M. Cohan
D. George Washington

101. Charles Coburn's character in what film was a caricature of playwright George Bernard Shaw?

A. *My Kingdom for a Cook* (1943)
B. *The Sea Hawk* (1940)
C. *The Star* (1952)
D. *Words and Music* (1948)

102. All of the following actors except which one starred in Zoltan Korda's 1948 film *A Woman's Vengeance*?

A. Ann Blyth
B. Charles Boyer
C. Jessica Tandy
D. Laurence Harvey

103. In 1948 Rex Harrison was involved in a scandal over the suicide of which actress?

A. Carole Landis
B. Dorothy Dandridge
C. Marilyn Monroe
D. Pier Angeli

104. In the 1941 film *Never Give a Sucker an Even Break*, W. C. Fields's character attempts to pitch a film story to what fictional studio?

A. Colossal Pictures
B. Esoteric Studios
C. Imagine That Studios
D. Monumental Pictures

105. Alan Ladd appears in what Orson Welles film?

A. *Citizen Kane* (1941)
B. *Moby Dick* (1956)
C. *Othello* (1952)
D. *The Third Man* (1949)

106. After *Jimmy the Gent* (1934), what was the only other movie in which Bette Davis worked with James Cagney?

A. *Juarez* (1939)
B. *Love Me or Leave Me* (1955)
C. *Shining Victory* (1941)
D. *The Bride Came C.O.D.* (1941)

107. Zoltan Korda's 1943 film *Sahara* was nominated for three Academy Awards. How many did it win?

A. 0
B. 1
C. 2
D. 3

108. Jack Carson was featured in what biopic about Broadway legends Nora Bayes and Jack Norworth?

A. *Let's Live a Little* (1948)
B. *Shine on Harvest Moon* (1944)
C. *The Great Caruso* (1951)
D. *The Student Prince* (1954)

answers found on page 544

109. Franz Waxman composed the musical score for *Nora Prentiss* in 1947. What actress played the title role?

A. Ann Sheridan

B. Ann Sothern

C. Jean Arthur

D. Patricia Neal

110. In what Lewis Milestone film does Barbara Stanwyck play an heiress trying to win back a lost lover years after a murder drove them apart?

A. *A Walk in the Sun* (1946)

B. *Of Mice and Men* (1940)

C. *The Strange Love of Martha Ivers* (1946)

D. *Two Arabian Knights* (1927)

111. Dalton Trumbo received his first Academy Award nomination for adapting the screenplay of what film starring Ginger Rogers?

A. *Kitty Foyle: The Natural History of a Woman* (1940)

B. *My Darling Clementine* (1946)

C. *Teresa* (1951)

D. *The Lady or the Tiger?* (1942)

112. The 1941 film *Dr. Jekyll and Mr. Hyde* was nominated for Academy Awards in all of the following categories except which one?

A. Best Cinematography

B. Best Editing

C. Best Musical Score

D. Best Supporting Actress

113. After playing Dracula in director Tod Browning's *Dracula* (1931), in what film did Bela Lugosi reprise the role?

A. *Bud Abbott and Lou Costello Meet Frankenstein* (1948)

B. *Dracula* (1958)

C. *House of Dracula* (1945)

D. *Son of Dracula* (1943)

114. In what film does Sir John Mills play the role of Pip?

A. *Cottage to Let* (1941)

B. *Great Expectations* (1946)

C. *In Which We Serve* (1942)

D. *O.H.M.S.* (1937)

Deception, 1946

115. In the 1946 film *Deception*, what instrument does Paul Henreid's character play?

A. Cello

B. Piano

C. Trumpet

D. Violin

116. In the 1949 film *John Loves Mary*, Ronald Reagan played John. Who played Mary?

A. Carole Lombard

B. Jane Wyman

C. Patricia Neal

D. Virginia Mayo

117. Rosalind Russell pretends to be married to a loser to win back her ex-husband, Robert Cummings, in what film?

A. *His Girl Friday* (1940)

B. *My Sister Eileen* (1942)

C. *Sister Kenny* (1946)

D. *Tell It to the Judge* (1949)

118. The 1941 Samuel Goldwyn production of *The Little Foxes* was based on a play by what author?

A. Carson McCullers
B. Eugene O'Neill
C. Lillian Hellman
D. Noel Coward

119. The 1949 Pedro Armendáriz film *Tulsa* was nominated for an Academy Award in what category?

A. Best Actress
B. Best Editing
C. Best Sound
D. Best Special Effects

120. On February 21, 1949, Louis Armstrong appeared on the cover of what magazine?

A. *Life*
B. *Newsweek*
C. *Time*
D. *Vanity Fair*

121. In what year did Hal Roach Studios become the first studio to switch to an all-color production schedule?

A. 1938
B. 1942
C. 1947
D. 1950

122. In what category did the 1947 film *The Bachelor and the Bobby-Soxer* win its only Academy Award?

A. Best Actress
B. Best Editing
C. Best Original Screenplay
D. Best Original Song

123. Bronislau Kaper composed the musical score of what film starring Ingrid Bergman and Charles Boyer?

A. *Gaslight* (1944)
B. *Jane Eyre* (1944)
C. *The Lady from Shanghai* (1947)
D. *Tomorrow Is Forever* (1946)

124. Jean Simmons was nominated for an Academy Award as Best Supporting Actress for her performance in what film?

A. *Footsteps in the Fog* (1955)
B. *Hamlet* (1948)
C. *Passage to Marseille* (1944)
D. *The Robe* (1953)

125. Mae West plays Flower Bell Lee in what 1940 film?

A. *Every Day's a Holiday*
B. *I'm No Angel*
C. *My Little Chickadee*
D. *She Done Him Wrong*

126. Roddy McDowall became lifelong friends with Peggy Ann Garner while making what film?

A. *Bye Bye Birdie* (1963)
B. *How Green Was My Valley* (1941)
C. *Macbeth* (1948)
D. *The Pied Piper* (1942)

127. In what city does the 1949 Anna May Wong film *Impact* take place?

A. London
B. Los Angeles
C. New York
D. San Francisco

128. Patricia Neal signed a seven-year contract with which studio in 1947?

A. MGM
B. United Artists
C. Universal
D. Warner Bros.

answers found on page 544

129. The 1948 Ethel Barrymore film *Moonrise* received only one Academy Award nomination. What was it for?

A. Best Actor
B. Best Editing
C. Best Original Song
D. Best Sound

130. In the 1943 Roddy McDowall film *My Friend Flicka*, what kind of animal is Flicka?

A. Dog
B. Duck
C. Horse
D. Mouse

131. The 1943 Benny Goodman film *The Gang's All Here* received its only Academy Award nomination in what category?

A. Best Art Direction
B. Best Editing
C. Best Picture
D. Best Sound

132. How many times in the 1940s did a film win exactly six Oscars?

A. 0
B. 1
C. 2
D. 3

133. Ronald Reagan acquired his nickname "The Gipper" from his role in what film?

A. *Dark Victory* (1939)
B. *Kings Row* (1942)
C. *Knute Rockne, All-American* (1940)
D. *Santa Fe Trail* (1940)

134. Melvyn Douglas plays a musician-composer in what film costarring Charles Coburn?

A. *Dancing in the Dark* (1949)
B. *Our Wife* (1941)
C. *Uncertain Glory* (1944)
D. *Words and Music* (1948)

135. In what film does Teresa Wright play Lark Ingoldsby?

A. *Enchantment* (1948)
B. *Mrs. Miniver* (1942)
C. *The Imperfect Lady* (1947)
D. *The Trouble with Women* (1947)

136. In the 1942 film *Son of Fury: The Story of Benjamin Blake*, Roddy McDowall plays a younger version of the character played by what actor?

A. Cary Grant
B. Tyrone Power
C. Vincent Price
D. William Powell

137. Cinematographer Freddie Young shot the 1948 film *Escape*. Who starred in it?

A. John Mills
B. Rex Harrison
C. Stewart Granger
D. Trevor Howard

Citizen Kane, 1941

138. The 1941 film *Citizen Kane* was nominated for Academy Awards in all of the following categories except which one?

A. Best Director
B. Best Musical Score
C. Best Picture
D. Best Supporting Actor

answers found on pages 544-545

Spotlight on
SPENCER **TRACY** (1900–1967)

Spencer Tracy was one of the screen's great independents. As a child, he struck out on his own several times, running away from home at seven, joining the navy at seventeen, and quitting college to become an actor after starring in a few school productions. He didn't think he had a future in movies until director John Ford spotted him playing a death row prisoner in *The Last Mile* and insisted Fox cast him in his own prison film, *Up the River* (1930). Tracy was so unhappy with most of his films there, however, that he grew increasingly rebellious, until the studio fired him. MGM production head Irving G. Thalberg came to the rescue, and when Tracy almost stole *San Francisco* (1936) from stars Clark Gable and Jeanette MacDonald, the studio started developing vehicles for him. With his performance as Father Flanagan in *Boys Town* (1938), he became a star in his own right. Tracy found his perfect screen partner when Katharine Hepburn requested he be cast as her leading man in *Woman of the Year* (1942). Through nine films together, his craggy stubbornness was the perfect foil for her fussiness as they matched wits in a series of sophisticated battles of the sexes.

Boys Town, 1938

Woman of the Year, 1942

1. **Spencer Tracy and Hedy Lamarr play husband and wife in what film?**
   A. *I Take This Woman* (1940)
   B. *Let's Live a Little* (1948)
   C. *My Favorite Spy* (1951)
   D. *The Strange Woman* (1946)

2. **For what film did Spencer Tracy win his first Academy Award as Best Actor?**
   A. *Bad Day at Black Rock* (1955)
   B. *Captains Courageous* (1937)
   C. *Father of the Bride* (1950)
   D. *Guess Who's Coming to Dinner* (1967)

3. **Spencer Tracy plays the title role in what biopic costarring Charles Coburn?**
   A. *Edison, the Man* (1940)
   B. *The Sea Hawk* (1940)
   C. *Young Tom Edison* (1940)
   D. *Young Winston* (1972)

4. **Which one of the following actresses costars with Spencer Tracy in the 1933 film *Man's Castle*?**
   A. Jean Harlow
   B. Jean Simmons
   C. Katharine Hepburn
   D. Loretta Young

answers found on page 545

139. The 1941 Kay Francis film *The Man Who Lost Himself* features what actor in a dual role?

A. Brian Aherne
B. David Niven
C. Gary Merrill
D. Ronald Colman

140. In the 1942 film *The Lady Is Willing*, Fred MacMurray costars with which of the following actresses?

A. Greta Garbo
B. Marlene Dietrich
C. Rita Hayworth
D. Susan Hayward

141. At the age of twenty-seven, what was Deanna Durbin's final film?

A. *In the Good Old Summertime* (1949)
B. *Something in the Wind* (1947)
C. *For the Love of Mary* (1948)
D. *Words and Music* (1948)

142. In the 1949 Jacques Tati film *The Big Day,* a postal worker becomes distracted from his duties when a what comes to town?

A. Motorcycle
B. Movie star
C. Movie theater
D. Traveling fair

143. Patricia Neal made her film debut in what film?

A. *Bright Leaf* (1950)
B. *John Loves Mary* (1949)
C. *The Fountainhead* (1949)
D. *The Hasty Heart* (1949)

144. How many Oscar nominations did *Yankee Doodle Dandy* (1942) receive?

A. 2
B. 4
C. 5
D. 8

145. The 1941 Claude Rains film *Here Comes Mr. Jordan* was remade as what contemporary film?

A. *Always* (2001)
B. *Heaven Can Wait* (1978)
C. *Kiss Me Goodbye* (1982)
D. *Seems Like Old Times* (1980)

146. Jean Simmons first appeared on screen at age fourteen in what film?

A. *Caesar and Cleopatra* (1945)
B. *Give Us the Moon* (1944)
C. *Great Expectations* (1946)
D. *The Way to the Stars* (1945)

147. Bronislau Kaper composed the musical score of what film starring Lana Turner and Donna Reed?

A. *Green Dolphin Street* (1947)
B. *Prince of Foxes* (1949)
C. *The Lady from Shanghai* (1947)
D. *Tomorrow Is Forever* (1946)

148. The 1941 film *Here Comes Mr. Jordan* received Academy Award nominations in all of the following categories except which one?

A. Best Actor
B. Best Picture
C. Best Supporting Actor
D. Best Supporting Actress

149. Leslie Brooks was featured in all of the following films starring Rita Hayworth except for which one?

A. *Cover Girl* (1944)
B. *Gilda* (1946)
C. *Tonight and Every Night* (1945)
D. *You Were Never Lovelier* (1942)

150. Merle Oberon and Cedric Hardwicke share the screen in what thriller?

A. *Escape* (1940)
B. *High Wall* (1947)
C. *Passage to Marseille* (1944)
D. *The Lodger* (1944)

answers found on page 545

151. John Dall was nominated for an Academy Award as Best Supporting Actor for his performance in what 1945 film?

A. *Spellbound*
B. *The Bells of St. Mary's*
C. *The Corn Is Green*
D. *The Lost Weekend*

152. Ingrid Bergman and Flora Robson costar in what film?

A. *Adventures of Don Juan* (1948)
B. *Saratoga Trunk* (1945)
C. *The Sea Hawk* (1940)
D. *Ziegfeld Follies* (1945)

153. Teresa Wright earned her first Academy nomination for what film?

A. *Mrs. Miniver* (1942)
B. *The Best Years of Our Lives* (1946)
C. *The Little Foxes* (1941)
D. *The Pride of the Yankees* (1942)

154. Cedric Hardwicke and which star of *My Fair Lady* (1964) shared the screen in 1947's *The Life and Adventures of Nicholas Nickleby* (1947)?

A. Audrey Hepburn
B. Rex Harrison
C. Stanley Holloway
D. Theodore Bikel

155. Alexander Korda produced the 1940 film *The Thief of Bagdad,* which won Academy Awards in all of the following categories except which one?

A. Best Art Direction
B. Best Cinematography
C. Best Editing
D. Best Special Effects

156. Gloria Grahame made her screen debut opposite Mary Astor in which film?

A. *Across the Pacific* (1942)
B. *Blonde Fever* (1944)

C. *The Maltese Falcon* (1941)
D. *Young Ideas* (1943)

157. The 1942 Kay Francis film *Always in My Heart* received its only Academy Award nomination in what category?

A. Best Art Direction
B. Best Original Score
C. Best Song
D. Best Supporting Actress

158. Ida Lupino was under contract with what studio during the 1940s?

A. MGM
B. Paramount
C. United Artists
D. Warner Bros.

159. Donna Reed made her screen debut in what film?

A. *Madame Curie* (1943)
B. *The Get-Away* (1941)
C. *Too Many Girls* (1940)
D. *Week-End at the Waldorf* (1945)

Two Sisters from Boston, 1946

160. *Cluny Brown* and *Two Sisters from Boston* opened days apart in 1946. Which actor starred in both?

A. James Stewart
B. Peter Lawford
C. David Niven
D. Fredric March

---

answers found on page 545

161. Richard Burton made his screen debut in what film?

A. *Love Happy* (1949)
B. *The Barkleys of Broadway* (1949)
C. *The Last Days of Dolwyn* (1949)
D. *The Sky's the Limit* (1943)

162. Teresa Wright signed a five-year contract with which studio in 1941?

A. MGM
B. RKO
C. United Artists
D. Warner Bros.

163. Natalie Wood played "Little Girl Who Drops Ice Cream Cone" in what film?

A. *Chicken Every Sunday* (1949)
B. *Happy Land* (1943)
C. *Miracle on 34th Street* (1947)
D. *The Bride Wore Boots* (1946)

164. Dorothy Dandridge plays Princess Malimi in what film?

A. *Drums of the Congo* (1942)
B. *Her Highness and the Bellboy* (1945)
C. *Sun Valley Serenade* (1941)
D. *Tamango* (1958)

165. In what film does Ida Lupino play a fugitive from justice who is picked up by a ship captained by Edward G. Robinson?

A. *High Sierra* (1941)
B. *Out of the Fog* (1941)
C. *The Sea Wolf* (1941)
D. *While the City Sleeps* (1956)

166. How many Oscar nominations did Michael Powell's *The Red Shoes* (1948) receive?

A. 2
B. 3
C. 4
D. 5

167. Kay Francis appears with which of the following actresses in the 1941 film *The Feminine Touch*?

A. Joan Crawford
B. Lana Turner
C. Loretta Young
D. Rosalind Russell

168. Esther Williams falls for a naval officer played by Peter Lawford in what film?

A. *Easter Parade* (1948)
B. *On an Island with You* (1948)
C. *The Picture of Dorian Gray* (1945)
D. *Ziegfeld Follies* (1946)

169. Joan Blondell costarred in the 1945 film *A Tree Grows in Brooklyn,* which won its only Academy Award in what category?

A. Best Actress
B. Best Musical Score
C. Best Picture
D. Best Supporting Actor

170. Anthony Quinn and Cedric Hardwicke costar in *Tycoon* (1947) and which other film?

A. *Stranger on the Third Floor* (1940)
B. *The Crowd Roars* (1938)
C. *The Imperfect Lady* (1947)
D. *To Each His Own* (1946)

171. In what film did Peter Lawford play a bully opposite Mickey Rooney?

A. *A Yank at Eton* (1942)
B. *Mrs. Miniver* (1942)
C. *Sahara* (1943)
D. *Ziegfeld Follies* (1946)

172. In the 1949 film *Everybody Does It,* based on a story by James M. Cain, a woman decides she wants to be a what?

A. Doctor
B. Lawyer
C. Opera singer
D. Painter

answers found on page 545

173. The 1942 film *My Sister Eileen* and what Broadway musical also starring Rosalind Russell were based on the same novel?

A. *Kismet*
B. *New Girl in Town*
C. *Plain and Fancy*
D. *Wonderful Town*

174. In 1948 Dorothy McGuire lost the Academy Award for Best Actress to whom?

A. Joan Crawford
B. Loretta Young
C. Rosalind Russell
D. Susan Hayward

175. When June Allyson married Dick Powell in 1945, how many years her senior was he?

A. 11
B. 13
C. 15
D. 8

176. Cedric Hardwicke is the voice of the narrator in what film featuring Donna Reed?

A. *Passage to Marseille* (1944)
B. *Stranger on the Third Floor* (1940)
C. *The Mask of Dimitrios* (1944)
D. *The Picture of Dorian Gray* (1945)

177. James Agee wrote and narrated which documentary short?

A. *Atomic Power* (1946)
B. *Passport to Nowhere* (1947)
C. *The Quiet One* (1948)
D. *The Rising Tide* (1949)

178. Robert Taylor and Charles Laughton costar in what espionage thriller?

A. *Hotel Berlin* (1945)
B. *Passage to Marseille* (1944)
C. *Strange Cargo* (1940)
D. *The Bribe* (1949)

179. Teresa Wright appeared as Lou Gehrig's wife in what film?

A. *Mrs. Miniver* (1942)
B. *The Best Years of Our Lives* (1946)
C. *The Little Foxes* (1941)
D. *The Pride of the Yankees* (1942)

180. The 1940 Rosalind Russell film *His Girl Friday* was based on what stage play?

A. *Hold Your Horses*
B. *The Bohemian Girl*
C. *The Front Page*
D. *The Ghost Writer*

181. Prior to the 1946 thriller *Notorious*, Claude Rains had worked with Cary Grant in what other film?

A. *Forever and a Day* (1943)
B. *Passage to Marseille* (1944)
C. *Strange Holiday* (1945)
D. *The Last Outpost* (1935)

182. In 1943, Alfred Newman recorded the first commercial multisided album of a film score for what movie?

A. *Beau Geste* (1939)
B. *South Pacific* (1958)
C. *The Robe* (1953)
D. *The Song of Bernadette* (1943)

183. Alexander Korda's 1941 film *That Hamilton Woman* won an Academy Award in which of the following categories?

A. Best Art Direction
B. Best Editing
C. Best Musical Score
D. Best Sound

184. In 1946 Rex Harrison was signed to a seven-year contract with which movie studio?

A. 20th Century-Fox
B. MGM
C. Paramount
D. Universal

answers found on page 545

185. Frank Loesser won an Academy Award for Best Music, Original Song in what film?

A. *Easter Parade* (1948)
B. *Neptune's Daughter* (1949)
C. *The Barkleys of Broadway* (1949)
D. *The Heavenly Body* (1944)

186. Peter Lorre costars with which of the following actors in the 1947 film *My Favorite Brunette*?

A. Bing Crosby
B. Bob Hope
C. Danny Kaye
D. Red Skelton

187. The 1943 Benny Goodman film *Stage Door Canteen* received two Academy Award nominations. One was for Best Original Song. What was the other for?

A. Best Art Direction
B. Best Editing
C. Best Original Score
D. Best Sound

Strange Cargo, 1940

188. The 1940 Frank Borzage film *Strange Cargo* is about a group of convicts escaping from what famous penitentiary?

A. Alcatraz
B. Attica
C. Devil's Island
D. Sing Sing

189. The 1942 film *Flying Tigers* received Academy Award nominations in all of the following categories except which one?

A. Best Editing
B. Best Original Score
C. Best Sound
D. Best Special Effects

190. The 1940 film *One Million B.C.* received two Academy Award nominations. One was for Best Special Effects. What was the other for?

A. Best Art Direction
B. Best Editing
C. Best Original Score
D. Best Supporting Actor

191. In the 1945 thriller *The Spiral Staircase*, Ethel Barrymore's young employee Helen suffers from what disorder?

A. Blindness
B. Deafness
C. Muteness
D. Paralysis

192. Jerry Austin appears in what film opposite Buster Keaton?

A. *Golden Boy* (1939)
B. *Strange Cargo* (1940)
C. *The Face Behind the Mask* (1941)
D. *The Lovable Cheat* (1949)

193. Irving Berlin himself sings in which of the following movies?

A. *Royal Wedding* (1951)
B. *The Barkleys of Broadway* (1949)
C. *The Sea Hawk* (1940)
D. *This Is the Army* (1943)

194. Deborah Kerr and Flora Robson portray Anglican nuns in which drama?

A. *Black Narcissus* (1947)
B. *Istanbul* (1957)
C. *Penny Serenade* (1941)
D. *The Sea Hawk* (1940)

answers found on page 545

195. In the 1940 film *Vigil in the Night,* Carole Lombard plays a what?

A. Judge
B. Nurse
C. Singer
D. Writer

196. Paul Muni and Gene Tierney share the screen in what adventure film?

A. *Hudson's Bay* (1941)
B. *Northern Pursuit* (1943)
C. *The Charge of the Light Brigade* (1936)
D. *The Sea Hawk* (1940)

197. Aline MacMahon received an Academy Award nomination as Best Supporting Actress for her role in what 1944 film?

A. *Dragon Seed*
B. *Gaslight*
C. *Since You Went Away*
D. *Wilson*

198. George Cukor directed Ronald Colman and Shelley Winters in what film?

A. *A Double Life* (1947)
B. *My Darling Clementine* (1946)
C. *The Constant Nymph* (1943)
D. *We Sail at Midnight* (1943)

199. Zoltan Korda's 1942 film *Jungle Book* received Academy Award nominations in all of the following categories except which one?

A. Best Cinematography
B. Best Editing
C. Best Musical Score
D. Best Special Effects

200. In the 1941 film *When Ladies Meet,* what actress plays the woman after Greer Garson's husband?

A. Barbara Stanwyck
B. Bette Davis
C. Joan Crawford
D. Rosalind Russell

201. Michael Curtiz directed Leslie Brooks and Doris Day in what film?

A. *A Piece of Cake* (1948)
B. *Love in Pawn* (1953)
C. *Romance on the High Seas* (1948)
D. *Room to Let* (1950)

202. The 1945 Alfred Hitchcock film *Spellbound* was nominated for six Academy Awards but only won one. In what category did it win?

A. Best Cinematography
B. Best Director
C. Best Musical Score
D. Best Supporting Actor

203. The 1949 Mark Robson film *My Foolish Heart* was based on a short story by which of the following authors?

A. Arthur Miller
B. Herman Melville
C. J. D. Salinger
D. John Steinbeck

204. In what film does Gene Kelly dream he is Louis XV?

A. *Du Barry Was a Lady* (1943)
B. *For Me and My Gal* (1942)
C. *Singin' in the Rain* (1952)
D. *Summer Stock* (1950)

205. The 1940 film *Dr. Ehrlich's Magic Bullet* received its only Academy Award nomination in what category?

A. Best Actor
B. Best Musical Score
C. Best Original Screenplay
D. Best Picture

206. Natalie Wood appeared in what film starring Gene Tierney and Rex Harrison?

A. *A New Kind of Love* (1963)
B. *The Ghost and Mrs. Muir* (1947)
C. *The Man from Laramie* (1955)
D. *The Shop Around the Corner* (1940)

answers found on page 545

Spotlight on
RITA **HAYWORTH** (1918–1987)

Rita Hayworth was born to dance. The child of a Spanish dancer and a Ziegfeld chorus girl, she had a lot of talent and little choice in the matter. "Instead of a rattle," she once said, "I had castanets." One night the head of Fox Studios, Winfield Sheehan, saw the teen beauty and brought her to Hollywood for screen tests. After a brief period at Fox, Hayworth began a twenty-year relationship with Columbia Pictures. Studio head Harry Cohn supervised the sometimes painful process that transformed her from Latin

Susan and God, 1940

dancer Margarita Cansino into love goddess Rita Hayworth. Her two musicals with Fred Astaire made her a star, and Hayworth reached the height of her popularity in her collaborations with Glenn Ford, particularly as the sultry femme fatale in *Gilda* (1946) who does a mock striptease while singing "Put the Blame on Mame." Husband Orson Welles saw her dramatic potential and put it on screen in *The Lady from Shanghai* (1948), but screen success did little to save that or any of her four other marriages. A goddess on the screen, the real Hayworth was probably closer to the high-spirited dancers she played in her films with Fred Astaire. As she would say late in her life, "Whatever you write about me, don't make it sad."

The Money Trap, 1965

1. **Though only for a few seconds, in what film do we hear Rita Hayworth sing in her own voice?**

    A. *Blonde Crazy* (1931)
    B. *Blondie on a Budget* (1940)
    C. *Gilda* (1946)
    D. *The Strawberry Blonde* (1941)

2. **Rita Hayworth appeared with James Cagney in only one film. What was it?**

    A. *Blonde Crazy* (1931)
    B. *Great Guy* (1936)
    C. *Kiss Tomorrow Goodbye* (1950)
    D. *The Strawberry Blonde* (1941)

3. **What was Rita Hayworth's nickname?**

    A. "The Brooklyn Bombshell"
    B. "The It Girl"

    C. "The Love Goddess"
    D. "The Sweater Girl"

4. **Rita Hayworth plays which Greek goddess in the 1947 musical *Down to Earth*?**

    A. Aphrodite
    B. Athena
    C. Hera
    D. Terpsichore

5. **Orson Welles caused a public outcry when he cropped Rita Hayworth's hair and dyed it platinum blonde for what film?**

    A. *Gilda* (1946)
    B. *Salome* (1953)
    C. *The Lady from Shanghai* (1948)
    D. *Touch of Evil* (1958)

answers found on page 545

207. Alfred Newman earned four Academy Award nominations in 1940. Which of the following was not one of his nominated films?

A. *Babes on Broadway*
B. *The Rains Came*
C. *They Shall Have Music*
D. *Wuthering Heights*

208. Cecil Kellaway plays Granet in what film based on the Original Dixieland Jazz Band of New Orleans?

A. *Birth of the Blues* (1941)
B. *Blue Skies* (1946)
C. *The Sky's the Limit* (1943)
D. *You Were Never Lovelier* (1942)

209. Lana Turner and Donna Reed share the screen in what film?

A. *Beyond Glory* (1948)
B. *Faithful in My Fashion* (1946)
C. *Green Dolphin Street* (1947)
D. *The Far Horizons* (1955)

210. John Garfield and Lana Turner costarred with Hume Cronyn in which of the following movies?

A. *Lifeboat* (1944)
B. *The Bride Goes Wild* (1948)
C. *The Postman Always Rings Twice* (1946)
D. *Top O' the Morning* (1949)

211. Jerry Austin appears in what film opposite Ingrid Bergman?

A. *Golden Boy* (1939)
B. *Saratoga Trunk* (1945)
C. *Strange Cargo* (1940)
D. *The Face Behind the Mask* (1941)

212. Edward Arnold played the role of Joe Lorgan in what baseball film starring Frank Sinatra, Esther Williams, and Gene Kelly?

A. *Angels in the Outfield* (1951)
B. *Take Me out to the Ball Game* (1949)

C. *The Pride of the Yankees* (1942)
D. *The Stratton Story* (1949)

213. Ida Lupino left Warner Bros. to start Arcadia Productions in what year?

A. 1945
B. 1947
C. 1949
D. 1951

The Yearling, 1946

214. Gregory Peck's 1946 film *The Yearling* was based on the novel by what author?

A. Edna Ferber
B. Harper Lee
C. John Steinbeck
D. Marjorie Kinnan Rawlings

215. Jean Renoir was nominated for an Academy Award as Best Director for what 1945 film?

A. *Mildred Pierce*
B. *The Bells of St. Mary's*
C. *The Lost Weekend*
D. *The Southerner*

216. On September 9, 1946, Jane Powell appeared on the cover of what magazine?

A. *Life*
B. *People*
C. *Time*
D. *Vanity Fair*

answers found on page 545

217. In the 1949 film *The Big Day*, Jacques Tati played a what?

    A. Furniture deliveryman
    B. Milkman
    C. Piano teacher
    D. Postman

218. Edward Arnold starred in the role of Daniel Webster, opposite Walter Huston, in which film?

    A. *All That Money Can Buy* (1941)
    B. *City That Never Sleeps* (1953)
    C. *Main Street After Dark* (1945)
    D. *Nothing but the Truth* (1941)

219. In the 1943 film *Forever and a Day*, Charles Laughton plays a what?

    A. Bum
    B. Butler
    C. Doctor
    D. Priest

220. James Stewart and Farley Granger costar in which Alfred Hitchcock thriller?

    A. *Foreign Correspondent* (1940)
    B. *Lifeboat* (1944)
    C. *Rope* (1948)
    D. *Spellbound* (1945)

221. Edward Arnold reprised the role of Diamond Jim Brady in which film costarring Henry Fonda and Don Ameche?

    A. *Fort Apache* (1948)
    B. *Honky Tonk* (1941)
    C. *It's in the Bag!* (1945)
    D. *Lillian Russell* (1940)

222. Marjorie Main appeared with James Cagney in only one film. What was it?

    A. *Dark Command* (1940)
    B. *Heaven Can Wait* (1943)
    C. *Johnny Come Lately* (1943)
    D. *The Bugle Sounds* (1942)

223. In 1943, Teresa Wright garnered dual Oscar nominations for her roles in what two films?

    A. *Shadow of a Doubt* and *Mrs. Miniver*
    B. *The Little Foxes* and *Mrs. Miniver*
    C. *The Little Foxes* and *Shadow of a Doubt*
    D. *The Pride of the Yankees* and *Mrs. Miniver*

224. The 1943 film *Sahara*, starring Humphrey Bogart, received Academy Award nominations in all of the following categories except which one?

    A. Best Cinematography
    B. Best Sound
    C. Best Supporting Actor
    D. Best Supporting Actress

225. Claude Rains was originally set to play Duke de Lorca in what film starring Errol Flynn?

    A. *Adventures of Don Juan* (1948)
    B. *Strange Cargo* (1940)
    C. *Streets of Laredo* (1949)
    D. *The Face Behind the Mask* (1941)

226. In 1940, Jane Russell signed a seven-year contract with which movie mogul?

    A. David O. Selznick
    B. Howard Hughes
    C. Jack L. Warner
    D. Louis B. Mayer

227. Bette Davis and Olivia de Havilland share the screen in what melodrama?

    A. *In This Our Life* (1942)
    B. *Old Acquaintance* (1943)
    C. *That Certain Woman* (1937)
    D. *The Man Who Came to Dinner* (1942)

228. Jane Russell made her film debut in what film?

    A. *His Kind of Woman* (1951)
    B. *The Outlaw* (1943)
    C. *The Paleface* (1948)
    D. *Young Widow* (1946)

229. Ralph Bellamy plays Dr. R. L. Davis, opposite Errol Flynn, in what film?

A. *Footsteps in the Dark* (1941)
B. *Stranger on the Third Floor* (1940)
C. *The Conspirators* (1944)
D. *The Maltese Falcon* (1941)

230. In 1948, Henry Fonda won a Tony Award for his performance in the title role of which stage production?

A. *Mister Roberts*
B. *Tea and Sympathy*
C. *The Chalk Garden*
D. *The Rose Tattoo*

231. Joan Leslie appeared with James Cagney in only one film. What is it?

A. *He Was Her Man* (1934)
B. *The Sky's the Limit* (1943)
C. *The Wagons Roll at Night* (1941)
D. *Yankee Doodle Dandy* (1942)

232. In 1949, which studio did John Sturges join?

A. Columbia
B. MGM
C. United Artists
D. Warner Bros.

233. Dorothy Lamour performs the song "Remember You" in what film?

A. *Blue Skies* (1946)
B. *Carefree* (1938)
C. *Love Affair* (1939)
D. *The Fleet's In* (1942)

234. Boris Karloff and Bela Lugosi appeared together for the last time in what Val Lewton film?

A. *Bedlam* (1946)
B. *Isle of the Dead* (1945)
C. *The Body Snatcher* (1945)
D. *The Seventh Victim* (1943)

235. How much was the blue bird featured in the Shirley Temple film *The Blue Bird* (1940) paid?

A. $1,000
B. $50 a day
C. 20 pounds of bird feed
D. No salary

236. Marlene Dietrich and Ronald Colman star in what film set in Baghdad?

A. *Kismet* (1944)
B. *The Long Voyage Home* (1940)
C. *The Plough and the Stars* (1936)
D. *We Sail at Midnight* (1943)

237. Marjorie Main appeared in which film starring Clark Gable as a reformed gambler?

A. *Boom Town* (1940)
B. *Honky Tonk* (1941)
C. *Love on the Run* (1936)
D. *Manhattan Melodrama* (1934)

238. James Cagney and Ann Sheridan costar in which film directed by William Keighley?

A. *Special Agent* (1935)
B. *The Green Pastures* (1936)
C. *The Old South* (1940)
D. *Torrid Zone* (1940)

239. Fay Wray married what screenwriter in 1942, who had written such films as *It Happened One Night* (1934) and *Lost Horizon* (1937)?

A. Don Mullaly
B. Erich von Stroheim
C. James Creelman
D. Robert Riskin

240. The 1940 Rita Hayworth film *Music in My Heart* received an Academy Award nomination for Best Original Song. What was the name of the song?

A. "Blue Is the Rain"
B. "Blue-Eyed Rosie"
C. "It's a Blue World"
D. "Paint Me in Blue"

241. Mary Astor won the Best Supporting Actress Oscar for what film?

A. *Dodsworth* (1936)
B. *Meet Me in St. Louis* (1944)
C. *The Great Lie* (1941)
D. *The Maltese Falcon* (1941)

242. Samuel Goldwyn's 1947 Best Picture nominee starring Loretta Young was remade in 1996 with what actress in the same part?

A. Halle Berry
B. Meg Ryan
C. Sandra Bullock
D. Whitney Houston

243. Cedric Hardwicke and Fredric March costar in what film adaptation of a Joseph Conrad novel?

A. *Hotel Berlin* (1945)
B. *Lest We Forget* (1937)
C. *Passage to Marseille* (1944)
D. *Victory* (1940)

244. Marjorie Main received an Academy Award nomination for her performance in which film?

A. *The Captain Is a Lady* (1940)
B. *The Egg and I* (1947)
C. *They Shall Have Music* (1939)
D. *Too Hot to Handle* (1938)

245. In the 1943 film *Stage Door Canteen*, Benny Goodman accompanies Peggy Lee as she sings what tune?

A. "Fever"
B. "Someone to Watch Over Me"
C. "Where or When"
D. "Why Don't You Do Right"

246. In the 1946 film *Sister Kenny*, Rosalind Russell plays the real-life title character who dedicated her life to finding a cure for what disease?

A. Cancer
B. Measles
C. Polio
D. Smallpox

247. Deborah Kerr received her first Oscar nomination when costarring with Spencer Tracy in what film?

A. *Edward, My Son* (1949)
B. *The End of the Affair* (1955)
C. *The Hucksters* (1947)
D. *The Proud and Profane* (1956)

248. In the 1947 film *Mine Own Executioner*, Burgess Meredith plays a what?

A. Lawyer
B. Police officer
C. Prison warden
D. Psychotherapist

249. In what film does David Niven play Eric Phillips?

A. *A Kiss in the Dark* (1949)
B. *Enchantment* (1948)
C. *The Dawn Patrol* (1938)
D. *The Prisoner of Zenda* (1937)

250. Anthony Asquith directed Cedric Hardwicke in what film?

A. *Lest We Forget* (1937)
B. *Passage to Marseille* (1944)
C. *The Winslow Boy* (1948)
D. *To Each His Own* (1946)

251. In what category did the 1945 film *Brewster's Millions* receive its only Academy Award nomination?

A. Best Art Direction
B. Best Original Score
C. Best Original Screenplay
D. Best Original Song

252. The 1946 film *Night and Day*, starring Cary Grant, was nominated for an Academy Award in what category?

A. Best Actor
B. Best Art Direction
C. Best Musical Score
D. Best Supporting Actress

Ben-Hur, 1959

Chapter 4

THE 1950s

The fifties opened with the camera looking up at a dead William Holden as he floated in the swimming pool in *Sunset Blvd.* (1950) and ended with Jack Lemmon sailing into an uncertain future in Joe E. Brown's speedboat in *Some Like It Hot* (1959). The years between were marked by one of Hollywood's greatest struggles—the fight to lure audiences away from their television sets. The studios fought back against the new medium with new technologies, stars, spectacles, and sins, but they lost as much as they won.

The entire landscape of stardom was changing. The megastars were losing their box-office power. After leaving Warner Bros., Bette Davis made a smashing comeback as an aging stage star in *All About Eve* (1950), but had trouble finding a suitable follow-up. Others, like Ann Sothern and Lucille Ball,

turned to television as the studios, faced with declining box office, cut their contract rolls. The most successful of the remaining stars turned to producing and packaging their own films. John Wayne created his own production company, Batjac, and Humphrey Bogart created Santana. Thinking him over the hill, MGM made the mistake of cutting Clark Gable loose, just before one of his last films there, *Mogambo* (1953), took off at the box office. There were new stars rising as well. Marilyn Monroe replaced Betty Grable as 20th Century-Fox's reigning blonde bombshell, while Audrey Hepburn and Grace Kelly stepped into Olivia de Havilland's ladylike shoes.

One lure for audiences was movies with more stars than could fit on a TV screen. MGM put William Holden, Barbara Stanwyck, June Allyson, Fredric March, Paul Douglas, and

Shelley Winters into *Executive Suite* (1954), and teamed Frank Sinatra, Bing Crosby, Grace Kelly, and Louis Armstrong for *High Society* (1956). But when Warner Bros. cast everyone from Hedy Lamarr to the Marx Brothers in *The Story of Mankind* (1957), they created a flop of epic proportions.

Making the movies bigger was one of Hollywood's most successful strategies, with audiences turning out for new technical wonders like CinemaScope, Cinerama, and 3-D. After years of creating the world on their back lots, the studios started sending productions out to real locations. Arthur Freed scored a Best Picture Oscar with the Paris-lensed musical *Gigi* (1958), while David Lean forced Holden, Jack Hawkins, and Alec Guinness to fight their way through the tropical heat of Sri Lanka to make *The Bridge on the River Kwai* (1957). And at decade's end, director William Wyler went to Rome to create the blockbuster hit *Ben-Hur* (1959).

The studios also realized that the need to make television family-friendly offered film a golden opportunity to produce more adult-oriented entertainment. Tennessee Williams's frankly sexual *A Streetcar Named Desire* (1951), *Baby Doll* (1956), and *Cat on a Hot Tin Roof* (1958) provided a critically respectable means of pushing the envelope. Inspired by European directors like Ingmar Bergman and Luchino Visconti, who worked outside the limits of Hollywood's restrictive Production Code, filmmakers here began fighting for more license. Otto Preminger led the way by releasing first the risqué comedy *The Moon Is Blue* (1953) and then *The Man with the Golden Arm* (1955), starring Sinatra as a recovering drug addict, without Code approval but to strong box office.

Outside the studios, low-budget and independent filmmakers were also suggesting new ways to keep the industry afloat. Burt Lancaster's production company turned an inexpensive adaptation of the television drama *Marty* (1955) into one of the most profitable movies ever made, suggesting there was an audience for smaller, more realistic pictures. Picking up on the success of Universal's science fiction films—the best, like *It Came from Outer Space* (1953) and *The Incredible Shrinking Man* (1957), directed by Jack Arnold—Roger Corman and other independents turned the drive-in circuit into a bonanza with cheaply shot science fiction and horror films aimed at the teen market, kids as eager to get out of the house as their parents were to stay home.

Before long, the studios jumped on the bandwagon. Singing sensation Elvis Presley signed to make *Jailhouse Rock* (1957) for MGM, outgrossing more traditional musicals starring Gene Kelly and Fred Astaire. Universal turned teen model Sandra Dee into a new kind of juvenile star who, even in fanciful vehicles like *Gidget* and *A Summer Place* (both 1959), faced the kinds of problems her teen fans dealt with in their own lives. As the decade closed, the studio contract ranks, once the home of adult stars like Davis and Bogart and character actors like Edward Arnold and Thelma Ritter, were now filled with younger actors like Troy Donahue and Connie Stevens, all hoping to become the next teen sensation.

1. The 1958 Sophia Loren comedy *Houseboat* was nominated for two Academy Awards. One was for Best Original Song. What was the other?

A. Best Actress
B. Best Cinematography
C. Best Original Screenplay
D. Best Sound

2. In 1953, who did Carolyn Jones marry and convert to Judaism for?

A. Aaron Spelling
B. Arthur Miller
C. John Astin
D. Woody Allen

3. How many times in the 1950s did a film win exactly eight Oscars?

A. 1
B. 2
C. 3
D. 4

4. In the 1958 Jacques Tati film *Mon Oncle,* the family has a fountain in the garden shaped like a what?

A. Fish
B. Giraffe
C. Question mark
D. Shoe

5. In *A Place in the Sun* (1951), what type of product is produced at the plant owned by Montgomery Clift's uncle?

A. Bathing suits
B. Paper
C. Sprockets
D. Umbrellas

6. In the 1959 film *A Summer Place,* what is the name of the island where the family vacations?

A. Magnolia Island
B. Pine Island
C. Spruce Island
D. Willow Island

7. What is the name of Mr. Hulot's nephew in the 1958 Jacques Tati film *Mon Oncle*?

A. Gerard
B. Philippe
C. Pierre
D. Yves

High Society, 1956

8. In the 1956 film *High Society,* what is the name of Bing Crosby's boat?

A. *Moonstar*
B. *Philadelphia*
C. *Tracy*
D. *True Love*

9. In the 1953 Ralph Meeker film *Jeopardy,* a family gets into trouble while on vacation in what country?

A. England
B. Mexico
C. Spain
D. Turkey

10. The 1952 film *Affair in Trinidad* received its only Academy Award nomination in what category?

A. Best Adapted Screenplay
B. Best Cinematography
C. Best Costume Design
D. Best Musical Score

answers found on pages 545–546

11. How many times in the 1950s did a film win exactly seven Oscars?

A. 0
B. 1
C. 2
D. 3

12. In the 1953 Delmer Daves film *Never Let Me Go*, actress Gene Tierney plays a what?

A. Ballet dancer
B. Fashion designer
C. Psychologist
D. Spy

13. The 1954 film *Seven Samurai* was nominated for two Academy Awards. One was for Best Art Direction. What was the other for?

A. Best Actor
B. Best Cinematography
C. Best Costume Design
D. Best Director

14. In the 1950 film *So Young, So Bad,* Paul Henreid played a what?

A. Animal trainer
B. Brain surgeon
C. Insurance salesman
D. Psychiatrist

15. The 1954 film *Susan Slept Here* received an Academy Award nomination for Best Song. What was the name of the song?

A. "Hold My Hand"
B. "Sleep to Dream"
C. "Something's Cooking"
D. "The Man That Got Away"

16. In Jack Arnold's *The Incredible Shrinking Man* (1957), what film's theme song plays on the radio in the background while Louise asks the operator for an unlisted number?

A. *Giant* (1956)
B. *Magnificent Obsession* (1954)

C. *Peyton Place* (1957)
D. *Written on the Wind* (1956)

17. The 1951 film *Fourteen Hours* was nominated for its only Academy Award in what category?

A. Best Actor
B. Best Art Direction
C. Best Editing
D. Best Musical Score

18. The 1950 Pedro Armendáriz film *The Torch* was a remake of one of his earlier films. What was the original title?

A. *Enamorada* (1946)
B. *Fort Apache* (1948)
C. *Maclovia* (1948)
D. *We Were Strangers* (1949)

19. In the 1955 film *Picnic*, Rosalind Russell plays a what?

A. Bank teller
B. Bar owner
C. Nurse
D. Schoolteacher

20. What film was not directed by John Sturges in 1958?

A. *Saddle the Wind*
B. *The Law and Jake Wade*
C. *The Old Man and the Sea*
D. *War of the Planets*

21. What hotel brand, founded in 1952, was named after a musical starring Bing Crosby and Fred Astaire?

A. Doubletree
B. Four Seasons
C. Holiday Inn
D. Homewood Suites

answers found on page 546

22. Thelma Ritter costars in the 1955 film *Daddy Long Legs,* which received an Academy Award nomination for Best Original Song. What was the name of the song?

A. "Happiness Is Just a Thing Called Joe"
B. "I Could Write a Book"
C. "It Had to Be You"
D. "Something's Gotta Give"

23. How many Academy Awards did the 1959 film *Ben-Hur* win?

A. 10
B. 11
C. 12
D. 9

24. Louis Malle's *The Lovers* (1958) and *Elevator to the Gallows* (1957) both starred what famous stage actress of the time?

A. Jeanne Balibar
B. Jeanne Garnier
C. Jeanne Moreau
D. Sarah Bernhardt

25. The 1958 Sophia Loren film *Desire Under the Elms* was based on a play by what author?

A. Arthur Miller
B. Edward Albee
C. Eugene O'Neill
D. Tennessee Williams

26. In the 1953 comedy *The Affairs of Dobie Gillis,* Charles Lane plays a professor of what?

A. Chemistry
B. Classics
C. Marine biology
D. Music theory

27. What Paris-set musical won the Academy Award for Best Picture in 1952?

A. *An American in Paris*
B. *French Can-Can*
C. *Funny Face*
D. *Gigi*

28. On March 31, 1952, Charles Laughton appeared on the cover of what magazine?

A. *Life*
B. *People*
C. *Time*
D. *Vanity Fair*

29. Chuck Jones directed the 1950 cartoon *The Ducksters.* What character played a game show contestant in it?

A. Bugs Bunny
B. Elmer Fudd
C. Porky Pig
D. Yosemite Sam

Silk Stockings, 1957

30. The 1957 Fred Astaire film *Silk Stockings* was a musical remake of what film?

A. *His Girl Friday* (1940)
B. *Ninotchka* (1939)
C. *The Philadelphia Story* (1940)
D. *The Women* (1939)

31. In the 1952 film *The Winning Team,* Ronald Reagan plays a what?

A. Baseball player
B. Football coach
C. Radio announcer
D. Sports writer

32. The 1956 Brigitte Bardot film *And God Created Woman* was remade in 1988 starring what actress?

A. Brooke Shields
B. Diane Lane
C. Kathleen Turner
D. Rebecca DeMornay

33. *Riding High* (1950) is a remake of what film also directed by Frank Capra?

A. *Broadway Bill* (1934)
B. *Forbidden* (1932)
C. *Pocketful of Miracles* (1961)
D. *Rain or Shine* (1930)

34. In the 1985 film *Back to the Future,* what Ronald Reagan film is playing at the Hill Valley movie theater in 1955?

A. *Brother Rat* (1938)
B. *Cattle Queen of Montana* (1954)
C. *Knute Rockne, All-American* (1940)
D. *Law and Order* (1953)

35. In the 1959 film *The Mouse That Roared,* how many roles does Peter Sellers play?

A. 1
B. 2
C. 3
D. 4

36. In the 1955 film *The Man with the Golden Arm,* Kim Novak costars with which of the following actors?

A. Frank Sinatra
B. Gene Kelly
C. Richard Harris
D. Sean Connery

37. In the 1951 film *Night into Morning,* Ray Milland plays a professor of what subject?

A. Chemistry
B. English
C. French
D. Music

38. In 1958, Claire Bloom and Yul Brynner starred in *The Brothers Karamazov* and what other film?

A. *Anastasia*
B. *Solomon and Sheba*
C. *The Buccaneer*
D. *The Man Between*

39. The "rain" in *Singin' in the Rain* (1952) consisted of water and what other ingredient?

A. Corn syrup
B. Milk
C. Vinegar
D. Whiskey

40. In 1956, which major film studio hired Gore Vidal as a screenwriter?

A. MGM
B. RKO
C. Universal
D. Warner Bros.

41. The soundtrack album to Leslie Caron's 1958 film *Gigi* is visible on the cover of another 1969 album by what famous band?

A. Pink Floyd
B. The Beatles
C. The Rolling Stones
D. Three Dog Night

42. The 1956 film *The King and I* was nominated for nine Academy Awards. How many did it win?

A. 1
B. 3
C. 5
D. 7

answers found on page 546

43. In which of the following categories was the 1950 film *Rashomon* nominated for an Academy Award?

A. Best Actor
B. Best Art Direction
C. Best Director
D. Best Special Effects

44. Which 1950s sci-fi movie did Jack Arnold not direct?

A. *Creature from the Black Lagoon* (1954)
B. *It Came from Outer Space* (1953)
C. *The Incredible Shrinking Man* (1957)
D. *Them!* (1954)

45. The 1952 film *Meet Me Tonight,* costarring Valerie Hobson, was based on a play by what author?

A. Anton Chekov
B. Arthur Miller
C. Noël Coward
D. Samuel Beckett

46. In 1953, Benny Goodman embarked on an ill-fated tour with what fellow jazz musician?

A. Count Basie
B. Glenn Miller
C. John Coltrane
D. Louis Armstrong

47. In *Gidget* (1959), who is the first of the surfers to call Sandra Dee by her eponymous nickname?

A. Kahuna
B. Lover Boy
C. Moondoggie
D. Stinky

48. In the 1955 film *Marty,* Ernest Borgnine portrays a shy what?

A. Butcher
B. Lawyer

C. Tailor
D. Veterinarian

49. What was the nickname of Julie Harris's character in the 1952 film *The Member of the Wedding*?

A. Belle
B. Frankie
C. Pumpkin
D. Rory

50. In 1953's *Roman Holiday*, Audrey Hepburn recites from the poem "Arethusa" by which poet?

A. John Keats
B. Percy Bysshe Shelley
C. William Blake
D. William Wordsworth

51. The 1958 Stanley Donen musical *Damn Yankees* featured which of the following songs?

A. "Baby, You Knock Me Out"
B. "Good Morning"
C. "Heart"
D. "Prehistoric Man"

52. What film won the Academy Award for Best Picture of 1953?

A. *From Here to Eternity*
B. *Roman Holiday*
C. *Shane*
D. *The Robe*

53. In the 1959 film *A Hole in the Head,* costarring Thelma Ritter, Frank Sinatra runs a hotel in what city?

A. Boston
B. Dallas
C. Miami
D. Seattle

Spotlight on
ESTHER **WILLIAMS** (1922–)

Like many young people, Esther Williams dreamed of fame and awards—but she was pining for Olympic, not Oscar, gold. An accomplished swimmer, Williams had to put Olympic fantasies to rest when Hitler's march on Europe caused the 1940 games to be canceled. She settled for joining showman Billy Rose's San Francisco Aquacade, where her looks and talents in water ballet caught the eye of MGM talent scouts. Despite her lack of experience, Williams was put under contract. After scoring in small roles, she was cast as a swimming gym teacher in the Red Skelton comedy *Mr. Coed*. MGM executives were so impressed with her performance they built up the role and changed the title to *Bathing Beauty* (1944). For eleven years, Williams swam through eighteen films shot on a stage with a large, specially equipped swimming pool built just for her. She was game for almost anything, yet the elaborate tricks her directors put her through were not without peril, and a fifty-foot dive at the climax of *Million Dollar Mermaid* (1952) resulted in half a year in a body cast. When the studio system fell apart in the 1950s, Williams became a successful businesswoman, marketing her own lines of swimsuits and swimming pools.

Million Dollar Mermaid, 1952

1. **In what category did the Esther Williams film *Million Dollar Mermaid* (1952) earn an Oscar nomination?**

   A. Best Color Cinematography

   B. Best Director

   C. Best Special Effects

   D. Best Supporting Actor

2. **Where on the MGM lot was Esther Williams's pool?**

   A. Stage 17

   B. Stage 30

   C. Stage 4

   D. Stage 10

3. **Esther Williams portrays an aquacade showgirl in which musical directed by Richard Thorpe?**

   A. *Bathing Beauty* (1944)

   B. *Easy to Love* (1953)

   C. *Her Highness and the Bellboy* (1945)

   D. *This Time for Keeps* (1947)

4. **What color was the furniture in Esther Williams's MGM dressing room?**

   A. Blue

   B. Gold

   C. Pink

   D. Silver

5. **Esther Williams falls for a naval officer played by Peter Lawford in what film?**

   A. *Easter Parade* (1948)

   B. *On an Island with You* (1948)

   C. *The Picture of Dorian Gray* (1945)

   D. *Ziegfeld Follies* (1946)

Bathing Beauty, 1944

answers found on page 546

54. Thelma Ritter costars in the 1959 film *A Hole in the Head*, which won an Academy Award for Best Original Song. What was the name of the song?
   A. "Chantilly Lace"
   B. "High Hopes"
   C. "Love Makes the World Go Round"
   D. "Personality"

55. The 1958 film *Cat on a Hot Tin Roof* was nominated for how many Oscars?
   A. 2
   B. 4
   C. 6
   D. 8

56. Which of these actors was not in *The World, the Flesh and the Devil* (1959)?
   A. Harry Belafonte
   B. Inger Stevens
   C. Mel Ferrer
   D. Vic Morrow

57. What is the name of Brigitte Bardot's character in the 1956 film *And God Created Woman*?
   A. Camille
   B. Colette
   C. Juliete
   D. Serena

58. The 1954 film *Human Desire,* starring Glenn Ford, was based on a novel by which writer?
   A. Émile Zola
   B. Gustave Flaubert
   C. Guy de Maupassant
   D. Victor Hugo

59. What 1954 short is edited from Deanna Durbin's *Mad About Music* (1938) and *Lady on a Train* (1945)?
   A. *Christmas Hymns*
   B. *Flight of the White Heron*
   C. *Gift for Gag*
   D. *House of History*

60. The 1958 film *Torpedo Run* received its only Academy Award nomination in what category?
   A. Best Director
   B. Best Editing
   C. Best Original Screenplay
   D. Best Special Effects

61. What is the name of Thelma Ritter's character in the 1959 film *Pillow Talk*?
   A. Alma
   B. Bitsy
   C. Dorothy
   D. Elsa

62. Angie Dickinson won a Golden Globe for Best New Female Star of the Year in what year?
   A. 1955
   B. 1957
   C. 1959
   D. 1961

63. Which Ealing comedy won an Oscar for its screenplay in 1953?
   A. *Kind Hearts and Coronets*
   B. *The Ladykillers*
   C. *The Lavender Hill Mob*
   D. *The Man in the White Suit*

64. In which of the following categories was the 1952 film *Above and Beyond* nominated for an Academy Award?
   A. Best Art Direction
   B. Best Director
   C. Best Editing
   D. Best Original Score

65. Charles Coburn was featured in 1953's *Gentlemen Prefer Blondes* and what other film opposite Marilyn Monroe?
   A. *Let's Dance* (1950)
   B. *Monkey Business* (1952)
   C. *Some Like It Hot* (1959)
   D. *Words and Music* (1948)

answers found on page 546

66. In *Gidget* (1959), what type of instrument does Gidget have in her room?
   A. A cello
   B. A harp
   C. A piano
   D. A violin

67. The title of the 1959 Jules Dassin film *The Law* refers to a what?
   A. Game
   B. Horse
   C. Schoolteacher
   D. Television show

68. Thelma Ritter costars in the 1955 film *Lucy Gallant*. Which actress portrays the title character?
   A. Bette Davis
   B. Esther Williams
   C. Grace Kelly
   D. Jane Wyman

69. Which of the following songs does not appear in *Gigi* (1958)?
   A. "I Remember It Well"
   B. "I'll Build a Stairway to Paradise"
   C. "Thank Heaven for Little Girls"
   D. "The Night They Invented Champagne"

70. In 1953's *Gentlemen Prefer Blondes*, Marilyn Monroe wears a gold dress previously worn by Ginger Rogers in what film?
   A. *Dreamboat* (1952)
   B. *The Barkleys of Broadway* (1949)
   C. *The Belle of New York* (1952)
   D. *Words and Music* (1948)

71. Which actress's role in the 1954 film *Human Desire* was originally intended for Rita Hayworth?
   A. Bette Davis
   B. Debbie Reynolds

C. Eleanor Powell
   D. Gloria Grahame

72. The 1958 film *The Young Lions* marked the only time that Marlon Brando costarred with which accomplished actor?
   A. James Dean
   B. Montgomery Clift
   C. Paul Newman
   D. Spencer Tracy

73. I wed Method actor Rod Steiger in 1959. Who am I?
   A. Claire Bloom
   B. Diana Dors
   C. Jane Greer
   D. Margaret Lockwood

74. In the 1953 film *The Actress*, starring Spencer Tracy, what actress plays his daughter?
   A. Elizabeth Taylor
   B. Eva Marie Saint
   C. Jean Simmons
   D. Jessica Tandy

75. In *Gidget* (1959), what two words do the surfers combine to come up with Sandra Dee's nickname?
   A. Gangly and fidget
   B. Gifted and widget
   C. Girl and midget
   D. Goof and digit

76. The 1953 Fay Wray film *Treasure of the Golden Condor* was a remake of what Tyrone Power film?
   A. *Blood and Sand* (1922)
   B. *Nightmare Alley* (1947)
   C. *Son of Fury: The Story of Benjamin Blake* (1942)
   D. *The Razor's Edge* (1946)

answers found on page 546

77. The 1955 Leslie Caron film *Daddy Long Legs* won an Academy Award for Best Original Song. What was the name of the song?

A. "Cry Me a River"
B. "Happiness Is Just a Thing Called Joe"
C. "Something's Gotta Give"
D. "The Way You Look Tonight"

78. In what year did Walter Mirisch found The Mirisch Corporation with his two brothers?

A. 1955
B. 1956
C. 1957
D. 1958

79. The 1959 comedy *Some Like It Hot* received Academy Award nominations in all of the following categories except which one?

A. Best Actor
B. Best Actress
C. Best Cinematography
D. Best Director

80. In the 1954 film *Seven Brides for Seven Brothers,* what does Jane Powell's character name her daughter?

A. Eve
B. Gina
C. Hannah
D. Laura

81. Sandra Dee's wholesome 1950s persona is the subject of the song "Look at Me, I'm Sandra Dee" from what musical?

A. *Chicago* (2002)
B. *Grease* (1978)
C. *Sweet Charity* (1969)
D. *West Side Story* (1961)

82. In what city does the action take place in the 1958 film *Vertigo*?

A. Boston

B. Honolulu
C. Philadelphia
D. San Francisco

83. Ronald Colman played Dr. William Hall on what 1950s radio program?

A. *Champion Spark Plug Hour*
B. *Our Miss Brooks*
C. *Suspense*
D. *The Halls of Ivy*

84. Natalie Wood appeared in how many episodes of the 1950s television show *Kings Row*?

A. 0
B. 1
C. 2
D. 3

85. In what city does the action take place in the 1950 Barbara Bel Geddes film *Panic in the Streets*?

A. Memphis
B. New Orleans
C. New York
D. San Francisco

86. Fay Wray played an understanding mother to the leader of a would-be rock group in 1956's *Rock, Pretty Baby*. Two years later she reprised her role in the sequel. What was its title?

A. *A Dangerous Age*
B. *Dragstrip Riot*
C. *Summer Love*
D. *The Rebel Set*

87. What actress portrays Queen Elizabeth I in 1957's *The Story of Mankind*?

A. Agnes Moorehead
B. Deborah Kerr
C. Ingrid Bergman
D. Olivia de Havilland

answers found on page 546

88. The 1950 Paul Henreid film *So Young, So Bad* marked the film debut of what actress?

A. Marilyn Monroe
B. Natalie Wood
C. Rita Moreno
D. Sophia Loren

89. In 1951, Bette Davis earned her first Best Actress nomination in six years for her performance in *All About Eve*. Who won the award that year?

A. Anne Baxter
B. Eleanor Parker
C. Gloria Swanson
D. Judy Holliday

Blackboard Jungle, 1955

90. How many Academy Award nominations did the 1955 film *Blackboard Jungle* receive?

A. 2
B. 4
C. 6
D. 8

91. From 1953 to 1957 Ann Sothern starred in a successful television series. What was it?

A. *December Bride*
B. *Father Knows Best*
C. *Private Secretary*
D. *The Real McCoys*

92. In 1953, who did Anne Bancroft marry?

A. Arthur Penn
B. Martin May
C. Mel Brooks
D. Warren Beatty

93. What is the name of Ralph Meeker's character in the 1952 film *Glory Alley*?

A. Peppi Donnato
B. Shadow Johnson
C. Socks Barbarrosa
D. Spider Domingo

94. In the mid-1950s, Anthony Asquith directed ballet productions for British television starring Rudolf Nureyev and which prima ballerina?

A. Alexandra Danilova
B. Cynthia Gregory
C. Margot Fonteyn
D. Sylvie Guillem

95. In his 1958 Hollywood debut, Sean Connery was featured in what film starring Lana Turner?

A. *Another Time, Another Place*
B. *The Frightened City*
C. *The Hill*
D. *Woman of Straw*

96. The 1957 musical *Funny Face*, starring Audrey Hepburn and Fred Astaire, received Academy Award nominations in all of the following categories except which one?

A. Best Actress
B. Best Art Direction
C. Best Cinematography
D. Best Original Screenplay

97. In the 1957 film *The Story of Mankind*, Napoleon Bonaparte is portrayed by which of the following actors?

A. Anthony Hopkins
B. Dennis Hopper
C. Gene Kelly
D. Ronald Colman

98. Sophia Loren won the Academy Award for Best Actress for her performance in the 1960 film *Two Women,* but she was not present at the ceremony when she won. Who accepted the award that night on her behalf?

    A. Angela Lansbury
    B. Greer Garson
    C. Jane Wyman
    D. Janet Leigh

99. Barbara Bel Geddes starred in the 1950 film *Panic in the Streets.* Who was the director?

    A. Elia Kazan
    B. George Stevens
    C. Robert Wise
    D. Sidney Lumet

100. The 1955 musical *Guys and Dolls* was nominated for Academy Awards in all of the following categories except which one?

    A. Best Actor
    B. Best Art Direction
    C. Best Cinematography
    D. Best Costume Design

101. The 1952 film *Scandal Sheet* was adapted from what novel written by Samuel Fuller?

    A. *Park Row*
    B. *The Dark Page*
    C. *The Last Laugh*
    D. *The Steel Helmet*

102. Luise Rainer appeared in the episode "A Bouquet for Caroline" of what 1950s television program?

    A. *Lux Video Theatre*
    B. *Kraft Suspense Theatre*
    C. *The Alfred Hitchcock Hour*
    D. *Wagon Train*

103. What Russ Tamblyn musical beat *Torpedo Run* for the Best Special Effects Oscar in 1959?

    A. *Seven Brides for Seven Brothers*
    B. *The Wonderful World of the Brothers Grimm*
    C. *tom thumb*
    D. *West Side Story*

104. In Chuck Jones's 1950 cartoon *The Hypo-Chondri-Cat* two mice harass a cat named what?

    A. Claude
    B. Max
    C. Sam
    D. Sylvester

105. The 1950 Dorothy McGuire film *Mister 880* is about a man who is a what?

    A. Arsonist
    B. Counterfeiter
    C. Murderer
    D. Spy

106. What is the name of Barbara Bel Geddes's character in the 1958 film *Vertigo*?

    A. Lila
    B. Madeleine
    C. Midge
    D. Sue

107. In *The Ten Commandments* (1956), Woody Strode played which character/s?

    A. A slave
    B. An Ethiopian king
    C. Both
    D. Neither

108. In the 1952 film *Clash by Night,* Barbara Stanwyck appears with which of the following actresses?

    A. Ingrid Bergman
    B. Lana Turner
    C. Marilyn Monroe
    D. Rita Hayworth

answers found on page 546

109. The 1956 film *Slightly Scarlet* was based on a James M. Cain story. What actress starred in it?

A. Barbara Stanwyck
B. Jean Arthur
C. Kim Novak
D. Rhonda Fleming

110. In Jack Arnold's *No Name on the Bullet* (1959), how many men has hired gunman John Grant killed?

A. 17
B. 23
C. 27
D. 32

111. Thelma Ritter cohosted the 1954 Academy Awards ceremony with which of the following people?

A. Bob Hope
B. Donald O'Connor
C. George Burns
D. Jerry Lewis

112. In the 1951 film *Mark of the Renegade*, Ricardo Montalban starred opposite which actress who was a former dancer with the Ballet Russe?

A. Ann Miller
B. Cyd Charisse
C. Ginger Rogers
D. Jane Powell

113. The 1959 film *The 400 Blows* was nominated for an Academy Award in what category?

A. Best Actor
B. Best Cinematography
C. Best Foreign Language Film
D. Best Original Screenplay

114. Who is Tony Curtis chained to throughout the 1958 film *The Defiant Ones*?

A. Burt Lancaster
B. Cary Grant
C. Glenn Ford
D. Sidney Poitier

115. For what 1950s movie was James Cagney nominated for Best Actor?

A. *Love Me or Leave Me* (1955)
B. *The Seven Little Foys* (1955)
C. *These Wilder Years* (1956)
D. *What Price Glory* (1952)

116. In the 1950s, Peter Lawford starred in a television series based on what film?

A. *Ocean's Eleven* (1960)
B. *Son of Lassie* (1945)
C. *The Picture of Dorian Gray* (1945)
D. *The Thin Man* (1934)

117. The 1958 Alfred Hitchcock thriller *Vertigo* was nominated for two Academy Awards. One was for Best Art Direction. What was the other for?

A. Best Director
B. Best Editing
C. Best Musical Score
D. Best Sound

An American in Paris, 1951

118. In *An American in Paris* (1951), Gene Kelly danced with a group of what while singing "I Got Rhythm"?

A. Nurses
B. Schoolchildren
C. Singers
D. Street vendors

Spotlight on
MARLON **BRANDO** (1924–2004)

Although Brando never considered himself a Method actor, he studied with New York teacher Stella Adler, who taught him to create impressively realistic performances by dredging up evocative past memories. He started acting at an early age to pull his mother out of frequent drunken stupors. Following his actress sister, Jocelyn, to New York in 1943, he did impressive stage work in *I Remember Mama* and *A Streetcar Named Desire* before signing to make his film debut as a paraplegic veteran in *The Men* (1950). He won raves for the performance, but the film that clearly carved his niche on screen was *A Streetcar Named Desire* (1951), in which animalistic Stanley Kowalski (Brando) menaced Vivien Leigh's faded Southern belle Blanche DuBois. The fifties were Brando's golden years, capped by an Oscar win for *On the Waterfront* (1954). By the sixties, however, indulgent on-set behavior (particularly during the filming of 1962's *Mutiny on the Bounty*) and offscreen excesses led to complaints that he was squandering his talent. He bounced back when young director Francis Ford Coppola fought to cast him as mafioso Vito Corleone in *The Godfather* (1972), which won Brando a second Best Actor Oscar.

A Streetcar Named Desire, 1951

Mutiny on the Bounty, 1962

1. Marlon Brando discovered and fell in love with Tahiti, where he kept a home until his death, while making which film?

   A. *Mutiny on the Bounty* (1962)
   B. *The Island of Dr. Moreau* (1996)
   C. *The Teahouse of the August Moon* (1956)
   D. *Viva Zapata!* (1952)

2. How many Academy Award nominations did Marlon Brando receive in his lifetime?

   A. 2
   B. 4
   C. 6
   D. 8

3. Marlon Brando plays Napoleon Bonaparte opposite Merle Oberon in which film?

   A. *Affectionately Yours* (1941)

   B. *Desiree* (1954)
   C. *Forever and a Day* (1943)
   D. *This Love of Ours* (1945)

4. The Marlon Brando classic *A Streetcar Named Desire* (1951) was based on a play by which famous author?

   A. Arthur Miller
   B. Eugene O'Neill
   C. Noel Coward
   D. Tennessee Williams

5. Marlon Brando surprised everyone by taking a large singing part in which of the following musicals?

   A. *An American in Paris* (1951)
   B. *Guys and Dolls* (1955)
   C. *Seven Brides for Seven Brothers* (1954)
   D. *The Best Little Whorehouse in Texas* (1982)

119. The 1956 Gregory Peck film *Moby Dick* was based on the classic novel by what author?

A. Ernest Hemingway
B. Herman Melville
C. John Steinbeck
D. Leo Tolstoy

120. In the 1957 film *Until They Sail*, Sandra Dee plays one of four sisters living in what country?

A. Australia
B. France
C. India
D. New Zealand

121. June Allyson made how many films in 1950 with her future husband Dick Powell?

A. 1
B. 2
C. 3
D. 4

122. In what category did the 1954 film *It Should Happen to You* receive its only Academy Award nomination?

A. Best Art Direction
B. Best Costume Design
C. Best Original Score
D. Best Supporting Actress

123. What is the name of the young protagonist in Ray Bradbury's 1957 novel *Dandelion Wine*?

A. Daniel
B. David
C. Donald
D. Douglas

124. In 1959, Sean Connery starred in which Greek drama at the Oxford playhouse?

A. *Hippolytus*
B. *Plutus*
C. *The Achamians*
D. *The Bacchae*

125. In the 1953 film *Mogambo*, who is Ava Gardner's rival for the affections of Clark Gable?

A. Grace Kelly
B. Janet Leigh
C. Marlene Dietrich
D. Susan Hayward

126. The 1951 film *Ace in the Hole* was nominated for an Academy Award in what category?

A. Best Actor
B. Best Editing
C. Best Original Score
D. Best Screenplay

127. Who was originally set to direct the 1957 film *The Garment Jungle* before he was replaced by Vincent Sherman?

A. Fritz Lang
B. Nicholas Ray
C. Robert Aldrich
D. Robert Siodmak

128. The 1952 film *With a Song in My Heart* costars Thelma Ritter and is a biopic of what singer?

A. Edith Piaf
B. Jane Froman
C. Lillian Roth
D. Ruth Etting

129. In *Voice in the Mirror* (1958), what is the profession of Walter Matthau's character?

A. Doctor
B. FBI agent
C. Journalist
D. Police chief

130. The 1950 film *Sunset Blvd.* was nominated for eleven Academy Awards. How many did it win?

A. 0
B. 1
C. 2
D. 3

answers found on page 546

131. In the 1950 film *Champagne for Caesar*, who is "Caesar"?

A. Beauregard's best friend
B. Beauregard's pet parrot
C. Happy's pet cat
D. Happy's pet iguana

132. In the 1951 film *The Mating Season,* Thelma Ritter's character is mistaken for a what?

A. Doctor
B. Maid
C. Queen
D. Thief

133. In Jack Arnold's *The Mouse That Roared* (1959), what is the name of the tiny country that declares war on the United States?

A. Grand Fenwick
B. Liechtenstein
C. Malta
D. Monaco

134. In what country is the 1958 Mark Robson film *The Inn of the Sixth Happiness* set?

A. China
B. Ireland
C. Spain
D. Turkey

135. Bing Crosby starred in the 1950 film *Riding High*. Who directed it?

A. Billy Wilder
B. Charles Walters
C. Frank Capra
D. Victor Fleming

136. Ricardo Montalban starred opposite Anne Bancroft in what 1955 thriller?

A. *A Life in the Balance*
B. *Border Incident*
C. *Don't Bother to Knock*
D. *Mystery Street*

137. Sophia Loren's 1959 film *That Kind of Woman* was a remake of what earlier film?

A. *Four Daughters* (1938)
B. *Pygmalion* (1938)
C. *The Shopworn Angel* (1928)
D. *You Can't Take It with You* (1938)

138. In 1953, Bette Davis had an operation to remove a section of what part of her body?

A. Her jaw
B. Her left ear
C. Her nose
D. Her right foot

139. In the 1954 film *Deep in My Heart*, Jane Powell performs the song "Will You Remember?" with whom?

A. Andy Williams
B. Frank Sinatra
C. Mel Torme
D. Vic Damone

140. In *Just for You* (1952), Ethel Barrymore plays headmistress to what famous young ingénue?

A. Debbie Reynolds
B. Leslie Caron
C. Natalie Wood
D. Shirley MacLaine

141. What is Gidget's real name in the 1959 Sandra Dee film *Gidget*?

A. Frances Fisher
B. Frances Fitzgerald
C. Frances Houseman
D. Frances Lawrence

142. What is the name of Louis Armstrong's character in *Glory Alley* (1952)?

A. Dizzy Simon
B. Notes Walker
C. Shadow Johnson
D. Socks Barbarrosa

143. The 1955 Kerwin Mathews film *5 Against the House* marked one of the first screen appearances of what sexy blonde star?

   A. Brigitte Bardot
   B. Jayne Mansfield
   C. Kim Novak
   D. Marilyn Monroe

144. Who was Ronald Reagan's best man when he married Nancy Davis in 1952?

   A. Burt Lancaster
   B. Edward G. Robinson
   C. Pat O'Brien
   D. William Holden

145. Ricardo Montalban made his Broadway debut in 1955 as Chico in the original version of what musical?

   A. *Fanny*
   B. *Kiss Me, Kate*
   C. *Seventh Heaven*
   D. *The Most Happy Fella*

146. In the 1953 film *The Glass Wall*, the title refers to what?

   A. Chrysler building
   B. Rockefeller Center
   C. The Louvre
   D. United Nations building

147. The 1957 film *Witness for the Prosecution* received Academy Award nominations in all of the following categories except which one?

   A. Best Director
   B. Best Original Screenplay
   C. Best Picture
   D. Best Supporting Actress

148. In 1959, Alfred Newman and his brother Lionel competed against each other for the Academy Award for Best Musical Score. Who won the award?

   A. Alfred Newman
   B. Andre Previn

   C. Lionel Newman
   D. Ray Heindorf

149. In *A Face in the Crowd* (1957), Walter Matthau's character is often referred to by the name of his alma mater. What school was it?

   A. Auburn
   B. Harvard
   C. Michigan State
   D. Vanderbilt

Gigi, 1958

150. The 1958 musical *Gigi* won Oscars in every category for which it was nominated. How many was that?

   A. 12
   B. 3
   C. 6
   D. 9

151. Fay Wray returned to films in the 1950s, after a long absence, with a role in what movie?

   A. *Hell on Frisco Bay* (1955)
   B. *Queen Bee* (1955)
   C. *Small Town Girl* (1953)
   D. *The Cobweb* (1955)

152. In the 1954 film *Sabrina*, the title character travels to Paris to become a what?

   A. Fashion designer
   B. Fashion model
   C. Gourmet chef
   D. Painter

153. The 1950 Jane Powell film *Nancy Goes to Rio* was a remake of what Deanna Durbin film?

A. *Hers to Hold* (1943)
B. *I'll Be Yours* (1947)
C. *It's a Date* (1940)
D. *That Certain Age* (1938)

154. The 1956 film *Gervaise* received an Academy Award nomination in what category?

A. Best Foreign Language Film
B. Best Musical Score
C. Best Original Screenplay
D. Best Supporting Actress

155. The 1955 film *Love Is a Many Splendored Thing* won Academy Awards in all of the following categories except which one?

A. Best Actress
B. Best Costume Design
C. Best Musical Score
D. Best Original Song

156. Who beat Deborah Kerr in the 1954 Best Actress Oscar race?

A. Audrey Hepburn
B. Ava Gardner
C. Elizabeth Taylor
D. Leslie Caron

157. In which one of the following categories did the 1951 film *The Great Caruso* win an Academy Award?

A. Best Art Direction
B. Best Director
C. Best Picture
D. Best Sound

158. John Sturges's *The Magnificent Yankee* (1950) was about what celebrated American jurist?

A. Annie Gough
B. Louis Brandeis
C. Oliver Wendell Holmes
D. Owen Wister

159. In the late 1940s and early 1950s, Edward Arnold portrayed a different president each week on what radio show?

A. *Imagination Theatre*
B. *Mr. President*
C. *The Rushmore Hour*
D. *The Twilight Zone*

160. What film was not directed by John Sturges in 1950?

A. *Mystery Street*
B. *Right Cross*
C. *The Magnificent Yankee*
D. *Timber Fury*

161. The 1951 film *It's a Big Country* features all of the following stars except for which one?

A. Gary Cooper
B. Gene Kelly
C. Spencer Tracy
D. Van Johnson

162. Sandra Dee starred in *Tammy Tell Me True* (1961) and *Tammy and the Doctor* (1963). What actress originated the Tammy character in the 1957 film *Tammy and the Bachelor*?

A. Ann-Margret
B. Annette Funicello
C. Connie Stevens
D. Debbie Reynolds

163. What is the name of Brigitte Bardot's character in the 1956 film *Nero's Mistress*?

A. Agrippina
B. Poppea
C. Seneca
D. Ursula

164. Which leading lady made her film debut with a small role in 1951's *Fourteen Hours*?

A. Grace Kelly
B. Kim Novak
C. Lana Turner
D. Patricia Neal

165. The 1959 Marlon Brando film *The Fugitive Kind* was based on what Tennessee Williams play?

A. *Orpheus Descending*
B. *Summer and Smoke*
C. *Sweet Bird of Youth*
D. *The Rose Tattoo*

166. Louis Calhern was nominated for an Academy Award as Best Actor for his performance in what 1950 film?

A. *All About Eve*
B. *Born Yesterday*
C. *King Solomon's Mines*
D. *The Magnificent Yankee*

167. The 1955 Peter Sellers film *The Ladykillers* received its only Academy Award nomination in what category?

A. Best Editing
B. Best Original Score
C. Best Original Screenplay
D. Best Supporting Actor

168. While filming *Singin' in the Rain* (1952), which screen legend, visiting the set one day, helped Debbie Reynolds master the dance choreography?

A. Audrey Hepburn
B. Buster Keaton
C. Fred Astaire
D. Ginger Rogers

169. What was the name of the socialite played by Elizabeth Taylor in *A Place in the Sun* (1951)?

A. Ann Vickers
B. Gloria Wandrous
C. Leslie Benedict
D. Susanna Drake

170. What actress received an Academy Award nomination for Best Actress for her performance in the 1950 John Cromwell film *Caged*?

A. Bette Davis
B. Eleanor Parker
C. Olivia de Havilland
D. Susan Hayward

171. In Jack Arnold's *The Incredible Shrinking Man* (1957), what does Grant Williams's wife assume killed her husband when she believes him to be dead?

A. A cat
B. A dog
C. A snake
D. A spider

172. In 1955, Bette Davis reprised her role as Queen Elizabeth for which Henry Koster drama?

A. *Elizabeth*
B. *Mrs. Brown*
C. *The Private Lives of Elizabeth and Essex*
D. *The Virgin Queen*

173. In Jack Arnold's *The Mouse That Roared* (1959), which role did Peter Sellers not play?

A. Duchess Gloriana XII
B. Prime Minister Count Rupert Mountjoy
C. Professor Alfred Kokintz
D. Tully Bascombe

174. In Chuck Jones's 1952 cartoon *Feed the Kitty*, what happens to the kitten?

A. It falls into a batch of cookie dough.
B. It falls into wet cement.
C. It falls out a window.
D. It gets stuck inside a bowling ball.

175. What film was not directed by John Sturges in 1955?

A. *Bad Day at Black Rock*
B. *King's Rhapsody*
C. *The Scarlet Coat*
D. *Underwater!*

answers found on page 547

176. In which one of the following categories did the 1951 film *The Man in the White Suit* receive its only Oscar nomination?

A. Best Cinematography

B. Best Director

C. Best Musical Score

D. Best Screenplay

177. The 1958 Rosalind Russell film *Auntie Mame* received Academy Award nominations in all the following categories except which one?

A. Best Actress

B. Best Art Direction

C. Best Director

D. Best Picture

Lust for Life, 1956

178. The 1956 film *Lust for Life*, shot by cinematographer Freddie Young, was about the life of what famous painter?

A. Degas

B. Matisse

C. Monet

D. van Gogh

179. In the 1953 film *The Story of Three Loves*, Moira Shearer plays a dancer who suffers from what ailment?

A. A heart condition

B. Deafness

C. Paralysis

D. Polio

180. The 1956 film *The Power and the Prize*, starring Robert Taylor, was nominated for an Academy Award in what category?

A. Best Actor

B. Best Costume Design

C. Best Director

D. Best Musical Score

181. Which of the following songs does Jane Powell sing in the 1958 film *The Girl Most Likely*?

A. "A Song Is a Song"

B. "I Don't Know What I Want"

C. "Make Mine Yours"

D. "Your Love"

182. The 1954 Mark Robson film *The Bridge at Toko-Ri* won an Academy Award in what category?

A. Best Director

B. Best Editing

C. Best Sound

D. Best Special Effects

183. A billboard for what Marx Brothers film appears in 1950's *Three Little Words*, starring Fred Astaire and Red Skelton?

A. *A Night in Casablanca* (1946)

B. *Animal Crackers* (1930)

C. *At the Circus* (1939)

D. *Duck Soup* (1933)

184. What film won the Academy Award for Best Picture of 1951?

A. *A Place in the Sun*

B. *A Streetcar Named Desire*

C. *An American in Paris*

D. *Quo Vadis*

Spotlight on
LESLIE **CARON** (1931–)

As a dancer, Leslie Caron has worked with Gene Kelly, Fred Astaire, Rudolf Nureyev, and Mikhail Baryshnikov. As an actress, she has matured from the spritely gamine of *Lili* (1953) to the world-weary woman in *The Man Who Loved Women* (1977) and *Damage* (1992). Her career spans over sixty years and, with credits in four media on two continents, defines international stardom. Kelly first spotted her in 1948 as the Sphinx in a Roland Petit ballet about Oedipus at the Ballet de Champs Elysées. Three years later, he was looking for a leading lady for *An American in Paris* (1951) and remembered her, leading to an MGM contract and a film debut in one of the most acclaimed musicals of all time. Musically, she followed with roles in *Daddy Long Legs* (1955), opposite Astaire, and *Gigi* (1958). But Caron also established her dramatic credentials by winning Oscar nominations as the young innocent in *Lili* and an unwed pregnant woman in *The L-Shaped Room* (1962). Since leaving Hollywood in the sixties, Caron has acted around the world, recently appearing with Johnny Depp and Judi Dench in *Chocolat* (2000) and in Emmy-winning television roles.

An American in Paris, 1951

Lili, 1953

1. **What musical features Leslie Caron and Farley Granger?**

    A. *Funny Face* (1957)

    B. *Silk Stockings* (1957)

    C. *The Band Wagon* (1953)

    D. *The Story of Three Loves* (1953)

2. **How many Academy Award nominations did the 1953 Leslie Caron film *Lili* receive?**

    A. 2

    B. 4

    C. 6

    D. 8

3. **In *Glory Alley* (1952), Leslie Caron plays the girlfriend to a boxer who goes by what name?**

    A. Haystacks Calhoun

    B. Kid Natural

    C. Mountain Rivera

    D. Socks Barbarrosa

4. **The 1958 Leslie Caron film *The Doctor's Dilemma* was based on a play by what author?**

    A. Arthur Miller

    B. Edward Albee

    C. Garson Kanin

    D. George Bernard Shaw

5. **For what film did Gene Kelly direct Leslie Caron's intro sequences?**

    A. *An American in Paris* (1951)

    B. *It's Always Fair Weather* (1955)

    C. *On the Town* (1949)

    D. *Singin' in the Rain* (1952)

185. In the 1953 Jacques Tati film *Mr. Hulot's Holiday,* where does Mr. Hulot spend his vacation?

A. At home
B. At a beach resort
C. At a Swiss chalet
D. In a mountain cabin

186. In Jack Arnold's *The Incredible Shrinking Man* (1957), what causes the title character to start shrinking?

A. An atomic bomb
B. Pesticide
C. Pollution
D. Radiation

187. What film won the Academy Award for Best Picture of 1959?

A. *Anatomy of a Murder*
B. *Ben-Hur*
C. *The Diary of Anne Frank*
D. *The Nun's Story*

188. In the 1956 film *Meet Me in Las Vegas,* Paul Henreid played the manager to which of the following actresses?

A. Cyd Charisse
B. Doris Day
C. Judy Garland
D. Kathryn Grayson

189. The 1952 musical *Singin' in the Rain* features all of the following songs except for which one?

A. "Make 'em Laugh"
B. "Moses Supposes"
C. "Steppin' Out with My Baby"
D. "Would You"

190. The 1954 epic *Demetrius and the Gladiators* is the sequel to what film that costarred Richard Burton?

A. *Ben-Hur* (1959)
B. *Julius Caesar* (1950)

C. *The Greatest Story Ever Told* (1965)
D. *The Robe* (1953)

191. In 1957, Sophia Loren moved to Hollywood under contract to which studio?

A. MGM
B. Paramount
C. Universal
D. Warner Bros.

192. The title of the 1957 Sophia Loren film *Boy on a Dolphin* refers to a what?

A. Boat
B. Necklace
C. Painting
D. Statue

193. In the 1951 Spencer Tracy film *Father's Little Dividend,* to what does the term "dividend" refer?

A. A baby
B. A business deal
C. A dog
D. A house

194. In 1955, Benny Goodman sang a duet of the song "It's Bad for Me" with which female vocalist?

A. Dinah Shore
B. Doris Day
C. Lena Horne
D. Rosemary Clooney

195. In the 1959 Sandra Dee film *Gidget,* what is Gidget's main hobby?

A. Basketball
B. Football
C. Skiing
D. Surfing

answers found on page 547

196. In the 1957 film *The Story of Mankind*, which actor portrays Sir Walter Raleigh?

A. Edward Everett Horton
B. Gary Cooper
C. Laurence Olivier
D. Walter Huston

197. Which well-known author wrote a famous profile of Marlon Brando for *The New Yorker* in 1957?

A. Dorothy Parker
B. Harper Lee
C. Tennessee Williams
D. Truman Capote

198. In the 1951 Thelma Ritter film *The Model and the Marriage Broker*, which of the following actresses played the model?

A. Doris Day
B. Elizabeth Taylor
C. Jeanne Crain
D. Susan Kohner

199. The 1958 film *Bell, Book and Candle* was nominated for two Academy Awards. One was for Best Art Direction. What was the other for?

A. Best Actress
B. Best Costume Design
C. Best Editing
D. Best Special Effects

200. The 1954 film *20,000 Leagues Under the Sea* won two Academy Awards. One was for Best Special Effects. What was the other for?

A. Best Actor
B. Best Art Direction
C. Best Original Song
D. Best Picture

201. In the 1952 film *Stolen Face*, Paul Henreid played a what?

A. Banker
B. Gambler
C. Makeup artist
D. Plastic surgeon

202. What film won the Academy Award for Best Picture of 1958?

A. *Auntie Mame*
B. *Cat on a Hot Tin Roof*
C. *Gigi*
D. *Separate Tables*

203. Leslie Caron made a splash in *Gigi* in 1958. Who originated the role on Broadway?

A. Audrey Hepburn
B. Julie Andrews
C. Lee Remick
D. Mary Martin

204. In the 1959 comedy *Some Like It Hot*, what instrument does Tony Curtis's character play?

A. Clarinet
B. Drums
C. Saxophone
D. Xylophone

205. Jean Simmons starred in the 1951 film *The Clouded Yellow*. What does the title refer to?

A. A butterfly
B. A car
C. A diamond
D. A disease

206. Luise Rainer appeared in the episode "Rosalind" of what 1950s television program?

A. *Lux Video Theatre*
B. *Kraft Suspense Theatre*
C. *The Alfred Hitchcock Hour*
D. *Wagon Train*

207. Who was Robert Wagner's mentor in the 1950s?

A. Clark Gable
B. Humphrey Bogart
C. Spencer Tracy
D. Warren Beatty

answers found on page 547

208. In what category did the 1952 film *The Atomic City* receive its only Academy Award nomination?

A. Best Actor
B. Best Original Score
C. Best Special Effects
D. Best Writing, Story, and Screenplay

209. In *King Creole* (1958), what is the name of Walter Matthau's nightclub?

A. Bongo Room
B. Club Conga
C. The Blue Shade
D. The Slow Club

North by Northwest, 1959

210. The 1959 thriller *North by Northwest* was nominated for Academy Awards in all of the following categories except which one?

A. Best Art Direction
B. Best Director
C. Best Editing
D. Best Original Screenplay

211. 1957's *White Nights* was the first film that director Luchino Visconti made with which actor?

A. Burt Lancaster

B. Farley Granger
C. Helmut Berger
D. Marcello Mastroianni

212. In 1953, James Wong Howe directed a short about artist Dong Kingman, who subsequently created the paintings for the title sequence of which of the following films?

A. *Bell, Book and Candle* (1958)
B. *Flower Drum Song* (1961)
C. *Terminal Station* (1953)
D. *The Outrage* (1964)

213. In the 1953 comedy *The Affairs of Dobie Gillis*, Debbie Reynolds attends what fictional college?

A. Grainbelt University
B. Pleasantville College
C. Sunbelt Institute of Technology
D. Sunnydale School of Design

214. In 1952, Ethel Barrymore was awarded an honorary doctorate by which university?

A. Columbia
B. Cornell
C. NYU
D. Yale

215. The 1954 musical *Seven Brides for Seven Brothers* won an Academy Award in what category?

A. Best Actress
B. Best Costume Design
C. Best Original Score
D. Best Picture

216. The 1956 film *The Harder They Fall* received its only Academy Award nomination in what category?

A. Best Art Direction
B. Best Cinematography
C. Best Director
D. Best Original Screenplay

answers found on page 547

217. What actress who starred opposite Richard Burton in 1951's *Green Grow the Rushes* went on to become a Bond girl?

A. Daniela Bianchi
B. Honor Blackman
C. Ursula Andress
D. Zena Marshall

218. The 1955 Kerwin Mathews film *5 Against the House* was based on a novel by what famous author?

A. George Orwell
B. Jack Finney
C. L. Ron Hubbard
D. Ray Bradbury

219. In the 1958 film *Touch of Evil*, Janet Leigh's character spends her honeymoon in what country?

A. England
B. Italy
C. Mexico
D. Spain

220. The 1952 classic *Singin' in the Rain* features all of the following stars except for which one?

A. Ann Miller
B. Cyd Charisse
C. Debbie Reynolds
D. Rita Moreno

221. The 1932 Jean Harlow film *Red Dust* was remade in 1953. What was the title of the remake?

A. *Elephant Walk*
B. *Mogambo*
C. *Taras Bulba*
D. *The Barefoot Contessa*

222. In the 1955 cartoon *One Froggy Evening*, directed by Chuck Jones, where is the singing frog first discovered?

A. In an old barn
B. In the cornerstone of an old building

C. Inside a shoe
D. Under a log

223. The 1951 musical *Royal Wedding* received an Academy Award nomination for Best Original Song. What was the name of the song?

A. "Open Your Eyes"
B. "The Happiest Day of My Life"
C. "Too Late Now"
D. "What a Lovely Day for a Wedding"

224. The 1952 Paul Henreid film *For Men Only* deals with what subject?

A. Fraternity hazing
B. Gang violence
C. Pornography
D. Teenage pregnancy

225. Which star of 1958's *Cat on a Hot Tin Roof* was the voice of Sam the Snowman in the television classic *Rudolph, the Red-Nosed Reindeer*?

A. Burl Ives
B. Hal Holbrook
C. Paul Newman
D. Vaughn Taylor

226. The 1958 film *The Girl Most Likely*, starring Jane Powell, was a remake of what Ginger Rogers film?

A. *Follow the Fleet* (1936)
B. *Kitty Foyle: The Natural History of a Woman* (1940)
C. *Tender Comrade* (1943)
D. *Tom, Dick and Harry* (1941)

227. Who plays Ann Sothern's daughter in the 1950 film *Nancy Goes to Rio*?

A. Debbie Reynolds
B. Esther Williams
C. Jane Powell
D. Julie Andrews

answers found on page 547

228. What film won the Oscar for Best Story and Screenplay in 1951?

A. *Adam's Rib*
B. *All About Eve*
C. *Born Yesterday*
D. *Sunset Blvd.*

229. In the 1957 film *The Story of Mankind*, Sir Isaac Newton is portrayed by which actor?

A. Groucho Marx
B. Harpo Marx
C. James Stewart
D. Stewart Granger

Athena, 1954

230. The 1954 film *Athena*, starring Jane Powell, was originally intended as a vehicle for what actress?

A. Ann Miller
B. Esther Williams
C. Janet Leigh
D. Judy Garland

231. Which of her costars did Bette Davis marry in 1950?

A. Errol Flynn
B. Gary Merrill
C. Herbert Marshall
D. James Mason

232. In the 1950 film *A Woman of Distinction*, what is the profession of Rosalind Russell's character?

A. College dean
B. Doctor
C. Nurse
D. Photographer

233. In 1958, Sandra Dee and Carolyn Jones shared the Golden Globe for Best Promising Newcomer with what *Peyton Place* actress?

A. Diane Varsi
B. Hope Lange
C. Tami Conner
D. Terry Moore

234. The title of Mark Robson's 1954 film *Phffft!* came from a term often used by which famous gossip columnist?

A. Hedda Hopper
B. Louella Parsons
C. Sheila Graham
D. Walter Winchell

235. Charles Laughton lost the Best Actor Academy Award in 1958 to whom?

A. Alec Guinness
B. Bing Crosby
C. Cary Grant
D. Humphrey Bogart

236. The 1953 Mark Robson film *Return to Paradise* was based on a short story by what author?

A. Ernest Hemingway
B. Herman Melville
C. James Michener
D. John Steinbeck

237. To which actress did Joan Blondell lose the Academy Award for Best Supporting Actress in 1952?

A. Kim Hunter
B. Lee Grant
C. Mildred Dunnock
D. Thelma Ritter

answers found on page 547

238. What was the name of Anna May Wong's short-lived television series in 1951?

A. *Chinatown Rose*
B. *Marvel of Miracles*
C. *Tales of the Dragon*
D. *The Gallery of Madame Liu-Tsong*

239. What actress portrays Cleopatra in 1957's *The Story of Mankind*?

A. Lena Horne
B. Marilyn Monroe
C. Sophia Loren
D. Virginia Mayo

240. During the 1950s, Gore Vidal wrote three mystery novels under what pseudonym?

A. Edgar Box
B. Edwin Cox
C. Erwin Fox
D. Ethan Nox

241. In 1953, Gene Krupa portrayed himself in a film biography of what famous musician?

A. Dizzy Gillespie
B. Duke Ellington
C. Glenn Miller
D. Harry James

242. How many times in the 1950s did a film win exactly six Oscars?

A. 0
B. 1
C. 2
D. 3

243. Ricardo Montalban portrayed a Blackfoot war chief opposite Clark Gable in which 1951 film?

A. *A Free Soul*
B. *Across the Wide Missouri*
C. *Fighting Blood*
D. *The Saracen Blade*

Raintree County, 1957

244. The 1957 film *Raintree County* was nominated for Academy Awards in all of the following categories except which one?

A. Best Actress
B. Best Costume Design
C. Best Musical Score
D. Best Picture

245. In my autobiography, I claim to have broken off my affair with actor Jeff Chandler after discovering he was a cross-dresser. Who am I?

A. Elizabeth Taylor
B. Esther Williams
C. Judy Garland
D. Lena Horne

2001: A Space Odyssey, 1968

Chapter 5

THE 1960s
AND BEYOND

The changes that had started in the fifties snowballed in subsequent decades, bringing the old method of making movies to an end but also heralding exciting new ways of reaching audiences. Careers and studios fell in the first waves of uncertainty, yet Hollywood survived by adapting to changing times.

Increasingly, the studios withdrew from the assembly-line production mentality of the studio era to become financiers and distributors of independent product. They also experienced major shifts in management as most became parts of international conglomerates that treated them as one of many subsidiaries. By the seventies, the studio moguls who loved the movies they made were replaced by businessmen, many with no Hollywood interests beyond their interest in profits.

One factor hastening the fall of the studios was the increasing reliance on big-budget blockbusters. Despite the success and high profit margins for more modest films like *The Apartment* (1960), everybody wanted the next *Ben-Hur* (1959) or *Lawrence of Arabia* (1962). As a result, high-budget films like 20th Century-Fox's *Cleopatra* (1963) almost sank the studios when they failed to deliver box-office returns approaching their production budgets. The same thing happened to musicals after *The Sound of Music* (1965) became the first film to topple *Gone With the Wind* (1939) as all-time box-office champ. Every studio launched its own location-shot tune fest, only to lose money on the likes of *Star!* (1968) and *Lost Horizon* (1973).

In the late sixties, a new type of moviemaking emerged as Hollywood realized there was a younger audience eager to see its values on screen. As the Vietnam War and a series of political scandals and assassinations shook people's faith in the American way of life, a new generation of fans embraced *Bonnie and Clyde* and *The Graduate* (both 1967), films with heroes far outside the Hollywood mold. When audiences flocked to watch the visually dazzling but structurally diffuse *2001: A Space Odyssey* (1968) and *Easy Rider* (1969), every studio set out to prove its movies were the hippest ever.

These movies brought with them new types of stars. Dustin Hoffman in *The Graduate* and Dennis Hopper and Jack Nicholson in *Easy Rider* were far from the conventionally handsome leading men Hollywood once cast. Transforming themselves into character was more important than making the fans swoon. They paved the way for other unconventional stars like Gene Hackman, Walter Matthau, and Barbra Streisand.

Stardom also became more of an international affair. At the height of the studios' power, each had employed its own foreign-born stars, creating virtual colonies of expatriates in Hollywood. But with the studio contract system declining, stars like Leslie Caron, Sophia Loren, and Sean Connery moved freely from country to country, going wherever they could find the best roles.

One distinct departure from the past was increasing diversity. Sidney Poitier's Best Actor Oscar for *Lilies of the Field* (1963), the first awarded to a black actor in a competitive category, marked his rise to become the screen's first black superstar, assuming the mantle of integrity previously reserved for white stars like Gregory Peck and Henry Fonda. The heir to his throne, Denzel Washington, has been able to perform within an even greater range, winning an Oscar as a corrupt police detective in *Training Day* (2001). The Academy Awards are one marker of this growing diversity. In the first decade of the twenty-first century, seven black actors won the coveted award in competitive categories, versus two in the first four decades of Academy history.

Now, a new generation of directors has drawn inspiration from the midcentury films that thrilled them in childhood. In 1975, Steven Spielberg recaptured the joys of monster movies past with *Jaws*, then mined his favorite adventure serials for the Indiana Jones films. His friend George Lucas brought back space heroes like Flash Gordon and Buck Rogers in the form of Luke Skywalker and Han Solo in *Star Wars* (1977), and suddenly the once-derided science fiction and horror genres were hot.

Hollywood has lost a lot since the sixties as old ways of doing business have faded. But it has also gained a lot in the form of new talents, new ways of telling stories, and new means of reflecting the diverse, global environment in which we live.

1. How many times in the 1990s did a film win exactly seven Oscars?
   A. 0
   B. 1
   C. 2
   D. 3

2. In 2004, Neil Simon received a kidney transplant from whom?
   A. Brother Danny Simon
   B. Daughter Nancy Simon
   C. Press agent Bill Evans
   D. Wife Elaine Joyce

3. In the 1965 film *The Slender Thread*, who tries desperately to keep Anne Bancroft's character from committing suicide?
   A. Charlton Heston
   B. James Earl Jones
   C. Sidney Poitier
   D. Tony Curtis

4. The title of 1998's *Naturally Native* refers to a product line of what?
   A. Cosmetics
   B. Soap
   C. Swimwear
   D. Wedding gowns

5. In 1972, Jackie Chan appeared in the film *Lady Kung Fu*. What actress played the title character?
   A. Angela Mao
   B. Li Gong
   C. Joan Chen
   D. Pam Grier

6. In 1984, Sophia Loren published a book on what topic?
   A. Animals
   B. Beauty
   C. Jewelry
   D. Travel

7. In the 1971 film *Cold Turkey*, starring Dick Van Dyke, an entire town tries to stop doing what?
   A. Drinking
   B. Gambling
   C. Lying
   D. Smoking

8. The 1975 film *The Stepford Wives*, starring Katharine Ross, was based on a novel by what author?
   A. Dean Koontz
   B. Ira Levin
   C. Peter Straub
   D. Stephen King

9. In the 1977 film *Oh, God!* what actor plays the role of God?
   A. Don Rickles
   B. George Burns
   C. Jerry Lewis
   D. Steve Lawrence

10. How many times in the 1960s did a film win exactly eight Oscars?
    A. 1
    B. 2
    C. 3
    D. 4

11. In 1989, what position did Roddy McDowall receive from the National Film Preservation Board?
    A. Chairman
    B. Director of Photography
    C. Honorary member
    D. Screen Actors Guild representative

12. In the 1977 film *The Turning Point*, Anne Bancroft plays a what?
    A. Ballet dancer
    B. Lawyer
    C. Nun
    D. Teacher

answers found on page 547

13. What was the title of the 1972 novel that Joan Blondell wrote?

A. *Center Door Fancy*
B. *Fancy Free Folks*
C. *Knock at the Door*
D. *Murder at Harker House*

14. Raymond Massey played which character in the 1969 film *Mackenna's Gold*?

A. Old Adams
B. The Editor
C. The Preacher
D. The Storekeeper

15. In what 1980s television show did Pam Grier become a regular?

A. *A Different World*
B. *MacGyver*
C. *Miami Vice*
D. *The Cosby Show*

16. In the 1979 comedy *Love at First Bite*, George Hamilton romances which of the following actresses?

A. Annie Potts
B. Jane Curtin
C. Jessica Lange
D. Susan Saint James

17. In 2000, Rita Moreno was presented an award by which organization recognizing her efforts in raising awareness as a champion of its cause?

A. Greenpeace
B. National Arthritis Foundation
C. National Osteoporosis Foundation
D. PETA

18. The 1978 Bruce Lee film *Game of Death* features what famous athlete in one of the roles?

A. Bruce Jenner
B. Jim Brown
C. Kareem Abdul-Jabbar
D. O. J. Simpson

19. Jane Powell had a recurring role on what popular 1980s sitcom?

A. *Gimme a Break*
B. *Growing Pains*
C. *The Cosby Show*
D. *The Facts of Life*

20. In the 1971 Jacques Tati film *Traffic*, an automobile inventor travels from Paris to an exhibition in what city?

A. Amsterdam
B. Florence
C. London
D. Rome

21. What film won the Academy Award for Best Picture of 1976?

A. *All the President's Men*
B. *Bound for Glory*
C. *Network*
D. *Rocky*

22. In the 1961 comedy *The Absent-Minded Professor*, Fred MacMurray plays a professor of what subject?

A. Chemistry
B. English
C. History
D. Math

23. The 1992 film *A River Runs Through It* won its only Academy Award in what category?

A. Best Art Direction
B. Best Cinematography
C. Best Director
D. Best Musical Score

24. In 1991, what award did Roddy McDowall receive from the Motion Picture and Television Fund?

A. Bronze Medal
B. Gold Box
C. Golden Popcorn
D. Silver Medallion Award

answers found on page 547

25. How many times in the 1960s did a film win exactly seven Oscars?

A. 0
B. 1
C. 2
D. 3

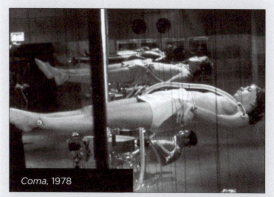

Coma, 1978

26. In the 1978 thriller *Coma*, Richard Widmark plays a what?

A. Detective
B. Janitor
C. Lawyer
D. Surgeon

27. In 1999, Franz Waxman was honored with what?

A. A U.S. postage stamp
B. A star on the Hollywood Walk of Fame
C. An honorary Oscar
D. Induction into the Composers' Hall of Fame

28. The 1962 film *Mutiny on the Bounty* was nominated for Academy Awards in all of the following categories except which one?

A. Best Actor
B. Best Cinematography
C. Best Musical Score
D. Best Picture

29. In the 2000 film *Remember the Titans*, Denzel Washington plays a what?

A. Boxer
B. Football coach

C. Lawyer
D. Police detective

30. In 1961, Robert Redford starred in what Broadway production?

A. *A Loss of Roses*
B. *Sunday in New York*
C. *Sweet Bird of Youth*
D. *The Long Dream*

31. In 1975, Meryl Streep made her Broadway debut in which production at Lincoln Center's Vivian Beaumont Theater?

A. *Man and Superman*
B. *Sunday in New York*
C. *Tartuffe*
D. *Trelawny of the "Wells"*

32. The 1963 Walter Matthau film *Charade* received only one Academy Award nomination. What was it for?

A. Best Actress
B. Best Cinematography
C. Best Editing
D. Best Song

33. In 1964, Ernest Borgnine had a month-long marriage to what actress?

A. Angela Lansbury
B. Eleanor Parker
C. Ethel Merman
D. Judy Garland

34. In the 2000 Leslie Caron film *The Last of the Blonde Bombshells*, "Blonde Bombshells" refers to what?

A. Hairdressers
B. Swing band
C. Tap dancers
D. Women's baseball team

35. In 1999, to what short did Deanna Durbin lend her singing voice?

A. *Fremde*
B. *Love Is All*
C. *Quiver*
D. *The Unfinished Journey*

36. The 1964 film *Kwaidan* was nominated for an Academy Award as Best Foreign Language Film. What country was it from?

A. Iran
B. Japan
C. Russia
D. Spain

37. The 1966 Roddy McDowall film *The Defector* was the last film ever made by what actor before his death?

A. James Dean
B. Montgomery Clift
C. Sal Mineo
D. Steve McQueen

38. Sally Field won an Emmy for her riveting portrayal of the title character in the 1976 television miniseries *Sybil*. Who was Field's costar?

A. Ellen Burstyn
B. Joanne Woodward
C. Linda Lavin
D. Louise Fletcher

39. Deborah Kerr made a brief return to feature films in what drama about a British widow's friendship with her East Indian neighbor?

A. *My Beautiful Laundrette* (1985)
B. *My Son the Fanatic* (1997)
C. *The Arrangement* (1997)
D. *The Assam Garden* (1985)

40. In 1964, what production company did Roddy McDowall form?

A. McDowell Inc.
B. RoddyCo.

C. Silver Lion Inc.
D. Studio of the Apes

41. The 1962 film *What Ever Happened to Baby Jane?* won its only Academy Award in which of the following categories?

A. Best Costume Design
B. Best Musical Score
C. Best Supporting Actor
D. Best Visual Effects

42. How old was Bruce Lee when he died in 1973?

A. 30
B. 31
C. 32
D. 33

43. In 1982, Ann Miller appeared with Van Johnson and Cab Calloway in a special episode of what television series?

A. *Dallas*
B. *Dynasty*
C. *M*A*S*H*
D. *The Love Boat*

44. The 1975 Nancy Kwan film *That Lady from Peking* revolves around the search for a missing what?

A. Child
B. Diamond
C. Diary
D. Statue

45. What film won the Best Picture Academy Award for 1962?

A. *Lawrence of Arabia*
B. *Mutiny on the Bounty*
C. *The Music Man*
D. *To Kill a Mockingbird*

answers found on page 548

46. The 1973 film *The Sting* is set in what city?

A. Chicago
B. Copenhagen
C. Kenosha
D. Syracuse

47. In which of the following categories did the 1960 film *Tunes of Glory,* starring Alec Guinness, receive its only Oscar nomination?

A. Best Actor
B. Best Adapted Screenplay
C. Best Cinematography
D. Best Musical Score

48. Samuel Fuller wrote the story for which episode of the 1960s television show *The Roaring 20's*?

A. "Burnett's Woman"
B. "Footlights"
C. "The Maestro"
D. "The Prairie Flower"

49. In the 1968 James Shigeta film *Nobody's Perfect,* what valuable item does the ship's crew steal?

A. A Buddha statue
B. A diamond necklace
C. A gold watch
D. An antique clock

50. The 1963 comedy classic *It's a Mad, Mad, Mad, Mad World* was nominated for Academy Awards in all of the following categories except which one?

A. Best Cinematography
B. Best Original Song
C. Best Picture
D. Best Sound

51. The 1965 Charlton Heston film *The Greatest Story Ever Told* received five Academy Award nominations. How many did it win?

A. 0
B. 1
C. 2
D. 3

Blow-Up, 1966

52. The 1966 film *Blow-Up* received an Academy Award nomination in which of the following categories?

A. Best Art Direction
B. Best Editing
C. Best Original Screenplay
D. Best Picture

53. When filming *The Graduate* (1967), actors Anne Bancroft and Dustin Hoffman were actually how many years apart in age?

A. 1
B. 15
C. 23
D. 6

54. In 1987, Moira Shearer published a book about what person?

A. Bob Fosse
B. George Balanchine
C. Margot Fonteyn
D. Mikhail Baryshnikov

55. In the 1978 film *Foul Play*, Burgess Meredith plays landlord to what young starlet?

A. Goldie Hawn
B. Karen Black
C. Meryl Streep
D. Susan Sarandon

56. In which of the following categories was the 1964 Leslie Caron film *Father Goose* not nominated for an Academy Award?

A. Best Cinematography
B. Best Editing
C. Best Original Screenplay
D. Best Sound

57. In the 1967 film *The Incident*, a group of people is held hostage where?

A. At the Empire State Building
B. At the Statue of Liberty
C. On a New York subway train
D. On an airplane

58. The 1965 Peter Sellers film *What's New, Pussycat?* features the Oscar-nominated title song made famous by what singer?

A. Andy Williams
B. Frank Sinatra
C. Mel Torme
D. Tom Jones

59. In the 1990 film *Heart Condition*, which of the following actors costars with Denzel Washington?

A. Anthony Hopkins
B. Bob Hoskins
C. Keifer Sutherland
D. Robert De Niro

60. In what American city does the action of Jules Dassin's 1968 film *Up Tight!* take place?

A. Atlanta
B. Biloxi
C. Cleveland
D. Detroit

61. In what city is Ray Bradbury's 2002 novel *Let's All Kill Constance* set?

A. Chicago
B. Los Angeles
C. Miami
D. New York

62. In 1997, Marlon Brando appeared in *The Brave*, which was the directorial debut of which actor?

A. Billy Bob Thornton
B. Johnny Depp
C. Sean Penn
D. Tim Robbins

63. In 1974, Leslie Caron starred in the television miniseries *QB VII*. What does the title refer to?

A. A courtroom
B. A person with amnesia
C. A planet
D. An unclaimed crate

64. The 1966 film *Who's Afraid of Virginia Woolf?*, photographed by cinematographer Haskell Wexler, won Academy Awards in all of the following categories except which?

A. Best Actress
B. Best Art Direction
C. Best Picture
D. Best Supporting Actress

65. On *Saturday Night Live*, Bill Murray replaced which famous comedian?

A. Chevy Chase
B. Dan Aykroyd
C. Gilda Radner
D. John Belushi

66. In the 1976 film *A Star Is Born*, Barbra Streisand's character is performing with a girl group when Kris Kristofferson's character discovers her. What is the name of the group?

A. The Floats
B. The Milkshakes
C. The Oreos
D. The Sundaes

answers found on page 548

67. In 1963, Bette Davis earned a Best Actress Oscar nomination for her role in what film?

A. *All About Eve*
B. *Hush . . . Hush, Sweet Charlotte*
C. *The Star*
D. *What Ever Happened to Baby Jane?*

68. The 1971 mystery-comedy *They Might Be Giants*, starring Joanne Woodward, is set in what city?

A. Chicago
B. London
C. New York
D. San Diego

69. What villain did George Sanders play on the 1960s *Batman* television series?

A. Mr. Freeze
B. The Joker
C. The Penguin
D. The Riddler

70. In 1969, Burt Lancaster appeared on television for the first time on what show?

A. *Laugh-In*
B. *Sesame Street*
C. *The Carol Burnett Show*
D. *The Lucy Show*

71. The 1963 Sandra Dee film *Take Her, She's Mine* was inspired by letters sent home from college by what real-life celebrity?

A. Diane English
B. Diane Keaton
C. Katharine Hepburn
D. Nora Ephron

72. In what year was *The Manchurian Candidate* (1962) remade with Denzel Washington?

A. 1994
B. 1999
C. 2004
D. 2006

73. The 1995 Marlon Brando film *Don Juan de Marco* received its only Academy Award nomination for the original song "Have You Ever Really Loved a Woman?" What singer scored a #1 hit with the song?

A. Bryan Adams
B. Peter Gabriel
C. Phil Collins
D. Randy Newman

74. In the 1967 Mark Robson film *Valley of the Dolls*, what does the word "dolls" refer to?

A. A band
B. A baseball team
C. Actresses
D. Pills

75. The title of 1974's *The Great McGonagall*, costarring Peter Sellers, is a reference to W. C. Fields's role in which film?

A. *Heavens Above!* (1963)
B. *Insomnia Is Good for You* (1957)
C. *The Old Fashioned Way* (1934)
D. *The Smallest Show on Earth* (1957)

The Hill, 1965

76. Sean Connery starred in the 1965 film *The Hill*, which was based on what play written by Ray Rigby and Ray Allen in 1964?

A. *Breaking Point*
B. *Honeymoon Hotel*
C. *Man in the Middle*
D. *Operation Crossbow*

Spotlight on

SIDNEY **POITIER** (1927–)

Poitier was raised in the Bahamas and moved to New York at eighteen, sleeping in a bus station men's room until he could earn a living. On a whim, he auditioned for the American Negro Theater, where he was soundly rejected. Instead of giving up, he worked as a janitor there in exchange for acting classes. On his second audition, he got in, quickly working his way up to leading roles on Broadway. These led to Hollywood, where he made his screen debut locking horns with racist gangster Richard Widmark in *No Way Out* (1950). Poitier's early battles for civil rights and his support of such blacklisted artists as Paul Robeson and Canada Lee made him politically suspect, forcing director Richard Brooks to fight to cast him in *Blackboard Jungle* (1955). When the film became a hit, however, Poitier started landing better parts, including that of the escaped convict in *The Defiant Ones* (1958), for which he became the first black male nominated for an acting Oscar. When *Lilies of the Field* became the sleeper hit of 1963, it brought him a Best Actor Oscar. Then three box-office smashes in 1967 made Poitier the nation's top-grossing star.

A Patch of Blue, 1965

Blackboard Jungle, 1955

1. Where does Sidney Poitier's character meet his fiancée Joanna for the first time in *Guess Who's Coming to Dinner* (1967)?

    A. Fiji

    B. Florida

    C. Hawaii

    D. Switzerland

2. 1967's *To Sir, With Love,* starring Sidney Poitier, was set in which city?

    A. London

    B. Los Angeles

    C. New York

    D. Paris

3. In *A Patch of Blue* (1965), Sidney Poitier falls in love with a girl who is what?

    A. Blind

    B. Dying

C. Mute

D. Paralyzed

4. Sidney Poitier garnered his first Oscar nomination as Best Actor in which film?

    A. *A Raisin in the Sun* (1961)

    B. *Band of Angels* (1957)

    C. *Porgy and Bess* (1959)

    D. *The Defiant Ones* (1958)

5. In *In the Heat of the Night* (1967), Sidney Poitier's character works as a homicide detective in what city?

    A. Boston

    B. Los Angeles

    C. New York

    D. Philadelphia

answers found on page 548

77. The 1963 Mark Robson film *Nine Hours to Rama* chronicles the life of the person who assassinated what famous figure?

    A. Abraham Lincoln
    B. John F. Kennedy
    C. Mahatma Gandhi
    D. Martin Luther King Jr.

78. In the 1962 film *Advise & Consent,* Charles Laughton plays a what?

    A. Judge
    B. Pilot
    C. Psychiatrist
    D. Senator

79. In 1972, Rita Moreno won a Grammy Award for her work on the soundtrack album of which children's educational program?

    A. *Animalia*
    B. *Sesame Street*
    C. *The Electric Company*
    D. *WordWorld*

80. The 1992 film *Enchanted April* received Academy Award nominations in all of the following categories except which one?

    A. Best Adapted Screenplay
    B. Best Costume Design
    C. Best Picture
    D. Best Supporting Actress

81. In 2001, Sally Field won an Emmy for Outstanding Guest Actress in a Drama for her work on what television show?

    A. *ER*
    B. *The Practice*
    C. *The Shield*
    D. *The West Wing*

82. In the 1966 film *After the Fox,* Peter Sellers plays a con man who poses as a what?

    A. Movie director
    B. Psychiatrist
    C. Race car driver
    D. Veterinarian

83. The 1970s television series *McCloud* was inspired by what film starring Clint Eastwood?

    A. *Coogan's Bluff* (1968)
    B. *High Plains Drifter* (1973)
    C. *The Beguiled* (1971)
    D. *Thunderbolt and Lightfoot* (1974)

84. Which star of *Harry Potter and the Half-Blood Prince* (2009) portrays Fyodor Dostoyevsky in the 1997 film *The Gambler*?

    A. Alan Rickman
    B. Gary Oldman
    C. Michael Gambon
    D. Ralph Fiennes

85. The 1964 Jules Dassin film *Topkapi* revolves around a theft of a jeweled dagger from a museum in what city?

    A. Istanbul
    B. London
    C. Paris
    D. Rome

86. In the 1968 film *Chitty Chitty Bang Bang,* starring Dick Van Dyke, what does the title refer to?

    A. A car
    B. A dog
    C. A drink
    D. A horse

87. How many times in the 1970s did a film win exactly six Oscars?

    A. 0
    B. 1
    C. 2
    D. 3

answers found on page 548

88. The 1965 Rex Harrison film *The Agony and the Ecstasy* was nominated for five Academy Awards. How many did it win?
A. 0
B. 1
C. 2
D. 3

89. How many times in the 1980s did a film win exactly six Oscars?
A. 0
B. 1
C. 2
D. 3

90. On May 1, 2006, Glenn Ford had a gala ninetieth birthday celebration. A newly restored print of what film was shown?
A. *A Pocketful of Miracles* (1961)
B. *Gilda* (1946)
C. *Texas* (1941)
D. *The Blackboard Jungle* (1955)

91. Sean Connery starred opposite what actor in the 1986 film *The Name of the Rose*?
A. Christian Slater
B. Keanu Reeves
C. Leonardo DiCaprio
D. Orlando Bloom

92. In the 1960 film *Elmer Gantry*, Jean Simmons plays a(n) what?
A. Divorce attorney
B. Evangelist
C. Fashion designer
D. Writer

93. In what city does the action of the 1974 Walter Matthau film *The Taking of Pelham One Two Three* take place?
A. London
B. New York
C. San Francisco
D. St. Louis

94. How many times in the 1970s did a film win exactly seven Oscars?
A. 0
B. 1
C. 2
D. 3

95. In Martin Scorsese's 2004 film *The Aviator*, which of the following actresses portrays Ava Gardner?
A. Emmy Rossum
B. Jennifer Connelly
C. Kate Beckinsale
D. Marcia Gay Harden

96. In 1980, Stanley Donen directed the science fiction thriller *Saturn 3* starring what seventies pinup girl?
A. Cheryl Ladd
B. Cheryl Tiegs
C. Farrah Fawcett
D. Loni Anderson

97. In the 1962 Delmer Daves film *Rome Adventure*, Suzanne Pleshette plays a teacher who leaves her teaching job over criticism that she gave a student what item?
A. A nude painting
B. A romance novel
C. A suggestive letter
D. Money

98. In 1994, Ray Bradbury won an Emmy for writing the teleplay for which of the following projects?
A. *Savannen*
B. *The Electric Grandmother*
C. *The Halloween Tree*
D. *The Martian Chronicles*

99. How many times in the 2000s did a film win exactly six Oscars?

A. 0
B. 1
C. 2
D. 3

100. In the 1967 film *Doctor, You've Got to Be Kidding!*, Sandra Dee's character has aspirations of being a what?

A. Dancer
B. Model
C. Painter
D. Singer

101. Jean Hagen appeared in what episode of the 1960s television show *Ben Casey*?

A. "A Story to Be Softly Told"
B. "Hang No Hats on Dreams"
C. "Mrs. McBroom and the Cloud Watcher"
D. "The Night That Nothing Happened"

102. The 1963 film *Yesterday, Today and Tomorrow* won the Academy Award for Best Foreign Language Film. What country was it from?

A. Italy
B. Mexico
C. Russia
D. Spain

103. The 1965 film *The Agony and the Ecstasy* received Academy Award nominations in all of the following categories except which one?

A. Best Art Direction
B. Best Cinematography
C. Best Director
D. Best Sound

104. In the 1961 film *A Majority of One*, Rosalind Russell's character falls in love with a man from what country?

A. Germany
B. Japan
C. Russia
D. Spain

105. Hume Cronyn costarred in the 1993 film *The Pelican Brief*, which was based on the novel by what author?

A. John Grisham
B. Michael Crichton
C. Sue Grafton
D. Tom Wolfe

Clash of the Titans, 1981

106. What actress portrayed Aphrodite in the 1981 film *Clash of the Titans*?

A. Faye Dunaway
B. Meryl Streep
C. Uma Thurman
D. Ursula Andress

107. How many times in the 1980s did a film win exactly seven Oscars?

A. 0
B. 1
C. 2
D. 3

108. In a 1996 *Vanity Fair* interview, what did Jackie Chan name as his favorite movie?

A. *Casablanca* (1942)
B. *Gone With the Wind* (1939)
C. *Raiders of the Lost Ark* (1981)
D. *The Sound of Music* (1965)

109. The 1960 film *Sons and Lovers,* costarring Donald Pleasence, was based on the novel by what author?

    A. Charles Dickens
    B. D. H. Lawrence
    C. Ernest Hemingway
    D. Thomas Hardy

110. In the 1969 film *Some Kind of a Nut*, Dick Van Dyke's character is fired from his job when he does what?

    A. Comes to work barefoot
    B. Grows a beard
    C. Punches a customer
    D. Wears a dress to work

111. Van Johnson portrayed what character in two episodes of the 1960s television show *Batman*?

    A. Harvey Dent
    B. The Clock King
    C. The Minstrel
    D. The Riddler

112. The 1971 film *Bedknobs and Broomsticks* received an Academy Award nomination for Best Original Song. What was the name of the song?

    A. "A Step in the Right Direction"
    B. "Nobody's Problems"
    C. "The Age of Not Believing"
    D. "The Beautiful Briny"

113. What film won the Academy Award for the Best Picture of 1964?

    A. *Zorba the Greek*
    B. *Becket*
    C. *Mary Poppins*
    D. *My Fair Lady*

114. Raymond Massey played Dr. Leonard Gillespie on what 1960s television series?

    A. *Dr. Kildare*
    B. *Kraft Mystery Theater*

    C. *Riverboat*
    D. *The Love Boat*

115. In the 1960 film *Swiss Family Robinson*, where does the family build their home?

    A. In a cave
    B. In a tree
    C. In an abandoned ship
    D. On a floating raft

116. The title of the 1978 Nancy Kwan film *Night Creature* refers to what?

    A. A bat
    B. A grizzly bear
    C. A leopard
    D. An alien

117. In the 1972 biopic *Young Winston,* who does Laurence Naismith portray?

    A. Captain Aylmer Haldane
    B. Lord Salisbury
    C. Mr. Welldon
    D. Winston Churchill

118. In the 1990 Leslie Caron television movie *Lenin: The Train,* what actor portrayed Lenin?

    A. Anthony Hopkins
    B. Ben Kingsley
    C. F. Murray Abraham
    D. Richard Harris

119. The 1972 film *1776* received its only Academy Award nomination in what category?

    A. Best Cinematography
    B. Best Editing
    C. Best Musical Score
    D. Best Supporting Actor

120. What film won the Academy Award for Best Picture of 1960?

    A. *Elmer Gantry*
    B. *Psycho*
    C. *Sons and Lovers*
    D. *The Apartment*

Spotlight on
ELIZABETH **TAYLOR** (1932–2011)

Elizabeth Taylor was born with such otherworldly beauty that she was never allowed to just be a child. She made her screen debut at age ten in *There's One Born Every Minute* (1942). A contract player with MGM at eleven, Taylor fought hard for the lead in *National Velvet* (1944), and her performance as the young rider led her to stardom. By the time she was sixteen, her grown-up beauty was bringing her adult roles opposite heartthrobs like Robert Taylor and Montgomery Clift. Her performance as the society beauty who falls for Clift in *A Place in the Sun* (1951) made critics aware of her mature acting abilities, which were further evidenced by such hits as *Cat on a Hot Tin Roof* (1958) and *BUtterfield 8* (1960). Her lavish star turn in *Cleopatra* (1963) changed her life when she took up with her costar, dashing Welsh actor Richard Burton. "Liz and Dick," as they were called, made several movies together (most notably 1966's *Who's Afraid of Virginia Woolf?*) while living large in the public eye. But some of the films they made to support their lifestyle, and her personal decision to take a backseat to his career, ended her reign as a box-office superstar.

National Velvet, 1944

1. Elizabeth Taylor won her first Academy Award as Best Actress in which film?

   A. *A Place in the Sun* (1951)
   B. *BUtterfield 8* (1960)
   C. *Cat on a Hot Tin Roof* (1958)
   D. *Giant* (1956)

2. Which of her husbands did Elizabeth Taylor marry twice?

   A. Eddie Fisher
   B. John W. Warner
   C. Michael Todd
   D. Richard Burton

3. Elizabeth Taylor plays a woman who falls in love with a gangster in which film directed by Richard Thorpe?

   A. *Conspirator* (1949)
   B. *Love Is Better Than Ever* (1952)
   C. *The Girl Who Had Everything* (1953)
   D. *Vengeance Valley* (1951)

4. George Stevens directed Elizabeth Taylor in all of the following films except for which one?

   A. *A Place in the Sun* (1951)
   B. *Giant* (1956)
   C. *The Last Hunt* (1956)
   D. *The Only Game in Town* (1970)

5. Elizabeth Taylor drove a Sunbeam Albine in what film?

   A. *A Place in the Sun* (1951)
   B. *BUtterfield 8* (1960)
   C. *Cat on a Hot Tin Roof* (1958)
   D. *The V.I.P.s* (1963)

BUtterfield 8, 1960

answers found on page 548

121. The 1961 George Hamilton film *Angel Baby* marked the film debut of what popular actor?

A. Burt Reynolds
B. Dustin Hoffman
C. Paul Newman
D. Robert Redford

122. In 1980, Burt Reynolds recorded a song for *Smokey and the Bandit 2* that made it to #88 on the Billboard Hot 100. What was the name of the song?

A. "Bandit Blues"
B. "East Bound and Down"
C. "Hard Candy Christmas"
D. "Let's Do Something Cheap and Superficial"

123. The 1963 film *Lilies of the Field* received Academy Award nominations in all of the following categories except which one?

A. Best Cinematography
B. Best Director
C. Best Picture
D. Best Supporting Actress

124. In 1960, Anthony Quinn played the role of King Henry II on Broadway in which play starring Laurence Olivier in the title role?

A. *Becket*
B. *Cyrano de Bergerac*
C. *Mister Roberts*
D. *The Entertainer*

125. In the 1963 thriller *Charade*, what is the occupation of Audrey Hepburn's character?

A. Book editor
B. Fashion designer
C. Interior decorator
D. Translator

126. The 1960 film *The Time Machine* won its only Academy Award in what category?

A. Best Art Direction
B. Best Editing

C. Best Sound
D. Best Special Effects

127. The 1974 Walter Mirisch–produced film *Mr. Majestyk* was based on a novel by what author?

A. Dashiell Hammett
B. Elmore Leonard
C. James Ellroy
D. James M. Cain

128. The 1970 film *Scrooge* received an Academy Award nomination for Best Original Song. What was the name of the song?

A. "Christmases Past"
B. "No One Knows Me"
C. "Thank You Very Much"
D. "What's Good for the Goose"

2001: A Space Odyssey, 1968

129. The 1968 film *2001: A Space Odyssey* received Academy Award nominations in all of the following categories except which one?

A. Best Art Direction
B. Best Director
C. Best Picture
D. Best Special Effects

answers found on page 548

130. In 1962, Sean Connery was cast as the lead actor in a West End production of which play by Jean Giraudoux?
A. *Electra*
B. *Intermezzo*
C. *Judith*
D. *Ondine*

131. The title of the 1971 film *They Might Be Giants*, costarring Joanne Woodward, was a line from what novel?
A. *Don Quixote*
B. *Gone with the Wind*
C. *The Great Gatsby*
D. *Vanity Fair*

132. Jean Hagen played Lilly de Milo in an episode of what 1960s television show?
A. *Gunsmoke*
B. *Kraft Suspense Theatre*
C. *Stagecoach West*
D. *The DuPont Show of the Week*

133. In 1968, Barbra Streisand shared the Oscar for Best Actress with whom?
A. Faye Dunaway
B. Jane Fonda
C. Katharine Hepburn
D. Vanessa Redgrave

134. In the 1963 comedy *The Thrill of It All*, Doris Day's character becomes a spokesperson for what fictional brand of soap?
A. Bubbly
B. Happy
C. Soapy
D. Zappy

135. In the 1974 film *Gold*, Susannah York stars opposite this "James Bond":
A. Pierce Brosnan
B. Roger Moore
C. Sean Connery
D. Timothy Dalton

136. The 1970 Sandra Dee film *The Dunwich Horror* is based on a short story by what author?
A. H. P. Lovecraft
B. Peter Straub
C. Stephen King
D. William Peter Blatty

137. In 1972's *Alice's Adventures in Wonderland*, Peter Sellers portrays which character?
A. Lewis Carroll
B. The Mad Hatter
C. The March Hare
D. Tweedledee

138. The 1977 John Frankenheimer film *Black Sunday* is about a terrorist plot to disrupt what major public event?
A. Mardi Gras
B. The Macy's Thanksgiving Day Parade
C. The Super Bowl
D. The World Series

139. In the 1971 Leslie Caron film *Chandler*, what actor plays the title character?
A. Glenn Ford
B. Henry Fonda
C. Kevin McCarthy
D. Warren Oates

140. In 2004, who directed the remake to George A. Romero's *Dawn of the Dead* (1978)?
A. John A. Russo
B. Tom Savini
C. Wes Craven
D. Zack Snyder

141. How many times in the 1970s did a film win exactly eight Oscars?
A. 1
B. 2
C. 3
D. 4

142. Jean Louis dressed Eva Gabor for episodes of which 1960s television show?

A. *Alfred Hitchcock Presents*
B. *Gilligan's Island*
C. *Green Acres*
D. *The Patty Duke Show*

143. In which of the following categories was the 1973 film *The Day of the Dolphin* nominated for an Academy Award?

A. Best Art Direction
B. Best Editing
C. Best Musical Score
D. Best Special Effects

144. In *Dragons Forever* (1988) Jackie Chan plays a what?

A. Doctor
B. Investment banker
C. Lawyer
D. Realtor

145. The 1968 Marlon Brando film *Candy* was a loose adaptation of what classic novel?

A. *Candide*
B. *Great Expectations*
C. *Siddhartha*
D. *Vanity Fair*

146. The set for the 1967 Jacques Tati film *Playtime* was nicknamed what?

A. "Circustown"
B. "Tativille"
C. "The Fort"
D. "The Playground"

147. The 1963 Walter Matthau film *Island of Love* was shot on location where?

A. Catalina
B. Greece
C. Nassau
D. Sicily

148. In what city does the action of the 1973 Walter Matthau film *The Laughing Policeman* take place?

A. Chicago
B. Minneapolis
C. New York
D. San Francisco

149. In 1982, Haskell Wexler served as the cinematographer on the live concert film starring what popular comedian?

A. Eddie Murphy
B. Richard Pryor
C. Robin Williams
D. Steve Martin

150. In the 1964 Sidney Lumet film *Fail-Safe*, who plays the president of the United States?

A. Burt Lancaster
B. Henry Fonda
C. Jack Palance
D. James Stewart

151. In the 1969 comedy *Staircase*, what is the name of the salon owned by Richard Burton's character?

A. Chez Harry
B. Chez Louis
C. Le Coiffeur
D. Mason Louis

152. In the 1973 film *Papillon*, Dustin Hoffman based his performance on which screenwriter?

A. Dalton Trumbo
B. James Webb
C. William Inge
D. William Rose

 answers found on page 548

153. The 1989 film *Glory* was nominated for Academy Awards in all of the following categories except which one?

A. Best Art Direction
B. Best Cinematography
C. Best Picture
D. Best Supporting Actor

154. The 1960 film *The Facts of Life* was nominated for five Academy Awards and won for Best Costume Design. Who were the lead actors?

A. Bob Hope and Lucille Ball
B. Gene Kelly and Esther Williams
C. Peter Lawford and June Allyson
D. Spencer Tracy and Katharine Hepburn

155. How many times in the 1980s did a film win exactly eight Oscars?

A. 1
B. 2
C. 3
D. 4

Shaft, 1971

156. The 1971 film *Shaft* won an Academy Award for its Best Original Song, "Theme from Shaft." Who performed it?

A. Herbie Hancock
B. Isaac Hayes
C. Ray Charles
D. Stevie Wonder

157. In the 2006 film *Inside Man*, Denzel Washington costars with all of the following actors except which one?

A. Christopher Plummer
B. Clive Owen
C. Jodie Foster
D. Julia Roberts

158. In which of the following categories was the 1977 Sophia Loren film *A Special Day* nominated for an Academy Award?

A. Best Actor
B. Best Actress
C. Best Original Score
D. Best Original Screenplay

159. The 1963 film *The Four Days of Naples* received an Academy Award nomination in what category?

A. Best Actress
B. Best Director
C. Best Editing
D. Best Original Screenplay

160. In the 1991 animated film *Beauty and the Beast*, which "object" character is the only one to address Belle by her name?

A. Chip
B. Cogsworth
C. Lumiere
D. Mrs. Potts

161. Sidney Lumet directed Sean Connery in 1965's *The Hill* and which other film?

A. *The Anderson Tapes* (1971)
B. *The Pawnbroker* (1964)
C. *The Sea Gull* (1968)
D. *The Wind and the Lion* (1975)

162. 1968's *Lady in Cement* is the sequel to which film starring Frank Sinatra?

A. *Not as a Stranger* (1955)
B. *The Man with the Golden Arm* (1955)
C. *Tony Rome* (1967)
D. *Von Ryan's Express* (1965)

163. Jean Louis' stepson Peter Lewis belonged to what 1960s musical group?

　　A. Jefferson Airplane
　　B. Lovin' Spoonful
　　C. Moby Grape
　　D. The Hollies

164. Meryl Streep's character in 1985's *Out of Africa* oversees the farming of what commodity?

　　A. Coffee
　　B. Corn
　　C. Rice
　　D. Tea

165. How many times in the 1960s did a film win exactly six Oscars?

　　A. 0
　　B. 1
　　C. 2
　　D. 3

166. In 2006, Rita Moreno starred in which Tennessee Williams play at the Berkeley Repertory Theater in Berkeley, California?

　　A. *A House Not Meant to Stand*
　　B. *Suddenly, Last Summer*
　　C. *Sweet Bird of Youth*
　　D. *The Glass Menagerie*

167. In the 1967 film *Fitzwilly*, starring Dick Van Dyke, what is Fitzwilly's real name?

　　A. Claude Fitzcaraldo
　　B. Claude Fitzgerald
　　C. Claude Fitzwilliam
　　D. Claude Fitzwilligen

168. The 1974 Hume Cronyn film *Conrack* was based on a novel by what author?

　　A. John Grisham
　　B. Pat Conroy
　　C. Sidney Sheldon
　　D. Tom Wolfe

169. In the 1962 thriller *The Manchurian Candidate*, where does Janet Leigh's character meet Frank Sinatra's for the first time?

　　A. In a diner
　　B. In an airport
　　C. On a train
　　D. On the subway

170. In the 1960s *Batman* television series, Otto Preminger played what character?

　　A. Mr. Freeze
　　B. The Joker
　　C. The Penguin
　　D. The Riddler

171. The 1984 film *The Pope of Greenwich Village* features all of the following stars except for which one?

　　A. Daryl Hannah
　　B. Geraldine Page
　　C. Meryl Streep
　　D. Mickey Rourke

172. The 1995 film *Crimson Tide* received Academy Award nominations in all of the following categories except which one?

　　A. Best Director
　　B. Best Editing
　　C. Best Sound
　　D. Best Sound Effects Editing

173. On October 24, 1960, Nancy Kwan appeared on the cover of what magazine?

　　A. *Life*
　　B. *Look*
　　C. *People*
　　D. *Time*

174. In 1961, André Previn competed in all three
Best Music Oscar categories with his contributions to *Elmer Gantry, Pepe*, and what other
film?

A. *Bells Are Ringing*
B. *Can-Can*
C. *Kiss Me, Stupid*
D. *Let's Make Love*

175. In the 1964 film *The Long Ships*, Richard
Widmark costars with which of the following
actors?

A. Burt Lancaster
B. John Wayne
C. Sidney Poitier
D. Spencer Tracy

176. The 1972 Roddy McDowall film *The Poseidon
Adventure* won an Academy Award for Best
Song. What was the name of the song?

A. "Blue Is the Ocean"
B. "For All We Know"
C. "Never Again"
D. "The Morning After"

177. Robert Benton's 1991 film *Billy Bathgate* was
based on the novel by what author?

A. E. L. Doctorow
B. John le Carré
C. Norman Mailer
D. Thomas Hardy

178. In the 1978 smash hit *Grease*, Joan Blondell
plays a waitress in the local soda shop. What is
its name?

A. Burger Palace
B. Frosty Freeze
C. Frosty Palace
D. Hamburger Hut

179. In the 1977 film *Smokey and the Bandit*, what
is the CB handle of Sally Field's character?

A. Chipmunk
B. Duck

C. Frog
D. Rabbit

180. In the 2005 remake of *The Bad News Bears*,
who plays the role originated by Walter
Matthau?

A. Adam Sandler
B. Billy Bob Thornton
C. Greg Kinnear
D. Jim Carrey

181. In 1967, Shirley Temple ran unsuccessfully for
what position?

A. Director of the Academy of Motion Picture
Arts and Sciences
B. Screen Actors Guild President
C. U.S. senator
D. U.S. congresswoman

Mister Buddwing, 1966

182. In the 1966 film *Mister Buddwing*, James
Garner's character suffers from what?

A. Amnesia
B. Blindness
C. Paralysis
D. Schizophrenia

183. The 1972 film *Slaughterhouse-Five,* directed by George Roy Hill, was based on a novel by what author?

A. Aldous Huxley
B. George Orwell
C. J. D. Salinger
D. Kurt Vonnegut

184. The 1961 film *The Absent-Minded Professor* received Academy Award nominations in all of the following categories except which one?

A. Best Art Direction
B. Best Cinematography
C. Best Editing
D. Best Special Effects

185. The title of the 1973 film *Papillon* is the French word for what?

A. Butterfly
B. Gold
C. Honeycomb
D. Paper

186. In the 1960s, what production company did George Romero form with friends?

A. Bloody Corps Productions
B. Image Ten Productions
C. Living Dead Productions
D. Romero Films

187. The 1963 George Hamilton film *Act One* depicted the life of what famous playwright?

A. Arthur Miller
B. Moss Hart
C. Noel Coward
D. Tennessee Williams

188. In 1995's *The Bridges of Madison County,* costarring Meryl Streep, Clint Eastwood's character is a photographer from which publication?

A. *Architectural Digest*
B. *National Geographic*

C. *Newsweek*
D. *Time*

189. All of the following actresses appear in 1984's *The Natural,* opposite Robert Redford, except for which one?

A. Barbara Hershey
B. Glenn Close
C. Kim Basinger
D. Meryl Streep

190. In what category did the 1963 film *The Great Escape* receive its only Academy Award nomination?

A. Best Actor
B. Best Editing
C. Best Musical Score
D. Best Original Screenplay

191. In 1969, James Shigeta starred in a television movie called *U.M.C.* This was a pilot for what future popular television series?

A. *Emergency*
B. *Marcus Welby, M.D.*
C. *Medical Center*
D. *Trapper John, M.D.*

192. Jean Louis designed more than fifty gowns for which actress's 1960s television show?

A. Donna Reed
B. Doris Day
C. Loretta Young
D. Lucille Ball

193. In 1978, Janet Gaynor presented the Academy Award for Best Actress to whom?

A. Anne Bancroft
B. Diane Keaton
C. Jane Fonda
D. Marsha Mason

answers found on page 549

194. The 1962 film *Phaedra,* directed by Jules Dassin, received its only Academy Award nomination in what category?

    A. Best Cinematography
    B. Best Costume Design
    C. Best Editing
    D. Best Original Score

195. The 1975 animated television special *Rikki-Tikki-Tavi,* directed by Chuck Jones, was based on a story by what author?

    A. E. M. Forster
    B. Ernest Hemingway
    C. John Steinbeck
    D. Rudyard Kipling

196. Joanne Woodward's role of Lila Green in 1963's *The Stripper* was originally intended for what other screen legend?

    A. Faye Dunaway
    B. Marilyn Monroe
    C. Meryl Streep
    D. Rita Hayworth

197. In the 1991 comedy *Soapdish*, what is the name of the soap opera in which Sally Field's character stars?

    A. *Pelican Trace*
    B. *Southwest General*
    C. *The Sun Also Sets*
    D. *The Valley*

198. In 1973's *The Way We Were*, what was the title of Hubbell's book?

    A. *A Country Made of Ice Cream*
    B. *A Country Made of Marshmallows*
    C. *Love in the Time of Disbelief*
    D. *Love in the Time of Politics*

199. John Carpenter's 1980 film *The Fog* quotes from what poem by Edgar Allan Poe?

    A. "A Dream Within a Dream"
    B. "Tamerlane"
    C. "The City in the Sea"
    D. "The Haunted Palace"

200. In *Die Hard* (1988), what is the name of the company that James Shigeta's character heads?

    A. Miyagi Corporation
    B. Morita Corporation
    C. Oshuro Corporation
    D. Takagi Corporation

201. The 1964 Marlon Brando comedy *Bedtime Story* was remade in 1988. What was it retitled?

    A. *All of Me*
    B. *Dirty Rotten Scoundrels*
    C. *Planes, Trains, and Automobiles*
    D. *Roxanne*

202. Ann Sothern provided the voice of mother Gladys Crabtree in the notorious 1960s television show *My Mother, the Car.* Who played her son?

    A. Alan Hale Jr.
    B. Dick Van Dyke
    C. Jerry Van Dyke
    D. Larry Hagman

203. The 1967 Kerwin Mathews television movie *Ghostbreakers* was originally intended as a pilot for which musical star's regular television theater show?

    A. Danny Kaye
    B. Dick Powell
    C. Donald O'Connor
    D. Gene Kelly

204. The 1967 Peter Sellers film *Casino Royale* received an Academy Award nomination for Best Song. What was the name of the song?

    A. "Nothing to Lose"
    B. "The Look of Love"
    C. "What the World Needs Now Is Love"
    D. "Wishin' and Hopin'"

Spotlight on
PETER **SELLERS** (1925–1980)

Often hailed as one of the most versatile comedians the film world has ever seen, Peter Sellers was also the ultimate character actor. His ability to adopt different voices and appearances, sometimes within a single film, left fans awestruck. Among his memorable gallery of characters are master of disguise Clare Quilty in *Lolita* (1962); a U.S. president, a British military man, and a deranged German scientist in *Dr. Strangelove* (1964); the harebrained Inspector Clouseau in five *Pink Panther* films starting in 1964; and the perpetually detached Chance the gardener in *Being There* (1979). When

Lolita, 1962

called on to play someone like himself in *The Mouse That Roared* (1959), the first film to cast him in multiple roles, he was at a loss. Later he would say, "If you ask me to play myself, I will not know what to do. I do not know who or what I am." But when he trusted his comic powers, as when he rose to prominence creating a series of voices for BBC Radio's *The Goon Show* in the fifties, or when director Stanley Kubrick let him improvise with three cameras running in *Lolita* and *Dr. Strangelove*, his talents were staggering.

Lolita, 1962

1. In the 1968 film *I Love You, Alice B. Toklas!,* Peter Sellers plays a middle-aged man who falls in love with a young hippie played by what actress?

    A. Cristina Ferrare
    B. Goldie Hawn
    C. Leigh Taylor-Young
    D. Susan Saint James

2. Peter Sellers is a singing bullfighter in what comedy?

    A. *The Bobo* (1967)
    B. *This Earth Is Mine* (1959)
    C. *Twilight for the Gods* (1958)
    D. *Waltz of the Toreadors* (1962)

3. In 1960, Sophia Loren and actor Peter Sellers recorded a hit novelty song called "Goodness Gracious Me" as a promotional device for what film?

    A. *Heller in Pink Tights*
    B. *It Started in Naples*
    C. *The Millionairess*
    D. *The Pink Panther*

4. The 1964 Peter Sellers film *Dr. Strangelove or: How I Learned to Stop Worrying and Love the Bomb* received Academy Award nominations in all of the following categories except which?

    A. Best Actor
    B. Best Director
    C. Best Original Score
    D. Best Picture

5. In the 1962 film *Only Two Can Play,* what is the profession of Peter Sellers's character?

    A. Accountant
    B. Hotel manager
    C. Librarian
    D. Waiter

answers found on page 549

205. In the 1972 film *They Only Kill Their Masters*, Katharine Ross costars with all of the following actors except which one?

A. Hal Holbrook
B. James Garner
C. June Allyson
D. Mickey Rooney

206. From 1993 to 1995, Claire Bloom appeared on which American soap opera?

A. *Another World*
B. *As the World Turns*
C. *Days of Our Lives*
D. *General Hospital*

207. Luchino Visconti's 1972 biopic *Ludwig* was about the king of what country?

A. Austria
B. Bavaria
C. England
D. France

The Loved One, 1965

208. The 1965 film *The Loved One*, shot by cinematographer Haskell Wexler, is about what?

A. A dog
B. A favorite uncle
C. A presidential candidate
D. The funeral industry

209. In 1994, Rudolph Valentino was commemorated on a U.S. postage stamp designed by what artist?

A. Al Hirschfeld
B. Andy Warhol
C. Norman Rockwell
D. Willem de Kooning

210. In the 2003 Leslie Caron film *Le Divorce*, what item does the family auction off?

A. A house
B. A map
C. A painting
D. An antique ring

211. What character did Roddy McDowall play in the 1960s *Batman* television show?

A. The Bookworm
B. The Joker
C. The Mad Hatter
D. The Riddler

212. Michael Caine made a splash as the title character in the 1966 film *Alfie*. Who played the same character in the 2004 remake?

A. Ewan McGregor
B. Hugh Grant
C. Jude Law
D. Rupert Everett

213. In 1985's *Out of Africa*, when Denys washes Karen's hair, he recites from which poem by Samuel Taylor Coleridge?

A. "Frost at Midnight"
B. "The Eolian Harp"
C. "The Nightingale: A Conversation Poem"
D. "The Rime of the Ancient Mariner"

answers found on page 549

214. In the late 1970s, Lee Marvin was involved in a sensational lawsuit that resulted in a landmark ruling on what subject?

A. Child custody
B. Domestic violence
C. Palimony
D. Stalkers

215. The 1960 film *Psycho* was nominated for Academy Awards in all of the following categories except which one?

A. Best Actor
B. Best Cinematography
C. Best Director
D. Best Supporting Actress

216. In 1995, Stanley Donen admitted that he had only one regret in life. What was it?

A. That he didn't buy real estate
B. That he didn't get bar mitzvahed
C. That he didn't win an Academy Award
D. That he had been divorced so many times

217. In the 1978 blockbuster *Superman: The Movie*, Marlon Brando plays Superman's father. What is his character's name?

A. General Zod
B. Jor-El
C. Kal-El
D. Rax Joris

218. In *The Odd Couple* (1968), what was the name of Walter Matthau's character?

A. Felix Ungar
B. John Gustafson
C. Max Goldman
D. Oscar Madison

219. In 1962, Jean Louis earned dual Oscar nominations for which two films?

A. *Gambit* and *Ship of Fools*
B. *Judgment at Nuremberg* and *Back Street*
C. *Pal Joey* and *Queen Bee*
D. *Thoroughly Modern Millie* and *Gambit*

220. In 1981, Sophia Loren launched a business focusing on what product?

A. Dolls
B. Eyewear
C. Lingerie
D. Wigs

221. In the 1963 film *The Stripper*, a tourist mistakes Joanne Woodward's character for which star of the silver screen?

A. Esther Williams
B. Jayne Mansfield
C. Kim Novak
D. Lana Turner

222. In 2007, Leslie Caron won an Emmy for Outstanding Guest Actress in a Drama Series for what television show?

A. *Brothers and Sisters*
B. *Desperate Housewives*
C. *Law and Order: Special Victims Unit*
D. *Without a Trace*

223. In 1965, Cary Grant married a much younger actress who gave him his only child. Who was she?

A. Dyan Cannon
B. Goldie Hawn
C. Natalie Wood
D. Samantha Eggar

224. How many times in the 1990s did a film win exactly six Oscars?

A. 0
B. 1
C. 2
D. 3

225. The 1966 film adaptation of Ray Bradbury's *Fahrenheit 451* was directed by whom?

A. Akira Kurosawa
B. François Truffaut
C. John Frankenheimer
D. Michelangelo Antonioni

226. The 1973 Kerwin Mathews film *The Boy Who Cried Werewolf* was one of the last theatrical double bills when it was released as a double feature with what other film?

A. *Empire of the Ants*
B. *Kingdom of the Spiders*
C. *Sssssss*
D. *The Severed Arm*

227. In the 1965 film *The Art of Love*, Dick Van Dyke costars with all of the following actors except who?

A. Angie Dickinson
B. Ethel Merman
C. James Garner
D. Shirley MacLaine

228. The 1971 Walter Mirisch–produced film *The Organization* stars which of the following actors?

A. Frank Sinatra
B. Lee Marvin
C. Sidney Poitier
D. Steve McQueen

229. The 1972 film *Sounder* was nominated for Academy Awards in all of the following categories except which one?

A. Best Actor
B. Best Actress
C. Best Director
D. Best Picture

230. In 1980, Glenn Ford offered to buy an NHL team to keep it in its home city. Which team was it?

A. Atlanta Flames
B. Los Angeles Kings
C. New York Rangers
D. Toronto Maple Leafs

231. In the 1972 film *What's Up, Doc?*, what song does Barbra Streisand sing on top of a piano?

A. "As Time Goes By"

B. "Come Rain or Come Shine"
C. "It Had to Be You"
D. "Who's Sorry Now?"

232. The 1990 Leslie Caron film *Courage Mountain* was based on what book?

A. *A Tree Grows in Brooklyn*
B. *Call of the Wild*
C. *Heidi*
D. *The Glass Castle*

233. In the 1970 film *There's a Girl in My Soup*, who is Peter Sellers's leading lady?

A. Goldie Hawn
B. Lily Tomlin
C. Natalie Wood
D. Shirley MacLaine

Soylent Green, 1973

234. In what year does the 1973 Charlton Heston film *Soylent Green* take place?

A. 2022
B. 2023
C. 2024
D. 2025

235. In a 1971 interview, Bruce Lee stated that the true meaning of martial arts was what?

A. Becoming one with the earth
B. Honestly expressing yourself
C. Mind over body
D. Speaking to God

answers found on page 549

236. Jane Russell appeared in commercials for what in the 1970s?

A. Chantelle
B. JC Penney
C. Playtex "Cross Your Heart" bras
D. Sears

237. The 1969 film *Paint Your Wagon* received its only Academy Award nomination in what category?

A. Best Costume Design
B. Best Editing
C. Best Musical Score
D. Best Original Song

238. In 1993, Gregory Peck costarred with real-life daughter Cecilia in the television movie *The Portrait*. It also reunited him with which of his previous leading ladies?

A. Audrey Hepburn
B. Lauren Bacall
C. Lee Remick
D. Sophia Loren

239. What villain did Burgess Meredith play in the original 1966 *Batman* movie and in the 1960s *Batman* television series?

A. Mr. Freeze
B. The Joker
C. The Penguin
D. The Riddler

240. In 1981's *Clash of the Titans*, Claire Bloom plays what character?

A. Andromeda
B. Hera
C. Oracle
D. Persephone

241. In 1984, David Mamet won the Pulitzer Prize for what play?

A. *American Buffalo*
B. *Glengarry Glen Ross*
C. *Sexual Perversity in Chicago*
D. *The Blue Hour*

242. I returned to acting in the 1980s as the head of an international crime circuit on television's *Falcon Crest*. Who am I?

A. Ava Gardner
B. Elizabeth Taylor
C. Kim Novak
D. Lana Turner

243. In the 1978 film *Sextette*, George Hamilton costars with which one of the former Beatles?

A. George Harrison
B. John Lennon
C. Paul McCartney
D. Ringo Starr

244. In 2005, what car manufacturer used Gene Kelly's likeness in one of their international commercials?

A. Audi
B. BMW
C. Mercedes Benz
D. Volkswagen

245. In 1982, Leslie Caron appeared in the "Run, Rabbit, Run" episode of the television series *Tales of the Unexpected*, which featured the work of what prominent author?

A. Dr. Seuss
B. Peter Straub
C. Roald Dahl
D. Stephen King

MOVIE
ICONS

Gone With the Wind, 1939

Chapter 6

LEADING
LADIES

Just to see them was to be transported into new worlds. Some embodied the fast-paced, brittle world of big business. Others lived in picturesque backstreet neighborhoods filled with wisecracking dames. Still others evoked the rarified atmosphere of haute couture and timeless glamour. One even seemed to live in a place where a swimming pool was always handy and smiling underwater was as natural as breathing on the surface.

Hollywood's greatest female stars achieved iconic status by bringing their own personal spin to the archetypes they embodied. There's no confusing Jean Harlow's blonde sexuality with Marilyn Monroe's. Rosalind Russell's career women were distinctly different from Katharine Hepburn's. As strongly as both registered on screen, Bette Davis and Barbara Stanwyck were not tough in the same way.

That said, the studio-era leading ladies were also distinctly products of the system. They were groomed to project a particular image, with everyone from directors and writers to costume designers, hair stylists, and makeup artists playing a vital role in their creation. As a dark-haired Latin type, Margarita Cansino was little more than set dressing, but with her hairline raised and her hair dyed red, she became Rita Hayworth, one of the screen's most sensual creations. In much the same way, MGM's makeup men covered up Lucille LeSueur's freckles and Adrian set off her athletic physique with shoulder pads and narrow waists to turn her into Joan Crawford.

But some also took a very strong hand in forging their own personal brand of stardom. Hepburn resolutely resisted studio grooming, projecting the image of a spirited iconoclast from the first. Faced with a future of drab, stock female leads at Warner Bros., Davis fought for a loan-out to RKO to play the slatternly waitress Mildred in *Of Human Bondage* (1934). Her boss, Jack Warner, and even her own family warned her that playing such an unpleasant character could sink her career. But she forged ahead, setting a new paradigm for female stars.

However they approached their careers, the silver-screen divas were an essential part of Hollywood economics. Their names sold movie tickets as surely as their faces in print ads engineered by the studios sold soap, toothpaste, and cosmetics. And they did it so well that the most profitable could get away with a little rebellion. Hayworth walked out on Columbia to marry Prince Aly Khan, but they welcomed her back when the marriage ended. Olivia de Havilland won a landmark decision limiting studio contracts to seven years, but even though Warner Bros., the studio she sued, tried to blacklist her, she was offered plum roles again as soon as she was available.

Studio publicists taught contract actresses certain basic lessons about how to handle stardom: never appear in public without movie-star grooming; never reveal too much in interviews, whether the topic be religion, politics, or even baseball; never make your private indiscretions public. But for all their reserve, the greatest female stars all revealed something very special about themselves,

Bombshell, 1933

giving an autobiographical twist to their most important roles. Elizabeth Taylor and Debbie Reynolds didn't just grow up on screen; films like *Father of the Bride* (1950) and *Bundle of Joy* (1956), respectively, coincided with their first forays into marriage and motherhood. Scarlett O'Hara's fight to save Tara was no less fierce than Leigh's own battles to land the role and survive making *Gone With the Wind* (1939). And when Davis, Stanwyck, and Crawford played women whose strength made keeping a man a challenge, one was reminded of the parallels to their own rocky romantic lives.

Some of these ladies seemed very much a product of their times. Lillian Gish's demure heroines captured the post-Victorian mores of the silent years. Clara Bow's flappers were the epitome of the twenties. And Greer Garson's British reserve reflected the tenacity of her homeland during World War II. Yet something about their images has maintained a hold on audiences even sixty, eighty, and ninety years later. Others—Davis, Hepburn, Crawford, and Stanwyck among them—managed to reinvent themselves as needed, becoming some of the most long-lived stars in history.

However long their careers lasted, these women were survivors, on and off screen. Their combined efforts represent a composite view of woman in the twentieth century at work and at play, in love and in war.

1. Before becoming a paid actress, I worked at an advertising company alongside George Sanders. Who am I?

   A. Audrey Hepburn
   B. Deborah Kerr
   C. Greer Garson
   D. Vivien Leigh

2. In what country was Hedy Lamarr born?

   A. Austria-Hungary
   B. England
   C. Hungary
   D. United States

3. In what year was Jean Harlow born?

   A. 1911
   B. 1912
   C. 1913
   D. 1914

4. How many times was Lana Turner married?

   A. 2
   B. 4
   C. 6
   D. 7

5. Jean Harlow was the first movie actress to appear on the cover of what magazine in May 1937?

   A. *Life*
   B. *New Yorker*
   C. *Time*
   D. *Vanity Fair*

6. Doris Day performs the song "Nobody's Sweetheart" in what film?

   A. *I'll See You in My Dreams* (1951)
   B. *Romance on the High Seas* (1948)
   C. *Tea for Two* (1950)
   D. *The Winning Team* (1952)

7. In which of the following films does Rosalind Russell costar with James Stewart?

   A. *A Majority of One* (1961)
   B. *My Sister Eileen* (1942)
   C. *No Time for Comedy* (1940)
   D. *This Thing Called Love* (1940)

8. What was Ava Gardner's star sign?

   A. Cancer
   B. Capricorn
   C. Leo
   D. Pisces

Love Me or Leave Me, 1955

9. In *Love Me or Leave Me* (1955), Doris Day starred with what great leading man (shown here)?

   A. Bing Crosby
   B. James Cagney
   C. Ronald Colman
   D. Laurence Olivier

10. In what film does Jean Harlow's character famously take a rain barrel bath?

    A. *Dinner at Eight* (1933)
    B. *Red Dust* (1932)
    C. *The Public Enemy* (1931)
    D. *Wife vs. Secretary* (1936)

11. In which of the following films did Audrey Hepburn costar with first husband Mel Ferrer?

    A. *The Lavender Hill Mob* (1951)
    B. *The Nun's Story* (1959)
    C. *Wait Until Dark* (1967)
    D. *War and Peace* (1956)

12. In which of the following films does Kim Novak costar with Jack Lemmon and Judy Holliday?

A. *Bell, Book and Candle* (1958)
B. *Jeanne Eagels* (1957)
C. *Kiss Me, Stupid* (1964)
D. *Phffft!* (1954)

13. Which leading lady was only twenty-six years old when she died of uremic poisoning?

A. Clara Bow
B. Jean Harlow
C. Lillian Gish
D. Susan Hayward

14. In what state was Rosalind Russell born and raised?

A. Connecticut
B. Minnesota
C. Rhode Island
D. Texas

15. Doris Day is mentioned in what song by the Beatles?

A. "Ain't She Sweet"
B. "All You Need Is Love"
C. "Dear Prudence"
D. "Dig It"

16. For what film was Audrey Hepburn not nominated for an Academy Award?

A. *Breakfast at Tiffany's* (1961)
B. *My Fair Lady* (1964)
C. *Roman Holiday* (1953)
D. *The Nun's Story* (1959)

17. F. Scott Fitzgerald based his famous story "Crazy Sunday" on a party at what actress's house?

A. Ava Gardner
B. Jean Harlow
C. Marilyn Monroe
D. Norma Shearer

18. Vivien Leigh made her screen debut in what British film?

A. *The 39 Steps* (1935)
B. *The Lady Vanishes* (1938)
C. *Things Are Looking Up* (1935)
D. *Waltzes from Vienna* (1934)

19. Marlene Dietrich had her legs painted gold for her role in what film?

A. *Kismet* (1944)
B. *My Darling Clementine* (1946)
C. *Stagecoach* (1939)
D. *The Sky's the Limit* (1943)

20. In which of the following films does Natalie Wood play Rosalind Russell's daughter?

A. *A Majority of One* (1961)
B. *Auntie Mame* (1958)
C. *Gypsy* (1962)
D. *Rosie!* (1967)

21. What was Rock Hudson's nickname for Doris Day?

A. "Dee Dee"
B. "Dodo"
C. "Eunice"
D. "Martha"

22. George Stevens directed Jean Arthur in all of the following films except for which one?

A. *Gunga Din* (1939)
B. *Shane* (1953)
C. *The More the Merrier* (1943)
D. *The Talk of the Town* (1942)

23. For which of the following films did Rosalind Russell not receive an Academy Award nomination as Best Actress?

A. *Auntie Mame* (1958)
B. *Gypsy* (1962)
C. *My Sister Eileen* (1942)
D. *Sister Kenny* (1946)

24. In which of the following films does Rosalind Russell play a judge?

   A. *Design for Scandal* (1941)
   B. *Flight for Freedom* (1943)
   C. *The Feminine Touch* (1941)
   D. *They Met in Bombay* (1941)

25. Gene Tierney's second husband, Howard Lee, was also married to which of the following actresses?

   A. Deborah Kerr
   B. Hedy Lamarr
   C. Rita Hayworth
   D. Rosalind Russell

26. What was the name of the only film to feature performances by Gene Tierney and Gary Merrill?

   A. *All About Eve* (1950)
   B. *Laura* (1944)
   C. *Shock Corridor* (1963)
   D. *Where the Sidewalk Ends* (1950)

27. Norma Shearer and Claire Danes have both portrayed which character on screen?

   A. Emma Woodhouse
   B. Juliet
   C. Marie Antoinette
   D. Natasha Rostova

28. When Claudette Colbert made *Imitation of Life* (1934) for Universal, she was on loan from which studio?

   A. Columbia
   B. MGM
   C. Paramount
   D. RKO

29. Rosalind Russell made her film debut in what film?

   A. *Evelyn Prentice* (1934)
   B. *My Sister Eileen* (1942)
   C. *Sister Kenny* (1946)
   D. *The Women* (1939)

30. Olivia de Havilland earned her second and final Oscar for her performance in what film?

   A. *Hold Back the Dawn* (1941)
   B. *The Heiress* (1949)
   C. *The Snake Pit* (1948)
   D. *To Each His Own* (1946)

31. After World War II put an end to my Olympic aspirations, I joined Billy Rose's San Francisco Aquacade. Who am I?

   A. Betty Grable
   B. Esther Williams
   C. Jayne Mansfield
   D. June Haver

32. Ingrid Bergman met second husband Roberto Rossellini while making what film?

   A. *Germany Year Zero* (1948)
   B. *Rome, Open City* (1945)
   C. *Stromboli* (1950)
   D. *Where Is Liberty?* (1962)

33. Audrey Hepburn made what film only a few months after giving birth to her son Sean Ferrer?

   A. *Breakfast at Tiffany's* (1961)
   B. *Charade* (1963)
   C. *Green Mansions* (1959)
   D. *The Children's Hour* (1961)

34. What was Hedy Lamarr's last film?

   A. *A Lady without Passport* (1950)
   B. *Copper Canyon* (1950)
   C. *My Favorite Spy* (1951)
   D. *The Female Animal* (1958)

35. In what film does Ginger Rogers play a night-club singer who has to adjust to her husband's conservative family?

   A. *A Damsel in Distress* (1937)
   B. *The More the Merrier* (1943)
   C. *Vigil in the Night* (1940)
   D. *Vivacious Lady* (1938)

Bombshell, 1933

36. What is the name of Jean Harlow's character in *Bombshell* (1933)?

A. Crystal Wetherby
B. Lola Burns
C. Rose Mason
D. Ruby Adams

37. Which leading lady began her showbiz career as one half of "The Dancing Cansinos"?

A. Debbie Reynolds
B. Ginger Rogers
C. Kim Novak
D. Rita Hayworth

38. For what film did Sophia Loren win her only Academy Award as Best Actress?

A. *A Countess from Hong Kong* (1967)
B. *El Cid* (1961)
C. *Two Women* (1960)
D. *Yesterday, Today and Tomorrow* (1963)

39. What actress did Dorothy McGuire replace in *A Tree Grows in Brooklyn* (1945) after that actress became pregnant?

A. Gene Tierney
B. Jane Wyman
C. Lana Turner
D. Merle Oberon

40. Doris Day was born in what city?

A. Chicago
B. Cincinnati
C. Honolulu
D. Palm Springs

41. Which leading lady died in Switzerland?

A. Audrey Hepburn
B. Ava Gardner
C. Greta Garbo
D. Rosalind Russell

42. In which of the following films does Susan Hayward not portray an alcoholic?

A. *I'll Cry Tomorrow* (1955)
B. *My Foolish Heart* (1949)
C. *Smash-Up: The Story of a Woman* (1947)
D. *The Lusty Men* (1952)

43. Joan Crawford won her only Academy Award as Best Actress for her role in which of the following films?

A. *A Woman's Face* (1941)
B. *Flamingo Road* (1949)
C. *Humoresque* (1946)
D. *Mildred Pierce* (1945)

44. Norma Shearer and Kirsten Dunst have what film role in common?

A. Elizabeth Barrett
B. Emma Woodhouse
C. Marie Antoinette
D. Queen Victoria

45. In which of the following films does Rosalind Russell not appear with William Powell?

A. *Evelyn Prentiss* (1934)
B. *Night Must Fall* (1937)
C. *Reckless* (1935)
D. *Rendezvous* (1935)

46. How old was Carole Lombard when she was tragically killed in a plane crash?

A. 28
B. 31
C. 33
D. 42

answers found on page 549–550

47. Marlene Dietrich learned to play the zither for her performance in what film directed by Mitchell Leisen?

A. *Golden Earrings* (1947)
B. *Let's Dance* (1950)
C. *Royal Wedding* (1951)
D. *The Belle of New York* (1952)

48. What year did Rosalind Russell die?

A. 1974
B. 1976
C. 1980
D. 1983

49. In which of the following films does Sophia Loren sport platinum blonde hair rather than her usual brunette?

A. *Boy on a Dolphin* (1957)
B. *Heller in Pink Tights* (1960)
C. *Houseboat* (1958)
D. *The Fall of the Roman Empire* (1964)

50. Lauren Bacall played Barbra Streisand's mother in what film?

A. *Funny Girl* (1968)
B. *Meet the Fockers* (2004)
C. *Nuts* (1987)
D. *The Mirror Has Two Faces* (1996)

51. What was Jean Harlow's real name?

A. Doris Kappelhoff
B. Harlean Carpenter
C. Jean Simmons
D. Lulamae Barnes

52. Hattie McDaniel appeared with Marlene Dietrich in what film?

A. *Blonde Venus* (1932)
B. *Quick Money* (1937)
C. *Saratoga* (1937)
D. *They Died with Their Boots On* (1941)

Little Women, 1933

53. In *Little Women* (1933), which sister did Katharine Hepburn play?

A. Amy
B. Beth
C. Jo
D. Meg

54. In what film did Barbara Bel Geddes costar with Irene Dunne?

A. *Fourteen Hours* (1951)
B. *I Remember Mama* (1948)
C. *Summertree* (1971)
D. *The Long Night* (1947)

55. What was Sophia Loren's nickname when she was growing up?

A. "Banana Girl"
B. "Potato Sack"
C. "The Stick"
D. "Va Va Voom"

56. What was Hedy Lamarr's character in *The Female Animal* (1958)?

A. Lily Frayne
B. Penny Windsor
C. Piggy
D. Vanessa Windsor

Spotlight on
BETTE **DAVIS** (1908–1989)

Bette Davis was shocked when Hollywood first came calling, never having thought a world that worshipped beauties like Jean Harlow would take an interest in her. Yet her confidence grew with each picture until she was like a boxer, going rounds with costars, directors, and studio executives. Ironically, her career took off when Warner Bros. reluctantly loaned her out to RKO to make *Of Human Bondage* (1934)—a role Jack Warner had cautioned would sink her career. But when critics hailed the performance, he had to admit he'd been wrong. She struggled for a time to find her niche at Warner Bros., but when Hal Wallis took over production the studio started making the kinds of moody dramas and unconventional romances that best suited Davis. *Jezebel* (1938); *Dark Victory* (1939); *The Letter* (1940); *Now, Voyager* (1942)—in each film she shattered the stereotype of the helpless female, so popular on screen at the time, bringing audiences spirited

Jezebel, 1938

women with inner resources and unwavering standards. These strong characters would allow her to make two comebacks in her decades-long career, first in the role of aging actress Margo Channing in *All About Eve* (1950), and later in the horror film *What Ever Happened to Baby Jane?* (1962) with offscreen rival Joan Crawford.

Fashions of 1934, 1934

1. **Bette Davis and Mary Astor first costarred in what drama?**

   A. *Bordertown* (1935)

   B. *Hush . . . Hush, Sweet Charlotte* (1964)

   C. *Red Dust* (1932)

   D. *The Great Lie* (1941)

2. **What was Bette Davis's real first name?**

   A. Cherry

   B. Dorothy

   C. Elsbeth

   D. Ruth

3. **Bette Davis drove costume designers crazy by refusing to wear what?**

   A. A bra

   B. Hats

   C. Stockings

   D. Wigs

4. **In 1935, an unnominated Bette Davis came close to winning the Best Actress Oscar through a write-in campaign. Who did win the award?**

   A. Claudette Colbert

   B. Fay Wray

   C. Grace Moore

   D. Norma Shearer

5. **Bette Davis won her first Academy Award as Best Actress in which film?**

   A. *All This, and Heaven Too* (1940)

   B. *Dangerous* (1935)

   C. *Kid Galahad* (1937)

   D. *Of Human Bondage* (1934)

answers found on page 550

57. Which leading lady did Fred Astaire admit was his favorite dancing partner?

A. Debbie Reynolds
B. Deborah Kerr
C. Judy Garland
D. Rita Hayworth

58. When Irene Dunne made *Back Street* (1932) for Universal, she was on loan from which studio?

A. Columbia
B. Paramount
C. RKO
D. Warner Bros.

59. Miriam Hopkins played Mrs. Mortar in which film starring Audrey Hepburn?

A. *Charade* (1963)
B. *Green Mansions* (1959)
C. *Sabrina* (1954)
D. *The Children's Hour* (1961)

60. How many Oscars did Rosalind Russell win?

A. 0
B. 1
C. 2
D. 3

61. For what film did Gloria Swanson offer William Haines a role that he turned down?

A. *Father Takes a Wife* (1941)
B. *Queen Kelly* (1929)
C. *Sadie Thompson* (1928)
D. *Sunset Blvd.* (1950)

62. MGM frequently used Rosalind Russell as a rival to and/or substitute for what actress?

A. Bette Davis
B. Joan Crawford
C. Myrna Loy
D. Norma Shearer

63. For which of her films did Carole Lombard receive her only Academy Award nomination for Best Actress?

A. *My Man Godfrey* (1936)
B. *Nothing Sacred* (1937)
C. *To Be or Not to Be* (1942)
D. *Twentieth Century* (1934)

64. In what film did Ingrid Bergman make her Oscar-winning triumphant return to the screen following her scandal with Roberto Rossellini?

A. *Anastasia* (1956)
B. *Goodbye Again* (1961)
C. *Indiscreet* (1958)
D. *The Yellow Rolls-Royce* (1964)

65. How were Audrey and Katharine Hepburn related?

A. Cousins
B. In-laws
C. Sisters
D. They weren't

66. *Every Sunday* (1936) was basically a screen test for two young actresses. One became Deanna Durbin, and the other became Judy Garland. What was Judy Garland's name in the short?

A. Edna Mae Garland
B. Frances Ethel Gumm
C. Judith Greenberg
D. Judy Garland

67. Myrna Loy and Rosalind Russell portray rivals for Franchot Tone's affections in which film directed by Richard Thorpe?

A. *Love Is Dangerous* (1933)
B. *Man-Proof* (1938)
C. *Notorious but Nice* (1933)
D. *Strange Wives* (1934)

answers found on page 550

68. Lana Turner portrays an alluring priestess in which film directed by Richard Thorpe?

A. *Dance Pretty Lady* (1932)
B. *On Such a Night* (1956)
C. *The Prodigal* (1955)
D. *Unfinished Symphony* (1934)

69. In which of the following Greta Garbo films does Marie Dressler costar?

A. *Anna Christie* (1931)
B. *Camille* (1936)
C. *Ninotchka* (1939)
D. *Queen Christina* (1933)

Christopher Strong, 1933

70. In the 1933 film *Christopher Strong*, Katharine Hepburn plays a famous what?

A. Aviator
B. Golfer
C. Race car driver
D. Swimmer

71. How many movies did Jean Harlow make during her career?

A. 15
B. 29
C. 36
D. 42

72. I was born Edythe Marrener on June 30, 1917, in Brooklyn, New York. Who am I?

A. Barbara Stanwyck
B. Claudette Colbert
C. Judy Garland
D. Susan Hayward

73. In what country was Ingrid Bergman born?

A. Finland
B. Germany
C. Iceland
D. Sweden

74. Loretta Young and Celeste Holm play French nuns trying to raise money for a New England children's hospital in what holiday film?

A. *Christmas in Connecticut* (1945)
B. *Come to the Stable* (1949)
C. *Holiday Inn* (1942)
D. *The Bishop's Wife* (1947)

75. How many Golden Globe Awards did Rosalind Russell receive?

A. 4
B. 5
C. 6
D. 7

76. Teresa Wright made her film debut as Bette Davis's daughter in what film?

A. *Mrs. Miniver* (1942)
B. *The Best Years of Our Lives* (1946)
C. *The Little Foxes* (1941)
D. *The Pride of the Yankees* (1942)

77. Which forty-three-year-old leading lady portrayed a thirteen-year-old in *Payment On Demand* (1951)?

A. Bette Davis
B. Ginger Rogers
C. Norma Shearer
D. Rosalind Russell

answers found on page 550

78. Jean Harlow's character is involved in a black-mail scheme in which of the following films?

A. *China Seas* (1935)
B. *Dinner at Eight* (1933)
C. *Hold Your Man* (1933)
D. *Wife vs. Secretary* (1936)

79. Which leading lady was Hitler's favorite actress?

A. Greta Garbo
B. Lana Turner
C. Mae West
D. Rita Hayworth

80. Which leading lady was born in Brooklyn on July 16, 1907?

A. Barbara Stanwyck
B. Claudette Colbert
C. Judy Garland
D. Mae West

81. In 1939, a UCLA student acting on a fraternity bet handcuffed himself to me and swallowed the key. Who am I?

A. Ann Sheridan
B. Barbara Stanwyck
C. Grace Kelly
D. Jean Harlow

82. Which leading lady landed her first agent by crashing her bike onto his front lawn?

A. Ann Sheridan
B. Hedy Lamarr
C. Norma Shearer
D. Susan Hayward

83. Doris Day suffered two broken ribs while filming what romantic comedy opposite James Garner and Don Knotts?

A. *Move Over, Darling* (1963)
B. *That Touch of Mink* (1962)
C. *The Glass Bottom Boat* (1966)
D. *The Thrill of It All* (1963)

84. Ann Sothern starred in the popular *Maisie* series for MGM. Who was originally intended to play Maisie?

A. Deanna Durbin
B. Ginger Rogers
C. Irene Dunne
D. Jean Harlow

85. What year did MGM release Deborah Kerr from her contract?

A. 1949
B. 1953
C. 1960
D. 1962

86. Who was Bette Davis's first husband?

A. Arthur Farnsworth
B. Gary Merrill
C. Harmon Nelson
D. William Grant Sherry

87. During World War II, Deborah Kerr was visiting my house in Denham, England, when the garden was bombed by a German aircraft. Who am I?

A. Basil Radford
B. James Mason
C. Michael Redgrave
D. Rex Harrison

88. Which leading lady cowrote the novel *Today Is Tonight*?

A. Carole Lombard
B. Jean Arthur
C. Jean Harlow
D. Myrna Loy

89. In which of the following films does Ava Gardner costar with Barbara Stanwyck and James Mason?

A. *Earthquake* (1974)
B. *East Side, West Side* (1949)
C. *Lone Star* (1952)
D. *The Great Sinner* (1949)

90. **Teresa Wright played Greer Garson's daughter-in-law in what film?**

A. *Mrs. Miniver* (1942)
B. *The Best Years of Our Lives* (1946)
C. *The Little Foxes* (1941)
D. *The Pride of the Yankees* (1942)

Mrs. Miniver, 1942

91. **Greer Garson won an Academy Award as Best Actress for *Mrs. Miniver* (1942). How many other Academy Awards did she win?**

A. 6
B. 4
C. 2
D. 0

92. **Several dancers of the Rome Opera ballet corps worked as costumed extras in which film starring Audrey Hepburn?**

A. *Breakfast at Tiffany's* (1961)
B. *Funny Face* (1957)
C. *My Fair Lady* (1964)
D. *The Nun's Story* (1959)

93. **Marjorie Main portrayed Lucy in which film opposite Norma Shearer?**

A. *A Free Soul* (1931)
B. *Escape* (1940)
C. *The Barretts of Wimpole Street* (1934)
D. *The Women* (1939)

94. **Which actress was born in Scotland?**

A. Charlize Theron
B. Deborah Kerr
C. Katharine Hepburn
D. Meryl Streep

95. **Where and when did Ava Gardner die?**

A. 1983 in Mexico City, Mexico
B. 1985 in Madrid, Spain
C. 1990 in London, England
D. 1996 in Paris, France

96. **Hattie McDaniel plays Mae West's maid in what film?**

A. *Alice Adams* (1935)
B. *Blonde Venus* (1932)
C. *I'm No Angel* (1933)
D. *Show Boat* (1936)

97. **What was Lana Turner's nickname?**

A. "The Brooklyn Bombshell"
B. "The It Girl"
C. "The Love Goddess"
D. "The Sweater Girl"

98. **In the 1932 film *Sinners in the Sun,* Carole Lombard portrays a what?**

A. Concert pianist
B. Fashion model
C. Lawyer
D. Nurse

99. **For what film did Katharine Hepburn win her first Academy Award for Best Actress?**

A. *Alice Adams* (1935)
B. *Morning Glory* (1933)
C. *The African Queen* (1951)
D. *Woman of the Year* (1942)

100. **What was Bette Davis's Massachusetts hometown?**
   A. Cambridge
   B. Cherry Hill
   C. Lowell
   D. Springfield

101. **Irene Dunne replaced Myrna Loy in what film that featured Natalie Wood?**
   A. *A New Kind of Love* (1963)
   B. *Never a Dull Moment* (1950)
   C. *The Happy Road* (1957)
   D. *The Man from Laramie* (1955)

102. **Jean Harlow makes an uncredited appearance as an extra in which Charles Chaplin film?**
   A. *City Lights* (1931)
   B. *The Gold Rush* (1925)
   C. *The Great Dictator* (1940)
   D. *The Kid* (1921)

103. **George Stevens got his first big break when he directed Katharine Hepburn in what film?**
   A. *Alice Adams* (1935)
   B. *Annie Oakley* (1935)
   C. *Laddie* (1935)
   D. *The Nitwits* (1935)

104. **Which English leading lady died in 1996 in Dallas, Texas?**
   A. Ava Gardner
   B. Deborah Kerr
   C. Greer Garson
   D. Vivien Leigh

105. **In which of the following films does Kim Novak costar with Kirk Douglas?**
   A. *Bell, Book and Candle* (1958)
   B. *Pushover* (1954)
   C. *Strangers When We Meet* (1960)
   D. *The Notorious Landlady* (1962)

Dancing Co-Ed, 1939

106. **The Lana Turner film *Dancing Co-Ed* (1939) was originally planned as a vehicle for what other actress?**
   A. Alexis Smith
   B. Doris Day
   C. Eleanor Powell
   D. Judy Garland

107. **My first husband was actor Jess Barker. Who am I?**
   A. Lana Turner
   B. Loretta Young
   C. Olivia de Havilland
   D. Susan Hayward

108. **I made my final film performance portraying Jean Harlow's mother in the 1965 biopic *Harlow*. Who am I?**
   A. Eleanor Parker
   B. Ginger Rogers
   C. Judy Garland
   D. Rita Hayworth

109. **What was Rosalind Russell's last feature film?**
   A. *Rosie* (1967)
   B. *The Trouble with Angels* (1966)
   C. *Mrs. Pollifax—Spy* (1971)
   D. *Where Angeles Go, Trouble Follows* (1968)

answers found on page 550

110. In what film did Doris Day receive top billing for the first time?

A. *April in Paris* (1952)
B. *Tea for Two* (1950)
C. *The West Point Story* (1950)
D. *Young Man with a Horn* (1950)

111. Rosalind Russell appears with Kirk Douglas in which of the following films?

A. *A Woman of Distinction* (1950)
B. *Mourning Becomes Electra* (1947)
C. *Picnic* (1955)
D. *The Guilt of Janet Ames* (1947)

112. A poster of Rita Hayworth plays a key part in what contemporary film?

A. *The Shawshank Redemption* (1994)
B. *The Silence of the Lambs* (1991)
C. *The Usual Suspects* (1995)
D. *Thelma & Louise* (1991)

113. In the 1930 film *Fast and Loose,* Carole Lombard costars with which of the following actresses?

A. Agnes Moorehead
B. Ann Miller
C. Miriam Hopkins
D. Myrna Loy

114. What leading lady played Betsy Booth in the Andy Hardy series?

A. Ava Gardner
B. Esther Williams
C. Judy Garland
D. Lana Turner

115. Which leading lady never kissed her leading men on screen?

A. Ginger Rogers
B. Lillian Gish
C. Mae West
D. Mary Pickford

116. What was Gloria Swanson's final film?

A. *Airport 1975* (1974)
B. *Male and Female* (1919)
C. *Queen Kelly* (1929)
D. *Sunset Blvd.* (1950)

117. In what year did Grace Kelly meet her husband while attending the Cannes Film Festival?

A. 1955
B. 1957
C. 1960
D. 1963

118. In which of the following films does Barbara Stanwyck costar with Elvis Presley?

A. *Change of Habit* (1969)
B. *G.I. Blues* (1960)
C. *Love Me Tender* (1956)
D. *Roustabout* (1964)

119. In what film is Jean Harlow's character married to a prizefighter?

A. *Goldie* (1931)
B. *Iron Man* (1931)
C. *The Girl from Missouri* (1934)
D. *The Secret Six* (1931)

120. I was born Virginia Katherine McMath in Independence, Missouri. Who am I?

A. Ginger Rogers
B. Irene Dunne
C. Rita Hayworth
D. Susan Hayward

121. Where was Loretta Young born?

A. Chicago, Illinois
B. Paramus, New Jersey
C. Pittsburgh, Pennsylvania
D. Salt Lake City, Utah

answers found on page 550

Spotlight on
GRETA **GARBO** (1905–1990)

In the 1926 film *Torrent*, the twenty-one-year-old Garbo dazzled audiences with her beauty and nuanced portrayal of emotions. Her films with silent-screen star John Gilbert (and their offscreen romance) made for big box office as well, and by the end of the silent era she was Hollywood royalty. With the advent of talkies, her career continued to rise; Greta's throaty, accented voice added to her provocative persona in such hits as *Anna Christie* (1930), *Grand Hotel* (1932), *Anna Karenina* (1935), and *Camille* (1936). In all these roles she was the "pained lady," wrapped in mysterious desire and lovely agony (qualities heightened by her varied and secretive offscreen love life) until director Ernst Lubitsch cast her in his mirthful *Ninotchka* (1939). "Garbo laughs!" the ads proclaimed, as though she had never chuckled in a film before. Yet the ploy worked—theaters filled with fans wanting to witness the miracle. Despite her successes, movie fame was challenging to Garbo. She was homesick for her beloved Sweden and valued her privacy like no other star of her magnitude. When the comedy follow-up to *Ninotchka*, entitled *Two-Faced Woman* (1941), turned into a humiliating debacle, Garbo decided not to make another movie until everything was just right. In the end, no script ever motivated her to leave her increasing reclusion, and she never made another picture.

Grand Hotel, 1932

Ninotchka, 1939

1. **In the 1933 film *Queen Christina*, Greta Garbo's character disguises herself as a what?**

    A. Circus clown
    B. Harem girl
    C. Maid
    D. Man

2. **Greta Garbo plays the ballerina who "vants to be alone" in what Vicki Baum adaptation?**

    A. *Camille* (1936)
    B. *Grand Hotel* (1932)
    C. *Ninotchka* (1939)
    D. *Queen Christina* (1933)

3. **What film earned Greta Garbo her final Oscar nomination for Best Actress?**

    A. *Camille* (1936)
    B. *Ninotchka* (1939)

    C. *Queen Christina* (1933)
    D. *Two-Faced Woman* (1941)

4. **Who said the following about Greta Garbo? "Her instinct, her mastery over the machine, was pure witchcraft. I cannot analyze this woman's acting. I only know that no one else so effectively worked in front of a camera."**

    A. Bette Davis
    B. Ginger Rogers
    C. Joan Crawford
    D. Katharine Hepburn

5. **Greta Garbo plays the title role in what film cowritten by Billy Wilder?**

    A. *Madame Curie* (1943)
    B. *Maisie Was a Lady* (1941)
    C. *Ninotchka* (1939)
    D. *Sabrina* (1954)

answers found on page 550

122. Vivian Mary Hartley was the birth name of which screen legend?
   A. Clara Bow
   B. Greer Garson
   C. Marlene Dietrich
   D. Vivien Leigh

123. What leading lady stars in *Ball of Fire* (1941)?
   A. Barbara Stanwyck
   B. Jean Simmons
   C. Lucille Ball
   D. Susan Hayward

124. What was the name of the character played by Deborah Kerr in *I See a Dark Stranger* (1946)?
   A. Bridie Quilty
   B. Jo McCracken
   C. Kitten Kavanagh
   D. Teresa McGrane

125. Which leading lady's MGM contract included a clause that prevented the studio from forcing her to make any public appearances?
   A. Claudette Colbert
   B. Greta Garbo
   C. Katharine Hepburn
   D. Louise Brooks

126. What was the first of eleven films to pair Elizabeth Taylor and Richard Burton?
   A. *Cleopatra* (1963)
   B. *El Cid* (1961)
   C. *Hamlet* (1964)
   D. *The Robe* (1953)

127. What was Greer Garson's nickname at the start of her stage career?
   A. "Garson of the West End"
   B. "Princess Garson"
   C. "Queen Greer"
   D. "The Duchess of Garson"

128. Jane Powell was cast in *Royal Wedding* (1951) after two actresses before her couldn't do the part. One of them was Judy Garland. Who was the other?
   A. Cyd Charisse
   B. Debbie Reynolds
   C. Ginger Rogers
   D. June Allyson

129. Audrey Hepburn and Olivia de Havilland have both portrayed what character on screen?
   A. Maid Marian
   B. Natasha Rostova
   C. Princess Aurora
   D. Sister Luke (Gabrielle van der Mal)

130. What was Lillian Gish's first film under her MGM contract?
   A. *Broken Blossoms* (1936)
   B. *La Bohème* (1926)
   C. *The Scarlet Letter* (1926)
   D. *The Wind* (1928)

131. Mae West's *She Done Him Wrong* (1933) saved which studio from bankruptcy?
   A. Columbia
   B. MGM
   C. Paramount
   D. Warner Bros.

132. In which of the following films does Doris Day sing her hit song "Que Sera, Sera (Whatever Will Be, Will Be)"?
   A. *Billy Rose's Jumbo* (1962)
   B. *Romance on the High Seas* (1948)
   C. *The Glass Bottom Boat* (1966)
   D. *Young at Heart* (1954)

133. In which of the following films does Rosalind Russell appear with Clark Gable?
   A. *Forsaking All Others* (1934)
   B. *Reckless* (1935)
   C. *Rendezvous* (1935)
   D. *West Point of the Air* (1935)

answers found on page 550

134. Marie Dressler appears with Norma Shearer in which of the following films?

A. *Dinner at Eight* (1933)
B. *Let Us Be Gay* (1930)
C. *Min and Bill* (1930)
D. *The Girl Said No* (1930)

135. Doris Day co-owns a beautiful hotel in what California city?

A. Carmel
B. San Diego
C. San Francisco
D. Santa Barbara

136. Who was Judy Garland's first husband?

A. David Rose
B. Mickey Rooney
C. Sidney Luft
D. Vincente Minnelli

137. What screen legend had already made twenty films by the age of sixteen?

A. Audrey Hepburn
B. Katharine Hepburn
C. Marilyn Monroe
D. Natalie Wood

138. Which leading lady connects *Death of a Gunfighter* (1969) and *Two Girls and a Sailor* (1944)?

A. Jean Arthur
B. Kim Novak
C. Lena Horne
D. Sophia Loren

139. Hedy Lamarr made a splash playing Delilah in *Samson and Delilah*. Who was the director?

A. Billy Wilder
B. Cecil B. DeMille
C. Howard Hawks
D. Orson Welles

Laugh, Clown, Laugh, 1928

140. I was only fourteen when Lon Chaney fell in love with me in *Laugh, Clown, Laugh* (1928). Who am I?

A. Clara Bow
B. Jean Arthur
C. Loretta Young
D. Louise Brooks

141. Greer Garson and Jean Hagen share the screen in what biopic about Franklin Delano Roosevelt?

A. *A Man for All Seasons* (1966)
B. *Pocketful of Miracles* (1961)
C. *Storm Center* (1956)
D. *Sunrise at Campobello* (1960)

142. In which of the following films does Greer Garson appear with Elizabeth Taylor?

A. *Julia Misbehaves* (1948)
B. *Mrs. Parkington* (1944)
C. *Pride and Prejudice* (1940)
D. *The Miniver Story* (1950)

143. Natalie Wood almost always wore what accessory around her left wrist?

A. Bracelet
B. Scrunchie
C. Silk scarf
D. Watch

144. **Who was Katharine Hepburn's first and only husband?**

A. Artie Shaw
B. Howard Hughes
C. Ludlow Ogden Smith
D. Spencer Tracy

145. **Sophia Loren and Cary Grant fell in love for real during the making of which film?**

A. *Desire Under the Elms* (1958)
B. *Houseboat* (1958)
C. *The Black Orchid* (1959)
D. *The Pride and the Passion* (1957)

146. **How many husbands has Sophia Loren had?**

A. 1
B. 2
C. 3
D. 4

147. **What year did Bette Davis die?**

A. 1965
B. 1977
C. 1989
D. 1991

148. **Maureen O'Sullivan was a childhood friend and classmate of which Oscar-winning actress?**

A. Audrey Hepburn
B. Loretta Young
C. Olivia de Havilland
D. Vivien Leigh

149. **In how many films did Bette Davis portray Queen Elizabeth I?**

A. 0
B. 1
C. 2
D. 3

150. **What was Susan Hayward's nickname?**

A. "The Brooklyn Bombshell"
B. "The It Girl"
C. "The Oompf Girl"
D. "The Sweater Girl"

151. **In which of the following films did Barbara Stanwyck costar with Ronald Reagan?**

A. *Cattle Queen of Montana* (1954)
B. *Clash by Night* (1952)
C. *Golden Boy* (1939)
D. *The Man with a Cloak* (1951)

152. **In which film did Hedy Lamarr not appear with Spencer Tracy?**

A. *Boom Town* (1940)
B. *Copper Canyon* (1950)
C. *I Take This Woman* (1940)
D. *Tortilla Flat* (1942)

153. **What was the last name Sophia Loren used before settling on Loren?**

A. Fiume
B. Fleming
C. Lazzaro
D. Matarazzo

154. **Rosalind Russell plays Mother Superior at a convent in what film?**

A. *My Sister Eileen* (1942)
B. *Sister Kenny* (1946)
C. *The Trouble with Angels* (1966)
D. *The Women* (1939)

155. **For what film did Ingrid Bergman win her first Academy Award as Best Actress?**

A. *Casablanca* (1942)
B. *For Whom the Bell Tolls* (1943)
C. *Gaslight* (1944)
D. *Murder on the Orient Express* (1974)

156. **What was the name of the nun played by Deborah Kerr in *Black Narcissus* (1947)?**

A. Sister Amanda
B. Sister Briony
C. Sister Clodagh
D. Sister Ruth

answers found on page 550

157. What actor was considered to be the love of Jean Harlow's life?

A. Clark Gable
B. Pat O'Brien
C. Robert Taylor
D. William Powell

158. What year did Audrey Hepburn die?

A. 1978
B. 1982
C. 1989
D. 1993

159. Maureen O'Hara plays Esmeralda in what film costarring Cedric Hardwicke?

A. *Flying Down to Rio* (1933)
B. *Les Misérables* (1935)
C. *Rose-Marie* (1936)
D. *The Hunchback of Notre Dame* (1939)

160. How many times was Rosalind Russell married?

A. 0
B. 1
C. 2
D. 3

161. What year did Lena Horne make her film debut?

A. 1920
B. 1926
C. 1931
D. 1938

162. Where was Jean Harlow born?

A. Birmingham, Alabama
B. Kansas City, Missouri
C. Toledo, Ohio
D. Yonkers, New York

163. In which of the following films does Walter Matthau costar with Tony Curtis and Debbie Reynolds?

A. *Charade* (1963)
B. *Ensign Pulver* (1964)
C. *Goodbye Charlie* (1964)
D. *Mirage* (1965)

164. What was Norma Shearer's final film?

A. *Her Cardboard Lover* (1942)
B. *Smilin' Through* (1932)
C. *The Women* (1939)
D. *Romeo and Juliet* (1936)

165. What Gene Kelly film did not costar Judy Garland?

A. *For Me and My Gal* (1942)
B. *On the Town* (1949)
C. *Thousands Cheer* (1943)
D. *Ziegfeld Follies* (1946)

166. In what film does Marlene Dietrich play Frenchy?

A. *Destry Rides Again* (1939)
B. *Shanghai Express* (1932)
C. *The Devil Is a Woman* (1935)
D. *The Lady Is Willing* (1942)

167. What was Susan Hayward's real name?

A. Doris Kappelhoff
B. Edythe Marrener
C. Frances Gumm
D. Norma Jean Baker

168. Simone Signoret was nominated for a Best Actress Oscar in what film opposite Vivien Leigh?

A. *Easter Parade* (1948)
B. *Ship of Fools* (1965)
C. *The Barkleys of Broadway* (1949)
D. *The House of the Seven Hawks* (1959)

169. What was Grace Kelly's final film before becoming the Princess of Monaco?

A. *High Society* (1956)
B. *Mogambo* (1953)
C. *Rear Window* (1954)
D. *To Catch a Thief* (1955)

Spotlight on
LANA **TURNER** (1921–1995)

It was difficult to tell Lana Turner the person from many of the characters she played—all of them beautiful and tragic. When she was eight, her father was murdered, triggering a family move to California in search of work. There she was "discovered" at the soda counter of the drugstore across from her high school, and the agent who spied her took her to see director Mervyn LeRoy, who was looking for a provocative young actress to fill the role of a murder victim in *They Won't Forget* (1937). Turner didn't stay long in such juvenile roles. At twenty she played torrid love scenes with gangster Robert Taylor in *Johnny Eager* (1941) and at twenty-five she seduced John Garfield in the classic film noir

The Postman Always Rings Twice, 1946

The Postman Always Rings Twice (1946). Critics often derided her acting, but her screen presence was electric. And the scandals that might have destroyed other careers—including her seven failed marriages—only made her more popular. As the 1957 hit *Peyton Place* was going into national release, Turner's abusive relationship with gangster Johnny Stompanato climaxed when her daughter, Cheryl Crane, killed the thug to protect her mother. The scandal drove ticket sales, and Turner launched a series of popular on-screen melodramas, including *Imitation of Life* (1959).

Johnny Eager, 1941

1. **Lana Turner falls for Richard Burton in what film set in 1930s India?**

   A. *My Cousin Rachel* (1952)

   B. *The Night of the Iguana* (1964)

   C. *The Rains of Ranchipur* (1955)

   D. *The Woman with No Name* (1950)

2. **In which Andy Hardy film does Lana Turner appear?**

   A. *Andy Hardy Meets Debutante* (1940)

   B. *Andy Hardy's Double Life* (1942)

   C. *Love Finds Andy Hardy* (1938)

   D. *Love Laughs at Andy Hardy* (1946)

3. **Lana Turner is employed by the Thomas Callaway Agency in what film?**

   A. *A Life of Her Own* (1950)

   B. *All About Eve* (1950)

   C. *Another Man's Poison* (1951)

   D. *The Star* (1952)

4. **What was Lana Turner's first Technicolor film?**

   A. *Betrayed* (1954)

   B. *Mr. Imperium* (1951)

   C. *Peyton Place* (1957)

   D. *The Three Musketeers* (1948)

5. **Lana Turner refused the lead role, that was ultimately played by Bette Davis, in what thriller?**

   A. *Confidential Agent* (1945)

   B. *Dead Ringer* (1964)

   C. *Hotel Berlin* (1945)

   D. *The Conspirators* (1944)

---

answers found on pages 550–551

170. Where was Norma Shearer born?

    A. Mexico City

    B. Montreal

    C. New Orleans

    D. Paris

171. Which leading lady appeared in nine films with "lady" or "ladies" in the title?

    A. Barbara Stanwyck

    B. Hedy Lamarr

    C. Rosalind Russell

    D. Sophia Loren

172. What was the first sound picture that Carole Lombard made?

    A. *High Voltage* (1929)

    B. *Motorboat Mamas* (1928)

    C. *Sinners in the Sun* (1932)

    D. *The Princess Comes Across* (1936)

173. Rosalind Russell plays a character named Hildy Johnson in what film?

    A. *Gypsy* (1962)

    B. *His Girl Friday* (1940)

    C. *Night Must Fall* (1937)

    D. *The Women* (1939)

174. Janet Gaynor costarred with Loretta Young in what film?

    A. *Ladies in Love* (1936)

    B. *State Fair* (1933)

    C. *The First Year* (1932)

    D. *Three Loves Has Nancy* (1938)

175. Claudette Colbert made her screen debut in what film directed by Frank Capra?

    A. *For the Love of Mike* (1927)

    B. *Forbidden* (1932)

    C. *Say It with Sables* (1928)

    D. *You Can't Take It with You* (1938)

The Divorcee, 1930

176. In 1930, Norma Shearer earned dual Best Actress nominations for *The Divorcee* and what other film?

    A. *Let Us Be Gay*

    B. *Marie Antoinette*

    C. *The Women*

    D. *Their Own Desire*

177. As Jean Harlow's career skyrocketed, so did the sale of what product?

    A. Fishnet stockings

    B. Peroxide

    C. Red lipstick

    D. White roses

178. What studio signed Grace Kelly to a seven-year contract?

    A. MGM

    B. Paramount

    C. Universal

    D. Warner Bros.

179. What was the name of the only film to costar Marilyn Monroe and Bette Davis?

    A. *All About Eve* (1950)

    B. *Beyond the Forest* (1949)

    C. *June Bride* (1948)

    D. *Mr. Skeffington* (1944)

180. Which leading lady received the Jean Hersholt Humanitarian Award in 1973?

A. Bette Davis

B. Ginger Rogers

C. Myrna Loy

D. Rosalind Russell

181. For what film did Barbara Stanwyck receive her first Oscar nomination for Best Actress?

A. *Ball of Fire* (1941)

B. *Double Indemnity* (1944)

C. *Sorry, Wrong Number* (1948)

D. *Stella Dallas* (1937)

182. What year was Lena Horne born?

A. 1899

B. 1917

C. 1926

D. 1945

183. What year did Loretta Young die?

A. 1983

B. 1995

C. 2000

D. 2004

184. Who was Lena Horne's second husband?

A. John Perlman

B. Lennie Hayton

C. Martin Smith

D. Orlando Stiller

185. Which one of the following actresses appears with Kay Francis in the 1930 film *Street of Chance*?

A. Carole Lombard

B. Fay Wray

C. Jean Arthur

D. Miriam Hopkins

186. In what film does Barbara Bel Geddes costar with Lana Turner?

A. *Fourteen Hours* (1951)

B. *By Love Possessed* (1961)

C. *I Remember Mama* (1948)

D. *Vertigo* (1958)

187. What was the name of the character played by Bette Davis in *The Little Foxes* (1941)?

A. Katharine Arden

B. Miriam Traherne

C. Regina Giddens

D. Tallulah Fontane

188. How many times was Hedy Lamarr married?

A. 3

B. 4

C. 5

D. 6

189. What was the name of the character played by Rosalind Russell in *The Women* (1939)?

A. Lisa Realto

B. Lydia Kilmer

C. Sylvia Fowler

D. Vivianne Sobcheck

190. Fay Wray plays Joan Crawford's neighbor in what film?

A. *Doctor X* (1932)

B. *Queen Bee* (1955)

C. *The Mystery of the Wax Museum* (1933)

D. *The Wedding March* (1928)

191. For which of the following films did Katharine Hepburn not win the Academy Award for Best Actress?

A. *Guess Who's Coming to Dinner* (1967)

B. *On Golden Pond* (1981)

C. *The African Queen* (1951)

D. *The Lion in Winter* (1968)

192. Which leading lady grew up in Holland during World War II?

A. Audrey Hepburn

B. Claudette Colbert

C. Greta Garbo

D. Lena Horne

193. Ann-Margret made her screen debut opposite Bette Davis in what film?

A. *Pocketful of Miracles* (1961)
B. *The Anniversary* (1968)
C. *The Nanny* (1965)
D. *Where Love Has Gone* (1964)

194. Which leading lady's daughter, Judy (born in 1936), was fathered out of wedlock by Clark Gable?

A. Carole Lombard
B. Doris Day
C. Grace Kelly
D. Loretta Young

195. Loretta Young and Jean Harlow share the screen in what Frank Capra film?

A. *Arsenic and Old Lace* (1944)
B. *Broadway Bill* (1934)
C. *It's a Wonderful Life* (1946)
D. *Platinum Blonde* (1931)

196. Ginger Rogers was a brunette in what film?

A. *A Certain Smile* (1958)
B. *Days of Wine and Roses* (1962)
C. *No Funny Business* (1933)
D. *Primrose Path* (1940)

197. What film earned Doris Day her only Oscar nomination?

A. *Lover Come Back* (1961)
B. *Pillow Talk* (1959)
C. *Please Don't Eat the Daisies* (1960)
D. *The Man Who Knew Too Much* (1956)

198. What leading lady is portrayed by Cate Blanchett in *The Aviator* (2004)?

A. Ava Gardner
B. Carole Lombard
C. Jean Harlow
D. Katharine Hepburn

199. Ingrid Bergman starred in all of the following Alfred Hitchcock films except which one?

A. *Notorious* (1946)
B. *Rebecca* (1940)
C. *Spellbound* (1945)
D. *Under Capricorn* (1949)

200. How old was Judy Garland when she starred in the *The Wizard of Oz* (1939)?

A. 11
B. 16
C. 23
D. 27

201. How many siblings did Rosalind Russell have?

A. 5
B. 6
C. 7
D. 8

202. In *Wife vs. Secretary* (1936), Jean Harlow plays the secretary. Who plays the wife?

A. Claudette Colbert
B. Donna Reed
C. Jane Wyman
D. Myrna Loy

203. Angela Lansbury plays Judy Garland's sultry rival in what film?

A. *In the Good Old Summertime* (1949)
B. *Summer Stock* (1950)
C. *The Harvey Girls* (1946)
D. *Ziegfeld Girl* (1941)

204. How much did it cost Universal Studios to "borrow" Claudette Colbert for *Imitation of Life* (1934)?

A. $120,000
B. $150,000
C. $50,000
D. $90,000

answers found on page 551

205. Jean Harlow died in the middle of production on what film?

A. *Dinner at Eight* (1933)
B. *Platinum Blonde* (1931)
C. *Saratoga* (1937)
D. *Suzy* (1936)

206. How many times was Jean Harlow married?

A. 1
B. 3
C. 5
D. 7

207. What was Rita Hayworth's last film?

A. *Circus World* (1964)
B. *The Money Trap* (1965)
C. *The Naked Zoo* (1971)
D. *The Wrath of God* (1972)

208. Where is Bette Davis interred?

A. Calvary Cemetery, in Los Angeles, California
B. Forest Lawn Memorial Park in Hollywood Hills, California
C. Holy Cross Cemetery in Culver City, California
D. Jordan-Fernald Funeral Home in Mount Desert, Maine

209. Katharine Hepburn's real-life niece plays her daughter in which film costarring Sidney Poitier?

A. *A Patch of Blue* (1965)
B. *A Warm December* (1973)
C. *Guess Who's Coming to Dinner* (1967)
D. *Little Nikita* (1988)

210. Thelma Ritter costars with Marilyn Monroe in which of the following films?

A. *As Young as You Feel* (1951)
B. *The Mating Season* (1951)
C. *The Model and the Marriage Broker* (1951)
D. *With a Song in My Heart* (1952)

Father of the Bride, 1950

211. Who played Spencer Tracy's wife and Elizabeth Taylor's mother in *Father of the Bride* (1950)?

A. Joan Bennett
B. Myrna Loy
C. Katharine Hepburn
D. Rosalind Russell

212. What was Ann Sheridan's birth name?

A. Clara Lou
B. Harlean Sky
C. Judy Mae
D. Pamela Jane

213. In what film did Doris Day have her first non-singing role?

A. *It Happened to Jane* (1959)
B. *Julie* (1956)
C. *Storm Warning* (1951)
D. *The Thrill of It All* (1963)

214. Which of the following actresses was not considered for Bette Davis's role in *All About Eve* (1950)?

A. Claudette Colbert
B. Donna Reed
C. Ingrid Bergman
D. Susan Hayward

3 Godfathers, 1948

Chapter 7

LEADING
MEN

How do you take your men? Do you like them dashing and athletic? Try a Douglas Fairbanks or Errol Flynn. Do you fancy a gent in fancy dress? How about Fred Astaire or Cary Grant? Do you want a man to sing you to sleep at night? You can choose between Bing Crosby and Frank Sinatra. Perhaps an all-American hero suits your palate? We have the latest in Gary Cooper, Henry Fonda, James Stewart, and John Wayne. Or if you want a touch of danger, you could always spend a few hours with Humphrey Bogart or James Cagney. During the studio era, Hollywood packaged leading men in all shapes, sizes, and flavors. The one thing the studio-bred male stars had in common was an almost irresistible magnetism. Pretty or plain, short or tall, audiences couldn't take their eyes off them.

Today, male stars dominate the industry. In many years it seems a minor miracle if even two women break into the box office top 20. During the studio era, the gender divide was more equitable, occasionally skewing toward the female. For a leading man to graduate to solo stardom took an extra dose of magic. George Brent may have made eleven films with Bette Davis, but few audiences would pay to see him without a powerhouse leading lady. Fonda, on the other hand, only squired her through two vehicles before proving he could carry a picture on his own.

But if leading men had a harder time getting to the top, they could stay there longer for one simple reason: Good looks were far less crucial for them. True, Tyrone Power and the young Robert Taylor were prettier than many of their leading ladies, but as their looks matured they continued to command top

Casablanca, 1942

go after the all-American lead in the musical *Yankee Doodle Dandy* (1942), and Edward G. Robinson saw his career crash and burn in the early fifties when he landed on the blacklist. Even more damaging was the suggestion that the star might be somewhat less than manly. When the influence of his designer wife Natacha Rambova started to feminize Latin lover Rudolph Valentino's on-screen image, leading one editorial to refer to him as a "pink powder puff," he cut her out of his career and, eventually, his life.

This is not to say that sensitivity was entirely off the table. Audiences loved watching tough guys like Bogart in *Casablanca* (1942) or Wayne in *3 Godfathers* (1948) show their softer side. Montgomery Clift's film debut in *The Search* (1948)—followed by the rise to stardom of Marlon Brando and James Dean—brought a new masculine archetype to the screen. Vulnerability was in. When Elizabeth Taylor held Clift's head in her hands in *A Place in the Sun* (1951) and said "Tell mama . . . tell mama all," women swooned and men started to realize that opening up emotionally might not be such a bad idea.

Sensitive or tough, image was at the heart of stardom. Nicknames like "The Man of a Thousand Faces" (Chaney), "The Great Profile" (John Barrymore), "The Little Tramp" (Charles Chaplin), and "Old Ski Nose" (Bob Hope) captured a specific brand that identified a performer as versatile, romantic, mischievous, or comical. And it was those images that kept audiences coming back for more every time they saw the right name above the title.

billing in compelling roles. It was also much easier for more ordinary-looking actors like Edward G. Robinson and Lon Chaney than for similar female types to emerge as character stars. And as actors grew older, nobody seemed to mind that their leading ladies kept getting younger. A fifty-eight-year-old Astaire could dance off into the sunset with twenty-eight-year-old Audrey Hepburn in *Funny Face* (1957), while Clark Gable proved a perfect match for Marilyn Monroe in *The Misfits* (1961) despite a quarter-century age difference.

The guys also got away with more off-screen peccadilloes than the ladies. Robert Mitchum came off a jail term for possession of marijuana to find even better roles waiting for him at RKO than those he'd had before. And even a charge of statutory rape failed to derail Errol Flynn's career; instead, it added the ironic phrase "in like Flynn" to the vernacular.

There were, however, a few charges that could threaten a male star. Suggestions that Cagney was some kind of subversive (triggered by labor activism and his support of President Roosevelt) helped inspire him to

1. Anthony Quinn was featured in which action film starring Arnold Schwarzenegger?

   A. *Commando* (1985)
   B. *Last Action Hero* (1993)
   C. *The Terminator* (1984)
   D. *True Lies* (1994)

2. Bing Crosby performed a total of how many different Oscar-winning songs in his film career?

   A. 1
   B. 2
   C. 3
   D. 4

3. What is the title of Edward G. Robinson's 1973 autobiography?

   A. *All My Yesterdays*
   B. *Before and After*
   C. *Me, Myself and I*
   D. *My Life on the Big Screen*

4. What was John Barrymore's nickname?

   A. "The Great Actor"
   B. "The Great Profile"
   C. "The Voice"
   D. "World's Sexiest Man"

5. Robert Taylor plays Dr. Ellis in what film costarring Billie Burke?

   A. *High Wall* (1947)
   B. *Society Doctor* (1935)
   C. *The Spectacle Maker* (1934)
   D. *Times Square Lady* (1935)

6. Alan Ladd was married to what silent film actress?

   A. Bessie Love
   B. Lillian Gish
   C. Mildred Harris
   D. Sue Carol

7. What film was Montgomery Clift in the midst of shooting when he was partially disfigured in a car accident?

   A. *Raintree County* (1957)
   B. *Suddenly, Last Summer* (1959)
   C. *The Heiress* (1949)
   D. *The Misfits* (1961)

8. Where did Montgomery Clift die?

   A. Las Vegas
   B. Los Angeles
   C. New York
   D. Paris

9. Gene Kelly met with what eighties pop star for tea every week until he passed away?

   A. Cindy Lauper
   B. Madonna
   C. Pat Benatar
   D. Paula Abdul

Ivanhoe, 1952

10. Robert Taylor played the title role in *Ivanhoe* (1952) and what other adventure film directed by Richard Thorpe?

    A. *El Cid* (1961)
    B. *Julius Caesar* (1950)
    C. *Quentin Durward* (1955)
    D. *The Buccaneer* (1958)

answers found on page 551

11. Frank Sinatra plays a detective in all of the following films except for which one?

   A. *Lady in Cement* (1968)
   B. *The Detective* (1968)
   C. *Tony Rome* (1967)
   D. *Von Ryan's Express* (1965)

12. Greenacres, an estate on the National Register of Historic Places, was the home of which film legend?

   A. Buster Keaton
   B. Clark Gable
   C. Harold Lloyd
   D. Humphrey Bogart

13. Rudolph Valentino costarred with Nita Naldi in *Blood and Sand* (1922), *A Sainted Devil* (1924), and what other film?

   A. *Beyond the Rocks* (1922)
   B. *Cobra* (1925)
   C. *The Eagle* (1925)
   D. *The Sheik* (1921)

14. After being lost for years, a print of the Rudolph Valentino film *Beyond the Rocks* (1922) was found where?

   A. Canada
   B. France
   C. Italy
   D. The Netherlands

15. Atticus Finch was the name of Gregory Peck's character in which of the following films?

   A. *Arabesque* (1966)
   B. *Moby Dick* (1956)
   C. *Roman Holiday* (1953)
   D. *To Kill a Mockingbird* (1962)

16. Harold Lloyd plays a shoe salesman with big dreams in which comedy?

   A. *Feet First* (1930)
   B. *Girl Shy* (1924)
   C. *Movie Crazy* (1932)
   D. *Now or Never* (1921)

17. Who starred in Jules Dassin's 1947 film *Brute Force*?

   A. Burt Lancaster
   B. Humphrey Bogart
   C. Richard Widmark
   D. Spencer Tracy

18. Anthony Quinn received his first Oscar for his role in what film?

   A. *Lust for Life* (1956)
   B. *Viva Zapata!* (1952)
   C. *Wild Is the Wind* (1957)
   D. *Zorba the Greek* (1964)

19. What is written on Jack Lemmon's tombstone?

   A. Go Away, I'm Sleeping
   B. He Did It the Hard Way
   C. Jack Lemmon in
   D. Nobody's Perfect

20. From what university did Jack Lemmon graduate in 1947?

   A. Harvard
   B. NYU
   C. University of Michigan
   D. University of Pennsylvania

21. A fencing tournament was staged in Los Angeles to promote what film starring Ronald Colman?

   A. *Forbidden Passage* (1941)
   B. *Forgotten Victory* (1939)
   C. *King Solomon's Mines* (1937)
   D. *The Prisoner of Zenda* (1937)

22. What was Clark Gable's first name?

   A. Beaufort
   B. Gerard
   C. Ryan
   D. William

23. Charles Chaplin won an honorary Oscar for what film?

A. *City Lights* (1931)
B. *Modern Times* (1936)
C. *The Circus* (1928)
D. *The Gold Rush* (1925)

24. What movie brought Henry Fonda his only competitive Oscar?

A. *12 Angry Men* (1957)
B. *On Golden Pond* (1981)
C. *The Grapes of Wrath* (1940)
D. *Young Mr. Lincoln* (1939)

25. In what film does Bing Crosby's character disguise himself as a waiter in order to be closer to the woman he loves?

A. *Double or Nothing* (1937)
B. *Here Is My Heart* (1934)
C. *She Loves Me Not* (1934)
D. *We're Not Dressing* (1934)

26. Peter O'Toole plays an English schoolteacher in what remake?

A. *Becket* (1964)
B. *Goodbye, Mr. Chips* (1969)
C. *Rosebud* (1975)
D. *The Lion in Winter* (1968)

27. What was Gene Kelly's last feature film as director?

A. *A Guide for the Married Man* (1967)
B. *Hello Dolly* (1969)
C. *The Cheyenne Social Club* (1970)
D. *Xanadu* (1980)

28. Although he has never won, how many times has Peter O'Toole been nominated for an Oscar?

A. 2
B. 5
C. 7
D. 8

29. For what film did Rock Hudson receive his only Oscar nomination for Best Actor?

A. *Giant* (1956)
B. *Magnificent Obsession* (1954)
C. *Pillow Talk* (1959)
D. *Written on the Wind* (1956)

30. How many times did Bob Hope host (or cohost) the Oscars?

A. 12
B. 18
C. 20
D. 9

31. In what city was Fred Astaire born?

A. Chicago, Illinois
B. New York, New York
C. Omaha, Nebraska
D. Pensacola, Florida

32. Anthony Quinn was best known for his acting career, but he was also a writer and a what?

A. Cinematographer
B. Director
C. Painter
D. Photographer

33. Although he never won, how many times was Charles Chaplin nominated for a Best Director Oscar?

A. 0
B. 1
C. 4
D. 6

34. Anthony Quinn's first role as executive producer was for which film?

A. *A Star for Two* (1991)
B. *A Walk in the Clouds* (1995)
C. *Across 110th Street* (1972)
D. *Only the Lonely* (1991)

answers found on page 551

No Time for Comedy, 1940

35. What does James Stewart's character do for a living in *No Time for Comedy* (1940)?

A. Lawyer
B. Playwright
C. Police officer
D. Stand-up comedian

36. In what film does Jack Lemmon play an alcoholic?

A. *Bell, Book and Candle* (1958)
B. *Days of Wine and Roses* (1962)
C. *Glengarry Glen Ross* (1992)
D. *The Apartment* (1960)

37. In the 1959 film *Pillow Talk,* costarring Thelma Ritter, Doris Day and Rock Hudson share a what?

A. Bathroom
B. Hotel room
C. Job
D. Telephone line

38. Ronald Colman portrays French poet François Villon in what adventure film?

A. *Forgotten Victory* (1939)
B. *If I Were King* (1938)
C. *The Lady or the Tiger?* (1942)
D. *They Live Again* (1938)

39. Edward G. Robinson starred in which of the following famous gangster films?

A. *Little Caesar* (1931)
B. *Scarface* (1932)
C. *The Public Enemy* (1931)
D. *White Heat* (1949)

40. In what film does Gene Kelly dance with a squeaky floorboard and a newspaper?

A. *Anchors Aweigh* (1945)
B. *It's Always Fair Weather* (1956)
C. *Singin' in the Rain* (1952)
D. *Summer Stock* (1950)

41. In what film does John Barrymore's character threaten to steal the Mona Lisa?

A. *Arsène Lupin* (1932)
B. *Svengali* (1931)
C. *The Thomas Crown Affair* (1968)
D. *True Confession* (1937)

42. Frank Sinatra replaced Marlon Brando in which film costarring Cary Grant and Sophia Loren?

A. *Houseboat* (1958)
B. *Once Upon a Honeymoon* (1942)
C. *The Bishop's Wife* (1947)
D. *The Pride and the Passion* (1957)

43. Peter O'Toole attended the Royal Academy of Dramatic Art in the same class as all of the following except whom?

A. Alan Bates
B. Albert Finney
C. Richard Harris
D. Roger Moore

44. In *Man's Favorite Sport?* (1964), Rock Hudson's character is the author of a book on what subject?

A. Bowling
B. Fishing
C. Golf
D. Hunting

answers found on page 551

45. Gene Kelly earned a degree in what subject in college?
    A. Economics
    B. English
    C. Physics
    D. Theater

46. For which of his films did Charles Chaplin compose the famous song "Smile"?
    A. *City Lights* (1931)
    B. *Limelight* (1952)
    C. *Modern Times* (1936)
    D. *The Kid* (1921)

47. Whose voice was the Chuck Jones cartoon character of Pepe Le Pew based on?
    A. Charles Boyer
    B. Louis Jourdan
    C. Maurice Chevalier
    D. Omar Sharif

48. Although he never won, how many times was Fred Astaire nominated for a competitive Oscar?
    A. 1
    B. 2
    C. 4
    D. 5

49. In what film does Alan Ladd play a blacksmith who fights evil in King Arthur's Camelot?
    A. *13 West Street* (1962)
    B. *The Badlanders* (1958)
    C. *The Black Knight* (1954)
    D. *Whispering Smith* (1949)

50. What was Robert Taylor's professed favorite of his own films?
    A. *All the Brothers Were Valiant* (1953)
    B. *Quo Vadis* (1951)
    C. *Undercurrent* (1946)
    D. *Waterloo Bridge* (1940)

51. Laurence Olivier and Ralph Fiennes have both portrayed which character in a feature film?
    A. Eugene Onegin
    B. Heathcliff
    C. Mr. Fitzwilliam Darcy
    D. Professor Moriarty

52. What disaster movie did Burt Lancaster star in?
    A. *Airport* (1970)
    B. *Airport '77*
    C. *Earthquake* (1974)
    D. *The Towering Inferno* (1974)

53. Buster Keaton makes a cameo appearance in the card game scene of what Oscar-winning film?
    A. *An American in Paris* (1951)
    B. *On the Waterfront* (1954)
    C. *Sunset Blvd.* (1950)
    D. *The Lost Weekend* (1945)

54. Anthony Quinn's first film opposite Sophia Loren was what?
    A. *Attila* (1955)
    B. *Heller in Pink Tights* (1960)
    C. *La Strada* (1954)
    D. *The Black Orchid* (1959)

55. Peter O'Toole made his stage debut at what age?
    A. 8
    B. 15
    C. 17
    D. 20

56. Gregory Peck played attorney Sam Bowden in the 1962 thriller *Cape Fear*. Who played the same role in Martin Scorsese's 1991 remake?
    A. Jeff Bridges
    B. Nick Nolte
    C. Robert De Niro
    D. Sam Shepard

answers found on page 551

Spotlight on
HUMPHREY **BOGART** (1899–1957)

Born into New York society, the son of a prominent doctor and a popular portrait artist, Bogart turned to acting after flunking out of school. Initially cast as callow young sophisticates, his failed attempt to break into films in the early thirties brought him back to Broadway, where he played a psychopathic gangster in *The Petrified Forest*. When the play became a movie in 1936, stage costar and close friend Leslie Howard refused to do the film without him, and Warner Bros. signed Bogie to a long-term contract. They kept him mainly in supporting roles until John Huston wrote *High Sierra* (1941) for him and then used his directorial debut, *The Maltese Falcon* (1941), to make Bogart a star. That was enough to win over producer Hal Wallis, who had the script for *Casablanca* (1942) written to showcase Bogart's world-weary cynicism. Bogie had already proved himself a surprisingly effective romantic lead, but it was a feisty newcomer who would really bring out the lover in him. Almost two decades his junior, Lauren Bacall was his match in cynicism and sass when director Howard Hawks paired them in *To Have and Have Not* (1944). The onscreen chemistry continued in three more films together. Offscreen, she provided a stability that had eluded him in three failed marriages.

To Have and Have Not, 1944

The Maltese Falcon, 1941

1. **For what film did Humphrey Bogart receive his only Academy Award for Best Actor?**
   A. *Casablanca* (1942)
   B. *The African Queen* (1951)
   C. *The Caine Mutiny* (1954)
   D. *The Treasure of the Sierra Madre* (1948)

2. **Which of the following Humphrey Bogart and Lauren Bacall films was directed by Delmer Daves?**
   A. *Dark Passage* (1947)
   B. *Key Largo* (1948)
   C. *The Big Sleep* (1946)
   D. *To Have and Have Not* (1944)

3. **At what age did Humphrey Bogart become a father for the first time?**
   A. 40
   B. 49

   C. 50
   D. 52

4. **What was the last film Humphrey Bogart made with director John Huston?**
   A. *Across the Pacific* (1942)
   B. *Beat the Devil* (1953)
   C. *Key Largo* (1948)
   D. *The African Queen* (1951)

5. **Humphrey Bogart and William Holden play two brothers as different as night and day in what film?**
   A. *My Brother Talks to Horses* (1947)
   B. *Sabrina* (1954)
   C. *The Member of the Wedding* (1952)
   D. *War and Peace* (1956)

answers found on page 551

57. The birth name of what star was Spangler Arlington Brugh?

A. Clark Gable
B. James Stewart
C. Robert Taylor
D. William Holden

58. What famous real-life person does Gregory Peck portray in the 1959 film *Beloved Infidel*?

A. Abraham Lincoln
B. Charles Lindbergh
C. F. Scott Fitzgerald
D. Ludwig von Beethoven

59. For what film did John Garfield receive his first Academy Award nomination?

A. *Body and Soul* (1947)
B. *Four Daughters* (1938)
C. *The Postman Always Rings Twice* (1946)
D. *They Made Me a Criminal* (1939)

60. In what film does Bing Crosby sing the song "Accentuate the Positive"?

A. *Blue Skies* (1946)
B. *Going My Way* (1944)
C. *Here Come the Waves* (1944)
D. *The Emperor Waltz* (1948)

61. For what movie did Gregory Peck win an Academy Award as Best Actor?

A. *Gentleman's Agreement* (1947)
B. *MacArthur* (1977)
C. *The Yearling* (1946)
D. *To Kill a Mockingbird* (1962)

62. Laurence Olivier and Richard Burton share the screen in what miniseries about the life and work of a legendary music composer?

A. *A Man for All Seasons* (1988)
B. *Noel* (1992)
C. *The Fifth Column* (1960)
D. *Wagner* (1983)

63. In 2000, who was honored as Entertainer of the Century?

A. Elvis Presley
B. Frank Sinatra
C. Gene Kelly
D. Judy Garland

64. How many times was Jack Lemmon nominated for an Oscar for Best Actor?

A. 3
B. 5
C. 7
D. 9

65. Mickey Rooney plays the kid brother to Van Johnson's character in what film?

A. *Beyond This Place* (1959)
B. *Holiday Inn* (1942)
C. *The Human Comedy* (1943)
D. *The Sky's the Limit* (1943)

66. Although he never won, how many times was Montgomery Clift nominated for an Oscar?

A. 1
B. 2
C. 3
D. 4

67. How many honorary Oscars did Charles Chaplin receive?

A. 0
B. 1
C. 2
D. 3

68. Peter O'Toole voiced a character in what animated film?

A. *Felix the Cat: The Movie* (1991)
B. *Hercules* (1997)
C. *The Hunchback of Notre Dame* (1996)
D. *The Nutcracker Prince* (1990)

answers found on page 551

69. Which James Dean film was the only one to be released during his lifetime?

A. *East of Eden* (1955)
B. *Giant* (1956)
C. *Magnificent Obsession* (1954)
D. *Rebel Without a Cause* (1955)

70. Douglas Fairbanks plays the title role in which film costarring Merle Oberon?

A. *The Cowboy and the Lady* (1938)
B. *The Private Life of Don Juan* (1934)
C. *The Private Life of Henry VIII* (1933)
D. *The Scarlet Pimpernel* (1934)

Green Light, 1937

71. In Frank Borzage's 1937 film *Green Light,* what is the profession of Errol Flynn's character?

A. Lawyer
B. Newspaper editor
C. Police officer
D. Surgeon

72. What film costarring Steve McQueen was based on the life of Henri Charrière?

A. *Papillon* (1973)
B. *The Getaway* (1972)
C. *The Honeymoon Machine* (1961)
D. *The MacKintosh Man* (1973)

73. AFI gave James Cagney the Lifetime Achievement Award in what year?

A. 1974
B. 1976

C. 1979
D. 1981

74. In the 1923 Charles Chaplin film *The Pilgrim,* Chaplin plays an escaped convict who gets mistaken for a what?

A. Boxer
B. Chicken thief
C. Circus clown
D. Pastor

75. How many times was Bing Crosby married?

A. 1
B. 2
C. 3
D. 4

76. Errol Flynn and Flora Robson share the screen in what adventure film?

A. *Adventures of Captain Fabian* (1951)
B. *The Master of Ballantrae* (1953)
C. *The Sea Hawk* (1940)
D. *The Whispering Shadow* (1933)

77. Gene Kelly romances Natalie Wood in what film?

A. *Invitation to the Dance* (1956)
B. *It's Always Fair Weather* (1955)
C. *Marjorie Morningstar* (1958)
D. *Paris Blues* (1961)

78. How old was Gene Kelly when he died?

A. 80
B. 81
C. 83
D. 85

79. In what film does Peter O'Toole play a character based on Errol Flynn?

A. *Club Paradise* (1986)
B. *My Favorite Year* (1982)
C. *Promise Her Anything* (1965)
D. *The Only Game in Town* (1970)

answers found on page 551

80. Ronald Colman plays "The Spirit of Man" in what film costarring Hedy Lamarr?

A. *The Story of Doctor Carver* (1938)
B. *The Story of Mankind* (1957)
C. *They Live Again* (1938)
D. *Weather Wizards* (1939)

81. Marlon Brando referred to his character as "The Old Lamplighter" in what film costarring Robert Redford?

A. *A Bridge Too Far* (1977)
B. *The Chase* (1966)
C. *The Great Gatsby* (1974)
D. *The Great Waldo Pepper* (1975)

82. In what film does Jack Lemmon's character suffer a nervous breakdown after he loses his job?

A. *Save the Tiger* (1973)
B. *The Front Page* (1974)
C. *The Odd Couple* (1968)
D. *The Prisoner of Second Avenue* (1975)

83. What was John Barrymore's final picture?

A. *A Guy Named Joe* (1943)
B. *Between Two Women* (1945)
C. *Playmates* (1941)
D. *The Invisible Woman* (1940)

84. Robert Mitchum stars opposite Deborah Kerr in *Heaven Knows, Mr. Allison* (1957). But who was director John Huston's first choice for the role?

A. Cary Grant
B. George C. Scott
C. Gregory Peck
D. Marlon Brando

85. Clark Gable seeks a career in advertising in what film costarring Deborah Kerr, Ava Gardner, and Edward Arnold?

A. *East Side, West Side* (1949)
B. *Manhattan Melodrama* (1934)
C. *The Easiest Way* (1931)
D. *The Hucksters* (1947)

86. In 1925, United Artists signed Rudolph Valentino to a contract that stipulated what?

A. He dance in all his movies
B. He make twelve films a year
C. He wear white in all his films
D. His wife not be allowed to visit any of his movie sets

87. Steve McQueen romances Natalie Wood in what film?

A. *A New Kind of Love* (1963)
B. *Days of Wine and Roses* (1962)
C. *Love with the Proper Stranger* (1963)
D. *Paris Blues* (1961)

88. How old was Rudolph Valentino when he died?

A. 20
B. 25
C. 31
D. 40

89. In which of the following films does Edward G. Robinson costar with Steve McQueen?

A. *Nightmare* (1956)
B. *Soylent Green* (1973)
C. *The Cincinnati Kid* (1965)
D. *Tight Spot* (1955)

90. How many children did Gene Kelly have?

A. 1
B. 2
C. 3
D. 4

91. Fredric March played the title role in which film costarring Olivia de Havilland?

A. *Anthony Adverse* (1936)
B. *Christopher Columbus* (1949)
C. *The Adventures of Mark Twain* (1944)
D. *The Buccaneer* (1938)

92. Gary Cooper romances Marion Davies in which film?

   A. *Beverly of Graustark* (1926)
   B. *Operator 13* (1934)
   C. *Peg O' My Heart* (1933)
   D. *The Fair Co-Ed* (1927)

93. James Dean made his film debut in which feature directed and adapted by Samuel Fuller?

   A. *Fixed Bayonets!* (1951)
   B. *Forty Guns* (1957)
   C. *Merrill's Marauders* (1962)
   D. *Park Row* (1952)

94. Gene Kelly received the National Medal of Arts from which president in 1994?

   A. Bill Clinton
   B. George Bush Sr.
   C. George W. Bush
   D. Jimmy Carter

95. Which Gregory Peck film was one of only two narrative features shot in the 3-Strip Cinerama process?

   A. *Ben-Hur* (1959)
   B. *How the West Was Won* (1962)
   C. *Lawrence of Arabia* (1962)
   D. *The Robe* (1953)

96. How many times did Frank Sinatra host (or cohost) the Oscars?

   A. 0
   B. 1
   C. 2
   D. 4

97. What was director Tod Browning and Lon Chaney's final collaboration?

   A. *The Blackbird* (1926)
   B. *The Devil-Doll* (1936)
   C. *The Thirteenth Chair* (1929)
   D. *Where East Is East* (1929)

98. Marlon Brando met his third wife, Tarita, when they appeared together in what film?

   A. *A Countess from Hong Kong* (1967)
   B. *Apocalypse Now* (1979)
   C. *Last Tango in Paris* (1972)
   D. *Mutiny on the Bounty* (1962)

99. What was Sidney Poitier's character's original profession in the 1967 film *To Sir, with Love*?

   A. Archaeologist
   B. Dentist
   C. Engineer
   D. Psychologist

100. Bing Crosby sang the Academy Award–winning song in the 1944 film *Going My Way*. What was the name of it?

   A. "Accentuate the Positive"
   B. "In the Cool, Cool, Cool of the Evening"
   C. "Swinging on a Star"
   D. "Zing a Little Zong"

101. Robert Taylor played the title role in all of the following films except for which one?

   A. *Ivanhoe* (1952)
   B. *Johnny Eager* (1941)
   C. *Quentin Durward* (1955)
   D. *The Remarkable Andrew* (1942)

102. In what film is Jack Lemmon's character constantly dodging the IRS?

   A. *Glengarry Glen Ross* (1992)
   B. *Grumpy Old Men* (1993)
   C. *My Fellow Americans* (1996)
   D. *That's Life!* (1986)

103. In what film does Jack Lemmon play a real-estate salesman?

   A. *Glengarry Glen Ross* (1992)
   B. *Grumpy Old Men* (1993)
   C. *Missing* (1982)
   D. *That's Life!* (1986)

answers found on page 552

Spotlight on
WILLIAM **HOLDEN** (1918–1981)

While performing at the Pasadena Playhouse, Holden was spotted by a Paramount talent scout and signed up as part of the Golden Circle, a group of talented newcomers that included Susan Hayward and Robert Preston. After just two bit parts, he won the title role in Columbia's film version of *Golden Boy* (1939) and then almost lost it when early rushes revealed his inexperience. Costar Barbara Stanwyck devoted her nights to coaching the young actor, who kept the role and also scored a major success with it. Columbia bought half his contract, and for the next several years typecast him in what he called "Smiling Jim" roles, good guys with little edge or sex appeal. But when Montgomery Clift turned down the role of a failed screenwriter turned gigolo in *Sunset Blvd.* (1950), writer-director Billy Wilder took a chance on Holden, whose performance made cynicism sexy. Another cynical role, in Wilder's World War II POW drama *Stalag 17* (1953), brought Holden an Oscar, and cynicism paid off again in *The Bridge on the River Kwai* (1957). Holden's struggles with alcohol nearly cost him his career, but he managed to pull it together for a few more great performances, including the aging outlaw in *The Wild Bunch* (1969), and the television news executive in *Network* (1976).

Network, 1976

Sunset Blvd., 1950

1. **William Holden and Ginger Rogers share the screen in what comedy?**

   A. *Forever Female* (1954)

   B. *Royal Wedding* (1951)

   C. *Serenade* (1956)

   D. *Silk Stockings* (1957)

2. **After *Golden Boy* (1939), William Holden was reunited with Barbara Stanwyck in what film?**

   A. *Born Yesterday* (1950)

   B. *Double Indemnity* (1944)

   C. *Executive Suite* (1954)

   D. *Sunset Blvd.* (1950)

3. **In *The World of Suzie Wong* (1960), William Holden's character moves to Hong Kong to be a what?**

   A. Architect

   B. Artist

   C. Doctor

   D. Professor

4. **Which romantic comedy pairing Audrey Hepburn and William Holden was based on the French film and story *La Fête à Henriette*?**

   A. *Charade* (1963)

   B. *Paris When It Sizzles* (1964)

   C. *Sabrina* (1954)

   D. *Two for the Road* (1967)

5. **After William Holden's death, actress Stefanie Powers became president of what foundation in his honor?**

   A. William Holden African Foundation

   B. William Holden Animal Preservation Society

   C. William Holden Foundation for African Relief

   D. William Holden Wildlife Foundation

answers found on page 552

104. Rudolph Valentino's body is interred in Hollywood Park Cemetery between what screenwriter and her husband?

A. Beulah Marie Dix
B. Frances Marion
C. Gene Gauntier
D. June Mathis

105. Anthony Quinn never graduated from high school, but he received a diploma in the 1990s from a high school in what state?

A. Arizona
B. California
C. Nevada
D. New Mexico

106. In 1948, Henry Fonda won a Tony Award for his performance in what play?

A. *All My Sons*
B. *Mister Roberts*
C. *The Heiress*
D. *The Importance of Being Earnest*

Mark of the Vampire, 1935

107. In director Tod Browning's *Mark of the Vampire* (1935), Lionel Barrymore and Bela Lugosi replaced whose roles?

A. Boris Karloff
B. Lon Chaney
C. Matt Moore
D. Warner Baxter

108. What was John Garfield's real name?

A. Jacob Garfinkle
B. Jacob Goldfarb
C. John Garfield
D. John Goldfarb

109. Ronald Colman plays Anthony Mason, a businessman with domestic problems, in what film based on a French play?

A. *Du Barry Was a Lady* (1943)
B. *Forgotten Victory* (1939)
C. *My Life with Caroline* (1941)
D. *They Live Again* (1938)

110. What graduate school did Gene Kelly drop out of to pursue an entertainment career?

A. Business school
B. Dental school
C. Law school
D. Medical school

111. AFI gave Gene Kelly the Lifetime Achievement Award in what year?

A. 1975
B. 1978
C. 1982
D. 1985

112. In which film does Gregory Peck play a compulsive gambler?

A. *Arabesque* (1966)
B. *Mackenna's Gold* (1969)
C. *The Big Country* (1958)
D. *The Great Sinner* (1949)

113. In the 1942 biopic *The Pride of the Yankees*, Lou Gehrig is portrayed by whom?

A. Clark Gable
B. Gary Cooper
C. James Stewart
D. Robert Taylor

answers found on page 552

114. Edward G. Robinson died two weeks after he completed filming what movie?

A. *Makenna's Gold* (1969)
B. *Never a Dull Moment* (1968)
C. *Song of Norway* (1970)
D. *Soylent Green* (1973)

115. In what film does William Holden play a boxer who aspired to be a violinist?

A. *Arizona* (1940)
B. *Golden Boy* (1939)
C. *Our Town* (1940)
D. *Texas* (1941)

116. Sidney Poitier made history when he won his first Academy Award as Best Actor for what film?

A. *In the Heat of the Night* (1967)
B. *Lilies of the Field* (1963)
C. *The Defiant Ones* (1958)
D. *To Sir, with Love* (1967)

117. In the 1919 Charles Chaplin film *Sunnyside,* where does Chaplin's character work?

A. In a barbershop
B. In a candy factory
C. In a restaurant
D. On a farm

118. What is Alan Ladd's most generally accepted height?

A. 5'
B. 5'5"
C. 6'
D. 6'2"

119. Robert Taylor plays an archaeologist in which adventure film set in Egypt?

A. *Many Rivers to Cross* (1955)
B. *Saddle the Wind* (1958)
C. *The Buccaneer* (1958)
D. *Valley of the Kings* (1954)

120. What notorious real-life person does Gregory Peck portray in *The Boys from Brazil* (1978)?

A. Adolf Hitler
B. Jack the Ripper
C. Josef Mengele
D. Joseph Stalin

121. In what film does Gene Kelly dance with his own reflection?

A. *Brigadoon* (1954)
B. *Cover Girl* (1944)
C. *Singin' in the Rain* (1952)
D. *Summer Stock* (1950)

122. In what movie does James Cagney play Lon Chaney?

A. *Man of a Thousand Faces* (1957)
B. *The Gallant Hours* (1960)
C. *The Seven Little Foys* (1955)
D. *Tribute to a Bad Man* (1956)

123. In 1923, a dispute with what film studio prohibited Rudolph Valentino from making films with other producers?

A. Columbia
B. Paramount
C. RKO
D. Universal

124. For what film did Burt Lancaster win his only Academy Award?

A. *A Child Is Waiting* (1963)
B. *Airport* (1970)
C. *Elmer Gantry* (1960)
D. *From Here to Eternity* (1953)

125. Anthony Quinn's first wife was the adopted daughter of which legendary film executive?

A. Cecil B. DeMille
B. David O. Selznick
C. Joseph L. Mankiewicz
D. King Vidor

126. What profession was Burt Lancaster in before he became an actor?

A. Circus acrobat
B. Construction worker
C. Plumber
D. Stuntman

127. Which of the following men was never married to Ava Gardner?

A. Artie Shaw
B. Clark Gable
C. Frank Sinatra
D. Mickey Rooney

128. In what film does Jack Lemmon's character work at a nuclear power plant?

A. *Missing* (1982)
B. *Save the Tiger* (1973)
C. *The China Syndrome* (1979)
D. *The Prisoner of Second Avenue* (1975)

129. For what film did Paul Muni receive his final Oscar nomination?

A. *Angel on My Shoulder* (1946)
B. *Hudson's Bay* (1941)
C. *Juarez* (1939)
D. *The Last Angry Man* (1959)

130. Errol Flynn plays Captain Lafe Barstow in what adventure film set in California and Nevada?

A. *A Way in the Wilderness* (1940)
B. *My Brother Talks to Horses* (1947)
C. *Rocky Mountain* (1950)
D. *The Search* (1948)

131. What was the one and only film that Jack Lemmon ever directed?

A. *It Should Happen to You* (1954)
B. *Kotch* (1971)
C. *Save the Tiger* (1973)
D. *The Detective* (1968)

132. Cinematographer Freddie Young shot the 1970 film *Ryan's Daughter*. Who starred in it?

A. Ernest Borgnine
B. Robert Mitchum
C. Tony Curtis
D. Victor Mature

133. Who stars in Robert Rossen's *The Hustler* (1961)?

A. Broderick Crawford
B. Paul Newman
C. Richard Burton
D. Warren Beatty

134. Sidney Poitier directed and starred in which film opposite Harry Belafonte?

A. *Buck and the Preacher* (1972)
B. *The Greatest Story Ever Told* (1965)
C. *The Organization* (1971)
D. *The Slender Thread* (1965)

135. Ronald Colman costars in what silent film that was later remade with Barbara Stanwyck in the title role?

A. *Cameo Kirby* (1923)
B. *Jackie* (1921)
C. *Little Miss Smiles* (1922)
D. *Stella Dallas* (1925)

136. Gene Kelly received a Golden Globe nomination for Best Director for what film?

A. *An American in Paris* (1951)
B. *Hello, Dolly!* (1969)
C. *It's Always Fair Weather* (1955)
D. *The Tunnel of Love* (1958)

137. In what year did Charles Chaplin pass away?

A. 1974
B. 1975
C. 1976
D. 1977

answers found on page 552

138. Gene Kelly directed what film starring Doris Day?

A. *It Happened to Jane* (1959)
B. *Pajama Game* (1957)
C. *Teacher's Pet* (1958)
D. *The Tunnel of Love* (1958)

139. Peter O'Toole was rejected from what school because he couldn't speak Gaelic?

A. Abbey Theatre's Drama School in Dublin
B. London Academy of Music and Drama
C. Royal Academy of Dramatic Art
D. UK Theatre School

140. How old was John Barrymore when he died?

A. 45
B. 57
C. 60
D. 63

141. In 1916, the New York District Attorney charged Rudolph Valentino with what crime?

A. Bigamy
B. Jaywalking
C. Murder
D. White slavery

142. Mickey Rooney and Donna Reed share the screen in what film?

A. *Beyond Glory* (1948)
B. *Faithful in My Fashion* (1946)
C. *The Far Horizons* (1955)
D. *The Human Comedy* (1943)

143. Errol Flynn plays a mystery writer and amateur detective in what film costarring Ralph Bellamy?

A. *A Lady Without Passport* (1950)
B. *Crossroads* (1942)
C. *Footsteps in the Dark* (1941)
D. *High Wall* (1947)

Humoresque, 1946

144. In *Humoresque* (1946), what instrument does John Garfield's character play?

A. Flute
B. Piano
C. Trumpet
D. Violin

145. In *I Confess* (1953), Montgomery Clift plays Anne Baxter's first love. Who plays her husband?

A. Robert Cummings
B. Roger Dann
C. Tom Helmore
D. Wendell Corey

146. In what film is John Barrymore's character Baron Felix von Geigern?

A. *Grand Hotel* (1932)
B. *Long Lost Father* (1934)
C. *Rasputin and the Empress* (1932)
D. *Reunion in Vienna* (1933)

147. Laurence Olivier starred in the 1943 film *The Demi-Paradise* and what other film directed by Anthony Asquith?

A. *Moscow Nights* (1935)
B. *On Such a Night* (1956)
C. *Two Fathers* (1944)
D. *We Dive at Dawn* (1943)

Spotlight on
GARY **COOPER** (1901–1961)

Gary Cooper's upbringing—born on a Montana ranch but sent to England for his education—provides a key to unlocking his screen persona. Although he achieved his greatest stardom as a simple man of few words, the offscreen Cooper was a sophisticated man of the world, respected for his taste in literature and modern art and notorious for his amorous exploits.

"Coop's" Western upbringing helped him get into movies, where he started out as a stunt rider, but it was his sophistication that gave his characters an edge that allowed him to take his career by the reins. His image as the ideal American was already established when director Frank Capra went after him to play small-town poet Longfellow Deeds in *Mr. Deeds Goes to Town* (1936), but that huge hit made him one of Hollywood's top stars. Parts like the World War I hero in *Sergeant York* (1941) and champion slugger Lou Gehrig in *The Pride of the Yankees* (1942) kept his career on the rise. By the late forties, however, Cooper was going through personal crises. In the midst of this period, he rejuvenated his career with the role of U.S. Marshal Will Kane in *High Noon* (1952), one of the most acclaimed westerns ever made.

Sergeant York, 1941

Sergeant York, 1941

1. **In which film did Gary Cooper have his first starring role?**

   A. *Arizona Bound* (1927)

   B. *Desire* (1936)

   C. *The Pride of the Yankees* (1942)

   D. *The Westerner* (1940)

2. **Gary Cooper romances Merle Oberon in which film?**

   A. *A Song to Remember* (1945)

   B. *Affectionately Yours* (1941)

   C. *Pardon My French* (1951)

   D. *The Cowboy and the Lady* (1938)

3. **In the 1933 film version of *Alice in Wonderland*, which character did Gary Cooper play?**

   A. The Cheshire Cat

   B. The White King

   C. The White Knight

   D. The White Rabbit

4. **How many films did Gary Cooper make with director Frank Capra?**

   A. 1

   B. 2

   C. 3

   D. 4

5. **What was Gary Cooper's final film before his death in 1961?**

   A. *The Fountainhead* (1949)

   B. *The Hanging Tree* (1959)

   C. *The Naked Edge* (1961)

   D. *They Came to Cordura* (1959)

answers found on page 552

148. Frank Sinatra reportedly threatened Peter Lawford with bodily harm after finding out that he had lunch with what actress?

A. Ava Gardner
B. Kim Novak
C. Lana Turner
D. Rita Hayworth

149. In what year did the American Film Institute give Jack Lemmon a Lifetime Achievement Award?

A. 1987
B. 1988
C. 1989
D. 1990

150. For what film did Cary Grant receive his first Oscar nomination for Best Actor?

A. *Father Goose* (1964)
B. *None but the Lonely Heart* (1944)
C. *North by Northwest* (1959)
D. *Penny Serenade* (1941)

151. James Stewart romances Ginger Rogers in what comedy directed by George Stevens?

A. *The More the Merrier* (1943)
B. *The Talk of the Town* (1942)
C. *Vivacious Lady* (1938)
D. *Woman of the Year* (1942)

152. James Cagney earned a black belt in what martial art?

A. Judo
B. Jujitsu
C. Karate
D. Tae kwon do

153. In the 1936 film *My Man Godfrey*, who plays the title character opposite Carole Lombard?

A. Fredric March
B. Ronald Colman
C. Spencer Tracy
D. William Powell

154. William Holden debuted as an extra in what Shirley Ross film?

A. *Prison Farm* (1938)
B. *Some Like It Hot* (1939)
C. *The Big Broadcast of 1938* (1937)
D. *Unexpected Father* (1939)

155. How many Oscar nominations had Gregory Peck earned before winning for *To Kill a Mockingbird* (1962)?

A. 0
B. 2
C. 4
D. 6

156. In 1961, Norman Z. McLeod directed an episode of *The Twilight Zone* that starred Buster Keaton as a janitor who travels through time. What is the episode called?

A. "A Certain Chemistry"
B. "Breakfast on Pluto"
C. "Intermission"
D. "Once Upon a Time"

157. Fredric March portrays Philip of Macedonia in which epic starring Richard Burton in the title role?

A. *Alexander the Great* (1956)
B. *Dark City* (1950)
C. *El Cid* (1961)
D. *The Buccaneer* (1958)

158. In which film does Anthony Quinn portray a character inspired by Aristotle Onassis?

A. *High Season* (1987)
B. *City Beneath the Sea* (1953)
C. *The Greek Tycoon* (1978)
D. *The Last Tycoon* (1976)

answers found on page 552

159. Fredric March originally began a career in what industry?

A. Academia
B. Finance
C. Medicine
D. Music

160. Douglas Fairbanks cast Lupe Velez in which film opposite himself and Mary Pickford?

A. *Lady of the Pavements* (1929)
B. *Stand and Deliver* (1928)
C. *The Gaucho* (1927)
D. *What Women Did for Me* (1927)

161. Paul Newman costarred opposite Joanne Woodward in all of the following films except for which one?

A. *A Fine Madness* (1966)
B. *A New Kind of Love* (1963)
C. *Paris Blues* (1961)
D. *Winning* (1969)

162. James Stewart portrays a rookie playwright in what film directed by William Keighley?

A. *No Time for Comedy* (1940)
B. *The Green Pastures* (1936)
C. *Torrid Zone* (1940)
D. *Varsity Show* (1937)

163. On the anniversary of *Golden Boy*'s (1939) premiere every year, William Holden would send what to his costar Barbara Stanwyck?

A. A card
B. Boxing gloves
C. Chocolates
D. Flowers

164. What was Bing Crosby's biggest-selling record?

A. "Accentuate the Positive"
B. "Pennies from Heaven"
C. "Swinging on a Star"
D. "White Christmas"

165. Marlon Brando plays a kidnapper in what gripping drama?

A. *A Countess from Hong Kong* (1967)
B. *The Fugitive Kind* (1960)
C. *The Night of the Following Day* (1968)
D. *The Nightcomers* (1971)

166. In which of the following films does Peter Lorre costar with Mickey Rooney?

A. *All Through the Night* (1941)
B. *Arsenic and Old Lace* (1944)
C. *Background to Danger* (1943)
D. *Quicksand* (1950)

167. Jack Lemmon won an Academy Award as Best Supporting Actor for his work in which of the following films?

A. *Bell, Book and Candle* (1958)
B. *Fire Down Below* (1957)
C. *Mister Roberts* (1955)
D. *My Sister Eileen* (1955)

168. Which film starring Fredric March premiered in New Orleans, Louisiana?

A. *Inherit the Wind* (1960)
B. *The Bridges at Toko-Ri* (1954)
C. *The Buccaneer* (1938)
D. *The Man in the Gray Flannel Suit* (1956)

169. Who starred in Henry Hathaway's 1948 film *Call Northside 777*?

A. Burt Lancaster
B. Cary Grant
C. James Stewart
D. Montgomery Clift

170. What is Burt Lancaster's character's name in *Field of Dreams* (1989)?

A. Crash Davis
B. Moonlight Graham
C. Roy Hobbs
D. Shoeless Joe Jackson

answers found on page 552

171. For what film did Gregory Peck receive his first Academy Award nomination?

A. *Moby Dick* (1956)
B. *The Keys of the Kingdom* (1944)
C. *The Yearling* (1946)
D. *To Kill a Mockingbird* (1962)

172. What 1962 film about a famous psychologist stars Montgomery Clift?

A. *Freud*
B. *Private Worlds*
C. *Shock Corridor*
D. *The Snake Pit*

173. Bing Crosby performs the song "It's Easy to Remember (And So Hard to Forget)" in what film costarring W. C. Fields?

A. *Mississippi* (1935)
B. *Shop Talk* (1935)
C. *The Barber Shop* (1933)
D. *Tillie and Gus* (1933)

174. What is Bob Hope's profession in George Marshall's *Monsieur Beaucaire* (1946)?

A. Barber
B. Candlestick maker
C. Dancer
D. Doctor

175. Peter O'Toole has conflicting birth certificates from both England and what other country?

A. Austria
B. France
C. Ireland
D. Scotland

176. Paul Muni was known for playing what instrument?

A. Guitar
B. Piano
C. Trumpet
D. Violin

177. In what film does Gene Kelly play a baseball player on a team taken over by Esther Williams?

A. *Anchors Aweigh* (1945)
B. *Singin' in the Rain* (1952)
C. *Summer Stock* (1950)
D. *Take Me Out to the Ballgame* (1949)

178. Ronald Colman costars in what film opposite both Lillian and Dorothy Gish?

A. *Kentucky Pride* (1925)
B. *Romola* (1924)
C. *Tudor Rose* (1936)
D. *Weather Wizards* (1939)

Network, 1976

179. William Holden plays a television executive who has to fire his best friend in the 1976 film *Network*. What is his character's name in that movie?

A. Howard Beale
B. Max Schumacher
C. Joe Gillis
D. J. J. Sefton

180. At the age of seventy-six, who was the oldest person to receive an Academy Award as Best Actor?

A. Henry Fonda
B. Humphrey Bogart
C. James Mason
D. Marlon Brando

answers found on page 552

181. In the 1954 film *Desirée,* which historical figure does Marlon Brando portray?

A. Christopher Columbus
B. Julius Caesar
C. King Henry VIII
D. Napoleon

182. Clark Gable proposed to Carole Lombard inside a phone booth at what famous restaurant?

A. Chasen's
B. Dan Tana's
C. Perino's
D. The Brown Derby

183. James Stewart plays a conservative father at odds with his liberal daughter Sandra Dee in what 1960s generation-gap comedy?

A. *Romanoff and Juilet*
B. *Rosie!*
C. *Take Her, She's Mine*
D. *The Grass Is Greener*

184. Alan Ladd plays a prisoner convicted for a gold robbery in what remake of *The Asphalt Jungle* (1950)?

A. *13 West Street* (1962)
B. *The Badlanders* (1958)
C. *The Carpetbaggers* (1964)
D. *Whispering Smith* (1949)

185. In the 1928 film *The Circus,* what act does Charles Chaplin do at the end of the film in order to impress his love interest?

A. Rides a motorcycle through a ring of fire
B. Swallows swords
C. Tames a lion
D. Walks the high wire

186. How many Oscars was John Barrymore nominated for?

A. 0
B. 2
C. 3
D. 8

187. Rudolph Valentino stars as a famous bullfighter trapped in a torrid affair with widow Nita Naldi in what 1922 silent film?

A. *Blood and Sand*
B. *Cobra*
C. *Eyes of Youth*
D. *Uncharted Seas*

188. In which of the following films does Henry Fonda play a ruthless villain?

A. *Fail-Safe* (1964)
B. *Meteor* (1979)
C. *Once Upon a Time in the West* (1968)
D. *The Boston Strangler* (1968)

189. Montgomery Clift died shortly before he was scheduled to begin shooting what film, which would have been his fourth collaboration with Elizabeth Taylor?

A. *Reflections in a Golden Eye* (1967)
B. *The Defector* (1966)
C. *The Last Time I Saw Paris* (1954)
D. *The Taming of the Shrew* (1967)

190. Gene Kelly received an honorary Oscar in what year?

A. 1952
B. 1965
C. 1972
D. 1980

191. Paul Muni's final film role was Dr. Sam Abelman in what drama?

A. *Across the Pacific* (1942)
B. *The Last Angry Man* (1959)
C. *The Oklahoma Kid* (1939)
D. *They Drive by Night* (1940)

192. Montgomery Clift plays the title role in what biopic opposite Susannah York?
    A. *Freud* (1962)
    B. *Harry & Son* (1984)
    C. *Mickey One* (1965)
    D. *The MacKintosh Man* (1973)

193. Fredric March portrays English poet Robert Browning in what film?
    A. *Nothing Sacred* (1937)
    B. *The Barretts of Wimpole Street* (1934)
    C. *The Best Years of Our Lives* (1946)
    D. *The Road to Glory* (1936)

194. What year did Henry Fonda die?
    A. 1979
    B. 1981
    C. 1982
    D. 1986

195. In the 1947 thriller *A Double Life*, Ronald Colman plays an actor starring in what Shakespeare play?
    A. *Hamlet*
    B. *King Lear*
    C. *Othello*
    D. *The Tempest*

196. In what Kirk Douglas film does Woody Strode fight him to the death?
    A. *Champion* (1949)
    B. *For Love or Money* (1963)
    C. *Spartacus* (1960)
    D. *The Vikings* (1958)

197. What was Cary Grant's real name?
    A. Archibald Leach
    B. Emmanuel Goldberg
    C. Marion Morrison
    D. Richard Jenkins

198. Anthony Quinn once studied architecture under the mentorship of which renowned architect?
    A. Antonio Gaudi
    B. Frank Lloyd Wright
    C. I. M. Pei
    D. Louis Isadore Kahn

199. In what film does James Stewart sing the Cole Porter song "Easy to Love"?
    A. *Born to Dance* (1936)
    B. *Of Human Hearts* (1938)
    C. *The Gorgeous Hussy* (1936)
    D. *Vivacious Lady* (1938)

200. Henry Fonda received his first Academy Award nomination as Best Actor for his performance in what film?
    A. *Mister Roberts* (1955)
    B. *My Darling Clementine* (1946)
    C. *Spencer's Mountain* (1963)
    D. *The Grapes of Wrath* (1940)

201. For which of the following films did Jack Lemmon win his only Academy Award as Best Actor?
    A. *Days of Wine and Roses* (1962)
    B. *Save the Tiger* (1973)
    C. *Some Like It Hot* (1959)
    D. *The Apartment* (1960)

202. How old was James Cagney when he died?
    A. 79
    B. 81
    C. 84
    D. 86

203. In what film does Frank Sinatra sing the Oscar-nominated song "All the Way"?
    A. *New York, New York* (1977)
    B. *Ocean's Eleven* (1960)
    C. *Robin and the 7 Hoods* (1964)
    D. *The Joker Is Wild* (1957)

answers found on page 552

204. In 1932, Paul Muni returned to Hollywood and signed with which studio?

A. Fox
B. MGM
C. Universal
D. Warner Bros.

205. Gregory Peck met his wife of over forty years, Veronique, while making which film?

A. *Cape Fear* (1962)
B. *Duel in the Sun* (1946)
C. *Roman Holiday* (1953)
D. *To Kill a Mockingbird* (1962)

206. What year did Mickey Rooney win an Oscar for "significant contribution in bringing to the screen the spirit and personification of youth"?

A. 1932
B. 1938
C. 1941
D. 1955

207. What was the nickname of Harold Lloyd's character in *The Milky Way* (1936)?

A. "Kid"
B. "Rascal"
C. "Sparky"
D. "Tiger"

208. Alan Ladd made his film debut with a bit part in what film?

A. *Island of Lost Souls* (1932)
B. *Once in a Lifetime* (1932)
C. *Saturday's Millions* (1933)
D. *Tom Brown in Culver* (1932)

209. For what film did Marlon Brando receive his last Academy Award nomination?

A. *A Dry White Season* (1989)
B. *Don Juan de Marco* (1995)
C. *Last Tango in Paris* (1972)
D. *The Godfather* (1972)

Camille, 1936

210. Robert Taylor plays Armand Duval opposite Greta Garbo in which classic?

A. *Camille* (1936)
B. *Society Doctor* (1935)
C. *The Spectacle Maker* (1934)
D. *Times Square Lady* (1935)

211. Although he never won, how many times was Edward G. Robinson nominated for an Oscar?

A. 0
B. 2
C. 4
D. 5

212. Bing Crosby received an Academy Award nomination as Best Actor for his work in all of the following films except which one?

A. *Going My Way* (1944)
B. *The Bells of St. Mary's* (1945)
C. *The Country Girl* (1936)
D. *White Christmas* (1954)

213. In what film does Jack Lemmon play a landlord who is entranced by one of his beautiful young tenants?

A. *Days of Wine and Roses* (1962)
B. *Save the Tiger* (1973)
C. *The Apartment* (1960)
D. *Under the Yum Yum Tree* (1963)

To Have and Have Not, 1924

Chapter 8
LEADING
COUPLES

If the Golden Age stars were the studios' stock in trade, then their teamings represented some of the most fascinating mergers in entertainment history. Every studio was on the lookout for the perfect pair to capture the fans' imagination. It didn't matter (except when billing issues were being decided) whether one star was bigger than the other. Together, teams like Fred Astaire and Ginger Rogers or William Powell and Myrna Loy were sheer magic.

The best teams established unique identities, a brand all their own. Mickey Rooney and Judy Garland were the ultimate gung-ho kids putting on a show; Wallace Beery and Marie Dressler were the timeworn couple facing their few remaining years (and more than a few drinks) together. Charles Farrell and Janet Gaynor epitomized youthful romance, while Powell and Loy provided a more sophisticated take, and Glenn Ford and Rita Hayworth captured the magnetic pull of illicit desires.

Their appeal was symbiotic as well, with each bringing out something in the other no other costar could. Spencer Tracy and Katharine Hepburn were never as sexy individually as they were when they played love scenes or fight scenes in nine films together, from *Woman of the Year* (1942) to *Guess Who's Coming to Dinner* (1967). Hepburn summed up Astaire and Rogers's appeal when she said, "He gave her class. She gave him sex." And Errol Flynn never seemed as noble, nor Olivia de Havilland as lighthearted, as they did in each other's arms.

Many great movie teams were the result of pairing a major star with somebody on the way up. John Gilbert was one of MGM's top stars when he agreed to work with studio newcomer Greta Garbo in *Flesh and the Devil* (1926). Making her first film, Lauren Bacall was so frightened to be working with Humphrey Bogart on *To Have and Have Not* (1944), she had to hold her chin down to keep her head from shaking. But when he looked at her as if she were the most desirable woman on earth, it made her a star.

Other teams were born by matching relatively unknown qualities in a way that helped build both careers. Dick Powell and Ruby Keeler were just getting started when *42nd Street* (1933) turned them into a top screen team. And *Red Dust* (1932), the birth of the Gable-Harlow partnership (they had earlier appeared together in 1931's *The Secret Six*, but not as a team), provided a huge boost to both careers.

In a few rare cases, established stars like Hepburn and Tracy or Rock Hudson and Doris Day brought out something in each other audiences had never really seen before. In the latter case, *Pillow Talk* (1959) resuscitated both stars' careers in the face of changing times. In addition to the two more films they made together (leading to a lifelong friendship), both would prolong their box-office reigns for a decade by adding romantic comedy to their repertoires.

Amazingly, some of the screen's greatest team-ups happened by accident. Dorothy Jordan was supposed to dance with Astaire in *Flying Down to Rio* (1933), but she fell in love with the studio head Merian C. Cooper, and was off on her honeymoon during filming when Rogers got her big break. Robert Donat was the original choice to play *Captain Blood* (1935) at Warner Bros., but when

illness prevented his taking part, the relatively unknown Flynn got the first of eight chances to work opposite de Havilland. Had Elizabeth Taylor not contracted pneumonia while filming *Cleopatra* (1963) in England, she might have gone on to make *The V.I.P.s* (1963) and *Who's Afraid of Virginia Woolf?* (1966) with Stephen Boyd instead of his replacement, Richard Burton.

Not every team captures the public's imagination, of course. Gary Cooper made four feature films with Fay Wray, more than any other of his costars, but these titles aren't as memorable as his three with Barbara Stanwyck or the two with Marlene Dietrich. And Wray's best-loved costar is King Kong.

There have also been one time pairings that have achieved legendary status. Some costars, like John Garfield and Lana Turner in *The Postman Always Rings Twice* (1946), or Cary Grant and Grace Kelly in *To Catch a Thief* (1955), were so well matched it's a crime they never worked together again. Others, like Bogart and Ingrid Bergman in *Casablanca* (1942) or Gable and Vivien Leigh in *Gone With the Wind* (1939), achieved such a level of perfection that any further work together would have been anticlimactic.

Whether they made a dozen films or just one, the screen's greatest teams had one thing in common. Their partnerships captured the dreams of a nation and created an image of romance no one will ever forget.

1. In which of the following films does Janet Leigh not costar with first husband Tony Curtis?
   A. *Houdini* (1953)
   B. *The Vikings* (1958)
   C. *Touch of Evil* (1958)
   D. *Who Was That Lady?* (1960)

2. Who is Cary Grant's leading lady in *Father Goose* (1964)?
   A. Deborah Kerr
   B. Ingrid Bergman
   C. Leslie Caron
   D. Sophia Loren

3. Who is Rex Harrison's leading lady in *The Citadel* (1938)?
   A. Carole Lombard
   B. Irene Dunne
   C. Jean Harlow
   D. Rosalind Russell

4. Which of the following actors does not costar in the 1942 film *Son of Fury: The Story of Benjamin Blake,* directed by John Cromwell?
   A. Fredric March
   B. Gene Tierney
   C. George Sanders
   D. Tyrone Power

5. Who is Claude Rains's Cleopatra in the 1945 film *Caesar and Cleopatra*?
   A. Bette Davis
   B. Elizabeth Taylor
   C. Greta Garbo
   D. Vivien Leigh

6. Who is Burt Reynolds's leading lady in *The Best Little Whorehouse in Texas* (1982)?
   A. Dolly Parton
   B. Joan Collins
   C. Loni Anderson
   D. Madeline Kahn

7. Which of the following actors appears with Rosalind Russell in the 1941 film *They Met in Bombay*?
   A. Clark Gable
   B. Kirk Douglas
   C. Michael Redgrave
   D. Spencer Tracy

8. Who is Joseph Cotten's costar in the 1973 film *A Delicate Balance*?
   A. Glenda Jackson
   B. Joanne Woodward
   C. Katharine Hepburn
   D. Maureen Stapleton

9. Who is Joseph Cotten's costar in the 1952 film *Untamed Frontier*?
   A. Joan Fontaine
   B. Marilyn Monroe
   C. Shelley Winters
   D. Teresa Wright

10. In which of the following films did Rita Hayworth not costar with Glenn Ford?
    A. *Gilda* (1946)
    B. *The Lady from Shanghai* (1947)
    C. *The Loves of Carmen* (1948)
    D. *The Money Trap* (1965)

11. Who is Joseph Cotten's costar in the 1947 film *The Farmer's Daughter*?
    A. Barbara Stanwyck
    B. Grace Kelly
    C. Ingrid Bergman
    D. Loretta Young

12. Ray Milland and Marlene Dietrich star in what film directed by Mitchell Leisen?
    A. *Above and Beyond* (1952)
    B. *Golden Earrings* (1947)
    C. *The Bribe* (1949)
    D. *To Each His Own* (1946)

Union Depot, 1932

13. Who is Joan Blondell's costar in *Union Depot* (1932)?
   A. Clark Gable
   B. Douglas Fairbanks Jr.
   C. James Cagney
   D. Melvyn Douglas

14. Anthony Asquith directed which film starring Sophia Loren and Peter Sellers that was an adaptation of a George Bernard Shaw play?
   A. *Boy on a Dolphin* (1957)
   B. *Pygmalion* (1938)
   C. *The Millionairess* (1960)
   D. *The Pride and the Passion* (1957)

15. Donna Reed appeared opposite William Powell and Myrna Loy in which film?
   A. *Escape* (1940)
   B. *High Wall* (1947)
   C. *Miss Grant Takes Richmond* (1949)
   D. *Shadow of the Thin Man* (1941)

16. Marjorie Main appeared in which film starring William Powell and Myrna Loy?
   A. *Another Thin Man* (1939)
   B. *Shadow of the Thin Man* (1941)
   C. *Song of the Thin Man* (1947)
   D. *The Thin Man Goes Home* (1944)

17. What couple dances to the Oscar-nominated song "The Carioca" in *Flying Down to Rio* (1933)?
   A. Fred Astaire and Ginger Rogers
   B. Fred Astaire and Ruby Keeler
   C. Gene Kelly and Dolores del Rio
   D. Gene Raymond and Virginia Mayo

18. In what film does Van Heflin not costar with Lana Turner?
   A. *Green Dolphin Street* (1947)
   B. *Johnny Eager* (1941)
   C. *Possessed* (1947)
   D. *The Three Musketeers* (1948)

19. Robert Taylor romances Betty Furness in what film?
   A. *A Wicked Woman* (1934)
   B. *Society Doctor* (1935)
   C. *The Spectacle Maker* (1934)
   D. *Times Square Lady* (1935)

20. Who married actress Fay Bainter?
   A. Claude Rains
   B. Henry Fonda
   C. Reginald Venable
   D. William Wyler

21. In which of the following films does Fred MacMurray not costar with Barbara Stanwyck?
   A. *Double Indemnity* (1944)
   B. *Face of a Fugitive* (1959)
   C. *The Moonlighter* (1953)
   D. *There's Always Tomorrow* (1956)

22. Who is Sophia Loren's leading man in *El Cid* (1961)?
   A. Burt Lancaster
   B. Charlton Heston
   C. George C. Scott
   D. John Wayne

answers found on page 553

23. Alan Ladd costarred in how many films with Veronica Lake?

A. 1
B. 2
C. 3
D. 4

24. Joanne Woodward costarred opposite Paul Newman in all of the following films except for which one?

A. *A Fine Madness* (1966)
B. *A New Kind of Love* (1963)
C. *Paris Blues* (1961)
D. *Winning* (1969)

25. Which one of the following actors costars with Kay Francis in the 1937 film *Another Dawn*?

A. Errol Flynn
B. Humphrey Bogart
C. Ian Hunter
D. Leslie Howard

26. Who was married to Ruby Dee for more than five decades?

A. Bill Cosby
B. Frank Dee Brown
C. Ossie Davis
D. Sidney Poitier

27. Jane Russell reunited with Robert Mitchum in what film?

A. *Double Dynamite* (1951)
B. *His Kind of Woman* (1951)
C. *Macao* (1952)
D. *The French Line* (1954)

28. Who was not married to Merle Oberon?

A. Bruno Pagliai
B. Leslie Howard
C. Lucien Ballard
D. Robert Wolders

29. Who is Rex Harrison's sultry costar in *The Happy Thieves* (1962)?

A. Ava Gardner
B. Elizabeth Taylor
C. Jean Harlow
D. Rita Hayworth

30. Who was never married to Robert Newton?

A. Debra Paget
B. Natalie Newhouse
C. Petronella Walton
D. Vera Budnik

Please Don't Eat the Daisies, 1960

31. While Doris Day frequently starred with Rock Hudson, who was her costar in *Please Don't Eat the Daisies* (1960)?

A. Robert Taylor
B. Peter O'Toole
C. David Niven
D. Gregory Peck

32. Rex Harrison and fourth wife Rachel Roberts made only one film together. What was the title?

A. *A Flea in Her Ear* (1968)
B. *A Time to Die* (1982)
C. *Escape* (1948)
D. *King Richard and the Crusaders* (1954)

33. Lucille Ball and Desi Arnaz share the screen in what film directed by Alexander Hall?

A. *Blue Skies* (1946)
B. *Forever, Darling* (1956)
C. *Neptune's Daughter* (1949)
D. *The Pleasure of His Company* (1961)

34. Who is Gary Cooper's beautiful blonde costar in *I Take This Woman* (1931)?

A. Carole Lombard
B. Grace Kelly
C. Jean Harlow
D. Marilyn Monroe

35. Who played the lead role opposite Merle Oberon in *The Scarlet Pimpernel* (1934)?

A. Bramwell Fletcher
B. Leslie Howard
C. Nigel Bruce
D. Raymond Massey

36. Who did Michael Caine marry in 1973?

A. Candice Bergen
B. Jane Asher
C. Julia Foster
D. Shakira Baksh

37. Which of the following films does not star Henry Fonda and Bette Davis?

A. *Jezebel* (1938)
B. *Land of Liberty* (1939)
C. *That Certain Woman* (1937)
D. *The Mad Miss Manton* (1938)

38. What film was the first on-screen pairing of Robert Taylor and Vivien Leigh?

A. *A Yank at Oxford* (1938)
B. *Broadway Melody of 1938* (1937)
C. *Camille* (1936)
D. *Lady of the Tropics* (1939)

39. Peter Sellers costarred with Sophia Loren in which film?

A. *A Shot in the Dark* (1964)
B. *The Ladykillers* (1955)
C. *The Millionairess* (1960)
D. *The Mouse That Roared* (1959)

40. Two of Glenn Ford's teeth were broken by which actress while filming a scene?

A. Bette Davis
B. Esther Williams
C. Ida Lupino
D. Rita Hayworth

41. Robert Taylor romances Hedy Lamarr in what film?

A. *Lady of the Tropics* (1939)
B. *Society Doctor* (1935)
C. *The Spectacle Maker* (1934)
D. *Times Square Lady* (1935)

42. What was the last film that Joan Blondell made with second husband Dick Powell?

A. *Gold Diggers of 1937* (1936)
B. *I Want a Divorce* (1940)
C. *Just Around the Corner* (1938)
D. *Model Wife* (1941)

43. In how many films did Fay Wray costar with Ralph Bellamy?

A. 1
B. 3
C. 5
D. 7

44. Which of the following actresses did Robert Wagner not marry?

A. Debbie Reynolds
B. Jill St. John
C. Marion Marshall
D. Natalie Wood

answers found on page 553

45. What film marked Glenn Ford's first time working with Rita Hayworth?

A. *Gilda* (1946)
B. *Loves of Carmen* (1948)
C. *The Lady in Question* (1940)
D. *The Renegade Ranger* (1938)

46. Who is Joseph Cotten's costar in the 1949 film *Beyond the Forest*?

A. Bette Davis
B. Lauren Bacall
C. Merle Oberon
D. Rita Hayworth

47. Richard Thorpe directed Katharine Alexander in what film opposite William Powell and Myrna Loy?

A. *Double Wedding* (1937)
B. *The Barretts of Wimpole Street* (1957)
C. *The Long Memory* (1952)
D. *The Valiant* (1962)

48. In what film dose Van Heflin costar with Patricia Neal?

A. *East Side, West Side* (1949)
B. *Madame Bovary* (1949)
C. *My Son John* (1952)
D. *Weekend with Father* (1951)

49. Who is Jack Lemmon's costar in the 1963 film *Irma la Douce*?

A. Grace Kelly
B. Kim Novak
C. Natalie Wood
D. Shirley MacLaine

50. What was the first film Cary Grant made with third wife Betsy Drake?

A. *Every Girl Should Be Married* (1948)
B. *Mr. Blandings Builds His Dream House* (1948)
C. *Room for One More* (1952)
D. *She Done Him Wrong* (1933)

51. What husband-and-wife screenwriting team earned an Oscar nomination for *Adam's Rib* (1949)?

A. Cindy and Donald H. Hewitt
B. Frances Goodrich and Albert Hackett
C. Garson Kanin and Ruth Gordon
D. Irving Ravetch and Harriet Frank Jr.

52. Which of the following actresses costars with Jack Lemmon in the 1969 film *The April Fools*?

A. Ann-Margret
B. Catherine Deneuve
C. Sandy Dennis
D. Sophia Loren

53. Mitchell Leisen directed William Holden and Veronica Lake in what drama?

A. *Above and Beyond* (1952)
B. *I Wanted Wings* (1941)
C. *The Bribe* (1949)
D. *To Each His Own* (1946)

54. Who is Burt Reynolds's leading lady in *Best Friends* (1982)?

A. Adrienne Barbeau
B. Goldie Hawn
C. Marilu Henner
D. Sally Field

55. Robert Taylor and Loretta Young share the screen in what film?

A. *Billy the Kid* (1941)
B. *Her Cardboard Lover* (1942)
C. *Lady of the Tropics* (1939)
D. *Private Number* (1936)

56. What film pairing Norma Shearer and Robert Taylor was based on a French play?

A. *Her Cardboard Lover* (1942)
B. *Society Doctor* (1935)
C. *The Spectacle Maker* (1934)
D. *Times Square Lady* (1935)

answers found on page 553

Spotlight on
FRED **ASTAIRE** (1899–1987)
AND GINGER **ROGERS** (1911–1995)

Film critic Arlene Croce called them the only screen musical team to transform dance into "a vehicle of serious emotion between a man and a woman." In nine films during the course of five years at RKO, followed by a curtain call at MGM a decade later, Astaire and Rogers were the epitome of grace, style, and fun. The Astaire-Rogers partnership was never supposed to be. When David O. Selznick first signed Astaire to an RKO contract, he was slated to dance "The Carioca" with Dorothy Jordan in *Flying Down to Rio* (1933). But Jordan's honeymoon coincided with *Rio*'s production dates and the studio rushed in recent contractee Rogers. She was billed fourth and he fifth, but their brief turn on the dance floor stole the picture and the studio's exhibitors demanded Fred and Ginger have a film of their own. Soon they were paired in *The Gay Divorcee* (1934), *Roberta* (1935), and *Top Hat* (1935), which went on to gross more than $3 million. RKO knew better than to meddle with success like that and most of the Astaire-Rogers musicals recycled the same plots, cast, and crew. But even at the height of their success together, they had other plans. When the box office for their films began to decline, Astaire moved on to new studios and dance partners—including Rita Hayworth and Judy Garland—and Rogers scored an Oscar for Best Actress in the dramatic *Kitty Foyle* (1940). They would reunite for *The Barkleys of Broadway* (1949) and again in 1967 as Oscar presenters. On the way to the podium, Astaire spun Rogers into an impromptu routine that brought the house down, a testament to their enduring popularity as the screen's greatest dancing team.

Top Hat, 1935

The Barkleys of Broadway, 1949

1. What film pairing Fred Astaire and Ginger Rogers features Irving Berlin's song "I'm Putting All My Eggs in One Basket"?

   A. *Flying Down to Rio* (1933)

   B. *Follow the Fleet* (1936)

   C. *Swing Time* (1936)

   D. *You Were Never Lovelier* (1942)

2. George Stevens did not direct Ginger Rogers and/or Fred Astaire in which of these films?

   A. *A Damsel in Distress* (1937)

   B. *Swing Time* (1936)

   C. *Vivacious Lady* (1938)

   D. *Woman of the Year* (1942)

3. What was Fred Astaire's nickname for Ginger Rogers?

   A. "Feathers"

   B. "Ginnie"

   C. "Little Lee Lee"

   D. "Taps"

4. What was the only feature pairing Fred Astaire and Ginger Rogers that was filmed in color?

   A. *Funny Face* (1957)

   B. *Silk Stockings* (1957)

   C. *The Barkleys of Broadway* (1949)

   D. *The Belle of New York* (1952)

5. The 1937 Fred Astaire and Ginger Rogers musical *Shall We Dance* received an Academy Award nomination for Best Original Song. What was the name of the song?

   A. "That Old Feeling"

   B. "The Continental"

   C. "The Way You Look Tonight"

   D. "They Can't Take That away from Me"

---

answers found on page 553

57. Errol Flynn and Olivia de Havilland shared the screen in a total of how many films?

A. 10
B. 3
C. 5
D. 8

58. Who is Van Heflin's costar in the 1941 film *H. M. Pulham, Esq.*?

A. Ava Gardner
B. Hedy Lamarr
C. Joan Crawford
D. Lana Turner

59. Who is Kenneth Branagh's Ophelia in *Hamlet* (1996)?

A. Emily Blunt
B. Helena Bonham Carter
C. Kate Winslet
D. Natalie Portman

60. James Ivory directed Paul Newman and Joanne Woodward in what film?

A. *Barefoot in the Park* (1967)
B. *Dear Brigitte* (1965)
C. *From the Terrace* (1960)
D. *Mr. and Mrs. Bridge* (1990)

61. Which of the following actresses does not costar with George Hamilton in the 1960 film *Where the Boys Are*?

A. Dolores Hart
B. Paula Prentiss
C. Sue Lyon
D. Yvette Mimieux

62. Which of the following actresses costars with Tony Curtis in the 1960 film *The Rat Race*?

A. Debbie Reynolds
B. Janet Leigh
C. Rosalind Russell
D. Sophia Loren

Woman of the Year, 1942

63. *Woman of the Year* (1942), directed by George Stevens, was the first film to pair what great screen couple?

A. Dick Powell and Ruby Keeler
B. Fred Astaire and Ginger Rogers
C. Jeanette MacDonald and Nelson Eddy
D. Katharine Hepburn and Spencer Tracy

64. Maurice Chevalier makes a cameo appearance in what film starring Paul Newman and Joanne Woodward?

A. *A New Kind of Love* (1963)
B. *Barefoot in the Park* (1967)
C. *Radio Days* (1987)
D. *Sometimes a Great Notion* (1970)

65. Gary Cooper costarred with Lauren Bacall in which of the following films?

A. *Blowing Wild* (1953)
B. *Bright Leaf* (1950)
C. *Distant Drums* (1951)
D. *Garden of Evil* (1954)

66. Stewart Granger and Jean Simmons star in what thriller set in Victorian London?

A. *Fanny by Gaslight* (1945)
B. *Footsteps in the Fog* (1955)
C. *The Lamp Still Burns* (1943)
D. *Waterloo Road* (1945)

67. What did Rita Hayworth and Orson Welles name their daughter?

A. Elizabeth
B. Lena
C. Lindsay
D. Rebecca

68. Who is Audrey Hepburn's costar in *Funny Face* (1957)?

A. Dan Dailey
B. Donald O'Connor
C. Fred Astaire
D. Gene Kelly

69. In which of the following films does Greer Garson not costar with Walter Pidgeon?

A. *Blossoms in the Dust* (1941)
B. *Madame Curie* (1943)
C. *That Forsyte Woman* (1949)
D. *When Ladies Meet* (1941)

70. Cecil Kellaway plays an aristocrat in what film opposite Greer Garson and Walter Pidgeon?

A. *Mrs. Parkington* (1944)
B. *The Barretts of Wimpole Street* (1957)
C. *The Long Memory* (1952)
D. *The Valiant* (1962)

71. Which of the following actresses costars with Henry Fonda in the 1938 film *Jezebel*?

A. Bette Davis
B. Irene Dunne
C. Katharine Hepburn
D. Norma Shearer

72. Which actor plays the role of Rex Harrison's lover in the 1969 film *Staircase*?

A. David Niven
B. George C. Scott
C. John Wayne
D. Richard Burton

73. In which of the following films did Jean Harlow not costar with Clark Gable?

A. *Dinner at Eight* (1933)
B. *Red Dust* (1932)
C. *Saratoga* (1937)
D. *The Secret Six* (1931)

74. Which of the following actresses was never married to George Sanders?

A. Benita Hume
B. Eva Gabor
C. Susan Larson
D. Zsa Zsa Gabor

75. Myrna Loy and Fredric March starred in what film directed by William Wyler?

A. *Carrie* (1952)
B. *The Best Years of Our Lives* (1946)
C. *The Heiress* (1949)
D. *The Westerner* (1940)

76. Who is Audrey Hepburn's leading man in *Robin and Marian* (1976)?

A. Burt Lancaster
B. Gene Hackman
C. Laurence Olivier
D. Sean Connery

77. Teresa Wright marries Gary Cooper in what film?

A. *Casanova Brown* (1944)
B. *Mrs. Miniver* (1942)
C. *The Best Years of Our Lives* (1946)
D. *The Pride of the Yankees* (1942)

78. With whom did Jane Russell not costar?

A. Clark Gable
B. Frank Sinatra
C. Marilyn Monroe
D. Paul Newman

79. In which of the following films did Rex Harrison costar with third wife Kay Kendall?

A. *King Richard and the Crusaders* (1954)
B. *The Constant Husband* (1955)
C. *The Happy Thieves* (1961)
D. *The Yellow Rolls-Royce* (1964)

80. Who is Van Heflin's costar in the 1936 film *A Woman Rebels*?

A. Bette Davis
B. Joan Crawford
C. Katharine Hepburn
D. Rosalind Russell

81. What was the last film that Gary Cooper made with Barbara Stanwyck?

A. *Ball of Fire* (1941)
B. *Blowing Wild* (1953)
C. *Meet John Doe* (1941)
D. *The Plainsman* (1936)

82. What was the first film Kay Francis made with frequent costar William Powell?

A. *Behind the Make-Up* (1930)
B. *For the Defense* (1930)
C. *Jewel Robbery* (1932)
D. *Street of Chance* (1930)

83. William Powell and Luise Rainer share the screen in all of the following films except for which one?

A. *Escapade* (1935)
B. *Star of Midnight* (1935)
C. *The Emperor's Candlesticks* (1937)
D. *The Great Ziegfeld* (1936)

84. In what film does Barbra Streisand costar with Kris Kristofferson?

A. *A Star Is Born* (1976)
B. *Funny Lady* (1975)
C. *The Mirror Has Two Faces* (1996)
D. *The Prince of Tides* (1991)

85. Frank Sinatra performed the song for the opening credits of what film pairing of Joanne Woodward and Paul Newman?

A. *A New Kind of Love* (1963)
B. *Cat on a Hot Tin Roof* (1958)
C. *The Prize* (1963)
D. *The Sting* (1973)

86. Which actor plays Sophia Loren's love interest in *That Kind of Woman* (1959)?

A. Anthony Perkins
B. Gene Hackman
C. Tab Hunter
D. Troy Donahue

87. In which of the following films does Rita Hayworth not costar with Glenn Ford?

A. *Affair in Trinidad* (1952)
B. *Down to Earth* (1947)
C. *Gilda* (1946)
D. *The Lady in Question* (1940)

88. In what film does Van Heflin costar with Rosalind Russell?

A. *A Woman Rebels* (1936)
B. *Seven Sweethearts* (1942)
C. *The Feminine Touch* (1941)
D. *The Strange Love of Martha Ivers* (1946)

89. Teresa Wright did not costar with what actor?

A. Gary Cooper
B. Humphrey Bogart
C. Marlon Brando
D. Robert Mitchum

90. Robert Taylor shares the screen with real-life love Barbara Stanwyck in which film?

A. *Society Doctor* (1935)
B. *The Spectacle Maker* (1934)
C. *This Is My Affair* (1937)
D. *Times Square Lady* (1935)

answers found on page 553

91. Who is Sophia Loren's love interest in
    The Key (1958)?

    A. Cary Grant
    B. Charlton Heston
    C. Marcello Mastroianni
    D. William Holden

92. William Powell stars in the title role of which
    film opposite Luise Rainer?

    A. *Baby Face Nelson* (1957)
    B. *Richard III* (1955)
    C. *The Great Ziegfeld* (1936)
    D. *Young Tom Edison* (1940)

The Thin Man Goes Home, 1945

93. In the 1945 film *The Thin Man Goes Home,*
    starring William Powell and Myrna Loy, who
    plays Dr. Bertram Charles (Powell's father)?

    A. Will Rogers
    B. W. C. Fields
    C. Harry Davenport
    D. Thomas Mitchell

94. Which of the following actresses costars with
    Paul Henreid in the 1946 film *Deception*?

    A. Bette Davis
    B. Eleanor Parker
    C. Hedy Lamarr
    D. Rita Hayworth

95. Which of the following actors costars with
    Katharine Hepburn in the 1956 film *The
    Rainmaker*?

    A. Burt Lancaster
    B. Humphrey Bogart
    C. Richard Burton
    D. Sidney Poitier

96. Who is Fred MacMurray's costar in the 1950
    film *Never a Dull Moment*?

    A. Ingrid Bergman
    B. Irene Dunne
    C. Lauren Bacall
    D. Loretta Young

97. Paul Muni and Luise Rainer play husband and
    wife in what film?

    A. *Penny Serenade* (1941)
    B. *Star of Midnight* (1935)
    C. *The Good Earth* (1937)
    D. *The Story of Vernon and Irene Castle* (1939)

98. What was the only film to star Irene Dunne and
    Robert Taylor?

    A. *Magnificent Obsession* (1935)
    B. *Small Town Girl* (1936)
    C. *The Age of Innocence* (1934)
    D. *The Gorgeous Hussy* (1936)

99. What picture pairing Gene Hackman and
    Barbara Hershey is among AFI's Ten Greatest
    Sports Films?

    A. *Breakfast of Champions* (1999)
    B. *Hoosiers* (1986)
    C. *Passion* (1999)
    D. *Tin Men* (1987)

100. Who is Jane Powell's costar in the 1951 film
     Royal Wedding?

    A. Fred Astaire
    B. Gene Kelly
    C. Michael Kidd
    D. Ricardo Montalban

101. Which of the following Fay Wray films does not costar Gary Cooper?

A. *One Sunday Afternoon* (1933)
B. *Pointed Heels* (1929)
C. *The Legion of the Condemned* (1928)
D. *The Texan* (1930)

102. Who is Burt Lancaster's costar in *Atlantic City* (1980)?

A. Kathleen Turner
B. Melanie Griffith
C. Meryl Streep
D. Susan Sarandon

103. What film pairing Fred Astaire and Ginger Rogers features Irving Berlin's song "Let's Face the Music and Dance"?

A. *Follow the Fleet* (1936)
B. *Silk Stockings* (1957)
C. *The Sky's the Limit* (1943)
D. *You Were Never Lovelier* (1942)

104. Miriam Hopkins replaced Olivia de Havilland in which film opposite Errol Flynn?

A. *Design for Living* (1933)
B. *Splendor* (1935)
C. *The Old Maid* (1939)
D. *Virginia City* (1940)

105. Ricardo Montalban and Madlyn Rhue played husband and wife in episodes of *Bonanza* and which other television series?

A. *Bracken's World*
B. *Star Trek*
C. *The High Chaparral*
D. *The Virginian*

106. What was the first film that paired Pedro Armendáriz with leading lady María Félix?

A. *Beyond All Limits* (1959)
B. *Café Colón* (1959)
C. *Enamorada* (1946)
D. *The Soldiers of Pancho Villa* (1959)

107. Gregory Peck and Susan Hayward portray the title characters in what film?

A. *David and Bathsheba* (1951)
B. *Solomon and Sheba* (1959)
C. *The Barretts of Wimpole Street* (1957)
D. *The Story of Vernon and Irene Castle* (1939)

108. Who is Fay Wray's leading man in *Shanghai Madness* (1933)?

A. Cary Grant
B. Clark Gable
C. Gregory Peck
D. Spencer Tracy

109. What was Hattie McDaniel's first film with Clark Gable?

A. *China Seas* (1935)
B. *Gone With the Wind* (1939)
C. *Saratoga* (1937)
D. *The Mad Miss Manton* (1938)

110. Who plays Rock Hudson's love interest in *Darling Lili* (1970)?

A. Audrey Hepburn
B. Doris Day
C. Dyan Cannon
D. Julie Andrews

111. In which of the following films did Sally Field not costar with longtime love Burt Reynolds?

A. *Hooper* (1978)
B. *Smokey and the Bandit* (1977)
C. *The Cannonball Run* (1981)
D. *The End* (1978)

112. Who is Tony Curtis's costar in the 1964 film *Sex and the Single Girl*?

A. Goldie Hawn
B. Mia Farrow
C. Natalie Wood
D. Tuesday Weld

answers found on page 553

113. Which of the following actors costars with Rosalind Russell in the 1961 film *A Majority of One*?

A. Alec Guinness
B. Karl Malden
C. Paul Newman
D. William Holden

114. Which of the following Jean Harlow films does not costar Clark Gable?

A. *Dinner at Eight* (1933)
B. *Red Dust* (1932)
C. *Saratoga* (1937)
D. *The Secret Six* (1931)

115. Stewart Granger stars in the title role of which film with Elizabeth Taylor as his love interest?

A. *Adam and Evelyne* (1949)
B. *Beau Brummel* (1954)
C. *Caesar and Cleopatra* (1945)
D. *Captain Boycott* (1947)

116. Louis Jourdan was the voice of the narrator in what film pairing Jack Lemmon and Shirley MacLaine?

A. *A Certain Smile* (1958)
B. *Days of Wine and Roses* (1962)
C. *Irma la Douce* (1963)
D. *Under the Yum Yum Tree* (1963)

117. In which of the following films did Janet Gaynor not costar with actor Charles Farrell?

A. *Change of Heart* (1934)
B. *Daddy Long Legs* (1931)
C. *Lucky Star* (1929)
D. *The First Year* (1932)

118. Which of the following actresses costars with Leslie Howard in the 1937 film *It's Love I'm After*?

A. Greer Garson
B. Katharine Hepburn
C. Merle Oberon
D. Olivia de Havilland

119. What film did not pair Paulette Goddard with Ray Milland?

A. *Kitty* (1945)
B. *On Our Merry Way* (1948)
C. *Reap the Wild Wind* (1942)
D. *The Lady Has Plans* (1942)

120. Who is Sally Field's leading man in the 1981 film *Absence of Malice*?

A. Beau Bridges
B. Burt Lancaster
C. Paul Newman
D. Richard Gere

121. Scenes in what film pairing Robert Taylor and Ava Gardner were filmed near Tintagel Castle?

A. *High Wall* (1947)
B. *Knights of the Round Table* (1953)
C. *Passage to Marseille* (1944)
D. *Undercurrent* (1946)

122. Who was not married to director Ingmar Bergman?

A. Ellen Lundstrom
B. Else Fisher
C. Gun Grut
D. Liv Ullmann

123. Frank Sinatra and Deborah Kerr are husband and wife in which film?

A. *High Society* (1956)
B. *Marriage on the Rocks* (1965)
C. *Not as a Stranger* (1955)
D. *The Tender Trap* (1955)

124. Who costars with Leslie Howard in the 1934 film *Of Human Bondage*?

A. Bette Davis
B. Joan Fontaine
C. Norma Shearer
D. Olivia de Havilland

answers found on page 553

Spotlight on
SPENCER **TRACY** (1900–1967) AND
KATHARINE **HEPBURN** (1907–2003)

Their first meeting set the tone for their on-screen partnership. Running into Spencer Tracy with producer and director Joseph L. Mankiewicz, Katharine Hepburn looked him up and down and said, "I'm afraid I'm a bit tall for Mr. Tracy." "Don't worry," the producer shot back, "he'll cut you down to size." Indeed, that was the theme of many of their films together, with the stern, unflappable Tracy standing by as Hepburn flitted around him, until he found an opening to shoot her down with a word or a glance. He was the most masculine leading man she had ever had, making her more appealing than she had been on screen since her tomboy performance in *Little Women* (1933). In return, when Hepburn finally melted to his charms, she gave him a sex appeal he had never had before. Their first picture together, *Woman of*

Woman of the Year, 1942

the Year (1942), crackles with sexual tension, reflecting their growing attraction to each other. Later films, culminating with *Guess Who's Coming to Dinner* (1967), show an abiding affection. Through three and a half decades, Tracy and Hepburn built an offscreen relationship that was unique in its tastefulness. The Catholic-raised Tracy hesitated to ask for a divorce and realized the importance of his marriage to wife Louise's charity work for the deaf (their son, John, was hearing impaired). Thus, he and Hepburn never appeared together in public or even shared the same living quarters. The press rarely referred to their relationship, joining in a gentlemen's agreement to honor the stars' discretion. This discretion, along with twenty-five years of screen magic, helped make them one of Hollywood's greatest duos.

Woman of the Year, 1942

1. **In which Spencer Tracy and Katharine Hepburn vehicle did Joan Blondell costar?**

   A. *Adam's Rib* (1949)
   B. *Desk Set* (1957)
   C. *Guess Who's Coming to Dinner* (1967)
   D. *Woman of the Year* (1942)

2. **Judy Holliday played a supporting role opposite Katharine Hepburn and Spencer Tracy in what film?**

   A. *Adam's Rib* (1949)
   B. *Bells Are Ringing* (1960)
   C. *Born Yesterday* (1950)
   D. *It Should Happen to You* (1954)

3. **What is the first Oscar nomination Katharine Hepburn earned for acting opposite Spencer Tracy?**

   A. *Adam's Rib* (1949)
   B. *Alice Adams* (1935)

   C. *Guess Who's Coming to Dinner* (1967)
   D. *Woman of the Year* (1942)

4. **Spencer Tracy wore glasses without lenses in which film costarring Katharine Hepburn and Sidney Poitier?**

   A. *For Love of Ivy* (1968)
   B. *Guess Who's Coming to Dinner* (1967)
   C. *The Lost Man* (1969)
   D. *To Sir, with Love* (1967)

5. **In what city does the action take place in the 1967 Hepburn-Tracy film *Guess Who's Coming to Dinner*?**

   A. Boston
   B. Los Angeles
   C. New York
   D. San Francisco

answers found on page 553

Top Hat, 1935

125. The 1935 film *Top Hat*, pairing Fred Astaire and Ginger Rogers, features which famous Irving Berlin song?

A. "Blue Skies"
B. "I'm Putting All My Eggs in One Basket"
C. "I've Got My Love to Keep Me Warm"
D. "No Strings (I'm Fancy Free)"

126. Gregory Peck is Sophia Loren's leading man in which of the following films?

A. *Angela* (1978)
B. *Arabesque* (1966)
C. *Judith* (1966)
D. *The Voyage* (1974)

127. What was the name of Ed Wood's first wife, who kicked him out when she found him wearing women's clothing?

A. Dolores Fuller
B. Kathleen O'Hara
C. Norma McCarty
D. Patricia Arquette

128. Harry Davenport was featured in 1945's *Adventure* and which other film costarring Greer Garson?

A. *That Forsyte Woman* (1949)
B. *The Barretts of Wimpole Street* (1957)
C. *The Long Memory* (1952)
D. *The Valiant* (1962)

129. Who is Robert Taylor's Guinevere in the 1953 film *Knights of the Round Table*?

A. Ava Gardner
B. Deborah Kerr
C. Hedy Lamarr
D. Vivien Leigh

130. Who inspired June Allyson to learn how to dance?

A. Fred Astaire and Cyd Charisse
B. Gene Kelly and Debbie Reynolds
C. Ginger Rogers and Fred Astaire
D. Mickey Rooney and Judy Garland

131. Which of the following on-screen couples meets while working at a factory?

A. Gary Cooper and Claudette Colbert in *Bluebeard's Eighth Wife* (1938)
B. Marlon Brando and Eva Marie Saint in *On the Waterfront* (1954)
C. Montgomery Clift and Shelley Winters in *A Place in the Sun* (1951)
D. Warren Beatty and Natalie Wood in *Splendor in the Grass* (1961)

132. Which Robert Wagner film did not star his wife Natalie Wood?

A. *All the Fine Young Cannibals* (1960)
B. *Cat on a Hot Tin Roof* (1976)
C. *In Love and War* (1958)
D. *The Affair* (1973)

133. Who is Sally Field's leading man in the 1985 film *Murphy's Romance*?

A. Henry Winkler
B. James Caan
C. James Garner
D. Paul Newman

134. Who is Gary Cooper's costar in *Meet John Doe* (1941)?

A. Audrey Hepburn
B. Barbara Stanwyck
C. Grace Kelly
D. Patricia Neal

135. What was the only film that Ronald Reagan made with second wife Nancy Davis?

A. *Hellcats of the Navy* (1957)
B. *John Loves Mary* (1949)
C. *Prisoner of War* (1954)
D. *The Killers* (1964)

136. Who is Doris Day's leading man in *That Touch of Mink* (1962)?

A. Cary Grant
B. Clark Gable
C. Frank Sinatra
D. Rock Hudson

137. Who was Gene Kelly's first leading lady?

A. Esther Williams
B. Jean Harlow
C. Judy Garland
D. Marlene Dietrich

138. In what film does Van Heflin costar with Judy Garland?

A. *East Side, West Side* (1949)
B. *Presenting Lily Mars* (1943)
C. *Seven Sweethearts* (1942)
D. *The Three Musketeers* (1948)

139. What was the first film to costar Claire Bloom and Richard Burton?

A. *The Man Between* (1953)
B. *Alexander the Great* (1956)
C. *Look Back in Anger* (1959)
D. *The Spy Who Came in from the Cold* (1965)

140. What film pairing Fred Astaire and Ginger Rogers features Irving Berlin's song "The Syncopated Walk"?

A. *Broadway Melody of 1940* (1940)
B. *Flying Down to Rio* (1933)
C. *Swing Time* (1936)
D. *The Story of Vernon and Irene Castle* (1939)

141. Who is Sophia Loren's leading man in *It Started in Naples* (1960)?

A. Clark Gable
B. Dean Martin
C. Frank Sinatra
D. Marlon Brando

142. What was the first film to star both Walter Matthau and Jack Lemmon?

A. *Grumpy Old Men* (1993)
B. *Out to Sea* (1997)
C. *The Fortune Cookie* (1966)
D. *The Odd Couple* (1968)

143. Which of the following actors costars with Barbara Stanwyck in the 1941 film *You Belong to Me*?

A. Henry Fonda
B. James Stewart
C. Ralph Bellamy
D. William Holden

144. What film did not pair Paulette Goddard with Fred MacMurray?

A. *Pot O' Gold* (1941)
B. *Standing Room Only* (1944)
C. *Suddenly, It's Spring* (1947)
D. *The Forest Rangers* (1942)

145. Who is Rita Hayworth's leading man in the 1948 film *The Loves of Carmen*?

A. Glenn Ford
B. Orson Welles
C. Ricardo Montalban
D. Walter Pidgeon

146. What actor earned his only two Oscar nominations for roles played opposite Greer Garson in *Mrs. Miniver* (1942) and *Madame Curie* (1943)?

A. Fredric March
B. Henry Travers
C. Robert Donat
D. Walter Pidgeon

147. What sexy actress appears with Bela Lugosi in *Ghosts on the Loose* (1943)?

A. Ava Gardner
B. Lana Turner
C. Maureen O'Hara
D. Zsa Zsa Gabor

148. Richard Burton starred opposite Elizabeth Taylor in all of the following films except for which one?

A. *Hammersmith Is Out* (1972)
B. *Ice Palace* (1960)
C. *The Comedians* (1967)
D. *The V.I.P.s* (1963)

149. In which of the following films did Rex Harrison costar with red-headed siren Maureen O'Hara?

A. *I Live in Grosvenor Square* (1945)
B. *Over the Moon* (1939)
C. *The Constant Husband* (1955)
D. *The Foxes of Harrow* (1947)

150. Groucho Marx once explained that the secret to his on-screen chemistry with what costar was that she never understood any of his jokes?

A. Hedy Lamarr
B. Margaret Dumont
C. Virginia Grey
D. Virginia Mayo

151. Rock Hudson, Doris Day, and Tony Randall share the screen in all of the following films except for which one?

A. *Lover Come Back* (1961)
B. *Pillow Talk* (1959)
C. *Please Don't Eat the Daisies* (1960)
D. *Send Me No Flowers* (1964)

152. Who was not married to Neil Simon?

A. Bess Armstrong
B. Diane Lander
C. Elaine Joyce
D. Marsha Mason

153. Which of the following actresses costars with Paul Henreid in the 1951 film *Pardon My French*?

A. Bette Davis
B. Greer Garson
C. Marlene Dietrich
D. Merle Oberon

Susan Lenox: Her Rise and Fall, 1931

154. Who plays Greta Garbo's love interest in the 1931 film *Susan Lenox: Her Fall and Rise*?

A. Clark Gable
B. John Barrymore
C. John Gilbert
D. Spencer Tracy

155. Which of the following actors costars with Ava Gardner in the 1954 film *The Barefoot Contessa*?

A. Gregory Peck
B. Humphrey Bogart
C. Orson Welles
D. Trevor Howard

156. Who is Ava Gardner's costar in the 1964 film *The Night of the Iguana*?

A. Burt Lancaster
B. Charlton Heston
C. Clark Gable
D. Richard Burton

157. Who was Ava Gardner's first husband?

A. Artie Shaw
B. Frank Sinatra
C. Gene Kelly
D. Mickey Rooney

158. Who was Barbra Streisand's first husband?

A. Don Johnson
B. Elliott Gould
C. Jeff Bridges
D. Ryan O'Neal

159. Who was Audrey Hepburn's first husband?

A. George Sanders
B. Gregory Peck
C. Mel Ferrer
D. William Holden

160. Who is Nancy Kwan's leading man in *The World of Suzie Wong* (1960)?

A. Burt Lancaster
B. David Niven
C. Marlon Brando
D. William Holden

161. Which of the following actresses does not costar with Joseph Cotten in the 1944 film *Since You Went Away*?

A. Claudette Colbert
B. Ginger Rogers
C. Jennifer Jones
D. Shirley Temple

162. Robert Wagner's wife Jill St. John starred in what James Bond film?

A. *Diamonds Are Forever* (1971)
B. *Never Say Never Again* (1983)
C. *The Living Daylights* (1987)
D. *Thunderball* (1965)

163. Who costars with Jean Simmons in the 1960 film *The Grass Is Greener*?

A. Cary Grant
B. Clark Gable
C. Karl Malden
D. Trevor Howard

164. What famous show biz couple named their daughter Leslie after Leslie Howard?

A. Eddie Fisher and Debbie Reynolds
B. Frank Sinatra and Ava Gardner
C. Humphrey Bogart and Lauren Bacall
D. Trevor Howard and Jean Simmons

165. Who is Greer Garson's costar in the 1945 film *The Valley of Decision*?

A. Cary Grant
B. Gregory Peck
C. James Stewart
D. Spencer Tracy

166. What husband-and-wife filmmaking team earned dual Oscar nominations for their work on *David and Lisa* (1962)?

A. Bruce Paltrow and Blythe Danner
B. Frank Perry and Eleanor Perry
C. Paul Newman and Joanne Woodward
D. Peter Jackson and Fran Walsh

167. Robert Taylor and real-life love interest Ava Gardner share the screen in all of the following films except for which one?

A. *Knights of the Round Table* (1953)
B. *Ride, Vaquero!* (1953)
C. *The Bribe* (1949)
D. *Westward the Women* (1951)

answers found on page 554

168. In what Nelson Eddy/Jeanette MacDonald film does John Barrymore appear?

A. *Maytime* (1937)
B. *Naughty Marietta* (1935)
C. *New Moon* (1940)
D. *Sweethearts* (1938)

169. Who was Sophia Loren's husband for more than forty years until his death?

A. Carlo Ponti
B. Franco Zeffirelli
C. Pier Paolo Pasolini
D. Roberto Rossellini

170. Who costars with Jean Harlow in the 1933 film *Hold Your Man*?

A. Clark Gable
B. Gary Cooper
C. Spencer Tracy
D. William Powell

171. In which film does Lana Turner appear with first husband Artie Shaw?

A. *Dancing Co-Ed* (1939)
B. *Rich Man, Poor Girl* (1938)
C. *These Glamour Girls* (1939)
D. *Ziegfeld Girl* (1941)

172. Who is Carole Lombard's leading man in *Swing High, Swing Low* (1937)?

A. Cary Grant
B. Clark Gable
C. Fred MacMurray
D. William Powell

173. Anna Magnani was Anthony Quinn's leading lady in *The Secret of Santa Vittoria* (1969) and which other film?

A. *Caravans* (1978)
B. *High Risk* (1981)
C. *The Salamander* (1981)
D. *Wild Is the Wind* (1957)

174. Fred Astaire and Ginger Rogers performed together in a total of how many feature films?

A. 10
B. 15
C. 30
D. 5

175. Who is Gary Cooper's costar in *Today We Live* (1933)?

A. Fay Wray
B. Hedy Lamarr
C. Joan Crawford
D. Veronica Lake

176. Who is Carole Lombard's leading man in the 1931 film *I Take This Woman*?

A. Clark Gable
B. Don Ameche
C. Gary Cooper
D. Melvyn Douglas

177. Who was Robert Wagner's first wife?

A. Debbie Reynolds
B. Jill St. John
C. Marion Marshall
D. Natalie Wood

178. William Powell and Luise Rainer costar in what espionage thriller?

A. *Star of Midnight* (1935)
B. *The Emperor's Candlesticks* (1937)
C. *The Magic Box* (1952)
D. *Uncertain Glory* (1944)

179. In which film does Rosalind Russell appear with William Powell and Myrna Loy?

A. *China Seas* (1935)
B. *Evelyn Prentice* (1934)
C. *Man-Proof* (1938)
D. *Trouble for Two* (1936)

180. What was the name of the only film that Jean Harlow and Robert Taylor made together?

A. *Personal Property* (1937)

answers found on page 554

B. *Red Dust* (1932)

C. *Saratoga* (1937)

D. *Wife vs. Secretary* (1936)

181. **What was the first film to costar Deborah Kerr and Cary Grant?**

    A. *An Affair to Remember* (1957)

    B. *Dream Wife* (1953)

    C. *The Awful Truth* (1937)

    D. *The Grass Is Greener* (1960)

182. **Who played opposite Walter Matthau in the original stage production of *The Odd Couple* (1968)?**

    A. Art Carney

    B. Burgess Meredith

    C. Jack Lemmon

    D. Ossie Davis

183. **Who was not married to Jane Fonda?**

    A. Donald Sutherland

    B. Roger Vadim

    C. Ted Turner

    D. Tom Hayden

184. **Which of the following actresses costars with Paul Henreid in the 1944 film *The Conspirators*?**

    A. Deborah Kerr

    B. Hedy Lamarr

    C. Lana Turner

    D. Maureen O'Hara

185. **Which actor plays Sandra Dee's love interest in the 1958 film *The Restless Years*?**

    A. Bill Bixby

    B. Eddie Fisher

    C. John Saxon

    D. Paul Newman

The V.I.P.s, 1963

186. **In the 1963 Anthony Asquith film *The V.I.P.s*, Richard Burton and Elizabeth Taylor star as what?**

    A. An estranged couple

    B. Unrequited lovers

    C. Father and daughter

    D. Coworkers having an affair

187. **Who is Walter Matthau's costar in *First Monday in October* (1981)?**

    A. Ann Bancroft

    B. Carol Burnett

    C. Jill Clayburgh

    D. Shirley MacLaine

188. **What film starring Robert Wagner and Natalie Wood was loosely adapted from a Rosamond Marshall novel?**

    A. *A New Kind of Love* (1963)

    B. *All the Fine Young Cannibals* (1960)

    C. *Bell, Book and Candle* (1958)

    D. *Something for the Girls* (1958)

189. **Who was Ed Wood's wife and featured player in several of his films?**

    A. Dolores Fuller

    B. Kathleen O'Hara

    C. Loretta King

    D. Vampira

Spotlight on
ELIZABETH **TAYLOR** (1932–2011)
AND RICHARD **BURTON** (1925–1984)

I f Elizabeth Taylor and Richard Burton had left their families for each other in the 1940s, it would have meant career suicide. But after years of postwar austerity, audiences around the world were ready for fun without shame— and from their high-profile affair to their penchant for living large, Burton and Taylor seemed to have none. Their chemistry began with 20th Century-Fox's notorious *Cleopatra* (1963). The role of Marc Antony originally went to another actor, but production delays left the role open for Burton. Before long, director Joseph L. Mankiewicz was having trouble getting the stars to stop their love scenes after he had cried, "Cut." When Taylor admitted to being in love with Burton, her husband, Eddie Fisher, left the location. Burton's wife wasn't far behind, triggering an uproar in the press. That coverage encouraged British producer

The V.I.P.s, 1963

Anatole de Grunwald to team them as an unhappily married wealthy couple in *The V.I.P.s* (1963). As they hashed through a failed on-screen marriage, fans began to wonder if they weren't simply playing themselves. That speculation increased with the screen adaptation of Edward Albee's *Who's Afraid of Virginia Woolf?* (1966). But the film was also their greatest triumph. For a while, critics thought their partnership might turn out for the best after all. But it wasn't to be. Their high-profile lifestyle began taking its toll, and supporting it made them accept the offers carrying the biggest pay rather than the best scripts. Though both would garner further acclaim separately, their screen pairings and private union never recovered.

Who's Afraid of Virginia Woolf?, 1966

1. **Richard Burton celebrated his fortieth birthday while filming what picture costarring Elizabeth Taylor?**

   A. *Anne of the Thousand Days* (1969)
   B. *Cleopatra* (1963)
   C. *The V.I.P.s* (1963)
   D. *Who's Afraid of Virginia Woolf?* (1966)

2. **In the 1963 film *The V.I.P.s*, Richard Burton and Elizabeth Taylor are stranded in the airport lounge in what city?**

   A. Geneva
   B. London
   C. New York
   D. Rome

3. **The 1963 film *The V.I.P.s,* starring Richard Burton and Elizabeth Taylor, was based on a true story involving what other legendary pair?**

   A. Cary Grant and Sophia Loren
   B. Frank Sinatra and Ava Gardner
   C. Paul Newman and Joanne Woodward
   D. Vivien Leigh and Laurence Olivier

4. **Orson Welles portrays Max Buda in what film costarring Richard Burton and Elizabeth Taylor?**

   A. *Doctor Faustus* (1967)
   B. *The Greatest Story Ever Told* (1965)
   C. *The Night of the Iguana* (1964)
   D. *The V.I.P.s* (1963)

5. **What film adaptation of a Tennessee Williams play pairs Elizabeth Taylor and Richard Burton?**

   A. *Boom!* (1968)
   B. *Candy* (1968)
   C. *The Comedians* (1967)
   D. *Villain* (1971)

answers found on page 554

East Side, West Side, 1949

190. Which of the following actresses does not costar with Van Heflin in the 1949 film *East Side, West Side*?

A. Ava Gardner
B. Barbara Stanwyck
C. Cyd Charisse
D. Vivien Leigh

191. Ray Milland and Gene Tierney star in what film directed by William Keighley?

A. *Big Hearted Herbert* (1934)
B. *Close to My Heart* (1951)
C. *No Time for Comedy* (1940)
D. *Yes, My Darling Daughter* (1939)

192. Sean Connery starred opposite Claire Bloom in the BBC adaptation of which literary work?

A. *Anna Karenina*
B. *Great Expectations*
C. *Sense and Sensibility*
D. *War and Peace*

193. What was Bette Davis's first starring role opposite Errol Flynn?

A. *The Petrified Forest* (1936)
B. *The Old Maid* (1939)
C. *The Private Lives of Elizabeth and Essex* (1939)
D. *The Sisters* (1938)

194. Who is Ingrid Bergman's costar in the 1945 classic *The Bells of St. Mary's*?

A. Bing Crosby
B. Dean Martin
C. Gregory Peck
D. Spencer Tracy

195. With what leading man did Jean Simmons not costar?

A. James Dean
B. Marlon Brando
C. Paul Newman
D. Richard Burton

196. Who was Henry Fonda's first wife?

A. Carole Lombard
B. Irene Dunne
C. Jean Arthur
D. Margaret Sullavan

197. What was the first movie James Cagney and Bette Davis worked on together?

A. *Blonde Crazy* (1931)
B. *Jimmy the Gent* (1934)
C. *Sinners' Holiday* (1930)
D. *The Bride Came C.O.D.* (1941)

198. Who is Kim Novak's costar in the 1956 film *The Eddy Duchin Story*?

A. Anthony Perkins
B. Trevor Howard
C. Tyrone Power
D. William Holden

199. Who is Robert Taylor's leading lady in *Broadway Melody of 1936* (1935) and *Broadway Melody of 1938* (1937)?

A. Barbara Stanwyck
B. Cyd Charisse
C. Eleanor Powell
D. Ginger Rogers

answers found on page 554

200. Who is Joseph Cotten's leading lady in the 1948 film *Portrait of Jennie*?

A. Bette Davis
B. Jennifer Jones
C. Katharine Hepburn
D. Maureen O'Hara

201. Stewart Granger appeared in which London stage production opposite Vivien Leigh?

A. *Romanoff and Juliet*
B. *Serena Blandish*
C. *The Cherry Orchard*
D. *The Disenchanted*

202. Glenn Ford starred opposite Rita Hayworth in all of the following films except for which one?

A. *Affair in Trinidad* (1952)
B. *Gilda* (1946)
C. *Interrupted Melody* (1955)
D. *The Loves of Carmen* (1948)

203. Who was Rita Hayworth's second husband?

A. Alfred Hitchcock
B. Glenn Ford
C. Joseph Cotten
D. Orson Welles

204. Who was never married to Paulette Goddard?

A. Bob Hope
B. Burgess Meredith
C. Charles Chaplin
D. Erich Maria Remarque

205. What was the first film to pair Robert Taylor and Barbara Stanwyck?

A. *Artists and Models Abroad* (1938)
B. *Behold My Wife* (1934)
C. *His Brother's Wife* (1936)
D. *Times Square Lady* (1935)

206. Playwright Noël Coward appears in what film opposite Richard Burton and Elizabeth Taylor?

A. *Bluebeard* (1972)
B. *Boom!* (1968)

C. *The V.I.P.s* (1963)
D. *Who's Afraid of Virginia Woolf?* (1966)

207. Who costars with Jean Simmons in the 1954 film *She Couldn't Say No*?

A. Farley Granger
B. Robert Mitchum
C. Van Johnson
D. Victor Mature

The Man with a Cloak, 1951

208. Who is Joseph Cotten's costar in the 1951 film *The Man with a Cloak*?

A. Barbara Stanwyck
B. Elizabeth Taylor
C. Maureen O'Hara
D. Shelley Winters

209. Who is Kim Novak's leading man in the 1964 film *Kiss Me, Stupid*?

A. Dean Martin
B. Jack Lemmon
C. Jerry Lewis
D. Tony Curtis

210. In which of the following films does Anne Bancroft costar with real-life husband Mel Brooks?

A. *Fatso* (1980)
B. *Garbo Talks* (1984)
C. *To Be or Not to Be* (1983)
D. *Young Frankenstein* (1974)

North by Northwest, 1959

Chapter 9

GREAT
DIRECTORS

If you noticed the chiaroscuro lighting in *Touch of Evil* (1958) or the long takes using deep focus in *The Best Years of Our Lives* (1946) or the precise editing of the crop-dusting sequence in *North by Northwest* (1959), you're probably attuned to the work of the screen's greatest directors. The director is the man or (not often enough) woman who calls the shots. Depending on the production, he or she supervises script preparation, casts and rehearses the actors, determines the camera setups, and supervises at least the first cut. It's a demanding, complicated job, particularly with studio executives breathing down his or her neck every time a film threatens to go over budget or underperforms at previews.

Not every director puts a personal style on his or her films. For many, like Henry Hathaway at 20th Century-Fox, or Richard Thorpe at MGM or Archie Mayo at Warner Bros., the focus was to produce solid pictures within the constraints of studio production. During the height of studio power, there were a few celebrity directors: Cecil B. DeMille, Alfred Hitchcock, Orson Welles. But most were unknown until the fifties, when a group of French critics, including future directors François Truffaut and Jean-Luc Godard, began promoting the idea that the director was the film's true author, the auteur.

The most celebrated directors clearly demonstrate a personal style, a brand that distinguishes them from anybody else. Although they're both romantics, it is clear Frank Borzage's *7th Heaven* (1927) is not directed by the same man as John Cromwell's *Of Human Bondage* (1934). Vincente Minnelli and John Huston both directed films about dreamers, but there's no mistaking the former's *Lust for Life* (1956) for the latter's *Moulin Rouge* (1952).

And Akira Kurosawa would never have shot a sword fight in *Seven Samurai* (1954) the way John Sturges shot the gunfights in its western adaptation, *The Magnificent Seven* (1960).

In some cases, what distinguishes directors is their choice of story materials. Frank Capra preferred sentimental, populist comedies like *You Can't Take It with You* (1938), while Billy Wilder liked a little acid mixed in with the laughs, as in *The Apartment* (1960). Other directors marked their films by creating a stock company of actors whom they worked with repeatedly. The presence of Victor McLaglen and Wallace Ford marks *The Informer* (1935) as a John Ford film as surely as Robert De Niro and Harvey Keitel brand *Taxi Driver* (1976) as Martin Scorsese's work.

There's no set career path that leads to directing. Although modern helmers like Steven Spielberg, George Lucas, and Martin Scorsese are film school graduates, their predecessors came from all over the career map. Stanley Kubrick started as a photographer, Norman Z. McLeod and Frank Tashlin as animators, and Robert Wise as a film editor. Elia Kazan and George Cukor came from the theater, while John Frankenheimer and Delbert Mann learned their craft directing live television. Screenwriting offered an opening to Wilder and Ingmar Bergman, but Alan J. Pakula stepped out of the producer's office. And though Robert Redford and Barbra Streisand's move from acting to directing seems like something new, Cromwell and Erich von Stroheim beat them to the punch by decades.

For a long time, directing has seemed an exclusive club to which women need not apply. Actually, women were more prominent in the silent era, when Alice Guy-Blaché pioneered in directing story films and Lois Weber directed some of the first films to deal with social issues. With the coming of sound, Dorothy Arzner and Ida Lupino were the only women directing at the major studios. The idea still seemed new when Streisand took up the megaphone, so much so that despite the success of films like *Yentl* (1983) and *The Prince of Tides* (1991), she has yet to earn a directing nomination from the Academy.

Nor has the situation been much better for racial minorities. Oscar Micheaux and Spencer Williams did outstanding work in independent "race movies," a movement that started in reaction to *The Birth of a Nation* (1915) in the silent era, but black directors made no inroads in Hollywood until Warner Bros. picked up Gordon Parks's *The Learning Tree* in 1969. Although Ang Lee became the first non-white to win a directing Oscar (for 2005's *Brokeback Mountain*), only one African American has even been nominated (John Singleton for 1991's *Boyz n the Hood*). Despite critical acclaim for the deeply personal *Do the Right Thing* (1989) and *Malcolm X* (1992), Spike Lee has only received nominations for writing the former and producing the 1997 documentary *4 Little Girls*.

Despite the ongoing need for greater equality behind the camera, directors have for more than a century drawn on their individual talents and proclivities to create a dazzlingly diverse array of films.

1. Director John Cromwell acted in which of the following Robert Altman films?
   A. *3 Women* (1977)
   B. *McCabe and Mrs. Miller* (1971)
   C. *Nashville* (1975)
   D. *Short Cuts* (1993)

2. Which of the following directors never received an Oscar nomination?
   A. Billy Wilder
   B. Carol Reed
   C. George Cukor
   D. George Marshall

3. Before directing films, what type of graduate degree did Otto Preminger receive?
   A. Accounting
   B. Art history
   C. Law
   D. Medical

4. Prior to collaborating on three installments of the James Bond franchise, Terence Young had directed Sean Connery in which film?
   A. *A Night to Remember* (1958)
   B. *Action of the Tiger* (1957)
   C. *Corridor of Mirrors* (1948)
   D. *Storm Over the Nile* (1955)

5. Alfred Hitchcock narrated the prologue for which one of his films?
   A. *Strangers on a Train* (1951)
   B. *The Man Who Knew Too Much* (1956)
   C. *The Wrong Man* (1956)
   D. *Vertigo* (1958)

6. What film directed by Henry Hathaway deals with a gambler with psychic powers?
   A. *Now and Forever* (1934)
   B. *The Lives of a Bengal Lancer* (1935)
   C. *The Witching Hour* (1934)
   D. *Woman Obsessed* (1959)

7. What was George Axelrod's directorial debut?
   A. *Breakfast at Tiffany's* (1961)
   B. *Lord Love a Duck* (1966)
   C. *Phffft!* (1954)
   D. *The Manchurian Candidate* (1962)

8. James Garner plays the title character in what film directed by Delbert Mann?
   A. *Father Is a Bachelor* (1950)
   B. *Fitzwilly* (1967)
   C. *Marty* (1955)
   D. *Mister Buddwing* (1966)

9. In how many films did Lloyd Bacon direct James Cagney?
   A. 2
   B. 6
   C. 7
   D. 9

10. Alan Arkin and Rita Moreno share the screen in what film directed by Arthur Hiller?
    A. *Plaza Suite* (1971)
    B. *Popi* (1969)
    C. *Romantic Comedy* (1983)
    D. *Taking Care of Business* (1990)

11. Frank Capra won the Academy Award for Best Director for all of the following films except which one?
    A. *It Happened One Night* (1934)
    B. *Mr. Deeds Goes to Town* (1936)
    C. *The Miracle Woman* (1931)
    D. *You Can't Take It with You* (1938)

12. What film starring Dorothy McGuire was directed by Elia Kazan?
    A. *A Tree Grows in Brooklyn* (1945)
    B. *I Want You* (1951)
    C. *The Enchanted Cottage* (1945)
    D. *The Spiral Staircase* (1945)

13. George Stevens directed Cary Grant in all of the following films except for which one?

A. *Gunga Din* (1939)
B. *Penny Serenade* (1941)
C. *The More the Merrier* (1943)
D. *The Talk of the Town* (1942)

14. Which of the following directors did not contribute segments for the film *Boccaccio '70* (1962)?

A. Federico Fellini
B. Mario Monicelli
C. Roberto Rossellini
D. Vittorio De Sica

15. John Frankenheimer directed Marlon Brando in which of the following films?

A. *Reflections in a Golden Eye* (1967)
B. *The Island of Dr. Moreau* (1996)
C. *The Men* (1950)
D. *The Wild One* (1953)

16. *Return of the Secaucus Seven* (1980) was whose directorial debut?

A. John Carpenter
B. John Sayles
C. Michael Mann
D. Ron Howard

17. Raquel Welch plays "Queenie" in what film directed by James Ivory?

A. *Mr. & Mrs. Bridge* (1990)
B. *Quartet* (1981)
C. *Roseland* (1977)
D. *The Wild Party* (1975)

18. Ray Milland won the Academy Award for Best Actor in what film directed by Billy Wilder?

A. *Sabrina* (1954)
B. *The Emperor Waltz* (1948)
C. *The Fortune Cookie* (1966)
D. *The Lost Weekend* (1945)

19. Jack Arnold directed Peter Sellers in what film?

A. *I'm All Right Jack* (1959)
B. *The Millionairess* (1960)
C. *The Mouse That Roared* (1959)
D. *tom thumb* (1958)

20. Who was the second woman to be inducted to the Director's Guild?

A. Carol Reed
B. Dorothy Arzner
C. Ida Lupino
D. Lina Wertmuller

21. Barbra Streisand received an Academy nod for Best Song for which film that she also directed?

A. *A Star Is Born* (1976)
B. *The Mirror Has Two Faces* (1996)
C. *The Prince of Tides* (1991)
D. *Yentl* (1983)

22. Arthur Hiller directed Ray Milland in what film?

A. *Love Story* (1970)
B. *Plaza Suite* (1971)
C. *Romantic Comedy* (1983)
D. *The Wheeler Dealers* (1963)

23. How many times was George Sanders married?

A. 1
B. 2
C. 3
D. 4

24. What film starring Bing Crosby was directed by Blake Edwards?

A. *High Time* (1960)
B. *Just for You* (1952)
C. *Robin and the 7 Hoods* (1964)
D. *The Road to Hong Kong* (1962)

25. Who became the youngest director ever to be signed to a long-term deal to a major Hollywood studio?
    A. George Lucas
    B. Martin Scorsese
    C. Orson Welles
    D. Steven Spielberg

26. In what film directed by Alan J. Pakula does Brad Pitt star?
    A. *Consenting Adults* (1992)
    B. *Presumed Innocent* (1990)
    C. *See You in the Morning* (1989)
    D. *The Devil's Own* (1997)

27. Alexander Hall directed Shirley Temple in what film?
    A. *Carefree* (1938)
    B. *Little Miss Marker* (1934)
    C. *Neptune's Daughter* (1949)
    D. *Roberta* (1935)

28. Alfred Hitchcock had a forest of pine trees planted on an MGM soundstage for which film featuring James Mason?
    A. *North by Northwest* (1959)
    B. *Strangers on a Train* (1951)
    C. *The Birds* (1963)
    D. *Vertigo* (1958)

29. What film directed by John Cromwell is about a newlywed couple struggling through their first year of marriage?
    A. *Banjo on My Knee* (1936)
    B. *Made for Each Other* (1939)
    C. *So Ends Our Night* (1941)
    D. *The Enchanted Cottage* (1945)

30. What film costarring Valerie Hobson was directed by Raoul Walsh?
    A. *Jump for Glory* (1937)
    B. *No Escape* (1936)
    C. *The Silent Battle* (1939)
    D. *This Man Is News* (1938)

31. Robert Redford directs and stars in what film opposite Meryl Streep and Tom Cruise?
    A. *A River Runs Through It* (1992)
    B. *Lions for Lambs* (2007)
    C. *Spy Game* (2001)
    D. *The Natural* (1984)

32. Raoul Walsh directed which of the following Fay Wray pictures?
    A. *Black Moon* (1934)
    B. *Once to Every Woman* (1934)
    C. *The Bowery* (1933)
    D. *The Countess of Monte Cristo* (1934)

33. Harry Belafonte created most of his characters' dialogue in what film directed by Robert Altman?
    A. *Beyond Therapy* (1987)
    B. *Kansas City* (1996)
    C. *Secret Honor* (1984)
    D. *Vincent & Theo* (1990)

34. Although he never won for Best Director, how many times was Arthur Penn nominated for an Oscar?
    A. 0
    B. 2
    C. 3
    D. 4

35. George Stevens made his directorial debut with what short film?
    A. *High Gear* (1931)
    B. *Ladies Last* (1930)
    C. *Mama Loves Papa* (1931)
    D. *The Laurel-Hardy Murder Case* (1930)

36. Robert Redford made his Oscar-winning directorial debut in what film?
    A. *A River Runs Through It* (1992)
    B. *Ordinary People* (1980)
    C. *Promised Land* (1987)
    D. *The Solar Film* (1980)

answers found on page 554

37. Director Michael Powell originally developed his skills making quota quickies that resulted from what United Kingdom Parliamentary Act to stimulate the declining film industry?

A. Cinematograph Films Act of 1927
B. Film Industry Act of 1928
C. Motion Picture Act of 1926
D. Quota Act of 1926

38. What film costarring Denzel Washington was directed by Mira Nair?

A. *Glory* (1989)
B. *Mississippi Masala* (1991)
C. *Mo' Better Blues* (1990)
D. *The Preacher's Wife* (1996)

39. All of the following films starring Burgess Meredith were directed by Otto Preminger except which one?

A. *Advise and Consent* (1962)
B. *Hurry Sundown* (1967)
C. *Of Mice and Men* (1939)
D. *The Cardinal* (1963)

40. What film starring Charles Laughton was directed by Jean Renoir?

A. *Forever and a Day* (1943)
B. *It Started with Eve* (1941)
C. *Stand by for Action* (1942)
D. *This Land Is Mine* (1943)

41. Elia Kazan directed which of the following John Garfield pictures?

A. *Body and Soul* (1947)
B. *Four Daughters* (1938)
C. *Gentleman's Agreement* (1947)
D. *Out of the Fog* (1941)

42. Alexander Korda directed all of the following films except which one?

A. *Lust for Life* (1956)
B. *Rembrandt* (1936)
C. *That Hamilton Woman* (1941)
D. *The Private Life of Henry VIII* (1933)

43. Daniel Mann directed what film about singer Lillian Roth's battle with alcoholism?

A. *BUtterfield 8* (1960)
B. *I'll Cry Tomorrow* (1955)
C. *The Rose Tattoo* (1955)
D. *The Teahouse of the August Moon* (1956)

44. How did director John Sturges start his career in Hollywood?

A. Actor
B. Busboy
C. Editor
D. Stuntman

45. Director Richard Boleslawski moved to New York City with what fellow émigré?

A. Maria Ouspenskaya
B. Olga Baclanova
C. Billy Wilder
D. Yevgeni Vakhtangov

BUtterfield 8, 1960

46. What role does Elizabeth Taylor play in the 1960 film *BUtterfield 8*?

A. A secretary who finds true love with a coworker
B. A party girl who falls for a married man
C. A small-town model who moves to New York
D. A hard-headed businesswoman

47. In which of the following films directed by John Cromwell does Gary Cooper star?

A. *The Texan* (1930)
B. *Spitfire* (1934)
C. *The Silver Cord* (1933)
D. *This Man Is Mine* (1934)

48. Who was the director of the 1974 James Shigeta film *The Yakuza*?

A. Alan Parker
B. Nicolas Roeg
C. Sidney Lumet
D. Sydney Pollack

49. François Truffaut called which of Jacques Tati's films a "film that comes from another planet, where they make films differently"?

A. *Mon Oncle* (1958)
B. *Mr. Hulot's Holiday* (1953)
C. *Playtime* (1967)
D. *Traffic* (1971)

50. In what film directed by Jules Dassin does Ruby Dee star?

A. *10:30 P.M. Summer* (1966)
B. *Phaedra* (1962)
C. *Promise at Dawn* (1970)
D. *Up Tight!* (1968)

51. Although he never won for Best Director, how many times was Howard Hawks nominated for an Oscar?

A. 1
B. 3
C. 5
D. 6

52. José Ferrer directed all of the following films except which one?

A. *Cyrano de Bergerac* (1950)
B. *I Accuse!* (1958)
C. *Return to Peyton Place* (1961)
D. *State Fair* (1962)

53. Bette Davis starred in which of the following films directed by William Wyler?

A. *How to Steal a Million* (1966)
B. *Mrs. Miniver* (1942)
C. *The Heiress* (1949)
D. *The Little Foxes* (1941)

54. In which of the following films directed by Robert Benton does Nicole Kidman star?

A. *Billy Bathgate* (1991)
B. *Nadine* (1987)
C. *Nobody's Fool* (1994)
D. *Twilight* (1998)

55. Louis Malle first studied what at the Sorbonne before turning to film studies?

A. Art history
B. Biology
C. Literature
D. Political science

56. George Lucas has expressed in interviews that his *Star Wars* trilogy was influenced by which Akira Kurosawa film?

A. *Drunken Angel* (1948)
B. *Rashomon* (1950)
C. *Seven Samurai* (1954)
D. *The Hidden Fortress* (1958)

57. During the fifties, sixties, and seventies, which of the following television series did Ida Lupino not work on as director?

A. *Bewitched*
B. *Gilligan's Island*
C. *I Love Lucy*
D. *Twilight Zone*

58. Director Robert Rossen won the Directors Guild of America Award for what film?

A. *All the King's Men* (1949)
B. *Edge of Darkness* (1943)
C. *Mambo* (1954)
D. *The Hustler* (1961)

answers found on page 555

Spotlight on
VINCENTE **MINNELLI** (1903–1986)

The trip from window dresser to major Hollywood director isn't a long one if you realize that both job descriptions include the capturing of dreams, and that's just what Vincente Minnelli did in a series of films that were among the most entertaining of his day. Whether helping MGM producer Arthur Freed reinvent the musical with sophisticated, visually witty productions like *An American in Paris* (1951) and *Gigi* (1958) or finding the emotional truth underlying intense melodramas like *Some Came Running* (1958) and family comedies like *Father of the Bride* (1950), Minnelli gave audiences the chance to move into a world that was

Lust for Life, 1956

somehow better than their own. Later critics have sometimes dismissed him as merely a "visual stylist," and certainly even his weakest films are impeccably designed and shot. But beneath the prettiness, there's a solid emotional base that bursts out most dramatically in moments like Margaret O'Brien's Halloween-night walk in *Meet Me in St. Louis* (1944), Lana Turner's car crash in *The Bad and the Beautiful* (1952), and Kirk Douglas's manic painting as Vincent van Gogh in *Lust for Life* (1956). It's a cinema of dreams and dreamers, where even the most violent moments can seem magical.

The Bad and the Beautiful, 1952

1. What film earned Vincente Minnelli his only Academy Award for directing?

   A. *An American in Paris* (1951)

   B. *Bells Are Ringing* (1960)

   C. *Gigi* (1958)

   D. *The Bad and the Beautiful* (1952)

2. Vincente Minnelli directed Gloria Grahame in what film set in a psychiatric clinic?

   A. *Not as a Stranger* (1955)

   B. *The Cobweb* (1955)

   C. *The Glass Wall* (1953)

   D. *The Man Who Never Was* (1956)

3. Vincente Minnelli directed Laurence Naismith in what film?

   A. *Escape from Fort Bravo* (1953)

   B. *Lust for Life* (1956)

   C. *The Gypsy and the Gentleman* (1958)

   D. *The Man Who Would Be King* (1975)

4. Deborah Kerr reprises her Broadway role in which film directed by Vincente Minnelli?

   A. *Kismet* (1955)

   B. *Love on the Dole* (1941)

   C. *Tea and Sympathy* (1956)

   D. *The Bad and the Beautiful* (1952)

5. Vincente Minnelli directed Harry Davenport and Mary Astor in what musical?

   A. *Daddy Long Legs* (1955)

   B. *Meet Me in St. Louis* (1944)

   C. *The Band Wagon* (1953)

   D. *The Belle of New York* (1952)

answers found on page 555

59. Samuel Fuller appeared in which film directed by Aki Kaurismaki?

A. *Gibellina, Metamorphosis of a Melody* (1992)
B. *La Vie de Bohème* (1992)
C. *Sons* (1989)
D. *The Madonna and the Dragon* (1990)

60. Jules Dassin directed his wife Melina Mercouri in all of the following films except which one?

A. *He Who Must Die* (1957)
B. *Never on Sunday* (1960)
C. *The Law* (1959)
D. *Up Tight!* (1968)

61. Alfred Hitchcock believed that he was under surveillance by the FBI during production of which film starring Cary Grant?

A. *North by Northwest* (1959)
B. *Notorious* (1946)
C. *Suspicion* (1941)
D. *To Catch a Thief* (1955)

62. What film earned David Lean his first Academy Award nomination for Best Director?

A. *Brief Encounter* (1945)
B. *Doctor Zhivago* (1965)
C. *Great Expectations* (1946)
D. *Lawrence of Arabia* (1962)

63. For what film did Alan J. Pakula receive his only Academy Award nomination as Best Director?

A. *All the President's Men* (1976)
B. *Klute* (1971)
C. *Presumed Innocent* (1990)
D. *Sophie's Choice* (1982)

64. Anthony Asquith directed and wrote the screenplay for what heist drama that featured a young Michael Crawford?

A. *Inside Out* (1975)
B. *The Games* (1970)
C. *The Window* (1949)
D. *Two Living, One Dead* (1961)

65. In his later life, director George Roy Hill taught at what university?

A. Columbia
B. Harvard
C. Northwestern
D. Yale

66. Who replaced director David O. Selznick on the set of *I'll Be Seeing You* (1944)?

A. Edwin L. Marin
B. George Cukor
C. Walter Lang
D. William Dieterle

67. Arthur Hiller directed Al Pacino in what film?

A. *Author! Author!* (1982)
B. *Nightwing* (1979)
C. *Plaza Suite* (1971)
D. *The Man in the Glass Booth* (1975)

68. "Can of Beans" was the code name during production on what film directed and cowritten by Billy Wilder?

A. *Some Like It Hot* (1959)
B. *Sunset Blvd.* (1950)
C. *The Apartment* (1960)
D. *The Emperor Waltz* (1948)

69. Norman Z. McLeod directed W. C. Fields and Alison Skipworth in which segment of *If I Had a Million* (1932)?

A. "Death Cell"
B. "Grandma"
C. "Road Hogs"
D. "The Forger"

70. Who was the first director to be nominated twice in the same year?

A. Clarence Brown
B. Ernst Lubitsch
C. Josef von Sternberg
D. King Vidor

answers found on page 555

71. What was Lucien Ballard's only feature-length collaboration with director Blake Edwards?

    A. *Darling Lili* (1970)
    B. *The Party* (1968)
    C. *The Pink Panther* (1963)
    D. *Victor/Victoria* (1995)

72. Samuel Fuller was featured as an actor in which film short directed by Robinson Savary?

    A. *Falstaff on the Moon* (1993)
    B. *Precious Images* (1986)
    C. *The Lunch Date* (1990)
    D. *Wild Wings* (1966)

73. In 1940 Jules Dassin apprenticed under what famous director?

    A. Alfred Hitchcock
    B. George Cukor
    C. John Ford
    D. William Wellman

74. Jean Simmons plays "The Blonde" in what film directed by Delbert Mann?

    A. *Lover Come Back* (1961)
    B. *Marty* (1955)
    C. *Mister Buddwing* (1966)
    D. *No Time for Love* (1943)

75. What film starring Nancy Carroll was directed by William Wellman?

    A. *Dangerous Paradise* (1930)
    B. *Honey* (1930)
    C. *Personal Maid* (1931)
    D. *The Shopworn Angel* (1928)

76. What famous actor made his directing debut with the 1957 Richard Widmark film *Time Limit*?

    A. Clint Eastwood
    B. Gene Kelly
    C. Karl Malden
    D. Marlon Brando

77. In which of the following films did director Henry Hathaway give Randolph Scott his first starring role?

    A. *Come On Marines* (1934)
    B. *Heritage of the Desert* (1932)
    C. *The Lives of a Bengal Lancer* (1935)
    D. *The Trail of the Lonesome Pine* (1936)

78. George Stevens formed Liberty Films with William Wyler, Frank Capra, and Samuel J. Briskin in what year?

    A. 1938
    B. 1945
    C. 1949
    D. 1952

79. Robert Duvall made his feature directorial debut with what film?

    A. *Angelo, My Love* (1983)
    B. *The Apostle* (1997)
    C. *The Great Santini* (1979)
    D. *The Natural* (1984)

80. Robert Aldrich directed all of the following films starring Ernest Borgnine except which one?

    A. *Barabba* (1961)
    B. *Hustle* (1975)
    C. *The Dirty Dozen* (1967)
    D. *The Flight of the Phoenix* (1965)

81. John Cromwell directed all of the following films starring Kay Francis except which one?

    A. *For the Defense* (1930)
    B. *In Name Only* (1939)
    C. *Scandal Sheet* (1931)
    D. *Stolen Holiday* (1937)

82. Jack Lemmon was the narrator in what film directed by Robert Redford?

    A. *A River Runs Through It* (1992)
    B. *Ordinary People* (1980)
    C. *The Horse Whisperer* (1998)
    D. *The Legend of Bagger Vance* (2000)

83. In what film directed by John Cromwell does Bette Davis star?

A. *Dead Reckoning* (1947)
B. *Made for Each Other* (1939)
C. *Of Human Bondage* (1934)
D. *Spitfire* (1934)

84. Anthony Hopkins and Anne Bancroft costar in which biopic directed by Richard Attenborough?

A. *King Creole* (1958)
B. *Lonely Are the Brave* (1962)
C. *Voice in the Mirror* (1958)
D. *Young Winston* (1972)

85. Robert Rossen was nominated for the Directors Guild of America Award for what film?

A. *A Walk in the Sun* (1945)
B. *Alexander the Great* (1956)
C. *Lilith* (1964)
D. *The Sea Wolf* (1941)

86. What was David Mamet's directorial debut?

A. *American Buffalo* (1996)
B. *Glengarry Glen Ross* (1992)
C. *House of Games* (1987)
D. *The Postman Always Rings Twice* (1981)

87. What film costarring Geraldine Page was adapted and directed by Francis Ford Coppola?

A. *Sweet Bird of Youth* (1962)
B. *The Day of the Locust* (1975)
C. *Walls of Glass* (1985)
D. *You're a Big Boy Now* (1966)

88. Alfred Hitchcock directed Ethel Barrymore in which of the following films?

A. *Rebecca* (1940)
B. *Strangers on a Train* (1951)
C. *The 39 Steps* (1935)
D. *The Paradine Case* (1947)

89. What film directed by Alexander Hall is a remake of 1941's *Tall, Dark and Handsome*?

A. *Excuse My Dust* (1951)
B. *Love That Brute* (1950)
C. *The Fuller Brush Man* (1948)
D. *The Pleasure of His Company* (1961)

90. Although he never won for Best Director, how many times was Ernst Lubitsch nominated for an Oscar?

A. 0
B. 2
C. 3
D. 5

91. Vincent Price played the title role in which film directed by Samuel Fuller?

A. *I Shot Jesse James* (1949)
B. *Merrill's Marauders* (1962)
C. *Run of the Arrow* (1957)
D. *The Baron of Arizona* (1950)

Blow-Up, 1966

92. Who was nominated for an Academy Award as Best Director for his work on the 1966 film *Blow-Up*?

A. Federico Fellini
B. Michelangelo Antonioni
C. Roberto Rossellini
D. Roman Polanski

answers found on page 555

93. What film directed by John Cromwell costarred Ronald Colman and David Niven?

A. *Algiers* (1938)
B. *Son of Fury: The Story of Benjamin Blake* (1942)
C. *The Prisoner of Zenda* (1937)
D. *The Racket* (1951)

94. In what film was Jean Simmons first directed by her second husband, Richard Brooks?

A. *Elmer Gantry* (1960)
B. *Spartacus* (1960)
C. *The Big Country* (1958)
D. *The Grass Is Greener* (1960)

95. What is the only film in which Sir John Mills is credited as director?

A. *Sky West and Crooked* (1966)
B. *The Baby and the Battleship* (1956)
C. *The Parent Trap* (1961)
D. *The Rocking Horse Winner* (1950)

96. Director Ingmar Bergman is sometimes credited by what name?

A. Buntel Eriksson
B. Eric Bergman
C. Irving Bergman
D. James Berg

97. Dick Van Dyke starred in the 1979 film *The Runner Stumbles*. Who directed it?

A. Blake Edwards
B. John Frankenheimer
C. Samuel Fuller
D. Stanley Kramer

98. How many films did George Axelrod direct?

A. 0
B. 2
C. 21
D. 8

99. Cary Grant starred in what film directed by John Cromwell?

A. *Anna and the King of Siam* (1946)
B. *In Name Only* (1939)
C. *So Ends Our Night* (1941)
D. *Son of Fury: The Story of Benjamin Blake* (1942)

100. Director Michael Powell worked where before entering the film industry?

A. A bank
B. A library
C. A pub
D. A theater

101. Which of the following is a true statement about director George Roy Hill?

A. He had an M.A. in zoology.
B. He was a pilot.
C. He was best friends with Clark Gable.
D. He was once married to Marilyn Monroe.

102. What film directed by Barbra Streisand was nominated for an Academy Award as Best Picture?

A. *Nuts* (1987)
B. *The Mirror Has Two Faces* (1996)
C. *The Prince of Tides* (1991)
D. *Yentl* (1983)

103. Anthony Quinn provided the voice narration for which documentary directed by Budd Boetticher?

A. *Arruza* (1972)
B. *Navajo* (1952)
C. *The Quiet One* (1948)
D. *Torero* (1962)

104. David Niven won a Best Actor Oscar for less than twenty minutes of screen time in what film directed by Delbert Mann?

A. *A Piece of Cake* (1948)
B. *Love in Pawn* (1953)
C. *Room to Let* (1950)
D. *Separate Tables* (1958)

105. In what film did Lewis Milestone direct scenes for Howard Hughes with no credit?

A. *Hell's Angels* (1930)
B. *Scarface* (1932)
C. *The Outlaw* (1943)
D. *Vendetta* (1950)

106. What famous actor directed the 1958 Charlton Heston film *The Buccaneer*?

A. Anthony Quinn
B. Karl Malden
C. Kirk Douglas
D. Sidney Poitier

107. Although he never won for Best Director, how many times was Stanley Kubrick nominated for an Oscar?

A. 0
B. 2
C. 3
D. 4

108. Although he never won for Best Director, how many times was Robert Altman nominated for an Oscar?

A. 3
B. 5
C. 6
D. 8

109. Roger Corman returned to directing after a brief retirement with what film?

A. *A Cry in the Wild* (1990)
B. *Frankenstein Unbound* (1990)
C. *Overexposed* (1990)
D. *Streets* (1990)

110. Two years after his death, Ed Wood was given what award for Worst Director of All Time?

A. Golden Raspberry
B. Golden Toilet Award
C. Golden Turkey Award
D. Infamy Award

111. For which of the following films did Robert Benton win the Academy Award for Best Director?

A. *Billy Bathgate* (1991)
B. *Kramer vs. Kramer* (1979)
C. *Nobody's Fool* (1994)
D. *Places in the Heart* (1984)

112. In which of the following films directed by Mark Robson does Edward G. Robinson star?

A. *From the Terrace* (1960)
B. *Limbo* (1972)
C. *The Prize* (1963)
D. *Von Ryan's Express* (1965)

113. Richard Dreyfuss and Holly Hunter costar in what film directed by Steven Spielberg?

A. *Close Encounters of the Third Kind* (1977)
B. *Always* (1989)
C. *Empire of the Sun* (1987)
D. *Raiders of the Lost Ark* (1981)

114. What film earned John Farrow his only Oscar nomination for Best Director?

A. *Around the World in Eighty Days* (1956)
B. *His Kind of Woman* (1951)
C. *Ride, Vaquero!* (1953)
D. *Wake Island* (1942)

115. Director Ingmar Bergman and Max von Sydow made how many films together?

A. 10
B. 13
C. 3
D. 7

116. Alan J. Pakula directed the 1974 thriller *The Parallax View*. Who starred in it?

A. Charlton Heston
B. Lee Marvin
C. Steve McQueen
D. Warren Beatty

117. What film earned George Lucas his first Academy Award nomination for Best Director?

A. *American Graffiti* (1973)
B. *Star Wars* (1977)
C. *Star Wars: Episode III—Revenge of the Sith* (2005)
D. *THX 1138* (1971)

118. Which director was known to make storyboards for his films in the form of full-scale paintings?

A. Akira Kurosawa
B. Alfred Hitchcock
C. Orson Welles
D. Sergei Eisenstein

119. Director George Marshall plays the villain in which Laurel and Hardy film?

A. *Babes in Toyland* (1934)
B. *Busy Bodies* (1933)
C. *On the Loose* (1931)
D. *Pack Up Your Troubles* (1932)

120. Robert Taylor starred in all of the following films directed by Richard Thorpe except which one?

A. *All the Brothers Were Valiant* (1953)
B. *Quentin Durward* (1955)
C. *The House of the Seven Hawks* (1959)
D. *The Prodigal* (1955)

121. What film starring Jean Simmons was directed by Robert Wise?

A. *Divorce American Style* (1967)
B. *Home Before Dark* (1958)
C. *The Big Country* (1958)
D. *This Could Be the Night* (1957)

122. Roger Corman made his directorial debut with what film?

A. *Five Guns West* (1955)
B. *Highway Dragnet* (1954)
C. *Monster from the Ocean Floor* (1954)
D. *The Fast and the Furious* (1954)

123. Richard Thorpe directed Elvis Presley in the 1963 film *Fun in Acapulco* and what other film, which was released in 1957?

A. *Follow the Boys*
B. *Jailhouse Rock*
C. *Kissin' Cousins*
D. *Viva Las Vegas*

124. Viewers of what William Castle film were given glasses with blue-and-red cellophane that allowed them to see or remove ghosts from the picture?

A. *13 Ghosts* (1960)
B. *House on Haunted Hill* (1959)
C. *Macabre* (1958)
D. *The Tingler* (1959)

125. What film directed by John Cromwell is about a feisty, independent mountain girl?

A. *Banjo on My Knee* (1936)
B. *Made for Each Other* (1939)
C. *Spitfire* (1934)
D. *This Man Is Mine* (1934)

126. Sam Wood directed Jerry Austin in what film?

A. *Saratoga Trunk* (1945)
B. *The Barretts of Wimpole Street* (1957)
C. *The Long Memory* (1952)
D. *The Valiant* (1962)

127. Steven Spielberg directed Audrey Hepburn in which film?

A. *Always* (1989)
B. *Robin and Marian* (1976)
C. *They All Laughed* (1981)
D. *Two for the Road* (1967)

128. Chuck Jones directed a short animated
sequence in what film starring Robin Williams?

A. *Jumanji* (1995)
B. *Mrs. Doubtfire* (1993)
C. *The World According to Garp* (1982)
D. *Toys* (1992)

129. In which of the following François Truffaut
films does Leslie Caron appear?

A. *Farenheit 451* (1966)
B. *Shoot the Piano Player* (1960)
C. *The Man Who Loved Women* (1977)
D. *The Wild Child* (1970)

130. What film starring Burgess Meredith was
directed by Ernst Lubitsch?

A. *Magnificent Doll* (1946)
B. *That Uncertain Feeling* (1941)
C. *The Cardinal* (1963)
D. *Tom, Dick and Harry* (1941)

131. Actor Dirk Bogarde made two films with director Luchino Visconti. One of them was *Death
in Venice* (1971). What was the other?

A. *Days of Glory* (1945)
B. *The Damned* (1969)
C. *The Leopard* (1963)
D. *White Nights* (1957)

132. Faye Dunaway has worked with all these directors except which one?

A. Elia Kazan
B. John Huston
C. Martin Scorsese
D. Norman Jewison

133. What film starring Jean Harlow was directed by
Tod Browning?

A. *Goldie* (1931)
B. *Iron Man* (1931)
C. *The Beast of the City* (1932)
D. *The Secret Six* (1931)

134. What picture directed by Delbert Mann was
the first commercial film shown on a United
Airlines flight?

A. *A Piece of Cake* (1948)
B. *Love in Pawn* (1953)
C. *Quick Before It Melts* (1964)
D. *Room to Let* (1950)

135. Katharine Ross appeared in what film directed
by Brian DePalma?

A. *Body Double* (1984)
B. *Dressed to Kill* (1980)
C. *Get to Know Your Rabbit* (1972)
D. *The Fury* (1978)

136. Director John Frankenheimer graduated from
what college?

A. Bowdoin College
B. College of William and Mary
C. Rollins College
D. Williams College

137. Gary Cooper starred in all of the following
films directed by Henry Hathaway except what?

A. *Garden of Evil* (1954)
B. *I Loved a Soldier* (1936)
C. *Lest We Forget* (1937)
D. *Now and Forever* (1934)

138. In what country did director Jules Dassin spend
the last thirty years of his life?

A. England
B. France
C. Greece
D. Spain

139. Billy Wilder owned more than sixty what?

A. Baseball caps
B. Cashmere sweaters
C. Golf shoes
D. Sunglasses

answers found on page 555

Mogambo, 1953

140. Cinematographer Freddie Young shot the 1953 film *Mogambo*. Who was the director?

A. George Cukor
B. John Ford
C. John Huston
D. Vincente Minnelli

141. Who replaced director Norman Z. McLeod for the third film in the Topper series, *Topper Returns* (1941)?

A. Alexander Hall
B. Richard Thorpe
C. Roy Del Ruth
D. W. S. Van Dyke

142. Donald Pleasence starred in the 1966 film *Cul-de-sac*. Who was the director?

A. George Roy Hill
B. Roman Polanski
C. Sam Peckinpah
D. William Friedkin

143. Deborah Kerr plays the role of Princess Flavia in what film directed by Richard Thorpe?

A. *Quo Vadis* (1951)
B. *The Prisoner of Zenda* (1952)
C. *The Prodigal* (1955)
D. *The Proud and Profane* (1956)

144. Katharine Hepburn starred in what film directed by John Cromwell?

A. *Ann Vickers* (1933)

B. *Anna and the King of Siam* (1946)
C. *Of Human Bondage* (1934)
D. *Spitfire* (1934)

145. Lupe Velez starred in which film directed by Cecil B. DeMille?

A. *Dynamite* (1929)
B. *Forbidden Fruit* (1921)
C. *The Squaw Man* (1914)
D. *This Day and Age* (1933)

146. What film costarring Ernest Borgnine was directed by Sam Peckinpah?

A. *Ice Station Zebra* (1968)
B. *Marty* (1955)
C. *The Dirty Dozen* (1967)
D. *The Wild Bunch* (1969)

147. Louis Malle made his U.S. film debut with what feature?

A. *Atlantic City* (1980)
B. *Murmur of the Heart* (1971)
C. *My Dinner with Andre* (1981)
D. *Pretty Baby* (1978)

148. Although he never won for Best Director, how many times was Akira Kurosawa nominated for an Oscar?

A. 1
B. 3
C. 4
D. 5

149. Arthur Hiller directed Rock Hudson in what film?

A. *Spartacus* (1960)
B. *The Beguiled* (1971)
C. *Tobruk* (1967)
D. *Walls of Glass* (1985)

answers found on page 555

150. Charles Coburn won an Oscar for Best Supporting Actor in what film directed by George Stevens?

A. *Gunga Din* (1939)
B. *The More the Merrier* (1943)
C. *The Talk of the Town* (1942)
D. *Woman of the Year* (1942)

151. What film directed by John Frankenheimer is about a middle-aged man who leaves his old life behind and is given a new identity?

A. *Seconds* (1966)
B. *Seven Days in May* (1964)
C. *The Fixer* (1968)
D. *The Train* (1964)

152. Rita Moreno played the role of Claudia Zimmer in what film written and directed by its star, Alan Alda?

A. *A New Life* (1988)
B. *Betsy's Wedding* (1990)
C. *Sweet Liberty* (1986)
D. *The Four Seasons* (1981)

153. Jack Lemmon starred in what film directed by Robert Altman?

A. *A Prairie Home Companion* (2006)
B. *Cookie's Fortune* (1999)
C. *Nashville* (1975)
D. *Short Cuts* (1993)

154. In which of the following films directed by Oliver Stone does Jack Lemmon star?

A. *JFK* (1991)
B. *Nixon* (1995)
C. *Platoon* (1986)
D. *Wall Street* (1987)

155. Richard Dreyfuss and Barbara Hershey share the screen in what film written and directed by Barry Levinson?

A. *Diner* (1982)
B. *Rain Man* (1988)
C. *Tin Men* (1987)
D. *Toys* (1992)

156. What was the first film featuring an Alfred Hitchcock cameo?

A. *The Farmer's Wife* (1928)
B. *The Lodger* (1927)
C. *The Mountain Eagle* (1926)
D. *The Pleasure Garden* (1925)

157. Frank Capra directed Fay Wray in which of the following films?

A. *Dirigible* (1931)
B. *Madame Spy* (1934)
C. *Master of Men* (1933)
D. *The Bowery* (1933)

158. What film was not directed by John Sturges in 1947?

A. *For the Love of Rusty*
B. *Glamour Girl*
C. *Keeper of the Bees*
D. *Thunderbolt*

159. What was John Sturges's mainstream directorial debut?

A. *Alias Mr. Twilight* (1946)
B. *For the Love of Rusty* (1947)
C. *The Magnificent Yankee* (1950)
D. *The Man Who Dared* (1946)

160. Rita Hayworth and Deborah Kerr share the screen in what film directed by Delbert Mann?

A. *A Piece of Cake* (1948)
B. *Love in Pawn* (1953)
C. *Room to Let* (1950)
D. *Separate Tables* (1958)

answers found on page 555

161. Kirk Douglas starred in what film directed by William Wyler?

A. *Carrie* (1952)
B. *Detective Story* (1951)
C. *Friendly Persuasion* (1956)
D. *The Desperate Hours* (1955)

162. Jane Fonda starred in all of the following films directed by Alan J. Pakula except which one?

A. *Comes a Horseman* (1978)
B. *Klute* (1971)
C. *Rollover* (1981)
D. *See You in the Morning* (1989)

163. Inger Stevens and Charles Boyer costar in what adventure film directed by Anthony Quinn?

A. *Many Rivers to Cross* (1955)
B. *Quentin Durward* (1955)
C. *The Buccaneer* (1958)
D. *Valley of the Kings* (1954)

164. Charles Laughton starred in the 1932 film *The Sign of the Cross*. Who directed it?

A. Alfred Hitchcock
B. Cecil B. DeMille
C. Erich von Stroheim
D. Victor Fleming

165. Barbra Streisand directed the 1991 film *The Prince of Tides*. How many Academy Award nominations did it receive?

A. 2
B. 3
C. 5
D. 7

166. Samuel Fuller made a cameo appearance in which film written and directed by Jean-Luc Godard?

A. *A Film Like Any Other* (1968)
B. *All's Well* (1972)
C. *Le Vent d'Est* (1970)
D. *Pierrot le Fou* (1965)

167. A woman's affair with her stepson is at the heart of what film directed by Jules Dassin?

A. *Circle of Two* (1980)
B. *Never on Sunday* (1960)
C. *Phaedra* (1962)
D. *The Affairs of Martha* (1942)

168. What was the first feature directed by George Marshall?

A. *Houdini* (1953)
B. *Love's Lariat* (1916)
C. *Scared Stiff* (1953)
D. *The Blue Dahlia* (1946)

169. What director lured Audrey Hepburn back to the screen after a nine-year hiatus to star in *Robin and Marian* (1976)?

A. Billy Wilder
B. Carol Reed
C. Michael Curtiz
D. Richard Lester

170. Ethel Waters and Julie Harris costar in what film directed by Fred Zinnemann?

A. *The Barretts of Wimpole Street* (1957)
B. *The Long Memory* (1952)
C. *The Member of the Wedding* (1952)
D. *The Valiant* (1962)

171. What film starring Janet Gaynor was directed by Raoul Walsh?

A. *Lucky Star* (1929)
B. *Paddy the Next Best Thing* (1933)
C. *Tess of the Storm Country* (1932)
D. *The Man Who Came Back* (1931)

172. What holiday film earned director Henry Koster his only Oscar nomination?

A. *A Christmas Carol* (1951)
B. *Holiday Affair* (1949)
C. *Miracle on 34th Street* (1947)
D. *The Bishop's Wife* (1947)

Spotlight on
JOHN **FORD** (1894–1973)

John Ford's films defined the image of the United States on screen. Whether turning the winning of the West into visual poetry, saluting the heroism of men at war, or celebrating the immigrant's (particularly the Irishman's) dream of a new life, he was a profoundly American film director. He was also one of the most acclaimed, winning more Best Director Oscars than anyone else—for *The Informer* (1935), *The Grapes of Wrath* (1940), *How Green Was My Valley* (1941), and *The Quiet Man* (1952)—along with two wins for his wartime documentaries. His style was unmistakable. If you saw a western with location footage in Utah's Monument Valley, if you heard "Shall We Gather at the River" on the soundtrack, if you saw actors like John Wayne, Maureen O'Hara, Victor McLaglen, or Ward Bond in long shot against a rugged landscape, you could be pretty certain it was a John Ford picture. Never one to brag about his art, the most Ford would say about directing was, "The secret is to make films that please the public and also allow the director to reveal his personality." That's exactly what he did, better than nearly anyone else.

The Informer, 1935

How the West Was Won, 1962

1. **Director John Ford gave Woody Strode the title role in what feature?**

   A. *African Treasure* (1952)

   B. *Caribbean* (1952)

   C. *Sergeant Rutledge* (1960)

   D. *Son of Sinbad* (1955)

2. **Besides *Mister Roberts* (1955), in what other movie did John Ford direct James Cagney?**

   A. *Mogambo* (1953)

   B. *The Fighting 69th* (1940)

   C. *Torpedo Squadron* (1942)

   D. *What Price Glory* (1952)

3. **Not including *How the West Was Won* (1962), how many films did Henry Fonda make with John Ford?**

   A. 5

   B. 6

   C. 7

   D. 9

4. **James Stewart and Shirley Jones share the screen in John Ford's *Two Rode Together* (1961) and what other film?**

   A. *Royal Wedding* (1951)

   B. *The Cheyenne Social Club* (1970)

   C. *The Notorious Landlady* (1962)

   D. *The Singer Not the Song* (1961)

5. **What film was the last western directed by John Ford?**

   A. *Cheyenne Autumn* (1964)

   B. *Escape from Fort Bravo* (1953)

   C. *The Wild Bunch* (1969)

   D. *Wild Rovers* (1971)

---

answers found on page 555

173. Robert Redford directed Brad Pitt and Brenda Blethyn in what film?

A. *A River Runs Through It* (1992)
B. *Ordinary People* (1980)
C. *The Electric Horseman* (1979)
D. *The Legend of Bagger Vance* (2000)

174. Although he has never won for Best Director, how many times has Spike Lee been nominated for an Oscar?

A. 0
B. 2
C. 3
D. 5

175. All of the following films in the Tarzan franchise were directed by Richard Thorpe except which one?

A. *Tarzan Finds a Son!* (1939)
B. *Tarzan, the Ape Man* (1932)
C. *Tarzan's New York Adventure* (1942)
D. *Tarzan's Secret Treasure* (1941)

176. Besides being a writer and director, Delmer Daves also earned a law degree from what university?

A. Harvard
B. Oxford
C. Stanford
D. Yale

177. What was director Jack Arnold's first science fiction film?

A. *Creature from the Black Lagoon* (1954)
B. *Girls in the Night* (1953)
C. *It Came from Outer Space* (1953)
D. *The Glass Web* (1953)

178. In which of the following films directed by Robert Benton does Bruce Willis appear?

A. *Nobody's Fool* (1994)
B. *Still of the Night* (1982)
C. *The Human Stain* (2003)
D. *Twilight* (1998)

179. How many times did John Cromwell receive an Academy Award nomination for Best Director?

A. 0
B. 1
C. 2
D. 3

180. Scenes in what picture directed by and starring Clint Eastwood were filmed at the Monterey Jazz Festival?

A. *High Plains Drifter* (1973)
B. *Play Misty for Me* (1971)
C. *The Gauntlet* (1977)
D. *Thunderbolt and Lightfoot* (1974)

181. Which of the following statements is true about film director John Cromwell?

A. He gave Paul Newman his first job in movies.
B. He was blacklisted in Hollywood.
C. He was once married to Carole Lombard.
D. He was one of the Hollywood Ten.

182. Arthur Hiller directed which biopic based on the life of a baseball legend?

A. *Honky Tonk Freeway* (1981)
B. *Taking Care of Business* (1990)
C. *The Babe* (1992)
D. *Walls of Glass* (1985)

183. Ronald Colman plays the title role in what film directed by Joseph L. Mankiewicz?

A. *Julius Caesar* (1953)
B. *The Late George Apley* (1947)
C. *The Mysterious Dr. Fu Manchu* (1929)
D. *Young Mr. Lincoln* (1939)

184. All of the following films starring Merle Oberon were directed by Alexander Korda except which one?

A. *The Lion Has Wings* (1939)
B. *The Private Life of Don Juan* (1934)
C. *The Scarlet Pimpernel* (1934)
D. *Wedding Rehearsal* (1932)

answers found on pages 555–556

Jezebel, 1938

185. What director purchased Bette Davis's Oscar for *Jezebel* (1938) at a Sotheby's auction in order to return it to the Academy?

A. Curtis Hanson
B. Quentin Tarantino
C. Steven Spielberg
D. William Wyler

186. All of the following characteristics were true of director Akira Kurosawa except for which one?

A. Edited his own films
B. Height of under six feet tall
C. Perfectionist
D. Required actors to live in their costumes prior to filming

187. George Roy Hill had a lifelong love of what?

A. Aviation
B. Deep-sea diving
C. Fishing
D. Restoring old houses

188. Norman Z. McLeod directed Bob Hope in five films. Which of the following is not one of them?

A. *Alias Jesse James* (1959)
B. *Road to Rio* (1947)
C. *The Great Lover* (1949)
D. *The Paleface* (1948)

189. Director Zoltan Korda made his English-language directorial debut with what film?

A. *Flight of Fancy* (1952)
B. *Men of Tomorrow* (1932)
C. *Queen Christina* (1933)
D. *The Magic Box* (1952)

190. Burt Lancaster starred in all of the following films directed by John Frankenheimer except which one?

A. *All Fall Down* (1962)
B. *Birdman of Alcatraz* (1962)
C. *Seven Days in May* (1964)
D. *The Train* (1964)

191. Otto Preminger received his first Academy nomination for Best Director for what film?

A. *Anatomy of a Murder* (1959)
B. *Bunny Lake Is Missing* (1965)
C. *Laura* (1944)
D. *The Cardinal* (1963)

192. Anthony Quinn made his directorial debut in which film that was a remake of the Cecil B. DeMille version in which Quinn was featured as an actor two decades earlier?

A. *Daughter of Shanghai* (1937)
B. *The Buccaneer* (1958)
C. *The Ghost Breakers* (1940)
D. *Waikiki Wedding* (1937)

193. Blake Edwards directed all of the following films starring Jack Lemmon except which one?

A. *Days of Wine and Roses* (1962)
B. *That's Life!* (1986)
C. *The Great Race* (1965)
D. *Under the Yum Yum Tree* (1963)

194. When did director Robert Rossen appear before the House Un-American Activities Committee?

A. 1949
B. 1953
C. 1957
D. 1961

answers found on page 556

195. Director Joseph L. Mankiewicz referred to what film as "the toughest three pictures I ever made"?

    A. *All About Eve* (1950)
    B. *Cleopatra* (1963)
    C. *Julius Caesar* (1953)
    D. *The Barefoot Contessa* (1954)

196. Robert Duvall starred in George Lucas's directorial debut. What was it called?

    A. *American Graffiti* (1973)
    B. *Lawman* (1971)
    C. *THX 1138* (1971)
    D. *Tomorrow* (1972)

197. David Lean directed James Donald in what film opposite William Holden?

    A. *The Barretts of Wimpole Street* (1957)
    B. *The Bridge on the River Kwai* (1957)
    C. *The Long Memory* (1952)
    D. *The Valiant* (1962)

198. Samuel Fuller directed James Hong in which film?

    A. *China Gate* (1957)
    B. *Park Row* (1952)
    C. *Shock Corridor* (1963)
    D. *Verboten!* (1959)

199. Paul Muni plays the title role in what film directed by William Dieterle?

    A. *Dr. Socrates* (1935)
    B. *Shane* (1953)
    C. *The Great Gatsby* (1949)
    D. *The Return of Doctor X* (1939)

200. What mystery thriller set in Scotland was directed by Anthony Asquith?

    A. *Cottage to Let* (1941)
    B. *On Such a Night* (1956)
    C. *The Millionairess* (1960)
    D. *The Runaway Princess* (1929)

201. Which of the following directors started out as an animator?

    A. Frank Borzage
    B. King Vidor
    C. Norman Z. McLeod
    D. Orson Welles

202. Ida Lupino received her first directing and cowriting credit for what film?

    A. *Forever and a Day* (1943)
    B. *Never Fear* (1949)
    C. *The Gay Desperado* (1936)
    D. *They Drive by Night* (1940)

203. George Romero directed a commercial in Japan for what popular video game?

    A. *Grand Theft Auto*
    B. *Hellblazer*
    C. *Mortal Kombat*
    D. *Resident Evil 2*

204. All of the following films starring Jane Powell were directed by Stanley Donen except which one?

    A. *Athena* (1954)
    B. *Deep in My Heart* (1954)
    C. *Royal Wedding* (1951)
    D. *Seven Brides for Seven Brothers* (1954)

205. In what year did director Ingmar Bergman receive the Irving G. Thalberg Memorial Award?

    A. 1965
    B. 1971
    C. 1976
    D. 1981

206. How many Academy Award nominations did Mark Robson receive for Best Director throughout the course of his career?

    A. 1
    B. 2
    C. 3
    D. 4

answers found on page 556

207. *The Name Above the Title* is the title of the auto-biography of which legendary film director?

A. David Lean
B. Frank Capra
C. George Cukor
D. John Ford

208. Michael Powell began his film career by working with what director in Nice, France?

A. David Lean
B. Emeric Pressburger
C. Max Anderson
D. Rex Ingram

209. Anthony Asquith directed Michael Redgrave in the 1951 film *The Browning Version* and which other movie?

A. *Channel Incident* (1940)
B. *Quiet Wedding* (1941)
C. *Rush Hour* (1941)
D. *The Way to the Stars* (1945)

210. All of the following films directed by Billy Wilder include card-playing scenes except for which one?

A. *Sabrina* (1954)
B. *Stalag 17* (1953)
C. *Sunset Blvd.* (1950)
D. *The Apartment* (1960)

211. All of the following films starring Denzel Washington were directed by Spike Lee except which one?

A. *Fallen* (1998)
B. *Inside Man* (2006)
C. *Malcolm X* (1992)
D. *Mo' Better Blues* (1990)

212. Director Mark Robson died during post-production on which of his films?

A. *Avalanche Express* (1979)
B. *Earthquake* (1974)

C. *The Inn of the Sixth Happiness* (1958)
D. *Valley of the Dolls* (1967)

213. How many actors received Academy Award nominations under the direction of Mark Robson?

A. 3
B. 5
C. 7
D. 9

214. A well-to-do community becomes unglued when a neighbor's maid writes a tell-all book is the plot to what film directed by Jules Dassin?

A. *Circle of Two* (1980)
B. *Phaedra* (1962)
C. *The Affairs of Martha* (1942)
D. *Two Smart People* (1946)

215. Ed Wood idolized, but never met, which legendary director?

A. Orson Welles
B. Tod Browning
C. Victor Fleming
D. Vincent Price

216. What film starring Julia Roberts did Alan J. Pakula direct?

A. *Erin Brockovich* (2000)
B. *Pretty Woman* (1990)
C. *Steel Magnolias* (1989)
D. *The Pelican Brief* (1993)

217. At sixteen, Steven Spielberg wrote and directed his first film, a science fiction adventure called *Firelight*, which later inspired what film?

A. *Back to the Future* (1985)
B. *Close Encounters of the Third Kind* (1977)
C. *E.T.: The Extra-Terrestrial* (1982)
D. *Poltergeist* (1982)

answers found on page 556

218. On which film did Anthony Asquith make his solo directing debut?

A. *French Without Tears* (1940)
B. *Quiet Wedding* (1941)
C. *Uncensored* (1942)
D. *Underground* (1928)

219. Walter Matthau's son Charlie directed him in which of the following films?

A. *Grumpier Old Men* (1995)
B. *Hanging Up* (2000)
C. *I'm Not Rappaport* (1996)
D. *The Grass Harp* (1995)

220. Robert Redford received an Oscar nomination as Best Director for what film featuring John Turturro and Ralph Fiennes?

A. *Lions for Lambs* (2007)
B. *Ordinary People* (1980)
C. *Quiz Show* (1994)
D. *The Legend of Bagger Vance* (2000)

221. Robert De Niro starred in what film directed by John Frankenheimer?

A. *52 Pick-Up* (1986)
B. *Reindeer Games* (2000)
C. *Ronin* (1998)
D. *The Fourth War* (1990)

222. In what film directed by John Frankenheimer does Omar Sharif star?

A. *All Fall Down* (1962)
B. *The Gypsy Moths* (1969)
C. *The Horsemen* (1971)
D. *The Iceman Cometh* (1973)

223. *Jaws* (1975), directed by Steven Spielberg, earned an Academy Award in all of the following categories except which one?

A. Best Picture
B. Best Editing
C. Best Original Score
D. Best Sound

224. For which of his films did Mark Robson receive his first Academy Award nomination for Best Director?

A. *From the Terrace* (1960)
B. *Peyton Place* (1957)
C. *The Inn of the Sixth Happiness* (1958)
D. *The Seventh Victim* (1943)

225. Director George Stevens also did all of the following during his career except which one?

A. Cinematography
B. Costume design
C. Producing
D. Writing

226. Although he never won for Best Director, how many times was Sidney Lumet nominated for an Oscar?

A. 0
B. 2
C. 4
D. 5

227. For what studio did Norman Z. McLeod direct *My Favorite Spy* (1951)?

A. MGM
B. Paramount
C. RKO
D. Warner Bros.

228. What film earned the Best Director Oscar the year that *Grand Hotel* (1932) won for Best Picture?

A. *Bad Girl*
B. *Cimarron*
C. *Grand Hotel*
D. *Skippy*

answers found on page 556

229. What film directed by Zoltan Korda is about a woman's relationship with a widowed opera singer?

A. *Cash* (1933)
B. *Forget Me Not* (1936)
C. *Men of Tomorrow* (1932)
D. *Sanders of the River* (1935)

Captain Blood, 1935

230. Which director earned an Oscar nomination as a write-in candidate for *Captain Blood* (1935)?

A. George Cukor
B. Howard Hawks
C. Leo McCarey
D. Michael Curtiz

231. John Cromwell directed actress Irene Dunne in all of the following films except which one?

A. *Ann Vickers* (1933)
B. *Anna and the King of Siam* (1946)
C. *Love Affair* (1939)
D. *The Silver Cord* (1933)

232. Although he never won for Best Director, how many times was Sam Peckinpah nominated for an Oscar?

A. 0
B. 2

C. 3
D. 5

233. What college did Steven Spielberg attend?

A. California State University Long Beach
B. Pepperdine University
C. UC Berkeley
D. UCLA

234. Who was the first British citizen to win Best Director?

A. Alfred Hitchcock
B. David Lean
C. Laurence Olivier
D. Tony Richardson

235. John Wayne starred in all of the following films directed by Henry Hathaway except which one?

A. *Circus World* (1964)
B. *Legend of the Lost* (1957)
C. *Nevada Smith* (1966)
D. *North to Alaska* (1960)

236. Director Louis Malle earned an Oscar nod for Best Writing how many times?

A. 0
B. 1
C. 2
D. 3

237. What film starring Dick Van Dyke was directed by Norman Jewison?

A. *Chitty Chitty Bang Bang* (1968)
B. *Cold Turkey* (1971)
C. *The Art of Love* (1965)
D. *The Comic* (1969)

238. What film starring Janet Gaynor was directed by John Ford?

A. *Daddy Long Legs* (1931)
B. *Servants' Entrance* (1934)
C. *7th Heaven* (1927)
D. *The Shamrock Handicap* (1925)

answers found on page 556

239. Jack Arnold made a cameo appearance in what John Landis film?

A. *Into the Night* (1985)
B. *National Lampoon's Animal House* (1978)
C. *The Blues Brothers* (1980)
D. *Trading Places* (1983)

240. James Garner falls for a stock market analyst in what film directed by Arthur Hiller?

A. *Nightwing* (1979)
B. *Plaza Suite* (1971)
C. *The Man in the Glass Booth* (1975)
D. *The Wheeler Dealers* (1963)

241. Steven Spielberg made his feature film directorial debut with what film?

A. *Close Encounters of the Third Kind* (1977)
B. *Duel* (1971)
C. *Jaws* (1975)
D. *The Sugarland Express* (1975)

242. The final film in which Sophia Loren appeared with Marcello Mastroianni was directed by Robert Altman. What was the title?

A. *Gosford Park* (2001)
B. *Ready to Wear* (1994)
C. *Short Cuts* (1993)
D. *The Player* (1992)

243. How old was William Castle when he directed his first feature?

A. 19
B. 23
C. 29
D. 40

244. What was Ida Lupino's last feature film as director?

A. *The Big Knife* (1955)
B. *The Hitch-Hiker* (1953)
C. *The Trouble with Angels* (1966)
D. *While the City Sleeps* (1956)

245. In which of his own films does George Marshall appear as himself?

A. *Monsieur Beaucaire* (1946)
B. *The Blue Dahlia* (1946)
C. *The Ghost Breakers* (1940)
D. *Variety Girl* (1947)

246. Laurence Olivier and Jean Simmons share the screen in what film directed by Stanley Kubrick?

A. *Lolita* (1962)
B. *Paths of Glory* (1957)
C. *Spartacus* (1960)
D. *The Seafarers* (1953)

247. What film directed by George Roy Hill was based on a play by Tennessee Williams?

A. *A Little Romance* (1979)
B. *Period of Adjustment* (1962)
C. *The World of Henry Orient* (1964)
D. *Toys in the Attic* (1963)

248. For which of the following films did Henry Hathaway receive an Academy Award nomination for Best Director?

A. *China Girl* (1942)
B. *Now and Forever* (1934)
C. *The Lives of a Bengal Lancer* (1935)
D. *To the Last Man* (1933)

249. Although he never won for Best Director, how many times was Cecil B. DeMille nominated for an Oscar?

A. 0
B. 1
C. 3
D. 7

250. What was Daniel Mann's first feature film as director?

A. *About Mrs. Leslie* (1954)
B. *Come Back, Little Sheba* (1952)
C. *I'll Cry Tomorrow* (1955)
D. *The Rose Tattoo* (1955)

251. What did Otto Preminger do in films besides direct?

    A. Act
    B. Cinematography
    C. Design costumes
    D. Write

252. What film starring Nancy Carroll was directed by Ernst Lubitsch?

    A. *Broken Lullaby* (1932)
    B. *Child of Manhattan* (1933)
    C. *Scarlet Dawn* (1932)
    D. *Wayward* (1932)

253. French director Anatole Litvak made his Hollywood debut directing what film starring Paul Muni?

    A. *Dr. Ehrlich's Magic Bullet* (1940)
    B. *Fog Over Frisco* (1934)
    C. *The Secret Bride* (1934)
    D. *The Woman I Love* (1937)

254. What film costarring Nancy Carroll was directed by James Whale?

    A. *After the Dance* (1935)
    B. *Child of Manhattan* (1933)
    C. *Jealousy* (1934)
    D. *The Kiss Before the Mirror* (1933)

255. Billy Wilder directed Jack Lemmon in all of the following films except for which one?

    A. *Irma la Douce* (1963)
    B. *Love in the Afternoon* (1957)
    C. *The Apartment* (1960)
    D. *The Fortune Cookie* (1966)

256. Director Ingmar Bergman and Liv Ullmann made how many films together?

    A. 10
    B. 13
    C. 3
    D. 7

257. James Cagney romances Bette Davis in what film directed by William Keighley?

    A. *Big Hearted Herbert* (1934)
    B. *No Time for Comedy* (1940)
    C. *The Bride Came C.O.D.* (1941)
    D. *The Green Pastures* (1936)

258. What film based on a James M. Cain story was directed by Douglas Sirk?

    A. *Interlude* (1957)
    B. *Serenade* (1956)
    C. *When Tomorrow Comes* (1939)
    D. *Wife, Husband and Friend* (1939)

259. What was the first film that Joan Blondell made with director Michael Curtiz?

    A. *Broadway Bad* (1933)
    B. *God's Gift to Women* (1931)
    C. *The Perfect Specimen* (1937)
    D. *Traveling Saleslady* (1935)

260. Barbra Streisand directed all of the following films except which one?

    A. *All Night Long* (1981)
    B. *The Mirror Has Two Faces* (1996)
    C. *The Prince of Tides* (1991)
    D. *Yentl* (1983)

261. Randolph Scott starred in all of the following films directed by Henry Hathaway except which one?

    A. *Go West Young Man* (1936)
    B. *Sunset Pass* (1933)
    C. *The Witching Hour* (1934)
    D. *To the Last Man* (1933)

262. Anthony Asquith directed which film starring Leslie Caron and David Niven?

    A. *A Kiss in the Dark* (1949)
    B. *Guns of Darkness* (1962)
    C. *Happy Go Lovely* (1951)
    D. *Promise Her Anything* (1965)

answers found on page 556

Spotlight on
GEORGE **CUKOR** (1899–1983)

If George Cukor hasn't gotten his due from critics and historians, blame his reputation. His ease at working with female stars—from Katharine Hepburn in *A Bill of Divorcement* (1932) to Candice Bergen in *Rich and Famous* (1981)—earned him a reputation as a "woman's director," a phrase often used dismissively. Yet he holds the record for directing Best Actor Oscar winners: James Stewart in *The Philadelphia Story* (1940), Ronald Colman in *A Double Life* (1947), and Rex Harrison in *My Fair Lady* (1964). Because he started on the stage before moving to Hollywood in 1929, and had some of his biggest

The Philadelphia Story, 1940

hits with stage adaptations, he has also been dismissed as someone who just filmed plays. But he filmed them well because he knew how to make them work on screen. By his earliest films he had mastered the art of moving the camera, and his first wide-screen, Technicolor film, *A Star Is Born* (1954), showed he was a master at guiding the cast and the camera. In truth, he was a master of cinema through and through, with a style that intrudes so little on his material and his stars it's easy to overlook his genius.

A Star Is Born, 1954

1. **George Cukor directed Robert Taylor and Norma Shearer in what romantic comedy?**

    A. *Her Cardboard Lover* (1942)

    B. *Society Doctor* (1935)

    C. *The Spectacle Maker* (1934)

    D. *Times Square Lady* (1935)

2. **Jean Hagen appears in what film directed by George Cukor?**

    A. *A Life of Her Own* (1950)

    B. *My Fair Lady* (1964)

    C. *We Were Strangers* (1949)

    D. *What Price Glory* (1952)

3. **What was the first musical directed by George Cukor?**

    A. *A Star Is Born* (1954)

    B. *Let's Dance* (1950)

    C. *Royal Wedding* (1951)

    D. *Three Little Words* (1950)

4. **Basil Rathbone earned an Oscar nomination for playing what character in George Cukor's *Romeo and Juliet* (1936)?**

    A. Lord Capulet

    B. Mercutio

    C. Paris

    D. Tybalt

5. **George Cukor directed James Donald in what film with Spencer Tracy and Deborah Kerr?**

    A. *Edward, My Son* (1949)

    B. *The Barretts of Wimpole Street* (1957)

    C. *The Long Memory* (1952)

    D. *The Valiant* (1962)

---

answers found on page 556

GREAT DIRECTORS **283**

263. George Marshall directed what Laurel and Hardy short about traveling fishmongers?

A. *County Hospital* (1932)
B. *Them Thar Hills* (1934)
C. *Tit for Tat* (1935)
D. *Towed in the Hole* (1932)

264. What film directed by John Frankenheimer was based on a novel by Elmore Leonard?

A. *52 Pick-Up* (1986)
B. *Black Sunday* (1977)
C. *Prophesy* (1979)
D. *The Manchurian Candidate* (1962)

265. How many Best Director Academy Awards did George Stevens win?

A. 0
B. 1
C. 2
D. 3

266. Claire Bloom starred in two films directed by Martin Ritt. What was their first big-screen collaboration?

A. *The Chapman Report* (1962)
B. *The Illustrated Man* (1969)
C. *The Outrage* (1964)
D. *The Spy Who Came in from the Cold* (1965)

267. Brigitte Bardot starred in the 1962 film *A Very Private Affair*. Who directed it?

A. Louis Malle
B. Robert Aldrich
C. Robert Wise
D. Roger Vadim

268. What film earned director Robert Rossen an Oscar nomination?

A. *All the King's Men* (1949)
B. *Mambo* (1954)
C. *Out of the Fog* (1941)
D. *The Roaring Twenties* (1939)

269. Sandra Dennis made her last on-screen appearance in what film directed by Sean Penn?

A. *Carlito's Way* (1993)
B. *The Crossing Guard* (1995)
C. *The Indian Runner* (1991)
D. *The Pledge* (2001)

270. Although he never won for Best Director, how many times was Orson Welles nominated for an Oscar in that category?

A. 1
B. 2
C. 3
D. 5

Royal Wedding, 1951

271. Who directed the 1951 film *Royal Wedding*, which contains the famous sequence of Fred Astaire dancing on the ceiling?

A. Stanley Donen
B. Vincente Minnelli
C. Joshua Logan
D. Robert Wise

272. Steven Spielberg filmed what Stanley Kubrick project that Kubrick was unable to finish during his lifetime?

A. *A.I.: Artificial Intelligence* (2001)
B. *Minority Report* (2002)
C. *Munich* (2005)
D. *Saving Private Ryan* (1998)

273. What was the last film Lewis Milestone completed as director?
   A. *Mutiny on the Bounty* (1962)
   B. *Ocean's Eleven* (1960)
   C. *PT 109* (1963)
   D. *The Dirty Game* (1965)

274. What film starring Van Heflin was directed by Fred Zinnemann?
   A. *H. M. Pulham, Esq.* (1941)
   B. *Johnny Eager* (1941)
   C. *Kid Glove Killer* (1942)
   D. *Presenting Lily Mars* (1943)

275. Robert Redford directed Donald Sutherland and Mary Tyler Moore in what film?
   A. *A River Runs Through It* (1992)
   B. *Lions for Lambs* (2007)
   C. *Ordinary People* (1980)
   D. *The Solar Film* (1980)

276. Although he has never won for Best Director, how many times has George Lucas been nominated for an Oscar?
   A. 0
   B. 1
   C. 2
   D. 3

277. Director Norman Z. McLeod reunited with his *Topper* (1937) stars Constance Bennett, Alan Mowbray, and Billie Burke for *Topper Takes a Trip* (1938) and which other film?
   A. *Holiday* (1938)
   B. *Let's Dance* (1950)
   C. *Merrily We Live* (1938)
   D. *Topper Returns* (1941)

278. What movie starring Errol Flynn was the last film directed by William Keighley?
   A. *Big Hearted Herbert* (1934)
   B. *My Brother Talks to Horses* (1947)
   C. *The Master of Ballantrae* (1953)
   D. *The Wings of Eagles* (1957)

279. What film costarring Jean Simmons was directed by Laurence Olivier?
   A. *Black Narcissus* (1947)
   B. *Great Expectations* (1946)
   C. *Hamlet* (1948)
   D. *Uncle Silas* (1947)

280. For which of the following films was Jules Dassin nominated for an Academy Award as Best Director?
   A. *Never on Sunday* (1960)
   B. *The Canterville Ghost* (1944)
   C. *The Law* (1959)
   D. *Topkapi* (1964)

281. For which film did Zoltan Korda win the Best Director prize at the Venice Film Festival?
   A. *Elephant Boy* (1937)
   B. *Men of Tomorrow* (1932)
   C. *The Drum* (1938)
   D. *The Four Feathers* (1939)

282. Jack Arnold's first effort as a feature director was the labor movement propaganda piece *With These Hands* (1950), which was courtesy of what union?
   A. American Federation of Labor
   B. Industrial Workers of the World
   C. International Ladies Garment Workers Union
   D. National Workers' Union

283. Who was the first person to win Best Director in consecutive years?
   A. Frank Capra
   B. John Ford
   C. John Huston
   D. William Wyler

FILM
GENRES

Bringing Up Baby, 1938

Chapter 10

COMEDIES

Audiences have loved laughing at the silver screen ever since Fred Ott sneezed in 1894. During the silent era, the studios produced almost every type of comedy audiences enjoy today. In romantic comedies like *It* (1927) Clara Bow looked for love as charmingly as Sandra Bullock does today. Even without sound, director Ernst Lubitsch captured the polished wit of Oscar Wilde's *Lady Windermere's Fan* (1925). And comic whizzes like Hal Roach and Mack Sennett spoofed popular films of the day with the same outrageous humor now found in the *Scary Movie* series.

The crowning glory of the silent screen was the work of slapstick geniuses like Charles Chaplin, Buster Keaton, and Harold Lloyd, who either directed their own pictures or exercised major artistic control over them. Popular films like Chaplin's *The Gold Rush* (1925), Keaton's *Sherlock, Jr.* (1924) and *The General* (1927), and Lloyd's *The Freshman* (1925) are now ranked among the greatest movies ever made.

With the coming of sound, the movies could crack wise thanks to a new school of writers imported from Broadway, radio, and burlesque. Screenwriters like Anita Loos and Robert Riskin made romance funny by putting carefully crafted lines and touching sentiment into the mouths of such stars as Jean Harlow, Claudette Colbert, and Jean Arthur. And Lubitsch could add knowing double entendres drafted by Samson Raphaelson and Ben Hecht to his already legendary comic touch in films like *Trouble in Paradise* (1932) and *Design for Living* (1933).

The immediate heirs to the slapstick clowns were the anarchic comics from Broadway and burlesque whose films set conventional notions of plot and propriety on their ear. The Marx Brothers deflated the pomposity of international diplomacy in *Duck Soup* (1933) and high culture in *A Night at the Opera* (1935). In irreverent comedies like *It's a Gift* (1934), W. C. Fields proved that "Any man who hates small dogs and children can't be all bad." And Mae West brought her disarming sexuality from stage to screen, saving Paramount Pictures from bankruptcy with *She Done Him Wrong* (1933).

The years of the Great Depression brought a new genre, screwball comedy, to the screen. Audiences had always enjoyed the antics of the upper classes, but with the once rich and powerful vying for spots in the breadlines, a new taste developed for films in which true love and sheer wackiness consistently trumped wealth and social standing. Whether it was hard-boiled reporter Clark Gable teaching snooty heiress Colbert to eat stolen carrots and thumb rides in *It Happened One Night* (1934) or pixilated socialite Katharine Hepburn wreaking havoc on paleontologist Cary Grant's career in *Bringing Up Baby* (1938), the message was the same—silliness conquers all.

The Daffy Duse who ruled the genre was Carole Lombard, a beautiful blonde who gleefully cavorted through some of the best films of Howard Hawks (1934's *Twentieth Century*) and Lubitsch (*To Be or Not to Be*, in 1942). The latter helped signal the end of the genre. With Jack Benny and Lombard teamed as husband-and-wife stage stars using screwball tactics against the Nazis, it pointed to the horrors that were quickly making such lightweight comedies seem irrelevant. Screwball comedy would resurface in later years—particularly in director Peter Bogdanovich's 1972 tribute to *Bringing Up Baby*, entitled *What's Up Doc?*—but only sporadically.

More recent, big-screen comedy has taken a more manic turn with gonzo comedies that combine outrageous parody with the off-the-cuff humor of stars like Steve Martin and Bill Murray, who trained doing stand-up comedy and improvisation. Their films *The Jerk* (1979) and *Caddyshack* (1980) offer nonstop laughs by leaving no sacred cow unstoned. Woody Allen directed and starred in a string of more intellectual anarchic comedies like *Bananas* (1971) and *Sleeper* (1973) modeled on the work of his idols, the Marx Brothers. But then he moved to more thoughtful films, mining the anxieties of modern life for laughs in *Annie Hall* (1977) and *Manhattan* (1979). His work has led the way for other contemporary clowns to attempt a more thoughtful approach.

Each generation discovers its own comic stars. The slapstick antics of Chaplin and Keaton are now the domain of Jackie Chan and Jim Carrey. Will Farrell has taken on the mantle of the Marx Brothers, Murray, and Martin. Just as Audrey Hepburn and Doris Day became the reigning romantic comediennes of the fifties and sixties, Meg Ryan has taken the place of Colbert and Arthur in *When Harry Met Sally* (1989). And twenty years later Bullock cemented her hold on the box office with her own romantic date-night hit, *The Proposal* (2009).

1. Robert Taylor made his film debut in what comedy starring Will Rogers?

   A. *Handy Andy* (1934)
   B. *Society Doctor* (1935)
   C. *The Spectacle Maker* (1934)
   D. *Times Square Lady* (1935)

2. Rosalind Russell costars in what romantic comedy directed by Alexander Hall?

   A. *Forever, Darling* (1956)
   B. *She Wouldn't Say Yes* (1945)
   C. *The Amazing Mr. Williams* (1939)
   D. *They All Kissed the Bride* (1942)

3. Writer Neil Simon originally planned for what film to be a segment of the 1971 comedy *Plaza Suite*?

   A. *Promise Her Anything* (1965)
   B. *The Entertainer* (1960)
   C. *The Out of Towners* (1970)
   D. *The Wheeler Dealers* (1963)

4. What is the only Woody Allen film with Mia Farrow and Diane Keaton?

   A. *Crimes and Misdemeanors* (1989)
   B. *Radio Days* (1987)
   C. *Stardust Memories* (1980)
   D. *The Purple Rose of Cairo* (1985)

5. Mitchell Leisen directed Betty Hutton and Patric Knowles in what romantic comedy?

   A. *Dream Girl* (1948)
   B. *Let's Dance* (1950)
   C. *Royal Wedding* (1951)
   D. *The Belle of New York* (1952)

6. The 1981 Walter Matthau/Jack Lemmon comedy *Buddy Buddy* was which famous director's final film?

   A. Arthur Hiller
   B. Billy Wilder
   C. Elia Kazan
   D. Vincente Minnelli

7. What Marlon Brando film was Glenn Ford's first foray into comedy?

   A. *Guys and Dolls* (1955)
   B. *Teahouse of the August Moon* (1956)
   C. *The Ugly American* (1963)
   D. *The Wild One* (1953)

8. Meryl Streep is featured in which Woody Allen film?

   A. *Broadway Danny Rose* (1984)
   B. *Bullets over Broadway* (1994)
   C. *Manhattan* (1979)
   D. *Stardust Memories* (1980)

9. Which of the following Carole Lombard films is about a woman pushed to marry into royalty in order to prevent her family from financial ruin?

   A. *From Hell to Heaven* (1933)
   B. *I Take This Woman* (1931)
   C. *No More Orchids* (1932)
   D. *Virtue* (1932)

10. Alan Arkin plays a single parent raising two sons in which comedy costarring Rita Moreno?

    A. *Boys' Night Out* (1962)
    B. *Freebie and the Bean* (1974)
    C. *Popi* (1969)
    D. *Untamed* (1955)

11. W. C. Fields originally wanted the title of what comedy short to be *W. C. Fields in a Drugstore*?

    A. *Six of a Kind* (1934)
    B. *The Pharmacist* (1933)
    C. *The Potters* (1927)
    D. *Tillie and Gus* (1933)

12. Marlon Brando's first comedic role was in what film opposite Shirley Jones?

    A. *Bedtime Story* (1964)
    B. *Casino Royale* (1967)
    C. *The Ladies Man* (1961)
    D. *The Valiant* (1962)

answers found on page 556

13. What comedy starring Jack Lemmon, Natalie Wood, and Tony Curtis features the largest, staged pie fight?

    A. *I Married an Angel* (1942)
    B. *Mister Roberts* (1955)
    C. *Some Like It Hot* (1959)
    D. *The Great Race* (1965)

The Big Hangover, 1950

14. Who is Van Johnson's costar in the 1950 comedy *The Big Hangover*?

    A. Rosalind Russell
    B. Ava Gardner
    C. Debbie Reynolds
    D. Elizabeth Taylor

15. Natalie Wood plays the daughter of James Stewart's character in what comedy?

    A. *It's Always Fair Weather* (1955)
    B. *The Happy Road* (1957)
    C. *The Jackpot* (1950)
    D. *The Man from Laramie* (1955)

16. Who played Barbra Streisand's husband in the 2004 comedy *Meet the Fockers*?

    A. Donald Sutherland
    B. Dustin Hoffman
    C. Gene Hackman
    D. Robert Redford

17. What leading lady was Howard Hawks's first choice to play Rosalind Russell's role in *His Girl Friday* (1940)?

    A. Carole Lombard
    B. Debbie Reynolds
    C. Jean Arthur
    D. Maureen O'Hara

18. Arthur Hiller directed Nick Nolte in what comedy?

    A. *Plaza Suite* (1971)
    B. *Promise Her Anything* (1965)
    C. *Teachers* (1984)
    D. *The Wheeler Dealers* (1963)

19. Gene Tierney plays the daughter of Miriam Hopkins's character in which comedy?

    A. *The Mating Season* (1951)
    B. *The Richest Girl in the World* (1934)
    C. *The Story of Temple Drake* (1933)
    D. *Woman Chases Man* (1937)

20. Burt Reynolds's first wife, Judy Carne, was a regular on what popular television comedy series?

    A. *Laugh-In*
    B. *The Carol Burnett Show*
    C. *The Lucy Show*
    D. *The Smothers Brothers*

21. Who does Jack Lemmon's character romance in the 1993 comedy *Grumpy Old Men*?

    A. Ann-Margret
    B. Julie Andrews
    C. Shirley MacLaine
    D. Sophia Loren

22. Bronislau Kaper composed the musical score of what comedy pairing Melvyn Douglas and Norma Shearer?

    A. *The Belle of New York* (1952)
    B. *The Sky's the Limit* (1943)
    C. *We Were Dancing* (1942)
    D. *You Were Never Lovelier* (1942)

answers found on page 556

23. What was the last film George Stevens made with comedic scenes?

    A. *I Remember Mama* (1948)
    B. *The More the Merrier* (1943)
    C. *Woman of the Year* (1942)
    D. *The Talk of the Town* (1942)

24. Janet Leigh made her screen debut in what romantic comedy opposite Van Johnson?

    A. *Blue Skies* (1946)
    B. *Once Upon a Honeymoon* (1942)
    C. *The Romance of Rosy Ridge* (1947)
    D. *Wives and Lovers* (1963)

25. Delbert Mann directed Doris Day in what comedy opposite Cary Grant?

    A. *A Piece of Cake* (1948)
    B. *Love in Pawn* (1953)
    C. *Room to Let* (1950)
    D. *That Touch of Mink* (1962)

26. Cary Grant plays a chemist in what comedy opposite Marilyn Monroe and Ginger Rogers?

    A. *Monkey Business* (1952)
    B. *Monsieur Beaucaire* (1946)
    C. *Penny Serenade* (1941)
    D. *Words and Music* (1948)

27. What was Carole Lombard's nickname?

    A. "The Blonde Cyclone"
    B. "The Brooklyn Bombshell"
    C. "The Ditzy Dynamo"
    D. "The Hoosier Tornado"

28. Fred MacMurray and Claudette Colbert share the screen in what romantic comedy directed by Mitchell Leisen?

    A. *No Time for Love* (1943)
    B. *Practically Yours* (1944)
    C. *The Girl Most Likely* (1958)
    D. *The Mating Season* (1951)

29. W. C. Fields plays a storekeeper who uses his inheritance to buy an orange grove in what Norman Z. McLeod comedy?

    A. *A Family Affair* (1937)
    B. *It's a Gift* (1934)
    C. *Live, Love and Learn* (1937)
    D. *The Potters* (1927)

30. In the 1938 comedy *Mr. Doodle Kicks Off*, the character Professor Minorous is among the faculty of what department?

    A. Art history
    B. Chemistry
    C. Greek mythology
    D. Mathematics

31. What was the first film that Carole Lombard ever made with Clark Gable?

    A. *Bolero* (1934)
    B. *No Man of Her Own* (1932)
    C. *Now and Forever* (1934)
    D. *We're Not Dressing* (1934)

32. Who does Walter Matthau romance in the 1978 comedy *House Calls*?

    A. Ann-Margret
    B. Glenda Jackson
    C. Goldie Hawn
    D. Ingrid Bergman

33. What is the name of Carole Lombard's character in the 1937 film *Nothing Sacred*?

    A. Hazel Flagg
    B. Linda Keane
    C. Millie Malloy
    D. Sally Simmons

34. What was Carole Lombard's last film?

    A. *Mr. and Mrs. Smith* (1941)
    B. *Nothing Sacred* (1937)
    C. *To Be or Not to Be* (1942)
    D. *Vigil in the Night* (1940)

35. Don Knotts made his feature film debut in what comedy opposite Andy Griffith?

    A. *Mr. Music* (1950)
    B. *My Favorite Spy* (1951)
    C. *No Time for Sergeants* (1958)
    D. *Riding High* (1950)

36. Arthur Hiller directed Leslie Caron in what romantic comedy?

    A. *I'm Dancing as Fast as I Can* (1982)
    B. *Promise Her Anything* (1965)
    C. *Taking Care of Business* (1990)
    D. *The Wheeler Dealers* (1963)

37. Where does Ingrid Bergman's character work in the 1969 comedy *Cactus Flower*?

    A. A bookstore
    B. A dentist's office
    C. A flower shop
    D. An insurance office

38. Jack Carson plays Chuck in what film? (Hint: It was the only romantic comedy directed by Alfred Hitchcock.)

    A. *A Guide for the Married Man* (1967)
    B. *Candy* (1968)
    C. *Mr. and Mrs. Smith* (1941)
    D. *Ten Thousand Bedrooms* (1957)

39. Who directed the 1937 Carole Lombard film *Nothing Sacred*?

    A. Ernst Lubtisch
    B. Howard Hawks
    C. Preston Sturges
    D. William A. Wellman

40. Rhonda Fleming plays Duchess Alexandria in what musical-romantic-comedy-thriller directed by Alexander Hall?

    A. *Forever, Darling* (1956)
    B. *The Great Lover* (1949)
    C. *They All Kissed the Bride* (1942)
    D. *Up Front* (1951)

41. Mariel Hemingway stars opposite Diane Keaton and Meryl Streep in which comedy?

    A. *Baby Boom* (1987)
    B. *Manhattan* (1979)
    C. *Radio Days* (1987)
    D. *The Lemon Sisters* (1989)

42. Charles Coburn plays Grampa in what comedy costarring Dorothy McGuire?

    A. *A Certain Smile* (1958)
    B. *Monsieur Beaucaire* (1946)
    C. *The Remarkable Mr. Pennypacker* (1959)
    D. *Until They Sail* (1957)

43. Lupe Velez's first comedic role was as the star of which 1932 film?

    A. *Big City Blues*
    B. *Bird of Paradise*
    C. *Movie Crazy*
    D. *The Half Naked Truth*

44. Which one of James Agee's former costars appeared in the 1956 comedy *The Ambassador's Daughter*?

    A. Dan Seymour
    B. Gene Lockhart
    C. Minor Watson
    D. Robert Preston

45. James Mason plays "The Guardian Angel" in what comedy directed by Alexander Hall?

    A. *Duchess of Idaho* (1950)
    B. *Forever, Darling* (1956)
    C. *Merton of the Movies* (1947)
    D. *Neptune's Daughter* (1949)

46. In which of the following Woody Allen films does José Ferrer costar?

    A. *A Midsummer Night's Sex Comedy* (1982)
    B. *Annie Hall* (1977)
    C. *Love and Death* (1975)
    D. *The Purple Rose of Cairo* (1985)

answers found on page 557

It's Love I'm After, 1937

47. Bette Davis stars opposite Leslie Howard and what famous actress in the 1937 screwball comedy *It's Love I'm After*?

A. Marion Davies
B. Olivia de Havilland
C. Rosalind Russell
D. Myrna Loy

48. Mary Wickes and Jean Hagen costar in what comedy?

A. *Beyond the Forest* (1949)
B. *Half a Hero* (1953)
C. *The Catered Affair* (1956)
D. *Winter Meeting* (1948)

49. Richard Burton and Walter Matthau costar in what comedy?

A. *A Guide for the Married Man* (1967)
B. *Candy* (1968)
C. *Hello, Dolly!* (1969)
D. *The Odd Couple* (1968)

50. Bronislau Kaper composed the musical score of what romantic comedy pairing William Powell and Hedy Lamarr?

A. *The Belle of New York* (1952)
B. *The Heavenly Body* (1944)
C. *The Sky's the Limit* (1943)
D. *You Were Never Lovelier* (1942)

51. Arthur Hiller directed Tom Arnold and Rod Steiger in what comedy?

A. *Carpool* (1996)
B. *I'm Dancing as Fast as I Can* (1982)
C. *Taking Care of Business* (1990)
D. *The Wheeler Dealers* (1963)

52. Jack Benny and Ann Sheridan attempt to renovate a dilapidated farmhouse in what comedy directed by William Keighley?

A. *Big Hearted Herbert* (1934)
B. *George Washington Slept Here* (1942)
C. *Kansas City Princess* (1934)
D. *The Green Pastures* (1936)

53. Tom Ewell reprised his Tony Award–winning Broadway role of Richard Sherman in what comedy directed by Billy Wilder?

A. *Love in the Afternoon* (1957)
B. *Some Like It Hot* (1959)
C. *The Apartment* (1960)
D. *The Seven Year Itch* (1955)

54. Which of the following Carole Lombard films was directed by Ernst Lubitsch?

A. *Made for Each Other* (1939)
B. *They Knew What They Wanted* (1940)
C. *To Be or Not to Be* (1942)
D. *True Confession* (1937)

55. Andy Griffith plays Alvin "Al" Woods in what comedy opposite Walter Matthau?

A. *Mr. Music* (1950)
B. *My Favorite Spy* (1951)
C. *Onionhead* (1958)
D. *Riding High* (1950)

56. Robert Taylor romances Greer Garson in what comedy?

A. *Remember?* (1939)
B. *Society Doctor* (1935)
C. *The Spectacle Maker* (1934)
D. *Times Square Lady* (1935)

answers found on page 557

57. Which star of *Gone With the Wind* (1939) was featured opposite Cedric Hardwicke in the 1934 comedy *The Lady Is Willing*?
   A. Clark Gable
   B. Leslie Howard
   C. Olivia de Havilland
   D. Vivien Leigh

58. What Moss Hart/George S. Kaufman comedy about a couple's frustrated attempts to improve their colonial-era farmhouse earned an Oscar nomination for Best Interior Decoration in 1943?
   A. *George Washington Slept Here*
   B. *Mr. Blandings Builds His Dream House*
   C. *The Amityville Horror*
   D. *The Money Pit*

59. Which comedy starring Harold Lloyd was uncharacteristically filmed in sequence?
   A. *An Eastern Westerner* (1920)
   B. *His Royal Slyness* (1920)
   C. *Movie Crazy* (1932)
   D. *The Freshman* (1925)

60. Donna Reed costars in what comedy pairing Dean Martin and Jerry Lewis?
   A. *No Leave, No Love* (1946)
   B. *The Caddy* (1953)
   C. *The Notorious Landlady* (1962)
   D. *Week-End at the Waldorf* (1945)

61. Which star of *His Girl Friday* (1940) was born in Chicago, Illinois?
   A. Cary Grant
   B. Gene Lockhart
   C. Ralph Bellamy
   D. Rosalind Russell

62. What year was Stan Laurel given an honorary Academy Award for his "creative pioneering in the field of cinema comedy"?
   A. 1960
   B. 1961
   C. 1962
   D. 1963

63. Who plays Sally Field's estranged husband in the 1993 comedy *Mrs. Doubtfire*?
   A. Pierce Brosnan
   B. Robin Williams
   C. Steve Martin
   D. Tom Hanks

64. Ann-Margret plays a fashion buyer in what romantic comedy opposite Louis Jourdan?
   A. *A Certain Smile* (1958)
   B. *Days of Wine and Roses* (1962)
   C. *Made in Paris* (1966)
   D. *Under the Yum Yum Tree* (1963)

65. What Eddie Murphy comedy features Pam Grier?
   A. *Boomerang* (1992)
   B. *Doctor Dolittle* (1998)
   C. *The Adventures of Pluto Nash* (2002)
   D. *The Nutty Professor* (1996)

66. Which Billy Wilder comedy was #1 on AFI's "100 Funniest Movies" list?
   A. *Irma la Douce* (1963)
   B. *Some Like It Hot* (1959)
   C. *The Fortune Cookie* (1966)
   D. *The Seven Year Itch* (1955)

67. What is the name of the comic played by Bob Hope in Norman Z. McLeod's *My Favorite Spy* (1951)?
   A. "Painless" Peter Potter
   B. Hubert "Fearless" Frazier
   C. Humphrey "Sorrowful" Jones
   D. Peanuts "Boffo" White

answers found on page 557

68. Ginger Rogers turns to David Niven's character for psychiatric help in what comedy?

    A. *Oh, Men! Oh, Women!* (1957)
    B. *Royal Wedding* (1951)
    C. *Serenade* (1956)
    D. *The Barkleys of Broadway* (1949)

69. Which Abbott and Costello comedy costarred Marjorie Main?

    A. *Abbott and Costello Go to Mars* (1953)
    B. *Bud Abbott and Lou Costello Meet Frankenstein* (1948)
    C. *Bud Abbott and Lou Costello in Hollywood* (1945)
    D. *The Wistful Widow of Wagon Gap* (1947)

70. What Laurel and Hardy film won the Oscar for Best Short Subject—Comedy in 1932?

    A. *A Fine Mess*
    B. *Chickens Come Home*
    C. *March of the Wooden Soldiers*
    D. *The Music Box*

71. Stewart Granger and Ava Gardner are shipwrecked in which romantic comedy?

    A. *Moonfleet* (1955)
    B. *On the Beach* (1959)
    C. *The Blue Bird* (1976)
    D. *The Little Hut* (1957)

72. What was the name of the improvisational comedy troupe that actor Bill Murray started out with?

    A. Broken Lizard
    B. Chicago Wisecrackers
    C. Second City Chicago
    D. The Groundlings

73. Who was Carole Lombard's costar in the 1938 film *Fools for Scandal*?

    A. Clark Gable
    B. Fred MacMurray
    C. James Stewart
    D. Ralph Bellamy

74. What Joan Blondell comedy stars Glenn Ford, Stella Stevens, and Melvyn Douglas?

    A. *Advance to the Rear* (1964)
    B. *Lizzie* (1957)
    C. *Stand Up and Be Counted* (1972)
    D. *The Courtship of Eddie's Father* (1963)

75. Who directed Kim Novak in the 1964 comedy *Kiss Me, Stupid*?

    A. Billy Wilder
    B. Blake Edwards
    C. Vincente Minnelli
    D. William Wyler

76. Beau Bridges made his feature film debut in what comedy starring Louis Jourdan?

    A. *No Funny Business* (1933)
    B. *No Minor Vices* (1948)
    C. *Personalities* (1942)
    D. *Words and Music* (1948)

77. Which up-and-coming comic actor starred in Stanley Donen's *Bedazzled* (1967)?

    A. Dudley Moore
    B. Gene Wilder
    C. Jack Lemmon
    D. Peter Sellers

78. Marilyn Monroe and Ginger Rogers share the screen in what comedy?

    A. *A Certain Smile* (1958)
    B. *Monkey Business* (1952)
    C. *Monsieur Beaucaire* (1946)
    D. *Until They Sail* (1957)

79. Charles Coburn plays the royal uncle of Olivia de Havilland's character in what comedy?

    A. *A Piece of Cake* (1948)
    B. *Old Acquaintance* (1943)
    C. *Princess O'Rourke* (1943)
    D. *Room to Let* (1950)

Spotlight on
THE **MARX BROTHERS**

GUMMO MARX (1882–1977), CHICO MARX (1887–1961),
HARPO MARX (1888–1964), GROUCHO MARX (1890–1977),
ZEPPO MARX (1901–1979)

Even their names were crazy. The Marx Brothers promoted anarchy in thirteen features, many of them considered among the funniest ever made. Whether building a series of puns into verbal lunacy or creating surrealistic sight gags, they kept audiences in stitches. Their calculated anarchy was most delightful when aimed at social doyenne Margaret Dumont, a peer-less straight woman often hailed as "the fifth Marx Brother." There actually were five brothers. Gummo retired at the outbreak of World War I, to be replaced by Zeppo. He stayed with the team through Broadway star-dom and their first five films, cul-minating in the madcap political satire *Duck Soup* (1933). When they left Paramount for MGM, he retired, to become a top Hollywood agent. The Marxs' first MGM film, *A Night at the Opera* (1935), is often hailed as their best. But when studio mentor Irving Thalberg died, the team found management

A Night at the Opera, 1935

much less sympathetic. They split up after finishing their contract in 1942, then reunited twice more to settle Chico's gambling debts. But thirteen films is enough for a legacy if they're the right thirteen films, and their work proved a major influence on later actors and filmmakers such as Peter Sellers and Woody Allen.

A Night at the Opera, 1935

1. In the 1933 comedy *Duck Soup*, Groucho Marx plays the leader of what fictitious nation?

    A. Amnesia

    B. Freedonia

    C. Harmonia

    D. Hedonia

2. Bronislau Kaper composed the song "Cosi Cosa" for what musical starring the Marx Brothers?

    A. *A Night at the Opera* (1935)

    B. *Copacabana* (1947)

    C. *Duck Soup* (1933)

    D. *Mr. Music* (1950)

3. According to Chico Marx's version of "Everyone Says I Love You," in Norman Z. McLeod's *Horse Feathers* (1932), what did Christopher "Columbo" say to Pocahontas?

    A. Achi Vachi Vachi Voo

    B. Icky Sicky Wicky Nicky

    C. Leeti Leeti Lela Loota

    D. Yasa Yasa Basa Fasa

4. What movie director said, "Groucho Marx was the best comedian this country ever produced"?

    A. Albert Brooks

    B. Martin Scorsese

    C. Mel Brooks

    D. Woody Allen

5. Norman Z. McLeod's first Marx Brothers film, *Horse Feathers* (1932), inspired which Surrealist to write a screenplay called "The Marx Brothers on Horseback Salad"?

    A. Jean Cocteau

    B. Luis Buñuel

    C. René Magritte

    D. Salvador Dalí

answers found on page 557

80. Debbie Reynolds plays a Broadway star in what comedy costarring Hans Conried?

A. *Caprice* (1967)
B. *My Six Loves* (1963)
C. *Rock-a-Bye Baby* (1958)
D. *The Thrill of It All* (1963)

81. Barbra Streisand starred in the 1972 comedy *What's Up, Doc?* In what city does the action take place?

A. Boston
B. New York
C. San Francisco
D. Seattle

82. Geraldine Page and Carol Burnett share the screen in what comedy?

A. *Pete 'n' Tillie* (1972)
B. *Some Like It Hot* (1959)
C. *The Notorious Landlady* (1962)
D. *Wives and Lovers* (1963)

83. Who won the Academy Award for Best Supporting Actor for his role in the 1966 film *The Fortune Cookie*?

A. George Burns
B. Jack Warden
C. Richard Benjamin
D. Walter Matthau

84. Walter Brennan appears in what comedy opposite W. C. Fields?

A. *Man on the Flying Trapeze* (1935)
B. *Shop Talk* (1935)
C. *The Big Wheel* (1949)
D. *The Human Comedy* (1943)

85. Natalie Wood plays the daughter of Margaret Sullavan's character in what film?

A. *Come Live with Me* (1941)
B. *No Sad Songs for Me* (1950)
C. *The Man from Laramie* (1955)
D. *The Shop Around the Corner* (1940)

86. Who directed Tony Curtis in the 1959 comedy *Operation Petticoat*?

A. Billy Wilder
B. Blake Edwards
C. Preston Sturges
D. Vincente Minnelli

87. Ronald Colman plays a quiz-show contestant in what comedy costarring Vincent Price?

A. *Champagne for Caesar* (1950)
B. *Excuse My Dust* (1951)
C. *Lovely to Look At* (1952)
D. *Watch the Birdie* (1950)

88. Ernest Laszlo was the cinematographer of what comedy starring William Holden and David Niven?

A. *Practically Yours* (1944)
B. *The Girl Most Likely* (1958)
C. *The Moon Is Blue* (1953)
D. *Tonight We Sing* (1953)

89. Maureen O'Hara and Lucille Ball share the screen in what comedy?

A. *Dance, Girl, Dance* (1940)
B. *No Time for Love* (1943)
C. *Practically Yours* (1944)
D. *Tonight We Sing* (1953)

90. Herbert Lom plays the role of Charles Dreyfus in which comedy opposite Peter Sellers?

A. *A Shot in the Dark* (1964)
B. *Casino Royale* (1967)
C. *Never Let Go* (1960)
D. *There's a Girl in My Soup* (1970)

91. Ginger Rogers plays a radio singer named Glory Eden in what comedy?

A. *Carefree* (1938)
B. *Professional Sweetheart* (1933)
C. *Rendezvous* (1935)
D. *Star of Midnight* (1935)

answers found on page 557

Arsenic and Old Lace, 1944

92. Who directed Cary Grant in the 1944 comedy *Arsenic and Old Lace*?

A. Charles Walters
B. Frank Capra
C. King Vidor
D. Victor Fleming

93. Arthur Hiller directed Steve Martin in what comedy?

A. *I'm Dancing as Fast as I Can* (1982)
B. *Taking Care of Business* (1990)
C. *The Lonely Guy* (1984)
D. *The Wheeler Dealers* (1963)

94. Ralph Bellamy romances Carole Lombard in what comedy?

A. *Fools for Scandal* (1938)
B. *Her Highness and the Bellboy* (1945)
C. *My Favorite Spy* (1951)
D. *The Heavenly Body* (1944)

95. Mae West was the star performer of Edward Arnold's traveling circus in which film costarring Cary Grant?

A. *Blonde Venus* (1932)
B. *Every Day's a Holiday* (1937)
C. *Go West Young Man* (1936)
D. *I'm No Angel* (1933)

96. Charles Coburn and Ronald Reagan star in what comedy directed by Alexander Hall?

A. *Louisa* (1950)

B. *Neptune's Daughter* (1949)
C. *The Fuller Brush Girl* (1950)
D. *Watch the Birdie* (1950)

97. Edward Arnold, as patriarch Senator Wilkins, attempts to rein in his daughter's antics in what comedy featuring Natalie Wood?

A. *Dear Brat* (1951)
B. *Father Was a Fullback* (1949)
C. *Never a Dull Moment* (1950)
D. *The Green Promise* (1949)

98. What was Carole Lombard's real name?

A. Betty Hought
B. Catherine Beeman
C. Jane Peters
D. Judy Vincent

99. Stanley Donen directed Richard Burton in what comedy?

A. *A Guide for the Married Man* (1967)
B. *Candy* (1968)
C. *Staircase* (1969)
D. *The Prince and the Showgirl* (1957)

100. James Cagney plays a corporate executive of what beverage company in Billy Wilder's comedy *One, Two, Three* (1961)?

A. Coca-Cola
B. Kool-Aid
C. Nestle Iced Tea
D. Sunny Delight

101. W. C. Fields's character masquerades as a missionary in what comedy?

A. *A Family Affair* (1937)
B. *Monsieur Beaucaire* (1946)
C. *The Potters* (1927)
D. *Tillie and Gus* (1933)

102. Anthony Quinn appeared as an extra in which Harold Lloyd comedy?

   A. *Feet First* (1930)
   B. *Movie Crazy* (1932)
   C. *The Cat's-Paw* (1934)
   D. *The Milky Way* (1936)

103. What comedy team stars in Norman Z. McLeod's *Here Comes Cookie* (1935)?

   A. Bing Crosby and Bob Hope
   B. Dean Martin and Jerry Lewis
   C. George Burns and Gracie Allen
   D. The Three Stooges

104. What comedy features Gary Cooper, W. C. Fields, and Charles Laughton?

   A. *If I Had a Million* (1932)
   B. *Shop Talk* (1935)
   C. *The Big Wheel* (1949)
   D. *The Human Comedy* (1943)

105. What comedy featuring Laurence Naismith is set during the Festival of Britain?

   A. *A Piece of Cake* (1948)
   B. *Love in Pawn* (1953)
   C. *Room to Let* (1950)
   D. *The Happy Family* (1952)

106. Which of the following is not one of the names of Walter Matthau's children?

   A. Albert
   B. Charlie
   C. David
   D. Jenny

107. What Neil Simon play was nominated for the Laurence Olivier Theatre Award for Best New Comedy?

   A. *Chapter Two*
   B. *Laughter on the 23rd Floor*
   C. *The Good Doctor*
   D. *The Odd Couple*

108. Fred MacMurray and Jean Hagen team up in what comedy?

   A. *Herbie Rides Again* (1974)
   B. *That Darn Cat!* (1965)
   C. *The Gnome-Mobile* (1967)
   D. *The Shaggy Dog* (1959)

109. Vivien Leigh and Rex Harrison star in what romantic comedy adapted from a Bruno Frank play?

   A. *Easy Living* (1937)
   B. *No Time for Love* (1943)
   C. *Practically Yours* (1944)
   D. *Storm in a Teacup* (1937)

110. Natalie Wood plays the daughter of Fred MacMurray's character in what comedy?

   A. *Never a Dull Moment* (1950)
   B. *On Our Merry Way* (1948)
   C. *Paris Blues* (1961)
   D. *Pot O' Gold* (1941)

111. At the end of the Sandra Dee/Bobby Darin comedy *If a Man Answers* (1962), what appears on the screen under the question "Finis?"

   A. Cherchez la femme
   B. Ha!
   C. We hardly think so
   D. You bet

112. Edward Arnold portrays the town mayor in what comedy opposite Dean Martin and Jerry Lewis?

   A. *Artists and Models* (1955)
   B. *Living It Up* (1954)
   C. *The Stooge* (1952)
   D. *You're Never Too Young* (1955)

answers found on page 557

113. What was the nickname of Natalie Wood's character in the 1948 comedy *Scudda Hoo! Scudda Hay!?*

A. "Bean"
B. "Pumpkin"
C. "Scout"
D. "Tater Tot"

114. Which of the following Carole Lombard films is about a socialite who marries a cowboy?

A. *I Take This Woman* (1931)
B. *Mr. and Mrs. Smith* (1941)
C. *Sinners in the Sun* (1932)
D. *To Be or Not to Be* (1942)

115. What Bob Hope film competed for the Best Scoring of a Dramatic or Comedy Picture Oscar in 1945?

A. *Road to Zanzibar*
B. *The Ghost Breakers*
C. *The Paleface*
D. *The Princess and the Pirate*

116. Thelma Ritter was nominated for an Academy Award as Best Supporting Actress in what comedy directed by Mitchell Leisen?

A. *Let's Dance* (1950)
B. *Royal Wedding* (1951)
C. *The Belle of New York* (1952)
D. *The Mating Season* (1951)

117. Bette Davis plays the daughter of an oil tycoon in what romantic comedy directed by William Keighley?

A. *Big Hearted Herbert* (1934)
B. *Kansas City Princess* (1934)
C. *Secrets of an Actress* (1938)
D. *The Bride Came C.O.D.* (1941)

118. The 1978 comedy *Rabbit Test*, costarring Roddy McDowall, was written and directed by what famous comic?

A. Alan King
B. George Carlin
C. Imogene Coca
D. Joan Rivers

119. Which of the following actresses does not appear with José Ferrer in the 1982 film *A Midsummer Night's Sex Comedy*?

A. Dianne Wiest
B. Julie Hagerty
C. Mary Steenburgen
D. Mia Farrow

120. Who was Carole Lombard's first husband?

A. Clark Gable
B. Gary Cooper
C. Leslie Howard
D. William Powell

121. In the 1936 comedy *Poppy*, W. C. Fields's character is a salesman of what questionable product?

A. Miracle-grow shampoo
B. Porcupine hair combs
C. Snake oil
D. Waterproof hair spray

122. Which of the following Carole Lombard films was directed by Garson Kanin?

A. *Hands Across the Table* (1935)
B. *Love Before Breakfast* (1936)
C. *They Knew What They Wanted* (1940)
D. *White Woman* (1933)

123. Who directed Peter Sellers in the 1963 comedy *The Pink Panther?*

A. Billy Wilder
B. Blake Edwards
C. Vincente Minnelli
D. Woody Allen

answers found on page 557

Spotlight on
WILLIAM **POWELL** (1892–1984)

Powell could deliver a withering bon mot while also making fun of himself, creating characters who were both sophisticated and totally unpretentious. With his most popular costar, Myrna Loy, Powell created an unprecedented image of marriage as a meeting of minds as well as hearts. Suavity was hardly in his blood; his father was an accountant who wanted William to become an attorney. But after a few weeks of law school, he switched to the American Academy of Dramatic Arts in New York. From 1912 to 1922 he struggled to build a stage career, finally hitting pay dirt as a dying romantic in 1922's *Spanish Love*. Strong reviews led to his screen debut as one of Moriarty's henchmen in *Sherlock Holmes* (1922), and to a contract with Paramount. Sound proved a boon to Powell, whose comic delivery was impeccable, and he finally became a star playing urbane sleuth

Manhattan Melodrama, 1934

Philo Vance in *The Canary Murder Case* (1929). A few years later he moved to MGM, where he scored the first time out in *Manhattan Melodrama* (1934), the first film to pair him with his perfect leading lady, Myrna Loy. Director W. S. Van Dyke reteamed them for *The Thin Man* (1934), and the surprise hit made them top stars.

1. William Powell's character in *The Thin Man Goes Home* (1945) reads a comic book called *Nick Carter Detective Magazine*. What is it about?

   A. A famous sleuth
   B. The husband of a beautiful heiress
   C. Powell's character himself
   D. All of the above

2. William Powell and Myrna Loy help an engaged couple make it to the altar in which comedy directed by Richard Thorpe?

   A. *Double Wedding* (1937)
   B. *Slightly Married* (1932)
   C. *The Toy Wife* (1938)
   D. *Too Many Kisses* (1925)

3. Gloria Grahame appeared in which film starring William Powell and Myrna Loy?

   A. *Merton of the Movies* (1947)
   B. *Song of the Thin Man* (1947)
   C. *The Glass Wall* (1953)
   D. *The Man Who Never Was* (1956)

4. Which of the following movies did not star William Powell and Carole Lombard?

   A. *Ladies' Man* (1931)
   B. *Man of the World* (1931)
   C. *My Man Godfrey* (1936)
   D. *Twentieth Century* (1934)

The Thin Man Goes Home, 1945

5. In what film did Jean Harlow wear the star sapphire ring given to her by her real-life beau William Powell?

   A. *High Wall* (1947)
   B. *Passage to Marseille* (1944)
   C. *Personal Property* (1937)
   D. *Society Doctor* (1935)

answers found on page 557

124. What leading lady made her film debut at age forty?

A. Irene Dunne
B. Loretta Young
C. Mae West
D. Myrna Loy

125. Rex Harrison and Richard Burton play hairdressers in the West End of London in what comedy?

A. *A Guide for the Married Man* (1967)
B. *Hello, Dolly!* (1969)
C. *Staircase* (1969)
D. *The Prince and the Showgirl* (1957)

126. Natalie Wood plays the daughter of Barbara Stanwyck's character in what comedy?

A. *Magic Town* (1947)
B. *Paris Blues* (1961)
C. *The Bride Wore Boots* (1946)
D. *You Gotta Stay Happy* (1948)

127. Which of the following actors does not appear with Henry Fonda in the 1955 comedy *Mister Roberts*?

A. Gregory Peck
B. Jack Lemmon
C. James Cagney
D. William Powell

128. Cecil Kellaway plays Professor Starkweather in what comedy?

A. *A Piece of Cake* (1948)
B. *A Very Young Lady* (1941)
C. *Love in Pawn* (1953)
D. *Room to Let* (1950)

129. Arthur Hiller directed Dudley Moore in what comedy?

A. *I'm Dancing as Fast as I Can* (1982)
B. *Romantic Comedy* (1983)
C. *Taking Care of Business* (1990)
D. *The Wheeler Dealers* (1963)

130. Gene Kelly directed Walter Matthau and Inger Stevens in what comedy?

A. *A Guide for the Married Man* (1967)
B. *Practically Yours* (1944)
C. *The Girl Most Likely* (1958)
D. *Tonight We Sing* (1953)

131. Daniel Mann branched out into comedy with what Dean Martin film?

A. *Come Back Little Sheba* (1952)
B. *The Rose Tattoo* (1955)
C. *The Teahouse of the August Moon* (1956)
D. *Who's Got the Action?* (1962)

132. Which of the following actors stars in the 1983 Walter Mirisch–produced film *Romantic Comedy*?

A. Alan Alda
B. Dudley Moore
C. Dustin Hoffman
D. James Caan

133. Rita Moreno appears in what romantic comedy starring Lana Turner and Ricardo Montalban?

A. *Dramatic School* (1938)
B. *Latin Lovers* (1953)
C. *Pagan Love Song* (1950)
D. *These Glamour Girls* (1939)

134. What comedy directed by Mitchell Leisen pairs Paulette Goddard and Fred MacMurray?

A. *No Time for Love* (1943)
B. *Practically Yours* (1944)
C. *Suddenly, It's Spring* (1947)
D. *The Girl Most Likely* (1958)

135. In what film did Paulette Goddard costar with Joan Crawford, Norma Shearer, and Rosalind Russell?

A. *Hold Back the Dawn* (1941)
B. *Kitty* (1945)
C. *The Women* (1939)
D. *Unconquered* (1947)

answers found on page 557

136. W. C. Fields and Louise Brooks costar in what comedy?

   A. *A Family Affair* (1937)
   B. *It's the Old Army Game* (1926)
   C. *Monsieur Beaucaire* (1946)
   D. *The Potters* (1927)

137. Vivien Leigh and Rex Harrison share the screen in *Storm in a Teacup* (1937) and what other comedy?

   A. *Artists and Models Abroad* (1938)
   B. *Sidewalks of London* (1938)
   C. *The Spectacle Maker* (1934)
   D. *Times Square Lady* (1935)

Merton of the Movies, 1947

138. What actress appears opposite Red Skelton in the 1947 comedy *Merton of the Movies*?

   A. Barbara Stanwyck
   B. Elizabeth Taylor
   C. Gloria Grahame
   D. Maureen O'Hara

139. What was Peter Lawford's first comedy?

   A. *My Brother Talks to Horses* (1947)
   B. *Royal Wedding* (1951)
   C. *Son of Lassie* (1945)
   D. *Ziegfeld Follies* (1948)

140. Robert Wagner portrays George Lytton in which comedy opposite Peter Sellers?

   A. *Casino Royale* (1967)
   B. *Simon Simon* (1970)
   C. *The Party* (1968)
   D. *The Pink Panther* (1963)

141. Which leading lady has her dress torn off in the Laurel and Hardy film *Double Whoopee* (1929)?

   A. Carole Lombard
   B. Gloria Swanson
   C. Jean Harlow
   D. Myrna Loy

142. Shirley Jones and Red Buttons share the screen in what romantic comedy?

   A. *A Ticklish Affair* (1963)
   B. *Bobbikins* (1959)
   C. *Mr. Music* (1950)
   D. *The Secret of My Success* (1965)

143. Cary Grant stars in what comedy directed by Alexander Hall?

   A. *Blue Skies* (1946)
   B. *Neptune's Daughter* (1949)
   C. *Once Upon a Time* (1944)
   D. *The Fuller Brush Man* (1948)

144. Who plays Helena Bonham Carter's mother in the Greek chorus scenes of Woody Allen's *Mighty Aphrodite* (1995)?

   A. Anna Massey
   B. Barbara Leigh-Hunt
   C. Claire Bloom
   D. Francesca Annis

145. Two manicurists hitchhike all the way to Paris, France, in what romantic comedy directed by William Keighley?

   A. *Babbitt* (1934)
   B. *Four Men and a Prayer* (1938)
   C. *Kansas City Princess* (1934)
   D. *The Green Pastures* (1936)

146. What was the only film in which Charles Chaplin and Buster Keaton appeared together?

A. *A Countess from Hong Kong* (1967)
B. *A King in New York* (1957)
C. *Limelight* (1952)
D. *The Great Dictator* (1940)

147. What is the name of Barbra Streisand's character in the 1979 comedy *The Main Event*?

A. Hillary
B. Ione
C. Pamela
D. Phyllis

148. What was the first comedy to win Best Picture?

A. *It Happened One Night* (1934)
B. *Lady for a Day* (1933)
C. *The Divorcee* (1930)
D. *The Thin Man* (1934)

149. William Holden strives to win the affections of Edward Arnold's daughter in which romantic comedy?

A. *Dear Ruth* (1947)
B. *Meet the Stewarts* (1942)
C. *Three Daring Daughters* (1948)
D. *Wallflower* (1948)

150. Hedda Hopper has a small role as snooty Grace Stuyvesant in what Norman Z. McLeod comedy?

A. *Bunker Bean* (1936)
B. *Early to Bed* (1936)
C. *If I Had a Million* (1932)
D. *Topper* (1937)

151. Peter Sellers plays "man with two cars" in what comedy short?

A. *Let's Go Crazy* (1951)
B. *Penny Points to Paradise* (1951)
C. *Simon Simon* (1970)
D. *The Smallest Show on Earth* (1957)

152. Rosalind Russell costars with Norma Shearer and Joan Crawford in what film?

A. *His Girl Friday* (1940)
B. *My Sister Eileen* (1942)
C. *Sister Kenny* (1946)
D. *The Women* (1939)

153. Miriam Hopkins and Fay Wray star in which comedy?

A. *Design for Living* (1933)
B. *The Mating Season* (1951)
C. *The Richest Girl in the World* (1934)
D. *Woman Chases Man* (1937)

154. Tony Randall and Burl Ives costar in what comedy featuring Barbara Eden?

A. *Love in Pawn* (1953)
B. *The Brass Bottle* (1964)
C. *The Magic Box* (1952)
D. *The Moon Is Blue* (1953)

155. What is the name of Carole Lombard's character in the 1934 film *Twentieth Century*?

A. Betsy Stafford
B. Hannah Brown
C. Lily Garland
D. Tiffany Lake

156. Who did Pam Grier play in the comedy *Jawbreaker* (1999)?

A. Courtney Alice Shayne
B. Detective Vera Cruz
C. Fern Mayo
D. Mrs. Purr

157. William Holden and David Niven vie for the affections of the same woman in what comedy?

A. *A Certain Smile* (1958)
B. *Goodbye, Mr. Chips* (1939)
C. *The Moon Is Blue* (1953)
D. *Words and Music* (1948)

answers found on pages 557–558

158. Which 1934 Mae West film was banned in Norway and Holland?

A. *Belle of the Nineties*
B. *I'm No Angel*
C. *Klondike Andy*
D. *She Done Him Wrong*

159. In which of the following films directed by Woody Allen did George Hamilton appear?

A. *Hollywood Ending* (2002)
B. *Match Point* (2005)
C. *Stardust Memories* (1980)
D. *Take the Money and Run* (1969)

160. Which romantic comedy stars John Candy, Maureen O'Hara, James Belushi, and Anthony Quinn?

A. *Betsey's Wedding* (1990)
B. *Boris and Natasha* (1992)
C. *Delirious* (1991)
D. *Only the Lonely* (1991)

161. Who won the Academy Award for Best Supporting Actor for his performance in the 1975 comedy *The Sunshine Boys*?

A. Bob Hope
B. George Burns
C. John Wayne
D. Peter O'Toole

162. Jack Lemmon and Jack Carson pal around in what comedy?

A. *A Guide for the Married Man* (1967)
B. *Candy* (1968)
C. *Phffft!* (1954)
D. *The Fortune Cookie* (1966)

163. In which of the following do Mel Brooks and Anne Bancroft not appear on screen together?

A. *Curb Your Enthusiasm*, "Opening Night" (2004)
B. *History of the World: Part I* (1981)
C. *Silent Movie* (1976)
D. *To Be or Not to Be* (1983)

164. Vince Edwards played the title role in what comedy opposite Jack Carson?

A. *Carbine Williams* (1952)
B. *Mr. Universe* (1951)
C. *The Great Caruso* (1951)
D. *The Prodigal* (1955)

165. Kathleen Freeman plays the babysitter in what comedy starring Jerry Lewis and Peter Lawford?

A. *A Piece of Cake* (1948)
B. *Hook, Line and Sinker* (1969)
C. *Love in Pawn* (1953)
D. *Room to Let* (1950)

166. Walter Matthau and Inger Stevens play husband and wife in what comedy?

A. *A Guide for the Married Man* (1967)
B. *No Time for Love* (1943)
C. *Practically Yours* (1944)
D. *The Mating Season* (1951)

167. In the 1933 comedy *International House*, the hotel guests clamor to buy the rights to what invention?

A. Airplane
B. Automobile
C. Space shuttle
D. Television

168. Red Skelton and Jean Hagen costar in what comedy?

A. *A Southern Yankee* (1948)
B. *Half a Hero* (1953)
C. *Son of Flubber* (1963)
D. *Watch the Birdie* (1950)

169. In the 1940 Laurel and Hardy comedy *Saps at Sea,* Oliver Hardy's character is advised to go on a sea cruise because he suffers from an aversion to what sound?

A. Bells
B. Horns
C. Laughter
D. Whistling

170. Which of the following Carole Lombard films is about an advertising executive who quits his job to become a writer?

A. *I Take This Woman* (1931)
B. *No More Orchids* (1932)
C. *Up Pops the Devil* (1931)
D. *Vigil in the Night* (1940)

171. William Holden stars in what comedy written by Dalton Trumbo?

A. *My Brother Talks to Horses* (1947)
B. *The Remarkable Andrew* (1942)
C. *Whistling in Brooklyn* (1943)
D. *Yes, My Darling Daughter* (1939)

172. What is the profession of Rex Harrison's character in the 1948 comedy *Unfaithfully Yours*?

A. College professor
B. Doctor
C. Pharmacist
D. Symphony conductor

173. Arthur Hiller directed Richard Pryor and Gene Wilder in what action-comedy?

A. *I'm Dancing as Fast as I Can* (1982)
B. *See No Evil, Hear No Evil* (1989)
C. *Taking Care of Business* (1990)
D. *The Wheeler Dealers* (1963)

174. What romantic comedy starring Ingrid Bergman, Rex Harrison, and Omar Sharif was directed by Anthony Asquith?

A. *A Walk in the Spring Rain* (1970)
B. *Over the Moon* (1939)
C. *School for Husbands* (1937)
D. *The Yellow Rolls-Royce* (1964)

175. Who was the director of the 1934 Carole Lombard film *Twentieth Century*?

A. Elia Kazan
B. Frank Capra
C. Howard Hawks
D. Vincente Minnelli

176. Who directed Carole Lombard in *Mr. and Mrs. Smith* (1941)?

A. Alfred Hitchcock
B. Ernst Lubitsch
C. Frank Capra
D. George Stevens

177. Which of the following leading ladies is not in *The Women* (1939)?

A. Joan Crawford
B. Loretta Young
C. Norma Shearer
D. Rosalind Russell

178. What is Van Johnson's character in the 1950 comedy *The Big Hangover* allergic to?

A. Alcohol
B. Chocolate
C. Coconut
D. Pineapple

179. Whose mother does Fay Wray play in the 1957 comedy *Tammy and the Bachelor*?

A. Debbie Reynolds
B. Leslie Nielsen
C. Peter Fonda
D. Sandra Dee

180. Tony Randall and Shirley Jones star in what comedy?

A. *Bobbikins* (1959)
B. *Fluffy* (1965)
C. *Let's Dance* (1950)
D. *The Secret of My Success* (1965)

181. Which actor makes a cameo appearance in the 1952 romantic comedy *Love Is Better Than Ever*, starring Elizabeth Taylor?

A. Clark Gable
B. Fred Astaire
C. Gene Kelly
D. William Holden

answers found on page 558

182. Ginger Rogers played a manicurist in what comedy?

A. *Don't Bet on Love* (1933)
B. *Flying Down to Rio* (1933)
C. *Perfect Understanding* (1933)
D. *Rose-Marie* (1936)

183. What romantic comedy directed by Billy Wilder was filmed at the actual home of Paramount Pictures chairman Barney Balaban?

A. *A Foreign Affair* (1948)
B. *Love in the Afternoon* (1957)
C. *Sabrina* (1954)
D. *The Emperor Waltz* (1948)

Bringing Up Baby, 1938

184. Who directed the 1938 screwball comedy *Bringing Up Baby*, starring Katharine Hepburn and Cary Grant?

A. Howard Hawks
B. W. S. Van Dyke
C. Leo McCarey
D. Norman McLeod

185. Cecil Kellaway appears in what comedy with Fred MacMurray?

A. *A Piece of Cake* (1948)
B. *Love in Pawn* (1953)
C. *New York Town* (1941)
D. *Room to Let* (1950)

186. W. C. Fields and George Burns costar in the 1934 film *Six of a Kind* and what other comedy?

A. *A Family Affair* (1937)
B. *International House* (1933)
C. *Monsieur Beaucaire* (1946)
D. *The Potters* (1927)

187. Carole Lombard directed Alfred Hitchcock's cameo in what comedy?

A. *Beau Geste* (1939)
B. *Let's Live a Little* (1948)
C. *Mr. and Mrs. Smith* (1941)
D. *The Cowboy and the Lady* (1938)

188. In the Joan Blondell comedy *Traveling Saleslady* (1935), she and her partner try to sell toothpaste that tastes like what?

A. Bubble gum
B. Chocolate ice cream
C. Liquor
D. Steak

189. Robert Taylor and Jean Harlow share the screen in what romantic comedy?

A. *Personal Property* (1937)
B. *Society Doctor* (1935)
C. *The Spectacle Maker* (1934)
D. *Times Square Lady* (1935)

190. Ralph Bellamy costars opposite Merle Oberon and Rita Hayworth in what romantic comedy?

A. *Affectionately Yours* (1941)
B. *Her Highness and the Bellboy* (1945)
C. *My Favorite Spy* (1951)
D. *No Time for Comedy* (1940)

191. Jack Carson and Kim Novak share the screen in what comedy?

A. *A Guide for the Married Man* (1967)
B. *Phffft!* (1954)
C. *The Fortune Cookie* (1966)
D. *Under the Yum Yum Tree* (1963)

answers found on page 558

Spotlight on
DORIS **DAY** (1924–)

Doris Day started out as a dancer, winning a dancing contest in her native Cincinnati and using the prize earnings for a trip to Hollywood. But on the drive back, she shattered her leg in a car accident. While recovering, she discovered she could sing and changed vocations, eventually winning a gig with the Les Brown Band. In 1948, director Michael Curtiz signed her to a personal contract (later sold to Warner Bros.) and gave her the lead in his next film, *Romance on the High Seas* (1948). There she introduced one of her signature songs, "It's Magic." Warner kept her mostly in lighthearted musicals, though they also loaned her to MGM for a rare dramatic turn as singer Ruth Etting in *Love Me or Leave Me* (1955). She even got to be one of director Alfred Hitchcock's trademark blondes in *The Man Who Knew Too Much* (1956), in which she introduced the song that would become her trademark, "Que Sera, Sera (Whatever Will Be, Will Be)." When Hollywood started cutting back on musicals in the late 1950s, Day switched to romantic comedies with *Pillow Talk* (1959), the first of three films she made with Rock Hudson and Tony Randall. Their success made her the nation's top box-office star.

The Tunnel of Love, 1958

1. **Which comedy paired Clark Gable and Doris Day?**

   A. *But Not for Me* (1959)
   B. *Teacher's Pet* (1958)
   C. *The Hucksters* (1947)
   D. *Too Hot to Handle* (1938)

2. **Doris Day plays the wife of a drama professor/critic in what comedy opposite David Niven?**

   A. *Pillow Talk* (1959)
   B. *Please Don't Eat the Daisies* (1960)
   C. *Teacher's Pet* (1958)
   D. *The Pajama Game* (1957)

3. **Delbert Mann directed Doris Day in 1962's *That Touch of Mink* and what other romantic comedy?**

   A. *Lover Come Back* (1961)
   B. *No Time for Love* (1943)
   C. *The Girl Most Likely* (1958)
   D. *The Moon Is Blue* (1953)

4. **Frank Sinatra romances Doris Day in which musical?**

   A. *Anchors Aweigh* (1945)
   B. *Guys and Dolls* (1955)
   C. *On the Town* (1949)
   D. *Young at Heart* (1954)

5. **Doris Day stars in what romantic comedy set off the shores of Catalina Island?**

   A. *By the Light of the Silvery Moon* (1953)
   B. *Caprice* (1967)
   C. *The Glass Bottom Boat* (1966)
   D. *The Tunnel of Love* (1958)

Love Me or Leave Me, 1955

answers found on page 558

192. Angela Lansbury and Dorothy Dandridge are both featured in what mystery-comedy?

A. *Remains to Be Seen* (1953)
B. *That Forsyte Woman* (1949)
C. *The Baroness and the Butler* (1938)
D. *The Pleasure of His Company* (1961)

193. Harry Davenport is featured in what comedy opposite Betty Grable and Cesar Romero?

A. *A Piece of Cake* (1948)
B. *Love in Pawn* (1953)
C. *Room to Let* (1950)
D. *That Lady in Ermine* (1948)

194. Paul Muni and Ned Sparks costar in what comedy directed by Mervyn LeRoy?

A. *A Piece of Cake* (1948)
B. *Hi, Nellie!* (1934)
C. *Love in Pawn* (1953)
D. *Room to Let* (1950)

195. In which of the following films does José Ferrer costar with Mel Brooks?

A. *A Midsummer Night's Sex Comedy* (1982)
B. *Fedora* (1978)
C. *The Big Brawl* (1980)
D. *To Be or Not to Be* (1983)

196. Rosalind Russell joins the army in order to keep tabs on her boyfriend in what Norman Z. McLeod comedy?

A. *Here Comes Cookie* (1935)
B. *Little Men* (1940)
C. *Merrily We Live* (1938)
D. *Never Wave at a WAC* (1953)

197. Joan Blondell costars as a murder victim in the comedy *Topper Returns* (1941). What actor plays Topper?

A. Cary Grant
B. Robert Young
C. Roland Young
D. William Powell

198. Bette Midler and Shelley Long star in what comedy directed by Arthur Hiller?

A. *Outrageous Fortune* (1987)
B. *Plaza Suite* (1971)
C. *Promise Her Anything* (1965)
D. *The Wheeler Dealers* (1963)

199. W. C. Fields plays a scheming carnival ringmaster in what comedy set during WWI?

A. *Babes on Broadway* (1941)
B. *Shop Talk* (1935)
C. *The Big Wheel* (1949)
D. *Tillie's Punctured Romance* (1928)

200. For what film did Rosalind Russell earn her first Academy Award nomination?

A. *His Girl Friday* (1940)
B. *My Sister Eileen* (1942)
C. *Sister Kenny* (1946)
D. *The Women* (1939)

201. The 1938 comedy *Mr. Doodle Kicks Off* takes place at what fictional college?

A. Butterscotch University
B. Doodle Institute
C. Taylor Tech
D. Toffee Tech

202. What is the only of Barbara Stanwyck's comedic performances to earn an Academy Award nomination?

A. Sugarpuss O'Shea in *Ball of Fire* (1941)
B. Elizabeth Lane in *Christmas in Connecticut* (1945)
C. Helen Hunt in *You Belong to Me* (1941)
D. Sally Warren in *The Bride Wore Boots* (1946)

203. Fred MacMurray's character in what comedy helps dig a tunnel under the Hudson River?

A. *Let's Dance* (1950)
B. *No Time for Love* (1943)
C. *The Belle of New York* (1952)
D. *The Moon Is Blue* (1953)

204. Which comedy pairs Goldie Hawn and Peter Sellers?

A. *Hoffman* (1970)
B. *The Party* (1968)
C. *There's a Girl in My Soup* (1970)
D. *Waltz of the Toreadors* (1962)

The Sunshine Boys, 1975

205. In *The Sunshine Boys* (1975), what is the name of the former comedy team played by Walter Matthau and George Burns?

A. Kane and Abel
B. Kupp and Saucer
C. Lewis and Clark
D. Walt and Willy

206. Merv Griffin makes a cameo appearance in what comedy starring Steve Martin?

A. *Plaza Suite* (1971)
B. *Promise Her Anything* (1965)
C. *The Lonely Guy* (1984)
D. *The Wheeler Dealers* (1963)

207. Walter Matthau and Carol Burnett play the title roles in what comedy?

A. *Mr. Peabody and the Mermaid* (1948)
B. *Pete 'n' Tillie* (1972)
C. *The Cat and the Canary* (1939)
D. *Tillie and Gus* (1933)

208. David Niven masquerades as an exiled prince in what comedy costarring Shirley Jones?

A. *Bedtime Story* (1964)
B. *Bobbikins* (1959)
C. *The Pleasure of His Company* (1961)
D. *The Secret of My Success* (1965)

209. The Burt Reynolds comedy *Switching Channels* (1988) was a remake of what classic film?

A. *A Face in the Crowd* (1957)
B. *His Girl Friday* (1940)
C. *It's a Wonderful Life* (1946)
D. *The Philadelphia Story* (1940)

210. What is the profession of Walter Matthau's character in *Cactus Flower* (1969)?

A. Acupuncturist
B. Chiropractor
C. Dentist
D. Surgeon

211. In what Abbott and Costello film did Charles Laughton costar?

A. *Abbott and Costello Go to Mars* (1953)
B. *Abbott and Costello Meet Captain Kidd* (1952)
C. *Abbott and Costello Meet the Mummy* (1953)
D. *Abbott and Costello in the Foreign Legion* (1950)

212. Bobby Van plays the title role in what comedy opposite Debbie Reynolds?

A. *Cinderfella* (1960)
B. *Merton of the Movies* (1947)
C. *The Affairs of Dobie Gillis* (1953)
D. *The Ladies Man* (1961)

213. Lucille Ball and Van Johnson share the screen in what romantic comedy?

A. *Clowning Around* (1992)
B. *Easy to Wed* (1946)
C. *The Notorious Landlady* (1962)
D. *Wives and Lovers* (1963)

answers found on page 558

214. W. C. Fields's character in what comedy ditches work to watch a wrestling match?

A. *A Family Affair* (1937)
B. *Live, Love and Learn* (1937)
C. *Man on the Flying Trapeze* (1935)
D. *The Potters* (1927)

215. Which Irving Berlin song was featured in the 1989 comedy *When Harry Met Sally*?

A. "I'm Putting All My Eggs in One Basket"
B. "It's a Lovely Day Today"
C. "Let Me Sing and I'm Happy"
D. "Say It Isn't So"

216. Walter Matthau and Geraldine Page costar in what comedy?

A. *Pete 'n' Tillie* (1972)
B. *Some Like It Hot* (1959)
C. *The Notorious Landlady* (1962)
D. *Wives and Lovers* (1963)

217. Charles Boyer and Louis Jourdan star in what comedy set in Quebec?

A. *A Certain Smile* (1958)
B. *Days of Wine and Roses* (1962)
C. *The Happy Time* (1952)
D. *Under the Yum Yum Tree* (1963)

218. W. C. Fields's character must win a boat race in what comedy?

A. *Mississippi* (1935)
B. *Shop Talk* (1935)
C. *The Big Wheel* (1949)
D. *Tillie and Gus* (1933)

219. What is the name of Carole Lombard's character in *My Man Godfrey* (1936)?

A. Irene Bullock
B. Jennie Pickaring
C. Kitty Packard
D. Louise Rinaldo

220. What is the only Mae West film to earn an Academy Award nomination for Best Picture?

A. *Belle of the Nineties* (1934)
B. *I'm No Angel* (1933)
C. *Klondike Annie* (1936)
D. *She Done Him Wrong* (1933)

221. Olivia de Havilland plays the role of Joan Fisk, daughter of Edward Arnold's character in what comedy?

A. *Lady in a Cage* (1964)
B. *The Ambassador's Daughter* (1956)
C. *The Proud Rebel* (1958)
D. *The Well-Groomed Bride* (1946)

222. Arthur Hiller directed Warren Beatty in what romantic comedy?

A. *I'm Dancing as Fast as I Can* (1982)
B. *Promise Her Anything* (1965)
C. *Taking Care of Business* (1990)
D. *The Wheeler Dealers* (1963)

223. Mae West and W. C. Fields starred in and cowrote what comedy?

A. *A Family Affair* (1937)
B. *Live, Love and Learn* (1937)
C. *Monsieur Beaucaire* (1946)
D. *My Little Chickadee* (1940)

224. What is the name of the company owned by W. C. Fields at the end of *It's a Gift* (1934)?

A. Bissonette's Bluebird Oranges
B. Canaby's Country Cheese
C. Dapper Dan's Pomade
D. Harold's Handsome Hats

225. Arthur Hiller directed Kevin Spacey in what comedy-thriller?

A. *I'm Dancing as Fast as I Can* (1982)
B. *See No Evil, Hear No Evil* (1989)
C. *Taking Care of Business* (1990)
D. *The Wheeler Dealers* (1963)

answers found on page 558

226. James Stewart and Rosalind Russell share the screen in what romantic comedy?

    A. *No Time for Comedy* (1940)
    B. *Secrets of an Actress* (1938)
    C. *The Green Pastures* (1936)
    D. *Varsity Show* (1937)

227. In which comedy did Carmen Miranda star opposite Dean Martin and Jerry Lewis?

    A. *Babes on Broadway* (1941)
    B. *Doll Face* (1945)
    C. *Scared Stiff* (1953)
    D. *Something for the Boys* (1944)

228. Dana Andrews is a child psychologist in what comedy costarring Louis Jourdan?

    A. *No Minor Vices* (1948)
    B. *The Big Wheel* (1949)
    C. *The Great Race* (1965)
    D. *The Human Comedy* (1943)

Never a Dull Moment, 1950

229. Irene Dunne plays a New York songwriter who marries a cowboy and must adjust to life on his Wyoming ranch in *Never a Dull Moment* (1950). Who plays the cowboy?

    A. Jack Lemmon
    B. Fred MacMurray
    C. Walter Matthau
    D. James Cagney

230. Who plays Carole Lombard's husband in the 1939 comedy *Made for Each Other*?

    A. Cary Grant
    B. Gary Cooper
    C. James Mason
    D. James Stewart

231. Michael Constantine and Natalie Wood costar in what comedy-mystery?

    A. *Escape to Burma* (1955)
    B. *Peeper* (1975)
    C. *The Man with a Cloak* (1951)
    D. *Trooper Hook* (1957)

232. Who plays Henry Fonda's new wife in the 1968 comedy *Yours, Mine and Ours*?

    A. Carol Channing
    B. Debbie Reynolds
    C. Ginger Rogers
    D. Lucille Ball

233. What blacklisted writer earned an Academy Award nomination for the McCarthy-era comedy *The Front* (1976)?

    A. Abraham Polonsky
    B. Dalton Trumbo
    C. Ring Lardner Jr.
    D. Walter Bernstein

234. Lupe Velez appeared in 1934's *Hollywood Party* and which other Laurel and Hardy comedy?

    A. *Monsieur Don't Care* (1924)
    B. *Sailors Beware* (1927)
    C. *Slipping Wives* (1927)
    D. *Sugar Daddies* (1927)

Cimarron, 1960

Chapter 11

WESTERNS

With breathtaking action and an epic sense of the landscape, the western was a natural for the movies. One of the first story films was a western, Edwin S. Porter's *The Great Train Robbery* (1903), shot in the wilds of New Jersey. The genre moved to Hollywood with Cecil B. DeMille's *The Squaw Man* (1914), originally slated to shoot in Arizona until bad weather drove DeMille's crew even farther west.

One constant through more than a century of film history has been the uniquely American quality to the genre. Even the Italian-made spaghetti westerns of the sixties and seventies were built around the American dream of conquering the land, however threatening. The Oklahoma land rush vividly captured in *Cimarron* (1931), the race to escape marauding Indians in *Stagecoach* (1939), and the climactic shoot-outs in *High Noon* (1952), *Rio Bravo* (1959), and hundreds of other films all reflect the same basic American theme: "Live Free or Die."

For early audiences, tales of the western expansion were recent history, and the shift to Hollywood put moviemaking in close proximity to sites of many a western legend. Early cowboy star William S. Hart had fallen in love with the area during his youthful travels. Paramount Studio chief Jesse L. Lasky based *The Covered Wagon* (1923) on his grandfather's stories about moving westward. Wyatt Earp even spent his last years in Hollywood.

The western flourished on all levels of production. The big studios created films featuring major stars like Gary Cooper and Errol Flynn and taking advantage of new developments like sound, Technicolor, and CinemaScope almost as soon as they were available. They also invested in the occasional epic western, pouring money, stars, and talent into films like DeMille's *Union Pacific* (1939). When MGM set out to make *How the West Was Won* (1962), an all-star Cinerama epic, it took three of the genre's best directors—John Ford, Henry Hathaway, and George Marshall—to get it all on screen. But the studios also churned out low-budget, formulaic westerns, many built around stars like Tom Mix, Roy Rogers, and Gene Autry, who essentially played the same character from one film to the next.

The proliferation of low-budget productions made the genre one of Hollywood's best training grounds for fresh talent. Phylis Isley made her screen debut opposite John Wayne in 1939's *New Frontier* before becoming dramatic star Jennifer Jones. Decades later future stars like Barbara Hershey, Jon Voight, and Robert Duvall would follow similar career trajectories. Director William Wyler cut his teeth on low-budget silent westerns and would return to the genre between Oscars for more upscale productions like *The Westerner* (1940) and *The Big Country* (1958).

The genre also developed its own A-list stars, actors whose natural athleticism and craggy determination made them a perfect fit for western legends. Former football player John Wayne was leader of a pack that included Montana-bred Gary Cooper, one-time stuntman Joel McCrea, fast-shooter Glenn Ford, and the mature James Stewart. Leading the distaff side was Barbara Stanwyck, who insisted on doing her own stunts, even when starring in *Forty Guns* (1957) at the age of fifty.

Epic wasn't the only variation available to the western. Studios big and small dabbled in western musicals (*Oklahoma!*, 1955), comedies (1939's *Destry Rides Again* and 1965's *Cat Ballou*), film noir (*Blood on the Moon*, 1948), and even a few horror films like the 1966 *Billy the Kid vs. Dracula*. They also increasingly explored social issues, with *Broken Arrow* (1950) pioneering in its sympathetic depiction of Native Americans, setting the stage for such later films as Ford's *Two Rode Together* (1961) and Kevin Costner's Oscar-winning *Dances with Wolves* (1990). Arthur Penn even used the form to comment on the Vietnam War in *Little Big Man* (1970).

In later years, one of the most intriguing themes for the genre has been the replacement of the Old West of outlaws and cowhands with a more civilized society. Hints of that can be found in such Ford classics as *Stagecoach* and *The Searchers* (1956), but Sam Peckinpah and Sergio Leone created some of the most striking images of changing times in *The Wild Bunch* (1969) and *Once Upon a Time in the West* (1968), respectively. The theme is even more vivid in attempts at modern-set westerns. The cowboys in *The Misfits* (1961) can only survive by driving trucks into the wilderness to catch horses for a dog food company, and Kirk Douglas's aging cowboy in *Lonely Are the Brave* (1962) learns that living free is a thing of the past in the modern West. Yet even at their lowest ebb, Hollywood's cowhands, lawmen, settlers, and outlaws present an image of the American character that continues to resonate with fans worldwide.

1. In which film does Gary Cooper play a devout Quaker?

    A. *Friendly Persuasion* (1956)
    B. *Springfield Rifle* (1952)
    C. *The Hanging Tree* (1959)
    D. *Vera Cruz* (1954)

2. Who plays the niece that John Wayne sets out to find in *The Searchers* (1956)?

    A. Julie Harris
    B. Kim Darby
    C. Margaret O'Brien
    D. Natalie Wood

3. Walter Matthau and Kirk Douglas costar in what western adapted for the screen by Dalton Trumbo?

    A. *Baby the Rain Must Fall* (1965)
    B. *Cheyenne Autumn* (1964)
    C. *Lonely Are the Brave* (1962)
    D. *Two Rode Together* (1961)

4. Though he acted in dozens of westerns, Stephen McNally only appeared in one film directed by Anthony Mann. What was it?

    A. *Bend of the River* (1953)
    B. *The Far Country* (1954)
    C. *Winchester '73* (1950)
    D. *Wyoming Mail* (1950)

5. The 1940 film *Arizona* was nominated for two Academy Awards. One was for Best Art Direction. What was the other for?

    A. Best Actor
    B. Best Cinematography
    C. Best Editing
    D. Best Musical Score

6. John Ireland plays Johnny Ringo in what western with Burt Lancaster?

    A. *A Walk in the Sun* (1945)
    B. *All the King's Men* (1949)
    C. *Gunfight at the O.K. Corral* (1957)
    D. *Red River* (1948)

7. Barbara Stanwyck starred on what popular 1960s television series?

    A. *Bewitched*
    B. *Bonanza*
    C. *Hogan's Heroes*
    D. *The Big Valley*

8. What was John Wayne's real name?

    A. Alfred Koppelhoffer
    B. Jake Ichabod
    C. Louis Culpepper
    D. Marion Morrison

9. Joan Blondell appears in the 1971 film *Support Your Local Gunfighter*. Who is the male lead?

    A. Clint Eastwood
    B. James Coburn
    C. James Garner
    D. Lee Marvin

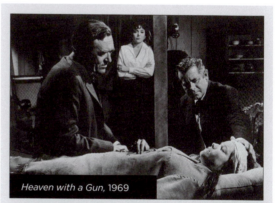

Heaven with a Gun, 1969

10. Which actress made one of her first appearances in the film *Heaven with a Gun* (1969), starring Glenn Ford?

    A. Barbara Hershey
    B. Goldie Hawn
    C. Sally Field
    D. Stockard Channing

answers found on page 558

11. Which actor plays the leader of the band of outlaws in the 1970 western *Barquero*?

   A. Charles Bronson
   B. Lee Marvin
   C. Lee Van Cleef
   D. Warren Oates

12. How many times did Pedro Armendáriz play Pancho Villa in a feature film?

   A. 1
   B. 3
   C. 5
   D. 7

13. What was the only western to earn an Oscar nomination for Best Story and Screenplay?

   A. *High Noon* (1952)
   B. *Hondo* (1953)
   C. *Ride the High Country* (1962)
   D. *The Naked Spur* (1953)

14. What actor won his/her only Oscar for his/her role in *The Big Country* (1958)?

   A. Burl Ives
   B. Carroll Baker
   C. Gregory Peck
   D. Jean Simmons

15. For which film did Lee Marvin win his only Academy Award?

   A. *Bad Day at Black Rock* (1955)
   B. *Cat Ballou* (1965)
   C. *Not as a Stranger* (1955)
   D. *Pillars of the Sky* (1956)

16. What character does Richard Dix play in *Badlands of Dakota* (1941)?

   A. Buffalo Bill Cody
   B. General George Custer
   C. Wild Bill Hickok
   D. Wyatt Earp

17. Who plays Gary Cooper's son in *Friendly Persuasion* (1956)?

   A. Anthony Perkins
   B. Montgomery Clift
   C. Russ Tamblyn
   D. Sal Mineo

18. What historical figure does Gary Cooper portray in *The Plainsman* (1936)?

   A. Abraham Lincoln
   B. General George Custer
   C. Wild Bill Hickok
   D. Wyatt Earp

19. In the 1966 film *The Professionals*, who are Lee Marvin and his team hired to rescue from a kidnapper?

   A. Claudia Cardinale
   B. Gina Lollobrigida
   C. Leslie Caron
   D. Sophia Loren

20. In which film adaptation of a James Fenimore Cooper novel did Rita Moreno star opposite Lex Barker?

   A. *The Deerslayer* (1957)
   B. *The Last of the Mohicans* (1992)
   C. *The Pathfinder* (1952)
   D. *The Pioneers* (1941)

21. Pedro Armendáriz made the 1955 film *The Littlest Outlaw* for which studio?

   A. Columbia
   B. Disney
   C. MGM
   D. RKO

22. Who stars in William Wyler's 1940 film *The Westerner*?

   A. Gary Cooper
   B. Henry Fonda
   C. James Stewart
   D. John Wayne

answers found on page 558

23. Who earned three Best Original Score Oscar nominations in the same year for the westerns *Arizona* (1940), *Dark Command* (1940), and *North West Mounted Police* (1940)?

A. Aaron Copland
B. Bernard Herrmann
C. Franz Waxman
D. Victor Young

24. Which of the following actors does not appear in the 1956 film *Jubal,* directed by Delmer Daves?

A. Anthony Perkins
B. Ernest Borgnine
C. Glenn Ford
D. Rod Steiger

25. What John Ford film earned Thomas Mitchell his first Oscar nomination?

A. *Stagecoach* (1939)
B. *The Hurricane* (1937)
C. *The Long Voyage Home* (1940)
D. *The Quiet Man* (1952)

26. Jean Hagen was featured in what episode of *Zane Grey Theatre*?

A. "Legacy of a Legend"
B. "The Empty Shell"
C. "The Tall Shadow"
D. "The Vaunted"

27. Anthony Quinn shared the screen with Henry Fonda in which western that was an Academy Award nominee for Best Picture?

A. *The Magnificent Matador* (1955)
B. *The Naked Street* (1955)
C. *The Ox-Bow Incident* (1943)
D. *The River's Edge* (1957)

28. Sterling Hayden portrays gunfighter Rick Martin in which film?

A. *Shotgun* (1955)
B. *The Iron Sheriff* (1957)

C. *Top Gun* (1955)
D. *Zero Hour!* (1957)

29. What famous actor costars with Claire Trevor in *Stagecoach* (1939)?

A. Clint Eastwood
B. Henry Fonda
C. John Wayne
D. Roy Rogers

30. Kirk Douglas and Gena Rowlands costar in what western?

A. *Baby the Rain Must Fall* (1965)
B. *Cheyenne Autumn* (1964)
C. *Lonely Are the Brave* (1962)
D. *Two Rode Together* (1961)

31. George Stevens directed Alan Ladd and Jack Palance in what western?

A. *Ride, Vaquero!* (1953)
B. *Saddle the Wind* (1958)
C. *Shane* (1953)
D. *The Last Hunt* (1956)

32. In the 1954 film *Cattle Queen of Montana,* Barbara Stanwyck costars with which of the following actors?

A. Glenn Ford
B. John Wayne
C. Ralph Bellamy
D. Ronald Reagan

33. Alan Ladd plays a railroad detective who tries to bring in a gang of train robbers in what film?

A. *13 West Street* (1962)
B. *Shane* (1953)
C. *The Badlanders* (1958)
D. *Whispering Smith* (1949)

Blood on the Moon, 1948

34. Who costars with Barbara Bel Geddes in the 1948 film *Blood on the Moon*?

A. Burt Lancaster
B. Henry Fonda
C. Marlon Brando
D. Robert Mitchum

35. John Ireland appears with Henry Fonda in what John Ford film?

A. *A Walk in the Sun* (1945)
B. *Gunfight at the O.K. Corral* (1957)
C. *My Darling Clementine* (1946)
D. *Red River* (1948)

36. Who directed the 1936 Gary Cooper film *The Plainsman*?

A. Cecil B. DeMille
B. John Ford
C. John Huston
D. William Wyler

37. Which of the following actors stars in the 1950 film *Broken Arrow*?

A. Gary Cooper
B. Glenn Ford
C. James Stewart
D. John Wayne

38. Jeff Corey plays Sheriff Bledsoe in what film opposite Paul Newman and Robert Redford?

A. *Butch Cassidy and the Sundance Kid* (1969)
B. *Escape from Fort Bravo* (1953)
C. *The Wild Bunch* (1969)
D. *Wild Rovers* (1971)

39. Which Pancho Villa biopic was shot by cinematographer James Wong Howe?

A. *Pancho Villa Returns* (1950)
B. *Under Strange Flags* (1937)
C. *Villa Rides* (1968)
D. *Viva Villa!* (1934)

40. Who earned Oscar nominations for *The Professionals* (1966), *Tequila Sunrise* (1988), and *American Beauty* (1999)?

A. Actor Jack Palance
B. Cinematographer Conrad L. Hall
C. Director Sam Mendes
D. Writer Robert Towne

41. The film *Along Came Jones* (1945) was Gary Cooper's first attempt at what?

A. Directing
B. Producing
C. Screenwriting
D. Singing

42. Who stars in Henry Hathaway's 1934 film *The Last Round-Up*?

A. Gary Cooper
B. James Stewart
C. John Wayne
D. Randolph Scott

43. In the 1930 film *The Arizona Kid*, who played the title character opposite Carole Lombard?

A. Gary Cooper
B. John Wayne
C. Wallace Beery
D. Warner Baxter

answers found on page 558

44. Who plays Dorothy McGuire's husband in *Friendly Persuasion* (1956)?
   A. Gary Cooper
   B. Glenn Ford
   C. Henry Fonda
   D. John Wayne

45. Henry Fonda portrayed which character in the 1946 film *My Darling Clementine*?
   A. Billy Clanton
   B. Dr. John "Doc" Holliday
   C. Peter Kirk
   D. Wyatt Earp

46. The 1960 film *The Alamo* received an Academy Award nomination for Best Original Song. What was the name of the song?
   A. "It Never Happened"
   B. "Near or Far"
   C. "The Green Leaves of Summer"
   D. "The Second Time Around"

47. Which of the following Henry Fonda films was not directed by John Ford?
   A. *Fort Apache* (1948)
   B. *My Darling Clementine* (1946)
   C. *The Ox-Bow Incident* (1943)
   D. *Young Mr. Lincoln* (1939)

48. In *Winchester '73* (1950), sharpshooters Stephen McNally and James Stewart compete for a rifle that is the same type of gun used by which U.S. president?
   A. James Polk
   B. John Adams
   C. Theodore Roosevelt
   D. Ulysses S. Grant

49. Who did Anthony Quinn play in John Sturges's *Last Train from Gun Hill* (1959)?
   A. Craig Belden
   B. Lee Smithers
   C. Matt Morgan
   D. Rick Belden

50. Who famously dedicated half of his Academy Award to a horse when he won Best Actor for his performance in the 1965 film *Cat Ballou*?
   A. Charles Bronson
   B. David Niven
   C. John Wayne
   D. Lee Marvin

51. Alan Ladd plays a drifter who helps farmers fight off a vicious gunman in what film?
   A. *Man in the Net* (1959)
   B. *Shane* (1953)
   C. *The Badlanders* (1958)
   D. *Whispering Smith* (1948)

52. Jeff Corey portrays Wild Bill Hickok in what film?
   A. *Escape from Fort Bravo* (1953)
   B. *Little Big Man* (1970)
   C. *The Wild Bunch* (1969)
   D. *Wild Rovers* (1971)

53. Who costars with Gary Cooper in *Vera Cruz* (1954)?
   A. Burt Lancaster
   B. Gregory Peck
   C. Humphrey Bogart
   D. James Cagney

54. Which of the following westerns earned only one Oscar nomination, which was for Best Editing?
   A. *Cimarron* (1931)
   B. *Colorado Territory* (1940)
   C. *Cowboy* (1958)
   D. *Stagecoach* (1939)

55. Who accepted Gary Cooper's Academy Award on his behalf for *High Noon* (1952)?
   A. Grace Kelly
   B. James Stewart
   C. John Wayne
   D. William Powell

answers found on pages 558–559

Spotlight on
JAMES **STEWART** (1908–1997)

That Stewart's films stand up to repeated viewing is a tribute to his ability to appear "unusually usual" (in the words of director W. S. Van Dyke) as everything from eternally tongue-tied small-town boys to ruthless, often obsessed heroes. Stewart himself was a small-town boy, whose acting career started when he went off to study architecture at Princeton. Classmate Josh Logan talked him into joining his University Players summer theater troupe on Cape Cod, where Stewart met lifelong friend Henry Fonda. He polished his craft on Broadway before signing with MGM. The studio didn't know what to do with him at first, even casting him as a villain in *After the Thin Man* (1936). It was director Frank Capra at Columbia Pictures who made him a star with *You Can't Take It with You* (1938) and *Mr. Smith Goes to Washington* (1939). After his Oscar-winning role in *The Philadelphia Story* (1940), Stewart signed up for World War II service. He came back a more mature and somewhat darker personality, as demonstrated in such works as Frank Capra's *It's a Wonderful Life* (1946), Stewart's four collaborations

The Naked Spur, 1953

with Alfred Hitchcock, and a series of top-notch westerns, such as *Winchester '73* (1950) and *The Naked Spur* (1953), wherein he played obsessively driven heroes.

The Philadelphia Story, 1940

1. In *Winchester '73* (1950), whom does James Stewart suspect Stephen McNally has murdered?

   A. His wife
   B. Their brother
   C. Their father
   D. Their mother

2. What film marked James Stewart's first role in a western?

   A. *City Streets* (1931)
   B. *Destry Rides Again* (1939)
   C. *Fighting Caravans* (1931)
   D. *The Cowboy and the Lady* (1938)

3. In George Marshall's *Destry Rides Again* (1939), James Stewart arrives into town carrying what?

   A. A flower pot and a ukulele
   B. A parasol and a birdcage
   C. A violin and a briefcase
   D. A rifle and a knife

4. Shirley Jones plays Marty Purcell in what western opposite James Stewart?

   A. *Only the Valiant* (1951)
   B. *The Bravados* (1958)
   C. *Twelve O'Clock High* (1949)
   D. *Two Rode Together* (1961)

5. In *Winchester '73* (1950), James Stewart and Stephen McNally compete in a marksman contest during the centennial celebration of what pioneer town?

   A. Carson City
   B. Dodge City
   C. Tombstone
   D. Virginia City

answers found on page 559

56. What western won the Oscar for Best Screenplay Written Directly for the Screen in 1964?

   A. *How the West Was Won* (1962)
   B. *Ride the High Country*
   C. *The Good, the Bad and the Ugly*
   D. *The Searchers*

57. In what popular television western did James Garner star?

   A. *Bonanza*
   B. *Have Gun—Will Travel*
   C. *Maverick*
   D. *Rough Riders*

58. Which of the following actors costars with Ernest Borgnine in the 1953 film *The Stranger Wore a Gun*?

   A. Gary Cooper
   B. James Stewart
   C. John Wayne
   D. Randolph Scott

59. Which of the following actresses costars with Bing Crosby in the 1966 film *Stagecoach*?

   A. Ann-Margret
   B. Jill St. John
   C. Sophia Loren
   D. Tuesday Weld

60. In the 1961 film *A Thunder of Drums*, George Hamilton costars with which of the following actors?

   A. Charles Bronson
   B. John Wayne
   C. Karl Malden
   D. Lee Marvin

61. In *Winchester '73* (1950), Stephen McNally's character uses the alias "Dutch Henry Brown." What is his real name?

   A. Jack Page

B. Jessie Gorman
C. Matthew McAdam
D. Sam Leeds

62. Lucien Ballard photographed John Wayne in three films. Which came first?

   A. *I Married a Woman* (1958)
   B. *The Searchers* (1956)
   C. *The Sons of Katie Elder* (1965)
   D. *True Grit* (1969)

63. Which of the following actors costars with Jack Palance in the 1966 film *The Professionals*?

   A. Alan Ladd
   B. Burt Lancaster
   C. John Wayne
   D. Yul Brenner

64. Richard Thorpe directed Lionel Barrymore in which western featuring Ronald Reagan?

   A. *Cowboy from Brooklyn* (1938)
   B. *Naughty but Nice* (1939)
   C. *The Bad Man* (1941)
   D. *West of Zanzibar* (1928)

65. In *Winchester '73* (1950), what character wins the eponymous gun from Stephen McNally in a card game?

   A. Joe Lamont
   B. Lin McAdam
   C. Wyatt Earp
   D. Young Bull

66. Who did Kirk Douglas play in John Sturges's *Last Train from Gun Hill* (1959)?

   A. Craig Belden
   B. Lee Smithers
   C. Matt Morgan
   D. Rick Belden

67. When Jack Palance won his Academy Award for Best Supporting Actor for his work in *City Slickers* (1991), what did he do onstage during his acceptance speech?

A. He did several one-armed push-ups.
B. He fainted.
C. He sang a song.
D. He took off his shirt.

The Naked Spur, 1953

68. Which of the following actors costars with James Stewart in the 1953 film *The Naked Spur*?

A. Henry Fonda
B. Ralph Meeker
C. John Wayne
D. Kirk Douglas

69. What 1972 western was Rita Hayworth's final film?

A. *My Name Is Nobody*
B. *Once Upon a Time in the West*
C. *The Wild Bunch*
D. *The Wrath of God*

70. Walter Matthau made his feature film debut in what western starring and directed by Burt Lancaster?

A. *Escape from Fort Bravo* (1953)
B. *The Kentuckian* (1955)
C. *The Wild Bunch* (1969)
D. *Wild Rovers* (1971)

71. The boots worn by Clint Eastwood in the television series *Rawhide* were the same ones he would later wear in what film?

A. *Bronco Billy* (1980)
B. *Escape from Alcatraz* (1979)
C. *The Beguiled* (1971)
D. *Unforgiven* (1992)

72. What U.S. state does Rock Hudson's character call home in *Giant* (1956)?

A. California
B. Louisiana
C. New York
D. Texas

73. Robert Redford portrays a rodeo star in what film?

A. *Brubaker* (1980)
B. *The Electric Horseman* (1979)
C. *The Natural* (1984)
D. *Up Close & Personal* (1996)

74. The 1965 film *The Hallelujah Trail*, costarring Donald Pleasence, concerns a wagon train carrying a load of what?

A. Cattle
B. Criminals
C. Liquor
D. Money

75. Which actor in John Sturges's *The Magnificent Seven* (1960) went on to voice Henry J. Waternoose in *Monsters, Inc.* (2001)?

A. Charles Bronson
B. James Coburn
C. Steve McQueen
D. Yul Brynner

76. Which segment of *How the West Was Won* (1962) was directed by George Marshall?

A. "The Civil War"
B. "The Outlaws"
C. "The Railroad"
D. "The Rivers"

answers found on page 559

77. Who wrote the screenplay for the 1961 film *The Misfits*?

A. Arthur Miller
B. Garson Kanin
C. Paddy Chayefsky
D. William Inge

78. The 1960 Sophia Loren film *Heller in Pink Tights* was based on a novel by what author?

A. Joseph Heller
B. Joseph Wambaugh
C. Larry McMurtry
D. Louis L'Amour

79. Laurence Naismith appears in what western costarring Dirk Bogarde?

A. *Escape from Fort Bravo* (1953)
B. *The Hill* (1965)
C. *The Singer Not the Song* (1961)
D. *The Wind and the Lion* (1975)

80. Which Glenn Ford film was not directed by George Marshall?

A. *Cowboy* (1958)
B. *Cry for Happy* (1961)
C. *Imitation General* (1958)
D. *Texas* (1941)

81. Which of the following Pedro Armendáriz films was not directed by John Ford?

A. *3 Godfathers* (1948)
B. *Fort Apache* (1948)
C. *The Conqueror* (1956)
D. *The Fugitive* (1947)

82. What film directed by Henry Hathaway costars Dean Martin?

A. *Nevada Smith* (1966)
B. *Shoot Out* (1971)
C. *The Last Safari* (1967)
D. *The Sons of Katie Elder* (1965)

83. The 1956 film *Friendly Persuasion* was nominated for Academy Awards in all of the following categories except which one?

A. Best Actor
B. Best Director
C. Best Original Song
D. Best Picture

84. Which of the following westerns is photographed by Lucien Ballard?

A. *Cheyenne Autumn* (1964)
B. *Ride the High Country* (1962)
C. *Rio Bravo* (1959)
D. *The Searchers* (1956)

85. During a hiatus from the 007 franchise, Sean Connery starred in which western that also featured Brigitte Bardot in her first film outside of France?

A. *Lone Star* (1952)
B. *Shalako* (1968)
C. *The Nevadan* (1950)
D. *Woman of Straw* (1964)

86. Who plays Wyatt Earp in John Sturges's *Gunfight at the O.K. Corral* (1957)?

A. Burt Lancaster
B. Dennis Hopper
C. Frank Faylen
D. Kirk Douglas

87. Stephen McNally plays a heartless rancher named McNulty in what 1956 western?

A. *40 Guns to Apache Pass*
B. *Devil's Canyon*
C. *Tribute to a Bad Man*
D. *Winchester '73*

88. What was Gary Cooper's first color feature?

A. *Along Came Jones* (1945)
B. *Friendly Persuasion* (1956)
C. *North West Mounted Police* (1940)
D. *Springfield Rifle* (1952)

89. James Cagney and Stephen McNally play ranchers vying for Irene Papas in what Robert Wise western?

A. *Badman's Country* (1958)
B. *Badman's Territory* (1946)
C. *Nevada Badmen* (1951)
D. *Tribute to a Bad Man* (1956)

90. What was the first western directed by and starring Clint Eastwood?

A. *Bronco Billy* (1980)
B. *Hang 'Em High* (1968)
C. *Hearts of the West* (1975)
D. *High Plains Drifter* (1973)

91. To whom did Henry Hathaway lose the Best Director Academy Award in 1936?

A. Frank Capra
B. George Cukor
C. John Ford
D. Michael Curtiz

92. Which one of the following actors starred with Pedro Armendáriz in *The Wonderful Country* (1959)?

A. Jack Palance
B. John Wayne
C. Ray Milland
D. Robert Mitchum

93. What famous actor stars in John Sturges's *McQ* (1974)?

A. Clint Eastwood
B. James Coburn
C. James Garner
D. John Wayne

94. Who costars with Jack Lemmon in the 1958 film *Cowboy*?

A. Glenn Ford
B. Henry Fonda
C. James Stewart
D. John Wayne

95. What actor won his third Academy Award for his role in William Wyler's *The Westerner* (1940)?

A. Dana Andrews
B. Forrest Tucker
C. Gary Cooper
D. Walter Brennan

96. Walter Mirisch was the executive producer on the 1960 film *The Magnificent Seven*. Which of the following actors does not appear in the film?

A. Charles Bronson
B. Lee Marvin
C. Steve McQueen
D. Yul Brynner

97. Lucien Ballard and Josef von Sternberg shared a Venice Film Festival Award for Best Cinematography for what 1935 film?

A. *Junior Bonner*
B. *Nevada Smith*
C. *Ride the High Country*
D. *The Devil Is a Woman*

98. All of the following westerns won Academy Awards as Best Picture except for which one?

A. *Cimarron* (1931)
B. *Dances with Wolves* (1990)
C. *The Plainsman* (1936)
D. *Unforgiven* (1992)

99. What *Star Trek* alum makes a brief appearance in John Sturges's *Gunfight at the O.K. Corral* (1957)?

A. DeForest Kelley
B. George Takei
C. Leonard Nimoy
D. William Shatner

answers found on page 559

100. Angie Dickinson plays Feathers in what Howard Hawks western?

   A. *Dressed to Kill* (1980)
   B. *Ocean's Eleven* (1960)
   C. *Point Blank* (1967)
   D. *Rio Bravo* (1959)

101. Anthony Quinn played Crazy Horse in what Raoul Walsh film?

   A. *Buffalo Bill* (1944)
   B. *The Ox-Bow Incident* (1943)
   C. *The Plainsman* (1936)
   D. *They Died with Their Boots On* (1941)

Cimarron, 1960

102. Franz Waxman composed the music for the 1960 film *Cimarron*. Who wrote the novel on which the film was based?

   A. Edna Ferber
   B. Fannie Hurst
   C. Larry McMurtry
   D. Louis L'Amour

103. What unlikely actor played an Indian chief in the 1947 Gary Cooper film *Unconquered*?

   A. Bela Lugosi
   B. Boris Karloff
   C. Claude Rains
   D. Lon Chaney Jr.

104. Robert Taylor and Stewart Granger star in what western?

   A. *Many Rivers to Cross* (1955)
   B. *Ride, Vaquero!* (1953)
   C. *Saddle the Wind* (1958)
   D. *The Last Hunt* (1956)

105. Who plays Sonny Crawford in *The Last Picture Show* (1971)?

   A. Ben Johnson
   B. Clu Gulager
   C. Jeff Bridges
   D. Timothy Bottoms

106. What was the first western to win Best Picture?

   A. *Cimarron* (1931)
   B. *In Old Arizona* (1928)
   C. *Ruggles of Red Gap* (1935)
   D. *Viva Villa!* (1934)

107. Warner Oland costars with which of the following actors in *Riders of the Purple Sage* (1925)?

   A. Gary Cooper
   B. John Wayne
   C. Roy Rogers
   D. Tom Mix

108. Marjorie Main portrayed Granny Becky in which film starring John Wayne?

   A. *How the West Was Won* (1962)
   B. *Rio Grande* (1950)
   C. *She Wore a Yellow Ribbon* (1949)
   D. *The Shepherd of the Hills* (1941)

109. Which of the following actors does not costar with Ralph Meeker in the 1957 film *Run of the Arrow*?

   A. Brian Keith
   B. Charles Bronson
   C. Paul Henreid
   D. Rod Steiger

110. Who stars in both John Sturges's *The Magnificent Seven* (1960) and Cecil B. DeMille's *The Ten Commandments* (1956)?

A. Charles Bronson
B. James Coburn
C. Steve McQueen
D. Yul Brynner

111. Which of the following actors costars with Janet Leigh in the 1953 western *The Naked Spur*?

A. Glenn Ford
B. Henry Fonda
C. Humphrey Bogart
D. James Stewart

112. In *Lonely Are the Brave* (1962), what is the profession of Walter Matthau's character?

A. Bank robber
B. Rancher
C. Saloon owner
D. Sheriff

113. What film earned Lucien Ballard a National Society of Film Critics Award for Best Cinematography?

A. *Don't Bother to Knock* (1952)
B. *Ride the High Country* (1962)
C. *The Searchers* (1956)
D. *The Wild Bunch* (1969)

114. *Yojimbo* (1961) was remade as what Clint Eastwood western?

A. *A Fistful of Dollars* (1964)
B. *Hang 'Em High* (1968)
C. *Paint Your Wagon* (1969)
D. *The Good, the Bad and the Ugly* (1966)

115. What was the first film in which Pedro Armendáriz portrayed Pancho Villa?

A. *Pancho Villa and Valentina* (1960)
B. *Pancho Villa Rides* (1968)
C. *This Was Pancho Villa* (1957)
D. *Vuelve Pancho Villa* (1950)

116. Which of the following Delmer Daves films costars Jack Lemmon?

A. *Cowboy* (1958)
B. *Kings Go Forth* (1958)
C. *Spencer's Mountain* (1963)
D. *The Hanging Tree* (1959)

117. What was the name of Lloyd Bridges's character in *High Noon* (1952)?

A. Deputy Marshal Harvey Pell
B. Judge Percy Mettrick
C. Marshal Will Kane
D. Mayor Jonas Henderson

118. In what Texas city is *The Last Picture Show* (1971) set?

A. Abilene
B. Anarene
C. Archer City
D. Arlington

119. In what film was the name of Katharine Ross's character Etta Place?

A. *Butch Cassidy and the Sundance Kid* (1969)
B. *The Graduate* (1967)
C. *The Stepford Wives* (1975)
D. *Voyage of the Damned* (1976)

120. In the opening sequence of what film does Woody Strode play a gunslinger in the Old West?

A. *African Treasure* (1952)
B. *Once Upon a Time in the West* (1968)
C. *The Gambler from Natchez* (1954)
D. *Two Rode Together* (1961)

121. For which film did John Wayne win his only Academy Award for Best Actor?

A. *Stagecoach* (1939)
B. *The Quiet Man* (1952)
C. *The Searchers* (1956)
D. *True Grit* (1969)

answers found on page 559

Spotlight on
JOHN **WAYNE** (1907-1979)

John Wayne said it best himself: "Goddamn, I'm the stuff men are made of!" His films gave the impression he had conquered the Old West and won World War II single-handedly. A good student, Wayne attended the University of Southern California on a football scholarship and got into the movies through a summer job arranged by team fan and western star Tom Mix. While doing crew work, he befriended director John Ford, who rec-

ommended him for the leading role in *The Big Trail* (1930), and the studio renamed him John Wayne. When the film flopped, however, Wayne found himself consigned to Poverty Row studios, where he gradually carved a niche in low-budget westerns. Ford came to the rescue by casting him as the Ringo Kid in *Stagecoach* (1939), a major hit that made Wayne a star. In 1948, director Howard Hawks gave him a chance to act as the tyrannical cattle baron in *Red River,* and he surprised everyone with a critically acclaimed performance. Wayne continued with a series of demanding roles, most notably in *She Wore a Yellow Ribbon* (1949) and *The Searchers* (1956). But it wasn't until Wayne took on a character role—the aging, one-eyed lawman in *True Grit* (1969)—that he earned an Oscar for Best Actor.

3 Godfathers, 1948

She Wore a Yellow Ribbon, 1949

1. **John Ireland appears in what John Wayne western directed by Howard Hawks?**

   A. *A Walk in the Sun* (1945)

   B. *All the King's Men* (1949)

   C. *Gunfight at the O.K. Corral* (1957)

   D. *Red River* (1948)

2. **In *3 Godfathers* (1948), what do John Wayne and his band of outlaws have to protect?**

   A. A baby

   B. A calf

   C. A puppy

   D. A sack of gold coins

3. **How many movies did Pedro Armendáriz make with John Wayne?**

   A. 1

   B. 2

   C. 3

   D. 4

4. **In which film did Claire Trevor not costar with John Wayne?**

   A. *Allegheny Uprising* (1939)

   B. *Dark Command* (1940)

   C. *Raw Deal* (1948)

   D. *Stagecoach* (1939)

5. **What award did Glenn Ford and John Wayne receive in recognition of their work as outstanding western stars?**

   A. Bronco Medal

   B. Golden Spur Award

   C. Lasso of Honor

   D. Silver Horseshoe

answers found on page 559

122. Which of the following actors starred with Roddy McDowall in the 1972 film *The Life and Times of Judge Roy Bean*?

   A. Clint Eastwood
   B. John Wayne
   C. Paul Newman
   D. Robert Redford

123. Who directed Roddy McDowall in the 1972 film *The Life and Times of Judge Roy Bean*?

   A. George Roy Hill
   B. John Ford
   C. John Huston
   D. Sergio Leone

124. What is the name of the sound technician who earned an Oscar nomination for *Shenandoah* (1965)?

   A. Bob Loblaw
   B. Cosmo Z. Kramer
   C. Rusty Ryan
   D. Waldon O. Watson

125. What Gary Cooper western earned an Academy Award nomination for the original song "The Cowboy and the Lady"?

   A. *The Cowboy and the Lady* (1938)
   B. *The Last Outlaw* (1927)
   C. *The Texan* (1930)
   D. *The Virginian* (1929)

126. The filmmaker who won the 1935 Best Assistant Director Oscar for *Viva Villa!* has the same name as a contemporary director. What is it?

   A. Curtis Hanson
   B. John Waters
   C. Steven Soderbergh
   D. Wes Anderson

127. What Claire Trevor film features John Wayne and Roy Rogers?

   A. *Crossroads* (1942)
   B. *Dark Command* (1940)
   C. *Stagecoach* (1939)
   D. *Texas* (1941)

128. Jean Hagen costars in what film about the life of a rodeo star?

   A. *Arena* (1953)
   B. *Mr. Skeffington* (1944)
   C. *My Brother Talks to Horses* (1947)
   D. *Pocketful of Miracles* (1961)

129. What film directed by Henry Hathaway concerns a long-standing family feud between the Haydens and the Colbys?

   A. *The Thundering Herd* (1933)
   B. *The Witching Hour* (1934)
   C. *To the Last Man* (1933)
   D. *Under the Tonto Rim* (1933)

130. All of the following actors appeared in Henry Hathaway's 1969 film *True Grit* except for whom?

   A. Dennis Hopper
   B. John Wayne
   C. Robert Duvall
   D. Robert Wagner

131. Which of the following 1961 Oscar nominees for Best Color Set Direction is a western?

   A. *Cimarron*
   B. *It Started in Naples*
   C. *Pepe*
   D. *Spartacus*

132. What is the name of the western town where George Marshall's *Destry* (1954) takes place?

   A. Daydream
   B. Napping
   C. Restful
   D. Sleepy

answers found on page 559

133. Stewart Granger starred in the title role of which western that was originally intended to be a trilogy?

    A. *Baby Face* (1933)

    B. *McQ* (1974)

    C. *Old Surehand* (1965)

    D. *The Shepherd of the Hills* (1941)

134. Billy the Kid and Doc Holliday fight over Jane Russell in what film?

    A. *Gentlemen Prefer Blondes* (1953)

    B. *Macao* (1952)

    C. *The Outlaw* (1943)

    D. *The Paleface* (1948)

135. Which actor was not featured in the 1962 film *How the West Was Won*?

    A. Clint Eastwood

    B. Gregory Peck

    C. James Stewart

    D. Raymond Massey

How the West Was Won, 1962

136. Which of the following was one of the directors of *How the West Was Won* (1962)?

    A. John Ford

    B. Ken Annakin

    C. King Vidor

    D. Sidney Lumet

137. What was the name of Buddy Ebsen's character in 1939's *The Kid from Texas*?

    A. Blanky

    B. Fifty

    C. Snifty

    D. Wild Bill

138. Before costarring in *Split Second* (1953), Stephen McNally and Alexis Smith played a former prizefighter and a dance-hall girl who fall in love in what western?

    A. *Cimarron* (1931)

    B. *The Far Country* (1954)

    C. *Tribute to a Bad Man* (1956)

    D. *Wyoming Mail* (1950)

139. Which is the only one of John Ford's major collaborations with John Wayne that won a Best Director Oscar?

    A. *Stagecoach* (1939)

    B. *The Quiet Man* (1952)

    C. *The Searchers* (1956)

    D. *They Were Expendable* (1945)

140. Rita Moreno appeared in which western starring Gary Cooper as an adventurer on a mission in the mountains of Mexico?

    A. *Garden of Evil* (1954)

    B. *Only the Brave* (1930)

    C. *The Cowboy and the Lady* (1939)

    D. *The Plainsman* (1936)

141. Which of the following actors received an Academy Award nomination as Best Supporting Actor for his work in the 1950 Delmer Daves film *Broken Arrow*?

    A. Broderick Crawford

    B. David Niven

    C. Jeff Chandler

    D. Ray Milland

142. Who is Ronald Reagan's costar in the 1954 film *Cattle Queen of Montana*?

    A. Barbara Bel Geddes

    B. Barbara Stanwyck

    C. Betty Hutton

    D. Donna Reed

143. Who is Gary Cooper's costar in *They Came to Cordura* (1959)?

    A. Katharine Hepburn
    B. Marlene Dietrich
    C. Rita Hayworth
    D. Shelley Winters

144. Who plays Doc Holliday to James Garner's Wyatt Earp in the 1967 film *Hour of the Gun*?

    A. Clint Eastwood
    B. Dennis Weaver
    C. Glenn Ford
    D. Jason Robards

145. George Marshall is one of the handful of directors to direct two films from the same story. What were they?

    A. *Destry Rides Again* (1939) and *Destry* (1954)
    B. *His Girl Friday* (1940) and *The Front Page* (1931)
    C. *The Good Thief* (1980) and *Bob le Flambeur* (1956)
    D. *The Man Who Knew Too Much* (1934) and *The Man Who Knew Too Much* (1956)

146. James Wong Howe earned his second of two Oscars for what Paul Newman western?

    A. *Butch Cassidy and the Sundance Kid* (1969)
    B. *Hombre* (1967)
    C. *Hud* (1963)
    D. *The Life and Times of Judge Roy Bean* (1972)

147. Who directed the Claire Trevor film *Stagecoach* (1939)?

    A. Allan Dwan
    B. John Ford
    C. Raoul Walsh
    D. William Wyler

148. What was John Wayne's nickname?

    A. "Duke"
    B. "Hondo"
    C. "Oak"
    D. "Rooster"

149. Ernest Borgnine costarred with Lee Marvin in all of the following films except which one?

    A. *Bad Day at Black Rock* (1955)
    B. *Jubal* (1956)
    C. *The Dirty Dozen* (1967)
    D. *The Stranger Wore a Gun* (1953)

150. What historical figure does John Wayne play in *How the West Was Won* (1962)?

    A. Abraham Lincoln
    B. General George A. Custer
    C. General William Tecumseh Sherman
    D. Robert E. Lee

151. Who directed Jack Palance in the 1973 film *Oklahoma Crude*?

    A. John Sturges
    B. Robert Aldrich
    C. Sam Peckinpah
    D. Stanley Kramer

152. Which Toshiro Mifune film uses Dashiell Hammett's novel *Red Harvest* as its inspiration?

    A. *I Live in Fear* (1967)
    B. *Red Beard* (1965)
    C. *Scandal* (1950)
    D. *Yojimbo* (1961)

153. In what film does Ernest Borgnine play a character named Coley Trimble?

    A. *Bad Day at Black Rock* (1955)
    B. *Run for Cover* (1955)
    C. *The Dirty Dozen* (1967)
    D. *Vera Cruz* (1954)

154. Who is Gary Cooper's leading lady in *High Noon* (1952)?

    A. Barbara Stanwyck
    B. Grace Kelly
    C. Marlene Dietrich
    D. Patricia Neal

answers found on page 559

155. Who plays Doc Holliday in John Sturges's *Gunfight at the O.K. Corral* (1957)?

A. Burt Lancaster
B. Dennis Hopper
C. Frank Faylen
D. Kirk Douglas

156. John Cromwell directed the 1930 film *The Texan*. Who starred in it?

A. Clark Gable
B. Gary Cooper
C. John Wayne
D. William Powell

157. Who plays Reno Smith in John Sturges's *Bad Day at Black Rock* (1955)?

A. Dean Jagger
B. Robert Ryan
C. Spencer Tracy
D. Walter Brennan

158. Who outfitted Marilyn Monroe for *The Misfits* (1961)?

A. Arnold Scaasi
B. Irene Sharaff
C. Jean Louis
D. William Travilla

159. Anita Ekberg played the title role in which western opposite Sterling Hayden?

A. *Stella Dallas* (1937)
B. *The Maverick Queen* (1956)
C. *Valerie* (1957)
D. *Virginia* (1941)

160. Which star of 1956's *Giant* was crowned Miss Florida Fruits & Vegetables in 1949?

A. Carroll Baker
B. Elizabeth Taylor
C. Jane Withers
D. Mercedes McCambridge

161. The 1960 Walter Mirisch–produced film *The Magnificent Seven* features an Oscar-nominated musical score by what composer?

A. Elmer Bernstein
B. Ennio Morricone
C. Henry Mancini
D. Quincy Jones

162. Jean Hagen appears opposite Robert Taylor in what western?

A. *Ambush* (1950)
B. *Rio Grande* (1950)
C. *The Quiet Man* (1952)
D. *Wagon Master* (1950)

163. Who plays Clint Canfield in *Santa Fe* (1951)?

A. Jerome Courtland
B. John Archer
C. Peter M. Thompson
D. Randolph Scott

164. Montgomery Clift spent a month attending rodeos across the Midwest in preparation for which film?

A. *Red River* (1948)
B. *The Defector* (1966)
C. *The Misfits* (1961)
D. *The Search* (1948)

165. In the 1962 film *How the West Was Won*, Raymond Massey portrays which historical figure?

A. Abraham Lincoln
B. Gen. William Tecumseh Sherman
C. Ulysses S. Grant
D. Wyatt Earp

166. Willie Nelson made his film debut in what western opposite Robert Redford and Jane Fonda?

A. *Barefoot in the Park* (1967)
B. *Cheyenne Autumn* (1964)
C. *The Electric Horseman* (1979)
D. *Young Cassidy* (1965)

167. What was Gary Cooper's first film in CinemaScope?

    A. *Blowing Wild* (1953)
    B. *Garden of Evil* (1954)
    C. *Love in the Afternoon* (1957)
    D. *Vera Cruz* (1954)

168. In the 1934 Fay Wray film *Viva Villa!,* what actor portrayed Pancho Villa?

    A. Fredric March
    B. Leon Ames
    C. Spencer Tracy
    D. Wallace Beery

169. In what film does Ernest Borgnine costar with Joan Crawford?

    A. *Johnny Guitar* (1954)
    B. *The Catered Affair* (1956)
    C. *The Stranger Wore a Gun* (1953)
    D. *Vera Cruz* (1954)

Fort Apache, 1948

170. What former child star played Henry Fonda's daughter in the Pedro Armendáriz film *Fort Apache* (1948)?

    A. Margaret O'Brien
    B. Natalie Wood
    C. Patty Duke
    D. Shirley Temple

171. Paul Newman and Robert Redford are leaders of what group in *Butch Cassidy and the Sundance Kid* (**1969**)?

    A. Big City Blues Gang
    B. Hole-in-the-Wall Gang
    C. Racket Busters
    D. The Invisible Stripes

172. Robert Taylor plays a rancher from Wyoming in what western?

    A. *Cattle King* (1963)
    B. *Many Rivers to Cross* (1955)
    C. *Ride, Vaquero!* (1953)
    D. *Saddle the Wind* (1958)

173. Van Johnson and Richard Boone star in what western?

    A. *Montana* (1950)
    B. *Rocky Mountain* (1950)
    C. *Siege at Red River* (1954)
    D. *The Baroness and the Butler* (1938)

174. Lucien Ballard photographed all of the following Sam Peckinpah films except which one?

    A. *Junior Bonner* (1972)
    B. *Major Dundee* (1965)
    C. *Ride the High Country* (1962)
    D. *The Ballad of Cable Hogue* (1970)

175. What did Howard Hughes have specially designed for Jane Russell in *The Outlaw* (1943), even though a much later autobiography revealed she did not wear it?

    A. Bra
    B. Dress
    C. Hose
    D. Wig

answers found on page 559

176. Ernest Laszlo was the cinematographer of what western starring and directed by Burt Lancaster?

A. *Many Rivers to Cross* (1955)
B. *Ride, Vaquero!* (1953)
C. *Saddle the Wind* (1958)
D. *The Kentuckian* (1955)

177. What film directed by Henry Hathaway stars Tyrone Power and Linda Darnell?

A. *Brigham Young* (1940)
B. *China Girl* (1942)
C. *Sundown* (1941)
D. *Ten Gentlemen from West Point* (1942)

178. Andy Griffith and Debbie Reynolds share the screen in what western?

A. *Escape from Fort Bravo* (1953)
B. *The Second Time Around* (1961)
C. *The Wild Bunch* (1969)
D. *Wild Rovers* (1971)

179. Which of the following westerns did not star Glenn Ford?

A. *Go West, Young Lady* (1941)
B. *In Old Oklahoma* (1943)
C. *The Desperadoes* (1943)
D. *The Man from Colorado* (1948)

180. What is James Stewart's relation to Stephen McNally in *Winchester '73* (1950)?

A. McNally married Stewart's sister.
B. Stewart is McNally's father.
C. They are brothers.
D. They married the same woman.

181. Joseph Cotten costarred in the 1961 film *The Last Sunset*. Who was the director?

A. John Ford
B. Robert Aldrich
C. Robert Wise
D. Sam Fuller

182. In *The Desperadoes* (1943), starring Glenn Ford, who plays the banker?

A. Claire Trevor
B. Edgar Buchanan
C. Porter Hall
D. Randolph Scott

183. Glenn Ford is credited with being the fastest gun in Hollywood westerns. How fast could he draw and fire?

A. 0.2 seconds
B. 0.3 seconds
C. 0.4 seconds
D. 0.6 seconds

184. What was John Ford's first color film?

A. *Drums Along the Mohawk* (1939)
B. *How Green Was My Valley* (1941)
C. *They Were Expendable* (1945)
D. *Tobacco Road* (1941)

185. In what film does Ernest Borgnine costar with Gary Cooper and Burt Lancaster?

A. *Bad Day at Black Rock* (1955)
B. *Johnny Guitar* (1954)
C. *The Bounty Hunter* (1954)
D. *Vera Cruz* (1954)

186. Dana Andrews plays a frontier scout trying to protect an Indian tribe from a bigoted cavalry officer in what film?

A. *Comanche* (1956)
B. *I Want You* (1951)
C. *The Best Years of Our Lives* (1946)
D. *The Devil's Brigade* (1968)

187. Who earned a Best Supporting Actor Oscar nomination for his role in *The Alamo* (1960)?

A. Chill Wills
B. Frankie Avalon
C. Laurence Harvey
D. Richard Widmark

Spotlight on
GLENN **FORD** (1916–2006)

Glenn Ford was more than just a western star: He was the real thing. In his many westerns, which constituted nearly half of his screen credits, he did all of his own riding and rarely required a double for even the more perilous horseback stunts. And although he may not have been *The Fastest Gun Alive* (1956), as was his character in the film, he was certainly the fastest gun in Hollywood, able to draw and fire a gun in 0.4 seconds. Ford started his film career in the thirties, but really came into his own when he returned from World War II. By that time his boyish good looks had matured, giving him the sexual swagger he needed to rise to stardom opposite Rita Hayworth in *Gilda* (1946). That new hardness also served him well in noir films like Fritz Lang's *The Big Heat* (1953) and helped him hold his own opposite dramatic divas like Bette Davis, Geraldine Page, and Eleanor Parker. Along with his western prowess, he was also a dedicated military man, serving with the marines from 1942 to 1945 and rising to the rank of captain in the Navy Reserve.

Cimarron, 1960

1. What western starring Glenn Ford was Columbia's first Technicolor film?

   A. *Go West, Young Lady* (1941)
   B. *Texas* (1941)
   C. *The Desperadoes* (1943)
   D. *The Loves of Carmen* (1948)

2. Glenn Ford and Angie Dickinson starred in what western directed by Richard Thorpe?

   A. *The Fastest Gun Alive* (1956)
   B. *The Last Challenge* (1967)
   C. *The Sheepman* (1958)
   D. *Vengeance Valley* (1951)

3. Nearly half of Glenn Ford's films were westerns. Which film below is not one of them?

   A. *3:10 to Yuma* (1957)
   B. *Teahouse of the August Moon* (1956)
   C. *The Desperadoes* (1943)
   D. *The Fastest Gun Alive* (1956)

4. Glenn Ford appears in all of the following Delmer Daves films except which one?

   A. *3:10 to Yuma* (1957)
   B. *Cowboy* (1958)
   C. *Jubal* (1956)
   D. *The Badlanders* (1958)

The Fastest Gun Alive, 1956

answers found on page 560

188. In the 1954 western *The Far Country,* Kathleen Freeman plays a co-owner of what establishment?

   A. Dawson Hash House
   B. Louisville Pancake House
   C. The Peach Pit
   D. The Roadside Diner

189. What actress earned Oscar nominations for both the Woody Allen film *Interiors* (1978) and the John Farrow western *Hondo* (1953)?

   A. Diane Keaton
   B. Geraldine Page
   C. Natalie Wood
   D. Thelma Ritter

190. Arthur Hunnicut earned his only Oscar nomination for playing what character in Howard Hawks's *The Big Sky* (1952)?

   A. Boone Caudill
   B. Jim Deakins
   C. Poordevil
   D. Zeb Calloway

191. Lucien Ballard photographed Charles Bronson for what 1975 Alistair MacLean western?

   A. *Breakheart Pass*
   B. *Buchanan Rides Alone*
   C. *Ride the High Country*
   D. *The Desert Rats*

192. Lee Marvin had a surprise hit record with a song he recorded for the 1969 western musical *Paint Your Wagon.* What was the name of the song?

   A. "Buttons and Bows"
   B. "Happy Trails"
   C. "They Call the Wind Maria"
   D. "Wand'rin Star"

193. William Haines gets caught conning cowboys and has to work off his debt on a ranch in what film?

   A. *Brown of Harvard* (1926)

   B. *Little Annie Rooney* (1925)
   C. *Show People* (1928)
   D. *Way Out West* (1930)

194. What George Stevens film is known as "The Greatest Story of the West Ever Filmed"?

   A. *Saddle the Wind* (1958)
   B. *Shane* (1953)
   C. *The Last Hunt* (1956)
   D. *The Man from Colorado* (1948)

195. What is the distinguishing feature of John Wayne's character Rooster Cogburn in *True Grit* (1969)?

   A. A hook for a hand
   B. A steel nose plate
   C. A wooden leg
   D. An eye patch

196. John Ireland compares the size of his gun with Montgomery Clift's in what Howard Hawks film?

   A. *A Walk in the Sun* (1945)
   B. *All the King's Men* (1949)
   C. *My Darling Clementine* (1946)
   D. *Red River* (1948)

197. What year was George Marshall's *Destry Rides Again* released in the United States?

   A. 1932
   B. 1939
   C. 1945
   D. 1953

198. Which star of *The Last of the Mohicans* (1992) played Eytukan in James Cameron's *Avatar* (2009)?

   A. Daniel Day-Lewis
   B. Eric Schweig
   C. Russell Means
   D. Wes Studi

answers found on page 560

199. Robert Taylor turned down the role of Langdon Towne in what film opposite Spencer Tracy?

A. *Drums Along the Mohawk* (1939)
B. *North by Northwest* (1959)
C. *Northwest Passage* (1940)
D. *The Westerner* (1940)

Day of the Evil Gun, 1968

200. Who directed the 1968 western *Day of the Evil Gun*?

A. David Swift
B. Jerry Thorpe
C. Lee H. Katzin
D. Richard Thorpe

201. Paul Muni plays a cowboy in what film opposite Mary Astor?

A. *All That Money Can Buy* (1941)
B. *Silver River* (1948)
C. *Stallion Road* (1947)
D. *The World Changes* (1933)

202. Who is Gary Cooper's lovely costar in *Along Came Jones* (1945)?

A. Carole Lombard
B. Lauren Bacall
C. Loretta Young
D. Norma Shearer

203. Robert Taylor plays the adopted brother of Anthony Quinn's character in what western?

A. *Many Rivers to Cross* (1955)
B. *Ride, Vaquero!* (1953)
C. *Saddle the Wind* (1958)
D. *The House of the Seven Hawks* (1959)

204. With which director did John Wayne make the most films?

A. Anthony Mann
B. Howard Hawks
C. John Ford
D. Robert Aldrich

205. Which of the following films is directed by Henry Hathaway and photographed by cinematographer Lucien Ballard?

A. *Junior Bonner* (1972)
B. *The Sons of Katie Elder* (1965)
C. *The Wild Bunch* (1969)
D. *Viridiana* (1961)

206. Which leading lady connects *Night Nurse* (1931) and *Forty Guns* (1957)?

A. Ann Sheridan
B. Barbara Stanwyck
C. Debbie Reynolds
D. Jean Arthur

207. Complete this Montgomery Clift line from *The Misfits* (1961): "How come you got such trust in your eyes, like . . .

A. . . . Gay's dumb puppy?"
B. . . . a doomed pig?"
C. . . . a little girl?"
D. . . . you was just born?"

208. How many Best Director Oscars has John Ford won?

A. 1
B. 2
C. 4
D. 5

---

answers found on page 560

An American in Paris, 1951

Chapter 12

MUSICALS

Despite some rough spots, the musical has been a Hollywood staple since the arrival of sound. The musical numbers by Al Jolson in *The Jazz Singer* (1927) established the new medium's popularity, and musicals have brought some of the greatest entertainers of all time, from Ethel Waters to Barbra Streisand, to audiences around the world.

Most musicals are set in a fantasy world where people sing and dance to express feelings that can't be contained in mere words. When Gene Kelly realizes he's in love with Debbie Reynolds in *Singin' in the Rain* (1952), he breaks into one of the greatest numbers of his career, cavorting through the rain like a five-year-old. Fred Astaire can't just tell Ginger Rogers he's attracted to her in *The Gay Divorcee* (1934), he has to sing "Night and Day" and then lead her into a dance so sensual that at the end she slaps his face.

The Hollywood musical developed certain distinctive forms over the years. It was ushered in with the backstage musical, stories about putting on a show that provided an obvious excuse for the musical numbers. Warner Bros. cornered the market on that subgenre in 1933 with *42nd Street*, the first of a series of popular tuners featuring a stock company that at various times included Dick Powell, Ruby Keeler, Joan Blondell, and Rogers. The best of them featured eye-popping choreography from Busby Berkeley, who quickly made his name by staging numbers too big to fit on any stage.

At MGM, producer Arthur Freed set out to create integrated musicals in which every number related to plot, character, and setting. With collaborators like directors Vincente

Minnelli and Stanley Donen, and writers Betty Comden and Adolph Green, he created a series of sophisticated films among the best in the business, including *The Wizard of Oz* (1939), *Meet Me in St. Louis* (1944), *An American in Paris* (1951), *Singin' in the Rain*, and *Gigi* (1958). It helped that the studio had under contract some of the best singers and dancers in the business, among them Astaire, Kelly, Judy Garland, Frank Sinatra, Ann Miller, and Lena Horne.

Indeed, one of the joys of the musical is the talent it has brought to the screen. Many, like Astaire and Kelly, came from Broadway, while Garland came from vaudeville, where her adult singing style had dazzled audiences even when she was a child performer. Recording led Sinatra and Bing Crosby to film stardom. Esther Williams swam in from Billy Rose's Aquacade. And Carmen Miranda brought her outlandish costumes and Latin rhythms from Brazil.

They didn't all have to sing and dance. The studios had no problems dubbing voices for performers like Rita Hayworth or Esther Williams who were too busy with other things to learn the songs. And they could always cut to a close-up of someone else's feet or torso if a dance number was too difficult. Some of the screen's greatest musicals included performers not known for their musical skills. Dramatic actors Marlon Brando and Jean Simmons proved effective choices to star in *Guys and Dolls* (1955), and Audrey Hepburn surprised and delighted audiences with her singing in *Funny Face* (1957).

Although many early musicals came direct from Broadway, Hollywood soon developed original works of its own. From then on, the relationship to Broadway was shaky. Hit shows like *Lady in the Dark* (1944) and *On the Town* (1949) routinely had songs cut and replaced by new numbers. And many of Broadway's greatest stars, including Ethel Merman and Mary Martin, rarely got the chance to re-create their most famous roles on screen. But Hollywood also fed Broadway, with popular films like *Sunset Blvd.* (1950) and *The Producers* (1968) becoming hit stage musicals.

As the studio system declined, however, more Broadway hits like *West Side Story* (1961) and *Oliver!* (1968) started making it to the screen with their scores intact. When *The Sound of Music* (1965) broke box-office records to become the top-grossing film to date, it started a trend toward ever-bigger musicals that eventually destroyed the genre with costly flops like *Star!* (1968) and the musical version of *Lost Horizon* (1973). At the same time, the new mega-musicals brought Hollywood one of its biggest stars, Barbra Streisand. It didn't matter how big or small the production was—all she had to do was open her mouth to sing and magic poured out. When she took the screen, she brought audiences the same excitement they had experienced from such other greats as Jolson and Crosby, Garland and Horne, and Astaire and Kelly.

1. Fred Astaire plays "Flying Tiger" Fred Atwell in what musical?

   A. *Blue Skies* (1946)
   B. *Love Affair* (1939)
   C. *The Sky's the Limit* (1943)
   D. *Top Hat* (1935)

2. Julie Andrews stars in what musical based on the life of stage actress Gertrude Lawrence?

   A. *No Time for Love* (1943)
   B. *Star!* (1968)
   C. *The Girl Most Likely* (1958)
   D. *Tonight We Sing* (1953)

3. Irving Berlin wrote the lyrics to which song featured in the 1943 musical *Hello Frisco, Hello*?

   A. "Am I in Love"
   B. "The Dance of the Grizzly Bear"
   C. "The High and the Mighty"
   D. "Zing a Little Zong"

4. Who plays Jack Lemmon's love interest in the 1955 musical *My Sister Eileen*?

   A. Ann Miller
   B. Betty Garrett
   C. Cyd Charisse
   D. Judy Holliday

5. What musical pairing Frank Sinatra and Doris Day is a remake of 1938's *Four Daughters*?

   A. *The Girl Most Likely* (1958)
   B. *The Sky's the Limit* (1943)
   C. *You Were Never Lovelier* (1942)
   D. *Young at Heart* (1954)

6. What film starring Ronald Colman was originally planned as a musical pairing Nelson Eddy and Jeanette MacDonald?

   A. *Forgotten Victory* (1939)
   B. *The Great Meddler* (1940)
   C. *The Prisoner of Zenda* (1937)
   D. *They Live Again* (1938)

7. What Oscar nomination did the Frank Sinatra musical *Step Lively* (1944) earn?

   A. Best Color Cinematography
   B. Best Interior Decoration—Black-and-White Film
   C. Best Scoring of a Musical Picture
   D. Best Song

8. Which of the following songs is not performed by Benny Goodman and His Orchestra in the 1937 film *Hollywood Hotel*?

   A. "Hooray for Hollywood"
   B. "I've Got a Heartful of Music"
   C. "On the Sunny Side of the Street"
   D. "Sing, Sing, Sing"

9. Thelma Ritter won the 1958 Tony Award for Best Actress in a musical in a tie with which of the following actresses?

   A. Ethel Merman
   B. Gwen Verdon
   C. Mary Martin
   D. Rosalind Russell

10. In 1930, Gene Krupa played along with Glenn Miller and Benny Goodman as part of the pit orchestra for what Broadway musical?

    A. *Anything Goes*
    B. *Dancing Partner*
    C. *Girl Crazy*
    D. *Strike Up the Band*

11. "Hernando's Hideaway" is the show-stopping number in what Stanley Donen musical?

    A. *Damn Yankees* (1958)
    B. *It's Always Fair Weather* (1955)
    C. *On the Town* (1949)
    D. *The Pajama Game* (1957)

answers found on page 560

12. What Al Jolson musical did Lewis Milestone direct?

A. *Hallelujah, I'm a Bum* (1933)
B. *The Heart of New York* (1932)
C. *The Jazz Singer* (1927)
D. *Wonder Bar* (1934)

13. Fred MacMurray and Greer Garson play husband and wife in what Disney musical?

A. *Honky Tonk Freeway* (1981)
B. *The Beguiled* (1971)
C. *The Happiest Millionaire* (1967)
D. *Toys in the Attic* (1963)

14. Who does Sally Sweetland sing for in *Yankee Doodle Dandy* (1942)?

A. Irene Manning
B. Jeanne Cagney
C. Joan Leslie
D. Rosemary DeCamp

15. Who earned a Best Dance Direction Oscar nomination for *Top Hat* (1935)?

A. Busby Berkeley
B. Gene Kelly
C. Hermes Pan
D. Stanley Donen

16. Fred Astaire performs the song "Piano Dance" in which film costarring Betty Hutton?

A. *Flying Down to Rio* (1933)
B. *Funny Face* (1957)
C. *Let's Dance* (1950)
D. *The Belle of New York* (1952)

17. Lena Horne was eighty years old when she appeared in an ad for what clothing company?

A. American Apparel
B. Banana Republic
C. Gap
D. Guess

18. What was Fred Zinnemann's first musical feature?

A. *Easter Parade* (1948)
B. *Oklahoma!* (1955)
C. *Royal Wedding* (1951)
D. *The Barkleys of Broadway* (1949)

19. The 1972 Sophia Loren musical *Man of La Mancha* starred which actor as Don Quixote?

A. Peter O'Toole
B. Richard Burton
C. Richard Harris
D. Robert Goulet

20. Ned Sparks plays press agent Inky Wells in what musical opposite Betty Grable?

A. *A Piece of Cake* (1948)
B. *Love in Pawn* (1953)
C. *Room to Let* (1950)
D. *This Way Please* (1937)

21. Fay Bainter's New York stage debut was in what musical?

A. *Arms and the Girl*
B. *The Kissing Burglar*
C. *The Rose of Panama*
D. *West Side Story*

22. Who served as music director for *The Goldwyn Follies* (1938)?

A. Alfred Newman
B. Jerry Goldsmith
C. Michael Kidd
D. Adolph Deutsch

23. Who sings "The Trolley Song" in *Meet Me in St. Louis* (1944)?

A. Doris Day
B. Irene Dunne
C. Judy Garland
D. Rosalind Russell

answers found on page 560

In the Good Old Summertime, 1949

24. What was the working title of the 1949 Van Johnson and Judy Garland movie *In the Good Old Summertime*?

A. *Summer, Summer, Summer!*
B. *The Girl from Chicago*
C. *The Girl That I Marry*
D. *Peas in a Pod*

25. Which of the following songs was a top ten hit that Barbra Streisand recorded as a duet with Barry Gibb in 1980?

A. "Guilty"
B. "Kiss Me in the Rain"
C. "The Main Event"
D. "Woman in Love"

26. What was the second of two musicals Rita Hayworth made with Fred Astaire?

A. *Cover Girl* (1944)
B. *Pal Joey* (1957)
C. *Top Hat* (1935)
D. *You Were Never Lovelier* (1942)

27. Mervyn LeRoy directed Howard Keel and Marjorie Main in which musical remake?

A. *Lovely to Look At* (1952)
B. *Rose Marie* (1954)
C. *Sweet Adeline* (1934)
D. *The Harvey Girls* (1946)

28. Which Barbra Streisand film is not based on a Broadway musical?

A. *Funny Girl* (1968)
B. *Hello, Dolly!* (1969)
C. *Nuts* (1987)
D. *On a Clear Day You Can See Forever* (1970)

29. What was the first film to win the Oscar for Best Original Song? (Hint: It was a Fred and Ginger musical.)

A. *Flying Down to Rio* (1933)
B. *Perfect Understanding* (1933)
C. *Rendezvous* (1935)
D. *The Gay Divorcee* (1934)

30. What two musicals won consecutive Best Picture Oscars?

A. *An American in Paris* and *Gigi*
B. *My Fair Lady* and *The Sound of Music*
C. *Singin' in the Rain* and *Oliver!*
D. *West Side Story* and *Chicago*

31. Jane Powell's character is engaged to three different men in what musical directed by Mitchell Leisen?

A. *Let's Dance* (1950)
B. *Royal Wedding* (1951)
C. *The Belle of New York* (1952)
D. *The Girl Most Likely* (1958)

32. Joan Blondell costarred in the 1956 musical *The Opposite Sex*. This was a remake of what popular film?

A. *His Girl Friday* (1940)
B. *Love Affair* (1939)
C. *The Philadelphia Story* (1940)
D. *The Women* (1939)

33. Who directed James Cagney in *Footlight Parade* (1933)?

A. Busby Berkeley
B. Lloyd Bacon
C. Ray Enright
D. Vincente Minnelli

answers found on page 560

34. Shirley Jones shares the screen with lifelong friend Eddie Albert in what musical?

   A. *Easter Parade* (1948)
   B. *Let's Dance* (1950)
   C. *Oklahoma!* (1955)
   D. *The Barkleys of Broadway* (1949)

35. Which of the following songs does Jean Simmons's character sing in the 1955 musical *Guys and Dolls*?

   A. "Adelaide's Lament"
   B. "If I Were a Bell"
   C. "Luck Be a Lady"
   D. "Sit Down, You're Rockin' the Boat"

36. Janet Gaynor starred in the 1931 film *Daddy Long Legs*. Who played her role in the 1955 musical remake?

   A. Audrey Hepburn
   B. Cyd Charisse
   C. Debbie Reynolds
   D. Leslie Caron

37. In the 1957 musical *Funny Face*, Fred Astaire and Kay Thompson masquerade as philosophy disciples from where?

   A. Baton Rouge, Louisiana
   B. Beverly Hills, California
   C. Palm Springs, Florida
   D. Tallahassee, Florida

38. Marjorie Main appeared in which musical adaptation starring Gloria Swanson?

   A. *Anchors Aweigh* (1945)
   B. *Babes on Broadway* (1941)
   C. *Music in the Air* (1934)
   D. *The Cowboy and the Lady* (1938)

39. Gordon MacRae and Shirley Jones costar in *Oklahoma!* (1955) and what other musical?

   A. *Carousel* (1956)
   B. *Easter Parade* (1948)
   C. *The Band Wagon* (1953)
   D. *The Barkleys of Broadway* (1949)

Hollywood Canteen, 1944

40. Delmer Daves's 1944 film *Hollywood Canteen* received an Academy Award nomination for Best Song. What was the name of the song?

   A. "Love for Two"
   B. "Love Is in the Stars"
   C. "Sweet Dreams, Sweetheart"
   D. "Take Me Back"

41. In the 1951 musical *Two Tickets to Broadway*, what is the hometown of Janet Leigh's character?

   A. Heron Lake
   B. Pelican Falls
   C. Pine Tree
   D. Poplar Bluff

42. Gloria Grahame starred in which film that was the first musical directed by Fred Zinnemann?

   A. *Du Barry Was a Lady* (1943)
   B. *Oklahoma!* (1955)
   C. *The Greatest Show on Earth* (1952)
   D. *Ziegfeld Follies* (1946)

43. What was Gene Kelly's last film as a performer for MGM?

   A. *Inherit the Wind* (1960)
   B. *Invitation to the Dance* (1956)
   C. *Les Girls* (1957)
   D. *The Happy Road* (1957)

44. The 1947 musical *Good News* was nominated for an Academy Award for Best Song. What was the name of the song?

A. "Lucky in Love"
B. "Pass the Peace Pipe"
C. "The Best Things in Life Are Free"
D. "Varsity Drag"

45. Louis Armstrong made his Broadway debut in the 1929 revue *Hot Chocolates*. What song did he sing that stopped the show almost every night?

A. "Ain't Misbehavin'"
B. "Heebie Jeebies"
C. "What a Wonderful World"
D. "When the Saints Go Marching In"

46. Fred Astaire's character in what musical was based on real-life photographer Richard Avedon?

A. *Funny Face* (1957)
B. *Royal Wedding* (1951)
C. *Silk Stockings* (1957)
D. *The Belle of New York* (1952)

47. Who directed Dick Powell in the 1937 film *Hollywood Hotel*?

A. Busby Berkeley
B. Edward Buzzell
C. Frank Capra
D. Robert Z. Leonard

48. Ron Howard played Winthrop Paroo in what musical opposite Shirley Jones?

A. *Mr. Music* (1950)
B. *The Music Man* (1962)
C. *The Singer Not the Song* (1961)
D. *Tonight We Sing* (1953)

49. In 1997, Barbra Streisand recorded "Tell Him" with what singer?

A. Celine Dion
B. Madonna
C. Sarah McLachlan
D. Whitney Houston

50. Edward Arnold shared the screen with Norma Shearer and Clark Gable in what 1939 musical?

A. *Idiot's Delight*
B. *Strange Interlude*
C. *Too Hot to Handle*
D. *We Were Dancing*

51. Who sings the Oscar-nominated song "Our Love Affair" in *Strike Up the Band* (1940)?

A. Dick Powell and Ruby Keeler
B. Ginger Rogers and Fred Astaire
C. Joe E. Brown and Virginia Mayo
D. Judy Garland and Mickey Rooney

52. In the Stanley Donen musical *It's Always Fair Weather* (1955), which of the following actors did not play one of the three best friends?

A. Dan Dailey
B. Frank Sinatra
C. Gene Kelly
D. Michael Kidd

53. Which film featuring James Mason was the first musical directed by George Cukor?

A. *A Star Is Born* (1954)
B. *Les Girls* (1957)
C. *My Fair Lady* (1964)
D. *The Actress* (1953)

54. Which musical star appeared with Walter Pidgeon in the 1946 film *Holiday in Mexico*?

A. Deanna Durbin
B. Jane Powell
C. Judy Garland
D. Kathryn Grayson

answers found on page 560

Spotlight on
BING **CROSBY** (1903-1977)

Crosby possessed an intimate singing style and laid-back attitude that were perfect for the movies. A set of mail-order drums started his career while he was still in college, and before long, he had dropped out of school and was singing with the era's most popular big band, the Paul Whiteman Orchestra. He made his screen debut when the band headlined the early musical *The King of Jazz* (1930). New, more sensitive microphones showcased Crosby's easygoing singing style on early recordings that caught the attention of CBS Radio head William S. Paley. He put Crosby on the air, which lead to a role as himself in Paramount's *The Big Broadcast* (1932). He stuck to that persona for the rest of his career. Crosby's casual air provided a perfect complement for Bob Hope's comic antics when they teamed for *Road to Singapore* (1940), the first of seven *Road* films in which they vied for Dorothy Lamour's affections while spoofing more serious adventure films, the movie business, and even their own images. Crosby's understated talents as an actor led to three Academy Award nominations and one win, as Best Actor for his portrayal of Father O'Malley, the singing priest in *Going My Way* (1944).

Going Hollywood (1933)

High Society, 1956

1. **All of the following songs sung by Bing Crosby won the Academy Award for Best Song except which one?**

    A. "Accentuate the Positive"

    B. "In the Cool, Cool, Cool of the Evening"

    C. "Sweet Leilani"

    D. "Swinging on a Star"

2. **Bing Crosby introduced what Academy Award–winning song in the 1942 film *Holiday Inn*?**

    A. "Easter Parade"

    B. "Have Yourself a Merry Little Christmas"

    C. "White Christmas"

    D. "Yankee Doodle Dandy"

3. **A song that Bing Crosby sang in the 1937 film *Waikiki Wedding* won the Academy Award for Best Song. What was the name of it?**

    A. "Love Has Never Seemed More Lovely"

    B. "Lovely Luau"

    C. "Sweet Leilani"

    D. "The Moon and the Ocean"

4. **Bing Crosby and Joan Fontaine share the screen in what musical directed and cowritten by Billy Wilder?**

    A. *Mr. Music* (1950)

    B. *No Time for Love* (1943)

    C. *Riding High* (1950)

    D. *The Emperor Waltz* (1948)

5. **Bing Crosby performs the Oscar-winning song "In the Cool, Cool, Cool of the Evening" in what musical?**

    A. *Here Comes the Groom* (1951)

    B. *Kiss Me Kate* (1953)

    C. *Lovely to Look At* (1952)

    D. *Shall We Dance* (1937)

---

answers found on page 560

55. What musical starring Bing Crosby and Rosemary Clooney features songs written by Irving Berlin?

    A. *Let's Dance* (1950)
    B. *The Band Wagon* (1953)
    C. *White Christmas* (1954)
    D. *You Were Never Lovelier* (1942)

56. Fred Astaire and Red Skelton star in which musical directed by Richard Thorpe that was loosely based on the Tin Pan Alley songwriting team of Bert Kalmar and Harry Ruby?

    A. *I Dood It* (1943)
    B. *Let's Dance* (1950)
    C. *Lovely to Look At* (1952)
    D. *Three Little Words* (1950)

57. Who sings the Academy Award–nominated song "Happiness Is a Thing Called Joe" in *Cabin in the Sky* (1943)?

    A. Dorothy Dandridge
    B. Duke Ellington
    C. Ethel Waters
    D. Lena Horne

58. Alfred Newman worked on two different film versions of which musical?

    A. *Alexander's Ragtime Band*
    B. *How to Marry a Millionaire*
    C. *Oklahoma!*
    D. *State Fair*

59. Luise Rainer won her first Academy Award as Best Actress for her performance in what musical?

    A. *Love Crazy* (1941)
    B. *The Baroness and the Butler* (1938)
    C. *The Great Ziegfeld* (1936)
    D. *The Lady from Shanghai* (1947)

60. Which musical actress plays Fay Wray's daughter in *Small Time Girl* (1953)?

    A. Ann Miller
    B. Ginger Rogers
    C. Jane Powell
    D. Judy Garland

Cabin in the Sky, 1943

61. Who was Ethel Waters's costar in *Cabin in the Sky* (1943)?

    A. Dorothy Dandridge
    B. Hattie McDaniel
    C. Lena Horne
    D. Cab Calloway

62. Bob Hope and Shirley Ross sing the song "Thanks for the Memory" in what film costarring W. C. Fields?

    A. *A Family Affair* (1937)
    B. *Live, Love and Learn* (1937)
    C. *Mrs. Wiggs of the Cabbage Patch* (1934)
    D. *The Big Broadcast of 1938* (1938)

63. Shirley Jones stars in all of the following musicals except for which one?

    A. *Carousel* (1956)
    B. *Guys and Dolls* (1955)
    C. *Oklahoma!* (1955)
    D. *The Music Man* (1962)

answers found on page 560

64. In which of the following musicals does Fred Astaire perform the number "Drum Crazy"?

A. *Easter Parade* (1948)
B. *Silk Stockings* (1957)
C. *The Band Wagon* (1953)
D. *Broadway Melody of 1940* (1940)

65. What film won the Oscar for Best Scoring of a Musical Picture in 1956?

A. *Guys and Dolls*
B. *Oklahoma!*
C. *South Pacific*
D. *Summer Stock*

66. Lena Horne made her film debut in what low-budget musical?

A. *Broadway Rhythm* (1944)
B. *State Fair* (1962)
C. *Stormy Weather* (1943)
D. *The Duke Is Tops* (1938)

67. The 1964 musical *The Pleasure Seekers* was a remake of what film starring Rossano Brazzi?

A. *Light in the Piazza* (1962)
B. *The Barretts of Wimpole Street* (1957)
C. *The Moon Is Blue* (1953)
D. *Three Coins in the Fountain* (1954)

68. Marjorie Main starred opposite Fred Astaire in which musical?

A. *Broadway Melody of 1940* (1940)
B. *Let's Dance* (1950)
C. *The Band Wagon* (1953)
D. *The Belle of New York* (1952)

69. Van Johnson and Kathryn Grayson share the screen in what musical?

A. *Blue Skies* (1946)
B. *Clowning Around* (1992)
C. *Grounds for Marriage* (1951)
D. *Holiday Inn* (1942)

70. Audrey Hepburn and Kay Thompson perform the song "On How to Be Lovely" in what musical directed by Stanley Donen?

A. *Funny Face* (1957)
B. *Silk Stockings* (1957)
C. *The Band Wagon* (1953)
D. *The Belle of New York* (1952)

71. To what university were Benny Goodman's musical papers donated following his death?

A. Columbia
B. NYU
C. Northwestern
D. Yale

72. All of the following Irving Berlin songs are featured in the musical *White Christmas* (1954) except for which one?

A. "Count Your Blessings Instead of Sheep"
B. "Let's Face the Music and Dance"
C. "Mandy"
D. "The Best Things Happen When You're Dancing"

73. Which musical won Frank Loesser and Abe Burrows a Pulitzer Prize?

A. *How to Succeed in Business Without Really Trying*
B. *It's a Bird . . . It's a Plane . . . It's Superman*
C. *No Strings*
D. *Promises, Promises*

74. What musical has won the most Academy Awards?

A. *My Fair Lady* (1964)
B. *On the Town* (1949)
C. *Singin' in the Rain* (1952)
D. *West Side Story* (1961)

answers found on page 560

75. Who was Bing Crosby's leading lady in the 1951 film *Here Comes the Groom*?

A. Debbie Reynolds
B. Doris Day
C. Jane Wyman
D. Rita Hayworth

76. In the 1962 musical *Gypsy*, Rosalind Russell plays Mama Rose. Who originated the role on Broadway?

A. Carol Channing
B. Ethel Merman
C. Judy Holliday
D. Mary Martin

77. Anthony Quinn reprised his starring role of Alexis Zorba in the 1983 Broadway musical revival by what name?

A. *The Dionysian*
B. *The Greek*
C. *Zorba*
D. *Zorba's Isle*

78. Harry Davenport made his Broadway debut in what musical?

A. *Follies*
B. *Quilters*
C. *The Voyage of Suzette*
D. *The Wiz*

79. In the 1986 comedy *Heartburn*, costarring Meryl Streep, Jack Nicholson performs a song from which Rodgers and Hammerstein musical?

A. *Carousel*
B. *Oklahoma!*
C. *The King and I*
D. *The Sound of Music*

80. The 1973 musical *Sugar* was inspired by which Billy Wilder film?

A. *Love in the Afternoon* (1957)
B. *Some Like It Hot* (1959)

C. *The Emperor Waltz* (1948)
D. *The Lost Weekend* (1945)

81. The hat rack used as a dance prop in what musical cost more than $900 to build?

A. *Royal Wedding* (1951)
B. *Serenade* (1956)
C. *Swing Time* (1936)
D. *The Gypsy and the Gentleman* (1958)

Rhapsody in Blue, 1945

82. Who shared an Oscar nomination with Ray Heindorf for scoring *Rhapsody in Blue* (1945)?

A. Alfred Newman
B. George Gershwin
C. Max Steiner
D. Werner Janssen

83. Who was Barbra Streisand's costar in the 1975 film *Funny Lady*?

A. James Caan
B. Keith Carradine
C. Nick Nolte
D. Ryan O'Neal

answers found on page 560

84. Peter Lawford admitted later in his career that his most terrifying experience was performing his first musical number, which was what?

   A. Jitterbug
   B. Mambo
   C. Salsa
   D. Tap

85. From what Danny Kaye film is the Oscar-nominated song "Now I Know"?

   A. *A Song Is Born* (1948)
   B. *The Court Jester* (1955)
   C. *Up in Arms* (1944)
   D. *Wonder Man* (1945)

86. Who was the first American to choreograph and stage a ballet at the Paris Opera?

   A. Fred Astaire
   B. Gene Kelly
   C. Ginger Rogers
   D. Judy Garland

87. Which of these Rogers and Hammerstein musicals was choreographed by Agnes de Mille?

   A. *Easter Parade* (1948)
   B. *Oklahoma!* (1955)
   C. *The Band Wagon* (1953)
   D. *The Barkleys of Broadway* (1949)

88. Claudette Colbert stars in what musical directed by Alexander Hall?

   A. *Neptune's Daughter* (1949)
   B. *Swing Time* (1936)
   C. *The Barkleys of Broadway* (1949)
   D. *Torch Singer* (1933)

89. In 1993, Andrew Lloyd Webber adapted which Billy Wilder classic into a London musical?

   A. *Sabrina* (1954)
   B. *Sunset Blvd.* (1950)
   C. *The Emperor Waltz* (1948)
   D. *The Lost Weekend* (1945)

90. Gene Krupa formed his own band following a four-year stint in what other famous bandleader's orchestra?

   A. Benny Goodman
   B. Glenn Miller
   C. Harry James
   D. Tommy Dorsey

91. In which of her films does Barbra Streisand sing the Academy Award–nominated song "Papa, Can You Hear Me?"

   A. *Funny Girl* (1968)
   B. *Funny Lady* (1975)
   C. *Nuts* (1987)
   D. *Yentl* (1983)

92. Which musical won the most Oscars without winning Best Picture?

   A. *Cabaret* (1972)
   B. *Gigi* (1958)
   C. *My Fair Lady* (1964)
   D. *West Side Story* (1961)

93. Irving Berlin's song "Puttin' on the Ritz" was performed in all of the following films except for which one?

   A. *Blue Skies* (1946)
   B. *Our Blushing Brides* (1930)
   C. *Puttin' on the Ritz* (1930)
   D. *The Sky's the Limit* (1943)

94. Fred MacMurray's character keeps a pet alligator in what musical?

   A. *Sweet Bird of Youth* (1962)
   B. *The Happiest Millionaire* (1967)
   C. *The Notorious Landlady* (1962)
   D. *Walls of Glass* (1985)

answers found on page 560

95. What musical based on a Charles Dickens novel won the Academy Award for Best Picture in 1969?

A. *Gigi*
B. *Great Expectations*
C. *Oliver!*
D. *Scrooge*

96. Bronislau Kaper received an Academy Award nomination for Best Music Scoring of a Musical for which film starring Nelson Eddy?

A. *No Time for Love* (1943)
B. *Practically Yours* (1944)
C. *The Chocolate Soldier* (1941)
D. *Tonight We Sing* (1953)

97. Frank Loesser wrote music and lyrics for which Tony Award–winning musical?

A. *Flower Drum Song*
B. *Guys and Dolls*
C. *My Fair Lady*
D. *The Most Happy Fella*

98. W. C. Fields and Dorothy Lamour share the screen in what musical?

A. *Hold That Kiss* (1938)
B. *Live, Love and Learn* (1937)
C. *Personalities* (1942)
D. *The Big Broadcast of 1938* (1938)

99. What was Barbra Streisand's featured song in the 1962 Broadway musical *I Can Get It for You Wholesale*?

A. "If They Could See Me Now"
B. "Miss Marmelstein"
C. "People"
D. "What's a Girl to Do?"

100. In the Stanley Donen film *Seven Brides for Seven Brothers* (1954), what is the last name of the brothers' family?

A. Bowen
B. Pontipee

C. Poppyberry
D. Roundtree

101. Mario Lanza stars in what musical directed by Alexander Hall?

A. *Because You're Mine* (1952)
B. *Blue Skies* (1946)
C. *Neptune's Daughter* (1949)
D. *The Sky's the Limit* (1943)

102. In 1979, Barbra Streisand recorded the hit song "No More Tears (Enough Is Enough)" as a duet with what performer?

A. Aretha Franklin
B. Donna Summer
C. Gloria Gaynor
D. Thelma Houston

103. Marjorie Main was featured in which musical starring Gene Kelly?

A. *Brigadoon* (1954)
B. *Les Girls* (1957)
C. *Summer Stock* (1950)
D. *The Belle of New York* (1952)

104. Shirley Jones made her film debut in what musical?

A. *Let's Dance* (1950)
B. *Oklahoma!* (1955)
C. *Royal Wedding* (1951)
D. *The Belle of New York* (1952)

105. What was the nickname of Ginger Rogers's character in the 1944 musical *Lady in the Dark*?

A. "Boss Lady"
B. "Lady Lovely"
C. "Pearl"
D. "Sweetheart"

answers found on pages 560–561

On the Town, 1949

106. Which song did Frank Sinatra make famous in *On the Town* (1949)?
   A. "Luck, Be a Lady"
   B. "Sit Down, You're Rockin' the Boat"
   C. "New York, New York"
   D. "My Way"

107. For what Broadway musical did Rosalind Russell win the Tony Award for Best Actress in 1953?
   A. *Annie, Get Your Gun*
   B. *Gypsy*
   C. *Hello, Dolly!*
   D. *Wonderful Town*

108. The 1971 musical *Fiddler on the Roof* was nominated for eight Academy Awards. How many did it win?
   A. 1
   B. 3
   C. 5
   D. 7

109. Ann Miller stars in what musical remake of Shakespeare's *The Taming of the Shrew*?
   A. *Easter Parade* (1948)
   B. *Kiss Me Kate* (1953)
   C. *On the Town* (1949)
   D. *Stage Door* (1937)

110. What comedy musical features both W. C. Fields and Bob Hope?
   A. *College Swing* (1938)
   B. *Monsieur Beaucaire* (1946)
   C. *Personalities* (1942)
   D. *The Big Broadcast of 1938* (1938)

111. What was Gene Kelly's first nonmusical film?
   A. *It's Always Fair Weather* (1955)
   B. *On the Town* (1949)
   C. *Pilot No. 5* (1943)
   D. *Singin' in the Rain* (1952)

112. In *Singin' in the Rain* (1952), what is the name of the disastrous silent film that Gene Kelly and friends turn into a musical?
   A. *The Crimson Pirate*
   B. *The Dueling Cavalier*
   C. *The Kissing Bandit*
   D. *The Surly Swordsman*

113. The 1947 Rita Hayworth film *Down to Earth* served as the basis for what film musical?
   A. *Can't Stop the Music* (1980)
   B. *Footloose* (1984)
   C. *The Apple* (1980)
   D. *Xanadu* (1980)

114. In 1979 Angela Lansbury won a Tony Award for her role in which Broadway musical?
   A. *A Little Night Music*
   B. *Candide*
   C. *Gypsy*
   D. *Sweeney Todd: The Demon Barber of Fleet Street*

115. Vivien Leigh won the 1963 Tony Award for Best Actress in what musical?
   A. *Camelot*
   B. *High Button Shoes*
   C. *No Strings*
   D. *Tovarich*

answers found on page 561

116. Ernest Laszlo was the cinematographer of what musical starring Julie Andrews?

A. *Practically Yours* (1944)
B. *Star!* (1968)
C. *The Girl Most Likely* (1958)
D. *Tonight We Sing* (1953)

117. Finish the title of this Lena Horne song from *The Duke Is Tops* (1938): "I Know You . . .

A. . . . Can"
B. . . . Don't"
C. . . . Remember"
D. . . . Will"

118. Audrey Hepburn turned down the title role in the film version of *Gigi* (1958) to make what musical instead?

A. *Funny Face* (1957)
B. *Let's Dance* (1950)
C. *Silk Stockings* (1957)
D. *The Band Wagon* (1953)

119. What was the profession of Ginger Rogers's character in the 1933 musical *Sitting Pretty*?

A. Concert pianist
B. Dance instructor
C. Fashion designer
D. Lunch-wagon proprietor

120. Which of the following musicals was shot by cinematographer James Wong Howe?

A. *Babes in Arms* (1939)
B. *Cabaret* (1927)
C. *How to Succeed in Business Without Really Trying* (1967)
D. *Yankee Doodle Dandy* (1942)

121. In what musical film starring Frank Sinatra and Kathryn Grayson was Ricardo Montalban featured as a dancer?

A. *Guys and Dolls* (1955)
B. *That Midnight Kiss* (1949)
C. *The Kissing Bandit* (1948)
D. *Young at Heart* (1954)

122. Andy Griffith starred in the 1959 Broadway musical adapted from what film?

A. *Destry Rides Again* (1939)
B. *Follow the Fleet* (1936)
C. *Swing Time* (1936)
D. *Top Hat* (1935)

The Gay Divorcee, 1934

123. For which original song did the 1934 Fred Astaire and Ginger Rogers musical *The Gay Divorcee* win an Academy Award?

A. "Cheek to Cheek"
B. "Let's Call the Whole Thing Off"
C. "The Continental"
D. "I'm Putting All My Eggs in One Basket"

124. Who sings Cole Porter's "Just One of Those Things" in Norman Z. McLeod's *Panama Hattie* (1942)?

A. Doris Day
B. Ethel Waters
C. Lena Horne
D. Peggy Lee

125. Which musical adaptation starring Dirk Bogarde was the film debut of Jane Seymour (in the chorus)?

A. *I Could Go On Singing* (1963)
B. *Oh! What a Lovely War* (1969)
C. *Silk Stockings* (1957)
D. *The Belle of New York* (1952)

answers found on page 561

126. Who was Barbra Streisand's costar in the 1970 film *The Owl and the Pussycat*?
    A. Donald Sutherland
    B. Elliott Gould
    C. Gene Hackman
    D. George Segal

127. In which category did *Yankee Doodle Dandy* (1942) not win an Oscar?
    A. Best Actor
    B. Best Director
    C. Best Music
    D. Best Sound, Recording

128. Who was Bing Crosby's costar in the 1942 film *Holiday Inn*?
    A. Dan Dailey
    B. Donald O'Connor
    C. Fred Astaire
    D. Gene Kelly

129. Vincente Minnelli directed Van Johnson in what musical?
    A. *Brigadoon* (1954)
    B. *On the Town* (1949)
    C. *That Forsyte Woman* (1949)
    D. *The Three Musketeers* (1948)

130. Which of the following songs from *Flower Drum Song* (1961) is performed by James Shigeta?
    A. "Don't Marry Me"
    B. "Sunday"
    C. "You Be the Rock"
    D. "You Are Beautiful"

131. In 1996, Rita Moreno was the first Latina actress to play the female lead in which Andrew Lloyd Webber musical rendition of a Hollywood film?
    A. *Sunset Blvd.*
    B. *The Phantom of the Opera*
    C. *The Sound of Music*
    D. *Whistle Down the Wind*

132. In the 1952 musical *Singin' in the Rain*, characters Don Lockwood and Lina Lamont are stars employed by what fictional studio?
    A. Cavalier Studios
    B. Monumental Pictures
    C. Sunbeam Studios
    D. Sunshine Pictures

133. Jeanette MacDonald stars as a single mother who finds romance while vacationing on a Cuban cruise in which musical featuring Edward Arnold?
    A. *I Married an Angel* (1942)
    B. *Sweethearts* (1938)
    C. *The Sun Comes Up* (1949)
    D. *Three Daring Daughters* (1948)

134. Doris Day made her film debut in what musical?
    A. *Romance on the High Seas* (1948)
    B. *The Girl Most Likely* (1958)
    C. *The Sky's the Limit* (1943)
    D. *You Were Never Lovelier* (1942)

135. Laurence Naismith made his stage debut in the chorus of what musical?
    A. *Hazel Flagg*
    B. *Kismet*
    C. *Oh, Boy*
    D. *The Most Happy Fella*

136. Who was offered the lead role in *Yankee Doodle Dandy* (1942) before James Cagney?
    A. Donald O'Connor
    B. Fred Astaire
    C. Gene Kelly
    D. Victor Moore

137. Paulette Goddard was the leading lady in what Fred Astaire musical?
    A. *Hold Back the Dawn* (1941)
    B. *Second Chorus* (1940)
    C. *The Great Dictator* (1940)
    D. *The Lady Has Plans* (1942)

Spotlight on
JUDY **GARLAND** (1922–1969)

Born into a hard-driving vaudeville family, Baby Frances was the youngest of the performing Gumm sisters (later, the Garland sisters), starting her stage career at age two. In 1935, MGM finally signed the spunky kid they'd been eyeing for more than a year. A born entertainer, she could do it all—sing, dance, and act with such verve that her portrayal of Dorothy in *The Wizard of Oz* (1939) elevated a children's film into a classic. After *Oz*, Garland gamely continued her teen persona in a series of highly successful "backyard musicals" with Mickey Rooney. Her personal struggles with addiction began during those years, but they didn't detract from the enormous presence she brought to the screen. At age twenty-one she appeared in *Meet Me in St. Louis* (1944), a huge hit for MGM, which introduced her to her second husband, director Vincente Minnelli. During the next few years, Garland lent her charisma to a number of films, but her personal problems had begun interfering with her work, and after *Summer Stock* (1950) MGM let her go. She bounced back with sell-out performances at New York's Palace Theater and the London Palladium. The concerts helped Garland win the lead role in *A Star Is Born* (1954)—a story of hard-won victories that in many ways paralleled her own.

In the Good Old Summertime, 1949

Meet Me in St. Louis, 1944

1. Finish the title of this Judy Garland song from *Summer Stock* (1950): "Get . . .

    A. . . . Going"
    B. . . . Happy"
    C. . . . Up and Get Out"
    D. . . . a Bloomin' Move On"

2. What song performed by Judy Garland in *The Wizard of Oz* (1939) won an Oscar for Best Music, Original Song?

    A. "Ding Dong! The Witch Is Dead"
    B. "If I Only Had a Heart"
    C. "We're Off to See the Wizard"
    D. "Over the Rainbow"

3. What musical pairing of Judy Garland and Van Johnson was based on the 1940 film *The Shop Around the Corner*?

    A. *Holiday Inn* (1942)
    B. *In the Good Old Summertime* (1949)

    C. *The Barkleys of Broadway* (1949)
    D. *You Were Never Lovelier* (1942)

4. Dirk Bogarde starred opposite Judy Garland in which musical?

    A. *Everybody Sing* (1938)
    B. *I Could Go on Singing* (1963)
    C. *The Pirate* (1948)
    D. *Till the Clouds Roll By* (1946)

5. Though Judy Garland happily sang "You Made Me Love You" to a photo of Clark Gable in *Broadway Melody of 1938* (1937), she claimed that she would have preferred to serenade which other actor?

    A. John Barrymore
    B. Robert Donat
    C. Rudolph Valentino
    D. William Powell

answers found on page 561

138. Ricardo Montalban earned a Tony nomination for what tropical-themed musical costarring Lena Horne?

A. *Birds of Paradise*
B. *Jamaica*
C. *Pacific Overtures*
D. *South Pacific*

139. Sammy Fain received an Academy Award nomination for composing the title song of what musical costarring Shirley Jones?

A. *April Love* (1957)
B. *Mr. Music* (1950)
C. *The Singer Not the Song* (1961)
D. *Tonight We Sing* (1953)

140. Who romances Jean Simmons's character in the 1955 film *Guys and Dolls*?

A. Frank Sinatra
B. Gene Kelly
C. Henry Fonda
D. Marlon Brando

141. In 1961, Richard Burton won the Best Actor (Musical) Tony Award for his performance in what production?

A. *Camelot*
B. *Finian's Rainbow*
C. *The Music Man*
D. *The Sound of Music*

142. Rita Moreno plays the role of Tuptim in what Rodgers and Hammerstein musical costarring Yul Brynner and Deborah Kerr?

A. *Carousel* (1956)
B. *Oklahoma!* (1955)
C. *South Pacific* (1958)
D. *The King and I* (1956)

Babes on Broadway, 1941

143. Which musical numbers from *Babes on Broadway* (1941) earned an Oscar nomination for Best Original Song?

A. "Anything Can Happen in New York"
B. "Babes on Broadway"
C. "How About You"
D. "Chin Up, Cherrio, Carry On"

144. Stanley Donen's film *On the Town* (1949) was notable for being the first musical ever to be what?

A. Shot in CinemaScope
B. Shot in Technicolor
C. Shot on a million-dollar budget
D. Shot on location

145. Dorothy Dandridge played the title role in what musical opposite Harry Belafonte?

A. *Carmen Jones* (1954)
B. *Rose-Marie* (1936)
C. *Solomon and Sheba* (1959)
D. *The Belle of New York* (1952)

146. Who sings the Oscar-nominated song "Whistling Away the Dark" in *Darling Lili* (1970)?

A. Donna Reed
B. Doris Day
C. Julie Andrews
D. Shirley MacLaine

answers found on page 561

147. Which "Green" earned an Oscar nomination for Best Scoring of a Musical Picture for *Fiesta* (1947)?
A. Adolph Green
B. Johnny Green
C. Tom Green
D. Walon Green

148. What stage adaptation of an Oscar-winning film won the Tony Award for Best Musical in 2001?
A. *Billy Elliot*
B. *Hairspray*
C. *The Producers*
D. *The Sweet Smell of Success*

149. In the 1943 film *The Gang's All Here*, Benny Goodman and Carmen Miranda sing a song about what city in Kentucky?
A. Bowling Green
B. Lexington
C. Louisville
D. Paducah

150. What musical stars Gene Kelly, Van Johnson, and Cyd Charisse?
A. *Brigadoon* (1954)
B. *Broadway Melody of 1940* (1940)
C. *Flying Down to Rio* (1933)
D. *It's Always Fair Weather* (1955)

151. Luise Rainer and Myrna Loy costar in what musical?
A. *Carefree* (1938)
B. *Holiday Inn* (1942)
C. *Swing Time* (1936)
D. *The Great Ziegfeld* (1936)

152. Who won an Academy Award for directing Rex Harrison and Audrey Hepburn in *My Fair Lady* (1964)?
A. Billy Wilder

B. David Lean
C. George Cukor
D. Stanley Donen

153. Ginger Rogers sings the Irving Berlin song "The Yam" in which musical?
A. *Carefree* (1938)
B. *Flying down to Rio* (1933)
C. *Follow the Fleet* (1936)
D. *Rose-Marie* (1936)

154. Who was Barbra Streisand's costar in the 1969 musical *Hello, Dolly!*?
A. Bob Newhart
B. Jack Lemmon
C. Kris Kristofferson
D. Walter Matthau

155. Who replaced Judy Garland in *Annie Get Your Gun* (1950)?
A. Betty Hutton
B. Deborah Kerr
C. Doris Day
D. Eleanor Powell

156. In the 1944 musical *Lady in the Dark*, Ginger Rogers plays editor of what magazine?
A. *Allure*
B. *Elle*
C. *Sassy*
D. *Vogue*

157. What screen legend appeared in and created the comedic stunts for the 1949 musical *In the Good Old Summertime*?
A. Buster Keaton
B. Harold Lloyd
C. Red Skelton
D. W. C. Fields

Spotlight on
GENE **KELLY** (1912–1996)

Kelly was at home hoofing it with children and cartoon figures or stomping in rain puddles, pioneering the use of real locations and special effects in musical numbers and stretching the genre's boundaries. After performing in vaudeville and nightclubs with his brother Fred during his youth, he landed roles on Broadway that ultimately led to a contract with producer David O. Selznick. With no musicals on his plate, however, Selznick sold the contract to MGM, where Kelly made his screen debut opposite Judy Garland in *For Me and My Gal* (1942). Working with Garland and producer Arthur Freed made him see the potential for dance, but he wouldn't get to explore it fully until MGM loaned him to Columbia to partner with Rita Hayworth in *Cover Girl* (1944). His "Alter Ego Ballet" in that film, in which special effects allowed him to dance with himself, was his first use of film technique to extend the language of dance. Kelly got to carry his ideas further and make his directing debut (with Stanley Donen as codirector) in *On the Town* (1949), the first musical with numbers shot on location. But he is best remembered for his performance in what might be the greatest movie musical ever, *Singin' in the Rain* (1952).

On the Town, 1949

Singin' in the Rain, 1952

1. In the 1949 musical *On the Town,* Gene Kelly searches for his dream girl, Miss Turnstiles. Who was the actress who played her?

   A. Ann Miller
   B. Cyd Charisse
   C. Jane Powell
   D. Vera-Ellen

2. Gene Kelly sings "The Heather on the Hill" in what musical?

   A. *Brigadoon* (1954)
   B. *The Sky's the Limit* (1943)
   C. *The Three Musketeers* (1948)
   D. *You Were Never Lovelier* (1942)

3. Rita Moreno dances the tango with Gene Kelly in which musical?

   A. *An American in Paris* (1951)
   B. *Brigadoon* (1954)
   C. *On the Town* (1949)
   D. *Singin' in the Rain* (1952)

4. In the Stanley Donen film *Singin' in the Rain* (1952), what is the name of Gene Kelly's movie star character?

   A. Cosmo Brown
   B. Danny McGuire
   C. Don Lockwood
   D. Jerry Mulligan

5. In 1993, Gene Kelly convinced what pop singer to perform an homage to Marlene Dietrich in her concert tour?

   A. Celine Dion
   B. Madonna
   C. Mariah Carey
   D. Whitney Houston

answers found on page 561

158. The Leonard Bernstein song "One Hand, One Heart," featured in *West Side Story* (1961), was originally written for what earlier musical?

A. *Candide*
B. *Kismet*
C. *New Girl in Town*
D. *Plain and Fancy*

159. Leslie Brooks was featured in what musical starring Gene Kelly?

A. *Cover Girl* (1944)
B. *Funny Face* (1957)
C. *Silk Stockings* (1957)
D. *The Band Wagon* (1953)

160. Who directed Benny Goodman in the 1943 film *The Gang's All Here*?

A. Busby Berkeley
B. Charles Walters
C. Michael Curtiz
D. Vincente Minnelli

161. Which one of the following actresses costars with Gene Kelly in the 1949 musical *Take Me Out to the Ball Game*?

A. Debbie Reynolds
B. Esther Williams
C. Judy Garland
D. Lucille Ball

162. Carmen Miranda shared the screen with Ann Sothern and Jane Powell in which musical?

A. *Nancy Goes to Rio* (1950)
B. *Seven Brides for Seven Brothers* (1954)
C. *Small Town Girl* (1953)
D. *The Girl Most Likely* (1958)

163. George Roy Hill's 1964 film *The World of Henry Orient* was turned into a Broadway musical in 1967. What was the title?

A. *Bet on Henry*
B. *Henry's Gals*
C. *Henry, Sweet Henry*
D. *Play One for Me, Henry*

High Society, 1956

164. Louis Armstrong made a memorable appearance in the 1956 film *High Society*, which was a musical remake of what film?

A. *His Girl Friday* (1940)
B. *Mr. Smith Goes to Washington* (1939)
C. *The Philadelphia Story* (1940)
D. *You Can't Take It with You* (1938)

165. Which musical pairing Fred Astaire and Ginger Rogers was directed by George Stevens?

A. *Blue Skies* (1946)
B. *Easter Parade* (1948)
C. *Swing Time* (1936)
D. *The Barkleys of Broadway* (1949)

166. Cary Grant whistles the theme song from which musical while pretending to take a shower in the 1959 film *North by Northwest*?

A. *Guys and Dolls* (1955)
B. *My Fair Lady* (1964)
C. *Singin' in the Rain* (1952)
D. *South Pacific* (1958)

167. Which of the following musicals was not nominated for a Best Picture Oscar?

A. *An American in Paris* (1951)
B. *Bye Bye Birdie* (1963)
C. *Gigi* (1958)
D. *Oliver!* (1969)

answers found on page 561

168. Johnny Mercer wrote the lyrics to the title song of what musical costarring Fred MacMurray?

A. *And the Angels Sing* (1944)
B. *Blue Skies* (1946)
C. *Carefree* (1938)
D. *Lovely to Look At* (1952)

169. Marjorie Main portrayed Mrs. Cabot opposite Lana Turner in which musical?

A. *Mr. Imperium* (1951)
B. *Summer Stock* (1950)
C. *The Harvey Girls* (1946)
D. *The Merry Widow* (1952)

170. Stanley Donen directed a musical number for an episode of what popular 1980s television show?

A. *Cheers*
B. *L.A. Law*
C. *Miami Vice*
D. *Moonlighting*

171. Hedy Lamarr costars with Judy Garland and Lana Turner in what 1941 musical?

A. *Dancing Lady* (1933)
B. *In the Good Old Summertime* (1949)
C. *Till the Clouds Roll By* (1946)
D. *Ziegfeld Girl* (1941)

172. Jane Powell made her Broadway debut in 1974 when she replaced Debbie Reynolds in what musical?

A. *A Little Night Music*
B. *Evita*
C. *Irene*
D. *Mame*

173. Irene Dunne plays the title role in what musical costarring Hugh Herbert and Ned Sparks?

A. *Roberta* (1935)
B. *Rose-Marie* (1936)
C. *Sweet Adeline* (1934)
D. *The Belle of New York* (1952)

174. Richard Thorpe directed what musical film starring Debbie Reynolds and Jane Powell as health-food-enthusiast sisters?

A. *Athena* (1954)
B. *Enchanted Island* (1958)
C. *The Gazebo* (1959)
D. *This Happy Feeling* (1958)

175. Which of the following musicals won only an Oscar for Best Sound?

A. *All That Jazz* (1979)
B. *Cabaret* (1927)
C. *Oklahoma!* (1955)
D. *South Pacific* (1958)

176. What film won the Oscar for Best Scoring of a Musical Picture in 1950?

A. *Funny Face*
B. *On the Town*
C. *Royal Wedding*
D. *Seven Brides for Seven Brothers*

177. In 1973 James Shigeta costarred in a musical version of what classic film?

A. *Gone With the Wind* (1939)
B. *Lost Horizon* (1937)
C. *Ninotchka* (1939)
D. *You Can't Take It with You* (1938)

178. What musical features both Luise Rainer and Fanny Brice?

A. *A Family Affair* (1937)
B. *Carefree* (1938)
C. *The Cat and the Canary* (1939)
D. *The Great Ziegfeld* (1936)

179. Katharine Hepburn portrayed what famous fashion designer in a 1969 Broadway musical?

A. Coco Chanel
B. Edith Head
C. Helen Rose
D. Vivienne Westwood

answers found on page 561

180. Audrey Hepburn's character plays what musical instrument in 1957's *Love in the Afternoon*?

A. Cello

B. Harp

C. Piano

D. Violin

181. Stanley Donen met lifelong friend and collaborator Gene Kelly while they were both appearing in what musical on Broadway?

A. *Anything Goes*

B. *Dubarry Was a Lady*

C. *Pal Joey*

D. *Take a Chance*

182. Ezio Pinza made his screen debut opposite Lana Turner in the title role of what musical?

A. *Mr. Imperium* (1951)

B. *Society Doctor* (1935)

C. *The Mask of Dimitrios* (1944)

D. *Young Tom Edison* (1940)

183. What was the only movie musical that William Wyler ever directed?

A. *Cabaret* (1927)

B. *Funny Girl* (1968)

C. *Seven Brides for Seven Brothers* (1954)

D. *The Music Man* (1962)

184. Doris Day performs what Oscar-nominated song in the 1948 musical *Romance on the High Seas*?

A. "I'm Sitting on Top of the World"

B. "It All Depends on You"

C. "It's Magic"

D. "Love Me or Leave Me"

185. Irving Berlin's song "Blue Skies" was featured in all of the following films except for which one?

A. *Blue Skies* (1946)

B. *The Jazz Singer* (1927)

C. *The Little Princess of Song* (1927)

D. *The Sky's the Limit* (1943)

Seven Brides for Seven Brothers, 1954

186. What Oscar did *Seven Brides for Seven Brothers* (1954) win?

A. Best Color Cinematography

B. Best Dance Direction

C. Best Picture

D. Best Scoring of a Musical Picture

187. In the 1963 film *Bye Bye Birdie,* what is the name of the song that Dick Van Dyke's character writes for Conrad Birdie to perform on *The Ed Sullivan Show*?

A. "Got a Lot of Living to Do"

B. "Honestly Sincere"

C. "One Last Kiss"

D. "Rosie"

188. Leslie Howard starred in the 1938 film of George Bernard Shaw's *Pygmalion*, which was turned into what famous musical?

A. *Gypsy* (1961)

B. *My Fair Lady* (1964)

C. *The Sound of Music* (1965)

D. *West Side Story* (1961)

189. During his opening monologue as host of *Saturday Night Live* in 2009, Joseph Gordon-Levitt performs the "Make 'Em Laugh" scene from what musical?

A. *It's Always Fair Weather* (1955)

B. *Singin' in the Rain* (1952)

C. *The Band Wagon* (1953)

D. *The Barkleys of Broadway* (1949)

190. In the Joan Blondell film *Gold Diggers of 1933* (1933), what actress performs the song "We're in the Money"?

A. Ann Miller
B. Ginger Rogers
C. Lucille Ball
D. Ruby Keeler

191. Rita Moreno won a Tony Award in 1975 for her performance in which musical?

A. *New Girl in Town*
B. *The Ritz*
C. *The Vamp*
D. *Wonderful Town*

192. Marion Davies falls for Bing Crosby in which musical?

A. *Anything Goes* (1936)
B. *East Side of Heaven* (1939)
C. *Going Hollywood* (1933)
D. *Too Much Harmony* (1933)

193. Which work earned Neil Simon a Best Book of a Musical Tony Award nomination in 1979?

A. *Fools*
B. *London Suite*
C. *The Prisoner of Second Avenue*
D. *They're Playing Our Song*

194. Leslie Caron plays Ella in what musical scored by Bronislau Kaper?

A. *Bedtime Story* (1964)
B. *Scent of Mystery* (1960)
C. *The Belle of New York* (1952)
D. *The Glass Slipper* (1955)

195. What musical starring Doris Day was adapted from the Broadway musical also choreographed by Bob Fosse?

A. *On Moonlight Bay* (1951)
B. *Please Don't Eat the Daisies* (1960)
C. *Tea for Two* (1950)
D. *The Pajama Game* (1957)

196. Who directed Benny Goodman in the 1948 film *A Song Is Born*?

A. Howard Hawks
B. Michael Curtiz
C. Preston Sturges
D. William Wellman

197. Peter O'Toole's character in what musical teaches at a prep school?

A. *Club Paradise* (1986)
B. *Goodbye, Mr. Chips* (1969)
C. *My Favorite Year* (1982)
D. *Promise Her Anything* (1965)

198. Which musical adaptation of the classic *Grand Hotel* (1932) features Van Johnson, Ginger Rogers, and Lana Turner?

A. *Blue Skies* (1946)
B. *Royal Wedding* (1951)
C. *Week-End at the Waldorf* (1945)
D. *Wives and Lovers* (1963)

199. Dean Martin portrays a hotel mogul in what musical comedy directed by Richard Thorpe and set in Rome, Italy?

A. *Artists and Models* (1955)
B. *Bells Are Ringing* (1960)
C. *Ten Thousand Bedrooms* (1957)
D. *That's My Boy* (1951)

200. Rossano Brazzi romances Mitzi Gaynor in what musical adapted from a Pulitzer Prize–winning play?

A. *Silk Stockings* (1957)
B. *Song of My Heart* (1948)
C. *South Pacific* (1958)
D. *Three Coins in the Fountain* (1954)

201. Bing Crosby performs the song "Down by the River" in what film costarring W. C. Fields?

A. *Babes on Broadway* (1941)
B. *Mississippi* (1935)
C. *Shop Talk* (1935)
D. *The Big Wheel* (1949)

answers found on page 561

202. Gene Krupa's drum solo on what song made him famous?

A. "Drum Crazy"
B. "Minnie's in the Money"
C. "Pennsylvania 6-5000"
D. "Sing, Sing, Sing"

203. What Judy Garland film won the Oscar for Best Scoring of a Musical Picture in 1949?

A. *Easter Parade*
B. *Summer Stock*
C. *The Harvey Girls*
D. *The Pirate*

204. Van Johnson plays the title role in what television musical costarring Claude Rains?

A. *Bill* (1981)
B. *Brothers' Destiny* (1995)
C. *Phantom of the Megaplex* (2000)
D. *The Pied Piper of Hamelin* (1957)

205. "Zing a Little Zong" was the name of the Academy Award–nominated song from the 1952 Jane Wyman musical *Just for You*. Who sings it in the film?

A. Bing Crosby
B. Danny Kaye
C. Dean Martin
D. Frank Sinatra

206. At sixteen, Lupe Velez debuted in which musical at Teatro Principal in Mexico?

A. *El Bruto*
B. *La Reina del Rio*
C. *Los Sonors*
D. *Ra-Ta-Plan*

207. Who directed the musical *At Long Last Love* (1975), starring Burt Reynolds and Cybill Shepherd?

A. Brian De Palma
B. Francis Ford Coppola
C. Peter Bogdanovich
D. Roger Corman

Royal Wedding, 1951

208. Jane Powell landed the female lead in *Royal Wedding* (1951) after what actress told Fred Astaire she wasn't interested in the part?

A. Deborah Kerr
B. Moira Shearer
C. Debbie Reynolds
D. Cyd Charisse

209. In which musical did Esther Williams star opposite both Peter Lawford and Ricardo Montalban?

A. *Easter Parade* (1948)
B. *Easy to Love* (1953)
C. *Million Dollar Mermaid* (1952)
D. *On an Island with You* (1948)

210. Joan Blondell starred in the 1933 musical *Footlight Parade*. Which of the following songs is not from that movie?

A. "Ah, the Moon Is Here"
B. "Honeymoon Hotel"
C. "Pettin' in the Park"
D. "Shanghai Lil"

211. Duke Ellington's song "Going Up" was featured in what musical starring Ethel Waters?

A. *Blue Skies* (1946)
B. *Cabin in the Sky* (1943)
C. *Easter Parade* (1948)
D. *The Barkleys of Broadway* (1949)

answers found on page 561

212. What was the first musical to win Best Picture?

    A. *42nd Street* (1933)
    B. *The Broadway Melody* (1929)
    C. *The Racket* (1928)
    D. *Top Hat* (1935)

213. Luise Rainer and Hugh Herbert share the screen in what musical?

    A. *Fashions of 1934* (1934)
    B. *Rendezvous* (1935)
    C. *The Girl Who Had Everything* (1953)
    D. *The Great Waltz* (1938)

214. Harry Belafonte won a Tony Award for his performance in what musical?

    A. *A Little Night Music*
    B. *John Murray Anderson's Almanac*
    C. *The Music Man*
    D. *Two Gentlemen of Verona*

215. W. C. Fields plays "The Great Man" in what musical comedy?

    A. *Never Give a Sucker an Even Break* (1941)
    B. *Shop Talk* (1935)
    C. *The Big Wheel* (1949)
    D. *The Human Comedy* (1943)

216. Which of the following songs from *Royal Wedding* (1951) was nominated for an Academy Award?

    A. "How Could You Believe Me When I Said I Love You When You Know I've Been a Liar All My Life"
    B. "Open Your Eyes"
    C. "Too Late Now"
    D. "You're All the World to Me"

217. Kathleen Freeman was nominated for a Best Actress Tony Award for her performance in what musical?

    A. *Dreamgirls*
    B. *Grand Hotel*
    C. *The Full Monty*
    D. *Woman of the Year*

218. Finish the title of this Lena Horne song from *Swing Fever* (1943): "You're So . . .

    A. . . . Beautiful"
    B. . . . Indifferent"
    C. . . . Wonderful"
    D. . . . Wrong"

219. Sidney Poitier and Dorothy Dandridge play the title roles in what musical adaptation of a Gershwin opera?

    A. *Porgy and Bess* (1959)
    B. *The Barkleys of Broadway* (1949)
    C. *The Gypsy and the Gentleman* (1958)
    D. *The Story of Vernon and Irene Castle* (1939)

220. What was the name of James Cagney's character in *Footlight Parade* (1933)?

    A. Chester Kent
    B. Dan Quigley
    C. Dizzy Davis
    D. Joe Greer

221. Which actor starred in the 1981 musical *Pennies from Heaven,* set in Depression-era Chicago?

    A. Al Pacino
    B. Robert De Niro
    C. Harrison Ford
    D. Steve Martin

222. Rita Moreno is featured in which Esther Williams musical set on the island of Tahiti?

    A. *Neptune's Daughter* (1949)
    B. *On an Island with You* (1948)
    C. *Pagan Love Song* (1950)
    D. *Thrill of a Romance* (1945)

Objective, Burma!, 1945

Chapter 13

WAR

The camaraderie of men and women under fire and the horrors of war are two themes underlying Hollywood's conflicted view of the military since the movies began. During the two world wars, the film capital supported the nation with patriotic epics, but in peacetime and with the more controversial engagements of later years, the viewpoint became increasingly jaded.

As one of the most dramatic expressions of human conflict, war has provided fertile material for filmmakers, and just about every major military action from biblical battles to the Russian Revolution has made it to the screen. The subject has provided action vehicles for such stars as John Wayne, Glenn Ford, Humphrey Bogart, and Gary Cooper. More critical treatments of military issues, from the human frailties of military leaders to the plight of returning veterans, have inspired Oscar-winning performances from the likes of Fredric March and Harold Russell in *The Best Years of Our Lives* (1946), Frank Sinatra in *From Here to Eternity* (1953), and Alec Guinness in *The Bridge on the River Kwai* (1957).

War films have brought out the best in some of the industry's top directors. Louis Malle used his memories of growing up in occupied France to create two of his most acclaimed films, *Lacombe, Lucien* (1974) and *Au revoir les enfants* (1987). Steven Spielberg finally entered the Academy's winners' circle with *Schindler's List* (1993) and repeated the trip with *Saving Private Ryan* (1998). One of the most talented and dedicated of all war movie directors was Lewis Milestone. His version of *All Quiet on the Western Front* (1930) taught other filmmakers how to use the new medium of talking pictures to depict the horrors of war, something he did so effectively the picture is often one of the first banned in nations gearing up for warfare. During World War II, he captured the fight of a Ukrainian village against Nazi invaders in *The North Star* (1943), the plight of U.S. POWs captured by the Japanese in *The Purple Heart* (1944), and the G.I.'s view of the action in *A Walk in the Sun* (1945).

Hollywood had some of its finest hours during World War II. Even before the Japanese attack on Pearl Harbor, studios were dramatizing the issues involved. Warner Bros. dealt with the Nazi menace so well in *Confessions of a Nazi Spy* (1939) that theater owners in Poland who dared to show it were hanged in their lobbies. William Wyler did such a fine job portraying the heroism of the British during the war's early days in *Mrs. Miniver* (1942) that it was credited with helping to sway U.S. sympathies in favor of its future allies.

Once the U.S. entered the war, Hollywood committed itself fully to the war effort. Between 1942 and 1945, the studios released five hundred films directly related to the war, from tales of international intrigue like *Casablanca* (1942) to home-front epics like *Since You Went Away* (1944). Films based on actual battles and locations—*Wake Island* (1942), *Thirty Seconds Over Tokyo* (1944), *Back to Bataan* (1945)—gave people at home a look at what was happening overseas in the years before television.

Offscreen, the studios and their employees were no less dedicated. Stars like Clark Gable and James Stewart enlisted, while directors like Frank Capra and John Ford made training films and military documentaries. Bette Davis founded the Hollywood Canteen to give soldiers a home away from home, Bob Hope led a phalanx of stars entertaining the troops around the world, and Carole Lombard became one of Hollywood's first war casualties when her plane crashed as she was returning home from a successful tour selling war bonds.

Once hostilities ended, more critical war films started to appear, particularly as controversy over later military policies grew. Samuel Fuller's *The Steel Helmet* (1951), though made on a shoestring, captured all the moral ambiguities of the Korean War even as the battle was raging overseas. Stanley Kubrick went even further with his blistering attack on military thinking in *Paths of Glory* (1957), then took on the Cold War and the arms race in *Dr. Strangelove* (1964).

As military actions continue to break out around the world, Hollywood keeps looking at both the glories of heroism under fire and the horrors of warfare. For every gung ho *The Green Berets* (1968), John Wayne's response to the Vietnam War, there seems to be an *Apocalypse, Now* (1979), Francis Ford Coppola's more jaundiced view of the action. Sometimes a single film can capture both sides of the argument, like Michael Cimino's Vietnam War epic *The Deer Hunter* (1978) or Kathryn Bigelow's recent *The Hurt Locker* (2009), two films that seem to sum up Hollywood's love-hate relationship with warfare.

1. Who was the first performer to be nominated for Best Actor and Best Writing Oscars for the same film?

   A. Charles Chaplin for *The Great Dictator* (1940)
   B. Orson Welles for *Citizen Kane* (1941)
   C. Sylvester Stallone for *Rocky* (1976)
   D. Warren Beatty for *Heaven Can Wait* (1978)

2. Paul Lukas played a man working against the Nazis in what film?

   A. *Berlin Express* (1948)
   B. *Confessions of a Nazi Spy* (1939)
   C. *The Ghost Breakers* (1940)
   D. *Watch on the Rhine* (1943)

3. What anti-Nazi film features Bonita Granville?

   A. *A Bridge Too Far* (1977)
   B. *Hitler's Children* (1943)
   C. *The Enemy Below* (1957)
   D. *The Longest Day* (1962)

4. In what film does Van Johnson play a military doctor whose sole ally is a nightclub singer?

   A. *Only Angels Have Wings* (1939)
   B. *Penny Serenade* (1941)
   C. *Subway in the Sky* (1959)
   D. *Suspicion* (1941)

5. Who directed the 1940 George Sanders film *Foreign Correspondent*?

   A. Alfred Hitchcock
   B. Robert Aldrich
   C. Robert Wise
   D. William Wyler

6. In which of the following films scored by Franz Waxman does John Garfield not appear?

   A. *Air Force* (1943)
   B. *Destination Tokyo* (1943)
   C. *He Ran All the Way* (1951)
   D. *That Hagen Girl* (1947)

7. Teresa Wright plays the daughter of a returning WWII veteran in what film?

   A. *Mrs. Miniver* (1942)
   B. *The Best Years of Our Lives* (1946)
   C. *The Little Foxes* (1941)
   D. *The Pride of the Yankees* (1942)

8. In 1960, *The Apartment* won Best Picture. What was the next film to win that utilized black-and-white photography?

   A. *Schindler's List* (1993)
   B. *The Elephant Man* (1980)
   C. *The Last Picture Show* (1971)
   D. *To Kill a Mockingbird* (1962)

9. Vincent Korda was the art director on the 1962 film *The Longest Day*, which starred all of the following actors except which one?

   A. Eddie Albert
   B. Richard Burton
   C. Richard Harris
   D. Sean Connery

Reunion in France, 1942

10. What actress stars in the 1942 film *Reunion in France,* directed by Jules Dassin?

    A. Ingrid Bergman
    B. Joan Crawford
    C. Joan Fontaine
    D. Vivien Leigh

11. Walter Mirisch produced the 1976 all-star film *Midway*. Which of the following actors does not appear in it?

A. Charlton Heston
B. Henry Fonda
C. James Coburn
D. Robert Duvall

12. Which of the following films directed by Jules Dassin centers around identical twins who go on to lead opposite lives?

A. *Brute Force* (1947)
B. *Nazi Agent* (1942)
C. *Phaedra* (1962)
D. *Reunion in France* (1942)

13. Which film featuring Dirk Bogarde included a cast of seven Academy Award–winning actors?

A. *A Bridge Too Far* (1977)
B. *Campbell's Kingdom* (1957)
C. *The Sea Shall Not Have Them* (1954)
D. *They Who Dare* (1954)

14. Who was nominated for an Academy Award as Best Director for his work on the 1981 film *Das Boot*?

A. Milos Forman
B. Richard Attenborough
C. Roman Polanski
D. Wolfgang Petersen

15. Peter Lawford plays a young WWII soldier in what film?

A. *Easter Parade* (1948)
B. *Mrs. Parkington* (1944)
C. *Cluny Brown* (1946)
D. *The White Cliffs of Dover* (1944)

16. Which of the following war films competed for the Best Original Story Oscar?

A. *Action in the North Atlantic* (1943)
B. *Bataan* (1943)
C. *Go Tell the Spartans* (1978)
D. *So Proudly We Hail!* (1943)

17. George Stevens directed Carole Lombard in what WWII film?

A. *Gunga Din* (1939)
B. *Penny Serenade* (1941)
C. *The Talk of the Town* (1942)
D. *Vigil in the Night* (1940)

18. What war film won the Academy Award for Best Story and Screenplay in 1950?

A. *Bataan*
B. *Battleground*
C. *The Longest Day*
D. *They Were Expendable*

19. In what George Stevens film does a young girl come of age while hiding from the Nazis?

A. *A Place in the Sun* (1951)
B. *I Remember Mama* (1948)
C. *The Diary of Anne Frank* (1959)
D. *The Talk of the Town* (1942)

20. What was the name of Sir John Mills's character in *The Midshipmaid* (1932)?

A. A. B. Pook
B. Golightly
C. Lt. Valentine
D. Sir Percy Newbiggin

21. Vincent Korda was the production designer on the 1941 film *Major Barbara*. Who starred in it?

A. Charles Boyer
B. James Cagney
C. John Mills
D. Rex Harrison

22. Which of the following actors starred in Delmer Daves's 1945 film *Pride of the Marines*?

A. Edward G. Robinson
B. Gary Cooper
C. Jeff Chandler
D. John Garfield

answers found on page 562

23. Which of the following Best Special Effects Oscar nominees is set in the Philippines during World War II?

A. *A Stolen Life* (1946)
B. *A Thousand and One Nights* (1945)
C. *Spellbound* (1945)
D. *They Were Expendable* (1945)

24. From what war film is the Oscar-nominated song "Linda"?

A. *Platoon* (1986)
B. *Saving Private Ryan* (1998)
C. *Flying Tigers* (1942)
D. *The Story of G.I. Joe* (1945)

25. Paul Henreid costarred in the 1962 film *The 4 Horsemen of the Apocalypse*. Who was the director?

A. Elia Kazan
B. Sam Fuller
C. Sam Peckinpah
D. Vincente Minnelli

26. In the 1966 Leslie Caron film *Is Paris Burning?*, what actor plays General George S. Patton?

A. George C. Scott
B. Glenn Ford
C. John Wayne
D. Kirk Douglas

27. What war is *What Price Glory* (1952) set in?

A. Civil War
B. Spanish Civil War
C. World War I
D. World War II

28. Who won the Academy Award as Best Supporting Actor for his performance in the 1953 film *From Here to Eternity*?

A. Frank Sinatra
B. Jack Lemmon
C. John Houseman
D. Tony Curtis

Gone With the Wind, 1939

29. Who won the Academy Award for Best Director for his work on the 1939 film *Gone With the Wind*?

A. Frank Capra
B. Howard Hawks
C. Mervyn LeRoy
D. Victor Fleming

30. Who shared the Best Screenplay Oscar nomination for *A Foreign Affair* (1948) with Charles Brackett and Billy Wilder?

A. I. A. L. Diamond
B. Leigh Brackett
C. Raymond Chandler
D. Richard L. Breen

31. The U.S. Navy's first aircraft carrier, the USS *Langley*, is seen in the background in what film directed by Frank Capra?

A. *Lost Horizon* (1937)
B. *Mr. Smith Goes to Washington* (1939)
C. *Rain or Shine* (1930)
D. *Submarine* (1928)

32. In what Lewis Milestone film does a platoon of American soldiers capture an Italian farmhouse?

A. *A Walk in the Sun* (1945)
B. *All Quiet on the Western Front* (1930)
C. *The Front Page* (1931)
D. *Two Arabian Knights* (1927)

33. Who plays Burt Lancaster's paramour in *From Here to Eternity* (1953)?

A. Audrey Hepburn
B. Deborah Kerr
C. Shirley Booth
D. Shirley Jones

34. Deanna Durbin was the favorite movie star of all of the following historical figures except which one?

A. Anne Frank
B. Benito Mussolini
C. Franklin Delano Roosevelt
D. Winston Churchill

35. Which U.S. city do Cary Grant and his navy pilot buddies visit in *Kiss Them for Me* (1957)?

A. Los Angeles
B. Miami
C. New York
D. San Francisco

36. Which of the following Ronald Reagan films is about a group of three cadets at the Virginia Military Institute who always find themselves in trouble?

A. *Boy Meets Girl* (1938)
B. *Brother Rat* (1938)
C. *Going Places* (1938)
D. *Knute Rockne, All-American* (1940)

37. Stanley Kubrick's 1964 film *Dr. Strangelove or: How I Learned to Stop Worrying and Love the Bomb* received Academy Award nominations in all of the following categories except which one?

A. Best Adapted Screenplay
B. Best Director
C. Best Original Song
D. Best Picture

38. In what film does Patricia Neal play a lieutenant in the navy opposite John Wayne and Kirk Douglas?

A. *A Face in the Crowd* (1957)
B. *Hud* (1963)
C. *In Harm's Way* (1965)
D. *The Fountainhead* (1949)

39. In which film set during the Spanish Civil War did Anthony Quinn star opposite both Gregory Peck and Omar Sharif?

A. *Behold a Pale Horse* (1964)
B. *Crosscurrent* (1981)
C. *Lion of the Desert* (1981)
D. *The Children of Sanchez* (1978)

40. What film won David Lean his first Oscar?

A. *Brief Encounter* (1945)
B. *Great Expectations* (1946)
C. *Lawrence of Arabia* (1962)
D. *The Bridge on the River Kwai* (1957)

41. What WWII movie featured Michael Caine?

A. *A Bridge Too Far* (1977)
B. *Letters from Iwo Jima* (2006)
C. *Saving Private Ryan* (1998)
D. *The Enemy Below* (1957)

42. Gary Cooper's 1932 film *A Farewell to Arms* was based on a novel by what famous author?

A. Edna Ferber
B. Ernest Hemingway
C. F. Scott Fitzgerald
D. John Steinbeck

43. What film starring Janet Gaynor is set during the Civil War Reconstruction?

A. *Carolina* (1934)
B. *Change of Heart* (1934)
C. *One More Spring* (1935)
D. *Servant's Entrance* (1934)

44. The 1987 film *Au revoir les enfants* was nominated for two Academy Awards. One was for Best Original Screenplay. What was the other for?

A. Best Actor
B. Best Art Direction
C. Best Cinematography
D. Best Foreign Language Film

45. In what category did *To Be or Not to Be* (1942) compete for an Oscar?

A. Best Actress
B. Best Director
C. Best Original Story
D. Best Scoring of a Dramatic or Comedy Picture

46. In the 1939 Zoltan Korda film *The Four Feathers*, what do the feathers symbolize?

A. Cowardice
B. Honor
C. Strength
D. Virility

47. Peter O'Toole plays a sadistic Nazi general in what film?

A. *Murphy's War* (1971)
B. *The Lion in Winter* (1968)
C. *The Night of the Generals* (1967)
D. *The Ruling Class* (1972)

48. Who costarred with Dorothy McGuire in the 1946 film *Till the End of Time*?

A. John Mills
B. Kirk Douglas
C. Robert Mitchum
D. Robert Taylor

49. What Oscar did *The Bridges at Toko-Ri* (1954) win?

A. Best Actor
B. Best Actress
C. Best Film Editing
D. Best Special Effects

50. In 1942, England's Royal Air Force named their inflatable life jackets after what buxom leading lady because of the way they made the wearer's chest bulge?

A. Doris Day
B. Joan Crawford
C. Mae West
D. Marilyn Monroe

51. Robert Duvall is a descendant of what famous Civil War general?

A. Robert E. Lee
B. Stonewall Jackson
C. Ulysses S. Grant
D. William Tecumseh Sherman

52. What was the only Academy Award category for which it was nominated that *The Best Years of Our Lives* (1946) failed to win?

A. Best Actor in a Leading Role
B. Best Director
C. Best Music, Scoring of a Dramatic or Comedy Picture
D. Best Sound, Recording

53. What film directed by John Frankenheimer is about U.S. military leaders who plot to overthrow the president over a nuclear disarmament treaty?

A. *Seconds* (1966)
B. *Seven Days in May* (1964)
C. *The Fixer* (1968)
D. *The Manchurian Candidate* (1962)

54. Which of the following war films earned an Oscar nomination for Best Special Effects?

A. *Back to Bataan* (1945)
B. *Desperate Journey* (1942)
C. *Paths of Glory* (1957)
D. *Sands of Iwo Jima* (1949)

answers found on page 562

Spotlight on
DANA **ANDREWS** (1909–1992)

If any actor's head shot could illustrate the phrase "unjustly forgotten" in the dictionary, it would be Dana Andrews's. Despite starring in one of the best early noir films, *Laura* (1944), the groundbreaking western *The Ox-Bow Incident* (1943), and two of the greatest films ever made about military men, *A Walk in the Sun* (1945) and *The Best Years of Our Lives* (1946), he faded from prominence in later years. (Many critics have suggested the never-nominated Andrews should have won the Best Actor Oscar that went to costar Fredric March for the latter film.) 20th Century-Fox and independent producer Sam Goldwyn shared his first contract, but neither came up with worthy follow-ups to his early classics. When he went freelance in the fifties, his projects were less prestigious, though some of them, like the offbeat horror film *Night of the Demon* (1958), have developed cult followings. Andrews retired from acting in the sixties, then made a killing in real estate. He battled a drinking problem throughout his career. In 1972, he became one of the first actors to film a public service announcement about alcoholism, an act that made him as much of a hero as many of the characters he had played.

Beyond a Reasonable Doubt, 1956

The Best Years of Our Lives, 1946

1. **Dana Andrews returns from WWII in what film?**

   A. *A Walk in the Sun* (1946)
   B. *Beyond a Reasonable Doubt* (1956)
   C. *The Best Years of Our Lives* (1946)
   D. *The Devil's Brigade* (1968)

2. **How many siblings did Dana Andrews have?**

   A. 6
   B. 7
   C. 8
   D. 9

3. **Dana Andrews's son is drafted to the Korean War in what film?**

   A. *A Walk in the Sun* (1946)
   B. *Hot Rods to Hell* (1967)

   C. *I Want You* (1951)
   D. *The Best Years of Our Lives* (1946)

4. **In which Academy Award–winning film did Dana Andrews appear?**

   A. *Gentleman's Agreement* (1947)
   B. *Going My Way* (1944)
   C. *The Best Years of Our Lives* (1946)
   D. *The Lost Weekend* (1945)

5. **Dana Andrews costarred in all of the following films directed by Mark Robson except which one?**

   A. *Edge of Doom* (1950)
   B. *Home of the Brave* (1949)
   C. *I Want You* (1951)
   D. *My Foolish Heart* (1949)

answers found on page 562

55. What film starring Charles Coburn is set during the Revolutionary War?
    A. *John Paul Jones* (1959)
    B. *The Sea Hawk* (1940)
    C. *Until They Sail* (1957)
    D. *Words and Music* (1948)

56. In which of the following films directed by Mark Robson did Alan Ladd star?
    A. *A Prize of Gold* (1955)
    B. *Hell Below Zero* (1954)
    C. *The Bridges at Toko-Ri* (1954)
    D. *The Little Hut* (1957)

57. Who directed James Cagney in *Here Comes the Navy* (1934)?
    A. Clarence Brown
    B. Lloyd Bacon
    C. Michael Curtiz
    D. William Dieterle

58. Who was nominated for an Academy Award as Best Director for his work on the 1951 film *The African Queen*?
    A. John Ford
    B. John Huston
    C. Orson Welles
    D. William Wyler

59. In what year was Hal Roach called to active military duty to make military training films?
    A. 1942
    B. 1944
    C. 1950
    D. 1968

60. June Allyson and her three sisters come of age during and after the Civil War in what film?
    A. *Good News* (1947)
    B. *Little Women* (1949)
    C. *Two Sisters from Boston* (1946)
    D. *You Can't Run Away from It* (1956)

Air Force, 1943

61. Howard Hawks's *Air Force* (1943) earned Oscar nominations in all of the following categories except which one?
    A. Best Black-and-White Cinematography
    B. Best Director
    C. Best Original Screenplay
    D. Best Special Effects

62. Who played the "The Cooler King" in John Sturges's *The Great Escape* (1963)?
    A. Charles Bronson
    B. James Garner
    C. Richard Attenborough
    D. Steve McQueen

63. In which film directed by Richard Thorpe did James Stewart star as the inventor of an automatic rifle used in WWII?
    A. *After the Thin Man* (1936)
    B. *Carbine Williams* (1952)
    C. *The Mortal Storm* (1940)
    D. *Thunder Bay* (1953)

64. Montgomery Clift and Marlon Brando play soldiers fighting on opposite sides during World War II in what film?
    A. *Morituri* (1965)
    B. *The Big Lift* (1950)
    C. *The Men* (1950)
    D. *The Young Lions* (1958)

65. Which Samuel Fuller film used tanks made of plywood?

A. *Fixed Bayonets!* (1951)
B. *Forty Guns* (1957)
C. *Merrill's Marauders* (1962)
D. *The Steel Helmet* (1951)

66. In which of the following films does Henry Fonda play the president of the United States?

A. *Fail-Safe* (1964)
B. *The Cheyenne Social Club* (1970)
C. *The Longest Day* (1962)
D. *The Tin Star* (1957)

67. Deborah Kerr portrays Roger Livesey's "ideal woman" in *The Life and Death of Colonel Blimp* (1943), but whom did Michael Powell originally want for the role?

A. Ann Todd
B. Maureen O'Hara
C. Petula Clark
D. Wendy Hiller

68. Which of the following actors starred in the 1943 film *Destination Tokyo,* directed by Delmer Daves?

A. Cary Grant
B. Edward G. Robinson
C. James Cagney
D. Spencer Tracy

69. Delbert Mann directed Tony Curtis in what war film?

A. *Bataan* (1943)
B. *Major Dundee* (1965)
C. *Miracle of the White Stallions* (1963)
D. *The Outsider* (1961)

70. Flora Robson appears in what WWII film starring Alec Guinness?

A. *Istanbul* (1957)
B. *Malta Story* (1953)

C. *Penny Serenade* (1941)
D. *The Sea Hawk* (1940)

71. Which of the following actors costars with Edward G. Robinson in the 1943 film *Destroyer*?

A. Glenn Ford
B. Humphrey Bogart
C. John Wayne
D. Kirk Douglas

72. Jean Harlow's film *Hell's Angels* (1930) received an Academy Award nomination in which of the following categories?

A. Best Cinematography
B. Best Director
C. Best Editing
D. Best Picture

73. Which of the following actors did not portray a member of Lee Marvin's team in *The Dirty Dozen* (1967)?

A. Charles Bronson
B. John Cassavetes
C. Steve McQueen
D. Telly Savalas

74. During World War II, which of the following divisions did Ray Harryhausen work for?

A. Air Force
B. Army Mobile Infantry
C. Army Motion Picture Unit
D. Naval Film Department

75. Meryl Streep received her first Oscar nomination for her performance in which film?

A. *The Deer Hunter* (1978)
B. *Julia* (1977)
C. *The French Lieutenant's Woman* (1981)
D. *Women in Love* (1970)

answers found on page 562

76. Who won an Academy Award as Best Supporting Actor costarring with Marlon Brando in *Sayonara* (1957)?

A. Bob Hope
B. Danny Kaye
C. Red Buttons
D. Sid Caesar

77. What actor earned Oscar nominations for his roles opposite Ingrid Bergman in *Notorious* (1946) and *Casablanca* (1942)?

A. Cary Grant
B. Claude Rains
C. Humphrey Bogart
D. Paul Henreid

78. What was William Haines's last film appearance?

A. *Are You Listening?* (1932)
B. *Fast Life* (1932)
C. *The Marines Are Coming* (1934)
D. *Young and Beautiful* (1934)

79. Glenn Ford fought in both WWII and Vietnam. What group did Ford not serve with?

A. British Foreign Legion
B. French Foreign Legion
C. Green Berets
D. Third Marine Amphibious Force

80. What actress stars in the 1936 film *I Loved a Soldier,* directed by Henry Hathaway?

A. Ann Sothern
B. Bette Davis
C. Claudette Colbert
D. Marlene Dietrich

81. Which of the following actors starred in Mark Robson's 1949 film *Home of the Brave*?

A. Gene Kelly
B. Kirk Douglas
C. Lloyd Bridges
D. Sidney Poitier

82. How many Academy Awards did the 1962 film *Lawrence of Arabia* win?

A. 1
B. 3
C. 5
D. 7

83. What Academy Award did *Thirty Seconds Over Tokyo* win in 1945?

A. Best Director
B. Best Picture
C. Best Scoring of a Dramatic or Comedy Picture
D. Best Special Effects

84. What film directed by John Cromwell is about a woman coping on the home front while her husband is off fighting in World War II?

A. *Night Song* (1947)
B. *Since You Went Away* (1944)
C. *The Company She Keeps* (1951)
D. *The Enchanted Cottage* (1945)

85. During WWII, Hal Roach Studios became known as "Fort Roach" when he leased them out to what organization?

A. U.S. Air Force
B. U.S. Army
C. U.S. Marines
D. U.S. Navy

86. Anthony Quinn plays the role of Italo Bombolini, the town drunk turned hero, in which film set during WWII?

A. *Captains of the Clouds* (1942)
B. *Dangerous Moonlight* (1941)
C. *The Long Voyage Home* (1940)
D. *The Secret of Santa Vittoria* (1969)

87. Which of the following films photographed by cinematographer Haskell Wexler deals with the fallout of the Vietnam War?

A. *Bound for Glory* (1976)
B. *Coming Home* (1978)
C. *Lookin' to Get Out* (1982)
D. *One Flew Over the Cuckoo's Nest* (1975)

88. What Abbott and Costello film introduced the Oscar-nominated song "Boogie Woogie Bugle Boy of Company B"?

A. *Buck Privates* (1941)
B. *Hold That Ghost* (1941)
C. *In the Navy* (1941)
D. *Pardon My Sarong* (1942)

Objective, Burma!, 1945

89. *Objective, Burma!* (1945) was shot by what famous cinematographer?

A. Rudolph Maté
B. Ernest Haller
C. James Wong Howe
D. Greg Toland

90. The 1961 film *The Guns of Navarone* was nominated for Academy Awards in all of the following categories except which one?

A. Best Actor
B. Best Adapted Screenplay
C. Best Picture
D. Best Sound

91. Which of the following actors does not appear with José Ferrer in the 1954 film *The Caine Mutiny*?

A. Fred MacMurray
B. Henry Fonda
C. Humphrey Bogart
D. Van Johnson

92. What was William Holden's entire acceptance speech when he won the Best Actor Oscar for *Stalag 17* (1953)?

A. "I'm shocked!"
B. "I'm speechless."
C. "Thank you!"
D. "You like me!"

93. In *The Life and Death of Colonel Blimp* (1943), what was Johnny's (Deborah Kerr's) occupation before the war?

A. Ballerina
B. Milkmaid
C. Photographic model
D. Seamstress

94. In the Cary Grant film *Operation Petticoat* (1959), what color does his submarine get painted?

A. Black
B. Pink
C. Purple
D. White

95. Paul Muni leads a group of resistance fighters in what film?

A. *Branded* (1950)
B. *Commandos Strike at Dawn* (1942)
C. *The World Changes* (1933)
D. *Uncertain Glory* (1944)

answers found on page 562

96. Jean Simmons plays one of four sisters in New Zealand who fall for WWII sailors in what film?

A. *Footsteps in the Fog* (1955)
B. *The Big Country* (1958)
C. *This Could Be the Night* (1957)
D. *Until They Sail* (1957)

97. In *Vacation from Marriage* (1945), Deborah Kerr and Robert Donat play a bored married couple whose relationship is revived by their separation during what war?

A. World War I
B. World War II
C. Boer War
D. Vietnam War

98. Donald Pleasence's real-life experience as a POW during World War II helped inform his performance in which of the following films?

A. *Killers of Kilimanjaro* (1959)
B. *Look Back in Anger* (1959)
C. *The Great Escape* (1963)
D. *The Man Inside* (1958)

99. Steve McQueen portrays navy officer Lieutenant Fergie Howard in what romantic comedy directed by Richard Thorpe?

A. *Love with the Proper Stranger* (1963)
B. *The Great Escape* (1963)
C. *The Honeymoon Machine* (1961)
D. *The War Lover* (1962)

100. Dirk Bogarde declined the role of Colonel Harker in what film directed by Arthur Hiller?

A. *A Bridge Too Far* (1977)
B. *Battle of Britain* (1969)
C. *The Treasure of Lost Canyon* (1952)
D. *Tobruk* (1967)

101. Who won his only Oscar for his work on *The African Queen* (1951)?

A. Humphrey Bogart
B. Jack Cardiff
C. James Agee
D. John Huston

102. In what Lewis Milestone film does Gregory Peck defend a vital hill in Korea?

A. *All Quiet on the Western Front* (1930)
B. *Of Mice and Men* (1940)
C. *Pork Chop Hill* (1959)
D. *The Front Page* (1931)

103. Marlon Brando starred in which of the following films scored by Franz Waxman?

A. *Crime in the Streets* (1956)
B. *Home Before Dark* (1958)
C. *Run Silent, Run Deep* (1958)
D. *Sayonara* (1957)

104. The 1966 film *The Battle of Algiers* received an Academy Award nomination in which of the following categories?

A. Best Actor
B. Best Director
C. Best Editing
D. Best Original Score

105. Jack Lemmon costarred with all of the following actors in the 1955 film *Mister Roberts* except for whom?

A. Henry Fonda
B. James Cagney
C. Walter Matthau
D. William Powell

106. John Frankenheimer took over directing the 1964 film *The Train* after what other director got fired?

A. Arthur Penn
B. George Cukor
C. Sidney Lumet
D. Warren Beatty

107. Clint Eastwood played Lt. Morris Schaffer in what film opposite Richard Burton?

A. *Away All Boats* (1956)
B. *Coogan's Bluff* (1968)
C. *Paint Your Wagon* (1969)
D. *Where Eagles Dare* (1968)

108. Ronald Reagan costarred with wife Nancy in what film?

A. *Hellcats of the Navy* (1957)
B. *Law and Order* (1953)
C. *She's Working Her Way Through College* (1952)
D. *The Winning Team* (1952)

109. In what Lewis Milestone silent film do two American soldiers try to escape German soldiers bickering over a girl during WWI?

A. *Garden of Eden* (1928)
B. *The Caveman* (1926)
C. *The Kid Brother* (1927)
D. *Two Arabian Nights* (1927)

110. J. Carrol Naish earned his first Oscar nomination for playing what character in *Sahara* (1943)?

A. Giuseppe
B. Jimmy Doyle
C. Tambul
D. Waco Hoyt

111. What is the name of Jean Harlow's character in the 1930 film *Hell's Angels*?

A. Ellen
B. Gwen
C. Helen
D. Sandra

112. John Mills stars as Captain Morgan in what film set during WWII?

A. *From Here to Eternity* (1953)
B. *The Valiant* (1962)
C. *The Wind and the Lion* (1975)
D. *Von Ryan's Express* (1965)

113. Who won the Academy Award as Best Supporting Actor for his work in the 1989 film *Glory*?

A. Denzel Washington
B. Kevin Kline
C. Morgan Freeman
D. Tim Robbins

114. In what Michael Powell film does the crew of a stranded German U-boat try to evade capture in Canada during World War II?

A. *49th Parallel* (1941)
B. *A Matter of Life and Death* (1946)
C. *Black Narcissus* (1947)
D. *The Life and Death of Colonel Blimp* (1943)

115. Which of the following actors did not costar with Donald Pleasence in the 1963 film *The Great Escape*?

A. Charles Bronson
B. James Garner
C. Richard Burton
D. Steve McQueen

Above and Beyond, 1952

116. What screenwriter earned Oscar nominations for the war films *Above and Beyond* (1952) and *Strategic Air Command* (1955)?

A. Beirne Lay Jr.
B. James Agee
C. James Jones
D. Robert Hardy Andrews

117. Who was Josh Logan's first choice to play Nellie in *South Pacific* (1958)?

A. Doris Day
B. Elizabeth Taylor
C. Grace Kelly
D. Judy Garland

118. Which of the following Gary Cooper films was based on an Ernest Hemingway novel?

A. *For Whom the Bell Tolls* (1943)
B. *Friendly Persuasion* (1956)
C. *Sergeant York* (1941)
D. *The Fountainhead* (1949)

119. What was the Academy Award category for which it was nominated that *The Bridge on the River Kwai* (1957) failed to win?

A. Best Actor in a Supporting Role
B. Best Cinematography
C. Best Director
D. Best Writing, Screenplay Based on Material from Another Medium

120. Which is not one of the reasons that Deborah Kerr gives for wanting to marry Roger Livesey in *The Life and Death of Colonel Blimp* (1943)?

A. She loves watching him play polo.
B. She wants sons with long mustaches.
C. She wants to join the army.
D. She wants to see the world.

121. What is the name of the officer that Glenn Ford's character impersonates in *Imitation General* (1958)?

A. Corporal Smothers
B. General Lane
C. Lieutenant Rags
D. Sergeant Decker

122. What actor costarred in Jules Dassin's 1942 film *Reunion in France*?

A. Gary Cooper
B. Henry Fonda

C. John Wayne
D. Robert Young

123. Meryl Streep and Tracey Ullman star in which film set in post-WWII England?

A. *Dancing at Lughnasa* (1998)
B. *Plenty* (1985)
C. *The River Wild* (1994)
D. *The Young Visitors* (1984)

124. In what division of the military did screenwriter George Axelrod serve during WWII?

A. U.S. Air Force
B. U.S. Army
C. U.S. National Guard
D. U.S. Navy

125. *The Great Escape* (1963) was nominated for an Academy Award in what category?

A. Best Adapted Screenplay
B. Best Cinematography
C. Best Film Editing
D. Best Musical Score

126. Humphrey Bogart starred in what film directed by Zoltan Korda?

A. *Sahara* (1943)
B. *Storm Over the Nile* (1955)
C. *The Four Feathers* (1939)
D. *The Macomber Affair* (1947)

127. Steven Spielberg received his first Academy Award for Best Director for what film?

A. *Close Encounters of the Third Kind* (1977)
B. *Raiders of the Lost Ark* (1981)
C. *Saving Private Ryan* (1998)
D. *Schindler's List* (1993)

128. Arthur Hiller directed George Peppard in what war film?

A. *A Bridge Too Far* (1977)
B. *Battle of Britain* (1969)
C. *The Treasure of Lost Canyon* (1952)
D. *Tobruk* (1967)

answers found on page 562

129. Otto Preminger was directed by Billy Wilder in what POW film?

A. *Anatomy of a Murder* (1959)
B. *Bunny Lake Is Missing* (1965)
C. *In Harm's Way* (1965)
D. *Stalag 17* (1953)

130. In 1942, Bette Davis cofounded what morale-building institution for World War II soldiers en route to the Pacific?

A. Doctors Without Borders
B. The Hollywood Canteen
C. The U.S.O.
D. The Veteran's Association

131. In which of the following Van Johnson films does June Allyson not appear?

A. *High Barbaree* (1947)
B. *Remains to Be Seen* (1953)
C. *Thirty Seconds Over Tokyo* (1944)
D. *Two Girls and a Sailor* (1944)

132. Which of the following actors does not appear with James Shigeta in *Midway* (1976)?

A. Charlton Heston
B. George Kennedy
C. Henry Fonda
D. James Coburn

133. In what Louis Malle film does a French boarding school harbor Jewish children during the Nazi occupation?

A. *Au revoir les enfants* (1987)
B. *Black Moon* (1975)
C. *Frantic* (1961)
D. *Pretty Baby* (1978)

134. June Allyson plays the wife of a baseball player who joins the Air Force in what film?

A. *Strategic Air Command* (1955)
B. *The Glenn Miller Story* (1954)
C. *The Opposite Sex* (1956)
D. *You Can't Run Away from It* (1956)

135. Which of the following actors costars with Kerwin Mathews in *The Last Blitzkrieg* (1959)?

A. Gary Cooper
B. James Stewart
C. Steve McQueen
D. Van Johnson

136. What British actress accepted Alec Guinness's Best Actor Oscar for *The Bridge on the River Kwai* (1957)?

A. Anna Massey
B. Greer Garson
C. Jean Simmons
D. Vanessa Redgrave

137. Rosalind Russell joins the army hoping to improve her love life in what film?

A. *His Girl Friday* (1940)
B. *Never Wave at a WAC* (1953)
C. *Sister Kenny* (1946)
D. *The Women* (1939)

138. Who costarred with Denzel Washington in the 1989 film *Glory*?

A. Bruce Willis
B. Dennis Hopper
C. Emilio Estevez
D. Matthew Broderick

139. Which star of *South Pacific* (1958) was previously an amateur boxer and stage director in Italy?

A. Archie Savage
B. Ken Clark
C. Ray Walston
D. Rossano Brazzi

140. Van Johnson and Jane Wyman share the screen in what wartime romance?

A. *Miracle in the Rain* (1956)
B. *Penny Serenade* (1941)
C. *Uncertain Glory* (1944)
D. *Wives and Lovers* (1963)

answers found on page 562

141. While Glenn Ford was in the U.S. Naval Reserve, to what rank did he rise?

    A. Commander
    B. Lieutenant
    C. Rear Admiral
    D. Vice Admiral

142. Which of the following actors costars with Leslie Howard in the 1941 film *49th Parallel*?

    A. John Wayne
    B. Laurence Olivier
    C. Rex Harrison
    D. Van Johnson

143. Which of the following films starring Dorothy McGuire concerns World War II veterans adjusting to civilian life?

    A. *A Summer Place* (1959)
    B. *Gentleman's Agreement* (1947)
    C. *Susan Slade* (1961)
    D. *Till the End of Time* (1946)

A Tale of Two Cities, 1935

144. The 1935 film *A Tale of Two Cities* was nominated for two Academy Awards. One was for Best Editing. What was the other for?

    A. Best Actor
    B. Best Art Direction
    C. Best Director
    D. Best Picture

145. What Louis Malle film is about collaboration with the Nazis in Vichy France during World War II?

    A. *Atlantic City* (1980)
    B. *Lacombe Lucien* (1974)
    C. *Murmur of the Heart* (1971)
    D. *My Dinner with Andre* (1981)

146. What is the surname of Leslie Howard's character in *Gone With the Wind* (1939)?

    A. Butler
    B. Holmes
    C. Mitchell
    D. Wilkes

147. What film directed by William Wyler is about three World War II veterans who must adjust to civilian life when they return home?

    A. *Mrs. Miniver* (1942)
    B. *The Best Years of Our Lives* (1946)
    C. *The Collector* (1965)
    D. *The Desperate Hours* (1955)

148. What action film features both Van Johnson and Sean Connery?

    A. *Action of the Tiger* (1957)
    B. *Objective, Burma!* (1945)
    C. *The Dark Avenger* (1955)
    D. *The Master of Ballantrae* (1953)

149. Ginger Rogers and Robert Ryan star in what WWII film written by Dalton Trumbo?

    A. *A Way in the Wilderness* (1940)
    B. *Tender Comrade* (1943)
    C. *The Wings of Eagles* (1957)
    D. *What Price Glory* (1952)

150. Which of the following films directed by Mark Robson is about a man who is blinded by a sniper's bullet during World War II?

    A. *Bright Victory* (1951)
    B. *Champion* (1949)
    C. *Nine Hours to Rama* (1963)
    D. *The Prize* (1963)

151. William Haines plays a private who rivals his drill sergeant for the same girl in what film?

    A. *Brown of Harvard* (1926)
    B. *Little Annie Rooney* (1925)
    C. *Show People* (1928)
    D. *Tell It to the Marines* (1927)

152. Which president did Jason Robards Jr. never play in a film?

    A. Abraham Lincoln
    B. Dwight Eisenhower
    C. Franklin Delano Roosevelt
    D. Ulysses S. Grant

153. After *The King and I* (1956), actors Deborah Kerr and Yul Brynner reunited in 1959 for which drama set during the 1956 Hungarian Revolution?

    A. *If Winter Comes*
    B. *The End of the Affair*
    C. *The Journey*
    D. *The Warning Shot*

154. What film directed by William Wyler is about a Quaker family during the Civil War?

    A. *Friendly Persuasion* (1956)
    B. *Roman Holiday* (1953)
    C. *The Big Country* (1958)
    D. *The Children's Hour* (1961)

155. Who was the first Asian actor or actress to win an Academy Award?

    A. Haing S. Ngor for *The Killing Fields* (1984)
    B. Ken Watanabe for *The Last Samurai* (2003)
    C. Miyoshi Umeki for *Sayonara* (1957)
    D. Sessue Hayakawa for *The Bridge on the River Kwai* (1957)

156. Which of the following films costarring Denzel Washington was nominated for an Academy Award as Best Picture?

    A. *A Soldier's Story* (1984)
    B. *Cry Freedom* (1987)
    C. *Glory* (1989)
    D. *Power* (1986)

157. Who was nominated for an Academy Award as Best Actor for his role in the 1954 film *The Caine Mutiny*?

    A. Clark Gable
    B. Henry Fonda
    C. Humphrey Bogart
    D. James Stewart

158. Stewart Granger portrayed Andre Moreau in which film set during the French Revolution?

    A. *A Tale of Two Cities* (1958)
    B. *Marie Antoinette* (1938)
    C. *Scaramouche* (1952)
    D. *The Scarlet Pimpernel* (1934)

159. One of the characters that Deborah Kerr portrays in *The Life and Death of Colonel Blimp* (1943) is nicknamed "Johnny." What is Johnny's real name?

    A. Angela
    B. Annabella
    C. Madeleine
    D. Maryanne

160. *Beau Geste* (1939) was Gary Cooper's last film under contract at which studio?

    A. Columbia
    B. MGM
    C. Paramount
    D. RKO

161. What newlyweds presented the Best Film Editing Oscar to Peter Taylor for *The Bridge on the River Kwai* (1957) in 1958?

    A. Debbie Reynolds and Eddie Fisher
    B. Janet Leigh and Tony Curtis
    C. Joanne Woodward and Paul Newman
    D. Natalie Wood and Robert Wagner

GREER **GARSON** (1904–1996)

MGM claimed for years that red-haired Greer Garson was Irish-born, yet in truth she was as properly British as many of the celebrated characters she played. Postcollege work with the Birmingham Repertory Theatre made Garson a popular star of London's West End, where MGM head Louis B. Mayer saw her (and some say fell in love with her) while scouting talent. Yet once Garson landed in Hollywood, she was largely ignored, until landing a part in a film being made back home, the poignant *Goodbye, Mr. Chips* (1939). As the main character's ill-fated wife she was only on screen for twenty minutes, but the role earned her a Best Actress Oscar nomination. Immediately, she was offered plum roles, sparring with Laurence Olivier in *Pride and Prejudice* (1940) and finding her perfect cinematic counterpart in Walter Pidgeon, with whom she made eight films. Their *Mrs. Miniver* (1942) was a triumph; she moved audiences to tears as a brave wife and mother trying to keep her family hopeful amid the perils of war, and earned a Best Actress Academy Award for her performance. After five straight years of receiving Oscar nominations, Garson found her brand of self-sacrificing heroines less popular in the postwar years, and retired in 1966 to focus on marriage and philanthropy.

Mrs. Miniver, 1942

Pride and Prejudice, 1940

1. **Approximately how long was Greer Garson's acceptance speech when she won the Best Actress Oscar for *Mrs. Miniver* (1942)?**

   A. 10 minutes

   B. 40 minutes

   C. 40 seconds

   D. 5 1/2 minutes

2. **Ronald Colman portrays an amnesiac WWI veteran in what film costarring Greer Garson?**

   A. *Forgotten Victory* (1939)

   B. *Random Harvest* (1942)

   C. *Stuffie* (1940)

   D. *The Greenie* (1942)

3. **In the 1939 film *Goodbye, Mr. Chips*, where does Greer Garson's character meet Mr. Chips?**

   A. In a schoolyard

   B. In the ocean

   C. On a mountain

   D. On a train

4. **How many Academy Award nominations did Greer Garson receive in her career?**

   A. 3

   B. 5

   C. 7

   D. 9

5. **In what Oscar-winning film did Walter Pidgeon and Greer Garson costar before *Mrs. Miniver* (1942)?**

   A. *Blossoms in the Dust* (1941)

   B. *Goodbye, Mr. Chips* (1939)

   C. *Random Harvest* (1942)

   D. *Yankee Doodle Dandy* (1942)

answers found on page 563

162. Jean Louis earned an Oscar nomination for which of the following black-and-white war films?

A. *Bataan* (1943)
B. *From Here to Eternity* (1953)
C. *So Proudly We Hail!* (1943)
D. *The Fighting Seabees* (1944)

163. Lewis Milestone directed what famous WWI film?

A. *All Quiet on the Western Front* (1930)
B. *Of Mice and Men* (1940)
C. *The Front Page* (1931)
D. *Two Arabian Knights* (1927)

164. Cinematographer Haskell Wexler shot the 1978 film *Coming Home*. What actress won the Academy Award for her role in the film?

A. Jane Fonda
B. Jill Clayburgh
C. Julie Christie
D. Sally Field

165. Who was nominated for an Academy Award as Best Supporting Actor for his performance in the 1946 film *Notorious*?

A. Charles Laughton
B. Claude Rains
C. Lionel Barrymore
D. Peter Lorre

166. What film won the Academy Award for Best Picture of 1942?

A. *Casablanca*
B. *For Whom the Bell Tolls*
C. *Madame Curie*
D. *The Song of Bernadette*

167. Which actor was Margaret Mitchell's original choice to portray Rhett Butler in 1939's *Gone With the Wind*?

A. Basil Rathbone
B. Burt Lancaster

C. Marlon Brando
D. Robert Taylor

168. Stephen McNally and John Hodiak fight over Linda Christian in what 1952 Korean War drama?

A. *Battle Circus*
B. *Battle Hymn*
C. *Battle Taxi*
D. *Battle Zone*

169. Robert Taylor portrays Colonel Alois Podhajsky of Austria in what film?

A. *High Wall* (1947)
B. *Miracle of the White Stallions* (1963)
C. *Passage to Marseille* (1944)
D. *Undercurrent* (1946)

170. In what category did the Randolph Scott war film *Bombardier* (1943) earn an Oscar nomination?

A. Best Actor
B. Best Dance Direction
C. Best Film Editing
D. Best Special Effects

171. William Wyler's 1946 film *The Best Years of Our Lives* won Academy Awards in all of the following categories except which one?

A. Best Actor
B. Best Actress
C. Best Editing
D. Best Director

172. In what film does David Niven play General Sir Roland "Rollo" Dane?

A. *Dodsworth* (1936)
B. *Enchantment* (1948)
C. *The Dawn Patrol* (1938)
D. *The Prisoner of Zenda* (1937)

The Four Horsemen of the Apocalypse, 1921

173. What screenwriter suggested Rudolph Valentino for the lead role in *The Four Horsemen of the Apocalypse* (1921)?

A. Anita Loos
B. Beta Breuil
C. Frances Marion
D. June Mathis

174. Which of the following actors did not costar with Ernest Borgnine in the 1967 film *The Dirty Dozen*?

A. Charles Bronson
B. Jim Brown
C. Lee Marvin
D. Tony Curtis

175. How did John Sturges participate in World War II?

A. Directed training films
B. Served in the navy
C. Sold scrap metal to the army
D. Toured as an army journalist

176. What film directed by Henry Hathaway deals with the atomic bomb?

A. *Home in Indiana* (1944)
B. *The Dark Corner* (1946)
C. *The House on 92nd Street* (1945)
D. *Wing and a Prayer* (1944)

177. The 1956 film *The Burmese Harp* received an Academy Award nomination for Best Foreign Language Film. What country was it from?

A. Israel
B. Italy
C. Japan
D. Sweden

178. Which "James" did not appear in the 1963 film *The Great Escape*?

A. James Coburn
B. James Donald
C. James Garner
D. James Stewart

179. What actor turned down Peter O'Toole's role in *Lawrence of Arabia* (1962)?

A. Albert Finney
B. Richard Harris
C. Roger Moore
D. Sean Connery

180. When Hal Roach produced military films for the First Motion Picture Unit, what future president did he work with?

A. Dwight D. Eisenhower
B. Lyndon Johnson
C. Richard Nixon
D. Ronald Reagan

181. Arthur Hiller directed Robert Taylor in what film set during WWII?

A. *Miracle of the White Stallions* (1963)
B. *Nightwing* (1979)
C. *Plaza Suite* (1971)
D. *The Man in the Glass Booth* (1975)

182. What comedian costarred with Ernest Borgnine in the 1964 film *McHale's Navy*?

A. Don Knotts
B. Harvey Korman
C. Mel Brooks
D. Tim Conway

Spotlight on
ERROL **FLYNN** (1909–1959)

A descendant of two key HMS *Bounty* mutineers who settled in the South Pacific, Flynn had adventure in his blood. From childhood, his one true love was the ocean, and as a young adult he jaunted around the Pacific in a variety of jobs. He accepted his first film role out of curiosity, playing his ancestor Fletcher Christian in the semidocumentary *In the Wake of the Bounty* (1933). Inspired, Flynn took off for London to pursue acting. Stage work brought him a Warner Bros. contract, but at first he had only minor roles. Then established star Robert Donat bowed out of Warner's first

historical adventure, *Captain Blood* (1935), and executives decided to take a chance on the young Australian. Cast opposite Olivia de Havilland, his costar in eight films, Flynn became an overnight sensation. With his roguish smile and the hint of an Australian accent, he triumphed in a series of swashbucklers, including *The Adventures of Robin Hood* (1938) and *The Sea Hawk* (1940), before turning to several high-profile war films such as *Edge of Darkness* (1943) and *Objective, Burma!* (1945). Offscreen, he indulged in his own brand of swashbuckling, with hard drinking and womanizing part of his daily routine. In 1959, he passed away, the victim of a heart attack at fifty.

The Adventures of Robin Hood, 1938

Objective, Burma!, 1945

1. **In what Lewis Milestone film do Errol Flynn and Ann Sheridan play resistance fighters against the Nazis in occupied Norway?**

   A. *Edge of Darkness* (1943)
   B. *Of Mice and Men* (1940)
   C. *Red Pony* (1949)
   D. *Two Arabian Knights* (1927)

2. **Errol Flynn plays a diamond smuggler in what adventure film?**

   A. *Istanbul* (1957)
   B. *The Wings of Eagles* (1957)
   C. *Torrid Zone* (1940)
   D. *What Price Glory* (1952)

3. **In which of the following films does Fred MacMurray costar with Errol Flynn?**

   A. *Dive Bomber* (1941)
   B. *Grand Old Girl* (1935)
   C. *Rangers of Fortune* (1940)
   D. *Too Many Husbands* (1940)

4. **Anthony Quinn was featured in what film that starred Errol Flynn as General Custer?**

   A. *Custer of the West* (1967)
   B. *Little Big Man* (1970)
   C. *Little Bighorn* (1951)
   D. *They Died with Their Boots On* (1941)

5. **In what film does Errol Flynn play a criminal set to be executed in WWII France?**

   A. *Desperate Journey* (1943)
   B. *Northern Pursuit* (1943)
   C. *Uncertain Glory* (1944)
   D. *Never Say Goodbye* (1946)

---

answers found on page 563

183. Deborah Kerr plays three different roles in what Powell-Pressburger film about a British Army officer?

A. *Beloved Infidel* (1959)
B. *Black Narcissus* (1947)
C. *The Fighting Pimpernel* (1950)
D. *The Life and Death of Colonel Blimp* (1943)

184. The 1940 Alfred Hitchcock film *Foreign Correspondent* was nominated for Academy Awards in all of the following categories except which one?

A. Best Cinematography
B. Best Director
C. Best Original Screenplay
D. Best Picture

185. In the 1934 Henry Hathaway film *Come On Marines*, a group of marines have the assignment of rescuing a group of children in what country?

A. Mexico
B. Philippines
C. Spain
D. Turkey

186. Frank Sinatra, Natalie Wood, and Tony Curtis star in what film set during WWII?

A. *Bell, Book and Candle* (1958)
B. *Kings Go Forth* (1958)
C. *Paris Blues* (1961)
D. *The Man from Laramie* (1955)

187. What cinematographer earned an Oscar nomination for *Waterloo Bridge* (1940)?

A. Georges Prinal
B. Gregg Toland
C. Jack Cardiff
D. Joseph Ruttenberg

188. What was the name of the revolutionary ape played by Roddy McDowall in *Conquest of the Planet of the Apes* (1972)?

A. Caesar
B. Cornelius
C. Milo
D. Taylor

189. What character did Anthony Quinn play in the 1941 film *They Died with Their Boots On*?

A. Charley Eagle
B. Crazy Horse
C. Prince Ramon
D. Wogan

190. Robert Duvall portrayed a relative of his in what film?

A. *A Civil Action* (1998)
B. *Gods and Generals* (2003)
C. *Lonesome Dove* (1989)
D. *The Great Santini* (1979)

191. In which film did Sean Connery share the screen with Richard Burton, Henry Fonda, and John Wayne?

A. *The Last of the Cowboys* (1977)
B. *The Longest Day* (1962)
C. *The Undefeated* (1969)
D. *Where Eagles Dare* (1968)

192. Michael Powell and Emeric Pressburger set out "The Archers' Manifesto" in a letter to what actress asking her to star in *The Life and Death of Colonel Blimp* (1943)?

A. Audrey Hepburn
B. Deborah Kerr
C. Ingrid Bergman
D. Olivia de Havilland

answers found on page 563

193. Which one of the following Samuel Goldwyn pictures did not feature actor Farley Granger?

A. *Edge of Doom* (1950)
B. *I Want You* (1951)
C. *Our Very Own* (1950)
D. *The Best Years of Our Lives* (1946)

194. In which film nominated for a Best Picture Oscar did Ricardo Montalban portray a Japanese Kabuki actor?

A. *Battleground* (1949)
B. *Sayonara* (1957)
C. *The Teahouse of the August Moon* (1956)
D. *Two Weeks with Love* (1950)

195. George Stevens and his crew filmed graphic scenes at what WWII concentration camp?

A. Auschwitz
B. Chelmno
C. Dachau
D. Treblinka

196. Ethel Barrymore was lifelong friends with what world leader?

A. Golda Meir
B. Mahatma Gandhi
C. Winston Churchill
D. Woodrow Wilson

197. What Steven Spielberg big-budget WWII farce flopped at the box office?

A. *1941* (1979)
B. *Always* (1989)
C. *Hook* (1991)
D. *Schindler's List* (1993)

198. Who was Susan Hayward's costar in *The Fighting Seabees* (1944)?

A. Dana Andrews
B. John Gavin
C. John Wayne
D. Robert Young

199. John Wayne earned his first Academy Award nomination for his performance in what war film?

A. *Flying Leathernecks* (1951)
B. *Sands of Iwo Jima* (1949)
C. *The Fighting Seabees* (1944)
D. *They Were Expendable* (1945)

200. Ricardo Montalban was featured in what World War II epic starring Van Johnson?

A. *Battleground* (1949)
B. *Decision Before Dawn* (1951)
C. *Edge of Darkness* (1943)
D. *Reach for the Sky* (1956)

Pride of the Marines, 1945

201. The 1945 Delmer Daves film *Pride of the Marines* was nominated for an Academy Award in what category?

A. Best Actor
B. Best Actress
C. Best Picture
D. Best Screenplay

202. The 1965 film *Doctor Zhivago* was nominated for ten Academy Awards. How many did it take home?

A. 1
B. 3
C. 5
D. 7

203. In what Roger Corman film does a lost soldier discover a mysterious beauty haunting a half-deserted castle?

A. *House of Usher* (1960)
B. *The Masque of the Red Death* (1964)
C. *The Terror* (1963)
D. *The Tomb of Ligeia* (1965)

204. For what film did George Stevens create an alternate ending for European audiences in recognition of WWII?

A. *Gunga Din* (1939)
B. *Penny Serenade* (1941)
C. *The Talk of the Town* (1942)
D. *Vigil in the Night* (1940)

205. In what category did the John Wayne film *The Fighting Seabees* (1944) earn an Oscar nomination?

A. Best Editing
B. Best Picture
C. Best Scoring of a Dramatic or Comedy Picture
D. Best Special Effects

206. Paul Muni and Miriam Hopkins starred in what film set in France during WWI?

A. *A Farewell to Arms* (1932)
B. *Journey's End* (1930)
C. *The Dawn Patrol* (1938)
D. *The Woman I Love* (1937)

207. Years before Stephen McNally appeared in Dick Powell's directing debut, *Split Second* (1953), the two actors costarred in what postwar espionage thriller?

A. *13 Rue Madeleine* (1947)
B. *Berlin Express* (1948)
C. *Foreign Correspondent* (1940)
D. *Rogues' Regiment* (1948)

208. Montgomery Clift lived with an army engineering unit located outside of Zurich to prepare for what film?

A. *A Place in the Sun* (1951)
B. *From Here to Eternity* (1953)
C. *The Misfits* (1961)
D. *The Search* (1948)

209. To whom was Deborah Kerr romantically linked while filming *From Here to Eternity* (1953)?

A. Burt Lancaster
B. Montgomery Clift
C. Tennessee Williams
D. Trevor Howard

210. Who starred in John Sturges's *The Great Escape* (1963) and Richard Donner's *Maverick* (1994)?

A. Charles Bronson
B. James Garner
C. Richard Attenborough
D. Steve McQueen

211. Which Samuel Fuller film used tanks made of plywood?

A. *Fixed Bayonets!* (1951)
B. *Forty Guns* (1957)
C. *Merrill's Marauders* (1962)
D. *The Steel Helmet* (1951)

212. In 1945, Neil Simon served in what division of the U.S. Armed Forces?

A. Air force
B. Army
C. Navy
D. Secret Service

213. Peter O'Toole plays a naval officer who tries to help Asian natives stage a revolution in what film?

A. *Lord Jim* (1965)
B. *The Lion in Winter* (1968)
C. *The Night of the Generals* (1967)
D. *The Ruling Class* (1972)

answers found on page 563

214. What WWII film featured an all-star cast including Roddy McDowall and Sean Connery?

A. *Attack* (1956)
B. *The Clay Pigeon* (1949)
C. *The Longest Day* (1962)
D. *The Thin Red Line* (1998)

215. What film starring Leslie Howard is about a man who goes back in time to meet his ancestors during the American Revolution?

A. *Berkeley Square* (1933)
B. *Of Human Bondage* (1934)
C. *Secrets* (1933)
D. *Smilin' Through* (1932)

216. Peter Sellers served in the Royal Air Force and toured in all of the following countries except for which one?

A. Burma
B. Germany
C. India
D. Italy

217. In what branch of the Armed Forces did Henry Fonda serve during WWII?

A. U.S. Air Force
B. U.S. Army
C. U.S. Coast Guard
D. U.S. Navy

218. In what category did the 1944 film *Thirty Seconds Over Tokyo* win its only Academy Award?

A. Best Cinematography
B. Best Editing
C. Best Sound
D. Best Special Effects

Gunga Din, 1939

219. In what category did the 1939 film *Gunga Din* receive its only Academy Award nomination?

A. Best Art Direction
B. Best Cinematography
C. Best Director
D. Best Supporting Actor

220. Which of the following actors did not costar with Paul Henreid in *Operation Crossbow* (1965)?

A. George Peppard
B. John Mills
C. Lee J. Cobb
D. Trevor Howard

221. Franz Waxman composed the music for the 1943 film *Air Force*. Who was the director?

A. Howard Hawks
B. John Ford
C. Robert Siodmak
D. William Wyler

222. Which of the following Oscar-nominated war films is about British soldiers?

A. *All Quiet on the Western Front* (1930)
B. *In Which We Serve* (1942)
C. *No Man's Land* (2001)
D. *So Proudly We Hail!* (1943)

Red Dust, 1932

Chapter 14
ROMANCE

When Thomas Edison unveiled his first slate of movie subjects in 1896, it included *The Kiss*, a recreation of the final moment from the Broadway hit *The Widow Jones*. Since then, romance has been a key element in nearly every film genre, from comedy to horror. Deborah Kerr's broken date to meet Cary Grant at the Empire State Building in *An Affair to Remember* (1957), princess Audrey Hepburn's *Roman Holiday* (1953) with Gregory Peck, Bette Davis's *Dark Victory* (1939) over death through marriage to George Brent, and *King Kong*'s (1933) unrequited love for Fay Wray have helped make a box of Kleenex as essential to moviegoing as popcorn.

No one type of actor or character has a monopoly on big-screen love stories. Clark Gable thrilled audiences with his virile love-making in *Red Dust* (1932) and *Gone With the Wind* (1939), but so did more sensitive types like Montgomery Clift in *A Place in the Sun* (1951) and *From Here to Eternity* (1953). James Stewart brought a gangly all-American appeal to romance in *It's a Wonderful Life* (1946) and even in a European-set story like *The Shop Around the Corner* (1940), but continental lovers like Charles Boyer in *Algiers* (1938) also carved a special niche. Fans loved Natalie Wood as the innocent girl discovering her heart in *West Side Story* (1961), the tomboy movie star in *Inside Daisy Clover* (1965), and the neurotic small-town girl in *Splendor in the Grass* (1961). Sandra Dee brought puppy love to life in *Imitation of Life* (1959), but audiences also fell in love with the septuagenarian lovebirds played by Henry Fonda and Katharine Hepburn in *On Golden Pond* (1981).

Nor is movie romance reserved for the pretty. Long after his years as a baby-food model, nobody would have accused Humphrey Bogart of having classical good looks, but he sure made a compelling suitor for Ingrid Bergman in *Casablanca* (1942), Lauren Bacall in *To Have and Have Not* (1944), and Audrey Hepburn in *Sabrina* (1954). For all her acting and singing talent, Barbra Streisand was no

Casablanca, 1942

conventional beauty, but she shared some sizzling love scenes with Robert Redford in *The Way We Were* (1973) and made audiences believe she was as magical as he thought she was.

Success as a romantic star can be achieved simply by looking at a costar with enough passion to sell the story (think Merle Oberon in 1939's *Wuthering Heights* and Rock Hudson in 1954's *Magnificent Obsession*) or through the subtle development of character and relationship, as when Audrey Hepburn parlayed her first romantic lead, in *Roman Holiday* (1953), into an Oscar. Meryl Streep has built a reputation as the screen's greatest living actress, at least in part by sharing romantic two-shots with Robert Redford in *Out of Africa* (1985) and Clint Eastwood in *The Bridges of Madison County* (1995). And dramatic heavyweight Marlon Brando likewise played some of the screen's hottest love scenes.

Some stars carved a special niche in romantic drama. Many of Bette Davis and Greta Garbo's best performances ended in heartbreak, with the leading lady dying or being left to live with her yearnings. Bubblier actresses like Doris Day and Irene Dunne seemed made for a final embrace. And Barbara Stanwyck was so strong, even as the seemingly heartless con artist in *The Lady Eve* (1941), that nobody could imagine her not getting her man once she set her mind to it.

Hollywood's romantic movies have also provided a barometer to changing times and shifting values. As the prejudices faced by minorities began to receive more attention, Hollywood responded by developing black romantic stars like Dorothy Dandridge in *Carmen Jones* (1954) and Sidney Poitier in *A Patch of Blue* (1965) and *For Love of Ivy* (1968). With the loosening of sexual taboos, Wood could play a pregnant single woman in *Love with the Proper Stranger* (1963) and Dustin Hoffman was able to land Katharine Ross at the end of *The Graduate* (1967) despite his having had an affair with her mother. Most recent, the screen has reflected new concepts of love and family, as evidenced by Heath Ledger's love scenes with Jake Gyllenhaal in *Brokeback Mountain* (2005) and the nontraditional marriage of Annette Bening and Julianne Moore in *The Kids Are All Right* (2010).

But however much society changes, romance seems to be a constant—at least at the box office. Love and the movies truly are a marriage made in heaven. As Dooley Wilson sings in *Casablanca*, "The world will always welcome lovers as time goes by."

1. What is the name of Fay Wray's character in *King Kong* (1933)?
   A. Ann Darrow
   B. Hope Reed
   C. Janie Tufts
   D. Kate Rivers

2. Who won the Academy Award for Best Supporting Actress playing Cher's mother in the 1987 film *Moonstruck*?
   A. Anne Bancroft
   B. Anne Ramsey
   C. Olympia Dukakis
   D. Shirley MacLaine

3. Who did Paul Henreid romance in the 1944 film *In Our Time*?
   A. Claire Trevor
   B. Ida Lupino
   C. Ingrid Bergman
   D. Joan Crawford

4. What Nora Ephron film earned an Oscar nomination for the song "A Wink and a Smile"?
   A. *Heartburn* (1986)
   B. *Sleepless in Seattle* (1993)
   C. *When Harry Met Sally* (1989)
   D. *You've Got Mail* (1998)

5. The 1948 film *The Red Shoes* won two Academy Awards. One was for Best Art Direction. What was the other for?
   A. Best Actress
   B. Best Editing
   C. Best Musical Score
   D. Best Picture

6. What actor plays Joan Blondell's leading man in *East Side of Heaven* (1939)?
   A. Bing Crosby
   B. Frank Sinatra
   C. James Mason
   D. James Stewart

Designing Woman, 1957

7. In *Designing Woman* (1957), which stylish actress is Gregory Peck's leading lady?
   A. Audrey Hepburn
   B. Grace Kelly
   C. Ingrid Bergman
   D. Lauren Bacall

8. Where does the action take place in the Rock Hudson film *Come September* (1961)?
   A. A school
   B. A villa
   C. A family member's house
   D. A summer camp

9. During production on 1985's *Out of Africa*, what was used to keep carnivorous wild animals at bay?
   A. Fire extinguishers
   B. Firecrackers
   C. Lemon juice
   D. Loud music

10. In *Brigadoon* (1954), Van Johnson and Gene Kelly get lost while on a hunting trip in what country?
    A. England
    B. France
    C. Ireland
    D. Scotland

11. The 1996 film *The Preacher's Wife* is a remake of the 1947 film *The Bishop's Wife*. Who played Denzel Washington's role in the original?

    A. Cary Grant
    B. James Stewart
    C. Spencer Tracy
    D. Van Johnson

12. Who plays Fay Wray's love interest in the 1931 film *The Unholy Garden*?

    A. Claude Rains
    B. John Barrymore
    C. John Gilbert
    D. Ronald Colman

13. The 1943 Spencer Tracy film *A Guy Named Joe* was remade by Steven Spielberg. What was the title of the remake?

    A. *Always* (1989)
    B. *Catch Me If You Can* (2002)
    C. *The Sugarland Express* (1974)
    D. *The Terminal* (2004)

14. Meryl Streep and Jack Nicholson star in which film based on its writer's (Nora Ephron) real-life marriage?

    A. *Falling in Love* (1984)
    B. *Heartburn* (1986)
    C. *Plenty* (1985)
    D. *The House of the Spirits* (1993)

15. Complete this Bette Davis line from *Of Human Bondage* (1934): "After you kissed me I always used to . . ."

    A. . . . faint."
    B. . . . thank my lucky stars."
    C. . . . wash my hair."
    D. . . . wipe my mouth."

16. Who does Sidney Poitier romance in *For Love of Ivy* (1968)?

    A. Abbey Lincoln
    B. Diahann Carroll
    C. Elizabeth Hartman
    D. Katharine Houghton

17. Who plays Katharine Hepburn's daughter in the 1981 film *On Golden Pond*?

    A. Jane Fonda
    B. Jill Clayburgh
    C. Julie Christie
    D. Meryl Streep

18. What is the name of the song that Ingrid Bergman asks Sam to play in the 1942 film *Casablanca*?

    A. "A Kiss to Build a Dream On"
    B. "As Time Goes By"
    C. "But Not for Me"
    D. "The Way You Look Tonight"

19. Jean Simmons starred in the 1960 film *The Grass Is Greener*. Who directed it?

    A. Blake Edwards
    B. Elia Kazan
    C. Robert Wise
    D. Stanley Donen

20. What song do Deborah Kerr and Cary Grant sing while dancing their last dance in *An Affair to Remember* (1957)?

    A. "A Lovely Way to Spend an Evening"
    B. "People Will Say We're in Love"
    C. "Put Your Head on My Shoulders"
    D. "You Make It Easy to Be True"

21. What actress played Fay Wray's part in the 1976 remake of *King Kong*?

    A. Dyan Cannon
    B. Jessica Lange
    C. Susan Sarandon
    D. Teri Garr

22. Who does Hedy Lamarr persuade to marry her in *Come Live with Me* (1941)?

A. Charles Boyer
B. Clark Gable
C. James Stewart
D. Robert Young

23. Jennifer Jones portrays Dr. Han Suyin opposite William Holden in which film?

A. *Good Morning, Miss Dove* (1955)
B. *Love Is a Many-Splendored Thing* (1955)
C. *Since You Went Away* (1944)
D. *The Man in the Gray Flannel Suit* (1956)

24. What special item did Fay Wray have to wear for her role in *King Kong* (1933)?

A. A blond wig
B. A bustle
C. A padded bra
D. False teeth

25. What film directed by John Cromwell is about a woman who falls in love with a blind pianist?

A. *Dead Reckoning* (1947)
B. *Double Harness* (1933)
C. *I Dream Too Much* (1935)
D. *Night Song* (1947)

26. In what country does the John Wayne classic *The Quiet Man* (1952) take place?

A. England
B. France
C. Ireland
D. Scotland

27. Bette Davis, Olivia de Havilland, and Vincent Price all appear in what 1939 historical romance?

A. *Brigham Young*
B. *The Adventures of Robin Hood*
C. *The Private Lives of Elizabeth and Essex*
D. *Tower of London*

28. *People in Love* was the working title for what film starring Ray Milland?

A. *Night Into Morning* (1951)
B. *Old Acquaintance* (1943)
C. *Pocketful of Miracles* (1961)
D. *The Catered Affair* (1956)

29. The 1957 Sophia Loren film *The Pride and the Passion* is based on a novel by which famous author?

A. C. S. Forester
B. Daphne du Maurier
C. Edith Wharton
D. Edna Ferber

30. What actor couldn't stand working with Audrey Hepburn on *Sabrina* (1954)?

A. Humphrey Bogart
B. John Williams
C. Walter Hampden
D. William Holden

31. Which film pairs Anthony Quinn and Lauren Bacall as a romantic couple in their twilight years?

A. *A Star for Two* (1991)
B. *A Walk in the Clouds* (1995)
C. *The Imperfect Lady* (1947)
D. *Waikiki Wedding* (1937)

32. What is the name of Barbra Streisand's character in *The Way We Were* (1973)?

A. Cleo
B. Katie
C. Maggie
D. Nora

33. William Holden loses the affections of Audrey Hepburn to Humphrey Bogart in what film?

A. *Executive Suite* (1954)
B. *Love Is a Many-Splendored Thing* (1955)
C. *Picnic* (1955)
D. *Sabrina* (1954)

34. What director accepted Katharine Hepburn's Academy Award for *Guess Who's Coming to Dinner* (1967)?

   A. Fritz Lang
   B. George Cukor
   C. John Huston
   D. Stanley Kramer

35. Who plays Barbra Streisand's love interest in the 1996 film *The Mirror Has Two Faces*?

   A. Daniel Day-Lewis
   B. Jeff Bridges
   C. Nick Nolte
   D. Robert Duvall

Now, Voyager, 1942

36. What is the name of Paul Henreid's character in *Now, Voyager* (1942)?

   A. Claude
   B. Henry
   C. Jerry
   D. Robert

37. William Haines falls in love with a professor's daughter, played by Mary Abbot, in what film?

   A. *Brown of Harvard* (1926)
   B. *Little Annie Rooney* (1925)
   C. *Show People* (1928)
   D. *Way Out West* (1930)

38. What actor stars in the 1938 film *Algiers,* directed by John Cromwell?

   A. Charles Boyer
   B. Humphrey Bogart
   C. James Cagney
   D. Leslie Howard

39. Complete this Bette Davis line from *Now, Voyager* (1942): "Jerry, don't let's ask for the moon; we have the . . ."

   A. . . . sky."
   B. . . . stars."
   C. . . . sun."
   D. . . . world."

40. The 1961 Sandra Dee film *Come September* is set in what country?

   A. England
   B. Ireland
   C. Italy
   D. Spain

41. In *Sabrina* (1954), Audrey Hepburn plays the daughter of what servant in the wealthy Larrabee family?

   A. Butler
   B. Chauffeur
   C. Cook
   D. Gardner

42. What is the name of Joseph Cotten's character in the 1948 film *Portrait of Jennie*?

   A. Dexter
   B. Eben
   C. Jeremiah
   D. John

43. The 1967 film *The Graduate* was nominated for seven Academy Awards but only took home one. In what category did it win?

   A. Best Adapted Screenplay
   B. Best Director
   C. Best Musical Score
   D. Best Supporting Actress

answers found on pages 563–564

44. What is the name of Leslie Caron's character in *An American in Paris* (1951)?

A. Colette
B. Fiona
C. Lise
D. Sasha

45. What color did Deborah Kerr dye her hair to play against type in *From Here to Eternity* (1953)?

A. Black
B. Blond
C. Brown
D. Red

46. Who plays Doris Day's husband in the 1954 film *Young at Heart*?

A. Dean Martin
B. Don Ameche
C. Frank Sinatra
D. Ralph Bellamy

47. Who do Marlon Brando and David Niven try to romance in *Bedtime Story* (1964)?

A. Eva Marie Saint
B. Janet Leigh
C. Shirley Jones
D. Sophia Loren

48. Who does Van Johnson romance in *The End of the Affair* (1955)?

A. Deborah Kerr
B. Elizabeth Taylor
C. Irene Dunne
D. June Allyson

49. I played Deborah Kerr's boyfriend, Kenneth, in *An Affair to Remember* (1957) and married actress Evelyn Ankers in real life. Who am I?

A. Paul Henreid
B. Ray Milland
C. Richard Denning
D. Van Heflin

The Red Danube, 1949

50. In *The Red Danube* (1949), Ethel Barrymore's character tries to help a young ballerina played by what actress?

A. Ann Miller
B. Cyd Charisse
C. Janet Leigh
D. Leslie Caron

51. Bob Hope romances Rhonda Fleming in what film directed by Alexander Hall?

A. *Blue Skies* (1946)
B. *Neptune's Daughter* (1949)
C. *The Great Lover* (1949)
D. *The Pleasure of His Company* (1961)

52. What character does Fay Bainter play in *Jezebel* (1938)?

A. Amy Bradford Dillard
B. Belle Massey
C. Julie Marsden
D. Mrs. Kendrick

53. The 1957 Luchino Visconti film *White Nights* is based on a novel by what author?

A. Alexandre Dumas
B. Fyodor Dostoyevsky
C. Victor Hugo
D. William Golding

answers found on page 564

Spotlight on
INGRID **BERGMAN** (1915–1982)

Many foreign stars were happy to come to America and be remade by Hollywood, but shy young orphan Ingrid Bergman would have none of it. When David O. Selznick brought her over to star in the 1939 American version of her earlier European hit *Intermezzo*, she insisted on maintaining her natural hair color and eyebrows. Selznick saw the publicity value in her position and sold her as a natural, fresh-faced heroine. *Intermezzo* was a hit, but Bergman soon chafed at being typecast as a good girl. Despite her attempts to vary her roles, her typecasting as "St. Ingrid" continued, thanks largely to her performances as a World War II resistance fighter in *Casablanca* (1942) and as a nun in *The Bells of St. Mary's* (1945). However, her reputation was changed when she and Italian director Roberto Rossellini, both married to other people, fell in love while filming *Stromboli* (1950) in Europe and had a child out of wedlock. They subsequently married, but it wasn't until their marriage was on its last legs that 20th Century-Fox asked her to star in *Anastasia* (1956). The same audiences who had rejected Bergman now welcomed her back, and she moved gracefully into mature roles— still radiating that emotional truth that had made her a star.

Saratoga Trunk, 1945

Casablanca, 1942

1. What film pairing Ingrid Bergman and Gary Cooper was adapted from an Edna Ferber novel?

   A. *Saratoga Trunk* (1945)

   B. *The Barretts of Wimpole Street* (1957)

   C. *The Long Memory* (1952)

   D. *The Valiant* (1962)

2. Who plays Ingrid Bergman's younger lover in the 1961 film *Goodbye Again*?

   A. Anthony Perkins

   B. Troy Donahue

   C. Van Johnson

   D. Warren Beatty

3. In *Cactus Flower* (1969), with whom does Ingrid Bergman have to compete for Walter Matthau's affections?

   A. Goldie Hawn

   B. Mia Farrow

   C. Sally Field

   D. Teri Garr

4. What is the name of Ingrid Bergman's character in *Casablanca* (1942)?

   A. Frida

   B. Ilsa

   C. Lise

   D. Marta

5. What is Ingrid Bergman's profession in *Indiscreet* (1958)?

   A. Actress

   B. Airline stewardess

   C. Cocktail waitress

   D. Interpreter

answers found on page 564

54. How does Barbra Streisand's character meet Robert Redford's character in the 1973 film *The Way We Were*?

A. At a restaurant
B. At a swimming pool
C. At college
D. At summer camp

55. Richard Burton plays what character in the 1981 film *Lovespell*?

A. Bishop
B. Gormond of Ireland
C. King Mark of Cornwall
D. Tristan

56. Which leading lady plays Warren Beatty's aunt in *Love Affair* (1994)?

A. Audrey Hepburn
B. Katharine Hepburn
C. Myrna Loy
D. Olivia de Havilland

57. The title of what film starring Natalie Wood came from a poem by William Wordsworth?

A. *Prince of Foxes* (1949)
B. *Splendor in the Grass* (1961)
C. *The Roots of Heaven* (1958)
D. *Tomorrow Is Forever* (1946)

58. In *The Ghost and Mrs. Muir* (1947), who is Rex Harrison's beautiful costar?

A. Carole Lombard
B. Claudette Colbert
C. Gene Tierney
D. Merle Oberon

59. Robert Redford and Natalie Wood shared the screen in what film?

A. *A New Kind of Love* (1963)
B. *Inside Daisy Clover* (1965)
C. *Prince of Foxes* (1949)
D. *The Roots of Heaven* (1958)

60. Who is Henry Fonda's leading lady in the 1941 film *The Lady Eve*?

A. Barbara Stanwyck
B. Greta Garbo
C. Lana Turner
D. Loretta Young

61. Who plays Ernest Borgnine's daughter in the 1956 film *The Catered Affair*?

A. Ann-Margret
B. Debbie Reynolds
C. Janet Leigh
D. Natalie Wood

62. Van Johnson costars with which first-time actress in *The Romance of Rosy Ridge* (1947)?

A. Ava Gardner
B. Elizabeth Taylor
C. Janet Leigh
D. June Allyson

63. Which of the following Carole Lombard films is about a family that is thrown into turmoil when the daughter falls in love with a chauffeur?

A. *Fast and Loose* (1930)
B. *Ladies' Man* (1931)
C. *Man of the World* (1931)
D. *Safety in Numbers* (1930)

64. What actor portrays Julius Caesar opposite Richard Burton and Elizabeth Taylor in the 1963 epic *Cleopatra*?

A. Charlton Heston
B. Peter O'Toole
C. Rex Harrison
D. Robert Taylor

answers found on page 564

65. At the end of *An Affair to Remember* (1957), Deborah Kerr tells Cary Grant that if he can paint, she can what?

A. Live
B. Sing
C. Walk
D. Watch

66. Besides *Romeo and Juliet* (1936), what is the only other film to star John Barrymore and Norma Shearer?

A. *Long Lost Father* (1934)
B. *Marie Antoinette* (1938)
C. *Strange Interlude* (1932)
D. *The Barretts of Wimpole Street* (1934)

67. I played Marguerite opposite Rudolph Valentino's Armand in the 1921 adaptation of *Camille*. Who am I?

A. Alice Terry
B. Alla Nazimova
C. Bebe Daniels
D. Nita Naldi

68. Who plays Leslie Howard's wife in the 1939 classic *Gone With the Wind*?

A. Greer Garson
B. Olivia de Havilland
C. Paulette Goddard
D. Vivien Leigh

69. Who does Merle Oberon play in *Wuthering Heights* (1939)?

A. Cathy
B. Ellen
C. Heathcliff
D. Isabella

70. Jules Dassin's 1960 film *Never on Sunday* is set in what country?

A. France
B. Greece
C. Italy
D. Turkey

Dark Victory, 1939

71. The 1939 film *Dark Victory*, starring Bette Davis, was nominated for Academy Awards in all of the following categories except which one?

A. Best Actress
B. Best Musical Score
C. Best Picture
D. Best Supporting Actor

72. Van Johnson appears in what film based on a poem by Alice Duer Miller?

A. *Beyond This Place* (1959)
B. *Blue Skies* (1946)
C. *Penny Serenade* (1941)
D. *The White Cliffs of Dover* (1944)

73. The 1989 film *Always* is a remake of what earlier film starring Spencer Tracy?

A. *A Guy Named Joe* (1943)
B. *The Mountain* (1956)
C. *The Sea of Grass* (1947)
D. *Without Love* (1945)

74. In the 1981 film *On Golden Pond*, what is the name of the elusive big fish that Henry Fonda's character is always trying to catch?

A. Dudley
B. Jasper
C. Stanley
D. Walter

answers found on page 564

75. Which star of 1985's *A Room with a View* appears opposite Richard Burton and Elizabeth Taylor in the 1963 film *The V.I.P.s*?

A. Daniel Day-Lewis
B. Denholm Elliott
C. Helena Bonham Carter
D. Maggie Smith

76. What actress won an Academy Award as Best Supporting Actress for portraying a man in the 1982 film *The Year of Living Dangerously*?

A. Geena Davis
B. Linda Hunt
C. Meryl Streep
D. Sigourney Weaver

77. Anthony Asquith directed what romantic drama set during the Cold War featuring Academy Award–nominated actor Theodore Bikel?

A. *A Cottage on Dartmoor* (1929)
B. *Moscow Nights* (1935)
C. *The Runaway Princess* (1929)
D. *The Young Lovers* (1954)

78. Sandra Dee and Bobby Darin met while filming the comedy *Come September* (1961). Who was the film's male lead?

A. James Darren
B. Robert Stack
C. Rock Hudson
D. Rod Taylor

79. Who plays the title character in the 1965 Roddy McDowall film *Inside Daisy Clover*?

A. Ann-Margret
B. Joanne Woodward
C. Natalie Wood
D. Tuesday Weld

80. Joseph Cotten stars in the 1944 film *Since You Went Away*, which won its only Academy Award in what category?

A. Best Cinematography
B. Best Director
C. Best Original Score
D. Best Picture

81. How many Academy Award categories for which it was nominated did *Gigi* (1958) lose?

A. 0
B. 1
C. 2
D. 3

82. *King Kong* (1933) used many of the sets from what other Fay Wray film?

A. *Below the Sea* (1933)
B. *The Most Dangerous Game* (1932)
C. *The Unholy Garden* (1931)
D. *The Vampire Bat* (1933)

83. What song does Audrey Hepburn sing in *Breakfast at Tiffany's* (1961)?

A. "Blue Moon"
B. "By the Light of the Silvery Moon"
C. "Moon River"
D. "Moonlight Bay"

84. William Wyler originally intended to make which film starring Audrey Hepburn as a sequel to his 1953 film *Roman Holiday*?

A. *How to Steal a Million* (1966)
B. *Love in the Afternoon* (1957)
C. *Paris When It Sizzles* (1964)
D. *Two for the Road* (1967)

85. In what film based on a James M. Cain story does a woman fall in love with a symphony conductor?

A. *Interlude* (1957)
B. *She Made Her Bed* (1934)
C. *Slightly Scarlet* (1956)
D. *Wife, Husband and Friend* (1939)

86. Which of the following stars does not appear in *Love in the Afternoon* (1957)?

A. Audrey Hepburn
B. Gary Cooper
C. Gregory Peck
D. Maurice Chevalier

87. Who is the only of *Doctor Zhivago's* (1965) actors to earn an Oscar nomination for his/her performance?

A. Geraldine Chaplin
B. Julie Christie
C. Omar Sharif
D. Tom Courtenay

88. What is the name of the de Winter house in *Rebecca* (1940)?

A. Manderley
B. Thornfield
C. Thrushcross Grange
D. Xanadu

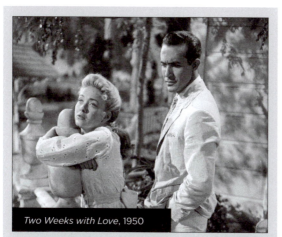

Two Weeks with Love, 1950

89. On whom did Jane Powell develop a big crush while making the film *Two Weeks with Love* (1950)?

A. Fred Astaire
B. Gene Kelly
C. Ricardo Montalban
D. Van Johnson

90. In *An Affair to Remember* (1957), what day and time do Deborah Kerr and Cary Grant plan to meet at the Empire State Building?

A. August 15 at 1 PM
B. December 24 at 11 PM
C. January 1 at 12 AM
D. July 1 at 5 PM

91. What is the name of the song that Sophia Loren performs in the film *Houseboat* (1958)?

A. "Bing! Bang! Bong!"
B. "Goodness Gracious Me"
C. "It's All the Same"
D. "What Does He Want of Me?"

92. Who plays the spirit that haunts Gene Tierney's cottage in *The Ghost and Mrs. Muir* (1947)?

A. Cary Grant
B. Dana Andrews
C. Don Ameche
D. Rex Harrison

93. What actress stars in Alexander Korda's 1941 film *That Hamilton Woman*?

A. Janet Leigh
B. Paulette Goddard
C. Rosalind Russell
D. Vivien Leigh

94. What character does Bonita Granville play in the film adaption of Lillian Hellman's *The Children's Hour*?

A. Karen
B. Lily
C. Martha
D. Mary

95. The 1950 Thelma Ritter film *I'll Get By* received its only Academy Award nomination in what category?

A. Best Art Direction
B. Best Editing
C. Best Musical Score
D. Best Screenplay

Spotlight on
DEBORAH **KERR** (1921–2007)

Deborah Kerr spent her lonely Scottish childhood dreaming of a life filled with color and drama, and got her chance while studying dance and acting. Her featured debut in a British film version of Shaw's *Major Barbara* (1941) typed Kerr as a genteel lady, but soon she would break through her typecasting and impress Hollywood with her portrayal of an arrogant nun in *Black Narcissus* (1947). MGM's Louis B. Mayer bought out Kerr's British film contract and offered her a seven-year deal. Yet despite her generous contract, MGM kept Kerr mostly in roles for which, as she recalled, "all I had to do was be high-minded, long-suffering, and decorative." But when Joan Crawford rejected the role of a promiscuous army wife in *From Here to Eternity* (1953), Kerr's agent convinced the film's producer that casting her against type would generate good publicity. She lost her British accent, her auburn hair color, and her inhibitions, rolling in the surf with Burt Lancaster in a scene that remains a classic depiction of unbridled passion (and earned her a second Oscar nomination). She continued to attract fans through the 1950s, particularly with the hit musical *The King and I* (1956) and the great romance *An Affair to Remember* (1957).

The Journey, 1959

The Prisoner of Zenda, 1952

1. **Van Johnson and Deborah Kerr costar in what film adapted from a Graham Greene novel?**

   A. *Arsenic and Old Lace* (1944)
   B. *Penny Serenade* (1941)
   C. *The End of the Affair* (1955)
   D. *Wives and Lovers* (1963)

2. **In *An Affair to Remember* (1957), Deborah Kerr meets Cary Grant when she finds his cigarette case. The inscription inside the case is written in what language?**

   A. Dutch
   B. French
   C. Italian
   D. Portuguese

3. **In *An Affair to Remember* (1957), what is Deborah Kerr's preferred drink?**

   A. Gin and tonic
   B. Pink champagne
   C. Scotch and soda
   D. Vodka

4. **In *The King and I* (1956), what does Deborah Kerr tell her son she does when she's afraid?**

   A. She blinks
   B. She scratches
   C. She stretches
   D. She whistles

5. **What is the name of the gossip columnist whose love affair with F. Scott Fitzgerald is the subject of the Deborah Kerr/Gregory Peck film *Beloved Infidel* (1959)?**

   A. Dorothy Kilgallen
   B. Hedda Hopper
   C. Liz Smith
   D. Sheilah Graham

answers found on page 564

96. While filming *Jezebel* (1938), Bette Davis had a dalliance with what director?

A. George Cukor
B. Howard Hawks
C. King Vidor
D. William Wyler

97. The 1945 film *Caesar and Cleopatra,* starring Vivien Leigh, received its only Academy Award nomination in what category?

A. Best Actress
B. Best Art Direction
C. Best Original Score
D. Best Picture

98. The 1952 William Wyler film *Carrie* stars Laurence Olivier and what actress?

A. Audrey Hepburn
B. Eleanor Parker
C. Jennifer Jones
D. Vivien Leigh

99. The popular 1940s song "Suddenly" was a reworded version of what song performed by Bing Crosby in *The Emperor Waltz* (1948)?

A. "Did You Ever See a Dream Walking"
B. "Moonlight Becomes You"
C. "Swinging on a Star"
D. "The Kiss in Your Eyes"

100. What actor stars in Henry Hathaway's 1934 film *Now and Forever?*

A. Don Ameche
B. Gary Cooper
C. John Barrymore
D. Melvyn Douglas

101. What is the first Jane Austen adaptation to win an Academy Award in any category?

A. *Emma* (1996)
B. *Mansfield Park* (1999)
C. *Pride and Prejudice* (1940)
D. *Sense and Sensibility* (1995)

102. I play the doctor who marries Bette Davis in *Dark Victory* (1939). Who am I?

A. George Brent
B. Henry Fonda
C. Humphrey Bogart
D. Leslie Howard

103. Anthony Quinn played Quasimodo in which version of *The Hunchback of Notre Dame?*

A. *The Hunchback of Notre Dame* (1923)
B. *The Hunchback of Notre Dame* (1939)
C. *The Hunchback of Notre Dame* (1957)
D. *The Hunchback of Notre Dame* (1982)

104. Which film starring Meryl Streep was adapted from a novel by Isabel Allende?

A. *Falling in Love* (1984)
B. *Still of the Night* (1982)
C. *The French Lieutenant's Woman* (1981)
D. *The House of the Spirits* (1993)

The Shop Around the Corner, 1940

105. What Van Johnson film is a remake of the 1940 James Stewart romance *The Shop Around the Corner?*

A. *Easy to Wed* (1946)
B. *In the Good Old Summertime* (1949)
C. *Mother Is a Freshman* (1949)
D. *Thrill of a Romance* (1945)

answers found on page 564

106. Who played Marlon Brando's wife in *A Streetcar Named Desire* (1951)?

A. Eva Marie Saint
B. Julie Harris
C. Kim Hunter
D. Vivien Leigh

107. What romantic drama directed by Anthony Asquith tells the love story of a working-class girl and aristocratic boy?

A. *Dance Pretty Lady* (1932)
B. *Fanny by Gaslight* (1945)
C. *Quiet Wedding* (1941)
D. *Two Fathers* (1944)

108. Samuel Goldwyn's 1944 film *The Princess and the Pirate* stars what comic actor?

A. Bob Hope
B. Danny Kaye
C. Eddie Cantor
D. Sid Caesar

109. Which star of *It's a Wonderful Life* (1946) was a star baseball player in high school?

A. Donna Reed
B. Frank Faylen
C. Gloria Grahame
D. Lionel Barrymore

110. How many Oscars did *Titanic* (1997) win?

A. 10
B. 11
C. 13
D. 9

111. In *Roman Holiday* (1953), Eddie Albert uses a photo camera disguised as a what?

A. Harmonica
B. Lighter
C. Pen
D. Pocket watch

112. Which star of 1987's *The Princess Bride* also appears in Frank Capra's *Pocketful of Miracles* (1961)?

A. Carol Kane
B. Cary Elwes
C. Mandy Patinkin
D. Peter Falk

113. What actor presented Olivia de Havilland with her Oscar for *The Heiress* (1949)?

A. Bing Crosby
B. Cary Grant
C. James Stewart
D. Robert Montgomery

114. The 1936 drama *These Three* was remade in 1961. What was its new title?

A. *Some Came Running*
B. *The Children's Hour*
C. *The Innocents*
D. *Three Coins in a Fountain*

115. Who plays Sophia Loren's young lover in 1958's *Desire Under the Elms*?

A. Anthony Perkins
B. Eddie Albert
C. Fernando Lamas
D. Jeff Chandler

116. In George Marshall's *Pot o' Gold* (1941), James Stewart falls for a singer portrayed by what actress?

A. Audrey Hepburn
B. Loretta Young
C. Paulette Goddard
D. Veronica Lake

117. What actress stars in the 1957 film *Interlude*, based on a James M. Cain story?

A. Ann Blyth
B. Joan Crawford
C. June Allyson
D. Kathryn Grayson

answers found on page 564

118. In *West Side Story* (1961), what was Russ Tamblyn?
   A. A Jet
   B. A Shark
   C. He wasn't in *West Side Story*
   D. Neither

119. Jane Russell plays a Texas heiress in search of true love in what film?
   A. *Double Dynamite* (1951)
   B. *Gentlemen Prefer Blondes* (1953)
   C. *Macao* (1952)
   D. *The French Line* (1954)

120. The 1977 film *Annie Hall* won Academy Awards in all of the following categories except which one?
   A. Best Actor
   B. Best Actress
   C. Best Director
   D. Best Picture

121. Sandra Dee and John Gavin costarred in *Imitation of Life* (1959) and what two subsequent films?
   A. *A Stranger in My Arms* (1959) and *The Restless Years* (1958)
   B. *Come September* (1961) and *That Funny Feeling* (1965)
   C. *Tammy Tell Me True* (1961) and *Romanoff and Juliet* (1961)
   D. *Written on the Wind* (1956) and *A Man Could Get Killed* (1966)

122. In *An Affair to Remember* (1957), what country are Deborah Kerr and Cary Grant visiting when they meet with his grandmother?
   A. England
   B. France
   C. Holland
   D. Italy

123. Katharine Hepburn modeled her performance in *The African Queen* (1951) after which first lady?
   A. Abigail Adams
   B. Eleanor Roosevelt
   C. Jacqueline Kennedy
   D. Nancy Reagan

124. Roddy McDowall had an uncredited role in what Peter Fonda action-romance?
   A. *Dirty Mary Crazy Larry* (1974)
   B. *Hello Down There* (1969)
   C. *The Third Day* (1965)
   D. *This England* (1941)

125. The 1937 tearjerker *Stella Dallas* starred Barbara Stanwyck in the title role. Who played her part in the 1990 remake?
   A. Bette Midler
   B. Glenn Close
   C. Michelle Pfeiffer
   D. Sally Field

126. What role in *West Side Story* (1961) did Russ Tamblyn originally try out for?
   A. Bernardo
   B. Doc
   C. Ice
   D. Tony

127. What is the name of the mission where Montgomery Clift's mother works in *A Place in the Sun* (1951)?
   A. Bethel Independent Mission
   B. Bucks Presbyterian Mission
   C. First Presbyterian Mission
   D. Grace Kansas City Mission

128. In *Roman Holiday* (1953), Princess Ann opts to drink what beverage for breakfast?
   A. Champagne
   B. Espresso
   C. Tea
   D. Wine

answers found on page 564

129. What is the name of Jack Lemmon's character in *The Apartment* (1960)?

A. C. K. Dexter Haven
B. C. C. Baxter
C. Felix Ungar
D. Weston Pringle

130. In *Desire* (1936), what stolen item does Marlene Dietrich plant on Gary Cooper?

A. Diamond
B. Earrings
C. Pearls
D. Statue

131. What actor stars in the 1934 film *This Man Is Mine,* directed by John Cromwell?

A. Don Ameche
B. Melvyn Douglas
C. Ralph Bellamy
D. Ronald Colman

132. In *That Midnight Kiss* (1949), Ethel Barrymore plays the wealthy grandmother to what beautiful singing star?

A. Jane Powell
B. Jeanette MacDonald
C. Kathryn Grayson
D. Shirley Jones

133. What actor plays the lead in Luchino Visconti's *The Leopard* (1963)?

A. Burt Lancaster
B. Marlon Brando
C. Peter O'Toole
D. Rex Harrison

134. In *Roman Holiday* (1953), what does Princess Ann routinely consume before going to sleep?

A. Gin and tonic
B. Milk and crackers
C. Milk and pudding
D. Pecan pie

135. In what European city does Audrey Hepburn's *Sabrina* (1954) undergo her shocking transformation?

A. Berlin
B. Madrid
C. Paris
D. Rome

136. How many Oscar nominations did *From Here to Eternity* (1953) earn in acting categories?

A. 0
B. 1
C. 3
D. 5

137. What was the real-life pen name of Meryl Streep's character in the 1985 Academy Award–winning film *Out of Africa*?

A. Isak Dinesen
B. Isak Westenholz
C. Karen Finch
D. Karen Rungstedlund

138. Who romances Greta Garbo in the 1936 film *Camille*?

A. Fredric March
B. John Gilbert
C. Melvyn Douglas
D. Robert Taylor

139. What is the name of Jean Harlow's character in the 1932 film *Red Dust*?

A. Valentine
B. Vantine
C. Veruca
D. Virgilia

140. What actress stars in the 1944 film *Since You Went Away,* directed by John Cromwell?

A. Claudette Colbert
B. Ginger Rogers
C. Lana Turner
D. Lauren Bacall

141. What Frank Capra film is ranked #1 Most Powerful Movie of All Time by the American Film Institute?

    A. *It Happened One Night* (1934)
    B. *It's a Wonderful Life* (1946)
    C. *Meet John Doe* (1941)
    D. *Pocketful of Miracles* (1961)

A Guy Named Joe, 1943

142. The 1943 film *A Guy Named Joe* received its only Academy Award nomination in what category?

    A. Best Cinematography
    B. Best Director
    C. Best Visual Effects
    D. Best Writing, Original Story

143. The theme of romance between royalty and a commoner pervades all of the following films directed by Richard Thorpe except for which one?

    A. *Her Highness and the Bellboy* (1945)
    B. *The Midnight Lady* (1932)
    C. *The Prisoner of Zenda* (1952)
    D. *The Student Prince* (1954)

144. What is the name of Katharine Ross's character in *The Graduate* (1967)?

    A. Cynthia
    B. Elaine
    C. Melanie
    D. Sarah

145. Who costarred with Leslie Howard in the 1939 film *Intermezzo: A Love Story*?

    A. Greer Garson
    B. Greta Garbo
    C. Ingrid Bergman
    D. Irene Dunne

146. For what film did Emma Thompson win her first Oscar in a nonacting category?

    A. *Portrait of a Lady* (1996)
    B. *Pride and Prejudice* (2005)
    C. *Remains of the Day* (1993)
    D. *Sense and Sensibility* (1995)

147. What actress stars in the 1939 film *Made for Each Other*, directed by John Cromwell?

    A. Carole Lombard
    B. Ginger Rogers
    C. Lucille Ball
    D. Rosalind Russell

148. What Oscar did *Operation Petticoat* (1959) vie for in 1960?

    A. Best Original Screenplay
    B. Best Picture
    C. Best Supporting Actor
    D. Best Supporting Actress

149. Who romances Hedy Lamarr in *Algiers* (1938)?

    A. Charles Boyer
    B. Robert Taylor
    C. Spencer Tracy
    D. Tom Mix

150. In the 1963 film *Love with the Proper Stranger*, Natalie Wood's character works at what department store?

    A. Bloomingdale's
    B. Macy's
    C. Neiman Marcus
    D. Saks Fifth Avenue

151. Jennifer Jones's character falls in love with poet Robert Browning in what biopic?

    A. *Love Is a Many-Splendored Thing* (1955)
    B. *The Barretts of Wimpole Street* (1957)
    C. *The Wild Heart* (1952)
    D. *We Were Strangers* (1949)

152. What was the only Academy Award category for which *West Side Story* (1961) was nominated that it failed to win?

    A. Best Actress in a Supporting Role
    B. Best Costume Design, Color
    C. Best Director
    D. Best Writing, Screenplay Based on Material from Another Medium

153. The 1964 Kim Novak film *Of Human Bondage* was based on a novel by what author?

    A. Charles Dickens
    B. Ernest Hemingway
    C. Victor Hugo
    D. W. Somerset Maugham

154. What film pairing Clark Gable and Doris Day was originally a drama that was later rewritten as a comedy?

    A. *Pillow Talk* (1959)
    B. *Tea for Two* (1950)
    C. *Teacher's Pet* (1958)
    D. *The Winning Team* (1952)

155. In the film *Wuthering Heights* (1939), featuring Merle Oberon, how many chapters from the thirty-four chapter book are covered?

    A. 16
    B. 22
    C. 3
    D. 34

156. Who plays Ernest Borgnine's wife in the 1956 film *The Catered Affair*?

    A. Angela Lansbury
    B. Bette Davis

C. Joan Crawford
D. Olivia de Havilland

157. Cornel Wilde romances Simone Signoret in what film?

    A. *Swiss Tour* (1950)
    B. *The Girl Who Had Everything* (1953)
    C. *The Spiral Staircase* (1945)
    D. *Tonight We Sing* (1953)

158. Who plays Paul Henreid's wife in the 1947 film *Song of Love*?

    A. Doris Day
    B. Joan Crawford
    C. Katharine Hepburn
    D. Kathryn Grayson

159. Truman Capote strongly disapproved of Audrey Hepburn's casting in *Breakfast at Tiffany's* (1961). Who was his first choice for the role?

    A. Anne Baxter
    B. Janet Leigh
    C. Kim Novak
    D. Marilyn Monroe

160. The 1960 film *The Apartment* was turned into a Broadway musical in 1968. What was it retitled?

    A. *Executive Washroom*
    B. *Keys to the Kingdom*
    C. *Promises, Promises*
    D. *Somebody's Knocking*

161. Who plays Janet Gaynor's love interest in the 1934 film *Carolina*?

    A. Clark Gable
    B. Gary Cooper
    C. Ralph Bellamy
    D. Robert Young

answers found on page 564

Spotlight on
CLARK **GABLE** (1901–1960)

Clark Gable was a star tailor-made for the thirties. Stage training gave him a perfect voice for talking pictures, while his size and rough features made him a fitting idol for Depression-weary Americans who wished they could stand up to adversity so well. His first important film assignment was as the gangster who roughs up Norma Shearer in *A Free Soul* (1931), and fans found his presence so exciting they didn't take offense to the role. For a while, Gable was so typecast in roughhouse roles he started refusing scripts in that vein. Studio head Louis B. Mayer decided to punish him with a loan-out to Columbia, a much less successful studio, for a film that seemed to be just another programmer. Instead, *It Happened One Night* (1934) was a huge hit that put director Frank Capra on the map and won Gable an Oscar. When the book *Gone with the Wind* became a runaway bestseller, fans clamored for him to play Rhett Butler. Gable initially resisted but gave in when MGM agreed to pay a divorce settlement to his second wife so he could marry Carole Lombard. Thus, his real-life romance landed him the ultimate romantic lead, and he would go on to play many such dashing rogues.

Red Dust, 1932

Gone With the Wind, 1939

1. Which Oscar-nominated actress once declared, "When Clark Gable kissed me, they had to carry me off the set"?

   A. Carroll Baker
   B. Eleanor Parker
   C. Natalie Wood
   D. Norma Shearer

2. In *Red Dust* (1932), Clark Gable has his eye on Jean Harlow and what other actress?

   A. Carole Lombard
   B. Grace Kelly
   C. Loretta Young
   D. Mary Astor

3. Mary Astor starred with Clark Gable in how many films?

   A. 4
   B. 3
   C. 2
   D. 1

4. Clark Gable danced and sang "Puttin' on the Ritz" in which film?

   A. *Boom Town* (1940)
   B. *Idiot's Delight* (1939)
   C. *Love on the Run* (1936)
   D. *They Met in Bombay* (1941)

5. In which of the following films does Clark Gable romance Doris Day?

   A. *Julie* (1956)
   B. *Teacher's Pet* (1958)
   C. *The Glass Bottom Boat* (1966)
   D. *With Six You Get Eggroll* (1968)

---

answers found on pages 564–565

ROMANCE **429**

162. *Sweet Charity* (1969) is a remake of a 1957 Oscar-winning film from what country?

A. Britain's *The Long Day Closes*
B. France's *Jules and Jim*
C. Germany's *Aguirre: The Wrath of God*
D. Italy's *Nights of Cabiria*

163. Franchot Tone romances Katharine Hepburn in what film directed by George Stevens?

A. *Quality Street* (1937)
B. *The More the Merrier* (1943)
C. *The Talk of the Town* (1942)
D. *Woman of the Year* (1942)

164. Which leading lady plays Elizabeth in 1940's *Pride and Prejudice*?

A. Deborah Kerr
B. Greer Garson
C. Katharine Hepburn
D. Vivien Leigh

165. Joseph Cotten costars in the 1941 film *Lydia*. What actress plays the title role?

A. Hedy Lamarr
B. Jennifer Jones
C. Loretta Young
D. Merle Oberon

166. What 1922 romance was the first of Rudolph Valentino's films for Famous Players-Lasky for which he received star billing?

A. *Blood and Sand*
B. *Cobra*
C. *Monsieur Beaucaire*
D. *The Four Horsemen of the Apocalypse*

167. The Sandra Dee film *The Reluctant Debutante* (1958) was remade into what 2003 comedy starring Colin Firth and Amanda Bynes?

A. *Hope Springs*
B. *Love Actually*
C. *The Importance of Being Earnest*
D. *What a Girl Wants*

168. The characters played by Van Johnson and Deborah Kerr in the 1955 film *The End of the Affair* were later portrayed by which pair in the 1999 remake?

A. Brad Pitt and Penelope Cruz
B. Daniel Day-Lewis and Nicole Kidman
C. George Clooney and Vera Farmiga
D. Ralph Fiennes and Julianne Moore

169. Which of the following actors did not appear in Samuel Goldwyn's big-screen version of *Porgy and Bess* (1959)?

A. Dorothy Dandridge
B. John Amos
C. Sammy Davis Jr.
D. Sidney Poitier

170. The 1960 Jules Dassin film *Never on Sunday* is about a woman who is a what?

A. Hairdresser
B. Nun
C. Prostitute
D. Teacher

171. The lead role in *Jezebel* (1938) was allegedly offered to Bette Davis as consolation for losing which part?

A. Lucie Dreyfus in *The Life of Emile Zola* (1937)
B. Lucy Warriner in *The Awful Truth* (1937)
C. Scarlett O'Hara in *Gone With the Wind* (1939)
D. Maid Marian in *The Adventures of Robin Hood* (1938)

172. Alexander Korda produced the 1948 film *Anna Karenina,* which was based on a novel by what author?

A. Charlotte Brontë
B. Henry James
C. James Joyce
D. Leo Tolstoy

answers found on page 565

173. In *Roman Holiday* (1953), Eddie Albert plays a what?

A. Barber
B. Musician
C. Photographer
D. Secret agent

174. What film starring Janet Gaynor is about a poor girl who falls in love with a wealthy man?

A. *Bernadine* (1957)
B. *Lucky Star* (1929)
C. *Sunnyside Up* (1929)
D. *Sunrise: A Song of Two Humans* (1927)

175. What actor appears with Moira Shearer in the 1953 film *The Story of Three Loves*?

A. Burt Lancaster
B. David Niven
C. James Mason
D. Sean Connery

Saratoga Trunk, 1945

176. The "trunk" in the title of 1945's *Saratoga Trunk* refers to what?

A. A railroad line
B. A special fashion show
C. A storage box
D. An elephant

177. The 1948 film *The Red Shoes* received Academy Award nominations in all of the following categories except which one?

A. Best Actress

B. Best Art Direction
C. Best Editing
D. Best Picture

178. What is the name of the play that the film *These Three* (1936), featuring Merle Oberon, was based upon?

A. *The Children's Hour*
B. *The Three Little Children*
C. *These Three Children of Mine*
D. *These Two*

179. Oscar-nominated *Love Story* (1970) scribe Erich Segal is also a respected scholar of what subject?

A. Classics
B. Film history
C. Physics
D. Statistics

180. Marni Nixon (dubbing for Deborah Kerr) sings the Oscar-nominated title song from *An Affair to Remember* (1957) in the film. Which crooner sings it over the credits?

A. Eddie Fisher
B. Paul Anka
C. Tony Bennett
D. Vic Damone

181. In *Christmas in Connecticut* (1945), Barbara Stanwyck's character writes a magazine article on what subject?

A. Beauty
B. Cooking
C. Shopping
D. Sports

182. Jean Hagen appears in what film opposite Ricardo Montalban?

A. *Latin Lovers* (1953)
B. *Mark of the Renegade* (1951)
C. *Sayonara* (1957)
D. *The Reluctant Saint* (1962)

answers found on page 565

183. What is the name of Paul Henreid's character in *Casablanca* (1942)?

A. Captain Renault
B. Rick Blaine
C. Ugarte
D. Victor Laszlo

184. Who is Audrey Hepburn's costar in *The Children's Hour* (1961)?

A. Anne Bancroft
B. Julie Andrews
C. Katharine Hepburn
D. Shirley MacLaine

185. Joseph Cotten costarred with Jennifer Jones in all of the following films except what?

A. *Duel in the Sun* (1946)
B. *Love Letters* (1945)
C. *Niagara* (1953)
D. *Portrait of Jennie* (1948)

186. The 1947 film *Green Dolphin Street* was nominated for four Academy Awards. How many did it win?

A. 0
B. 1
C. 2
D. 3

187. Who romances Kim Novak in the 1955 film *Picnic*?

A. Burt Lancaster
B. John Gavin
C. Kirk Douglas
D. William Holden

188. Sandy Dennis plays a lonely woman in love with another woman in what film?

A. *Splendor in the Grass* (1961)
B. *Sweet November* (1968)
C. *The Fox* (1968)
D. *The Out-of-Towners* (1970)

189. The 1935 film *The Farmer Takes a Wife*, starring Janet Gaynor, marked the feature film debut of what actor?

A. Clark Gable
B. Henry Fonda
C. James Stewart
D. John Wayne

190. In *An Affair to Remember* (1957), Deborah Kerr tells Cary Grant that her mother told her never to enter a man's room during months ending in what letter?

A. E
B. H
C. R
D. Y

191. The 1927 film *7th Heaven*, starring Janet Gaynor, is set in what city?

A. Florence
B. London
C. Paris
D. Rome

192. Van Johnson appears in what Woody Allen film?

A. *Broadway Danny Rose* (1984)
B. *Celebrity* (1998)
C. *Mighty Aphrodite* (1995)
D. *The Purple Rose of Cairo* (1985)

193. What is the only film to star Ava Gardner and Humphrey Bogart?

A. *Mogambo* (1953)
B. *Sabrina* (1954)
C. *The Barefoot Contessa* (1954)
D. *The Killers* (1946)

194. The 1948 film *The Red Shoes*, starring Moira Shearer, was based on a story by what author?

A. Dr. Seuss
B. Hans Christian Andersen
C. L. Frank Baum
D. Roald Dahl

answers found on page 565

195. What film pairing Fred Astaire and Ginger Rogers was based on a true story?

A. *For Me and My Gal* (1942)
B. *It's Always Fair Weather* (1955)
C. *The Happy Road* (1957)
D. *The Story of Vernon and Irene Castle* (1939)

196. The "Mouth of Truth" scene from *Roman Holiday* (1953) is either shown or referenced in all of the following films except for which one?

A. *L.A. Confidential* (1997)
B. *Only You* (1994)
C. *The Twilight Saga: New Moon* (2009)
D. *You, Me and Dupree* (2006)

197. Who plays Anne Bancroft's daughter in the 1967 film *The Graduate*?

A. Ann-Margret
B. Katharine Ross
C. Patty Duke
D. Shelley Fabares

198. In which of the following films does Fred MacMurray play Katharine Hepburn's love interest?

A. *Alice Adams* (1935)
B. *Little Women* (1933)
C. *Pat and Mike* (1952)
D. *The Philadelphia Story* (1940)

199. In *One Sunday Afternoon* (1933), what is the profession of Gary Cooper's character?

A. Architect
B. Banker
C. Dentist
D. Preacher

200. Audrey Hepburn sings "La Vie en Rose" in a scene in which film?

A. *Breakfast at Tiffany's* (1961)
B. *Paris When It Sizzles* (1964)
C. *Roman Holiday* (1953)
D. *Sabrina* (1954)

201. The 1963 epic *Cleopatra* was primarily filmed on location in what city?

A. Alexandria, Egypt
B. Nice, France
C. Rome, Italy
D. Tangier, Morocco

202. Which actress plays Rex Harrison's love interest in *Storm in a Teacup* (1937)?

A. Dorothy McGuire
B. Ingrid Bergman
C. Jane Wyman
D. Vivien Leigh

203. In the 1979 film *A Little Romance,* directed by George Roy Hill, two young lovers travel to what city in order to share a kiss?

A. Berlin
B. Florence
C. Venice
D. Vienna

204. What actor stars in Alexander Korda's 1945 film *Perfect Strangers*?

A. David Niven
B. Robert Donat
C. Spencer Tracy
D. William Powell

205. Thelma Ritter stars in the 1963 film *A New Kind of Love*. In what city does the story take place?

A. Cairo
B. Florence
C. London
D. Paris

206. The 1932 Frank Borzage film *A Farewell to Arms* is based on the novel by what famous author?

A. Charles Dickens
B. Ernest Hemingway
C. F. Scott Fitzgerald
D. John Steinbeck

answers found on page 565

207. In the 1991 film *The Prince of Tides*, Barbra Streisand plays a what?

A. Chef
B. Poet
C. Psychiatrist
D. Violinist

208. What film starring Merle Oberon was later remade as a two-hour episode of the television series *The Love Boat*?

A. *'Til We Meet Again* (1940)
B. *Big Hearted Herbert* (1934)
C. *No Time for Comedy* (1940)
D. *Yes, My Darling Daughter* (1939)

None but the Lonely Heart, 1944

209. The 1944 Ethel Barrymore film *None but the Lonely Heart* marked the directorial debut of which famous screenwriter?

A. Clifford Odets
B. Dalton Trumbo
C. Garson Kanin
D. Henry Ephron

210. In which production did Stewart Granger portray Prince Philip, Duke of Edinburgh?

A. *Diana: Her True Story* (1992)
B. *The Queen's Sister* (2005)
C. *The Royal Romance of Charles and Diana* (1982)
D. *Young Bess* (1953)

211. Who wrote the novel that inspired the Bette Davis film *Now, Voyager* (1942)?

A. Gore Vidal
B. John Updike
C. Olive Higgins Prouty
D. W. Somerset Maugham

212. Sandra Dee played Susie in *Imitation of Life* (1959), but who was Universal's first choice for the role?

A. Deanna Durbin
B. Elizabeth Taylor
C. Jeanne Crain
D. Natalie Wood

213. What is the name of the character portrayed by Bette Davis in *Jezebel* (1938)?

A. Judith Traherne
B. Julie Mardsen
C. Katherine Porter
D. Margo Channing

214. Who plays Juliet to Leslie Howard's Romeo in the 1936 film *Romeo and Juliet*?

A. Irene Dunne
B. Merle Oberon
C. Norma Shearer
D. Olivia de Havilland

215. The 1936 film *Ladies in Love*, starring Janet Gaynor, is set in what city?

A. Budapest
B. Istanbul
C. Moscow
D. Vienna

216. In which category did the Rex Harrison hit *The Ghost and Mrs. Muir* (1947) receive its only Academy Award nomination?

A. Best Adapted Screenplay
B. Best Cinematography
C. Best Director
D. Best Supporting Actor

217. The 1961 film *The Children's Hour* received Academy Award nominations in all of the following categories except which one?

A. Best Actress
B. Best Art Direction
C. Best Cinematography
D. Best Supporting Actress

218. Ava Gardner's character in *The Barefoot Contessa* (1954) is loosely based on what other leading lady?

A. Grace Kelly
B. Jean Harlow
C. Marion Davies
D. Rita Hayworth

219. Who was the only actress to play Elvis Presley's love interest in three films?

A. Ann-Margret
B. Natalie Wood
C. Shelley Fabares
D. Ursula Andress

220. The 1942 film *Now, Voyager* won one Academy Award. What was it for?

A. Best Actress
B. Best Editing
C. Best Original Score
D. Best Picture

221. Which French actor had the lead role in the 1990 film *Cyrano de Bergerac?*

A. Daniel Auteuil
B. Gérard Depardieu
C. Vincent Cassel
D. Jean Renaud

222. Who plays Jane Powell's love interest in *Two Weeks with Love* (1950)?

A. Desi Arnaz
B. Howard Keel
C. Ricardo Montalban
D. Van Johnson

223. In the title of the 1947 film *The Ghost and Mrs. Muir*, the word "Muir" means what in Gaelic?

A. Cloud
B. Lighthouse
C. Mirror
D. Sea

224. Who won an Academy Award for the score to *Love Is a Many-Splendored Thing* (1955)?

A. Alfred Newman
B. Charles Henderson
C. Irving Berlin
D. Ken Darby

225. What Oscar did *I Married a Witch* vie for in 1943?

A. Best Actress
B. Best Director
C. Best Picture
D. Best Scoring of a Dramatic or Comedy Picture

226. What actor did not costar with Jean Harlow in the 1937 film *Saratoga*?

A. Clark Gable
B. Lionel Barrymore
C. Spencer Tracy
D. Walter Pidgeon

Angels with Dirty Faces, 1938

Chapter 15
CRIME

Killers and crooks, private eyes and public enemies—the movies have a long-standing love affair with people who shoot, stab, poison, and punch. The public's fascination with illegal activities can be traced to the earliest days of Greek tragedy, when all good dramas had a body count. Twenty-five hundred years later, some of the screen's most famous criminals—Tony Camonte in 1932's *Scarface* (called Tony Montana in the 1983 remake), Cody Jarrett in *White Heat* (1949), and Michael Corleone in *The Godfather* saga—have achieved tragic stature in their battles against society and personal demons.

When criminals get organized, it almost always spells big box office. Gangster figures turned up throughout the silent years, most notably in D. W. Griffith's 1912 *The Musketeers of Pig Alley*. But the genre didn't really take

shape until the coming of sound made it possible to enhance the drama with screeching tires, fast-clipped speech, and the rattle of tommy guns. With Prohibition still in force, the organizations that trafficked in illegal liquor were often viewed as a social necessity, so the first gangster films tended to view their protagonists sympathetically, as victims of social inequality. As a result, the three pictures that established the form's popularity—*Little Caesar* (1931), *The Public Enemy* (1931), and *Scarface* (1932)—made stars of their leading men, Edward G. Robinson, James Cagney, and Paul Muni, respectively.

The gangster has proven to be one of the screen's most versatile character types. Films like *Dead End* (1937), with Humphrey Bogart, and Cagney's *White Heat* focused on the psychology of the criminals, while *The Roaring Twenties* (1939) and *High Sierra* (1941) made him a victim of changing times, the last honorable man in an increasingly corrupt world. Lee J. Cobb's mob-controlled union boss in *On the Waterfront* (1954) symbolized a corrupt system out to get the little man. And Billy Wilder made gang leaders the butt of some of his best jokes in *Some Like It Hot* (1959). Legendary gangsters even became counterculture figures in the sixties when *Bonnie and Clyde* (1967) turned robbing banks into a social revolution.

Francis Ford Coppola created the ultimate gangster epic with his three *Godfather* films, released in 1972, 1974, and 1990. Tracing the history of the Corleone family from their emigration at the turn of the century through the late seventies, he painted a picture of organized crime as just another American business, neither less deadly nor less corrupt than those operating under full public scrutiny.

Corruption is at the center of another classic crime genre, the film noir. Set in a world of crooked politicians, duplicitous females, and mostly honest private eyes, the form rose to prominence shortly after World War II, as people began to raise doubts about what we had really been fighting for. Detective fiction proved a particularly fertile source for film noir, which brought to life the works of such acclaimed crime writers as Dashiell Hammett and Raymond Chandler. But the spirit of corruption and desolation could pervade almost any genre, including romance in *The Postman Always Rings Twice* (1946) and the woman's picture in *Mildred Pierce* (1945).

Shot with oppressive camera angles, usually in deeply shadowed black and white, the genre produced a memorable gallery of twisted characters. Humphrey Bogart in *The Big Sleep* (1946) and Ralph Meeker in *Kiss Me Deadly* (1955) epitomized the tough, opportunistic yet still honorable private eye picking away at society's scabs. Orson Welles took the corrupt politico to new heights in *Touch of Evil* (1958), while Ronald Reagan left the movies for politics after a memorable turn as a gangland chief in *The Killers* (1964). But the most memorable were the femmes fatales, some of the toughest ladies ever to saunter across the screen. What man could stand up to Barbara Stanwyck as the icy blonde murderess in *Double Indemnity* (1944)? Or resist the twisted pleasures offered by Rita Hayworth in *Gilda* (1946)? Or see through Claire Trevor's seductive lies in *Murder, My Sweet* (1944)?

A few shades down the color palette from film noir are the suspense thrillers, covering a range of crimes from blackmail to grand larceny, all of them leading inevitably to murder most foul. Murder lifted the lid on sexual hypocrisy in Otto Preminger's *Anatomy of a Murder* (1959) and exposed racial prejudice in Norman Jewison's *In the Heat of the Night* (1967). But it was never as entertaining as in the hands of Alfred Hitchcock. The Master of Suspense made crime intriguing, slightly absurd, and unsettlingly seductive, even tricking audiences into identifying with twisted killers like Bruno Antony in *Strangers on a Train* (1951) and Norman Bates in *Psycho* (1960). His classic studies in mystery and mayhem proved conclusively that in Hollywood, at least, crime always pays.

1. Jean Hagen appears in what film noir drama opposite Ida Lupino?

   A. *Hotel Berlin* (1945)
   B. *Mysterious Mr. Moto* (1938)
   C. *Stranger on the Third Floor* (1940)
   D. *The Big Knife* (1955)

2. Ida Lupino falls in love with John Garfield in what film?

   A. *High Sierra* (1941)
   B. *Out of the Fog* (1941)
   C. *The Sea Wolf* (1941)
   D. *While the City Sleeps* (1956)

3. Who designed the strapless gown worn by Rita Hayworth in *Gilda* (1946)?

   A. Christian Dior
   B. Ernest Dryden
   C. Jean Louis
   D. Odette Myrtil

4. Franz Waxman composed the suspenseful music for the 1936 thriller *Fury* starring Spencer Tracy. Who was the director?

   A. Alfred Hitchcock
   B. Billy Wilder
   C. Fritz Lang
   D. Josef von Sternberg

5. Which of the following films edited by Anne V. Coates does not star Peter O'Toole?

   A. *Becket* (1964)
   B. *Great Catherine* (1968)
   C. *Lawrence of Arabia* (1962)
   D. *Murder on the Orient Express* (1974)

6. In which of his films did director Jules Dassin act under the name of "Perlo Vita"?

   A. *Never on Sunday* (1960)
   B. *Night and the City* (1950)
   C. *Topkapi* (1964)
   D. *Rififi* (1955)

King of the Underworld, 1939

7. What is the profession of Kay Francis's character in the 1939 film *King of the Underworld*?

   A. Doctor
   B. Fashion designer
   C. Singer
   D. Waitress

8. What was the first Alfred Hitchcock film in which James Stewart starred? (Film dates hidden to conceal answer.)

   A. *Rear Window*
   B. *Rope*
   C. *The Man Who Knew Too Much*
   D. *Vertigo*

9. What actress presented Marlon Brando with his 1954 Best Actor Oscar for *On the Waterfront*?

   A. Bette Davis
   B. Grace Kelly
   C. Ingrid Bergman
   D. Katharine Hepburn

10. Who is Jean Harlow's costar in *The Public Enemy* (1931)?

   A. Humphrey Bogart
   B. James Cagney
   C. John Garfield
   D. Spencer Tracy

11. What actress costarred in the 1950 film *Night and the City,* directed by Jules Dassin?

    A. Barbara Stanwyck
    B. Gene Tierney
    C. Loretta Young
    D. Maureen O'Hara

12. In what film does Dick Van Dyke play an actor who finds himself in the company of a notorious gangster when he is mistaken for a killer?

    A. *Cold Turkey* (1971)
    B. *Fitzwilly* (1967)
    C. *Never a Dull Moment* (1968)
    D. *Some Kind of a Nut* (1969)

13. Which actor portrayed Marlon Brando's Vito Corleone character as a young man in *The Godfather Part II* (1974)?

    A. Al Pacino
    B. James Caan
    C. Robert De Niro
    D. Robert Duvall

14. George Raft and Edward Arnold star in what film noir?

    A. *Stranger on the Third Floor* (1940)
    B. *The Glass Key* (1935)
    C. *The Maltese Falcon* (1941)
    D. *The Spiral Staircase* (1945)

15. What is the name of Thelma Ritter's character in the 1954 film *Rear Window*?

    A. Charlotte
    B. Joan
    C. Molly
    D. Stella

16. Who directed James Cagney in *Angels with Dirty Faces* (1938)?

    A. Clarence Brown
    B. George Cukor
    C. Michael Curtiz
    D. Tod Browning

17. The 1981 film version of James M. Cain's *The Postman Always Rings Twice* stars what actress?

    A. Cathy Moriarty
    B. Jessica Lange
    C. Jill Clayburgh
    D. Kathleen Turner

18. The 1934 Fay Wray film *Woman in the Dark* was based on a story by what famous author?

    A. Agatha Christie
    B. Dashiell Hammett
    C. Mickey Spillane
    D. Raymond Chandler

19. How many times did Pat O'Brien, Frank McHugh, and James Cagney work together?

    A. 2
    B. 4
    C. 5
    D. 7

20. In which of the following films directed by Fritz Lang does Roddy McDowall appear?

    A. *Fury* (1936)
    B. *Man Hunt* (1941)
    C. *Scarlet Street* (1945)
    D. *Western Union* (1941)

21. What film jump-started Glenn Ford's career after he returned from service in WWII?

    A. *A Stolen Life* (1946)
    B. *Framed* (1947)
    C. *Gallant Journey* (1946)
    D. *Gilda* (1946)

22. How old was James Cagney when he made *Ragtime* (1981)?

    A. 77
    B. 79
    C. 81
    D. 83

answers found on page 565

Murder, My Sweet, 1944

23. The 1944 film *Murder, My Sweet,* starring Dick Powell and Claire Trevor, is based on which Raymond Chandler novel?
A. *The Little Sister*
B. *The High Window*
C. *The Long Goodbye*
D. *Farewell, My Lovely*

24. Farley Granger stars in *Rope* (1948) and what other film directed by Alfred Hitchcock?
A. *Foreign Correspondent* (1940)
B. *Notorious* (1946)
C. *Spellbound* (1945)
D. *Strangers on a Train* (1951)

25. In which film does Marlon Brando parody his role as Don Corleone in *The Godfather* (1972)?
A. *A Dry White Season* (1989)
B. *Don Juan de Marco* (1995)
C. *The Freshman* (1990)
D. *The Island of Dr. Moreau* (1996)

26. Stephen McNally plays Sydney Poitier's mentor in what social drama about an African-American doctor's run-in with a racist gangster?
A. *Bad for Each Other* (1953)
B. *Bedlam* (1946)
C. *No Way Out* (1950)
D. *Not as a Stranger* (1955)

27. What was the name of George Hamilton's character in *The Godfather III* (1990)?
A. Al Neri
B. Anthony Corleone
C. B. J. Harrison
D. Vincent Mancini

28. Boris Karloff plays the character Gaffney in what film starring Paul Muni?
A. *Glory Alley* (1952)
B. *Scarface* (1932)
C. *The Breaking Point* (1950)
D. *They Drive by Night* (1940)

29. Vincente Minnelli directed Robert Taylor and Katharine Hepburn in what film noir thriller?
A. *High Wall* (1947)
B. *Hotel Berlin* (1945)
C. *Passage to Marseille* (1944)
D. *Undercurrent* (1946)

30. Teresa Wright has a murderer for an uncle in what Alfred Hitchcock film?
A. *Mrs. Miniver* (1942)
B. *Shadow of a Doubt* (1943)
C. *The Best Years of Our Lives* (1946)
D. *The Little Foxes* (1941)

31. Part of a quote from Rudyard Kipling's poem "If" is visible in what Alfred Hitchcock thriller?
A. *Rear Window* (1954)
B. *Strangers on a Train* (1951)
C. *The Birds* (1963)
D. *Vertigo* (1958)

32. Who was James Cagney's character in *White Heat* (1949)?
A. Arthur "Cody" Jarrett
B. Johnny "Red" Cave
C. Nick "Nicky" Butler
D. Richard "Patsy" Gargan

answers found on page 565

33. Jack Carson plays Wally Fay in what film noir classic?
   A. *A Lady Without Passport* (1950)
   B. *Mildred Pierce* (1945)
   C. *The Conspirators* (1944)
   D. *The Strange Woman* (1946)

34. In the 1953 film *Niagara*, who plays Joseph Cotten's wife?
   A. Ava Gardner
   B. Grace Kelly
   C. Kim Novak
   D. Marilyn Monroe

35. Who directed the film *Dead End* (1937)?
   A. Allan Dwan
   B. John Ford
   C. Raoul Walsh
   D. William Wyler

36. Ava Gardner double-crosses the former boxer played by Burt Lancaster in what 1946 Hemingway adaptation?
   A. *Night and the City*
   B. *The Big Sleep*
   C. *The Killers*
   D. *The Maltese Falcon*

37. Which film noir is directed by Jules Dassin and stars Richard Widmark and Gene Tierney?
   A. *Cat People* (1942)
   B. *Laura* (1944)
   C. *Night and the City* (1950)
   D. *Panic in the Streets* (1950)

38. What James Cagney film had the characters Mamie, Putty Nose, and Nails Nathan?
   A. *Angels with Dirty Faces* (1938)
   B. *The Public Enemy* (1931)
   C. *The Roaring Twenties* (1939)
   D. *White Heat* (1949)

39. What is the name of Barbara Stanwyck's character in the 1944 film *Double Indemnity*?
   A. Cora Smith
   B. Matty Walker
   C. Phyllis Dietrichson
   D. Sheila Simpson

40. What item of jewelry is Barbara Stanwyck famous for wearing in *Double Indemnity* (1944)?
   A. A belly ring
   B. A tiara
   C. An ankle bracelet
   D. An arm band

41. Shirley MacLaine made her screen debut in what Hitchcock film for which Bernard Herrmann wrote the musical score?
   A. *Strangers on a Train* (1951)
   B. *The Man Who Knew Too Much* (1956)
   C. *The Trouble with Harry* (1955)
   D. *Vertigo* (1958)

42. Which of the following films based on a Ray Bradbury story concerns two boys who meet a mysterious character at a carnival?
   A. *Something Wicked This Way Comes* (1983)
   B. *The Beast from 20,000 Fathoms* (1953)
   C. *The Illustrated Man* (1969)
   D. *The Picasso Summer* (1969)

43. George Raft plays "Spats" in what comedy directed by Billy Wilder?
   A. *Love in Pawn* (1953)
   B. *Some Like It Hot* (1959)
   C. *The Fortune Cookie* (1966)
   D. *The Moon Is Blue* (1953)

44. Henry Fonda and Marlene Dietrich both make cameo appearances in which film noir?
   A. *High Sierra* (1941)
   B. *Jigsaw* (1949)
   C. *The Maltese Falcon* (1941)
   D. *To Have and Have Not* (1944)

answers found on page 565

45. Name the accused murderess portrayed by Susan Hayward in *I Want to Live!* (1958)

A. Barbara Graham
B. Kitty O'Shea
C. Lena Jennings
D. Maggie Cutler

46. For what film did Jules Dassin win the Best Director Award at the Cannes Film Festival?

A. *Never on Sunday* (1960)
B. *Rififi* (1955)
C. *The Naked City* (1948)
D. *Thieves' Highway* (1949)

Johnny Eager, 1941

47. Who costarred with Lana Turner in the 1941 crime classic *Johnny Eager*?

A. David Niven
B. Clark Gable
C. Robert Taylor
D. Henry Fonda

48. For what film did Claire Trevor receive an Oscar nomination, despite only appearing in one scene?

A. *Crossroads* (1942)
B. *Dark Command* (1940)
C. *Dead End* (1937)
D. *Stagecoach* (1939)

49. Mary Astor plays a scheming temptress who commits murder in what John Huston film?

A. *Dodsworth* (1936)
B. *Meet Me in St. Louis* (1944)
C. *The Maltese Falcon* (1941)
D. *The Prisoner of Zenda* (1937)

50. The 1933 Anna May Wong film *A Study in Scarlet* features what famous detective character?

A. Charlie Chan
B. Hercule Poirot
C. Miss Marple
D. Sherlock Holmes

51. Edward Arnold and Donna Reed costar in what mystery-thriller?

A. *Escape* (1940)
B. *Eyes in the Night* (1942)
C. *Scandal Sheet* (1952)
D. *They Were Expendable* (1945)

52. What was the name of the television show hosted by George Sanders?

A. *Crimes and Sleuths*
B. *The Falcon*
C. *The George Sanders Mystery Theater*
D. *The Mystery Hour*

53. In what film does Jean Harlow costar with James Cagney?

A. *Hell's Angels* (1930)
B. *Saratoga* (1937)
C. *The Public Enemy* (1931)
D. *The Secret Six* (1931)

54. Marlon Brando refused to accept the Best Actor Academy Award for *The Godfather* (1972), but he did accept the award when he won for what other film?

A. *A Streetcar Named Desire* (1951)
B. *Julius Caesar* (1953)
C. *Mutiny on the Bounty* (1962)
D. *On the Waterfront* (1954)

answers found on page 565

Spotlight on
PAUL **MUNI** (1895–1967)

Paul Muni never wanted to be a star, saying, "I think 'star' is what you call actors who can't act." But ultimately, his unerring talent for humanizing characters brought him screen stardom in a wide variety of roles. The child of actors, he rose to prominence at New York's Yiddish Art Theater, debuting there at the age of twelve in the role of an eighty-year-old man. He made his Broadway debut in 1926, the first he had performed in English. Stage work brought him to Fox, where he won an Oscar nomination for his film debut in *The Valiant* and then played seven characters, including Napoleon and Franz Schubert, in *Seven Faces* (both 1929). When other screen offers didn't meet his expectations, he returned to Broadway and scored a major hit in *Counsellor at Law*. Muni returned to Hollywood in 1932, starring both as a vicious gangster in *Scarface: The Shame of the Nation* and an escaped convict in *I Am a Fugitive from a Chain Gang* that same year. Warner Bros. was so impressed, they signed him to a long-term contract, publicizing him as the screen's greatest actor. In 1936, Muni convinced them to take a chance on a historical biography, *The Story of Louis Pasteur* (1936), and he won an Oscar for his performance.

I Am a Fugitive from a Chain Gang, 1932

The Story of Louis Pasteur, 1936

1. **Anne Baxter and Paul Muni share the screen in what film?**

   A. *Angel on My Shoulder* (1946)
   B. *Bright Leaf* (1950)
   C. *Flamingo Road* (1949)
   D. *The Vagabond King* (1956)

2. **Paul Muni turned down the role of Roy Earle in what film noir?**

   A. *Across the Pacific* (1942)
   B. *High Sierra* (1941)
   C. *The Maltese Falcon* (1941)
   D. *They Drive by Night* (1940)

3. **Bette Davis falls for Paul Muni in what film noir drama?**

   A. *Bordertown* (1935)
   B. *Dark Victory* (1939)

   C. *King of the Underworld* (1939)
   D. *The Big Shot* (1942)

4. **Paul Muni's character rises from bouncer to casino owner in what crime drama?**

   A. *Across the Pacific* (1942)
   B. *Bordertown* (1935)
   C. *High Sierra* (1941)
   D. *To Have and Have Not* (1944)

5. **Howard Hawks directed Paul Muni in what film noir drama?**

   A. *Angels with Dirty Faces* (1938)
   B. *Gentleman Jim* (1942)
   C. *Salty O'Rourke* (1945)
   D. *Scarface* (1932)

---

answers found on page 565

55. In what film does Ronald Reagan play an insurance adjuster who gets caught up with an insurance fraud gang?

A. *Accidents Will Happen* (1938)
B. *Going Places* (1938)
C. *Hell's Kitchen* (1939)
D. *Night unto Night* (1949)

56. Who is George Sanders's costar in *Witness to Murder* (1954)?

A. Barbara Stanwyck
B. Elizabeth Taylor
C. Joan Crawford
D. Joan Fontaine

57. Who directed James Cagney in *White Heat* (1949)?

A. Anthony Mann
B. Norman Taurog
C. Raoul Walsh
D. William Wyler

58. Which of the following actors does not appear with Fay Wray in the 1957 drama *Crime of Passion*?

A. Barbara Stanwyck
B. Raymond Burr
C. Sterling Hayden
D. Virginia Mayo

59. What was Marlon Brando's character named in *On the Waterfront* (1954)?

A. Fletcher Christian
B. Sky Masterson
C. Stanley Kowalski
D. Terry Malloy

60. Who costars with Dick Van Dyke in the 1968 film *Never a Dull Moment*?

A. Edward G. Robinson
B. Humphrey Bogart
C. James Cagney
D. John Garfield

61. How many movies did James Cagney make after *One, Two, Three* (1961)?

A. 0
B. 1
C. 2
D. 4

62. Paul Muni is given a second chance at life in what film costarring Claude Rains?

A. *Angel on My Shoulder* (1946)
B. *Beyond Glory* (1948)
C. *It's a Great Feeling* (1949)
D. *The Unsuspected* (1947)

63. What film directed by Ida Lupino attacked the controversial topic of rape?

A. *Hard, Fast and Beautiful* (1951)
B. *Outrage* (1950)
C. *The Bigamist* (1953)
D. *The Hitch-Hiker* (1953)

64. Raymond Chandler makes a cameo appearance in what film pairing Barbara Stanwyck and Fred MacMurray?

A. *Deception* (1946)
B. *Double Indemnity* (1944)
C. *Hotel Berlin* (1945)
D. *Three Strangers* (1946)

65. In which Orson Welles film does Joseph Cotten make an uncredited cameo appearance as a coroner?

A. *Mr. Arkadin* (1955)
B. *The Lady from Shanghai* (1947)
C. *The Stranger* (1946)
D. *Touch of Evil* (1958)

66. What was Roddy McDowall's first film appearance at the age of ten?

A. *His Brother's Keeper* (1940)
B. *How Green Was My Valley* (1941)
C. *Murder in the Family* (1938)
D. *You Will Remember* (1941)

answers found on pages 565–566

67. Robert Taylor and Cyd Charisse share the screen in what crime drama?

A. *High Wall* (1947)
B. *Hotel Berlin* (1945)
C. *Party Girl* (1958)
D. *Passage to Marseille* (1944)

68. Who directed James Cagney in *The Strawberry Blonde* (1941)?

A. Cecil B. DeMille
B. Leo McCarey
C. Raoul Walsh
D. Robert Wise

69. What is the only film directed by James Cagney?

A. *Shake Hands with the Devil* (1959)
B. *Short Cut to Hell* (1957)
C. *Tribute to a Bad Man* (1956)
D. *You, John Jones!* (1943)

High Sierra, 1941

70. Who was Ida Lupino's costar in the 1941 Raoul Walsh film *High Sierra*?

A. Colin Clive
B. Lon Chaney
C. Boris Karloff
D. Humphrey Bogart

71. In which of the following Alfred Hitchcock films does Kim Novak star?

A. *Dial M for Murder* (1954)
B. *Family Plot* (1976)
C. *North by Northwest* (1959)
D. *Vertigo* (1958)

72. Who was the producer for 1932's *Scarface*, starring Paul Muni?

A. Alfred Hitchcock
B. Howard Hughes
C. Orson Welles
D. William Castle

73. What does Rita Hayworth take off while singing "Put the Blame on Mame" in *Gilda* (1946)?

A. Her earrings
B. Her glove
C. Her stockings
D. Her top

74. Thelma Ritter stars in which of the following Alfred Hitchcock films?

A. *North by Northwest* (1959)
B. *Psycho* (1960)
C. *Rear Window* (1954)
D. *The Birds* (1963)

75. In which of the following films does Joseph Cotten play a Scotland Yard detective?

A. *Gaslight* (1944)
B. *Niagara* (1953)
C. *Shadow of a Doubt* (1943)
D. *The Steel Trap* (1952)

76. Who is Barbara Stanwyck's partner in crime in *Double Indemnity* (1944)?

A. Fred MacMurray
B. John Garfield
C. Robert Mitchum
D. Spencer Tracy

answers found on page 566

77. Paul Muni received his second Oscar nomination for what film?

A. *I Am a Fugitive from a Chain Gang* (1932)
B. *Seven Faces* (1929)
C. *The Valiant* (1929)
D. *The World Changes* (1933)

78. Marjorie Main appears in which film noir thriller starring Katharine Hepburn and Robert Taylor?

A. *Conspirator* (1949)
B. *High Wall* (1947)
C. *The House of the Seven Hawks* (1959)
D. *Undercurrent* (1946)

79. What film earned Lana Turner her only Oscar nomination?

A. *Imitation of Life* (1959)
B. *Madame X* (1966)
C. *Peyton Place* (1957)
D. *They Won't Forget* (1937)

80. What portrait served as Jean Louis's inspiration for the black satin strapless gown he created for Rita Hayworth's character in *Gilda* (1946)?

A. *Isabella Brant* by Peter Paul Rubens
B. *Mona Lisa* by Leonardo Da Vinci
C. *Madame X* by John Singer Sargent
D. *The Cheat* by Georges de La Tour

81. What was the name of Jean Harlow's character in *The Public Enemy* (1931)?

A. Anne Courtland
B. Gwen Allen
C. Mona Leslie
D. Vantine Jefferson

82. James Cagney made his film acting debut in what Joan Blondell movie?

A. *My Past* (1931)
B. *Sinners' Holiday* (1930)
C. *The Public Enemy* (1931)
D. *The Office Wife* (1930)

83. In what film does Alfred Hitchcock make his cameo as a passenger carrying a double bass fiddle?

A. *North by Northwest* (1959)
B. *Spellbound* (1945)
C. *Strangers on a Train* (1951)
D. *Vertigo* (1958)

84. In *Rear Window* (1954), what does Grace Kelly go looking for in Raymond Burr's apartment?

A. A death certificate
B. A hacksaw
C. A suitcase
D. A wedding ring

85. What two crime dramas earned writer Virginia Kellogg Oscar nominations?

A. *T-Men* (1947) and *Pickup on South Street* (1953)
B. *The Big Sleep* (1946) and *Gilda* (1946)
C. *The Postman Always Rings Twice* (1946) and *Laura* (1944)
D. *White Heat* (1949) and *Caged* (1950)

86. Angie Dickinson gets slapped by Ronald Reagan in what film?

A. *Dressed to Kill* (1980)
B. *Ocean's Eleven* (1960)
C. *Rio Bravo* (1959)
D. *The Killers* (1964)

87. What was Claire Trevor's nickname for all her "bad girl" roles in films noir?

A. "'The First Lady of Dark Cinema"
B. "The Queen of Film Noir"
C. "The Queen of Floozies"
D. "The Thriller Queen"

answers found on page 566

88. Valerie Hobson costarred in the 1935 film *Mystery of Edwin Drood*, which was based on an unfinished novel by what author?

A. Charles Dickens
B. George Eliot
C. Gustave Flaubert
D. Victor Hugo

89. Cinematographer Haskell Wexler shot the 1967 film *In the Heat of the Night*. Who directed it?

A. Arthur Hiller
B. Franco Zeffirelli
C. Norman Jewison
D. Stanley Kramer

90. What film earned Lana Turner her famous nickname "The Sweater Girl"?

A. *A Star Is Born* (1976)
B. *Slightly Dangerous* (1943)
C. *The Postman Always Rings Twice* (1946)
D. *They Won't Forget* (1937)

91. Ida Lupino stars as a columnist in what Fritz Lang film?

A. *High Sierra* (1941)
B. *The Sea Wolf* (1941)
C. *They Drive by Night* (1940)
D. *While the City Sleeps* (1956)

92. What film based on a James M. Cain story stars Lana Turner and John Garfield?

A. *Everybody Does It* (1949)
B. *Mildred Pierce* (1945)
C. *Serenade* (1956)
D. *The Postman Always Rings Twice* (1946)

93. Flora Robson stars in which of the following mysteries?

A. *Murder at the Gallop* (1963)
B. *Shadow of the Thin Man* (1941)
C. *The Dark Avenger* (1955)
D. *Uncertain Glory* (1944)

Angel Face, 1952

94. Jean Simmons starred in the 1952 film noir *Angel Face*. Who directed it?

A. Billy Wilder
B. George Sidney
C. John Frankenheimer
D. Otto Preminger

95. Kathleen Freeman appears in what film noir thriller opposite Tony Curtis?

A. *Hotel Berlin* (1945)
B. *Passage to Marseille* (1944)
C. *The Face Behind the Mask* (1941)
D. *The Midnight Story* (1957)

96. Who directed the 1944 film noir classic *Double Indemnity*?

A. Alfred Hitchcock
B. Billy Wilder
C. Howard Hawks
D. Michael Curtiz

97. When was the original play of *Dead End* (1937), featuring Claire Trevor, written?

A. 1919
B. 1926
C. 1931
D. 1935

answers found on page 566

98. In which Bogie and Bacall film does Claire Trevor appear?

A. *Dark Passage* (1947)
B. *Key Largo* (1948)
C. *The Big Sleep* (1946)
D. *To Have and Have Not* (1944)

99. Jean Hagen and Jack Palance costar in what film noir drama?

A. *Strange Cargo* (1940)
B. *Stranger on the Third Floor* (1940)
C. *The Big Knife* (1955)
D. *The Face Behind the Mask* (1941)

100. What was the last movie James Cagney made?

A. *Brewster's Millions* (1985)
B. *Cocoon* (1985)
C. *On Golden Pond* (1981)
D. *Ragtime* (1981)

101. Raymond Massey portrayed Sherlock Holmes in how many feature films?

A. 0
B. 1
C. 2
D. 3

102. George Raft plays the title role, opposite Nina Foch, in what film?

A. *Ivanhoe* (1952)
B. *Johnny Allegro* (1949)
C. *Johnny Eager* (1941)
D. *Quentin Durward* (1955)

103. What studio borrowed Ava Gardner from MGM for *The Killers* (1946)?

A. Columbia
B. RKO
C. Universal
D. Warner Bros.

104. Gloria Grahame stars opposite Robert Mitchum in which film noir thriller?

A. *Crossfire* (1947)
B. *Man on a Tightrope* (1953)
C. *Roughshod* (1949)
D. *The Big Heat* (1953)

105. Dana Andrews investigates the murder of a young woman, and ultimately falls in love with her, in what Otto Preminger film?

A. *Anatomy of a Murder* (1959)
B. *Bunny Lake Is Missing* (1965)
C. *In Harm's Way* (1965)
D. *Laura* (1944)

106. What actor starred in the 1981 remake of *The Postman Always Rings Twice*?

A. Jack Nicholson
B. Mel Gibson
C. Nick Nolte
D. Robert De Niro

107. Faye Dunaway costars with Warren Beatty as his partner in crime in what film?

A. *Bonnie and Clyde* (1967)
B. *The Arrangement* (1969)
C. *The Thomas Crown Affair* (1968)
D. *Three Days of the Condor* (1975)

108. In *Gilda* (1946), whose child was used for the picture of Johnny Farrell as a baby?

A. Charles Vidor (director)
B. Glenn Ford
C. Rita Hayworth
D. Virginia Van Upp (producer)

109. Which of the following films based on a James M. Cain story was nominated for an Academy Award as Best Picture?

A. *Double Indemnity* (1944)
B. *Interlude* (1957)
C. *The Postman Always Rings Twice* (1946)
D. *When Tomorrow Comes* (1939)

110. What actress plays Cody Jarrett's "Ma" in *White Heat* (1949)?

A. Arlene Francis

B. Glynis Johns

C. Margaret Wycherly

D. Milly Vitale

111. Gene Tierney plays an obsessive wife who destroys the life of all those who come between her and her husband in what 1945 film?

A. *Heaven Can Wait*

B. *Laura*

C. *Leave Her to Heaven*

D. *The Razor's Edge*

112. Who earned an Academy Award nomination for his supporting role in *The Maltese Falcon* (1941)?

A. Elisha Cook Jr.

B. Humphrey Bogart

C. Peter Lorre

D. Sydney Greenstreet

113. Who directed Denzel Washington in the 2007 film *American Gangster*?

A. Oliver Stone

B. Ridley Scott

C. Spike Lee

D. Tony Scott

114. Ida Lupino supervises a prison in what film?

A. *High Sierra* (1941)

B. *The Sea Wolf* (1941)

C. *While the City Sleeps* (1956)

D. *Women's Prison* (1955)

115. The 1967 James Shigeta film *The Mystery of the Chinese Junk* features what famous detective(s)?

A. Charlie Chan

B. Hercule Poirot

C. Miss Marple

D. The Hardy Boys

The Public Enemy, 1931

116. In what category did the 1931 gangster classic *The Public Enemy* receive its only Academy Award nomination?

A. Best Actor

B. Best Art Direction

C. Best Director

D. Best Writing, Original Story

117. Who directed James Cagney in *The Doorway to Hell* (1930)?

A. Archie Mayo

B. Frank Capra

C. King Vidor

D. Sam Wood

118. Ralph Meeker starred in the 1955 film *Kiss Me Deadly*. Who was the director?

A. Elia Kazan

B. John Huston

C. Robert Aldrich

D. Sam Fuller

119. The 1944 film *Double Indemnity* was based on a novel by James M. Cain. What actress starred in it?

A. Barbara Stanwyck

B. Jennifer Jones

C. Joan Crawford

D. Lana Turner

answers found on page 566

Spotlight on
IDA **LUPINO** (1918–1995)

Although she often joked that she was "the poor man's Bette Davis," Ida Lupino was much more than that. A pioneering director, her issue-oriented independent films anticipated the work of later women like Penny Marshall and Gillian Armstrong. The child of a British theatrical family, she started making movies in England at age thirteen, then came to Hollywood in 1934. Lupino languished in ingénue roles until she fought to play a less than reputable gal in *The Light That Failed* (1939). That brought her a contract at Warner Bros., where she was groomed as the next Davis. Although she excelled at tough-girl roles in films like *High Sierra* (1941), specializing in gangster's molls and lady crooks, she refused to accept scripts Davis had rejected. Instead, she spent her time at the studio studying directors as they worked. When she launched her own production company in the late 1940s, she was ready to take on directing, tackling controversial issues like adoption in *Not Wanted* (1949) and rape in *Outrage* (1950). With *The Hitch-Hiker* (1953), she became the first woman to direct a film noir. Moving into television in the 1950s, she would often appear as a guest on one episode of series such as *The Twilight Zone*, then direct others.

The Light That Failed, 1939

High Sierra, 1941

1. **Ida Lupino performed her own songs as a nightclub singer in what film?**

   A. *Deep Valley* (1947)

   B. *Forever and a Day* (1943)

   C. *Road House* (1948)

   D. *Woman in Hiding* (1949)

2. **Bernard Herrmann composed the score for what film noir drama starring Ida Lupino?**

   A. *Endless Night* (1972)

   B. *Mysterious Island* (1961)

   C. *On Dangerous Ground* (1952)

   D. *Zaza* (1939)

3. **Ida Lupino plays the blind sister to a killer in what film?**

   A. *High Sierra* (1941)

   B. *On Dangerous Ground* (1952)

   C. *The Sea Wolf* (1941)

   D. *While the City Sleeps* (1956)

4. **Ernest Laszlo was the cinematographer of what film noir drama featuring real-life couple Howard Duff and Ida Lupino?**

   A. *Models, Inc.* (1952)

   B. *Spaceways* (1953)

   C. *The Lady from Texas* (1951)

   D. *While the City Sleeps* (1956)

5. **Ida Lupino plays opposite George Raft, Ann Sheridan, and Humphrey Bogart in what film?**

   A. *High Sierra* (1941)

   B. *The Sea Wolf* (1941)

   C. *They Drive by Night* (1940)

   D. *While the City Sleeps* (1956)

answers found on page 566

120. What film shot by cinematographer Haskell Wexler is about gang violence?

A. *Colors* (1988)
B. *Lookin' to Get Out* (1982)
C. *Medium Cool* (1969)
D. *Three Fugitives* (1989)

121. In *Vertigo* (1958), who is James Stewart hired to follow?

A. Eva Marie Saint
B. Grace Kelly
C. Kim Novak
D. Tippi Hedren

122. Where does the Glenn Ford/Rita Hayworth film *Gilda* (1946) take place?

A. Argentina
B. Brazil
C. Colombia
D. Cuba

123. Anne V. Coates edited the 1974 film *Murder on the Orient Express*. Which of the following actors did not appear in it?

A. Albert Finney
B. Anthony Perkins
C. Diana Rigg
D. Ingrid Bergman

124. John Huston earned three consecutive Oscar nominations for Best Director from 1951 to 1953. What film began this streak?

A. *Moulin Rouge*
B. *The African Queen*
C. *The Asphalt Jungle*
D. *The Treasure of the Sierra Madre*

125. Starring in the title role of the 1936 film *Meet Nero Wolfe*, who was the first actor to portray Rex Stout's famed detective Nero Wolfe?

A. Edward Arnold
B. Maury Chaykin
C. Walter Connolly
D. William Conrad

126. What was Marlon Brando's first feature film? (Film dates hidden to conceal answer.)

A. *A Streetcar Named Desire*
B. *The Men*
C. *The Ugly American*
D. *The Wild One*

127. James Garner plays a detective in the title role of which film costarring Rita Moreno?

A. *Marlowe* (1969)
B. *Mister Buddwing* (1966)
C. *Popi* (1969)
D. *The Vagabond King* (1956)

128. How many times did James Cagney work with Mervyn LeRoy?

A. 1
B. 4
C. 5
D. 7

129. Luchino Visconti's first film *Ossessione* (1943) and what later American movie are both adaptations of a popular James M. Cain novel?

A. *Dark Passage* (1947)
B. *Double Indemnity* (1944)
C. *The Big Sleep* (1946)
D. *The Postman Always Rings Twice* (1946)

130. Jules Dassin's 1950 film *Night and the City* was remade in 1992 starring what contemporary actor?

A. Harvey Keitel
B. Nick Nolte
C. Robert De Niro
D. Sean Penn

131. In which of the following films directed by Alfred Hitchcock does Hume Cronyn appear?

A. *North by Northwest* (1959)
B. *Rebecca* (1940)
C. *Shadow of a Doubt* (1943)
D. *Strangers on a Train* (1951)

132. Which Oscar-nominated film originated from a story by Kubec Glasmon and John Bright called "Blood and Sand"?

    A. *Blood and Sand* (1922)
    B. *Duel in the Sun* (1946)
    C. *Hell and High Water* (1954)
    D. *The Public Enemy* (1931)

133. In *Sunset Blvd.* (1950), Norma Desmond has a funeral for one of her pets. What kind of pet is it?

    A. Bird
    B. Cat
    C. Dog
    D. Monkey

134. In which of the following films does Edward G. Robinson costar with Humphrey Bogart and Bette Davis?

    A. *Barbary Coast* (1935)
    B. *Brother Orchid* (1940)
    C. *I Loved a Woman* (1933)
    D. *Kid Galahad* (1937)

135. Who directed James Cagney in *Sinners' Holiday* (1930)?

    A. George Cukor
    B. John G. Adolfi
    C. King Vidor
    D. Michael Curtiz

136. What famous detective did Ralph Meeker play in the 1955 film *Kiss Me Deadly*?

    A. Mike Hammer
    B. Philip Marlowe
    C. Sam Spade
    D. Sherlock Holmes

137. Ida Lupino directed the first film noir by a woman. What was it?

    A. *Hard, Fast and Beautiful* (1951)
    B. *Outrage* (1950)
    C. *The Bigamist* (1953)
    D. *The Hitch-Hiker* (1953)

138. Who does Thelma Ritter play nurse to in the 1954 thriller *Rear Window*?

    A. Cary Grant
    B. Gregory Peck
    C. James Stewart
    D. Joseph Cotten

Angels with Dirty Faces, 1938

139. James Cagney and Humphrey Bogart play racketeers in the 1938 film *Angels with Dirty Faces*. Who plays the straight and narrow Jerry Connolly?

    A. Karl Malden
    B. Pat O'Brien
    C. Bing Crosby
    D. William Powell

140. In which of the following Alfred Hitchcock films does Gregory Peck star?

    A. *Rebecca* (1940)
    B. *Spellbound* (1945)
    C. *The Birds* (1963)
    D. *To Catch a Thief* (1955)

141. What writer earned an Oscar nomination for *The Strange Love of Martha Ivers* (1946)?

    A. Ben Hecht
    B. Charles Brackett
    C. John Patrick
    D. Raymond Chandler

142. Who directed the John Garfield film *They Made Me a Criminal* (1939)?

    A. Anthony Mann
    B. Busby Berkeley
    C. Nicholas Ray
    D. Vincente Minnelli

143. In what Woody Allen film does Claire Bloom's husband have his mistress murdered?

    A. *Crimes and Misdemeanors* (1989)
    B. *Husbands and Wives* (1992)
    C. *Love and Death* (1975)
    D. *Take the Money and Run* (1969)

144. In what film directed by Stanley Kubrick does Ralph Meeker costar?

    A. *2001: A Space Odyssey* (1968)
    B. *Barry Lyndon* (1975)
    C. *Paths of Glory* (1957)
    D. *The Killing* (1956)

145. Paul Newman plays detective Lew Harper in what thriller costarring Joanne Woodward?

    A. *A Fine Madness* (1966)
    B. *The Drowning Pool* (1975)
    C. *The Sting* (1973)
    D. *The Three Faces of Eve* (1957)

146. The 1954 Alfred Hitchcock thriller *Rear Window* received Academy Award nominations in all of the following categories except which one?

    A. Best Actor
    B. Best Cinematography
    C. Best Director
    D. Best Sound

147. For what film did Claire Trevor receive her first Oscar nomination?

    A. *Dead End* (1937)
    B. *Johnny Angel* (1945)
    C. *Key Largo* (1948)
    D. *The High and the Mighty* (1954)

148. What real-life murderer was the inspiration for Montgomery Clift's character in *A Place in the Sun* (1951)?

    A. Chester Gillette
    B. Ed Gein
    C. Hawley Harvey Crippen
    D. Peter Sutcliffe

149. Russell Metty photographed Lana Turner for what 1966 film about a fallen woman, on trial for murder, who is defended by her estranged son?

    A. *Madame X*
    B. *The Appaloosa*
    C. *The War Lord*
    D. *The Thrill of It All*

150. Paul Muni plays Antonio "Tony" Camonte in what film noir drama?

    A. *High Sierra* (1941)
    B. *Scarface* (1932)
    C. *The Big Sleep* (1946)
    D. *To Have and Have Not* (1944)

151. In the Fay Wray thriller *Doctor X* (1932), what is the nickname of the murderer roaming the streets of New York?

    A. "New York Night Stalker"
    B. "The Bat"
    C. "The Green River Killer"
    D. "The Moon Killer"

152. Cedric Hardwicke was featured in what Alfred Hitchcock thriller opposite Cary Grant?

    A. *Notorious* (1946)
    B. *Spellbound* (1945)
    C. *Suspicion* (1941)
    D. *Vertigo* (1958)

153. Who directed James Cagney in his final film?

    A. Billy Wilder
    B. Edgar G. Ulmer
    C. Milos Forman
    D. Roger Vadim

154. Mickey Rooney plays the title role in what film costarring Cedric Hardwicke?

A. *Baby Face Nelson* (1957)
B. *The Errand Boy* (1961)
C. *Uncle Vanya* (1963)
D. *Young Tom Edison* (1940)

155. Who plays Charlton Heston's wife in the 1958 film *Touch of Evil*?

A. Hedy Lamarr
B. Janet Leigh
C. Jean Simmons
D. Rita Hayworth

156. Who was nominated for an Academy Award as Best Supporting Actor for his performance in the 1959 film *Anatomy of a Murder*?

A. George C. Scott
B. Omar Sharif
C. Spencer Tracy
D. Tyrone Power

157. Which of the following actresses starred in the 1953 film *Niagara*, directed by Henry Hathaway?

A. Eva Marie Saint
B. Lana Turner
C. Marilyn Monroe
D. Susan Hayward

158. Harry Belafonte stars in what film noir drama opposite Shelley Winters and Gloria Grahame?

A. *Bell, Book and Candle* (1958)
B. *Odds Against Tomorrow* (1959)
C. *The Angel Levine* (1970)
D. *The Loners* (1972)

159. In *The Maltese Falcon* (1941), what famous detective does Humphrey Bogart portray?

A. Hercule Poirot
B. Philip Marlowe
C. Sam Spade
D. Sherlock Holmes

160. Claire Trevor heads a gang of criminals in what film?

A. *My Man and I* (1952)
B. *Raw Deal* (1948)
C. *Stagecoach* (1939)
D. *The Amazing Dr. Clitterhouse* (1938)

161. Who starred in the remake of *Scarface* (1932), which originally starred Paul Muni?

A. Al Pacino
B. Dustin Hoffman
C. Joe Pesci
D. Robert De Niro

Little Caesar, 1931

162. In what Oscar category did *Little Caesar* (1931) compete?

A. Best Actor
B. Best Adaptation
C. Best Director
D. Best Supporting Actress

163. What is the only film to credit both George Raft and James Cagney?

A. *Each Dawn I Die* (1939)
B. *Madame Racketeer* (1932)
C. *Scarface* (1932)
D. *Spawn of the North* (1938)

answers found on page 566

Spotlight on
JAMES **CAGNEY** (1899–1986)

By the early thirties, America was up to its eyes in crime, and the gangster genre was more prominent than ever. The studios needed leading men who weren't afraid to portray these very human monsters, and James Cagney was the man for the job. He knew these characters all too well, having grown up in one of New York's toughest neighborhoods, where he learned to fight at an early age. While some of his playmates turned to crime, however, he worked to support his family. Acting at the local settlement house was a way to let off steam, and led to his first professional job as part of the ladies' chorus in an all-male musical. His ticket to Hollywood came when Warner Bros. bought the screen rights to his 1929 Broadway flop *Penny Arcade* and signed him and leading lady Joan Blondell for the film version, *Sinner's Holiday* (1930). Then, Cagney's venomous portrayal of gangster Tom Powers in *The Public Enemy* (1931) made him a star. Though best remembered as a tough guy, Cagney always described himself as "just a song-and-dance man." He got to show off those talents in his only Oscar-winning performance, as musical star George M. Cohan in *Yankee Doodle Dandy* (1942).

The Public Enemy, 1931

Angels with Dirty Faces, 1938

1. **In *The Public Enemy* (1931), what actress gets the famous grapefruit in the kisser from James Cagney?**

    A. Beryl Mercer

    B. Jean Harlow

    C. Joan Blondell

    D. Mae Clark

2. **How many times was James Cagney credited as "Jimmy" Cagney?**

    A. 0

    B. 1

    C. 3

    D. 7

3. **What is James Cagney's original family name?**

    A. Cagne

    B. Kagney

    C. O'Caigne

    D. O'Kagney

4. **In what film does James Cagney's character say "Made it, Ma! Top of the world!"?**

    A. *Run for Cover* (1955)

    B. *The Crowd Roars* (1932)

    C. *The Roaring Twenties* (1939

    D. *White Heat* (1949)

5. **How many films did James Cagney make with Humphrey Bogart?**

    A. 0

    B. 2

    C. 3

    D. 5

answers found on page 566

164. Who directed James Cagney in *The Public Enemy* (1931)?

A. Alexander Korda
B. John Ford
C. Michael Curtiz
D. William Wellman

165. What was Walter Matthau's first attempt at directing?

A. *Bigger Than Life* (1956)
B. *The Fortune Cookie* (1966)
C. *Gangster Story* (1959)
D. *Voice in the Mirror* (1958)

166. What Oscar did *The Third Man* win in 1951?

A. Best Actor
B. Best Black-and-White Cinematography
C. Best Director
D. Best Picture

167. Who directed Edward G. Robinson in the 1948 film *Key Largo*?

A. Howard Hawks
B. John Huston
C. Mervyn LeRoy
D. Michael Curtiz

168. Howard Hawks's *Criminal Code* (1931) was shot by James Wong Howe and what other cinematographer?

A. Charles Lang
B. Gilbert Taylor
C. Stanley Cortez
D. Ted Tetzlaff

169. What was Alfred Hitchcock's first feature film in color (film dates hidden to conceal answer)?

A. *North by Northwest*
B. *Rope*
C. *Spellbound*
D. *Vertigo*

170. Albert Finney plays a Belgian detective investigating a murder in what film?

A. *Murder on the Orient Express* (1974)
B. *Gumshoe* (1971)
C. *The Picasso Summer* (1969)
D. *Night Must Fall* (1964)

171. Which of the following films directed by Alan J. Pakula is about a private investigator's relationship with a call girl?

A. *Klute* (1971)
B. *See You in the Morning* (1989)
C. *The Devil's Own* (1997)
D. *The Sterile Cuckoo* (1969)

172. Which of the following actors costars with Kay Francis in the 1939 film *King of the Underworld*?

A. Clark Gable
B. Edward G. Robinson
C. Humphrey Bogart
D. John Garfield

173. What performance earned James Cagney his first Academy Award nomination for Best Actor?

A. George M. Cohan in *Yankee Doodle Dandy* (1942)
B. Lon Chaney in *Man of a Thousand Faces* (1957)
C. Martin Snyder in *Love Me or Leave Me* (1955)
D. William "Rocky" Sullivan in *Angels with Dirty Faces* (1938)

174. Who plays Barbara Stanwyck's meek husband in the 1948 thriller *Sorry, Wrong Number*?

A. Burt Lancaster
B. Humphrey Bogart
C. James Cagney
D. Kirk Douglas

answers found on page 566

175. What crime novelist earned his only Oscar nomination for adapting the Bette Davis film *Watch on the Rhine* (1943)?

A. Dashiell Hammett
B. Edgar Wallace
C. James M. Cain
D. Raymond Chandler

176. Who directed the 1974 film *Murder on the Orient Express*?

A. Arthur Penn
B. John Schlesinger
C. Mike Nichols
D. Sidney Lumet

177. Who was nominated for an Academy Award as Best Actress for her performance in the 1944 film noir classic *Double Indemnity*?

A. Barbara Stanwyck
B. Lana Turner
C. Lauren Bacall
D. Loretta Young

178. What was the first film to earn three Oscar nominations for Best Supporting Actor?

A. *12 Angry Men* (1957)
B. *Fail-Safe* (1964)
C. *On the Waterfront* (1954)
D. *The Caine Mutiny* (1954)

179. Billy Wilder directed Barbara Stanwyck in what film noir thriller?

A. *Double Indemnity* (1944)
B. *Invisible Agent* (1942)
C. *The Conspirators* (1944)
D. *The Mask of Dimitrios* (1944)

180. In what film directed by John Cromwell does Robert Mitchum star?

A. *Anna and the King of Siam* (1946)
B. *Caged* (1950)
C. *Dead Reckoning* (1947)
D. *The Racket* (1951)

181. Ronald Reagan plays a violent crime kingpin in what film that proved to be his final feature role?

A. *Hellcats of the Navy* (1957)
B. *Tennessee's Partner* (1955)
C. *The Killers* (1964)
D. *The Young Doctors* (1961)

182. Which star played master detective Ellery Queen in four films?

A. Humphrey Bogart
B. Ralph Bellamy
C. Robert Taylor
D. William Powell

183. What William Powell/Myrna Loy film won the Best Original Story Oscar in 1935?

A. *Libeled Lady* (1936)
B. *Manhattan Melodrama* (1934)
C. *The Great Ziegfeld* (1936)
D. *The Thin Man* (1934)

184. Leslie Brooks plays an alluring femme fatale in what film costarring Robert Paige?

A. *Blonde Ice* (1948)
B. *Hotel Berlin* (1945)
C. *The Conspirators* (1944)
D. *The Maltese Falcon* (1941)

185. Which of the following films directed by Jules Dassin revolves around a jewel heist?

A. *Phaedra* (1962)
B. *Reunion in France* (1942)
C. *Rififi* (1955)
D. *The Law* (1959)

186. Which of the following actors stars in the 1937 Samuel Goldwyn production of *Dead End*?

A. Fred MacMurray
B. Humphrey Bogart
C. James Cagney
D. John Garfield

answers found on page 566

187. What is the only movie Cagney made with Edward G. Robinson?

A. *Blackmail* (1939)
B. *Little Caesar* (1931)
C. *Smart Money* (1931)
D. *The Sea Wolf* (1941)

188. Walter Matthau directed only one movie in which he also starred. What was it?

A. *Bigger Than Life* (1956)
B. *Gangster Story* (1959)
C. *Onionhead* (1958)
D. *Ride a Crooked Trail* (1958)

The Maltese Falcon, 1941

189. Who directed the 1941 film *The Maltese Falcon*?

A. Alfred Hitchcock
B. Elia Kazan
C. John Ford
D. John Huston

190. Which of the *Key Largo* (1948) stars won an Academy Award for his or her role in the film?

A. Humphrey Bogart
B. Lionel Barrymore
C. Claire Trevor
D. Lauren Bacall

191. Who is James Cagney's female costar in *The Public Enemy* (1931)?

A. Ann Dvorak
B. Jean Harlow
C. Loretta Young
D. Mary Astor

192. Jean Harlow was godmother to what notorious gangster's daughter, Millicent?

A. Al Capone
B. Bugsy Siegel
C. Legs Diamond
D. Lucky Luciano

193. What semiprofessional baseball team did James Cagney play for?

A. Bronx P-Nuts
B. Brooklyn Gloves
C. New York Knots
D. Yorkville Nut Club

194. Which of the following Anna May Wong films features the fictional detective Charlie Chan?

A. *Impact* (1949)
B. *King of Chinatown* (1939)
C. *The Chinese Parrot* (1927)
D. *Tiger Bay* (1934)

195. What famous female detective does Angela Lansbury portray in *The Mirror Crack'd* (1980)?

A. Miss Jane Marple
B. Nancy Drew
C. Nora Charles
D. V. I. Warshawski

196. In what film does Van Heflin costar with Janet Leigh?

A. *Act of Violence* (1948)
B. *Airport* (1970)
C. *B. F.'s Daughter* (1948)
D. *Madame Bovary* (1949)

197. In which of the following films does Barbara Stanwyck costar with Sterling Hayden and Raymond Burr?

A. *Baby Face* (1933)

B. *Crime of Passion* (1957)

C. *The Bride Walks Out* (1936)

D. *Witness to Murder* (1954)

198. James Stewart defends a man on trial for murdering a rapist in what Otto Preminger film?

A. *Anatomy of a Murder* (1959)

B. *Bunny Lake Is Missing* (1965)

C. *In Harm's Way* (1965)

D. *Stalag 17* (1953)

199. Glenn Ford and Cedric Hardwicke costar in what film noir mystery?

A. *Hotel Berlin* (1945)

B. *Passage to Marseille* (1944)

C. *The Green Glove* (1952)

D. *The Mask of Dimitrios* (1944)

200. What film starring Paul Muni was director Archie Mayo's last picture before his retirement?

A. *All That Money Can Buy* (1941)

B. *Angel on My Shoulder* (1946)

C. *I'll See You in My Dreams* (1951)

D. *The Secret Bride* (1934)

201. George Sanders plays a scheming blackmailer in what Alfred Hitchcock thriller?

A. *Family Plot* (1976)

B. *Notorious* (1946)

C. *Rebecca* (1940)

D. *Strangers on a Train* (1951)

202. Peter Lorre costars in the 1941 film *The Maltese Falcon*, which was based on the novel by what author?

A. Agatha Christie

B. Dashiell Hammett

C. James Ellroy

D. Raymond Chandler

203. Ann Sheridan plays a sultry nightclub singer who drives a doctor to fake his own death in what film noir?

A. *Gilda* (1946)

B. *Laura* (1944)

C. *Mildred Pierce* (1945)

D. *Nora Prentiss* (1947)

204. Robert Taylor and Edward Arnold appear in what film noir classic?

A. *High Wall* (1947)

B. *Hotel Berlin* (1945)

C. *Johnny Eager* (1941)

D. *Passage to Marseille* (1944)

I Am a Fugitive from a Chain Gang, 1932

205. Who earned an Oscar nomination for his role in *I Am a Fugitive from a Chain Gang* (1932)?

A. Howard Keel

B. John Garfield

C. Paul Muni

D. Walter Pidgeon

206. Richard Widmark stars in what film directed by Jules Dassin?

A. *Circle of Two* (1980)

B. *Night and the City* (1950)

C. *Thieves' Highway* (1949)

D. *Two Smart People* (1946)

answers found on page 567

VARIETY
SHOW

Stage Door, 1937

Chapter 16

HE SAID/
SHE SAID

One of the many ironies in *Sunset Blvd.* (1950), Billy Wilder's definitive dissection of the movies, is that when Norma Desmond decries the arrival of talking pictures and the "words, words, mere words" that she says are strangling the film industry, she does it with some of the best dialogue ever crafted for the screen. "There once was a time in this business when it had the eyes of the whole world!" says Gloria Swanson, as Desmond. "But that wasn't good enough for them, oh no! They had to have the ears of the whole world too. So they opened their big mouths and out came talk. Talk! TALK!" The truth is that though the movies are very much a visual art form, they also depend on words for survival—words said from the screen, words used in interviews and advertising campaigns, and even the words celebrities write years later in their memoirs.

Sound did not introduce words to the movies. Even in the silent days, the intertitles played a major role in cinema's success. Audiences may best remember the building rhythm of D. W. Griffith's editing in *Intolerance* (1916), but a simple quote from Walt Whitman, "Out of the cradle, endlessly rocking . . ." puts the film's four plots in their proper context.

With sound came an influx of writers who knew how to create great lines and stage-trained actors who knew how to breathe life into the words. The movies' greatest quotes represent the perfect merging of actor and writer to create a moment that lives on in the memory. If Ronald Reagan had said, "Here's looking at you, kid" in *Casablanca* (1942), it's possible nobody would remember it today. In all likelihood, without Humphrey Bogart, the line might never even have made it into the movie, as behind-the-scenes accounts suggest it was one of his contributions.

Hollywood imported any number of great writers, some of whom, like Ben Hecht and Anita Loos, made it as screenwriters, while some (most notably F. Scott Fitzgerald) never developed the knack for bringing words to the screen. And a special group of writers took on directing as well. Wilder claimed he did it after getting tired of watching other directors massacre his scripts. Among his peers were Preston Sturges, John Huston, and Joseph L. Mankiewicz. When the latter was lucky enough to get Bette Davis to replace an injured Claudette Colbert in *All About Eve* (1950), the result was a classic. One of the wittiest scripts ever written, its crackling dialogue continues to delight audiences.

The greatest lines have even become a part of the language. Nobody thought of slipping into "something more comfortable" until Jean Harlow used the phrase in *Hell's Angels* (1930). Nor did politicians and editorials refer to "creative accounting" until Mel Brooks introduced the phrase in his script for *The Producers* (1968). And thanks to Bette Davis, everybody knows the words "Fasten your seatbelts" signal a bumpy night to come.

But the words aren't confined to the screen. Under the studio system, everybody who had to deal with the press learned to give good quote. Erudite stars like Davis, Fred Astaire, and, when she was still giving interviews, Greta Garbo, reached out to their fans through movie magazines, gossip columns, and other interviews. W. C. Fields, Groucho Marx, and Mae West were among the great comics whose public pronouncements reinforced their screen images. And the few directors who developed celebrity status—Frank Capra and Alfred Hitchcock, for example—helped educate the public about the industry and their own working methods.

Filmmakers have also created a library of memoirs about the experience of making movies in the golden age. Hume Cronyn's *A Terrible Liar* included personal insights of such coworkers as Richard Burton and Katharine Hepburn. *Where's the Rest of Me?*, Ronald Reagan's 1965 memoir, revealed an affable character similar to those he had played in most of his films. Claire Bloom's *Limelight and After* and *Leaving a Doll's House* shed light on her famous costars, husbands, and romantic partners.

In the end, all of it comes back to one thing—selling the movies. Just as the tag lines created by publicity departments brought in audiences when Hollywood's greatest films were first released, so our movie memories bring us back to revisit our favorites. Whether it's a fondly remembered line, a killer quote about filmmaking, or a memoir we just can't put down, Hollywood's words continue to lead us back to the movies that have become the language of our lives.

1. About whom was Joseph Cotten speaking when he said the following? "He was the easiest, most inspiring man I've ever worked with."
   A. Alfred Hitchcock
   B. George Cukor
   C. Orson Welles
   D. Robert Wise

2. At his fifty-fifth birthday party, what famous writer said the following when asked what he wanted to be when he grew up? "I want to be fourteen years old like Chuck Jones."
   A. Kurt Vonnegut
   B. Ray Bradbury
   C. Stephen King
   D. Tom Wolfe

3. What William Castle film had early advertisements that claimed theaters would have seatbelts for those who would be scared out of their seats?
   A. *Homicidal* (1961)
   B. *I Saw What You Did* (1965)
   C. *Mr. Sardonicus* (1961)
   D. *Straight Jacket* (1964)

4. Which screen legend once said, "Only the gentle are ever really strong"?
   A. Clark Gable
   B. Gary Cooper
   C. James Dean
   D. Marlon Brando

5. Who was Clark Gable talking about when he told his wife, "Well, baby, I told you I was going to kiss a mermaid today"?
   A. Esther Williams
   B. Jean Harlow
   C. Mamie Van Doren
   D. Vivien Leigh

6. James Mason once said of which actress, "I have never met someone so badly behaved"?
   A. Cybill Shepherd
   B. Esther Williams
   C. Loretta Young
   D. Raquel Welch

7. According to Lucien Ballard, a wild party at what actress's house convinced him that he was perfect for show business?
   A. Ava Gardner
   B. Clara Bow
   C. Lana Turner
   D. Marion Davies

8. What famous musician said the following about Benny Goodman? "Benny used to practice fifteen times more than the whole band combined"
   A. Artie Shaw
   B. Harry James
   C. Les Brown
   D. Lionel Hampton

9. Which cinematographer said, "I'm their man if they want more than a cameraman"?
   A. Charles Lang
   B. Conrad Hall
   C. Joseph Ruttenberg
   D. Lucien Ballard

10. In what film does Bette Davis claim, "The only fun I get is feeding the goldfish, and they only eat once a day"?
    A. *Bordertown* (1935)
    B. *Jezebel* (1938)
    C. *Now, Voyager* (1942)
    D. *Old Acquaintance* (1943)

11. Cary Grant said that his role in which film was most similar to his real self?
    A. *Father Goose* (1964)
    B. *Houseboat* (1958)
    C. *North by Northwest* (1959)
    D. *The Philadelphia Story* (1940)

12. With which of his cartoon characters did Chuck Jones say he most identified with?

A. Daffy Duck
B. Pepe Le Pew
C. Porky Pig
D. Wile E. Coyote

13. "She didn't want to be famous. She wanted to be happy," was said of what actress?

A. Jean Harlow
B. Audrey Hepburn
C. Clara Bow
D. Carole Lombard

14. What actress said the following? "Scarlett O'Hara is going to be a thankless and difficult role. The part I'd like to play is Rhett Butler."

A. Carole Lombard
B. Joan Crawford
C. Katharine Hepburn
D. Norma Shearer

15. In Jack Arnold's *No Name on the Bullet* (1959), hired assassin John Grant says everyone does what?

A. Dies
B. Gets a little crazy sometimes
C. Lies
D. Runs away

16. Which actor is on the receiving end of this James Cagney insult from *Tribute to a Bad Man* (1956)? "You act like a man with a lot of ideas. But all of them second-rate . . . and not one honorable."

A. Ed Begley
B. Robert Walker
C. Stephen McNally
D. Ward Bond

17. Who said the following about Jean Harlow? "Jean was always cheerful, full of fun, but she also happened to be a sensitive woman with a great deal of self-respect. All that other stuff—that was put on. She just happened to be a good actress who created a lively characterization that exuded sex appeal."

A. Ann Miller
B. Ginger Rogers
C. Lucille Ball
D. Myrna Loy

18. Which Academy Award winner once said, "Every movie I make teaches me something, and that's why I keep making them"?

A. Ang Lee
B. Clint Eastwood
C. Martin Scorsese
D. Oliver Stone

19. Which screen legend once said, "I wish I were supernaturally strong so I could put right everything that is wrong"?

A. Greta Garbo
B. Merle Oberon
C. Olivia de Havilland
D. Vivien Leigh

20. Which screen legend once said that any romantic comedy script he was given seemed to have "had the fingerprints of Cary Grant on it"?

A. Gary Cooper
B. Gregory Peck
C. James Stewart
D. Orson Welles

21. Who called Jack Lemmon "a director's dream, a writer's savior, and a gift to the audience from a Harvard man who decided to turn actor"?

A. Billy Wilder
B. Janet Leigh
C. Lee Remick
D. Neil Simon

answers found on page 567

22. According to composer Jerry Goldsmith, what film score was the hardest and most complex?

    A. *Basic Instinct* (1992)
    B. *L.A. Confidential* (1997)
    C. *Lionheart* (1986)
    D. *Rudy* (1993)

23. Who said the following about Bing Crosby? "He could do anything better than almost anyone. He may well have been the most versatile human in the history of the world or of Paramount, whichever comes first"?

    A. Bob Hope
    B. Danny Kaye
    C. Donald O'Connor
    D. Dorothy Lamour

24. Which of Stewart Granger's costars in the 1952 western *The Wild North* was referred to as "beautiful dynamite" by Fred Astaire?

    A. Audrey Hepburn
    B. Cyd Charisse
    C. Ginger Rogers
    D. Rita Hayworth

25. Who referred to James Cagney as "the professional against-er"?

    A. David O. Selznick
    B. Jack Warner
    C. Jeanne Cagney
    D. Lloyd Bacon

26. Which screen legend once said, "Life would be so wonderful if we only knew what to do with it"?

    A. Ava Gardner
    B. Greta Garbo
    C. Olivia de Havilland
    D. Vivien Leigh

27. What Oscar-winning film was known in Hollywood as "John's Folly," as most believed it to be unadaptable for the screen?

    A. *Around the World in 80 Days* (1956)

    B. *From Here to Eternity* (1953)
    C. *Marty* (1955)
    D. *On the Waterfront* (1954)

28. Director George Roy Hill once said that the only music he played for pleasure was by what composer?

    A. Bach
    B. Beethoven
    C. Chopin
    D. Mozart

29. What did Chuck Jones say was "the essence, the spine, and the electrical magic of humor, and of animation"?

    A. Color
    B. Movement
    C. Timing
    D. Voices

30. In which George Marshall film does the following line occur? "The girls call me Pilgrim, because every time I dance with one I make a little progress."

    A. *Destry* (1954)
    B. *Imitation General* (1958)
    C. *Never a Dull Moment* (1950)
    D. *The Ghost Breakers* (1940)

31. Who was director John Cromwell talking about when he said the following? "[He] never understood a thing about real acting but had the most marvelous presence."

    A. Gary Cooper
    B. James Stewart
    C. Raymond Massey
    D. Ronald Colman

32. Which of his cartoons did Chuck Jones say was the one on which he "learned how to be funny"?
   A. *My Favorite Duck* (1942)
   B. *Outpost* (1944)
   C. *The Dover Boys* (1942)
   D. *The Unbearable Bear* (1943)

33. What actress accepted her Oscar for Best Supporting Actress by thanking her "dad, who paid the bills"?
   A. Ann-Margret for *Carnal Knowledge* (1971)
   B. Cloris Leachman for *The Last Picture Show* (1971)
   C. Ellen Burstyn for *Alice Doesn't Live Here Anymore* (1974)
   D. Maggie Smith for *The Prime of Miss Jean Brodie* (1969)

34. When someone left open this comedy legend's bottle of whiskey, he responded by saying, "Who took the cork out of my lunch?"
   A. Bob Hope
   B. Jack Lemmon
   C. Red Skelton
   D. W. C. Fields

35. In what film do you hear the line, "Life in this family is one subpoena after another"?
   A. *Bringing Up Baby* (1938)
   B. *It Happened One Night* (1934)
   C. *My Man Godfrey* (1936)
   D. *The Awful Truth* (1937)

36. Who was director John Cromwell talking about when he said the following? "She was a nice girl, or she was then. [She] didn't make trouble, didn't have an ego problem. The problem was that she couldn't act."
   A. Hedy Lamarr
   B. Jean Arthur
   C. Lana Turner
   D. Rita Hayworth

37. What fellow director gave Robert Benton the following advice, which he said was the truest he ever got? "Movies are not written on a typewriter. They're written in a camera."
   A. Francis Ford Coppola
   B. Martin Scorsese
   C. Richard Donner
   D. Robert Altman

38. Who said of Jean Harlow, "She didn't want to be famous. She just wanted to be happy"?
   A. Clark Gable
   B. Louis B. Mayer
   C. Spencer Tracy
   D. William Powell

39. At what silent film comedian's funeral did Dick Van Dyke deliver the eulogy?
   A. Buster Keaton
   B. Charles Chaplin
   C. Harold Lloyd
   D. Stan Laurel

40. Which screen legend once said the following? "They say marriages are made in heaven. But so is thunder and lightning."
   A. Clint Eastwood
   B. Laurence Olivier
   C. Marlon Brando
   D. Richard Burton

41. Who did Groucho Marx call "a very nice guy, and a fairly good director, but no genius"?
   A. Norman Z. McLeod
   B. Sam Wood
   C. Victor Heerman
   D. William A. Seiter

answers found on page 567

42. The following lyric is to which song sung by Deborah Kerr's character in *The King and I* (1956)? "I know how it feels to have wings on your heels, and to fly down the street in a trance."
   A. "Getting to Know You"
   B. "Hello, Young Lovers"
   C. "I Whistle a Happy Tune"
   D. "Shall We Dance"

43. Who was Fay Wray talking about when she said the following? "I just thought [he] was mostly sleepy and un-alive! He did have the capacity to fall asleep in between scenes. And he almost never talked."
   A. Charles Boyer
   B. Farley Granger
   C. Gary Cooper
   D. Richard Dix

44. The memoirs of which Oscar-nominated actress were released in 1983 under the title *Baby Doll: An Autobiography*?
   A. Carroll Baker
   B. Eleanor Parker
   C. Gene Tierney
   D. Natalie Wood

45. Sally Field made her famous "You like me!" speech after she won the Best Actress Academy Award for what film?
   A. *Absence of Malice* (1981)
   B. *Norma Rae* (1979)
   C. *Places in the Heart* (1984)
   D. *Steel Magnolias* (1989)

46. In her 1998 memoir, *Leaving a Doll's House*, Claire Bloom claims to have had romantic relationships with all of the following actors except which one?
   A. Cary Grant
   B. Laurence Olivier
   C. Richard Burton
   D. Yul Brynner

47. Who did Ronald Reagan describe as "a pro, but an affable, easy person, fond of gentle ribbing"?
   A. Cary Grant
   B. Errol Flynn
   C. Humphrey Bogart
   D. William Powell

48. Orson Welles said of which costar, "She was so good, she frightened me"?
   A. Deborah Kerr
   B. Ingrid Bergman
   C. Joanne Woodward
   D. Natalie Wood

49. Which leading lady famously annoyed her costars by creating a "swear box" and fining them for using curse words?
   A. Carole Lombard
   B. Claudette Colbert
   C. Loretta Young
   D. Mary Pickford

50. What very pregnant actress accepted her 1955 Best Supporting Actress Oscar by quipping, "I think I may have the baby right here"?
   A. Claire Trevor for *The High and the Mighty*
   B. Donna Reed for *From Here to Eternity*
   C. Eva Marie Saint for *On the Waterfront*
   D. Grace Kelly for *Mogambo*

51. In what film does Deborah Kerr say, "Winter must be cold for those with no warm memories . . . And we've already missed the spring"?
   A. *An Affair to Remember* (1957)
   B. *Separate Tables* (1958)
   C. *The Arrangement* (1969)
   D. *The King and I* (1956)

52. About what leading lady's death did Ray Bolger say "She just plain wore out"?
   A. Jean Harlow
   B. Judy Garland
   C. Marilyn Monroe
   D. Rita Hayworth

answers found on page 567

53. According to his 1987 autobiography, what nickname did Joseph Cotten give the 1949 film *Under Capricorn*?

A. "Cornucopia"
B. "Under Capricornball"
C. "Under Corny Crap"
D. "Underwear Crappycorn"

54. Which comedy legend once said, "I am the most fortunate self-taught harpist and non-speaking actor who has ever lived"?

A. Buster Keaton
B. Charles Chaplin
C. Harold Lloyd
D. Harpo Marx

55. Who said the following about Bing Crosby? "Bing's voice has a mellow quality that only Bing's got. It's like gold being poured out of a cup."

A. Bob Hope
B. Frank Sinatra
C. Louis Armstrong
D. Rosemary Clooney

56. Robert Duvall has been reported to say that his favorite character to play was Gus McCrae in what television miniseries?

A. *Apocalypse Now* (1979)
B. *Lonesome Dove* (1989)
C. *M*A*S*H* (1970)
D. *True Grit* (1969)

57. Walter Matthau arranged to be credited as "Walter Matuschanskayasky" in mock protest to which of his films?

A. *Earthquake* (1974)
B. *Hello, Dolly!* (1969)
C. *Pete 'n' Tillie* (1972)
D. *Pirates* (1968)

58. What actress did William Wyler call "a director's dream"?

A. Bette Davis
B. Goldie Hawn
C. Greer Garson
D. Sophia Loren

59. According to the Kinks song "Celluloid Heroes," which silent film star "looks up ladies' dresses as they sadly pass him by"?

A. Buster Keaton
B. Fatty Arbuckle
C. Rudolph Valentino
D. Wallace Beery

60. Who did Ronald Reagan call "one of the warmest-hearted, truly kind people in the world"?

A. Edward G. Robinson
B. James Cagney
C. John Barrymore
D. Kirk Douglas

61. Which comedy legend once said that upon his visit to a Havana cigar factory, "There were four hundred people there rolling cigars, and when they saw me, they all stood up and applauded"?

A. Groucho Marx
B. Milton Berle
C. Red Skelton
D. W. C. Fields

62. To whom was he referring when Ernest Borgnine said the following? "I've got the Oscar, he's got a therapist. Checkmate."

A. Danny Kaye
B. Frank Sinatra
C. Mickey Rooney
D. Paul Newman

Stage Door, 1937

63. What actress referred to *Stage Door* (1937) as her "big break"?

A. Gail Patrick
B. Ginger Rogers
C. Katharine Hepburn
D. Lucille Ball

64. My real name was Julia Jean, but growing up most people called me "Judy." Who am I?

A. Carole Lombard
B. Esther Williams
C. Lana Turner
D. Lauren Bacall

65. Samuel Goldwyn claimed what Merle Oberon film to be his favorite production?

A. *The Dark Angel* (1935)
B. *The Lion Has Wings* (1939)
C. *The Private Life of Henry VIII* (1933)
D. *Wuthering Heights* (1939)

66. Ricardo Montalban was a commercial spokesman for which automobile company that used "rich, Corinthian leather"?

A. BMW
B. Chrysler
C. Porsche
D. Renault

67. To which of his films was Ronald Reagan referring when he said the following? "The entire picture was a sentimental journey and a thrilling experience."

A. *Brother Rat* (1938)
B. *Kings Row* (1942)
C. *Knute Rockne, All-American* (1940)
D. *The Girl from Jones Beach* (1949)

68. Which legendary filmmaker once said the following? "My advice to young filmmakers is this: Don't follow trends. Start them!"

A. Frank Capra
B. Fred Zinnemann
C. John Ford
D. Orson Welles

69. About which leading lady did Louis B. Mayer say, "She can't act, she can't talk, she's terrific"?

A. Ava Gardner
B. Jean Harlow
C. Lana Turner
D. Marilyn Monroe

70. When criticized about the violence in his film *The Big Boss* (1971), Bruce Lee said that the real violence was where?

A. Inner city
B. On the streets
C. The schools
D. Vietnam

71. To whom does Marlon Brando make his famous "I coulda been a contender" speech in *On the Waterfront* (1954)?

A. Karl Malden
B. Lee J. Cobb
C. Lee Marvin
D. Rod Steiger

answers found on page 567

72. Who was Jane Powell talking about when she said the following in her autobiography? "He had a snappy kind of arrogance I didn't appreciate"?

A. Fred Astaire
B. Howard Keel
C. Peter Lawford
D. Ricardo Montalban

73. Which film starring Moira Shearer has director George Romero called "the movie that made me want to make movies"?

A. *Peeping Tom* (1960)
B. *The Man Who Loved Redheads* (1955)
C. *The Red Shoes* (1948)
D. *The Tales of Hoffman* (1951)

74. Which star once said, "My own name, I never did understand"?

A. Buster Keaton
B. Charles Chaplin
C. Groucho Marx
D. W. C. Fields

75. Which leading lady delivered the line, "Nature, Mr. Allnut, is what we are put in this world to rise above"?

A. Barbara Stanwyck
B. Katharine Hepburn
C. Myrna Loy
D. Rosalind Russell

76. Who said of Jack Lemmon, "He was ugly as a woman"?

A. Frank Sinatra
B. Shirley MacLaine
C. Tony Curtis
D. Walter Matthau

77. In what film can you hear the famous line, "Would you be shocked if I changed into something more comfortable?"

A. *Hell's Angels* (1930)

B. *Libeled Lady* (1936)
C. *The Public Enemy* (1931)
D. *Three Wise Girls* (1932)

78. Jack Nicholson once said of which actor, "Acting is life study, and [his] classes got me into looking at life as an artist"?

A. Jeff Corey
B. Laurence Naismith
C. Laurence Olivier
D. William Holden

79. Who was Jean Harlow talking about when she said the following? "Being in the same cast with [her] was a break for me. She's one trouper I'd never try to steal a scene from. It'd be like trying to carry Italy against Mussolini."

A. Loretta Young
B. Marie Dressler
C. Mary Astor
D. Rosalind Russell

80. In what Gore Vidal novel does he reference Richard Cromwell as being "so satisfyingly tortured in *The Lives of a Bengal Lancer* (1935)"?

A. Julian
B. Myra Breckinridge
C. The City and the Pillar
D. Washington, D.C.

81. Which Academy Award winner once said, "People think of me as an intellectual actor. Yet I have always trusted almost entirely to observation, emotion, and instinct"?

A. Alec Guinness
B. Gary Cooper
C. John Gielgud
D. Laurence Olivier

82. According to George Sanders's voice-over, how old was Bette Davis's character in *All About Eve* (1950) when she made her first stage appearance?

A. 10
B. 15
C. 19
D. 4

83. Who said the following about the movies? "The only thing wrong with the silent picture was that mouths opened, and nothing came out. The talking picture only partially solved that problem."

A. Alfred Hitchcock
B. Charles Chaplin
C. King Vidor
D. Sam Goldwyn

84. In his memoirs, director Franco Zeffirelli said that working on what film with Elizabeth Taylor and Richard Burton was the most fun he ever had in his career?

A. *Cleopatra* (1963)
B. *Doctor Faustus* (1967)
C. *The Taming of the Shrew* (1967)
D. *The V.I.P.s* (1963)

85. Faye Dunaway exclaims "No more wire hangers!" in what film?

A. *Chinatown* (1974)
B. *Mommie Dearest* (1981)
C. *Network* (1976)
D. *The Arrangement* (1969)

86. According to Groucho Marx, who are the "people who feel that they don't dance enough"?

A. Comedians
B. Husbands
C. Musicians
D. Wives

87. Who said the following about Sandra Dee? "When she did the love scenes, she surprised me that she knew how to kiss."

A. John Gavin
B. John Saxon
C. Peter Fonda
D. Troy Donahue

88. What actress, when told she'd earned her big break after a contest judge threw the contestants' photos in the air and hers landed right-side-up, replied, "And I've been on my back ever since"?

A. Ann Sheridan
B. Ava Gardner
C. Joan Crawford
D. Loretta Young

89. Irving Berlin once said of what screen legend, "He knew the value of a song and his heart was in it before his feet took over"?

A. Buster Keaton
B. Clark Gable
C. Fred Astaire
D. Gene Kelly

90. Who was he talking about when Ernest Borgnine said the following? "[He] was the first actor I've seen who could just look down into the dirt and command a scene."

A. Lee Marvin
B. Montgomery Clift
C. Robert De Niro
D. Spencer Tracy

91. To whom was Carole Lombard referring when she said the following? "If the picture's a huge hit he'll get the credit, and if it's a flop, I'll be blamed."

A. Alfred Hitchcock
B. Frank Capra
C. George Cukor
D. Orson Welles

answers found on page 567

92. Who was he talking about when Jack Lemmon said the following? "Difficult? Yes. But she was a wonderful comedienne and she had a charisma like no one before or since."
   A. Judy Holliday
   B. Lucille Ball
   C. Marilyn Monroe
   D. Shirley MacLaine

93. Frank Capra once said that what film star's "appeal lay in being so unusually usual"?
   A. Gary Cooper
   B. Glenn Ford
   C. James Stewart
   D. Peter O'Toole

94. Which screen legend once said, "Success only breeds a new goal"?
   A. Bette Davis
   B. Deborah Kerr
   C. Elizabeth Taylor
   D. Katharine Hepburn

95. Which *The Night of the Iguana* (1964) star joked that he/she was the only cast member who "wasn't having an affair with somebody" during production?
   A. Ava Gardner
   B. Deborah Kerr
   C. Richard Burton
   D. Sue Lyon

96. Roddy McDowall was well loved in the acting community. All of the following claimed McDowall was one of their best friends except who?
   A. Carol Lawrence
   B. Elizabeth Taylor
   C. Marilyn Monroe
   D. Peggy Ann Garner

97. Which Academy Award winner once said the following? "I don't believe in pessimism. If something doesn't come up the way you want, forge ahead."
   A. Anthony Hopkins
   B. Clint Eastwood
   C. Gary Cooper
   D. Spencer Tracy

98. About whom was she speaking when Rosalind Russell made the following statement in her autobiography? "He was terrific to work with because he's a true comic, in the sense that comedy is in the mind, the brain, the cortex."
   A. Cary Grant
   B. George Cukor
   C. James Stewart
   D. Karl Malden

99. What actress was Rex Harrison talking about when he said the following? "Working with [her] was rather like being a very well-trained hundred-yard sprinter, waiting in the starting position for the gun to go off."
   A. Audrey Hepburn
   B. Elizabeth Taylor
   C. Rita Hayworth
   D. Vivien Leigh

100. A critic once said of what composer, "His was the music of Gothic and gaslight"?
   A. Antonio Vivaldi
   B. Bernard Herrmann
   C. Dimitri Tiomkin
   D. Johann Strauss

101. About whom was Robert Benton talking when he said the following in an interview? "She's like a woman in a Howard Hawks film."
   A. Melanie Griffith
   B. Meryl Streep
   C. Nicole Kidman
   D. Susan Sarandon

102. In which of her films did Barbra Streisand utter her famous line, "Hello, gorgeous"?

A. *Funny Girl* (1968)
B. *Funny Lady* (1975)
C. *The Main Event* (1979)
D. *The Way We Were* (1973)

103. When asked at the first Academy Awards ceremony what the most exciting part of her night was, Janet Gaynor replied that it was meeting what actor?

A. Buster Keaton
B. Charles Chaplin
C. Douglas Fairbanks
D. Lon Chaney

104. What actor called Jean Harlow "a square shooter if ever there was one"?

A. Cary Grant
B. Fredric March
C. James Stewart
D. Spencer Tracy

105. Who did Ronald Reagan describe in his 1965 autobiography as "a strange person, terribly unsure of himself"?

A. Errol Flynn
B. Gary Cooper
C. Humphrey Bogart
D. Wallace Beery

106. What Republican actress refused to read the "subversive" line, "Share and share alike, that's the American way," in *Tender Comrade* (1943)?

A. Ginger Rogers
B. Jean Arthur
C. Loretta Young
D. Ruth Hussey

107. Which leading lady said the following about acting? "Career is too pompous a word. It was a job."

A. Barbara Stanwyck
B. Lillian Gish

C. Myrna Loy
D. Rosalind Russell

108. Who referred to Benny Goodman as America's "International Ambassador with Clarinet"?

A. Henry Kissinger
B. John F. Kennedy
C. Richard Nixon
D. Ronald Reagan

109. Whom did Marilyn Monroe describe as "the only person I know who is in worse shape than I am"?

A. Arthur Miller
B. John F. Kennedy
C. Montgomery Clift
D. Tony Curtis

110. Which director kept a note to himself in a desk drawer for thirty years that said, "No More Goldwyn Pictures"?

A. John Ford
B. King Vidor
C. Victor Fleming
D. William Wyler

111. In what film does Bette Davis utter the line, "Everybody has a heart, except some people"?

A. *All About Eve* (1950)
B. *Beyond the Forest* (1949)
C. *Now, Voyager* (1942)
D. *The Great Lie* (1941)

112. Which legendary actor once said, "Home is where the books are"?

A. Humphrey Bogart
B. Laurence Olivier
C. Marlon Brando
D. Richard Burton

answers found on page 567

113. Who was Jack Lemmon talking about when he said the following? "She hated rehearsals and had a bad habit of ad-libbing . . . But we got used to each other, because mainly she's a helluva girl."

A. Judy Holliday
B. Kim Novak
C. Marilyn Monroe
D. Shirley MacLaine

114. To whom was Hume Cronyn referring when he wrote the following in his autobiography? "She was tall, slim, beautiful and very direct, and her look was as firm as her handshake."

A. Ingrid Bergman
B. Jessica Tandy
C. Katharine Hepburn
D. Lauren Bacall

115. After meeting James Dean on the set of what film did John Steinbeck proclaim, "He *is* Cal!"

A. *East of Eden* (1955)
B. *Many Rivers to Cross* (1955)
C. *Saddle the Wind* (1958)
D. *Valley of the Kings* (1954)

116. Which director is sometimes called "King of the Bs"?

A. Ed Wood
B. Edgar G. Ulmer
C. Roger Corman
D. Val Lewton

117. The memoir of which screen legend is titled *Steps in Time*?

A. Bing Crosby
B. Fred Astaire
C. Gene Kelly
D. Harold Lloyd

118. To which of his films was William Haines referring when he made the following comment? "I didn't have to act. I was just myself."

A. *Brown of Harvard* (1926)
B. *Little Annie Rooney* (1925)
C. *Show People* (1928)
D. *Way Out West* (1930)

119. Whom did Hume Cronyn refer to as "one of the very few actors I've known who was truly touched by the finger of God"?

A. Laurence Olivier
B. Orson Welles
C. Richard Burton
D. Spencer Tracy

120. Ida Lupino described herself as the "poor man's" what?

A. Bette Davis
B. Carole Lombard
C. Jean Harlow
D. Judy Garland

121. In her 1972 autobiography, Ingrid Bergman said the following about what actor? "He was polite naturally, but I always felt there was a distance; he was behind a wall. I was intimidated by him."

A. Cary Grant
B. Charles Boyer
C. Gregory Peck
D. Humphrey Bogart

122. In the opening scene of *It Started with Eve* (1941), a character comments that if Jonathan Reynolds had lived two centuries earlier, he would have made a great pirate; three years later, the actor who played Jonathan Reynolds in that film would play the title role in *Captain Kidd* (1945). Who was that actor?

A. Charles Laughton
B. Guy Kibbee
C. Robert Cummings
D. Walter Catlett

123. About whom did Robert Benton make the following statement in an interview? "I think he's like this generation's Jack Lemmon; he makes you cry, he's funny, he never lets you see the acting."

A. Bruce Willis
B. Greg Kinnear
C. Vince Vaughn
D. William H. Macy

124. Which of Bette Davis's costars of the 1930s said, "Even when I was carrying a gun, she scared the bejesus out of me"?

A. Edward G. Robinson
B. Errol Flynn
C. Humphrey Bogart
D. Leslie Howard

125. Which one of Bette Davis's classmates at John Murray Anderson's Dramatic School was sent packing for being "too shy"?

A. Cyd Charisse
B. Debbie Reynolds
C. Doris Day
D. Lucille Ball

126. Which famous boxer said, "I wanted to do in boxing what Bruce Lee was able to do in karate"?

A. George Foreman
B. Mike Tyson
C. Muhammed Ali
D. Sugar Ray Leonard

127. Which actress claimed to have nicknamed the Academy Award statuette "Oscar" because its shapely buttocks resembled those of her husband Harmon Oscar Nelson?

A. Bette Davis
B. Irene Dunne
C. Joan Crawford
D. Norma Shearer

The Letter, 1940

128. During the filming of *The Letter* (1940), director William Wyler and Bette Davis had a bitter disagreement over how to say which line?

A. "Frankly, my dear, I don't give a damn."
B. "With all my heart, I still love the man I killed."
C. "If you love a person, you can forgive anything."
D. "Thou shalt not kill."

129. What director was Ronald Reagan talking about when he said the following in his 1965 autobiography? "When he was shooting a picture, [he]—who was normally a kind, good-natured soul—became a ruthless tyrant, as hard on himself as anyone else."

A. Michael Curtiz
B. Raoul Walsh
C. Robert Wise
D. William Wyler

130. Which film director once said the following? "There are no rules in filmmaking. Only sins. And the cardinal sin is dullness."

A. Alfred Hitchcock
B. Frank Capra
C. Michael Curtiz
D. Orson Welles

131. Which Oscar-winning songwriter once said, "The song has ended, but the melody lingers on"?
A. Harry Warren
B. Irving Berlin
C. Max Steiner
D. Ralph Rainger

132. Ann Miller claimed that she was able to tap dance at what speed?
A. 200 taps per minute
B. 300 taps per minute
C. 400 taps per minute
D. 500 taps per minute

133. Who was Jack Lemmon talking about when he said the following? "He could have just been the beautiful young leading man, handsome and charming as hell, with a great personality, sensitive, all of those qualities he has. But he didn't. He wanted to be a good actor, and he's the only guy I know who learned his craft successfully—literally, learned how to act—on film. Nobody else comes to my mind who did this."
A. Burt Lancaster
B. James Dean
C. Michael Douglas
D. Tony Curtis

134. To which director was Michael Caine referring when he wrote the following in his autobiography? "He was a very quiet and sensitive man who liked to work in a very quiet atmosphere, so even the crew on his pictures were the quietest crew with whom I have ever worked."
A. Brian De Palma
B. Richard Attenborough
C. Sidney Lumet
D. Woody Allen

135. According to *The Man Who Came to Dinner* (1942), what would it take for a girl to fall for Richard Travis?
A. A set of dishes
B. Blindness
C. Complete desperation
D. Diamonds, pearls, and an analyst

136. Who said the following about Jackie Chan? "He is one of the greatest physical comedians since sound came into films. If I could be any actor, I would have the life Jackie Chan has."
A. Quentin Tarantino
B. Spike Lee
C. Steven Soderbergh
D. Steven Spielberg

137. What was the only thing Frank Sinatra said he could do better than Groucho Marx?
A. Act
B. Dance
C. Play golf
D. Sing

138. To whom does Humphrey Bogart say his famous line, "Here's looking at you, kid"?
A. Audrey Hepburn
B. Ingrid Bergman
C. Katharine Hepburn
D. Lauren Bacall

139. Who said the following about Jean Harlow? "I loved her, and oh she was a stunning creature! I remember sitting under a hair dryer in a beauty parlor one day, and sitting next to me was a child, also under a dryer . . . suddenly the hood of the dryer went back and the child stood up and it was Jean. She was probably twenty-three at the time but without makeup and no eyebrows, she looked exactly like a little kid."
A. Gloria Swanson
B. Joan Crawford
C. Loretta Young
D. Rosalind Russell

140. Whom was Hume Cronyn talking about when he made the following statement in his autobiography? "He thought in images. The story was to be pictorially revealed, not just told."

A. Alan J. Pakula
B. Alfred Hitchcock
C. Ron Howard
D. Sydney Pollack

141. About which leading lady's acting talents did Dorothy Parker comment, "She ran the gamut of emotions from A to B"?

A. Ava Gardner
B. Bette Davis
C. Katharine Hepburn
D. Lillian Gish

142. According to Cyd Charisse, of all the films she made with Gene Kelly, which one was her favorite?

A. *Anchors Aweigh* (1945)
B. *Brigadoon* (1954)
C. *Silk Stockings* (1957)
D. *The Three Musketeers* (1948)

143. Who claimed that Peter Lawford was homosexual and needed supervision in order to convince Louis B. Mayer that he needed to pay him/her a salary as Lawford's personal assistant?

A. Brother
B. Mother
C. Sister
D. Wife

144. Who called Chuck Jones "the Orson Welles of cartoons"?

A. Dr. Seuss
B. Jimmy Carter
C. Robin Williams
D. Stephen King

145. Who said, "There are two kinds of merchandise that can be made profitably in this business, either the very cheap pictures or the very expensive pictures"?

A. David O. Selznick
B. Howard Hughes
C. Louis Mayer
D. Sam Goldwyn

146. Which comedy legend once quipped, "I drink to make other people interesting"?

A. Groucho Marx
B. Martin Short
C. Redd Foxx
D. Stan Laurel

147. What man does Lana Turner name as the love of her life in her 1983 autobiography?

A. Artie Shaw
B. Johnny Stompanato
C. Stephen Crane
D. Tyrone Power

148. In which film does Robert Duvall utter the line, "I love the smell of napalm in the morning"?

A. *Apocalypse Now* (1979)
B. *M*A*S*H* (1970)
C. *The Godfather* (1972)
D. *Tomorrow* (1972)

149. According to the feminist motto, "Ginger Rogers did everything Fred Astaire did, but . . ."

A. . . . backward and in high heels"
B. . . . better and with her eyes closed"
C. . . . faster and in pinafores"
D. . . . first and with all her hair"

150. Deborah Kerr utters the following line in which film? "Years from now when you talk about this—and you will—be kind."

A. *Tea and Sympathy* (1956)
B. *The End of the Affair* (1955)
C. *The Innocents* (1961)
D. *The Night of the Iguana* (1964)

151. Who said the following quote about Bing Crosby? "He was the father of my career, the idol of my youth and a dear friend of my maturity."
   A. Dean Martin
   B. Eddie Fisher
   C. Frank Sinatra
   D. Robert Goulet

152. According to the famous line from *I'm No Angel* (1933), what does Mae West want "Beulah" to peel for her?
   A. A banana
   B. A grape
   C. An apple
   D. An orange

153. The memoir of which actor was published in 2007 under the title *Include Me Out: My Life from Goldwyn to Broadway*?
   A. Farley Granger
   B. Frederic March
   C. Mel Ferrer
   D. Richard Burton

154. Who did Fay Wray describe as "a fascinating combination of high imagination, an implicitly rebellious nature, a political conservative, an intellect, an adventurer, and a visionary"?
   A. Louis B. Mayer
   B. Merian C. Cooper
   C. Mike Todd
   D. Ted Turner

155. Which of her costars did Claire Bloom describe in the following manner? "It was obvious that he was going to be a huge star, which is not the same as being a great actor. He has confused them."
   A. Charles Chaplin
   B. Laurence Olivier
   C. Richard Burton
   D. Yul Brynner

156. In which Norman Z. McLeod film does the following line of dialogue occur? "Afraid? Me? A man who's licked his weight in wild caterpillars?"
   A. *Casanova's Big Night* (1954)
   B. *Jackass Mail* (1942)
   C. *Monkey Business* (1931)
   D. *The Kid from Brooklyn* (1946)

157. To whom was Ronald Reagan referring when he wrote the following in his autobiography? "I was one of thousands who were drawn to this very kind man, and who would think of him as a best friend."
   A. Dick Powell
   B. Eddie Albert
   C. Pat O'Brien
   D. Peter Lawford

158. Jean Harlow is referenced in the first line of which of these popular songs?
   A. "Bette Davis Eyes"
   B. "Girls on Film"
   C. "Glamorous"
   D. "Heart of Glass"

159. The quote, "It looks as if Hollywood brides keep the bouquets and throw away the grooms," is attributed to whom?
   A. Bing Crosby
   B. Dean Martin
   C. Groucho Marx
   D. W. C. Fields

160. Who was Ronald Reagan talking about when he said the following? "I was warned that [he] was an inveterate scene-stealer and would even get his face in the camera when it was a close-up on other players."
   A. Dick Powell
   B. Edward G. Robinson
   C. James Cagney
   D. Wallace Beery

answers found on page 568

161. In Jack Arnold's *No Name on the Bullet* (1959), who does hired gunman John Grant tell he is in "a similar line of work"?

A. The local banker
B. The local blacksmith
C. The town doctor
D. The town mayor

162. What William Castle film had advertisements that said a "million dollar insurance policy had been taken out for the film's star Hercules the cockroach"?

A. *Bug* (1975)
B. *Homicidal* (1961)
C. *Mr. Sardonicus* (1961)
D. *Straight Jacket* (1964)

163. In his song "Lonesome Day Blues," Bob Dylan quotes a line from what short film starring W. C. Fields?

A. *International House* (1933)
B. *Six of a Kind* (1934)
C. *That Royle Girl* (1925)
D. *The Fatal Glass of Beer* (1933)

164. In *She Done Him Wrong* (1933), what actor is on the receiving end of the famous Mae West line, "Why don't you come up sometime and see me?"

A. Cary Grant
B. Clark Gable
C. Gary Cooper
D. George Raft

165. Which Hollywood mogul said that Bette Davis had as much sex appeal as Slim Summerville?

A. Carl Laemmle
B. Irving Thalberg
C. Jack Warner
D. Louis B. Meyer

166. All her life, Merle Oberon denied her mixed heritage by claiming what country as her homeland?

A. Australia
B. Canada
C. England
D. Greece

167. Who said, after watching *The Sound of Music* (1965), "That was the only time I've ever rooted for the Nazis"?

A. Carol Reed
B. Charlton Heston
C. Gene Tierney
D. Rex Harrison

168. After his performance in *Stalag 17* (1953) earned him the Best Actor Oscar, who did William Holden say he felt actually deserved to win?

A. Burt Lancaster for *From Here to Eternity* (1953)
B. Marlon Brando for *Julius Caesar* (1953)
C. Montgomery Clift for *From Here to Eternity* (1953)
D. Richard Burton for *The Robe* (1953)

169. Who delivers the following line of dialogue in *The Haunting* (1936)? "Just the thing to give a child at bedtime. No family should be without one."

A. Carolyn Craig
B. Claire Bloom
C. Julie Harris
D. Russ Tamblyn

170. In *An Affair to Remember* (1957), what landmark does Deborah Kerr call "the nearest thing to heaven we have in New York"?

A. Grant's Tomb
B. Chrysler Building
C. Empire State Building
D. Statue of Liberty

answers found on page 568

171. In what film does Jean Harlow say, "You can get another 'if' girl, a 'but' girl, a 'how when and where girl,' I'm clearing out"?
    A. *Bombshell* (1933)
    B. *Hold Your Man* (1933)
    C. *Red Dust* (1932)
    D. *Red-Headed Woman* (1932)

172. Which Academy Award–winner once said, "Anytime anybody tells me the trend is such and such, I go the opposite direction"?
    A. Al Pacino
    B. Clint Eastwood
    C. Jack Nicholson
    D. Marlon Brando

173. To what movie star did Charles Chaplin say the following? "Acting is ninety-nine percent sweat and one percent talent. But that talent had better be good."
    A. Cary Grant
    B. Errol Flynn
    C. Gregory Peck
    D. Mickey Rooney

174. Which of his costars was Marlon Brando talking about when he said the following? "He made me laugh so hard. We got the giggles like two girls at a boarding school."
    A. David Niven
    B. Frank Sinatra
    C. Johnny Depp
    D. Karl Malden

175. Which of his films did Ronald Reagan call "the finest picture I've ever been in"?
    A. *Brother Rat* (1938)
    B. *Kings Row* (1942)
    C. *Knute Rockne, All-American* (1940)
    D. *The Girl from Jones Beach* (1949)

176. Where did MGM falsely claim that Greer Garson was born?
    A. Australia
    B. Canada
    C. Ireland
    D. Paris

177. Which screen legend once said the following? "Every one of us lives his life just once; if we are honest, to live once is enough."
    A. Audrey Hepburn
    B. Barbara Stanwyck
    C. Elizabeth Taylor
    D. Greta Garbo

178. Which Academy Award winner once said, "The toughest thing about success is that you've got to keep on being a success"?
    A. Clark Gable
    B. Humphrey Bogart
    C. Irving Berlin
    D. Johnny Mercer

179. Who was Fay Wray talking about when she said the following? "He had grace, style, wit and technique. He was not absolutely handsome, so that he was believable as a leading man or as a villain."
    A. Gary Cooper
    B. Melvyn Douglas
    C. Ralph Bellamy
    D. William Powell

180. What actor was approached to portray Professor Henry Higgins in the film version of *My Fair Lady* (1964), but refused it by saying the following? "Not only will I not play Higgins, if you don't put Rex Harrison in it, I won't go see it!"
    A. Cary Grant
    B. Gregory Peck
    C. Howard Keel
    D. James Cagney

answers found on page 568

181. Which actress described her on-screen voice as sounding "like an angry Minnie Mouse"?

A. Gene Tierney
B. Irene Dunne
C. Kim Novak
D. Mary Pickford

182. Who was Jane Powell referring to when she made the following statement in her autobiography? "He ignored everybody and everything. He never said hello. He never said goodbye. He never smiled."

A. Howard Keel
B. Mickey Rooney
C. Ralph Bellamy
D. Wallace Beery

183. Chuck Jones said the following about which of his cartoons? "This was, for me, the first cartoon in which the music absolutely determined the action."

A. *Baton Bunny* (1959)
B. *The Cats Bah* (1954)
C. *The Rabbit of Seville* (1950)
D. *What's Opera, Doc?* (1957)

184. In what James Cagney movie does a character say, "One of you's gonna get married and the other one's going to jail, so you really got a lot in common"?

A. *Great Guy* (1936)
B. *He Was Her Man* (1934)
C. *The Bride Came C.O.D.* (1941)
D. *The Strawberry Blonde* (1941)

185. In what James Cagney movie does a character say, "My mother thanks you. My father thanks you. My sister thanks you. And I thank you"?

A. *Ragtime* (1981)
B. *The Time of Your Life* (1948)
C. *White Heat* (1949)
D. *Yankee Doodle Dandy* (1942)

186. Whom did Hume Cronyn refer to as "a lady with whom it is best not to trifle"? Then he added, "Beneath that beautiful exterior is a repository of tempered steel."

A. Joan Crawford
B. Katharine Hepburn
C. Lana Turner
D. Lauren Bacall

187. What contemporary film did Ray Bradbury call "brilliant" and "absolutely perfect" in a 2001 interview?

A. *As Good as It Gets* (1997)
B. *Shakespeare in Love* (1998)
C. *The Matrix* (1999)
D. *The Shawshank Redemption* (1994)

188. In which of her films does Bette Davis deliver the oft-quoted line, "Fasten your seat belts—it's going to be a bumpy night"?

A. *All About Eve* (1950)
B. *Jezebel* (1938)
C. *Now, Voyager* (1942)
D. *The Letter* (1940)

189. In a 2002 interview with Sam Donaldson for ABCNews.com, Sean Connery stated his favorite Bond film was what?

A. *Dr. No* (1962)
B. *From Russia with Love* (1963)
C. *Goldfinger* (1964)
D. *Thunderball* (1965)

190. Whom did Rosalind Russell refer to in her autobiography as "a demon"? Then she added, "She used to stick out her tongue whenever I passed (she couldn't stand me) and she was bursting at the seams with repressed sexuality."

A. Hayley Mills
B. Kim Novak
C. Natalie Wood
D. Sandra Dee

191. Who said the following quote about Robert Benton? "He's the kind of director you can work with time and time again, because he loves actors and he cares about the integrity of small stories."
A. Bruce Willis
B. Dustin Hoffman
C. Greg Kinnear
D. Paul Newman

192. Which film starring Cary Grant and Audrey Hepburn was popularly known as "the best Hitchcock film that Hitchcock never made"?
A. *Arsenic and Old Lace* (1944)
B. *Charade* (1963)
C. *The Children's Hour* (1961)
D. *Wait Until Dark* (1967)

193. Which Oscar-winning director once said, "Anyone who doesn't believe in miracles isn't a realist"?
A. Billy Wilder
B. Frank Capra
C. George Cukor
D. George Stevens

194. Which star once joked that the ideal woman is, "Short and tall, and slim and stout, and blonde and brunette"?
A. Clark Gable
B. Dean Martin
C. Groucho Marx
D. W. C. Fields

195. Fred Astaire once said about what costar, "When you dance with her you stay danced"?
A. Cyd Charisse
B. Doris Day
C. Ginger Rogers
D. Rita Hayworth

196. Which screen legend once said the following about modern films? "They tend to overdo the vulgarity. I'm not embarrassed by the language itself, but it's embarrassing to be listening to it, sitting next to perfect strangers."
A. Clark Gable
B. Fred Astaire
C. Gene Kelly
D. Rex Harrison

197. What is written on Jean Harlow's crypt at Forest Lawn Cemetery?
A. "Baby Blonde"
B. "Our Baby"
C. "The Original Blonde Bombshell"
D. "Platinum Blonde "

198. In which Norman Z. McLeod film does the following line of dialogue occur? "It's nights like these that drive men like me to women like you for nights like this."
A. *Casanova's Big Night* (1954)
B. *Monkey Business* (1931)
C. *My Favorite Spy* (1951)
D. *Road to Rio* (1947)

199. Which comedy legend said, "Once during Prohibition, I was forced to live for days on nothing but food and water"?
A. Groucho Marx
B. Harold Lloyd
C. Stan Laurel
D. W. C. Fields

200. Marilyn Monroe appears for a moment on screen with the line "Hi, Rad" in what film?
A. *Magic Town* (1947)
B. *On Our Merry Way* (1948)
C. *Pot O' Gold* (1941)
D. *Scudda Hoo! Scudda Hay!* (1948)

201. John Steinbeck said that Henry Fonda's performance in which film adaptation made Steinbeck "believe [his] own words"?
   A. *East of Eden* (1955)
   B. *La Perla* (1947)
   C. *The Forgotten Village* (1941)
   D. *The Grapes of Wrath* (1940)

Kings Row, 1942

202. Which actor who starred in *King's Row* (1942) called the picture "a slightly sordid but moving yarn about the antics in a small town?"
   A. Ronald Reagan
   B. Robert Cummings
   C. Charles Coburn
   D. Claude Rains

203. Who was Moira Shearer talking about when she said the following? "His dancing was of a totally different style, of course, but I think he was probably the best dancer I've ever seen in my life."
   A. Fred Astaire
   B. Gene Kelly
   C. Mikhail Baryshnikov
   D. Peter Martins

204. In *The Spy Who Came in from the Cold* (1965), Claire Bloom defines the word "lycanthrope" for Richard Burton. What does it mean?
   A. A man who has been transformed into a wolf
   B. One who donates to charitable causes

C. The hatred of mankind
D. The study of algae

205. About whom was Ethel Barrymore speaking when she made the following statement? "He is so relaxed, so nice, just being around him is heaven."
   A. Bing Crosby
   B. Cary Grant
   C. Gregory Peck
   D. Humphrey Bogart

206. Which leading lady is famous for the following line of dialogue? "It's not the men in my life, but the life in my men."
   A. Carole Lombard
   B. Clara Bow
   C. Mae West
   D. Marilyn Monroe

207. In *If a Man Answers* (1962), what does Sandra Dee claim her father considered "adequate sex education"?
   A. Jane Austen
   B. "Me Tarzan, you Jane"
   C. Church
   D. Slow dancing

208. According to a 2004 interview, what novel by F. Scott Fitzgerald does Ray Bradbury reread every July?
   A. *Tender Is the Night*
   B. *The Beautiful and Damned*
   C. *The Great Gatsby*
   D. *This Side of Paradise*

209. Which leading lady said, "Whatever you write about me, don't make it sad"?
   A. Clara Bow
   B. Jean Harlow
   C. Rita Hayworth
   D. Rosalind Russell

210. "I thought drama was when the actors cried. But drama is when the audience cries," are the words of which Oscar-winning film director?

A. Frank Capra
B. Fred Zinnemann
C. Victor Fleming
D. William Wyler

211. Who was considered "the greatest actress of all time" by James Mason?

A. Bette Davis
B. Greta Garbo
C. Ingrid Bergman
D. Olivia de Havilland

212. Who said of Jackie Chan, "My dog likes Jackie more, and so does my mother"?

A. Bruce Lee
B. Chris Tucker
C. Owen Wilson
D. Sylvester Stallone

213. I claimed to have kept busy during my 1941 strike from Warner Bros. by rebuilding abandoned cars in a friend's garage. Who am I?

A. Ann Sheridan
B. Bette Davis
C. Gene Tierney
D. Loretta Young

214. Which actress wrote in the first paragraph of her 1961 autobiography, *The Lonely Life*, "I have been at war from the beginning"?

A. Bette Davis
B. Katharine Hepburn
C. Mary Pickford
D. Maureen O'Sullivan

215. In what film does Katharine Hepburn deliver the line, "The calla lilies are in bloom again"?

A. *Mary of Scotland* (1936)
B. *Stage Door* (1937)
C. *The Iron Petticoat* (1956)
D. *The Lion in Winter* (1968)

216. Marlon Brando clashed bitterly with the director of *A Countess from Hong Kong* (1967), whom he often called "sadistic." Who was it?

A. Alfred Hitchcock
B. Busby Berkeley
C. Charles Chaplin
D. Stanley Kubrick

217. Bruce Lee said no to which famous rocker when asked to appear in a movie with him?

A. Bob Dylan
B. Elvis Presley
C. Frank Zappa
D. Mick Jagger

218. Circa 1926, which leading lady said the following about Hollywood? "Here, it is boring, incredibly boring, so boring I can't believe it is true."

A. Clara Bow
B. Gloria Swanson
C. Greta Garbo
D. Louise Brooks

219. Who was Charles Laughton talking about when he said the following: "All the tough talk is blind. He's a literate, gracious, kind man and he speaks beautifully—when he wants to"?

A. Charles Bronson
B. Marlon Brando
C. Robert Mitchum
D. Sylvester Stallone

220. Which actor once said, "By temperament, a young actor needs to be mercurial"?

A. Cedric Hardwicke
B. Leslie Howard
C. Raymond Burr
D. Richard Burton

221. Who did Jane Powell describe as "the only actor I ever had problems with"?

A. Ann Sothern
B. Carmen Miranda
C. Hedy Lamarr
D. Jeanette MacDonald

222. To whom was Michael Caine referring when he wrote the following in his autobiography? "I had rarely worked with an actor so unselfish and generous, so much so that you could experiment and take chances and not expect to find a knife in your back if it went wrong."

A. Christopher Plummer
B. Christopher Reeve
C. Donald Sutherland
D. Sean Connery

223. After watching what film at the Venice Film Festival did Jean-Luc Godard declare "Le cinema, c'est Nicholas Ray" (the cinema is Nicholas Ray)?

A. *Alexander the Great* (1956)
B. *Bitter Victory* (1957)
C. *The Night of the Iguana* (1964)
D. *The Rains of Ranchipur* (1955)

answers found on page 568

Doctor Zhivago, 1965

Chapter 17

MAKING MOVIE MAGIC:
ARTISTS, TECHNICIANS, PRODUCERS

Actors may be the most visible aspect of the movie-going experience, but before they can cast their spell on the audience, a troop of unseen, often unsung magicians have to create the worlds in which they move. From producers and writers to technicians and hairdressers, Hollywood's studios kept hundreds of artists and craftspeople on their payrolls during the studio era. Their names flash by in the credits, and, with luck, they were nominated for and even won the Oscars that only the most serious movie buffs pay attention to. But they are a vital part of creating the mystique of the movies.

They came from everywhere. Some were native Californians who got into the movie business because it was literally in their backyards. Others came from all over the world to add luster to Hollywood's films, including hundreds of artists who emigrated from Europe during two world wars. Many came from related fields—photographers who learned to run a movie camera, newspaper reporters who took to scriptwriting, couturiers who moved into studio wardrobe departments. And some belonged to families that became Hollywood dynasties. While Norma Shearer emoted on screen, her brother Douglas supervised the recording and editing of her dialogue. The Westmores—Perc, Ern, Bud, Frank, Monty, and Wally—dominated the makeup field. And three Hungarian brothers—producer-directors Alexander and Zoltan Korda and art director Vincent—were a virtual family studio, traveling to England and later Hollywood for lavish productions like *The Thief of Bagdad* (1940).

Rarely did any of these artists enter the public consciousness. For every Sam Goldwyn or David O. Selznick who generated personal publicity to help sell the pictures they produced, there were dozens of largely unknown producers like Walter Mirisch, who labored for years producing quality productions like *Some Like It Hot* (1959) and *In the Heat of the Night* (1967), who were more associated with their stars and directors. In the earlier years, producers weren't even credited on screen. Producer Ross Hunter might have referred to Lana Turner's lavish costumes in ads for *Imitation of Life* (1959), but only the most dedicated fans knew they had been designed by Jean Louis. And F. Scott Fitzgerald was always better known for the great novels he wrote, many of which were turned into good (and not-so-good) films, than for any of the screenplays on which he worked.

Yet the writers, cinematographers, designers, editors, and technicians who worked in Hollywood helped set the tone for the studios at which they worked. The irreverent wit of Philip and Julius Epstein was a key element to Warner Bros.' best films of the thirties and forties, as was the gritty cinematography of James Wong Howe, Tony Gaudio, and Sol Polito. Joseph Ruttenberg and William Daniels's creamy cinematography helped define the MGM look, as did Adrian's trendsetting costumes. Paramount's exoticism in the thirties owed a great deal to gowns Travis Banton put on stars like Marlene Dietrich and Mae West, just as its contemporary films in the forties and fifties were a perfect match for Edith Head's fashion sensibility.

The people behind the scenes also helped shape the work of major directors. Robert Riskin's screenplays for *It Happened One Night* (1934) and *Mr. Deeds Goes to Town* (1936) helped create the Frank Capra brand. Edith Head and composer Bernard Herrmann played a key role in making Alfred Hitchcock's fifties films classics. Freddie Young was the man behind the camera for such David Lean epics as *Lawrence of Arabia* (1962) and *Ryan's Daughter* (1970).

Historical films, particularly epics, have traditionally provided the greatest showcases for behind-the-scenes work. The challenges of hiring, dressing, photographing, and putting words into the mouths of a cast of thousands are as daunting as the task of finding and/or designing dozens of international locations. Little wonder productions like *Joan of Arc* (1948) and *Doctor Zhivago* (1965) dominate the design and technical Oscars.

Yet, as Sandy Powell pointed out accepting her Oscar for *Young Victoria* (2009), it's no less a challenge to costume a small-scale contemporary film. Nor does a production's size or lack thereof make any other behind-the-scenes job easier or harder. Haskell Wexler faced no more challenges creating a period look for the Woody Guthrie biopic *Bound for Glory* (1976) than he did shooting the ensemble cast of the contemporary drama *Who's Afraid of Virginia Woolf?* (1966). Finding the right words for a group of World War II fliers in *A Guy Named Joe* (1943) drew on Dalton Trumbo's talents no less than finding the idiom for ancient Rome in *Spartacus* (1960). In each case, it's a question of creating an entire world, a world composed of words, images, and sounds.

1. What costume designer earned an Oscar nomination for his work on *Bell, Book and Candle* (1958)?

   A. Bob Mackie
   B. Cecil Beaton
   C. Jean Louis
   D. Travis Banton

2. Who shared *Funny Face*'s (1957) Oscar nomination for Best Costume Design with Hubert de Givenchy?

   A. Audrey Hepburn
   B. Cecil Beaton
   C. Christian Dior
   D. Edith Head

3. What three films earned composer Miklos Rozsa consecutive Oscar nominations between 1952 and 1954?

   A. *A Song to Remember*, *The Lost Weekend*, and *Spellbound*
   B. *Quo Vadis*, *Ivanhoe*, and *Julius Caesar*
   C. *The Killers*, *A Double Life*, and *Quo Vadis*
   D. *The Lost Weekend*, *Spellbound*, and *The Killers*

4. What was Roger Corman's first film as producer for his own production company?

   A. *Five Guns West* (1955)
   B. *Highway Dragnet* (1954)
   C. *Monster from the Ocean Floor* (1954)
   D. *The Fast and the Furious* (1954)

5. Deborah Kerr's second husband, Peter Viertel, wrote the screenplay to what Hitchcock film?

   A. *Saboteur* (1942)
   B. *Shadow of a Doubt* (1943)
   C. *The 39 Steps* (1935)
   D. *The Wrong Man* (1956)

6. What film shot by cinematographer Freddie Young starred Clark Gable and Lana Turner?

   A. *Betrayed* (1954)
   B. *Knights of the Round Table*
   C. *Mogambo* (1953)
   D. *Time Bomb* (1953)

7. In which of the following films shot by cinematographer Haskell Wexler did Danny DeVito star?

   A. *Mulholland Falls* (1996)
   B. *Other People's Money* (1991)
   C. *The Rich Man's Wife* (1996)
   D. *Three Fugitives* (1989)

8. Who wrote the Oscar-nominated title song to *Blues in the Night* (1941)?

   A. Cole Porter
   B. Gene Autry
   C. Harold Arlen and Johnny Mercer
   D. Paul Anka and Jerome Kern

9. How old was Orson Welles when he won the Best Original Screenplay Oscar for *Citizen Kane* (1941)?

   A. 21
   B. 26
   C. 30
   D. 32

10. In which of the following categories did the 1961 comedy *The Parent Trap* receive an Academy Award nomination?

    A. Best Actress
    B. Best Editing
    C. Best Musical Score
    D. Best Original Song

11. Julie Andrews costars in what film adapted for the screen by Dalton Trumbo?

    A. *A Hatful of Rain* (1957)
    B. *Hawaii* (1966)
    C. *The Getaway* (1972)
    D. *The Honeymoon Machine* (1961)

answers found on page 568

12. Merle Oberon owes much of her early work to what producer and eventual husband?

A. Alexander Korda
B. Louis B. Mayer
C. Rex Ingram
D. Samuel Goldwyn

13. James Wong Howe earned his first Academy Award nomination for Best Color Cinematography for his work on what adventure film?

A. *Gunga Din* (1939)
B. *North by Northwest* (1959)
C. *The Old Man and the Sea* (1958)
D. *The Rose Tattoo* (1955)

14. James M. Cain's novella *Two Can Sing* was the basis for what film?

A. *Gypsy Wildcat* (1944)
B. *She Made Her Bed* (1934)
C. *When Tomorrow Comes* (1939)
D. *Wife, Husband and Friend* (1939)

15. Cinematographer Freddie Young shot all of the following films starring Robert Donat except which one?

A. *Goodbye, Mr. Chips* (1939)
B. *The Citadel* (1938)
C. *The Inn of the Sixth Happiness* (1958)
D. *The Young Mr. Pitt* (1942)

16. What was cinematographer Russell Metty's first film?

A. *Annabel Takes a Tour* (1938)
B. *Annapolis Salute* (1937)
C. *They Wanted to Marry* (1937)
D. *West of the Pecos* (1934)

17. How many Golden Globe nominations did film composer Jerry Goldsmith receive?

A. 0
B. 13
C. 6
D. 9

18. Johnny Mercer wrote the lyrics to the song "Hooray for Spinach," which was featured in what film?

A. *Blue Skies* (1946)
B. *Love Affair* (1939)
C. *Naughty but Nice* (1939)
D. *Top Hat* (1935)

19. Bernard Herrmann wrote the musical score for what film adapted from a Ray Bradbury novel?

A. *Fahrenheit 451* (1966)
B. *Strangers on a Train* (1951)
C. *The Man from Laramie* (1955)
D. *Vertigo* (1958)

20. Jean Louis designed costumes for Rita Hayworth in a total of how many films?

A. 10
B. 2
C. 3
D. 5

21. Director Alexander Mackendrick and cinematographer James Wong Howe emulated the look of New York tabloid photography for what black-and-white film?

A. *Ace in the Hole* (1951)
B. *Deadline—U.S.A.* (1952)
C. *Scandal Sheet* (1931)
D. *Sweet Smell of Success* (1957)

22. Cinematographer James Wong Howe photographed John Garfield in nine films. What was their first collaboration?

A. *Body and Soul* (1947)
B. *He Ran All the Way* (1951)
C. *They Made Me a Criminal* (1939)
D. *The Brave Bulls* (1951)

23. Which of the following producers was not an original founder of the Academy?

A. Harry Rapf
B. Jack Warner
C. Louis B. Mayer
D. Sam Goldwyn

24. Vincent Korda was the production designer on the 1955 film *Summertime*. In what city does the action take place?

A. London
B. Paris
C. Rome
D. Venice

25. Jean Louis designed costumes for Kim Novak in all of the following films except which one?

A. *Bell, Book and Candle* (1958)
B. *Pal Joey* (1957)
C. *Picnic* (1955)
D. *Who Was That Lady* (1960)

26. Where did composer Miklos Rozsa move when he first left his home city?

A. Berlin
B. Leipzig
C. London
D. Prague

27. Which costume designer was nominated for an Academy Award for his work in both *A Star Is Born* (1954) and *From Here to Eternity* (1953)?

A. Helen Rose
B. Jean Louis
C. Marcel Vertes
D. Walter Plunkett

28. What was Ray Harryhausen's first foray into color films?

A. *20 Million Miles to Earth* (1957)
B. *First Men in the Moon* (1964)
C. *Jason and the Argonauts* (1963)
D. *The 7th Voyage of Sinbad* (1958)

29. Composer-songwriter Frank Loesser won a total of how many Tony Awards?

A. 1
B. 2
C. 3
D. 5

30. What film starring Richard Burton and Elizabeth Taylor was adapted from a Christopher Marlowe play?

A. *Bluebeard* (1972)
B. *Cleopatra* (1963)
C. *Doctor Faustus* (1967)
D. *The Taming of the Shrew* (1967)

31. Cinematographer James Wong Howe used mirrors, matte work, and various other tricks to make Ronald Colman appear to be dueling with himself in which 1937 adventure film?

A. *The Man in the Iron Mask*
B. *The Prisoner of Zenda*
C. *The Scarlet Pimpernel*
D. *Under the Red Robe*

32. Who won the Best Costume Design Oscar for *Les Girls* (1957)?

A. Charles LeMaire
B. Jean Louis
C. Orry-Kelly
D. Walter Plunkett

33. Deborah Kerr's pleated gowns in *The King and I* (1956) reportedly weighed between thirty and forty pounds each. Who designed these heavy dresses?

A. Edith Head
B. Helen Rose
C. Irene Sharaff
D. Travilla

answers found on page 568

34. Norman Z. McLeod's *Topper* (1937) is based on a novel by what writer?

A. Anthony Trollope
B. James Thurber
C. Laurence Stern
D. Thorne Smith

35. Who designed the white, daisy-covered party dress worn by Elizabeth Taylor in *A Place in the Sun* (1951)?

A. Cecil Beaton
B. Edith Head
C. Helen Rose
D. Travis Banton

36. *Over 21* (1945) marked Irene Dunne's final official collaboration with what costume designer?

A. Cecil Beaton
B. Charles LeMaire
C. Jean Louis
D. Pierre Balmain

37. Cinematographer Haskell Wexler collaborated with director Norman Jewison on all of the following films except which one?

A. *Blaze* (1989)
B. *In the Heat of the Night* (1967)
C. *Other People's Money* (1991)
D. *The Thomas Crown Affair* (1968)

38. Cinematographer Freddie Young shot the 1956 film *Invitation to the Dance*. Who directed it?

A. Gene Kelly
B. Michael Kidd
C. Stanley Donen
D. Vincente Minnelli

39. Mary Astor was the author of how many novels?

A. 2
B. 3
C. 4
D. 5

The Philadelphia Story, 1940

40. *The Philadelphia Story* (1940) earned an Academy Award for which screenwriter who would later be blacklisted?

A. Dalton Trumbo
B. Alva Bessie
C. Adrian Scott
D. Donald Ogden Stewart

41. What was George Romero's first film that was adapted from a Stephen King novel?

A. *Creepshow* (1982)
B. *Hungry Wives* (1972)
C. *Knightriders* (1981)
D. *The Crazies* (1973)

42. What film starring Van Johnson was based on the short story "Babylon Revisited" by F. Scott Fitzgerald?

A. *That Forsyte Woman* (1949)
B. *The Last Time I Saw Paris* (1954)
C. *When in Rome* (1952)
D. *Wives and Lovers* (1963)

43. What costume designer shared an Oscar nomination with Helen Rose for his work on *Dream Wife* (1953)?

A. Adrian
B. Charles LeMaire
C. Herschel McCoy
D. Walter Plunkett

44. What instrument did composer Miklos Rozsa begin playing at age five?

A. Guitar
B. Piano
C. Viola
D. Violin

45. What producer put Tod Browning in single-reel nickelodeon comedies until he started working at Reliance-Majestic Studios?

A. Carl Laemmle
B. Charles Murray
C. D. W. Griffith
D. William Fox

46. Joan Blondell starred in the film *A Tree Grows in Brooklyn* (1945). Who wrote the novel on which it was based?

A. Betty Smith
B. Carson McCullers
C. Harper Lee
D. Willa Cather

47. Fay Wray's first husband, screenwriter John Monk Saunders, wrote two of her films. The first one was *The Legion of the Condemned* (1928). What was the second?

A. *Cheating Cheaters* (1934)
B. *One Sunday Afternoon* (1933)
C. *The Affairs of Cellini* (1934)
D. *The Finger Points* (1931)

48. Which film starring Deborah Kerr was adapted from the memoirs of Sheilah Graham?

A. *An Affair to Remember* (1957)
B. *Beloved Infidel* (1959)
C. *The Innocents* (1961)
D. *The Sundowners* (1960)

49. Which Oscar-winning songwriter lived to be 101 years old?

A. Franz Waxman

B. Herbert Stothart
C. Irving Berlin
D. Leo F. Forbstein

50. Vincent Korda was the production designer on what film starring Laurence Olivier and Vivien Leigh?

A. *21 Days Together* (1940)
B. *Fire Over England* (1937)
C. *Rembrandt* (1936)
D. *Wuthering Heights* (1939)

51. Miriam Hopkins starred in the title role of which film adapted from William Makepeace Thackeray's novel *Vanity Fair*?

A. *Becky Sharp* (1935)
B. *Carrie* (1952)
C. *The Home Girl* (1928)
D. *The Story of Temple Drake* (1933)

52. What film shot by cinematographer Freddie Young won the Academy Award for Best Picture?

A. *Doctor Zhivago* (1965)
B. *Lawrence of Arabia* (1962)
C. *Lord Jim* (1965)
D. *Ryan's Daughter* (1970)

53. Dalton Trumbo received his first Academy Award nomination for adapting the screenplay of what film starring Ginger Rogers?

A. *Kitty Foyle: The Natural History of a Woman* (1940)
B. *My Darling Clementine* (1946)
C. *Teresa* (1951)
D. *The Lady or the Tiger?* (1942)

54. Before becoming a film director, how did Jack Arnold get his start in the entertainment industry?

A. As a cinematographer
B. As a producer
C. As a screenwriter
D. As an actor

answers found on page 569

55. William Keighley directed what film adaptation of a Sinclair Lewis novel?

A. *Babbitt* (1934)
B. *The Man Who Came to Dinner* (1942)
C. *The Wings of Eagles* (1957)
D. *What Price Glory* (1952)

56. In what category did the Tennessee Williams adaptation *Period of Adjustment* (1962) earn an Oscar nomination?

A. Best Actress
B. Best Adapted Screenplay
C. Best Art Decoration, Black-and-White
D. Best Director

57. What producer from Victorine Studios first cast Merle Oberon in films as an extra?

A. Lupino Lane
B. Rex Ingram
C. Victor Saville
D. W. P. Kellino

58. Jean Louis designed the famous clingy, flesh-colored, beaded gown that made what fifty-two-year-old actress appear almost naked in her 1953 Vegas show?

A. Ann-Margret
B. Judy Garland
C. Marilyn Monroe
D. Marlene Dietrich

59. Ernest Laszlo was the cinematographer of what sci-fi adventure starring Stephen Boyd and Raquel Welch?

A. *Fantastic Voyage* (1966)
B. *Solar Crisis* (1990)
C. *Soylent Green* (1973)
D. *The Earthling* (1980)

60. What cinematographer earned Oscar nominations for *The Uninvited* (1944), *The Ghost and Mrs. Muir* (1947), *Sabrina* (1954), and *Butterflies Are Free* (1972)?

A. Charles Lang

B. Hal Mohr
C. James Wong Howe
D. Joseph LaShelle

61. Which of the following Peter Sellers films has an original screenplay written by Woody Allen?

A. *Heavens Above!* (1963)
B. *The Mouse That Roared* (1959)
C. *The Wrong Box* (1966)
D. *What's New, Pussycat?* (1965)

62. What George Stevens film earned cinematographer Robert De Grasse his only Oscar nomination?

A. *A Place in the Sun* (1951)
B. *Gunga Din* (1939)
C. *Vivacious Lady* (1938)
D. *Woman of the Year* (1942)

63. Tony Award–winning composer-songwriter Frank Loesser appeared in what film opposite Betty Hutton?

A. *Follow the Fleet* (1936)
B. *Red, Hot and Blue* (1949)
C. *Swing Time* (1936)
D. *Top Hat* (1935)

64. Who is the first cinematographer to win back-to-back Oscars?

A. Gregg Toland for *The Long Voyage Home* and *Citizen Kane*
B. Jack Cardiff for *Black Narcissus* and *War and Peace*
C. John Toll for *Legends of the Fall* and *Braveheart*
D. Winton C. Hoch for *Joan of Arc* and *She Wore a Yellow Ribbon*

65. What composer earned his only Academy Award for the original song "Sooner or Later (I Always Get My Man)" from Warren Beatty's *Dick Tracy* (1990)?
    A. Andrew Lloyd Webber
    B. James Horner
    C. John Williams
    D. Stephen Sondheim

66. What American screenwriter earned an Oscar nomination for penning the Ealing comedy *The Ladykillers* (1955)?
    A. Charles Brackett
    B. David Mamet
    C. Ernest Lehman
    D. William Rose

67. What was Ray Harryhausen's first project with producer Charles H. Schneer?
    A. *First Men in the Moon* (1964)
    B. *It Came from Beneath the Sea* (1955)
    C. *The 3 Worlds of Gulliver* (1960)
    D. *Tulips Shall Grow* (1942)

68. For what film did Alan J. Pakula receive an Academy Award nomination for Best Adapted Screenplay?
    A. *Klute* (1971)
    B. *Sophie's Choice* (1982)
    C. *The Parallax View* (1974)
    D. *The Sterile Cuckoo* (1969)

69. What cinematographer photographed George Marshall's *The Goldwyn Follies* (1938)?
    A. Gregg Toland
    B. Jack Cardiff
    C. James Wong Howe
    D. John F. Seitz

70. Jean Louis designed costumes for Lana Turner in what film?
    A. *Bell, Book and Candle* (1958)
    B. *Imitation of Life* (1959)
    C. *Middle of the Night* (1959)
    D. *Strangers When We Meet* (1960)

71. What film starring Paul Muni was dedicated to producer Irving Thalberg as "his last great achievement"?
    A. *Gold Is Where You Find It* (1938)
    B. *Intermezzo: A Love Story* (1939)
    C. *The Good Earth* (1937)
    D. *The Life of Emile Zola* (1937)

72. James Agee shared an Academy Award nomination with John Huston for cowriting the adapted screenplay of which film?
    A. *Gentleman's Agreement* (1947)
    B. *The African Queen* (1951)
    C. *The Quiet Man* (1952)
    D. *The Snake Pit* (1948)

73. Who designed the diagonally placed hat worn by Greta Garbo in *Romance* (1930)?
    A. Adrian
    B. Helen Rose
    C. Irene
    D. Walter Plunkett

74. Robert Taylor and Burl Ives star in what film adapted from a Howard Swigett novel?
    A. *High Wall* (1947)
    B. *Many Rivers to Cross* (1955)
    C. *Saddle the Wind* (1958)
    D. *The Power and the Prize* (1956)

75. F. Scott Fitzgerald worked on the screenplay for which film featuring Marjorie Main?
    A. *Lucky Night* (1939)
    B. *The Angels Wash Their Faces* (1939)
    C. *The Shepherd of the Hills* (1941)
    D. *The Women* (1939)

answers found on page 569

76. **What was composer Jerry Goldsmith's final film?**

A. *Hollow Man* (2000)
B. *Looney Tunes: Back in Action* (2003)
C. *Star Trek: Nemesis* (2002)
D. *The Sum of all Fears* (2002)

77. **Where was screenwriter David Mamet born?**

A. Atlanta
B. Boston
C. Chicago
D. New York

The Good Earth, 1937

78. ***The Good Earth*** **(1937), starring Luise Rainer, was adapted from a novel of what famous writer?**

A. Pearl S. Buck
B. Robert Louis Stevenson
C. Ayn Rand
D. F. Scott Fitzgerald

79. **Jean Louis worked as head designer for what studio from 1944 to 1958?**

A. Columbia
B. MGM
C. Universal
D. Warner Bros.

80. **How many Academy Award nominations did cinematographer Freddie Young receive over the course of his career?**

A. 1
B. 3
C. 5
D. 7

81. **What film was adapted from the Tennessee Williams play *The Milk Train Doesn't Stop Here Anymore*?**

A. *Boom!* (1968)
B. *Hammersmith Is Out* (1972)
C. *Mirage* (1965)
D. *The Comedians* (1967)

82. **Sean Connery was both lead actor and executive producer for all of the following films except which one?**

A. *Medicine Man* (1992)
B. *Rising Sun* (1993)
C. *The Avengers* (1998)
D. *The Rock* (1996)

83. **Alexander Korda sold his "shares" of Merle Oberon's contract to what famous producer?**

A. Carl Laemmle
B. Louis B. Mayer
C. Rex Ingram
D. Samuel Goldwyn

84. **At what age did Freddie Young win his first Academy Award for Best Cinematography?**

A. 30
B. 40
C. 50
D. 60

answers found on page 569

85. Cinematographer Haskell Wexler won an Academy Award for his work on which of the following films?

A. *Bound for Glory* (1976)
B. *Colors* (1988)
C. *One Flew Over the Cuckoo's Nest* (1975)
D. *The Babe* (1992)

86. The Franz Waxman–scored *Beloved Infidel* (1959) is about writer F. Scott Fitzgerald's affair with which famous Hollywood gossip columnist?

A. Hedda Hopper
B. Liz Smith
C. Louella Parsons
D. Sheilah Graham

87. For what studio did cinematographer Russell Metty work for two decades?

A. Columbia
B. 20th Century-Fox
C. Universal
D. Warner Bros.

88. Who wrote the Oscar-nominated title song from *Charade* (1963)?

A. Burt Bacharach
B. Johnny Mercer and Henry Mancini
C. Paul Anka
D. Randy Newman

89. For which of the following Warren Beatty movies did Robert Benton cowrite the screenplay?

A. *Bonnie and Clyde* (1967)
B. *Bugsy* (1991)
C. *Heaven Can Wait* (1978)
D. *Reds* (1981)

90. Cinematographer Freddie Young won all of his Academy Awards working under what director?

A. Bob Fosse
B. David Lean
C. John Ford
D. Steven Spielberg

91. Ralph Bellamy stars in what thriller adapted from an E. Phillips Oppenheim novel?

A. *Escape* (1940)
B. *High Wall* (1947)
C. *The Conspirators* (1944)
D. *The Great Impersonation* (1942)

92. Jerry Goldsmith was the composer for what production company logo theme?

A. Amblin Entertainment
B. Carolco Pictures
C. Orion Pictures
D. Warner Bros.

93. Basil Rathbone and W. C. Fields costar in what film adaptation of a Charles Dickens classic?

A. *David Copperfield* (1935)
B. *Monsieur Beaucaire* (1946)
C. *Penny Serenade* (1941)
D. *The Cat and the Canary* (1939)

94. Cinematographer Russell Metty began his career as a what?

A. Cameraman
B. Editor
C. Janitor
D. Lab assistant

95. In which of the following categories did the 1979 film *The Black Hole* receive an Academy Award nomination?

A. Best Cinematography
B. Best Original Song
C. Best Sound
D. Best Supporting Actor

96. Who designed the green sequined gown that Susan Hayward wore to the 1974 Academy Awards and was later buried in?

A. Bob Mackie
B. Calvin Klein
C. Nolan Miller
D. Vivienne Westwood

answers found on page 569

97. Leslie Caron appears in the 1999 film *The Reef*, which is based on a novel by what author?

A. Edith Wharton
B. John Steinbeck
C. Louisa May Alcott
D. Norman Mailer

98. In 1930, Lucien Ballard served as which cinematographer's assistant on *Morocco*?

A. Erwin Hillier
B. Lee Garmes
C. Roger Deakins
D. Ronald Neame

99. Jean Louis designed Joan Crawford's gowns for what 1957 melodrama?

A. *Autumn Leaves*
B. *Jeanne Eagles*
C. *The Garment Jungle*
D. *The Story of Esther Costello*

100. Roald Dahl wrote the screenplay for which James Bond film starring Sean Connery?

A. *From Russia with Love* (1963)
B. *Goldfinger* (1964)
C. *Thunderball* (1965)
D. *You Only Live Twice* (1967)

101. Who shared the Best Black-and-White Costume Design Oscar for *The Facts of Life* (1960) with Edith Head?

A. Edward Stevenson
B. Hubert de Givenchy
C. Moss Mabry
D. Orry-Kelly

102. Claudette Colbert wore costumes designed by Jean Louis in what film? (Hint: It costarred Orson Welles.)

A. *Middle of the Night* (1959)
B. *The Sky's the Limit* (1943)
C. *Tomorrow Is Forever* (1946)
D. *You Were Never Lovelier* (1942)

103. When was cinematographer Lucien Ballard born?

A. 1898
B. 1908
C. 1918
D. 1928

104. Stirling Silliphant won an Academy Award for Best Screenplay for what film?

A. *The Grass Harp* (1996)
B. *In the Heat of the Night* (1967)
C. *The Towering Inferno* (1974)
D. *Village of the Damned* (1960)

105. How many Best Original Screenplay Oscar nominations did Louis Malle receive?

A. 0
B. 1
C. 2
D. 3

106. What film brought composer Miklos Rozsa to Hollywood?

A. *Jungle Book* (1942)
B. *Sahara* (1943)
C. *The Green Cockatoo* (1937)
D. *The Thief of Bagdad* (1940)

107. What film directed and coadapted by Billy Wilder was based on a Claude Anet novel?

A. *Love in the Afternoon* (1957)
B. *Some Like It Hot* (1959)
C. *The Apartment* (1960)
D. *The Lost Weekend* (1945)

108. What was George Axelrod's final screenplay?

A. *Lord Love a Duck* (1966)
B. *The Fourth Protocol* (1987)
C. *The Holcroft Covenant* (1985)
D. *The Secret Life of an American Wife* (1968)

answers found on page 569

109. Which of the following films earned costume designer Irene Sharaff an Oscar nomination, but not the award?

A. *Brigadoon* (1954)
B. *Cleopatra* (1963)
C. *West Side Story* (1961)
D. *Who's Afraid of Virginia Woolf?* (1966)

110. Which legendary costumer designed the sheer, crystal-studded gown worn by Marilyn Monroe when she sang "Happy Birthday, Mr. President"?

A. Helen Rose
B. Jean Louis
C. Marcel Vertes
D. Walter Plunkett

111. Tom Stoppard adapted the screenplay for which film starring Dirk Bogarde and based on a Vladimir Nabokov novel?

A. *Dear Mr. Prohack* (1949)
B. *Despair* (1978)
C. *Doctor at Sea* (1955)
D. *The Sleeping Tiger* (1954)

112. Cinematographer James Wong Howe earned his first Academy Award nomination for his work on what film?

A. *Algiers* (1938)
B. *Kings Row* (1942)
C. *The North Star* (1943)
D. *The Thin Man* (1934)

113. William Holden and Kim Novak star in what film adaptation of a William Inge play?

A. *Bus Stop* (1956)
B. *Come Back, Little Sheba* (1952)
C. *Picnic* (1955)
D. *Splendor in the Grass* (1961)

114. How many scores for the *Star Trek* movie franchise were produced by composer Jerry Goldsmith?

A. 10

B. 2
C. 5
D. 8

115. Which of the following is a true statement about producer/director Alexander Korda?

A. He had a Ph.D. in physics.
B. He was a motorcycle racing champion.
C. He was also a singer and had a hit record in 1930.
D. He was the first film director ever to be knighted by the Queen.

116. What cinematographer photographed *The Killing* (1956)?

A. Gregg Toland
B. Jack Cardiff
C. Joseph LaShelle
D. Lucien Ballard

117. At what studio did cinematographer Russell Metty get his start?

A. Columbia
B. MGM
C. RKO
D. Warner Bros.

118. Robert Benton cowrote the screenplay for which of the following Kirk Douglas films?

A. *Cast a Giant Shadow* (1966)
B. *Lonely Are the Brave* (1962)
C. *The Arrangement* (1969)
D. *There Was a Crooked Man . . .* (1970)

119. Which of the following men is not part of the Newman family of film composers?

A. Alfred Newman
B. Emil Newman
C. Jonathan Newman
D. Lionel Newman

answers found on page 569

For Me and My Gal, 1942

120. What composer earned Oscar nominations for *Meet Me in St. Louis* (1944), *For Me and My Gal* (1942), and *Babes in Arms* (1939)?

A. Alfred Newman
B. George E. Stoll
C. Max Steiner
D. Percy Faith

121. Which of the following designers was not competing against Edith Head the year she won the Oscar for *Sabrina* (1954)?

A. Christian Dior
B. Helen Rose
C. Jean Louis
D. Travis Banton

122. Ray Bradbury cowrote the screenplay for which of the following films directed by John Huston?

A. *Moby Dick* (1956)
B. *The African Queen* (1951)
C. *The Misfits* (1961)
D. *The Night of the Iguana* (1964)

123. At what age did composer Miklos Rozsa start performing and composing?

A. 12
B. 17
C. 5
D. 8

124. What Russian-born art director earned an Oscar nomination for Josef von Sternberg's *The Shanghai Gesture* (1941)?

A. Boris Leven
B. Hans Dreier
C. Lionel Banks
D. Vincent Korda

125. Cinematographer Freddie Young invented the process of pre-exposing color film in order to mute the colors. On what film was this process first used?

A. *Bhowani Junction* (1956)
B. *Edward, My Son* (1949)
C. *Ryan's Daughter* (1970)
D. *The Deadly Affair* (1966)

126. Which Oscar-winning cinematographer was born in Budapest, Hungary?

A. Boris Kaufman
B. Ernest Laszlo
C. Guy Green
D. William C. Mellor

127. For what film did film composer Jerry Goldsmith win an Oscar?

A. *Chinatown* (1974)
B. *Rambo III* (1988)
C. *The Omen* (1976)
D. *The Secret of N.I.M.H.* (1982)

128. What was Anne Bancroft's debut as a screenwriter and director?

A. *Agnes of God* (1985)
B. *Bert Rigby, You're a Fool* (1989)
C. *Fatso* (1980)
D. *Great Expectations* (1998)

129. Alec Guinness and Burl Ives costar in what film adapted by Graham Greene from his own novel?

A. *Footsteps in the Fog* (1955)
B. *Our Man in Havana* (1959)
C. *Passage to Marseille* (1944)
D. *The Magic Box* (1952)

answers found on page 569

130. On what film did Glenn Ford serve as an associate producer?

A. *Day of the Evil Gun* (1968)
B. *Pocketful of Miracles* (1961)
C. *The Courtship of Eddie's Father* (1963)
D. *The Money Trap* (1965)

131. Jean Louis earned his first Academy Award nomination for dressing Judy Holliday in what George Cukor film?

A. *Bells Are Ringing* (1960)
B. *Born Yesterday* (1950)
C. *It Should Happen to You* (1954)
D. *The Solid Gold Cadillac* (1956)

132. Which of the following films produced by Walter Mirisch stars Shirley MacLaine?

A. *By Love Possessed* (1961)
B. *Hawaii* (1966)
C. *Scorpio* (1973)
D. *Two for the Seesaw* (1962)

133. The 1942 film *Jungle Book* received Academy Award nominations in all of the following categories except which one?

A. Best Art Direction
B. Best Cinematography
C. Best Editing
D. Best Musical Score

134. In what category did Ray Enright's *The Spoilers* compete at the 1943 Academy Awards?

A. Best Actor
B. Best Director
C. Best Interior Decoration, Black-and-White
D. Best Picture

135. Who is the only composer besides Alfred Newman to earn four Oscar nominations in the same year?

A. George Gershwin
B. Lionel Newman

C. Max Steiner
D. Victor Young

136. What screenplay earned Warren Beatty his first Oscar nomination in a writing category?

A. *Bulworth* (1998)
B. *Heaven Can Wait* (1978)
C. *Reds* (1981)
D. *Shampoo* (1975)

137. In addition to Best Art Direction, what other Oscar was *Captains of the Clouds* (1942) up for?

A. Best Cinematography
B. Best Musical Score
C. Best Picture
D. Best Supporting Actress

138. Who designed the costumes worn by Rudolph Valentino in *The Young Rajah* (1922)?

A. Cecil B. DeMille
B. Mitchell Leisen
C. Natacha Rambova
D. Travis Banton

139. What composer won the 1950 Oscar for Best Scoring of a Dramatic or Comedy Picture?

A. Aaron Copland for *The Heiress*
B. Alfred Newman for *Come to the Stable*
C. Max Steiner for *Beyond the Forest*
D. Roger Edens for *On the Town*

140. Which film starring Bette Davis was adapted from Lillian Hellman's sequel to her play *Another Part of the Forest*?

A. *Beyond the Forest* (1949)
B. *The Corn Is Green* (1945)
C. *The Little Foxes* (1941)
D. *Watch on the Rhine* (1943)

answers found on page 569

141. What was Jack Arnold's first fiction feature as a producer?

A. *Creature from the Black Lagoon* (1954)
B. *Girls in the Night* (1953)
C. *It Came from Outer Space* (1953)
D. *No Name on the Bullet* (1959)

142. Where was screenwriter George Axelrod when he passed away?

A. London
B. Los Angeles
C. Rome
D. Tokyo

143. What film costarring Ronald Colman was adapted from a George Eliot novel?

A. *Romola* (1924)
B. *The Greenie* (1942)
C. *The Long Voyage Home* (1940)
D. *The Quiet Man* (1952)

144. Which film costarring Peter Sellers was adapted from a George Bernard Shaw play?

A. *A Shot in the Dark* (1964)
B. *The Millionairess* (1960)
C. *The Party* (1968)
D. *There's a Girl in My Soup* (1970)

145. What Ridley Scott film only featured composer Jerry Goldsmith's work in the European release?

A. *Alien Nation* (1988)
B. *Legend* (1985)
C. *Poltergeist* (1982)
D. *Ransom* (1975)

146. What film costarring Ethel Waters was adapted from a Carson McCullers play?

A. *The Barretts of Wimpole Street* (1957)
B. *The Long Memory* (1952)
C. *The Member of the Wedding* (1952)
D. *The Valiant* (1962)

147. Ida Lupino received her first credit as a producer for what film?

A. *Deep Valley* (1947)
B. *Road House* (1948)
C. *The Judge* (1948)
D. *Woman in Hiding* (1949)

148. Composer Saul Chaplin earned Oscar nominations for all the following films. Which did not win him the award?

A. *An American in Paris* (1951)
B. *Kiss Me Kate* (1953)
C. *Seven Brides for Seven Brothers* (1954)
D. *West Side Story* (1961)

149. Which of the following actresses has starred in adaptations of works by James Jones, George Bernard Shaw, and Tennessee Williams?

A. Audrey Hepburn
B. Ava Gardner
C. Deborah Kerr
D. Jennifer Jones

150. Which Neil Simon work was not originally a screenplay for film?

A. *Murder by Death* (1976)
B. *The Goodbye Girl* (1977)
C. *The Odd Couple* (1968)
D. *The Out of Towners* (1970)

151. How many Grammy nominations did film composer Jerry Goldsmith receive?

A. 0
B. 12
C. 21
D. 5

152. Vincent Korda was the production designer on the 1941 film *Old Bill and Son*. Which of the following actors starred in it?

A. Cary Grant
B. John Mills
C. Laurence Olivier
D. Leslie Howard

answers found on page 569

153. What Frank Capra film was adapted from the Philip Van Doren Stern short story "The Greatest Gift"?

   A. *It Happened One Night* (1934)
   B. *It's a Wonderful Life* (1946)
   C. *Pocketful of Miracles* (1961)
   D. *You Can't Take It with You* (1938)

154. James Goldman, screenwriter for the 1968 film *The Lion in Winter*, also wrote the screenplay for what film starring Sean Connery?

   A. *Diamonds Are Forever* (1971)
   B. *Robin and Marian* (1976)
   C. *The Molly Maguires* (1970)
   D. *Zardoz* (1974)

155. Luchino Visconti received his one and only Academy Award nomination for cowriting the screenplay to which film?

   A. *Ludwig* (1972)
   B. *The Damned* (1969)
   C. *The Innocent* (1976)
   D. *The Witches* (1967)

156. Which member of the Newman family of film composers devised the "Newman System" for film synchronization?

   A. Alfred Newman
   B. Emil Newman
   C. Randy Newman
   D. Thomas Newman

157. Stewart Granger starred opposite David Niven in what adventure-comedy adapted from a Rudyard Kipling novel?

   A. *Cage of Gold* (1950)
   B. *Soldiers Three* (1951)
   C. *The Jungle Book* (1967)
   D. *Waterloo Road* (1945)

158. Who wrote the novel and screenplay for John Sturges's *The Capture* (1950)?

   A. Don McGuire
   B. Ernest Hemingway

   C. Millard Kaufman
   D. Niven Busch

159. Samuel Fuller wrote the story and screenplay for which musical comedy?

   A. *Cinderfella* (1960)
   B. *Everybody Sing* (1938)
   C. *Girl Crazy* (1943)
   D. *Hats Off* (1936)

The Bachelor and the Bobby-Soxer, 1947

160. Who won an Oscar for Best Original Screenplay for *The Bachelor and the Bobby-Soxer* (1947)?

   A. William Faulkner
   B. Sidney Sheldon
   C. Abraham Polonsky
   D. Norman Panama

161. What Neil Simon film earned a Golden Globe for Best Screenplay?

   A. *Biloxi Blues* (1988)
   B. *The Goodbye Girl* (1978)
   C. *The Heartbreak Kid* (1972)
   D. *The Sunshine Boys* (1975)

162. Which of the following films starring Donald Pleasence was based on a novel by F. Scott Fitzgerald?

   A. *Journey into Fear* (1975)
   B. *The Black Windmill* (1974)
   C. *The Eagle Has Landed* (1976)
   D. *The Last Tycoon* (1976)

answers found on page 569

163. Louis Malle's *Zazie in the Metro* (1960) was an adaptation of what author's novel?

A. Albert Camus
B. Gilbert Cesbron
C. Michel Houellebecq
D. Raymond Queneau

164. Which Daniel Mann film was adapted from a novel?

A. *BUtterfield 8* (1960)
B. *Come Back, Little Sheba* (1952)
C. *The Rose Tattoo* (1955)
D. *The Teahouse of the August Moon* (1956)

165. Vincent Korda was the art director on the 1939 film *Q Planes*, which starred which of the following actors?

A. Laurence Olivier
B. Leslie Howard
C. Rex Harrison
D. Robert Donat

166. With help from fellow composer Joel McNeely, Jerry Goldsmith composed and recorded the score for what film in three weeks?

A. *Air Force One* (1997)
B. *First Blood* (1982)
C. *Logan's Run* (1976)
D. *Star Trek: The Motion Picture* (1979)

167. What was William Castle's last film as a producer?

A. *Bug* (1975)
B. *Macabre* (1977)
C. *Shampoo* (1975)
D. *Shanks* (1974)

168. Who adapted the version of *Alice in Wonderland* (1933) directed by Norman Z. McLeod?

A. Billy Wilder and Charles Brackett
B. Franz Schulz and Robert Riskin

C. Howard Koch and Samson Raphaelson
D. Joseph L. Mankiewicz and William Cameron Menzies

169. Bernard Herrmann composed the score for what film adaptation of a novel by F. Scott Fitzgerald?

A. *Night Passage* (1957)
B. *Tender Is the Night* (1962)
C. *The Great Gatsby* (1974)
D. *Vertigo* (1958)

170. Luise Rainer appears in what adaptation of a Fyodor Dostoyevsky novel?

A. *Midnight in Saint Petersburg* (1996)
B. *The Gambler* (1997)
C. *The Good Night* (2007)
D. *The Innocent Sleep* (1996)

171. Which James Bond film did cinematographer Freddie Young shoot?

A. *Dr. No* (1962)
B. *For Your Eyes Only* (1981)
C. *From Russia with Love* (1963)
D. *You Only Live Twice* (1967)

172. What famous writer wrote the first draft of the screenplay for the Jean Harlow film *Red-Headed Woman* (1932)?

A. Clare Booth Luce
B. F. Scott Fitzgerald
C. John Steinbeck
D. Truman Capote

173. Jean Louis earned an Academy Award nomination for dressing Joan Crawford in what 1955 film?

A. *Affair in Trinidad*
B. *Mildred Pierce*
C. *Queen Bee*
D. *What Ever Happened to Baby Jane?*

answers found on page 569

174. Cinematographer Haskell Wexler photographed the 1996 film *Mulholland Falls*. Which of the following actors did not costar in it?

A. Billy Bob Thornton
B. Jennifer Connelly
C. Melanie Griffith
D. Nick Nolte

175. What actress allegedly offended costume designer Erté so profoundly that he left MGM and fled back to Paris?

A. Clara Bow
B. Lillian Gish
C. Marion Davies
D. Norma Shearer

176. Who was the first film composer to match Alfred Newman's record of forty-five Academy Award nominations?

A. Danny Elfman
B. James Horner
C. Jerry Goldsmith
D. John Williams

177. What year did composer Victor Young earn three separate Oscar nominations for his work on *Flying Tigers*, *Silver Queen*, and *Take a Letter, Darling*?

A. 1939
B. 1941
C. 1943
D. 1955

178. In which of the following categories did the 1967 film *Divorce American Style* receive its only Academy Award nomination?

A. Best Actress
B. Best Costume Design
C. Best Editing
D. Best Original Screenplay

179. What was David Mamet's first screenplay?

A. *The Postman Always Rings Twice* (1981)
B. *The Untouchables* (1987)

C. *The Verdict* (1982)
D. *We're No Angels* (1989)

180. William Keighley directed Errol Flynn and Claude Rains in what adaptation of a Mark Twain novel?

A. *The Green Pastures* (1936)
B. *The Old South* (1940)
C. *The Prince and the Pauper* (1937)
D. *The Singing Kid* (1936)

181. Who wrote the book adapted into John Sturges's *The Old Man and the Sea* (1958)?

A. Arthur Miller
B. Don McGuire
C. Ernest Hemingway
D. J. D. Salinger

182. Film producer Hal Roach lived to be how old?

A. 100
B. 77
C. 82
D. 95

183. What film earned composer Conrad Salinger his only Oscar nomination?

A. *Alice in Wonderland* (1933)
B. *An American in Paris* (1951)
C. *Show Boat* (1951)
D. *The Great Caruso* (1951)

184. The 1938 film *The Great Waltz* won an Academy Award in what category?

A. Best Art Direction
B. Best Cinematography
C. Best Editing
D. Best Original Song

185. What composer earned Academy Award nominations for his work on the Laurel and Hardy films *Way Out West* (1937) and *Block-Heads* (1938)?
A. Alfred Newman
B. Frank Churchill
C. Marvin Hatley
D. Max Steiner

186. I dropped out of high school and worked as a boxer, a busboy, and a janitor before becoming the world's highest-paid cinematographer in 1933. Who am I?
A. Gregg Toland
B. Haskell Wexler
C. James Wong Howe
D. Joseph Ruttenberg

187. For which of the following films did Robert Benton not receive an Academy Award nomination for Best Screenplay?
A. *Bonnie and Clyde* (1967)
B. *Nobody's Fool* (1994)
C. *The Human Stain* (2003)
D. *The Late Show* (1977)

188. Dalton Trumbo wrote the screenplay for what espionage thriller costarring Burt Lancaster and Robert Ryan?
A. *Executive Action* (1973)
B. *Scorpio* (1973)
C. *The Getaway* (1972)
D. *The Midnight Man* (1974)

189. James Agee was one of three cinematographers for which documentary short set in New York?
A. *Adventure in the Bronx* (1941)
B. *In the Street* (1948)
C. *Life at the Zoo* (1946)
D. *The Living City* (1953)

190. Ray Harryhausen received the Gordon E. Sawyer Lifetime Achievement Award in what year?
A. 1964
B. 1979
C. 1986
D. 1992

191. What was the only film for which cinematographer James Wong Howe photographed Cary Grant?
A. *His Girl Friday* (1940)
B. *Mr. Blandings Builds His Dream House* (1948)
C. *My Favorite Wife* (1940)
D. *None But the Lonely Heart* (1944)

192. Vincent Korda was the art director/production designer on all of the following films except which one?
A. *Perfect Strangers* (1945)
B. *The Lion Has Wings* (1939)
C. *The Longest Day* (1962)
D. *The Red Shoes* (1948)

193. Jean Louis was married to which of the following actresses?
A. Carol Channing
B. Judy Garland
C. Kim Novak
D. Loretta Young

194. The highest price paid at auction in the twentieth century for part of a costume was $165,000. What did the bidder purchase?
A. Audrey Hepburn's cigarette holder from *Breakfast at Tiffany's* (1961)
B. Barbara Stanwyck's ankle bracelet from *Double Indemnity* (1944)
C. Jean Harlow's wig from *Saratoga* (1937)
D. Judy Garland's ruby slippers from *The Wizard of Oz* (1939)

answers found on page 570

The Great Waltz, 1938

195. *The Great Waltz* (1938) earned which cinematographer his first of four Academy Awards?

A. James Wong Howe
B. Joseph Walker
C. Ernest Haller
D. Joseph Ruttenberg

196. Cinematographer James Wong Howe rollerskated around a prizefighting ring with a handheld camera in order to shoot John Garfield in which boxing film?

A. *Body and Soul* (1947)
B. *Fat City* (1972)
C. *Raging Bull* (1980)
D. *Somebody Up There Likes Me* (1956)

197. Alexander Korda produced the 1939 film *The Four Feathers*, which received an Academy Award nomination in what category?

A. Best Art Direction
B. Best Cinematography
C. Best Costume Design
D. Best Editing

198. For which of the following films did Walter Mirisch receive the Academy Award for Best Picture as producer?

A. *In the Heat of the Night* (1967)
B. *One Flew Over the Cuckoo's Nest* (1975)
C. *Terms of Endearment* (1983)
D. *The Apartment* (1960)

199. Dirk Bogarde costars in what drama adapted for the screen by Dalton Trumbo?

A. *A Hatful of Rain* (1957)
B. *The Fixer* (1968)
C. *The Midnight Man* (1974)
D. *The Nun's Story* (1959)

200. How many Academy Award nominations did composer Miklos Rozsa receive?

A. 11
B. 17
C. 4
D. 7

201. What comedy directed and coadapted by Billy Wilder was based on a Ferenc Molnár play?

A. *Love in the Afternoon* (1957)
B. *One, Two, Three* (1961)
C. *Some Like It Hot* (1959)
D. *The Front Page* (1974)

202. Where was film composer Jerry Goldsmith originally from?

A. Los Angeles
B. New York City
C. Poland
D. Russia

203. Cinematographer Haskell Wexler apprenticed as a camera operator under which of the following people to learn his craft?

A. Billy Bitzer
B. Charles Lang
C. James Wong Howe
D. William Daniels

204. Who wrote the book that was adapted into the Shirley Temple film *Rebecca of Sunnybrook Farm* (1938)?

A. Kate Douglas Wiggin
B. Louisa May Alcott
C. Margaret Mitchell
D. Mary Shelley

answers found on page 570

205. Henry Hathaway's 1941 film *Sundown* received Academy Award nominations in all of the following categories except which one?

A. Best Actress
B. Best Art Direction
C. Best Cinematography
D. Best Original Score

206. In what category did George E. Stoll and Johnny Green earn an Oscar nomination for their work on *Meet Me in Las Vegas* (1956)?

A. Best Director
B. Best Film Editing
C. Best Original Screenplay
D. Best Scoring of a Musical Picture

207. What art director collaborated with cinematographer James Wong Howe to create the period look of *Kings Row* (1942)?

A. Alfred Herman
B. Cedric Gibbons
C. Hans Dreier
D. William Cameron Menzies

208. Judy Holliday was credited as a composer for what film?

A. *A Thousand Clowns* (1965)
B. *Adam's Rib* (1949)
C. *Born Yesterday* (1950)
D. *It Should Happen to You* (1954)

209. Ernest Laszlo was the cinematographer of what biopic starring Tony Curtis in the title role?

A. *Edison, the Man* (1940)
B. *Houdini* (1953)
C. *Young Tom Edison* (1940)
D. *Young Winston* (1972)

210. What costume designer earned an Oscar nomination for *Pal Joey* (1957)?

A. Helen Rose
B. Jean Louis
C. Orry-Kelly
D. Walter Plunkett

211. Cinematographer Freddie Young photographed all of the following films costarring John Mills except which one?

A. *Escape* (1948)
B. *Ryan's Daughter* (1970)
C. *So Well Remembered* (1947)
D. *The Young Mr. Pitt* (1942)

212. How many Emmys did film composer Jerry Goldsmith win?

A. 0
B. 2
C. 5
D. 9

213. Composer Alfred Newman was born in what New England state?

A. Connecticut
B. Massachusetts
C. New Hampshire
D. Vermont

214. William Keighley directed what adaptation of a W. Somerset Maugham play?

A. *Babbitt* (1934)
B. *Four Men and a Prayer* (1938)
C. *The Green Pastures* (1936)
D. *The Right to Live* (1935)

215. In what year did Zoltan Korda pass away?

A. 1960
B. 1961
C. 1962
D. 1963

216. Freddie Young won the Academy Award for Best Cinematography for his work on all of the following films except which one?

A. *Doctor Zhivago* (1965)
B. *Ivanhoe* (1952)
C. *Lawrence of Arabia* (1962)
D. *Ryan's Daughter* (1970)

217. William Inge won an Oscar for writing the story and screenplay of what film starring Natalie Wood?

A. *A New Kind of Love* (1963)
B. *Prince of Foxes* (1949)
C. *Splendor in the Grass* (1961)
D. *Thousands Cheer* (1943)

218. Which of the following films did cinematographer Haskell Wexler both shoot and direct?

A. *Bound for Glory* (1976)
B. *Coming Home* (1978)
C. *Medium Cool* (1969)
D. *Second-Hand Hearts* (1981)

219. Richard Thorpe directed Robert Taylor in what mystery adapted from a Victor Canning novel?

A. *High Wall* (1947)
B. *Passage to Marseille* (1944)
C. *The House of the Seven Hawks* (1959)
D. *Undercurrent* (1946)

220. Preston Sturges received an Academy Award nomination for Best Original Screenplay for what film released in 1944?

A. *Going My Way*
B. *Mr. Skeffington*
C. *Since You Went Away*
D. *The Miracle of Morgan's Creek*

221. At what age did film composer Jerry Goldsmith learn how to play the piano?

A. 11
B. 14
C. 19
D. 6

222. Johnny Mercer wrote the lyrics to what song in 1940 that was made famous by Elvis Presley in 1971?

A. "Fools Rush In"
B. "Love of My Life"
C. "Over Forever"
D. "Too Much in Love"

223. Music composer Friedrich Hollaender makes a cameo appearance as a piano player in what film directed and cowritten by Billy Wilder?

A. *A Foreign Affair* (1948)
B. *Some Like It Hot* (1959)
C. *The Apartment* (1960)
D. *The Spirit of St. Louis* (1957)

224. Marion Davies wrote the screenplay for which film that also marked her screen debut?

A. *Beauty's Worth* (1922)
B. *Enchantment* (1921)
C. *Runaway Romany* (1917)
D. *The Belle of New York* (1918)

225. Carl Foreman had Humphrey Bogart in mind for the role of "Shears" when adapting the screenplay for what film?

A. *The Barretts of Wimpole Street* (1957)
B. *The Bridge on the River Kwai* (1957)
C. *The Long Memory* (1952)
D. *The Valiant* (1962)

226. Michael Powell received his first Oscar nomination for Best Screenplay for what film?

A. *A Matter of Life and Death* (1946)
B. *Black Narcissus* (1947)
C. *One of Our Aircraft Is Missing* (1942)
D. *The Red Shoes* (1948)

227. Director Jack Clayton adapted my nineteenth-century Gothic novel about a tormented governess into *The Innocents* (1961) starring Deborah Kerr. Who am I?

A. Charlotte Brontë
B. Henry James
C. Jane Austen
D. Mary Shelley

answers found on page 570

228. Paul Lukas costars with Walter Huston in which film based on a novel by Sinclair Lewis?

    A. *Dodsworth* (1936)
    B. *Grand Slam* (1933)
    C. *The Lady Vanishes* (1938)
    D. *Watch on the Rhine* (1943)

229. Which feature coadapted by James Agee was Katharine Hepburn's first Technicolor film?

    A. *Holiday* (1938)
    B. *Song of Love* (1947)
    C. *The African Queen* (1951)
    D. *The Rainmaker* (1956)

230. What was cinematographer James Wong Howe's final film?

    A. *Funny Lady* (1975)
    B. *Seconds* (1966)
    C. *Macabre* (1977)
    D. *The Molly Maguires* (1970)

231. All of the following actors costarred in the adaptation of Ray Bradbury's *Something Wicked This Way Comes* (1983) except which one?

    A. Diane Ladd
    B. Ellen Burstyn
    C. Jason Robards
    D. Jonathan Pryce

232. Who wrote the lyrics to the Oscar-nominated song "Wonder Why" from *Rich, Young and Pretty* (1951)?

    A. Alan Jay Lerner
    B. Eliot Daniel
    C. Johnny Mercer
    D. Sammy Cahn

233. Which Academy Award–winner was the cinematographer of *Road to Rio* (1947)?

    A. Burnett Guffey
    B. Ernest Laszlo
    C. Freddie Young
    D. Loyal Griggs

Bringing Up Baby, 1938

234. The Howard Hawks film *Bringing Up Baby* (1938) featured the work of what cinematographer?

    A. Robert De Grasse
    B. Russell Metty
    C. Ernest Miller
    D. Joseph A. Valentine

235. Jean Louis earned his second Academy Award nomination for dressing Rita Hayworth's nightclub singer in what 1952 film?

    A. *A Star Is Born*
    B. *Affair in Trinidad*
    C. *Gilda*
    D. *Pal Joey*

236. When did screenwriter George Axelrod pass away?

    A. 1981
    B. 1996
    C. 2000
    D. 2003

237. What famous composer created the musical score for Luchino Visconti's *The Damned* (1969)?

    A. Bernard Herrmann
    B. Elmer Bernstein
    C. John Williams
    D. Maurice Jarre

answers found on page 570

238. **Lucien Ballard earned his only Oscar nomination for Best Black-and-White Cinematography in 1964. Who won the award?**

A. Ernest Haller for *Lilies of the Field*

B. Ernest Laszlo for *It's a Mad, Mad, Mad, Mad World*

C. James Wong Howe for *Hud*

D. Joseph LaShelle for *Irma La Douce*

239. **Ronald Colman and Ida Lupino costar in what film adapted from a Rudyard Kipling novel?**

A. *Forbidden Passage* (1941)

B. *Forgotten Victory* (1939)

C. *My Brother Talks to Horses* (1947)

D. *The Light That Failed* (1939)

240. **Which of Woody Allen's longtime collaborators earned an Academy Award nomination for Best Costume Design for his/her work on *Zelig* (1983)?**

A. Gordon Willis

B. Mia Farrow

C. Ralph Rosenblum

D. Santo Loquasto

241. ***Drums Along the Mohawk* (1939), *Dive Bomber* (1941), and *Blood and Sand* (1941) all earned Oscar nominations in what category?**

A. Best Actor

B. Best Color Cinematography

C. Best Director

D. Best Special Effects

answers found on page 570

Chapter 18
EXPERTS ONLY

1. What was Kerwin Mathews's job before getting involved with movies?

   A. Botanist
   B. Mailman
   C. Teacher
   D. Tire salesman

2. How long is Montgomery Clift's Oscar-nominated performance in *Judgment at Nuremburg* (1961)?

   A. 15 minutes
   B. 20 minutes
   C. 3 minutes
   D. 7 minutes

3. On September 4, 1939, Rosalind Russell appeared on the cover of what magazine?

   A. *Life*
   B. *Newsweek*
   C. *Time*
   D. *Vanity Fair*

4. What did Humphrey Bogart name both his sailboat and his production company?

   A. Betty
   B. Casablanca
   C. Santana
   D. Slim

5. *The Last American Hero* (1973) is based on the life of what NASCAR driver?

   A. Benny Parsons
   B. Bobby Allison
   C. Junior Johnson
   D. Richard Petty

6. What is Ernest Borgnine's real name?

   A. Ermes Borgnino
   B. Ernesto Gulch
   C. Mladen Sekulovich
   D. Thomas Mapother

answers found on page 570

7. James Wong Howe went to Britain to shoot *Fire Over England* (1937) for Alexander Korda and what German film producer?

A. Erich Pommer
B. Paul Davidson
C. Rudolf Meinert
D. William Dieterle

8. What clothing brand featured Audrey Hepburn's dance sequence from *Funny Face* (1957) in its "Skinny Black Pant" commercial?

A. Gucci
B. Guess
C. Lacoste
D. Gap

9. What is Meryl Streep's birth name?

A. Mary Alena Streep
B. Mary Louise Streep
C. Meryl Eleanora Streep
D. Meryl Louise Streep

10. What is the name of Jack Lemmon's feminine alter ego in *Some Like It Hot* (1959)?

A. Buffy
B. Daphne
C. Hildegard
D. Josephine

11. How tall was Woody Strode?

A. 5'10"
B. 6'1"
C. 6'10"
D. 6'5"

12. Which leading lady's uncle wrote the Pulitzer Prize–winning play *Craig's Wife*?

A. Grace Kelly
B. Lena Horne
C. Olivia de Havilland
D. Rosalind Russell

13. When did Rosalind Russell decide to not renew her contract with MGM?

A. 1941
B. 1945
C. 1949
D. 1951

14. How did Lucien Ballard die?

A. Car accident
B. Heart attack
C. Malaria
D. Pneumonia

15. *The Lost Weekend* (1945) and what other film were the only two movies to win Best Picture and the Palme d'Or?

A. *Brief Encounter* (1945)
B. *Friendly Persuasion* (1956)
C. *Marty* (1955)
D. *The Third Man* (1949)

16. Glenn Ford took his stage name from a town in his native Canada. What was the name of the town?

A. Fordham
B. Glenbrooke
C. Glendale
D. Glenford

17. Which of the following was not one of George Axelrod's professions?

A. Director
B. Editor
C. Producer
D. Screenwriter

18. What is the name of the Elsa Schiaparelli perfume inspired by Mae West?

A. I'm No Angel
B. La Vogue Mae West
C. Sex
D. Shocking

answers found on page 570

19. From which magazine was Robert Benton fired from his job as art director in the 1960s?
    A. *Esquire*
    B. *New York*
    C. *Time*
    D. *Vanity Fair*

20. After George Sanders handed off the role of the Falcon to his brother, how many more films were there in the series?
    A. 1
    B. 4
    C. 7
    D. 9

21. What was Rex Harrison's much-hated nickname?
    A. "Rex the Hex"
    B. "Rex the Runt"
    C. "Sexy Rexy"
    D. "Tyrannosaurus Rex"

22. Which is not one of Roddy McDowall's middle names?
    A. Andrew
    B. Anthony
    C. Edward
    D. Jude

23. What card game do Jack Lemmon and Shirley MacLaine play to pass the time in *The Apartment* (1960)?
    A. Crazy eights
    B. Gin rummy
    C. Go fish
    D. Poker

24. What NFL team was Burt Reynolds drafted by before he suffered a career-ending injury?
    A. Baltimore Colts
    B. Dallas Cowboys
    C. Los Angeles Rams
    D. Miami Dolphins

25. Raymond Massey was featured in what episode of *Alfred Hitchcock Presents*?
    A. "Into Thin Air"
    B. "Our Cook's a Treasure"
    C. "Place of Shadows"
    D. "Road Hog"

26. What is Neil Simon's nickname?
    A. "Doc"
    B. "Rabbi"
    C. "The Pen"
    D. "Yonkers"

27. In what Mario Van Peebles film did Woody Strode play "The Storyteller"?
    A. *Gunmen* (1994)
    B. *Hotshot* (1987)
    C. *New Jack City* (1991)
    D. *Posse* (1993)

28. British rock legend Sting appeared in which film opposite Meryl Streep and Sam Neill?
    A. *Music of the Heart* (1999)
    B. *Plenty* (1985)
    C. *Postcards from the Edge* (1990)
    D. *The House of the Spirits* (1993)

29. What were the names of the two children under Deborah Kerr's charge in *The Innocents* (1961)?
    A. D. J. and Michelle
    B. Francis and Malcolm
    C. Michael and Lindsay
    D. Miles and Flora

30. Groucho Marx's daughter Melinda made her screen debut in what film opposite Ronald Colman?
    A. *Friend Indeed* (1937)
    B. *One Against the World* (1939)
    C. *Pilgrimage* (1933)
    D. *The Story of Mankind* (1957)

answers found on page 570

31. Carmen Miranda worked in which profession before she was invited to display her singing talents at a music academy?
    A. Catering
    B. Hat making
    C. Nursing
    D. Race car driving

32. What was James Cagney's nickname for Jack Warner?
    A. "Meshugener"
    B. "The Bupkis"
    C. "The Nudnik"
    D. "The Shvontz"

33. In what year did Cecil B. DeMille win an honorary Oscar?
    A. 1949
    B. 1950
    C. 1955
    D. 1960

34. How many children did composer Miklos Rozsa have?
    A. 0
    B. 2
    C. 5
    D. 8 (including twins)

35. The 1999 Bollywood film *Mann* was inspired by which film pairing Cary Grant and Deborah Kerr?
    A. *An Affair to Remember* (1957)
    B. *Indiscreet* (1958)
    C. *Once Upon a Time* (1944)
    D. *The Grass Is Greener* (1960)

36. Judy Holliday's first job was as an assistant switchboard operator at the Mercury Theater, run by what future famous director?
    A. Cecil B. DeMille
    B. George Cukor
    C. Orson Welles
    D. William Wellman

37. The Elizabeth Taylor film *National Velvet* (1944) is about what horse race?
    A. The Belmont Stakes
    B. The Epsom Derby
    C. The Grand National
    D. The Preakness Stakes

38. What Montgomery Clift film was also released as a director's cut titled *Terminal Station*?
    A. *Indiscretion of an American Wife* (1953)
    B. *Lonelyhearts* (1958)
    C. *The Heiress* (1949)
    D. *The Search* (1948)

39. What is the name of the butler played by Alan Mowbray in Norman Z. McLeod's *Topper* (1937) and *Topper Takes a Trip* (1938)?
    A. Dimsdale
    B. Pilkington
    C. Rowley
    D. Wilkins

40. The prop octopus used in Ed Wood's *Bride of the Monster* (1955) was meant for what film?
    A. *Citizen Kane* (1941)
    B. *Drums of Fu Manchu* (1940)
    C. *The Cat and the Mermouse* (1949)
    D. *Wake of the Red Witch* (1948)

41. In what city was Chuck Jones born?
    A. Marietta, Georgia
    B. Phoenix, Arizona
    C. Spokane, Washington
    D. St. Louis, Missouri

42. I was Lana Turner's fourth husband. Who am I?
    A. Artie Shaw
    B. Lex Barker
    C. Otto Preminger
    D. Stephen Crane

answers found on page 570

43. What was the name of Anne Bancroft and Mel Brooks's one son?

A. Alexander
B. Christian
C. Jebediah
D. Maximillian

44. What was Walter Matthau's nickname as a child?

A. "Jake"
B. "John"
C. "Waldo"
D. "Walt"

45. Jane Powell is currently married to which former child star?

A. Dickie Moore
B. Freddie Bartholomew
C. Jackie Coogan
D. Roddy McDowall

46. The Jean Harlow film *Reckless* (1935) was based on a scandal surrounding what real-life singer?

A. Libby Holman
B. Lillian Roth
C. Ruth Etting
D. Sophie Tucker

47. In 1939, which department store developed a line of hats and jewelry inspired by Carmen Miranda's signature style?

A. Bergdorf Goodman
B. Bloomingdale's
C. Neiman Marcus
D. Saks Fifth Avenue

48. All of the following celebrities were members of the Van Nuys High School Class of 1954 except for which one?

A. Don Drysdale
B. Doris Day
C. Natalie Wood
D. Robert Redford

49. Famed columnist Sidney Skolsky makes a cameo appearance in what film starring Paul Muni?

A. *All That Money Can Buy* (1941)
B. *Hi, Nellie!* (1934)
C. *The Great Gatsby* (1949)
D. *The World Changes* (1933)

50. Who threw a star-studded Las Vegas bash to celebrate Rosalind Russell's twenty-fifth anniversary of marriage to husband Freddie Brisson in 1966?

A. Cary Grant
B. Dean Martin
C. Frank Sinatra
D. James Stewart

51. How is Cary Grant driving his car in the first scene of Norman Z. McLeod's *Topper* (1937)?

A. Backward
B. Blindfolded
C. Upside down
D. With his feet

52. What was Rossano Brazzi's profession prior to acting?

A. Doctor
B. Investment banker
C. Lawyer
D. Musician

53. What is the name of the 1979 song by the band The Clash about actor Montgomery Clift?

A. "Brand New Cadillac"
B. "Death or Glory"
C. "The Right Profile"
D. "Train in Vain"

54. In what country did Merle Oberon first appear in films (as an extra)?

A. England
B. France
C. India
D. United States

55. Mary Astor was a two-time finalist as a teenager in a beauty contest for what magazine?

A. *Modern Screen*

B. *Motion Picture*

C. *Movie Story*

D. *Picture Play*

56. What was Oliver Hardy's nickname?

A. "Babe"

B. "Bean"

C. "Bear"

D. "Big Top"

57. Which of the following is a true statement about Chuck Jones?

A. He never learned how to drive.

B. He occasionally appeared in Mack Sennett film comedies when he was a child.

C. He once ran for governor of California.

D. He once was roommates with Charles Chaplin.

58. Ronald Colman appears in all of the following episodes of *Four Star Playhouse* except for which one?

A. "Man in the Cellar"

B. "The Ladies on His Mind"

C. "The Lost Silk Hat"

D. "The Man Who Walked out on Himself"

59. In the 1936 film *They Met in a Taxi*, what is Fay Wray wearing when she meets Chester Morris in the taxi?

A. A bathrobe

B. A top hat

C. A wedding dress

D. Diamond earrings

60. Where did composer Miklos Rozsa study music?

A. Juilliard

B. Leipzig Conservatory

C. Paris Conservatoire

D. University of Berlin

61. What was Merle Oberon's nickname?

A. "Essie"

B. "Mer"

C. "Mumu"

D. "Obie"

62. What was the title of cinematographer Freddie Young's 1998 autobiography?

A. *Light and Shadows*

B. *Seventy Light Years*

C. *The Light at the End of the Tunnel*

D. *Visions of Light*

63. Peter Lawford's first wife was the sister of what U.S. president?

A. Gerald Ford

B. John F. Kennedy

C. Lyndon B. Johnson

D. Richard Nixon

64. At what popular university was Woody Strode a decathlete and football star?

A. Notre Dame

B. Stanford

C. UCLA

D. USC

65. Ian Fleming's James Bond was partly modeled after which screen legend?

A. Cary Grant

B. Humphrey Bogart

C. James Stewart

D. Robert Taylor

66. Which Katharine Hepburn film had the tag line, "The dangerous age for women is from three to seventy"?

A. *Adam's Rib* (1949)

B. *Bringing Up Baby* (1938)

C. *Desk Set* (1957)

D. *The Philadelphia Story* (1940)

67. What was the title of the first book that Bruce Lee published?

    A. *Chinese Gung-Fu: The Philosophical Art of Self-Defense*
    B. *Karate-Do: My Way of Life*
    C. *Ki and the Way of the Martial Arts*
    D. *The Canon of Judo*

68. How much does Sandra Dee pay for her surfboard in *Gidget* (1959)?

    A. $10
    B. $12
    C. $25
    D. $60

69. James Agee was editor of which publication at Harvard University?

    A. *Harvard Advocate*
    B. *Harvard Business Press*
    C. *The Gamut*
    D. *The Harvard Independent*

70. Richard Thorpe directed what film that contained eight episodes featuring Gary Cooper, Gene Kelly, Ethel Barrymore, and Janet Leigh?

    A. *City Park* (1934)
    B. *It's a Big Country* (1951)
    C. *Lest We Forget* (1937)
    D. *Strange Wives* (1934)

71. How much was W. C. Fields paid for starring in *You Can't Cheat an Honest Man* (1939)?

    A. $100,000
    B. $125,000
    C. $70,000
    D. 25 percent of gross

72. "Tammy goes to college . . ." is the beginning of the tag line to what Sandra Dee film?

    A. *Doctor, You've Got to Be Kidding* (1967)
    B. *If a Man Answers* (1962)
    C. *Tammy and the Doctor* (1963)
    D. *Tammy Tell Me True* (1961)

73. In what profession did Dana Andrews work briefly before moving to Los Angeles?

    A. Accounting
    B. Marketing
    C. Pharmacy
    D. Tailoring

74. A scene in what feature directed by Robert Redford was filmed at the Original House of Pancakes in Wilmette, Illinois?

    A. *A River Runs Through It* (1992)
    B. *Lions for Lambs* (2007)
    C. *Ordinary People* (1980)
    D. *Quiz Show* (1994)

75. In Merle Oberon's will, she left $1 million to what organization?

    A. Academy of Motion Picture Arts and Sciences
    B. Calcutta Amateur Dramatic Society
    C. Motion Picture Country Home and Hospital
    D. Smile Foundation

76. According to her contract, Teresa Wright was not to be photographed in any of the following situations except which one?

    A. Assuming an athletic stance while pretending to hit something with a bow and arrow
    B. Playing tennis in a tennis skirt
    C. Running on the beach with her hair flying in the wind
    D. Twinkling on prop snow in a skiing outfit while a fan blows her scarf

77. For screenings of what William Castle feature did an inflatable skeleton hover above the audience during the final moments of the film?

    A. *13 Ghosts* (1960)
    B. *House on Haunted Hill* (1959)
    C. *Macabre* (1958)
    D. *The Tingler* (1959)

answers found on pages 570–571

78. Which of the following is a true statement about Leslie Howard?

A. He paid to have his body cryogenically frozen upon his death.
B. He was killed when a plane he was flying in was shot down during World War II.
C. He was married four times.
D. He was once ranked as one of the best golfers in the world.

79. In the 1980s, Sophia Loren launched a fragrance. What was it called?

A. Bella
B. La Donna
C. Loren
D. Sophia

80. Fredric March and Val Kilmer have which role in common?

A. Aristotle
B. Harry Hope
C. Philip of Macedonia
D. Sir Lancelot

81. Gore Vidal is a fifth cousin to what former U.S. president?

A. Bill Clinton
B. George Bush Sr.
C. Jimmy Carter
D. Ronald Reagan

82. How many children did Teresa Wright have when she was married to writer Niven Busch?

A. 0
B. 1
C. 2
D. 3

83. What was the name of the cabaret group Judy Holliday cofounded?

A. The Reeves
B. The Revelers
C. The Reviewers
D. The Revuers

84. Glenn Ford's father, Newton Ford, was an executive for what Canadian industry?

A. Manufacturing
B. Maple syrup
C. Mining
D. Railroad

85. How many stars does Ida Lupino have on the Hollywood Walk of Fame?

A. 1
B. 2
C. 3
D. 4

86. Which leading lady's publicity photo was pasted on the atomic bomb that was dropped on Bikini Atoll?

A. Ava Gardner
B. Betty Grable
C. Lana Turner
D. Rita Hayworth

87. In his youth, Robert Wagner was a caddie for what famous actor?

A. Charles Chaplin
B. Clark Gable
C. Errol Flynn
D. Humphrey Bogart

88. For what Thornton Wilder stage production did Teresa Wright understudy and eventually take over the role of Emily?

A. *Our Town*
B. *The Matchmaker*
C. *The Merchant of Yonkers*
D. *The Skin of Our Teeth*

89. What beautiful actress suggested that George Sanders enter the acting profession when he was still working at an ad agency?

A. Deborah Kerr
B. Greer Garson
C. Jeanette MacDonald
D. Katharine Hepburn

90. Which is not one of director Richard Boleslawski's books?

A. *Lance Down*
B. *Methods to Acting*
C. *Six Lessons of Dramatic Art*
D. *The Way of the Lancer*

91. In what year did Hal Roach sell his debt-ridden studios to his son?

A. 1948
B. 1955
C. 1962
D. 1980

92. How many short films did Tod Browning direct for Reliance-Majestic Studios?

A. 11
B. 23
C. 3
D. 46

93. As the youngest child in his family, film director Anthony Asquith was given what nickname?

A. "Parker"
B. "Prodigy"
C. "Puffin"
D. "Pumpkin"

94. What was the name of the kidnapped mare in 1939's *Two Thoroughbreds* starring Marjorie Main?

A. Coral
B. Daffodil
C. Larkspur
D. Spirit

95. The snow globe from *Citizen Kane* (1941) was later used in what film directed by Alexander Hall?

A. *Blue Skies* (1946)
B. *Down to Earth* (1947)
C. *Neptune's Daughter* (1949)
D. *The Pleasure of His Company* (1961)

96. Director Michael Powell was born in what county in England?

A. Hampshire
B. Kent
C. London
D. West Sussex

97. In what country was Moira Shearer born?

A. Germany
B. Ireland
C. Scotland
D. Sweden

98. What was James Cagney's favorite flower?

A. Iris
B. Lily
C. Morning glory
D. Orchid

99. What was Angie Dickinson's first job?

A. Commercial acting
B. Modeling
C. Selling Hershey's Kisses
D. Singing

100. What was director Robert Rossen's profession before making films?

A. Kosher baker
B. Novelist
C. Pianist
D. Professional boxer

101. Steven Spielberg directed what actress in a segment for the television pilot episode of *Night Gallery*?

A. Audrey Hepburn
B. Faye Dunaway
C. Joan Crawford
D. Katharine Hepburn

answers found on page 571

102. What job did Ronald Reagan have for seven summers as a young man?

    A. Department store salesman
    B. Lifeguard
    C. Movie usher
    D. Newspaper delivery boy

103. What is cinematographer Russell Metty's middle name?

    A. Edward
    B. Israel
    C. James
    D. Louis

104. George Marshall was expelled from which of the following Midwestern universities?

    A. Northwestern
    B. Notre Dame
    C. University of Chicago
    D. University of Michigan

105. Cary Grant appears in the 1970 concert documentary *That's the Way It Is*, which is about what music legend?

    A. Bob Dylan
    B. Elvis Presley
    C. Frank Sinatra
    D. Willie Nelson

106. Norma Shearer and Jennifer Jones have both portrayed which figure?

    A. Amelia Earhart
    B. Cleopatra
    C. Elizabeth Barrett
    D. Queen Victoria

107. What is Andy Griffith's middle name?

    A. Owen
    B. Samuel
    C. Todd
    D. Winston

108. Miklos Rozsa's "Violin Concerto No. 2" was the source material for what film?

    A. *E.T.: The Extra-Terrestrial* (1982)
    B. *Star Wars* (1977)
    C. *The Private Life of Sherlock Holmes* (1970)
    D. *The Towering Inferno* (1974)

109. Actor Glenn Ford is the direct descendant of which U.S. president?

    A. Franklin Pierce
    B. Gerald R. Ford
    C. John Tyler
    D. Martin Van Buren

110. What was the name of the real-life entertainer played by Ann Sheridan in *Shine On, Harvest Moon* (1944)?

    A. Ethel Barrymore
    B. Irene Castle
    C. Maxene Andrews
    D. Nora Bayes

111. What business is Barbra Streisand's character in at the beginning of the 1979 film *The Main Event*?

    A. Candles
    B. Lingerie
    C. Perfume
    D. Wigs

112. What was the profession of composer Bernard Herrmann's father?

    A. Anesthesiologist
    B. Cinematographer
    C. Optometrist
    D. Orchestra conductor

113. *Passage to Cairo* was the working title for what Norman Z. McLeod film?

    A. *It's a Gift* (1934)
    B. *My Favorite Spy* (1951)
    C. *Panama Hattie* (1942)
    D. *Road to Rio* (1947)

114. Ringo Starr gave Peter Sellers a rough mix of songs from what Beatles album that was later auctioned after Sellers's death?

A. *Abbey Road*
B. *Sgt. Pepper's Lonely Hearts Club Band*
C. *The Beatles*
D. *White Album*

115. In which Marx Brothers film does Kay Francis appear?

A. *A Day at the Races* (1937)
B. *A Night at the Opera* (1935)
C. *Duck Soup* (1933)
D. *The Cocoanuts* (1929)

116. In the 1992 film *Sneakers*, Robert Redford's jacket is the same one he wore in which other film?

A. *A Bridge Too Far* (1977)
B. *Butch Cassidy and the Sundance Kid* (1969)
C. *The Natural* (1984)
D. *The Sting* (1973)

117. In 1935 Benny Goodman and His Orchestra received a big break playing regularly on what popular radio program?

A. *Big Bandstand*
B. *Let's Dance*
C. *Pop Show*
D. *Under the Stars*

118. How many films did Walter Matthau appear in that were written by Neil Simon?

A. 2
B. 4
C. 6
D. 8

119. Which rock group named two of their albums after Marx Brothers movies?

A. Abba
B. Queen
C. U2
D. Van Halen

120. After decades at the top, Deanna Durbin retired to a life of seclusion. What French village has she resided in ever since?

A. Champagne-Ardenne
B. Neauphle-le-Château
C. Nord-Pas-de-Calais
D. Provence-Alpes-Côte d'Azur

121. What college did film composer Jerry Goldsmith attend?

A. Cal State Long Beach
B. NYU
C. UCLA
D. USC

122. During production on what film did the cast wear out two hundred pairs of shoes?

A. *Singin' in the Rain* (1952)
B. *Thousands Cheer* (1943)
C. *West Side Story* (1961)
D. *Ziegfeld Follies* (1945)

123. Oscar-winning film director Delbert Mann graduated from which university?

A. NYU
B. Oxford
C. Vanderbilt
D. Yale

124. Jacques Tati began his career performing as a what?

A. Magician
B. Mime
C. Radio announcer
D. Stand-up comedian

125. Gloria Grahame appeared in two episodes of *Tales of the Unexpected*, a series adapted from short stories by which writer?

A. H. G. Wells
B. Mark Twain
C. Ray Bradbury
D. Roald Dahl

answers found on page 571

126. Gloria Hallward was the real name of which actress?

A. Gloria Grahame
B. Gloria Swanson
C. Greer Garson
D. Rita Hayworth

127. Angie Dickinson gave Burt Reynolds his first on-screen kiss in what film?

A. *Dressed to Kill* (1980)
B. *Ocean's Eleven* (1960)
C. *Rio Bravo* (1959)
D. *Sam Whiskey* (1959)

128. In the 1994 film *Ready to Wear*, Sophia Loren re-creates her famous striptease from which one of her earlier films?

A. *It Started in Naples* (1960)
B. *Marriage Italian-Style* (1964)
C. *The Millionairess* (1960)
D. *Yesterday, Today and Tomorrow* (1963)

129. Neil Simon received an honorary D.H.C. from what college?

A. Hofstra
B. NYU
C. UC Berkeley
D. Williams

130. What was the name of the album that won Ruby Dee the Grammy Award for Best Spoken Word Album?

A. *A Black History*
B. *Dee and Davis: Kindred*
C. *Love and Color: The Ruby Dee Story*
D. *With Ossie and Ruby: In This Life Together*

131. Roger Moore celebrated his fiftieth birthday while filming what picture costarring Richard Burton?

A. *Bluebeard* (1972)
B. *Lovespell* (1981)
C. *The Wild Geese* (1978)
D. *Where Eagles Dare* (1968)

132. What was Pam Grier's first job after moving to Los Angeles?

A. Grocery store clerk
B. Receptionist
C. Stuntwoman
D. Waitress

133. The Kerwin Mathews film *The 3 Worlds of Gulliver* (1960) is based on a novel by what author?

A. Daniel Defoe
B. Edgar Rice Burroughs
C. Jack London
D. Jonathan Swift

134. When Humphrey Bogart was a baby, his face was used in an advertising campaign for what product?

A. Baby food
B. Diapers
C. Milk
D. Shoes

135. Which leading lady was the inspiration for Hannibal Lecter's voice in *The Silence of the Lambs* (1991)?

A. Bette Davis
B. Greta Garbo
C. Katharine Hepburn
D. Lauren Bacall

136. Which of the following professions did Glenn Ford never hold?

A. Bus driver
B. Delivery man
C. Phone repairman
D. Stable boy

137. Stan Laurel appears on the cover of what Beatles album?

A. *Abbey Road*
B. *Let It Be*
C. *Rubber Soul*
D. *Sgt. Pepper's Lonely Hearts Club Band*

138. Audrey Hepburn adopted a pet deer for her role in what film?
    A. *Charade* (1963)
    B. *Green Mansions* (1959)
    C. *The Nun's Story* (1959)
    D. *Two for the Road* (1967)

139. Jane Powell sang at the inauguration ball of which U.S. president?
    A. Dwight D. Eisenhower
    B. Harry Truman
    C. John F. Kennedy
    D. Ronald Reagan

140. A role as an extra on the set of what film starring Sophia Loren was given away as a prize on an early episode of *The Price Is Right*?
    A. *Beau Brummel* (1954)
    B. *The Fall of the Roman Empire* (1964)
    C. *The Master of Ballantrae* (1953)
    D. *Uncle Vanya* (1963)

141. Judy Garland took the first part of her stage name from a song by what musician?
    A. Hoagy Carmichael
    B. Johnny Mercer
    C. Paul Anka
    D. Sammy Fain

142. What song did Peter Sellers request to be played at his funeral because he hated it and found it wonderfully inappropriate for the occasion?
    A. "I Could Have Danced All Night"
    B. "In the Mood"
    C. "It's a Great Feeling"
    D. "Whatever Will Be, Will Be (Que Sera, Sera)"

143. Sophia Loren costarred with O. J. Simpson in two films. One of them was 1979's *Firepower*. What was the other?
    A. *Angela* (1978)
    B. *The Cassandra Crossing* (1976)
    C. *The Towering Inferno* (1974)
    D. *Verdict* (1982)

144. Louis Jourdan and Gary Oldman have both portrayed what character?
    A. D'Artagnan
    B. Dracula
    C. Rosencrantz
    D. Van Helsing

145. When did Shirley Temple officially retire from motion pictures?
    A. 1949
    B. 1955
    C. 1981
    D. 1997

146. Which of the following is true about the painting of Gene Tierney in *Laura* (1944)?
    A. It was a Tierney family heirloom.
    B. It was a photograph.
    C. It was painted by Vincent Price.
    D. It was stolen after the first day of shooting.

147. What was the name of the Italian tailor played by Bob Hope in Norman Z. McLeod's *Casanova's Big Night* (1954)?
    A. Fasso Fassolada
    B. Pesce Panzanella
    C. Pippo Popolino
    D. Zica Ziccato

148. How much money did writer James Thurber allegedly offer Samuel Goldwyn to stop production on Norman Z. McLeod's *The Secret Life of Walter Mitty* (1947)?
    A. $1,000
    B. $10,000
    C. $50,000
    D. $500,000

149. At the age of nineteen, Sean Connery was employed at a dance hall in what capacity?

A. Bartender
B. Bouncer
C. Dance instructor
D. Saxophone player

150. What Lionel Richie music video did Stanley Donen direct in the 1980s?

A. "All Night Long"
B. "Dancing on the Ceiling"
C. "Hello"
D. "Running with the Night"

151. What is Lloyd Bridges's middle name?

A. Cassius
B. Floyd
C. Vernet
D. Vernon

152. George Sanders is mentioned in what song by the rock band The Kinks?

A. "Arthur"
B. "Celluloid Heroes"
C. "Lola"
D. "Shangrila"

153. Audrey Hepburn's earliest career ambition was to be a what?

A. Ballerina
B. Doctor
C. Painter
D. Violinist

154. What legendary actor portrays Richard Wagner in the 1983 miniseries *Wagner*?

A. Anthony Hopkins
B. Marlon Brando
C. Richard Burton
D. Robert Taylor

155. What is Montgomery Clift's medical specialty in *Suddenly, Last Summer* (1959)?

A. Cardiology
B. Endocrinology
C. Nuclear medicine
D. Psychosurgery

156. What is the name of the makeup shade Max Factor created especially for Lena Horne?

A. Dark Honey
B. Golden Tan
C. Light Egyptian
D. Sweet Brown

157. How did James Cagney's father die?

A. Bus accident
B. Influenza
C. Scarlet fever
D. Yellow fever

158. What was the name of the jazzy 1946 Disney short set to the music of Benny Goodman?

A. *All the Cats Join In*
B. *Babes in the Woods*
C. *The Dancing Toys*
D. *The Three Little Pigs*

159. Frank Loesser was inducted into the Songwriters Hall of Fame in what year?

A. 1955
B. 1960
C. 1970
D. 1983

160. What was the first film in the *Falcon* series starring George Sanders?

A. *A Date with the Falcon* (1942)
B. *The Falcon's Brother* (1942)
C. *The Hooded Falcon* (1924)
D. *The Gay Falcon* (1941)

answers found on page 571

161. Geraldine Page's real-life twin sons appear with her in a scene in what film?

    A. *Honky Tonk Freeway* (1981)
    B. *I'm Dancing as Fast as I Can* (1982)
    C. *Sweet Bird of Youth* (1962)
    D. *The Trip to Bountiful* (1985)

162. Director Stanley Donen's own car (a Mercedes 230) was used in which film starring Audrey Hepburn?

    A. *Funny Face* (1957)
    B. *Green Mansions* (1959)
    C. *Love in the Afternoon* (1957)
    D. *Two for the Road* (1967)

163. What football team did Woody Strode play for before moving to Los Angeles?

    A. Atlanta Falcons
    B. Chicago Bears
    C. Cleveland Rams
    D. Dallas Texans

164. What did Sandra Dee and Bobby Darin name their only son?

    A. Damon
    B. David
    C. Dirk
    D. Dodd

165. Elvis performs the tango song "The Walls Have Ears" in which film?

    A. *Follow That Dream* (1962)
    B. *Fun in Acapulco* (1963)
    C. *Girls! Girls! Girls!* (1962)
    D. *Roustabout* (1964)

166. What was director John Sturges's middle name?

    A. Edward
    B. Eliot
    C. Israel
    D. Jason

167. What was James Dean's middle name?

    A. Byron
    B. Calvin
    C. Pierce
    D. Vincent

168. Which of the following is not one of Elizabeth Taylor's perfumes?

    A. Black Pearls
    B. Passion
    C. Red Emeralds
    D. White Diamonds

169. On the television show *I Love Lucy*, what John Wayne item did Lucy steal while visiting Hollywood?

    A. His car
    B. His footprints
    C. His mailbox
    D. His statue

170. What is Michael Caine's original given name?

    A. Matthew
    B. Maurice
    C. Melvin
    D. Michael

171. What job did Franz Waxman have before pursuing a music career?

    A. Bank teller
    B. Farmer
    C. Mechanic
    D. Teacher

172. Which Hollywood screenwriter was the brother-in-law of Anthony Quinn?

    A. Allan Scott
    B. Ben Hecht
    C. Martin Goldsmith
    D. Philip Yordan

answers found on page 571

173. Which screen legend studied medicine in college?

A. Cary Grant
B. Clark Gable
C. Humphrey Bogart
D. Robert Taylor

174. Which Oscar-winning screenwriter once worked at the Davis Perfection Bakery in Los Angeles?

A. Dalton Trumbo
B. Orson Welles
C. Preston Sturges
D. William Inge

175. What is Bill Murray's middle name?

A. Edward
B. James
C. Michael
D. William

176. In what year did Meryl Streep receive Harvard University's Hasty Pudding Award as Woman of the Year?

A. 1970
B. 1980
C. 1990
D. 2000

177. What Academy Awards tradition began the same year that James Stewart won his Oscar for *The Philadelphia Story* (1940)?

A. The presentation of the Best Actor Award by the previous year's Best Actress
B. The projection of a short film dedicated to recently deceased entertainers
C. The red carpet "preshow"
D. The use of sealed envelopes to keep the identities of the winners secret

178. At the age of eighteen, what was Deanna Durbin's salary?

A. $100,000 a year
B. $20,000 a year
C. $250,000 a year
D. $50,000 a year

179. Jane Fonda and Donald Sutherland star in what documentary?

A. *Alaska Wilderness Lake* (1971)
B. *FTA* (1972)
C. *Sky Above and Mud Beneath* (1961)
D. *The War Game* (1965)

180. What company does James Cagney's character work for in *One, Two, Three* (1961)?

A. AT&T
B. Coca-Cola
C. IBM
D. TWA

181. Which of the following films starring Jack Lemmon was turned into a popular television series?

A. *Grumpy Old Men* (1993)
B. *Save the Tiger* (1973)
C. *The April Fools*
D. *The Odd Couple* (1968)

182. Vivien Leigh made her professional stage debut in what play?

A. *House of Flowers*
B. *The Green Sash*
C. *The Rose Tattoo*
D. *Wonderful Town*

183. How old was Ann Miller when she first signed with RKO?

A. 13
B. 15
C. 18
D. 21

answers found on page 571

184. What was the name of Barbara Bel Geddes's character on the popular television show *Dallas*?

A. Miss Ellie
B. Miss Helen
C. Miss Lila
D. Miss Rosie

185. Michael Powell and Emeric Pressburger dubbed their partnership, and named their production company, what?

A. The Archers
B. The Blacksmiths
C. The Duo
D. The Film Jockeys

186. In what year did Paul Muni retire from stage and screen?

A. 1949
B. 1952
C. 1959
D. 1966

187. From which university did director Alan J. Pakula graduate?

A. Georgetown
B. Harvard
C. Princeton
D. Yale

188. Which of the following is a true statement about Barbara Bel Geddes?

A. She designed a line of women's clothes.
B. She had a degree in physics.
C. She had a hit record in 1961.
D. She wrote two children's books.

189. Which play inspired Clark Gable to become an actor?

A. *A Streetcar Named Desire*
B. *Inherit the Wind*
C. *Point of No Return*
D. *The Bird of Paradise*

190. What was the first film of the 1940s *Lassie* series to earn an Academy Award nomination?

A. *Challenge to Lassie* (1949)
B. *Courage of Lassie* (1946)
C. *Lassie Come Home* (1943)
D. *Son of Lassie* (1945)

191. What was the title of the children's book that Chuck Jones wrote and published in 1986?

A. *Bart the Beaver*
B. *Johnson, the Cat Who Wouldn't Climb Trees*
C. *Samson Bear Gets His Hair Cut*
D. *William, the Backwards Skunk*

192. Cary Grant's character, Peter Joshua, in 1963's *Charade* was named after Stanley Donen's two what?

A. Agents
B. Brothers
C. Cinematographers
D. Sons

193. Jacques Tati's uncompleted film *Forza Bastia* (2002) was intended to be a short documentary about what?

A. A circus act
B. A mime
C. A soccer team
D. An airline pilot

194. Which of the following is a true statement about Ernest Borgnine?

A. He has been nominated for six Academy Awards.
B. He has written two cookbooks.
C. He was once married to Judy Garland.
D. He was the original center square when the game show *Hollywood Squares* first premiered in 1966.

195. What rock group named their first album after Lillian Gish?

A. New Order
B. Oasis
C. Radiohead
D. Smashing Pumpkins

196. After a serious car accident, Merle Oberon suffered even further damage to her complexion as a result of an allergic reaction to what?

A. Heavy cloths
B. Penicillin
C. Sulfa drugs
D. Tomatoes

197. In what Coen Brothers' film does actor Steve Buscemi's character not die?

A. *Barton Fink* (1991)
B. *Fargo* (1996)
C. *Miller's Crossing* (1990)
D. *The Big Lebowski* (1998)

198. What was Roddy McDowall's main hobby/profession outside of acting?

A. Gardening
B. Music
C. Photography
D. Writing

199. What actress plays Sandra Dee's roommate, Audrey, in *That Funny Feeling* (1965)?

A. Nancy Walker
B. Nita Talbot
C. Stefanie Powers
D. Sue George

200. In the James Bond film series what was the full character name of gadgets expert "Q"?

A. Colonel Prescott
B. Colonel Quinn
C. Major Boothroyd
D. Major Quartermain

201. In the Deanna Durbin film *Three Smart Girls Grow Up* (1939), who replaced Barbara Read for the character of Kay Craig?

A. Alice Brady
B. Helen Parrish
C. Nan Grey
D. Nella Walker

202. Benny Goodman's wife was a descendant of what prominent family?

A. The Hearsts
B. The Peabodys
C. The Rockefellers
D. The Vanderbilts

203. Who escorted Susan Hayward onstage at the 1974 Oscars?

A. Cary Grant
B. George Sanders
C. John Wayne
D. Paul Henreid

204. Who bought the rights to *The Philadelphia Story* (1940) as a gift to Katharine Hepburn?

A. Cary Grant
B. Howard Hughes
C. Louis B. Mayer
D. Spencer Tracy

205. What is Anne Bancroft's full birth name?

A. Anna Maria Louisa Italiano
B. Anna Nicole Bancropolos
C. Anne Michelle Berkowitz
D. Anne Michelle Bancroft

206. Humphrey Bogart's only son was named after which one of his movie characters?

A. Charlie in *The African Queen* (1951)
B. Linus in *Sabrina* (1954)
C. Rick in *Casablanca* (1942)
D. Steve in *To Have and Have Not* (1944)

answers found on page 571

207. *Brooks Wilson, Ltd.* was the working title of which film starring Sterling Hayden?

A. *Bahama Passage* (1941)
B. *Kansas Pacific* (1953)
C. *Loving* (1970)
D. *Shotgun* (1955)

208. What was the last Hal Roach short subject film?

A. *Hide and Shriek* (1938)
B. *Merrily We Live* (1938)
C. *Roamin' Holiday* (1937)
D. *Rushin' Ballet* (1937)

209. What two actors served as the best man and matron of honor at Mae Murray's wedding to Prince David Mdivani?

A. Clark Gable and Carole Lombard
B. Gary Merrill and Betty Davis
C. Rudolph Valentino and Pola Negri
D. William Powell and Jean Harlow

210. In *Take Me Out to the Ball Game* (1949), what is the name of the baseball team that Esther Williams inherits?

A. The Coyotes
B. The Wildcats
C. The Wolverines
D. The Wolves

211. Which leading lady has a Hermès bag named in her honor?

A. Grace Kelly
B. Joan Crawford
C. Kim Novak
D. Louise Brooks

212. Anne Bancroft shares a birthday with all of the following celebrities except which one?

A. Cliff Montgomery
B. Jennifer Love Hewitt
C. John Ritter
D. Roddy McDowall

213. Benny Goodman was awarded honorary doctorates from all of the following universities except which one?

A. Columbia
B. Harvard
C. NYU
D. Yale

214. Felix Aylmer portrayed Lord Palmerston in all of the following films except for which one?

A. *Sixty Glorious Years* (1938)
B. *The Lady with the Lamp* (1951)
C. *The Years Between* (1946)
D. *Victoria the Great* (1937)

215. Boxer Max Baer's younger brother, Buddy, saves Deborah Kerr from being gored by a bull in what 1951 MGM epic?

A. *Ben-Hur*
B. *Cleopatra*
C. *El Cid*
D. *Quo Vadis*

216. Ronald Reagan worked as an announcer for what baseball team?

A. Boston Red Sox
B. Chicago Cubs
C. Chicago White Sox
D. New York Yankees

217. On New Year's Eve of what year did Angie Dickinson make her acting debut in an episode of *Death Valley Days*?

A. 1950
B. 1954
C. 1956
D. 1958

218. How did Merle Oberon's father die?

A. Falling off a train
B. In a bar fight in Burma
C. In prison
D. On the Western Front of World War I

219. In his teens, Andre Previn played the piano offscreen in which film starring Frank Sinatra?
   A. *It Happened in Brooklyn* (1947)
   B. *Meet Danny Wilson* (1951)
   C. *Till the Clouds Roll By* (1946)
   D. *Young at Heart* (1954)

220. Future First Lady Nancy Reagan (as Nancy Davis) made her first on-screen appearance in which Ethel Barrymore film?
   A. *Pinky* (1949)
   B. *Portrait of Jennie* (1948)
   C. *The Red Danube* (1949)
   D. *The Secret of Convict Lake* (1951)

221. How long did James Cagney's only marriage last?
   A. 20 years
   B. 63 years
   C. 7 years
   D. 1 day

222. What film featuring Natalie Wood was played at the theater next door to the Piggly Wiggly grocery store in 1989's *Driving Miss Daisy*?
   A. *It's Always Fair Weather* (1955)
   B. *Scudda Hoo! Scudda Hay!* (1948)
   C. *The Happy Road* (1957)
   D. *The Silver Chalice* (1954)

223. What was the name of Alan Ladd's company that produced many of his radio programs such as *Box 13*?
   A. Ladd Productions
   B. Mayfield Productions
   C. Oasis Productions
   D. The Ladd Company

224. In what city was Stanley Donen born and raised?
   A. Buffalo, New York
   B. Charleston, West Virginia
   C. Cleveland, Ohio
   D. Columbia, South Carolina

225. What was the name of the Rock Island, Tennessee, lingerie factory owned by Ginger Rogers?
   A. Form Fit Rogers
   B. Ginger's Lace
   C. Lela's Garments
   D. Spice Unmentioned

226. What was the title of the book by bestselling author Harold Robbins based on Lana Turner's love affair with Johnny Stompanato?
   A. *Imitation of Lives*
   B. *Love and Other Killing Experiences*
   C. *Madame X*
   D. *Where Love Has Gone*

227. Asta from the *Thin Man* series appears as a ghost dog in what Norman Z. McLeod film?
   A. *The Kid from Brooklyn* (1946)
   B. *The Paleface* (1948)
   C. *The Secret Life of Walter Mitty* (1947)
   D. *Topper Takes a Trip* (1938)

228. Which leading lady starred in the first movie to have Sensurround?
   A. Ava Gardner
   B. Debbie Reynolds
   C. Gloria Swanson
   D. Lana Turner

229. What was the name of the spoof of Deanna Durbin's *Three Smart Girls* (1936)?
   A. *Four Smart Girls* (1938)
   B. *Three Dumb Clucks* (1937)
   C. *Three Not-So-Smart Women* (1944)
   D. *Three Silly Nillies* (1943)

230. What other Shirley Temple film is referenced in *Just Around the Corner* (1938)?
   A. *Bright Eyes* (1934)
   B. *Curly Top* (1935)
   C. *Dimples* (1936)
   D. *Our Little Girl* (1935)

answers found on page 572

231. What color are Sandra Dee's snorkel mask and flippers in *Gidget* (1959)?

    A. Baby blue

    B. Lemon yellow

    C. Lime green

    D. Pastel pink

232. From which university did Meryl Streep receive her M.F.A. degree?

    A. Harvard

    B. NYU

    C. Princeton

    D. Yale

233. In the 1931 film *Man of the World*, Carole Lombard's character meets William Powell's while visiting what city?

    A. Cairo

    B. London

    C. Paris

    D. Rome

234. Buddy Ebsen's performance in which film won him the role of Jed Clampett in *The Beverly Hillbillies*?

    A. *Behold a Pale Horse* (1964)

    B. *Breakfast at Tiffany's* (1961)

    C. *The Sundowners* (1960)

    D. *Two for the Road* (1967)

235. Actor John Ireland was a professional athlete in what sport before becoming an actor?

    A. Baseball

    B. Running

    C. Skiing

    D. Swimming

236. Whose birthday did Katharine Hepburn adopt as her own?

    A. Sarah Bernhardt's

    B. Spencer Tracy's

    C. Her brother's

    D. Her grandmother's

237. When Jack Lemmon was alive, what could you expect to see him doing at any Hollywood party?

    A. Doing a tap dance number

    B. Doing magic tricks

    C. Playing the piano

    D. Singing a song

238. Portions of what film directed by Arthur Hiller were included in *Raid on Rommel* (1971), starring Richard Burton?

    A. *Hamlet* (1948)

    B. *Richard III* (1955)

    C. *Spartacus* (1960)

    D. *Tobruk* (1967)

239. What future leading man made his screen debut in the 1961 film *Angel Baby* with Joan Blondell?

    A. Burt Reynolds

    B. John Travolta

    C. Tom Selleck

    D. Warren Beatty

240. Which is not a part of Glenn Ford's full legal name?

    A. Gwyllyn

    B. Henry

    C. Newton

    D. Samuel

241. Elvis Presley graduated from Humes High School in which city?

    A. Buffalo, New York

    B. East Tupelo, Mississippi

    C. Memphis, Tennessee

    D. Orlando, Florida

242. In what city was cinematographer Haskell Wexler born?

    A. Austin, Texas

    B. Brooklyn, New York

    C. Chicago, Illinois

    D. San Francisco, California

answers found on page 572

243. What was cinematographer James Wong Howe's nickname?

A. "Deep Focus Jimmie"
B. "Long Lens Jim"
C. "Low Key Hoe"
D. "Wide Shot Wong"

244. Which Agatha Christie novel is allegedly inspired by Gene Tierney?

A. *Cards on the Table*
B. *Death Comes as an End*
C. *Death in the Clouds*
D. *The Mirror Crack'd from Side to Side*

245. Director Ingmar Bergman's father was of what profession?

A. Banker
B. Clergy
C. Doctor
D. Filmmaker

246. Which Academy Award–nominated actress is the grandniece of film director Anthony Asquith?

A. Helena Bonham Carter
B. Keira Knightley
C. Natalie Portman
D. Uma Thurman

247. What was the name of the team Woody Strode played for in the Canadian Football League?

A. Calgary Stampeders
B. Edmonton Eskimos
C. Montreal Alouettes
D. Toronto Argonauts

248. In what important way did the film *Wee Willie Winkie* (1937) deviate from the original Rudyard Kipling story?

A. Nothing significant was changed.
B. The ethnicities of the characters were changed.
C. The sex of the character was changed for Shirley Temple.
D. The story was expanded to be a full-length film.

249. Which screen legend was Vivien Leigh's maid of honor at her wedding to Laurence Olivier?

A. Barbara Stanwyck
B. Katharine Hepburn
C. Norma Shearer
D. Olivia de Havilland

250. Woody Strode posed for a painting commissioned by whom?

A. Adolf Hitler
B. Franklin D. Roosevelt
C. John Ford
D. Richard Nixon

answers found on page 572

ANSWERS

CHAPTER 1

1. A. *Frühjahrsparade* (1934)
2. A. *Beyond the Rocks* (1922)
3. C. *The Wicked Darling* (1919)
4. C. *Follow the Fleet* (1936)
5. A. Circus
6. D. Poland
7. A. *Cud nad Wisla* (1921)
8. A. *Sadie Thompson* (1928)
9. D. Rudolph Valentino
10. D. Warner Bros.
11. D. Virginia
12. C. Harold Lloyd
13. A. *Camille* (1936)
14. B. Lillian Gish
15. B. "Rose Tint My World"
16. A. *Brothers Under the Skin* (1922)
17. D. *The Mill on the Floss* (1937)
18. D. *Two Arabian Knights* (1927)
19. B. *Khleb* (1918)
20. D. *Seven Faces* (1929)
21. D. *The Trespasser* (1929)
22. C. Philadelphia
23. B. A cheetah
24. D. Rodeo star
25. A. Clara Bow
26. A. 1882
27. B. Jean Acker
28. C. 3
29. B. Greta Garbo
30. C. *The Valiant* (1929)
31. B. Raoul Walsh
32. C. Lon Chaney
33. C. *7th Heaven* (1927)
34. B. In a church

Spotlight on Marion Davies

1. A. Basketball
2. D. *Show People* (1928)
3. B. *Polly of the Circus* (1932)
4. A. *The Pilgrim* (1923)
5. A. Mary Tudor

35. D. Rosebud Blondell
36. A. *Betrayal* (1929)
37. B. Fox
38. C. 1962
39. B. R. Di Volentina
40. A. *John Smith* (1922)
41. B. Harold Lloyd
42. D. *Wings*
43. C. *The Gamblers* (1929)
44. B. *The Havoc* (1916)
45. B. *Navy Blues* (1929)
46. C. Laurel and Hardy
47. B. *Jim Bludso* (1917)
48. B. *The Adventures of Huckleberry Finn* (1939)
49. D. The Weintraub Syncopaters
50. C. Russian Empire
51. D. Wallace Beery
52. D. Harold Lloyd
53. D. Bette Davis
54. A. Agricultural science
55. B. London, England
56. D. Robert Henri
57. A. Bette Davis
58. C. *The Temptress* (1926)
59. A. *Alias Jimmy Valentine* (1928)
60. C. 14
61. A. Alexander Pushkin
62. C. London's Film Society
63. C. *Khleb* (1918)
64. A. 1895
65. C. George Fitzmaurice
66. A. 0
67. C. Greta Garbo
68. D. *The White Sister* (1923)

69. C. Gary Cooper
70. A. Alfred Hitchcock
71. C. 5
72. B. Dorothy Gish
73. C. *Monsieur Beaucaire* (1924)
74. D. William Wellman
75. A. He challenged the writer to a boxing match.
76. B. King Vidor
77. B. MGM
78. B. *Mark of the Vampire* (1935)

Spotlight on John Barrymore
1. A. 0
2. C. *The Mad Genius* (1931)
3. B. 3
4. B. *Rasputin and the Empress* (1932)
5. A. *Beau Brummel* (1924)

79. D. Prime Minister
80. B. Paramount
81. C. Mormon
82. B. Charles Chaplin
83. B. 2
84. D. *The Kid Brother* (1927)
85. D. *The Hooded Falcon* (1924)
86. A. Fox
87. B. MGM
88. A. A bass drum pedal
89. A. Cecil B. DeMille
90. B. Kabar
91. C. Joan Crawford
92. C. *The Day of Faith* (1923)
93. C. 1926
94. C. Norman Kerry's
95. D. *Young Mr. Lincoln* (1939)
96. D. "Spurs"
97. B. 5
98. D. Rudyard Kipling
99. A. *Camille*
100. D. 1937
101. C. *The Valiant* (1929)
102. B. *Champagne* (1928)
103. B. 26
104. D. *The Shamrock Handicap*
105. C. Gary Cooper
106. A. *A Sainted Devil*
107. B. Metro Studios
108. C. Interior designer
109. A. Billy Wilder

110. B. *Day Dreams*
111. D. Ronald Colman
112. B. *Little Annie Rooney* (1925)
113. A. Fox
114. C. Pola Negri
115. D. Norman Kerry
116. C. 1893
117. B. Armand
118. A. Acted in English
119. C. *Seven Sinners* (1925)
120. C. *Sally, Irene and Mary* (1925)
121. D. *The Wolf Song* (1929)
122. D. *West Point* (1928)
123. B. Scraps
124. C. *Sentimental Tommy* (1921)
125. A. 4'11"
126. B. Cary Grant
127. B. Gloria Swanson
128. B. The Duke de Chandre
129. C. Natacha Rambova
130. B. *Running Wild* (1927)
131. A. The Ben Pollack Orchestra
132. C. Rodolfo Alfonso Raffaello Piero Filiberto Guglielmi di Valentino d'Antoguolla
133. A. 1891
134. A. Charles Chaplin
135. A. *Dracula* (1931)
136. B. Texas
137. D. *White Tiger* (1923)
138. C. His chest circumference was one inch too small.
139. D. *The Outcasts of Poker Flat* (1919)
140. A. *A Man's Man*
141. D. Lon Chaney
142. C. Dorothy Burgess
143. D. Warner Bros.
144. C. Laurence Olivier
145. C. Myrna Loy
146. D. *Who Is the Man?* (1924)
147. B. Sheik
148. B. 3
149. A. Actor
150. B. Hungary
151. B. Best Cinematography
152. C. Greta Garbo
153. D. Virgo
154. A. *Disraeli* (1929)
155. A. Buster Keaton

156. D. Rita Hayworth
157. C. *Sally of the Sawdust* (1925)
158. A. Centaur Pendragon
159. C. Kate Hudson
160. B. Joseph P. Kennedy
161. D. Sweden
162. C. Joan Crawford
163. B. *Broken Blossoms* (1919)
164. D. Rudolph Valentino
165. D. $6,500
166. D. *Way Out West* (1930)
167. C. Greta Garbo
168. D. Hal Roach
169. C. *Seven Faces* (1929)

Spotlight on Anna May Wong
1. B. J. M. Barrie
2. C. *Peter Pan*
3. B. Loo Song
4. A. "After the Ball"
5. B. *Piccadilly* (1929)

170. D. *Submarine* (1928)
171. C. *The Front Page* (1931)
172. A. Clifton Webb
173. D. Margaret Sullavan
174. B. *Pool Sharks* (1915)
175. A. *Gasoline Love* (1923)
176. D. *The Eagle*
177. A. *Beau Geste* (1926)
178. A. Lotus Blossom
179. D. "Speedy"
180. B. Charles Chaplin
181. B. Indiana
182. A. *London After Midnight* (1927)
183. B. Gloria Swanson
184. A. *Four Walls*
185. A. Fred Niblo
186. D. William Collier Jr.
187. C. *The Midnight Express* (1924)
188. B. *Queen Kelly* (1929)
189. D. *The Kiss* (1929)
190. C. Phroso "Dead-Legs"
191. A. 1880
192. D. *Tom Thumb's Wedding*
193. A. Lillian Gish
194. D. *The Young Rajah* (1922)
195. B. *Janice Meredith* (1924)
196. B. Chemical/electrical engineering
197. B. *Montana Moon* (1930)

198. B. Greta Garbo
199. D. Norma Shearer for *Marie Antoinette* (1938)
200. B. Lillian Gish
201. D. *The Wedding March* (1928)
202. B. Museum of Fine Arts in Boston
203. A. The crab dolly
204. B. 1902
205. C. Janet Gaynor for *7th Heaven* (1927), *Sunrise* (1927), and *Street Angel* (1928)
206. A. *Character Studies*
207. B. *Lady Windermere's Fan* (1925)
208. A. Douglas Fairbanks
209. D. *The Thirteenth Chair* (1929)
210. C. 1925
211. A. Clara Bow
212. C. *The Sporting Venus* (1925)
213. C. *The Nightingale* (1914)
214. C. Seaweed
215. B. *Laugh, Clown, Laugh* (1928)
216. B. *The Unholy Three* (1925)
217. D. *The Virginian* (1929)
218. D. *Romola* (1924)
219. C. He refused to hide his homosexuality.
220. A. Alberto
221. B. Playing an extra in silent films
222. B. Fourth
223. D. 1927
224. B. American Laboratory Theatre
225. A. 1913
226. A. Hadrian
227. B. *Rain* (1932)
228. A. William Haines
229. C. *The Story of Alexander Graham Bell* (1939)
230. A. Douglas Fairbanks

CHAPTER 2

1. A. Edmund Gwenn
2. C. Best Screenplay
3. B. *This Marriage Business* (1938)
4. A. *Change of Heart* (1934)
5. B. *Heidi* (1937)
6. D. William Wellman
7. B. 1935
8. A. Best Art Direction

9. A. "Remember My Forgotten Man"
10. D. Rex Harrison
11. C. *The Mystery of the Wax Museum* (1933)
12. A. *Gone With the Wind* (1939)
13. A. *One Precious Year* (1933)
14. D. *The Voice of Bugle Ann* (1936)
15. C. 1974
16. D. Tyrone Power
17. D. Myrna Loy
18. B. India
19. A. 1935
20. A. *The Roaring Twenties* (1939)
21. D. Sea captain
22. B. James Cagney
23. C. Norma Shearer
24. B. *Find the Lady* (1936)
25. A. *David Copperfield* and *A Tale of Two Cities*
26. A. *Her First Affaire* (1932)
27. D. *Westward Passage* (1932)
28. B. George Raft
29. D. *Ninotchka* (1939)
30. D. *Stand-In* (1937)
31. A. *Dirigible* (1931)
32. C. 3
33. D. *The Prince and the Pauper* (1937)
34. C. The prize-winning 1915 racehorse
35. D. *The Little Colonel* (1935)
36. B. *Going Places* (1938)
37. B. *Curly Top* (1935)
38. B. *The Private Life of Henry VIII* (1933)
39. C. A horse race
40. A. Franz Schubert
41. D. Tania
42. B. *The Heiress* (1949)
43. D. *Tudor Rose* (1936)
44. A. *Animal Crackers* (1930)
45. D. *The Strawberry Blonde*
46. B. 1906
47. B. Saxophone
48. B. Marlene Dietrich
49. A. *Calling All Girls* (1942)
50. A. Adolphe Menjou
51. A. Alice Brady
52. C. *Splendor* (1935)
53. C. 1935
54. D. *The Good Earth* (1937)

Spotlight on Cary Grant

1. B. The Mock Turtle
2. C. Randolph Scott
3. D. *Topper* (1937)
4. C. 2
5. C. *His Girl Friday* (1940)

55. D. Mary Pickford
56. C. *The Citadel*
57. A. Fredric March
58. C. United Artists
59. C. *Reunion* (1932)
60. C. Katharine Hepburn
61. C. *The Prince and the Pauper* (1937)
62. B. *The Rise of Catherine the Great* (1934)
63. D. *Wuthering Heights* (1939)
64. B. Bob Hope
65. B. 2
66. B. *It's a Wonderful World* (1939)
67. A. Academy Juvenile Award
68. B. A broken leg
69. D. *One Hundred Men and a Girl* (1937)
70. A. *David Copperfield* (1935)
71. C. *Hearts Divided* (1936)
72. A. *Christopher Bean* (1933)
73. A. 0
74. B. Bela Lugosi
75. A. 0
76. D. Nella Walker
77. C. Ginger Rogers
78. C. *Million Dollar Legs* (1932)
79. C. *The Story of Vernon and Irene Castle* (1939)
80. D. Loretta Young
81. A. *Having Wonderful Time* (1938)
82. B. Paramount
83. D. *Too Much Harmony* (1933)
84. B. Jewelry
85. C. Leslie Howard
86. B. Jessica Tandy
87. B. *Love Is on the Air* (1937)
88. B. *There Goes My Heart* (1938)
89. A. *Below the Sea* (1933)
90. A. Gloria Stuart
91. A. *King Kong* (1933)
92. D. William Holden
93. B. Constance Bennett

94. C. Shirley Temple
95. D. Princess
96. A. Claudette Colbert
97. B. *Andy Hardy's Blonde Trouble* (1944)
98. B. Greta Garbo
99. C. Best Cinematography
100. B. *Nelson* (1926)
101. A. Charles Laughton
102. A. Caterpillar
103. A. 0
104. C. *Judge Priest* (1934)
105. B. *Little Women* (1933)
106. D. *The Love Race* (1931)
107. C. *Swing That Music*
108. A. *The Crowd Roars* (1938)
109. B. *A Tale of Two Cities* (1935)
110. A. *Bored of Education*
111. C. *Paris Herald*
112. C. For sounding too mature
113. C. *The Impatient Maiden* (1932)
114. D. $60,000
115. D. *Yankee Doodle Dandy* (1942)
116. C. Mae West
117. A. Bela Lugosi
118. A. *I, Claudius* (1937)
119. B. *Morocco*
120. A. *The Three Passions* (1928)
121. D. Leslie Howard
122. A. 0

Spotlight on Carole Lombard
1. D. William Powell
2. D. William Powell
3. D. A train
4. D. *We're Not Dressing* (1934)
5. B. *No Man of Her Own* (1932)

123. D. *Showboat* (1936)
124. B. *The Chase and Sanborn Hour*
125. C. Best Original Screenplay
126. C. Klopstokia
127. A. *Conquest* (1937)
128. B. Fredric March
129. C. *The Lady Vanishes* (1938)
130. B. *The Casino Murder Case* (1935)
131. D. *The Champ*
132. D. *The Little Princess* (1939)
133. A. *Les Misérables* (1935)
134. C. *This Side of Heaven* (1934)
135. D. Myrna Loy

136. A. $129,000
137. B. Gas meters
138. D. *Splendor* (1935)
139. C. *Meet John Doe* (1941)
140. A. Carmelita
141. D. Victor Fleming
142. C. Johnny Eck
143. A. *Life in the Raw* (1933)
144. A. *Doctor X* (1932)
145. D. 8
146. A. Humpty Dumpty
147. B. $40,000
148. B. *Mississippi* (1935)
149. B. McGargle's daughter
150. D. *West of Zanzibar* (1928)
151. D. Warner Bros.
152. C. RKO
153. C. 1935
154. A. *Anthony Adverse* (1936)
155. C. Best Musical Score
156. B. John Cardwell
157. A. December 4
158. A. *Eddie Cantor Radio Hour*
159. B. *David Copperfield* (1935)
160. A. *Bright Eyes* (1934)
161. A. *Cardinal Richelieu* (1935)
162. B. *Folies Bergère de Paris*
163. C. Best Picture nomination
164. C. 1931
165. B. Jean Harlow
166. A. *I, Claudius* (1937)
167. D. *The Wizard of Oz* (1939)
168. A. *Becky Sharp* (1935)
169. A. *Enchanted April* (1935)
170. C. Claude Rains
171. C. *The Emperor's Candlesticks* (1937)
172. D. *The Great Waltz* (1938)
173. D. *The Wedding March* (1928)
174. A. *Cardinal Richelieu* (1935)
175. A. *Grand Hotel*
176. D. Lawrence Tibbett
177. C. Maureen O'Hara
178. A. *Dramatic School* (1938)
179. B. Gale Sondergaard
180. D. Rita Hayworth
181. B. Convention
182. D. James Mason
183. A. *Dimples* (1936)
184. A. H. G. Wells

185. D. Vicki Lester
186. C. 1935

Spotlight on Leslie Howard
1. C. Norma Shearer
2. D. Writer
3. D. *The Scarlet Pimpernel* (1934)
4. D. *The Petrified Forest* (1936)
5. A. Concert violinist

187. B. Charles Laughton
188. D. *These Three* (1936)
189. B. *Mr. Doodle Kicks Off* (1938)
190. B. Eugene Ormandy
191. C. *Pardon Us* (1931)
192. D. *You Can't Take It with You* (1938)
193. C. Princeton
194. B. *Goodbye, Mr. Chips*
195. A. *One Million B.C.* (1940)
196. A. *King Kong* (1933)
197. B. Humphrey Bogart
198. D. 4
199. C. Jane Wyman
200. B. Luise Rainer
201. B. *Just Around the Corner* (1938)
202. B. John Ford
203. B. *The Most Dangerous Game* (1932)
204. C. *Jesse James* (1939)
205. B. *I, Claudius* (1937)
206. A. Australia
207. B. *The Sea Hawk* (1940)
208. D. Kay Francis
209. A. Deanna Durbin
210. C. *The Jewess* (1897)
211. D. *Duck Soup* (1933)
212. C. Maureen O'Hara
213. B. MGM
214. D. Spencer Tracy
215. D. *Trade Winds* (1938)
216. C. On a golf course
217. C. Mae Clark
218. A. Basil Rathbone
219. A. Ameche
220. A. *Folies Bergère de Paris* (1935)
221. B. *Road Show* (1941)
222. D. *The Wizard of Oz* (1939)
223. B. *Gone With the Wind* (1939)
224. D. Walter Huston
225. D. Irving Berlin
226. D. *You Can't Take It with You* (1938)

227. C. Empress Elisabeth
228. B. *Dance Pretty Lady* (1932)
229. C. *Having Wonderful Time* (1938)
230. A. *Anything Goes* (1936)
231. A. 0

CHAPTER 3

1. C. Ray Collins
2. D. *The Lost Weekend* (1945)
3. D. Louisa May Alcott
4. D. Norma Shearer
5. D. Robert Louis Stevenson
6. B. *Miss Annie Rooney* (1942)
7. C. Best Supporting Actor
8. B. Chopin
9. B. Ma Kettle
10. C. *Madame Bovary* (1949)
11. C. *Nine Girls* (1944)
12. B. *Kings Row* (1942)
13. D. Loretta Young
14. B. Best Original Screenplay
15. C. Harry
16. B. Joan Crawford
17. A. Barbara Stanwyck
18. C. *Pinky* (1949)
19. A. *Caesar and Cleopatra* (1946)
20. D. Best Writing, Original Story
21. A. *Brother Orchid* (1940)
22. C. *Time*
23. A. Brian Aherne
24. C. *Princess O'Rourke* (1943)
25. A. *Hotel Berlin* (1945)
26. B. Greta Garbo
27. C. Loretta Young
28. A. *It Happened in Brooklyn* (1947)
29. C. *Road to Singapore* (1940)
30. B. *Grandpa Goes to Town* (1940)
31. C. *Spellbound* (1945)
32. A. International Screenplays

Spotlight on Barbara Stanwyck
1. B. Panther
2. B. *Magnificent Obsession* (1935)
3. A. *Ball of Fire* (1941)
4. B. *Banjo on My Knee* (1936)
5. C. *Stella Dallas* (1937)

33. B. Best Art Direction
34. A. Bugs Bunny

35. D. Best Sound
36. B. Ernest Hemingway
37. D. Mother superior
38. B. Eugene O'Neill
39. B. Best Editing
40. D. *Lorenzo Goes to Hollywood*
41. A. Frank Sinatra
42. D. Best Original Screenplay
43. C. "I'm Making Believe"
44. D. *Star Spangled Rhythm* (1943)
45. D. "We Mustn't Say Goodbye"
46. B. Clark Gable
47. C. Nathaniel Hawthorne
48. A. *Frenchman's Creek* (1944)
49. A. *A Guy Named Joe* (1943)
50. D. *Tomorrow Is Forever* (1946)
51. D. *The Song of Bernadette* (1943)
52. C. Rita Hayworth
53. B. Best Editing
54. A. Alfred Hitchcock
55. A. Bicycle
56. B. *Present Laughter*
57. A. *A Walk in the Sun* (1945)
58. B. *Enchantment* (1948)
59. C. *Down Argentine Way*
60. D. Teacher
61. B. *Experiment Perilous* (1944)
62. B. Best Editing
63. C. *The Westerner* (1940)
64. C. Norman Krasna
65. D. "White Christmas"
66. B. Elizabeth Taylor
67. B. Best Director
68. B. Hypnotist
69. D. Australia
70. B. Humphrey Bogart
71. D. Niccolo Paganini
72. C. *The Yearling*
73. B. *My Sister Eileen* (1942)
74. A. 0
75. A. *Adventure* (1945)
76. C. "Joshua Fit the Battle of Jericho"
77. D. *Wyoming* (1940)
78. D. Wisconsin
79. A. Elia Kazan
80. A. *Driftwood* (1947)
81. A. James Cagney
82. A. *Hold Back the Dawn* (1941)
83. A. 13

84. C. 15
85. D. *Springtime in the Rockies*
86. A. *Her Highness and the Bellboy* (1945)
87. D. "Some Sunday Morning"
88. A. *Fire Over England* (1937)
89. A. *Lady on a Train* (1945)
90. A. *A Place of One's Own* (1945)
91. B. Frederic Chopin
92. C. Best Musical Score
93. D. Raymond Massey
94. D. Ruth Gordon
95. A. *Caesar and Cleopatra* (1945)
96. C. *Miracle on 34th Street* (1947)
97. A. *Her Cardboard Lover*
98. C. Monterey Pictures
99. B. *Conspirator* (1949)
100. C. George M. Cohan
101. A. *My Kingdom for a Cook* (1943)
102. D. Laurence Harvey
103. A. Carole Landis
104. B. Esoteric Studios
105. A. *Citizen Kane* (1941)
106. D. *The Bride Came C.O.D.* (1941)
107. A. 0
108. B. *Shine on Harvest Moon* (1944)
109. A. Ann Sheridan
110. C. *The Strange Love of Martha Ivers* (1946)
111. A. *Kitty Foyle: The Natural History of a Woman* (1940)
112. D. Best Supporting Actress
113. A. *Bud Abbott and Lou Costello Meet Frankenstein* (1948)
114. B. *Great Expectations* (1946)
115. A. Cello
116. C. Patricia Neal
117. D. *Tell It to the Judge* (1949)
118. C. Lillian Hellman
119. D. Best Special Effects
120. C. *Time*
121. C. 1947
122. C. Best Original Screenplay
123. A. *Gaslight* (1944)
124. B. *Hamlet* (1948)
125. C. *My Little Chickadee*
126. D. *The Pied Piper* (1942)
127. D. San Francisco
128. D. Warner Bros.
129. D. Best Sound

130. C. Horse
131. A. Best Art Direction
132. B. 1
133. C. *Knute Rockne, All-American* (1940)
134. B. *Our Wife* (1941)
135. A. *Enchantment* (1948)
136. B. Tyrone Power
137. B. Rex Harrison
138. D. Best Supporting Actor

Spotlight on Spencer Tracy
1. A. *I Take This Woman* (1940)
2. B. *Captains Courageous* (1937)
3. A. *Edison, the Man* (1940)
4. D. Loretta Young

139. A. Brian Aherne
140. B. Marlene Dietrich
141. C. *For the Love of Mary* (1948)
142. D. Traveling fair
143. B. *John Loves Mary* (1949)
144. D. 8
145. B. *Heaven Can Wait* (1978)
146. B. *Give Us the Moon* (1944)
147. A. *Green Dolphin Street* (1947)
148. D. Best Supporting Actress
149. B. *Gilda* (1946)
150. D. *The Lodger* (1944)
151. C. *The Corn is Green*
152. B. *Saratoga Trunk* (1945)
153. C. *The Little Foxes* (1941)
154. C. Stanley Holloway
155. C. Best Editing
156. B. *Blonde Fever* (1944)
157. C. Best Song
158. D. Warner Bros.
159. B. *The Get-Away* (1941)
160. B. Peter Lawford
161. C. *The Last Days of Dolwyn* (1949)
162. B. RKO
163. B. *Happy Land* (1943)
164. A. *Drums of the Congo* (1942)
165. C. *The Sea Wolf* (1941)
166. D. 5
167. D. Rosalind Russell
168. B. *On an Island with You* (1948)
169. D. Best Supporting Actor
170. C. *The Imperfect Lady* (1947)
171. A. *A Yank at Eton* (1942)

172. C. Opera singer
173. D. *Wonderful Town*
174. B. Loretta Young
175. B. 13
176. D. *The Picture of Dorian Gray* (1945)
177. C. *The Quiet One* (1948)
178. D. *The Bribe* (1949)
179. D. *The Pride of the Yankees* (1942)
180. C. *The Front Page*
181. D. *The Last Outpost* (1935)
182. D. *The Song of Bernadette* (1943)
183. D. Best Sound
184. A. 20th Century-Fox
185. B. *Neptune's Daughter* (1949)
186. B. Bob Hope
187. C. Best Original Score
188. C. Devil's Island
189. A. Best Editing
190. C. Best Original Score
191. C. Muteness
192. D. *The Lovable Cheat* (1949)
193. D. *This Is the Army* (1943)
194. A. *Black Narcissus* (1947)
195. B. Nurse
196. A. *Hudson's Bay* (1941)
197. A. *Dragon Seed*
198. A. *A Double Life* (1947)
199. B. Best Editing
200. C. Joan Crawford
201. C. *Romance on the High Seas* (1948)
202. C. Best Musical Score
203. C. J. D. Salinger
204. A. *Du Barry Was a Lady* (1943)
205. C. Best Original Screenplay
206. B. *The Ghost and Mrs. Muir* (1947)

Spotlight on Rita Hayworth
1. D. *The Strawberry Blonde* (1941)
2. D. *The Strawberry Blonde* (1941)
3. C. "The Love Goddess"
4. D. Terpsichore
5. C. *The Lady from Shanghai* (1948)

207. A. *Babes on Broadway*
208. A. *Birth of the Blues* (1941)
209. C. *Green Dolphin Street* (1947)
210. C. *The Postman Always Rings Twice* (1946)
211. B. *Saratoga Trunk* (1945)

212. B. *Take Me out to the Ball Game* (1949)
213. B. 1947
214. D. Marjorie Kinnan Rawlings
215. D. *The Southerner*
216. A. *Life*
217. D. Postman
218. A. *All That Money Can Buy* (1941)
219. B. Butler
220. C. *Rope* (1948)
221. D. *Lillian Russell* (1940)
222. C. *Johnny Come Lately* (1943)
223. D. *The Pride of the Yankees* and *Mrs. Miniver*
224. D. Best Supporting Actress
225. A. *Adventures of Don Juan* (1948)
226. B. Howard Hughes
227. A. *In This Our Life* (1942)
228. B. *The Outlaw* (1943)
229. A. *Footsteps in the Dark* (1941)
230. A. *Mister Roberts*
231. D. *Yankee Doodle Dandy* (1942)
232. B. MGM
233. D. *The Fleet's In* (1942)
234. C. *The Body Snatcher* (1945)
235. B. $50 a day
236. A. *Kismet* (1944)
237. B. *Honky Tonk* (1941)
238. D. *Torrid Zone* (1940)
239. D. Robert Riskin
240. C. "It's a Blue World"
241. C. *The Great Lie* (1941)
242. D. Whitney Houston
243. D. *Victory* (1940)
244. B. *The Egg and I* (1947)
245. D. "Why Don't You Do Right"
246. C. Polio
247. A. *Edward, My Son* (1949)
248. D. Psychotherapist
249. A. *A Kiss in the Dark* (1949)
250. C. *The Winslow Boy* (1948)
251. B. Best Original Score
252. C. Best Musical Score

CHAPTER 4

1. C. Best Original Screenplay
2. A. Aaron Spelling
3. B. 2

4. A. Fish
5. A. Bathing suits
6. B. Pine Island
7. A. Gerard
8. D. *True Love*
9. B. Mexico
10. C. Best Costume Design
11. B. 1
12. A. Ballet dancer
13. C. Best Costume Design
14. D. Psychiatrist
15. A. "Hold My Hand"
16. D. *Written on the Wind* (1956)
17. B. Best Art Direction
18. A. *Enamorada* (1946)
19. D. Schoolteacher
20. D. *War of the Planets*
21. C. Holiday Inn
22. D. "Something's Gotta Give"
23. B. 11
24. C. Jeanne Moreau
25. C. Eugene O'Neill
26. A. Chemistry
27. A. *An American in Paris*
28. C. *Time*
29. C. Porky Pig
30. B. *Ninotchka* (1939)
31. A. Baseball player
32. D. Rebecca DeMornay
33. A. *Broadway Bill* (1934)
34. B. *Cattle Queen of Montana* (1954)
35. C. 3
36. A. Frank Sinatra
37. B. English
38. C. *The Buccaneer*
39. B. Milk
40. A. MGM
41. A. Pink Floyd
42. C. 5
43. B. Best Art Direction
44. D. *Them!* (1954)
45. C. Noël Coward
46. D. Louis Armstrong
47. C. Moondoggie
48. A. Butcher
49. B. Frankie
50. B. Percy Bysshe Shelley
51. C. "Heart"
52. A. *From Here to Eternity*

53. C. Miami

Spotlight on Esther Williams
1. A. Best Color Cinematography
2. B. Stage 30
3. D. *This Time for Keeps* (1947)
4. A. Blue
5. B. *On an Island with You* (1948)

54. B. "High Hopes"
55. C. 6
56. D. Vic Morrow
57. C. Juliete
58. A. Émile Zola
59. A. *Christmas Hymns*
60. D. Best Special Effects
61. A. Alma
62. C. 1959
63. C. *The Lavender Hill Mob*
64. D. Best Original Score
65. B. *Monkey Business* (1952)
66. A. A cello
67. A. Game
68. D. Jane Wyman
69. B. "I'll Build a Stairway to Paradise"
70. A. *Dreamboat* (1952)
71. D. Gloria Grahame
72. B. Montgomery Clift
73. A. Claire Bloom
74. C. Jean Simmons
75. C. Girl and midget
76. C. *Son of Fury: The Story of Benjamin Blake* (1942)
77. C. "Something's Gotta Give"
78. C. 1957
79. B. Best Actress
80. C. Hannah
81. B. *Grease* (1978)
82. D. San Francisco
83. D. *The Halls of Ivy*
84. C. 2
85. B. New Orleans
86. C. *Summer Love*
87. A. Agnes Moorehead
88. C. Rita Moreno
89. D. Judy Holliday
90. B. 4
91. C. *Private Secretary*
92. B. Martin May
93. C. Socks Barbarrosa

94. C. Margot Fonteyn
95. A. *Another Time, Another Place*
96. A. Best Actress
97. B. Dennis Hopper
98. B. Greer Garson
99. A. Elia Kazan
100. A. Best Actor
101. B. *The Dark Page*
102. A. *Lux Video Theatre*
103. C. *tom thumb*
104. A. Claude
105. B. Counterfeiter
106. C. Midge
107. C. Both
108. C. Marilyn Monroe
109. D. Rhonda Fleming
110. B. 23
111. A. Bob Hope
112. B. Cyd Charisse
113. D. Best Original Screenplay
114. D. Sidney Poitier
115. A. *Love Me or Leave Me* (1955)
116. D. *The Thin Man* (1934)
117. D. Best Sound
118. B. Schoolchildren

Spotlight on Marlon Brando
1. A. *Mutiny on the Bounty* (1962)
2. D. 8
3. B. *Desiree* (1954)
4. D. Tennessee Williams
5. B. *Guys and Dolls* (1955)

119. B. Herman Melville
120. D. New Zealand
121. B. 2
122. B. Best Costume Design
123. D. Douglas
124. D. *The Bacchae*
125. A. Grace Kelly
126. D. Best Screenplay
127. C. Robert Aldrich
128. B. Jane Froman
129. A. Doctor
130. D. 3
131. B. Beauregard's pet parrot
132. B. Maid
133. A. Grand Fenwick
134. A. China
135. C. Frank Capra

136. A. *A Life in the Balance*
137. C. *The Shopworn Angel* (1928)
138. A. Her jaw
139. D. Vic Damone
140. C. Natalie Wood
141. D. Frances Lawrence
142. C. Shadow Johnson
143. C. Kim Novak
144. D. William Holden
145. C. *Seventh Heaven*
146. D. United Nations building
147. B. Best Original Screenplay
148. B. Andre Previn
149. D. Vanderbilt
150. D. 9
151. C. *Small Town Girl* (1953)
152. C. Gourmet chef
153. C. *It's a Date* (1940)
154. A. Best Foreign Language Film
155. A. Best Actress
156. A. Audrey Hepburn
157. D. Best Sound
158. C. Oliver Wendell Holmes
159. B. *Mr. President*
160. D. *Timber Fury*
161. C. Spencer Tracy
162. D. Debbie Reynolds
163. B. Poppea
164. A. Grace Kelly
165. A. *Orpheus Descending*
166. D. *The Magnificent Yankee*
167. C. Best Original Screenplay
168. C. Fred Astaire
169. A. Ann Vickers
170. B. Eleanor Parker
171. A. A cat
172. D. *The Virgin Queen*
173. C. Professor Alfred Kokintz
174. A. It falls into a batch of cookie dough.
175. B. *King's Rhapsody*
176. D. Best Screenplay
177. C. Best Director
178. D. van Gogh
179. A. A heart condition
180. B. Best Costume Design
181. B. "I Don't Know What I Want"
182. D. Best Special Effects
183. B. *Animal Crackers* (1930)

184. C. *An American in Paris*

Spotlight on Leslie Caron
1. D. *The Story of Three Loves* (1953)
2. C. 6
3. D. Socks Barbarrosa
4. D. George Bernard Shaw
5. A. *An American in Paris* (1951)

185. B. At a beach resort
186. B. Pesticide
187. B. *Ben-Hur*
188. A. Cyd Charisse
189. C. "Steppin' Out with My Baby"
190. D. *The Robe* (1953)
191. B. Paramount
192. D. Statue
193. A. A baby
194. D. Rosemary Clooney
195. D. Surfing
196. A. Edward Everett Horton
197. D. Truman Capote
198. C. Jeanne Crain
199. B. Best Costume Design
200. B. Best Art Direction
201. D. Plastic surgeon
202. C. *Gigi*
203. A. Audrey Hepburn
204. C. Saxophone
205. A. A butterfly
206. A. *Lux Video Theatre*
207. C. Spencer Tracy
208. D. Best Writing, Story, and Screenplay
209. C. The Blue Shade
210. B. Best Director
211. D. Marcello Mastroianni
212. B. *Flower Drum Song* (1961)
213. A. Grainbelt University
214. C. NYU
215. C. Best Original Score
216. B. Best Cinematography
217. B. Honor Blackman
218. B. Jack Finney
219. C. Mexico
220. A. Ann Miller
221. B. *Mogambo*
222. B. In the cornerstone of an old building
223. C. "Too Late Now"

224. A. Fraternity hazing
225. A. Burl Ives
226. D. *Tom, Dick and Harry* (1941)
227. C. Jane Powell
228. D. *Sunset Blvd.*
229. B. Harpo Marx
230. B. Esther Williams
231. B. Gary Merrill
232. A. College dean
233. A. Diane Varsi
234. D. Walter Winchell
235. A. Alec Guinness
236. C. James Michener
237. A. Kim Hunter
238. D. *The Gallery of Madame Liu-Tsong*
239. D. Virginia Mayo
240. A. Edgar Box
241. C. Glenn Miller
242. D. 3
243. B. *Across the Wide Missouri*
244. D. Best Picture
245. B. Esther Williams

CHAPTER 5

1. D. 3
2. C. Press agent Bill Evans
3. C. Sidney Poitier
4. A. Cosmetics
5. A. Angela Mao
6. B. Beauty
7. D. Smoking
8. B. Ira Levin
9. B. George Burns
10. A. 1
11. D. Screen Actors Guild representative
12. A. Ballet dancer
13. A. *Center Door Fancy*
14. C. The Preacher
15. C. *Miami Vice*
16. D. Susan Saint James
17. C. National Osteoporosis Foundation
18. C. Kareem Abdul-Jabbar
19. B. *Growing Pains*
20. A. Amsterdam
21. D. *Rocky*
22. A. Chemistry
23. B. Best Cinematography
24. D. Silver Medallion Award

25. B. 1
26. D. Surgeon
27. A. A U.S. postage stamp
28. A. Best Actor
29. B. Football coach
30. B. *Sunday in New York*
31. D. *Trelawny of the "Wells"*
32. D. Best Song
33. C. Ethel Merman
34. B. Swing band
35. B. *Love Is All*
36. B. Japan
37. B. Montgomery Clift
38. B. Joanne Woodward
39. D. *The Assam Garden* (1985)
40. C. Silver Lion Inc.
41. A. Best Costume Design
42. C. 32
43. D. *The Love Boat*
44. C. Diary
45. A. *Lawrence of Arabia*
46. A. Chicago
47. B. Best Adapted Screenplay
48. A. "Burnett's Woman"
49. A. A Buddha statue
50. C. Best Picture
51. A. 0
52. C. Best Original Screenplay
53. D. 6
54. B. George Balanchine
55. A. Goldie Hawn
56. A. Best Cinematography
57. C. On a New York subway train
58. D. Tom Jones
59. B. Bob Hoskins
60. C. Cleveland
61. B. Los Angeles
62. B. Johnny Depp
63. A. A courtroom
64. C. Best Picture
65. A. Chevy Chase
66. C. The Oreos
67. D. *What Ever Happened to Baby Jane?*
68. C. New York
69. A. Mr. Freeze
70. B. *Sesame Street*
71. D. Nora Ephron
72. C. 2004
73. A. Bryan Adams

74. D. Pills
75. C. *The Old Fashioned Way* (1934)
76. A. *Breaking Point*

Spotlight on Sidney Poitier
1. C. Hawaii
2. A. London
3. A. Blind
4. D. *The Defiant Ones* (1958)
5. D. Philadelphia

77. C. Mahatma Gandhi
78. D. Senator
79. C. *The Electric Company*
80. C. Best Picture
81. A. *ER*
82. A. Movie director
83. A. *Coogan's Bluff* (1968)
84. C. Michael Gambon
85. A. Istanbul
86. A. A car
87. B. 1
88. A. 0
89. A. 0
90. B. *Gilda* (1946)
91. A. Christian Slater
92. B. Evangelist
93. B. New York
94. C. 2
95. C. Kate Beckinsale
96. C. Farrah Fawcett
97. B. A romance novel
98. C. *The Halloween Tree*
99. B. 1
100. D. Singer
101. A. "A Story to Be Softly Told"
102. A. Italy
103. C. Best Director
104. B. Japan
105. A. John Grisham
106. D. Ursula Andress
107. B. 1
108. D. *The Sound of Music* (1965)
109. B. D. H. Lawrence
110. B. Grows a beard
111. C. The Minstrel
112. C. "The Age of Not Believing"
113. D. *My Fair Lady*
114. A. *Dr. Kildare*
115. B. In a tree

116. C. A leopard
117. B. Lord Salisbury
118. B. Ben Kingsley
119. A. Best Cinematography
120. D. *The Apartment*

Spotlight on Elizabeth Taylor
1. B. *BUtterfield 8* (1960)
2. D. Richard Burton
3. C. *The Girl Who Had Everything* (1953)
4. C. *The Last Hunt* (1956)
5. B. *BUtterfield 8* (1960)

121. A. Burt Reynolds
122. D. "Let's Do Something Cheap and Superficial"
123. B. Best Director
124. A. *Becket*
125. D. Translator
126. D. Best Special Effects
127. B. Elmore Leonard
128. C. "Thank You Very Much"
129. C. Best Picture
130. C. *Judith*
131. A. *Don Quixote*
132. C. *Stagecoach West*
133. C. Katharine Hepburn
134. B. Happy
135. B. Roger Moore
136. A. H. P. Lovecraft
137. C. The March Hare
138. C. The Super Bowl
139. D. Warren Oates
140. D. Zack Snyder
141. A. 1
142. C. *Green Acres*
143. C. Best Musical Score
144. C. Lawyer
145. A. *Candide*
146. B. "Tativille"
147. B. Greece
148. D. San Francisco
149. B. Richard Pryor
150. B. Henry Fonda
151. A. Chez Harry
152. A. Dalton Trumbo
153. C. Best Picture
154. A. Bob Hope and Lucille Ball
155. B. 2
156. B. Isaac Hayes

157. D. Julia Roberts
158. A. Best Actor
159. D. Best Original Screenplay
160. A. Chip
161. A. *The Anderson Tapes* (1971)
162. C. *Tony Rome* (1967)
163. C. Moby Grape
164. A. Coffee
165. C. 2
166. D. *The Glass Menagerie*
167. C. Claude Fitzwilliam
168. B. Pat Conroy
169. C. On a train
170. A. Mr. Freeze
171. C. Meryl Streep
172. A. Best Director
173. A. *Life*
174. A. *Bells Are Ringing*
175. C. Sidney Poitier
176. D. "The Morning After"
177. A. E. L. Doctorow
178. C. Frosty Palace
179. C. Frog
180. B. Billy Bob Thornton
181. D. U.S. congresswoman
182. A. Amnesia
183. D. Kurt Vonnegut
184. C. Best Editing
185. A. Butterfly
186. B. Image Ten Productions
187. B. Moss Hart
188. B. *National Geographic*
189. D. Meryl Streep
190. B. Best Editing
191. C. *Medical Center*
192. C. Loretta Young
193. B. Diane Keaton
194. B. Best Costume Design
195. D. Rudyard Kipling
196. B. Marilyn Monroe
197. C. *The Sun Also Sets*
198. A. *A Country Made of Ice Cream*
199. A. "A Dream Within a Dream"
200. D. Takagi Corporation
201. B. *Dirty Rotten Scoundrels*
202. C. Jerry Van Dyke
203. B. Dick Powell
204. B. "The Look of Love"

Spotlight on Peter Sellers

1. C. Leigh Taylor-Young
2. A. *The Bobo* (1967)
3. C. *The Millionairess*
4. C. Best Original Score
5. C. Librarian

205. D. Mickey Rooney
206. B. *As the World Turns*
207. B. Bavaria
208. D. The funeral industry
209. A. Al Hirschfeld
210. C. A painting
211. A. The Bookworm
212. C. Jude Law
213. D. "The Rime of the Ancient Mariner"
214. C. Palimony
215. A. Best Actor
216. B. That he didn't get bar mitzvahed
217. B. Jor-El
218. D. Oscar Madison
219. B. *Judgment at Nuremberg* and *Back Street*
220. B. Eyewear
221. B. Jayne Mansfield
222. C. *Law and Order: Special Victims Unit*
223. A. Dyan Cannon
224. B. 1
225. B. François Truffaut
226. C. *Sssssss*
227. D. Shirley MacLaine
228. C. Sidney Poitier
229. C. Best Director
230. A. Atlanta Flames
231. A. "As Time Goes By"
232. C. *Heidi*
233. A. Goldie Hawn
234. A. 2022
235. B. Honestly expressing yourself
236. C. Playtex "Cross Your Heart" bras
237. C. Best Musical Score
238. B. Lauren Bacall
239. C. The Penguin
240. B. Hera
241. B. *Glengarry Glen Ross*
242. D. Lana Turner
243. D. Ringo Starr
244. D. Volkswagen
245. C. Roald Dahl

CHAPTER 6

1. C. Greer Garson
2. A. Austria-Hungary
3. A. 1911
4. D. 7
5. A. *Life*
6. A. *I'll See You in My Dreams* (1951)
7. C. *No Time for Comedy* (1940)
8. B. Capricorn
9. B. James Cagney
10. B. *Red Dust* (1932)
11. D. *War and Peace* (1956)
12. D. *Phffft!* (1954)
13. B. Jean Harlow
14. A. Connecticut
15. D. "Dig It"
16. B. *My Fair Lady* (1964)
17. D. Norma Shearer
18. C. *Things Are Looking Up* (1935)
19. A. *Kismet* (1944)
20. C. *Gypsy* (1962)
21. C. "Eunice"
22. A. *Gunga Din* (1939)
23. B. *Gypsy* (1962)
24. A. *Design for Scandal* (1941)
25. B. Hedy Lamarr
26. D. *Where the Sidewalk Ends* (1950)
27. B. Juliet
28. C. Paramount
29. A. *Evelyn Prentice* (1934)
30. B. *The Heiress* (1949)
31. B. Esther Williams
32. C. *Stromboli* (1950)
33. A. *Breakfast at Tiffany's* (1961)
34. D. *The Female Animal* (1958)
35. D. *Vivacious Lady* (1938)
36. B. Lola Burns
37. D. Rita Hayworth
38. C. *Two Women* (1960)
39. A. Gene Tierney
40. B. Cincinnati
41. A. Audrey Hepburn
42. D. *The Lusty Men* (1952)
43. D. *Mildred Pierce* (1945)

44. C. Marie Antoinette
45. B. *Night Must Fall* (1937)
46. C. 33
47. A. *Golden Earrings* (1947)
48. B. 1976
49. B. *Heller in Pink Tights* (1960)
50. D. *The Mirror Has Two Faces* (1996)
51. B. Harlean Carpenter
52. A. *Blonde Venus* (1932)
53. C. Jo
54. B. *I Remember Mama* (1948)
55. C. "The Stick"
56. D. Vanessa Windsor

Spotlight on Bette Davis
1. D. *The Great Lie* (1941)
2. D. Ruth
3. A. A bra
4. A. Claudette Colbert
5. B. *Dangerous* (1935)

57. D. Rita Hayworth
58. C. RKO
59. D. *The Children's Hour* (1961)
60. A. 0
61. D. *Sunset Blvd.* (1950)
62. C. Myrna Loy
63. A. *My Man Godfrey* (1936)
64. A. *Anastasia* (1956)
65. D. They weren't
66. B. Frances Ethel Gumm
67. B. *Man-Proof* (1938)
68. C. *The Prodigal* (1955)
69. A. *Anna Christie* (1931)
70. A. Aviator
71. C. 36
72. D. Susan Hayward
73. D. Sweden
74. B. *Come to the Stable* (1949)
75. B. 5
76. C. *The Little Foxes* (1941)
77. A. Bette Davis
78. C. *Hold Your Man* (1933)
79. A. Greta Garbo
80. A. Barbara Stanwyck
81. A. Ann Sheridan
82. D. Susan Hayward
83. A. *Move Over, Darling* (1963)
84. D. Jean Harlow
85. B. 1953

86. C. Harmon Nelson
87. D. Rex Harrison
88. C. Jean Harlow
89. B. *East Side, West Side* (1949)
90. A. *Mrs. Miniver* (1942)
91. D. 0
92. D. *The Nun's Story* (1959)
93. D. *The Women* (1939)
94. B. Deborah Kerr
95. C. 1990 in London, England
96. C. *I'm No Angel* (1933)
97. D. "The Sweater Girl"
98. B. Fashion model
99. B. *Morning Glory* (1933)
100. C. Lowell
101. B. *Never a Dull Moment* (1950)
102. A. *City Lights* (1931)
103. A. *Alice Adams* (1935)
104. C. Greer Garson
105. C. *Strangers When We Meet* (1960)
106. C. Eleanor Powell
107. D. Susan Hayward
108. B. Ginger Rogers
109. C. *Mrs. Pollifax—Spy* (1971)
110. B. *Tea for Two* (1950)
111. B. *Mourning Becomes Electra* (1947)
112. A. *The Shawshank Redemption* (1994)
113. C. Miriam Hopkins
114. C. Judy Garland
115. C. Mae West
116. A. *Airport 1975* (1974)
117. A. 1955
118. D. *Roustabout* (1964)
119. B. *Iron Man* (1931)
120. A. Ginger Rogers
121. D. Salt Lake City, Utah

Spotlight on Greta Garbo
1. D. Man
2. B. *Grand Hotel* (1932)
3. B. *Ninotchka* (1939)
4. A. Bette Davis
5. C. *Ninotchka* (1939)

122. D. Vivien Leigh
123. A. Barbara Stanwyck
124. A. Bridie Quilty
125. B. Greta Garbo
126. A. *Cleopatra* (1963)

127. D. "The Duchess of Garson"
128. D. June Allyson
129. A. Maid Marian
130. B. *La Bohème* (1926)
131. C. Paramount
132. C. *The Glass Bottom Boat* (1966)
133. A. *Forsaking All Others* (1934)
134. B. *Let Us Be Gay* (1930)
135. A. Carmel
136. A. David Rose
137. D. Natalie Wood
138. C. Lena Horne
139. B. Cecil B. DeMille
140. C. Loretta Young
141. D. *Sunrise at Campobello* (1960)
142. A. *Julia Misbehaves* (1948)
143. A. Bracelet
144. C. Ludlow Ogden Smith
145. D. *The Pride and the Passion* (1957)
146. A. 1
147. C. 1989
148. D. Vivien Leigh
149. C. 2
150. A. "The Brooklyn Bombshell"
151. A. *Cattle Queen of Montana* (1954)
152. B. *Copper Canyon* (1950)
153. C. Lazzaro
154. C. *The Trouble with Angels* (1966)
155. B. *For Whom the Bell Tolls* (1943)
156. C. Sister Clodagh
157. D. William Powell
158. D. 1993
159. D. *The Hunchback of Notre Dame* (1939)
160. B. 1
161. D. 1938
162. B. Kansas City, Missouri
163. C. *Goodbye Charlie* (1964)
164. A. *Her Cardboard Lover* (1942)
165. B. *On the Town* (1949)
166. A. *Destry Rides Again* (1939)
167. B. Edythe Marrener
168. B. *Ship of Fools* (1965)
169. A. *High Society* (1956)

Spotlight on Lana Turner
1. C. *The Rains of Ranchipur* (1955)
2. C. *Love Finds Andy Hardy* (1938)
3. A. *A Life of Her Own* (1950)
4. D. *The Three Musketeers* (1948)

5. B. *Dead Ringer* (1964)

170. B. Montreal
171. A. Barbara Stanwyck
172. A. *High Voltage* (1929)
173. B. *His Girl Friday* (1940)
174. A. *Ladies in Love* (1936)
175. A. *For the Love of Mike* (1927)
176. D. *Their Own Desire*
177. B. Peroxide
178. A. MGM
179. A. *All About Eve* (1950)
180. D. Rosalind Russell
181. D. *Stella Dallas* (1937)
182. B. 1917
183. C. 2000
184. B. Lennie Hayton
185. C. Jean Arthur
186. B. *By Love Possessed* (1961)
187. C. Regina Giddens
188. D. 6
189. C. Sylvia Fowler
190. B. *Queen Bee* (1955)
191. C. *The African Queen* (1951)
192. A. Audrey Hepburn
193. A. *Pocketful of Miracles* (1961)
194. D. Loretta Young
195. D. *Platinum Blonde* (1931)
196. D. *Primrose Path* (1940)
197. B. *Pillow Talk* (1959)
198. D. Katharine Hepburn
199. B. *Rebecca* (1940)
200. B. 16
201. B. 6
202. D. Myrna Loy
203. C. *The Harvey Girls* (1946)
204. D. $90,000
205. C. *Saratoga* (1937)
206. B. 3
207. D. *The Wrath of God* (1972)
208. B. Forest Lawn Memorial Park in
      Hollywood Hills, California
209. C. *Guess Who's Coming to Dinner*
      (1967)
210. A. *As Young as You Feel* (1951)
211. A. Joan Bennett
212. A. Clara Lou
213. C. *Storm Warning* (1951)
214. B. Donna Reed

CHAPTER 7

1. B. *Last Action Hero* (1993)
2. D. 4
3. A. *All My Yesterdays*
4. B. "The Great Profile"
5. B. *Society Doctor* (1935)
6. D. Sue Carol
7. A. *Raintree County* (1957)
8. C. New York
9. D. Paula Abdul
10. C. *Quentin Durward* (1955)
11. D. *Von Ryan's Express* (1965)
12. C. Harold Lloyd
13. B. *Cobra* (1925)
14. D. The Netherlands
15. D. *To Kill a Mockingbird* (1962)
16. A. *Feet First* (1930)
17. A. Burt Lancaster
18. B. *Viva Zapata!* (1952)
19. C. Jack Lemmon in
20. A. Harvard
21. D. *The Prisoner of Zenda* (1937)
22. D. William
23. C. *The Circus* (1928)
24. B. *On Golden Pond* (1981)
25. B. *Here Is My Heart* (1934)
26. B. *Goodbye, Mr. Chips* (1969)
27. C. *The Cheyenne Social Club* (1970)
28. D. 8
29. A. *Giant* (1956)
30. C. 20
31. C. Omaha, Nebraska
32. C. Painter
33. B. 1
34. C. *Across 110th Street* (1972)
35. B. Playwright
36. B. *Days of Wine and Roses* (1962)
37. D. Telephone line
38. B. *If I Were King* (1938)
39. A. *Little Caesar* (1931)
40. D. *Summer Stock* (1950)
41. A. *Arsène Lupin* (1932)
42. D. *The Pride and the Passion* (1957)
43. D. Roger Moore
44. B. Fishing
45. A. Economics
46. C. *Modern Times* (1936)
47. A. Charles Boyer

48. A. 1
49. C. *The Black Knight* (1954)
50. D. *Waterloo Bridge* (1940)
51. B. Heathcliff
52. A. *Airport* (1970)
53. C. *Sunset Blvd.* (1950)
54. A. *Attila* (1955)
55. C. 17
56. B. Nick Nolte

Spotlight on Humphrey Bogart

1. B. *The African Queen* (1951)
2. A. *Dark Passage* (1947)
3. B. 49
4. B. *Beat the Devil* (1953)
5. B. *Sabrina* (1954)

57. C. Robert Taylor
58. C. F. Scott Fitzgerald
59. B. *Four Daughters* (1938)
60. C. *Here Come the Waves* (1944)
61. D. *To Kill a Mockingbird* (1962)
62. D. *Wagner* (1983)
63. B. Frank Sinatra
64. C. 7
65. C. *The Human Comedy* (1943)
66. D. 4
67. C. 2
68. D. *The Nutcracker Prince* (1990)
69. A. *East of Eden* (1955)
70. B. *The Private Life of Don Juan* (1934)
71. D. Surgeon
72. A. *Papillon* (1973)
73. A. 1974
74. D. Pastor
75. B. 2
76. C. *The Sea Hawk* (1940)
77. C. *Marjorie Morningstar* (1958)
78. C. 83
79. B. *My Favorite Year* (1982)
80. B. *The Story of Mankind* (1957)
81. B. *The Chase* (1966)
82. D. *The Prisoner of Second Avenue*
      (1975)
83. C. *Playmates* (1941)
84. D. Marlon Brando
85. D. *The Hucksters* (1947)
86. D. His wife not be allowed to visit any
      of his movie sets
87. C. *Love with the Proper Stranger* (1963)

88. C. 31
89. C. *The Cincinnati Kid* (1965)
90. C. 3
91. A. *Anthony Adverse* (1936)
92. B. *Operator 13* (1934)
93. A. *Fixed Bayonets!* (1951)
94. A. Bill Clinton
95. B. *How the West Was Won* (1962)
96. C. 2
97. D. *Where East Is East* (1929)
98. D. *Mutiny on the Bounty* (1962)
99. C. Engineer
100. C. "Swinging on a Star"
101. D. *The Remarkable Andrew* (1942)
102. B. *Grumpy Old Men* (1993)
103. A. *Glengarry Glen Ross* (1992)

Spotlight on William Holden

1. A. *Forever Female* (1954)
2. C. *Executive Suite* (1954)
3. B. Artist
4. B. *Paris When It Sizzles* (1964)
5. D. William Holden Wildlife
   Foundation

104. D. June Mathis
105. A. Arizona
106. B. *Mister Roberts*
107. B. Lon Chaney
108. A. Jacob Garfinkle
109. C. *My Life with Caroline* (1941)
110. C. Law school
111. D. 1985
112. D. *The Great Sinner* (1949)
113. B. Gary Cooper
114. D. *Soylent Green* (1973)
115. B. *Golden Boy* (1939)
116. B. *Lilies of the Field* (1963)
117. D. On a farm
118. B. 5'5"
119. D. *Valley of the Kings* (1954)
120. C. Josef Mengele
121. B. *Cover Girl* (1944)
122. A. *Man of a Thousand Faces* (1957)
123. B. Paramount
124. C. *Elmer Gantry* (1960)
125. A. Cecil B. DeMille
126. A. Circus acrobat
127. B. Clark Gable
128. C. *The China Syndrome* (1979)

129. D. *The Last Angry Man* (1959)
130. C. *Rocky Mountain* (1950)
131. B. *Kotch* (1971)
132. B. Robert Mitchum
133. B. Paul Newman
134. A. *Buck and the Preacher* (1972)
135. D. *Stella Dallas* (1925)
136. B. *Hello, Dolly!* (1969)
137. D. 1977
138. D. *The Tunnel of Love* (1958)
139. A. Abbey Theatre's Drama School
   in Dublin
140. C. 60
141. D. White slavery
142. D. *The Human Comedy* (1943)
143. C. *Footsteps in the Dark* (1941)
144. D. Violin
145. B. Roger Dann
146. A. *Grand Hotel* (1932)
147. A. *Moscow Nights* (1935)

Spotlight on Gary Cooper

1. A. *Arizona Bound* (1927)
2. D. *The Cowboy and the Lady* (1938)
3. C. The White Knight
4. B. 2
5. C. *The Naked Edge* (1961)

148. A. Ava Gardner
149. B. 1988
150. D. *Penny Serenade* (1941)
151. C. *Vivacious Lady* (1938)
152. A. Judo
153. D. William Powell
154. A. *Prison Farm* (1938)
155. C. 4
156. D. "Once Upon a Time"
157. A. *Alexander the Great* (1956)
158. C. *The Greek Tycoon* (1978)
159. B. Finance
160. C. *The Gaucho* (1927)
161. A. *A Fine Madness* (1966)
162. A. *No Time for Comedy* (1940)
163. D. Flowers
164. D. "White Christmas"
165. C. *The Night of the Following Day*
   (1968)
166. D. *Quicksand* (1950)
167. C. *Mister Roberts* (1955)
168. C. *The Buccaneer* (1938)

169. C. James Stewart
170. B. Moonlight Graham
171. B. *The Keys of the Kingdom* (1944)
172. A. *Freud*
173. A. *Mississippi* (1935)
174. A. Barber
175. C. Ireland
176. D. Violin
177. D. *Take Me Out to the Ballgame*
   (1949)
178. B. *Romola* (1924)
179. B. Max Schumacher
180. A. Henry Fonda
181. D. Napoleon
182. D. The Brown Derby
183. C. *Take Her, She's Mine*
184. B. *The Badlanders* (1958)
185. D. Walks the high wire
186. A. 0
187. A. *Blood and Sand*
188. C. *Once Upon a Time in the West*
   (1968)
189. A. *Reflections in a Golden Eye* (1967)
190. A. 1952
191. B. *The Last Angry Man* (1959)
192. A. *Freud* (1962)
193. B. *The Barretts of Wimpole Street*
   (1934)
194. C. 1982
195. C. *Othello*
196. C. *Spartacus* (1960)
197. A. Archibald Leach
198. B. Frank Lloyd Wright
199. A. *Born to Dance* (1936)
200. D. *The Grapes of Wrath* (1940)
201. B. *Save the Tiger* (1973)
202. D. 86
203. D. *The Joker Is Wild* (1957)
204. D. Warner Bros.
205. C. *Roman Holiday* (1953)
206. B. 1938
207. D. "Tiger"
208. B. *Once in a Lifetime* (1932)
209. A. *A Dry White Season* (1989)
210. A. *Camille* (1936)
211. A. 0
212. D. *White Christmas* (1954)
213. D. *Under the Yum Yum Tree* (1963)

CHAPTER 8

1. C. *Touch of Evil* (1958)
2. C. Leslie Caron
3. D. Rosalind Russell
4. A. Fredric March
5. D. Vivien Leigh
6. A. Dolly Parton
7. A. Clark Gable
8. C. Katharine Hepburn
9. C. Shelley Winters
10. B. *The Lady from Shanghai* (1947)
11. D. Loretta Young
12. B. *Golden Earrings* (1947)
13. B. Douglas Fairbanks Jr.
14. C. *The Millionairess* (1960)
15. D. *Shadow of the Thin Man* (1941)
16. A. *Another Thin Man* (1939)
17. A. Fred Astaire and Ginger Rogers
18. C. *Possessed* (1947)
19. A. *A Wicked Woman* (1934)
20. C. Reginald Venable
21. B. *Face of a Fugitive* (1959)
22. B. Charlton Heston
23. D. 4
24. A. *A Fine Madness* (1966)
25. A. Errol Flynn
26. C. Ossie Davis
27. C. *Macao* (1952)
28. B. Leslie Howard
29. D. Rita Hayworth
30. A. Debra Paget
31. C. David Niven
32. A. *A Flea in Her Ear* (1968)
33. B. *Forever, Darling* (1956)
34. A. Carole Lombard
35. B. Leslie Howard
36. D. Shakira Baksh
37. D. *The Mad Miss Manton* (1938)
38. A. *A Yank at Oxford* (1938)
39. C. *The Millionairess* (1960)
40. D. Rita Hayworth
41. A. *Lady of the Tropics* (1939)
42. D. *Model Wife* (1941)
43. C. 5
44. A. Debbie Reynolds
45. C. *The Lady in Question* (1940)
46. A. Bette Davis
47. A. *Double Wedding* (1937)
48. D. *Weekend with Father* (1951)
49. D. Shirley MacLaine
50. A. *Every Girl Should Be Married* (1948)
51. C. Garson Kanin and Ruth Gordon
52. B. Catherine Deneuve
53. B. *I Wanted Wings* (1941)
54. B. Goldie Hawn
55. D. *Private Number* (1936)
56. A. *Her Cardboard Lover* (1942)

Spotlight on Fred Astaire and Ginger Rogers

1. B. *Follow the Fleet* (1936)
2. D. *Woman of the Year* (1942)
3. A. "Feathers"
4. C. *The Barkleys of Broadway* (1949)
5. D. "They Can't Take That away from Me"

57. D. 8
58. B. Hedy Lamarr
59. C. Kate Winslet
60. D. *Mr. and Mrs. Bridge* (1990)
61. C. Sue Lyon
62. A. Debbie Reynolds
63. D. Katharine Hepburn and Spencer Tracy
64. A. *A New Kind of Love* (1963)
65. B. *Bright Leaf* (1950)
66. B. *Footsteps in the Fog* (1955)
67. D. Rebecca
68. C. Fred Astaire
69. D. *When Ladies Meet* (1941)
70. A. *Mrs. Parkington* (1944)
71. A. Bette Davis
72. D. Richard Burton
73. A. *Dinner at Eight* (1933)
74. B. Eva Gabor
75. B. *The Best Years of Our Lives* (1946)
76. D. Sean Connery
77. A. *Casanova Brown* (1944)
78. D. Paul Newman
79. B. *The Constant Husband* (1955)
80. C. Katharine Hepburn
81. B. *Blowing Wild* (1953)
82. A. *Behind the Make-Up* (1930)
83. B. *Star of Midnight* (1935)
84. A. *A Star Is Born* (1976)
85. A. *A New Kind of Love* (1963)

86. C. Tab Hunter
87. B. *Down to Earth* (1947)
88. C. *The Feminine Touch* (1941)
89. B. Humphrey Bogart
90. C. *This Is My Affair* (1937)
91. D. William Holden
92. C. *The Great Ziegfeld* (1936)
93. C. Harry Davenport
94. A. Bette Davis
95. A. Burt Lancaster
96. B. Irene Dunne
97. C. *The Good Earth* (1937)
98. A. *Magnificent Obsession* (1935)
99. B. *Hoosiers* (1986)
100. A. Fred Astaire
101. B. *Pointed Heels* (1929)
102. D. Susan Sarandon
103. A. *Follow the Fleet* (1936)
104. D. *Virginia City* (1940)
105. B. *Star Trek*
106. C. *Enamorada* (1946)
107. A. *David and Bathsheba* (1951)
108. D. Spencer Tracy
109. C. *Saratoga* (1937)
110. D. Julie Andrews
111. C. *The Cannonball Run* (1981)
112. C. Natalie Wood
113. A. Alec Guinness
114. A. *Dinner at Eight* (1933)
115. B. *Beau Brummel* (1954)
116. C. *Irma la Douce* (1963)
117. B. *Daddy Long Legs* (1931)
118. D. Olivia de Havilland
119. B. *On Our Merry Way* (1948)
120. C. Paul Newman
121. B. *Knights of the Round Table* (1953)
122. D. Liv Ullmann
123. B. *Marriage on the Rocks* (1965)
124. A. Bette Davis

Spotlight on Spencer Tracy and Katharine Hepburn

1. B. *Desk Set* (1957)
2. A. *Adam's Rib* (1949)
3. D. *Woman of the Year* (1942)
4. B. *Guess Who's Coming to Dinner* (1967)
5. D. San Francisco

125. D. "No Strings (I'm Fancy Free)"
126. B. *Arabesque* (1966)

127. C. Norma McCarty
128. A. *That Forsyte Woman* (1949)
129. A. Ava Gardner
130. C. Ginger Rogers and Fred Astaire
131. C. Montgomery Clift and Shelley
Winters in *A Place in the Sun* (1951)
132. C. *In Love and War* (1958)
133. C. James Garner
134. B. Barbara Stanwyck
135. A. *Hellcats of the Navy* (1957)
136. A. Cary Grant
137. C. Judy Garland
138. B. *Presenting Lily Mars* (1943)
139. B. *Alexander the Great* (1956)
140. D. *The Story of Vernon and Irene
Castle* (1939)
141. A. Clark Gable
142. C. *The Fortune Cookie* (1966)
143. A. Henry Fonda
144. A. *Pot O' Gold* (1941)
145. A. Glenn Ford
146. D. Walter Pidgeon
147. A. Ava Gardner
148. B. *Ice Palace* (1960)
149. D. *The Foxes of Harrow* (1947)
150. B. Margaret Dumont
151. C. *Please Don't Eat the Daisies* (1960)
152. A. Bess Armstrong
153. D. Merle Oberon
154. A. Clark Gable
155. B. Humphrey Bogart
156. D. Richard Burton
157. D. Mickey Rooney
158. B. Elliott Gould
159. C. Mel Ferrer
160. D. William Holden
161. B. Ginger Rogers
162. A. *Diamonds Are Forever* (1971)
163. A. Cary Grant
164. C. Humphrey Bogart and
Lauren Bacall
165. B. Gregory Peck
166. B. Frank Perry and Eleanor Perry
167. D. *Westward the Women* (1951)
168. A. *Maytime* (1937)
169. A. Carlo Ponti
170. A. Clark Gable
171. A. *Dancing Co-Ed* (1939)
172. C. Fred MacMurray

173. D. *Wild Is the Wind* (1957)
174. A. 10
175. C. Joan Crawford
176. C. Gary Cooper
177. D. Natalie Wood
178. B. *The Emperor's Candlesticks* (1937)
179. B. *Evelyn Prentice* (1934)
180. A. *Personal Property* (1937)
181. B. *Dream Wife* (1953)
182. A. Art Carney
183. A. Donald Sutherland
184. B. Hedy Lamarr
185. C. John Saxon
186. A. An estranged couple
187. C. Jill Clayburgh
188. B. *All the Fine Young Cannibals*
(1960)
189. B. Kathleen O'Hara

**Spotlight on Elizabeth Taylor and
Richard Burton**
1. D. *Who's Afraid of Virginia Woolf?*
(1966)
2. B. London
3. D. Vivien Leigh and Laurence Olivier
4. D. *The V.I.P.s* (1963)
5. A. *Boom!* (1968)

190. D. Vivien Leigh
191. B. *Close to My Heart* (1951)
192. A. *Anna Karenina*
193. D. *The Sisters* (1938)
194. A. Bing Crosby
195. A. James Dean
196. D. Margaret Sullavan
197. B. *Jimmy the Gent* (1934)
198. C. Tyrone Power
199. C. Eleanor Powell
200. B. Jennifer Jones
201. B. *Serena Blandish*
202. C. *Interrupted Melody* (1955)
203. D. Orson Welles
204. A. Bob Hope
205. C. *His Brother's Wife* (1936)
206. B. *Boom!* (1968)
207. B. Robert Mitchum
208. A. Barbara Stanwyck
209. A. Dean Martin
210. C. *To Be or Not to Be* (1983)

CHAPTER 9

1. A. *3 Women* (1977)
2. D. George Marshall
3. C. Law
4. B. *Action of the Tiger* (1957)
5. C. *The Wrong Man* (1956)
6. C. *The Witching Hour* (1934)
7. B. *Lord Love a Duck* (1966)
8. D. *Mister Buddwing* (1966)
9. D. 9
10. B. *Popi* (1969)
11. C. *The Miracle Woman* (1931)
12. A. *A Tree Grows in Brooklyn* (1945)
13. C. *The More the Merrier* (1943)
14. C. Roberto Rossellini
15. B. *The Island of Dr. Moreau* (1996)
16. B. John Sayles
17. D. *The Wild Party* (1975)
18. D. *The Lost Weekend* (1945)
19. C. *The Mouse That Roared* (1959)
20. C. Ida Lupino
21. B. *The Mirror Has Two Faces* (1996)
22. A. *Love Story* (1970)
23. D. 4
24. A. *High Time* (1960)
25. D. Steven Spielberg
26. D. *The Devil's Own* (1997)
27. B. *Little Miss Marker* (1934)
28. A. *North by Northwest* (1959)
29. B. *Made for Each Other* (1939)
30. A. *Jump for Glory* (1937)
31. B. *Lions for Lambs* (2007)
32. C. *The Bowery* (1933)
33. B. *Kansas City* (1996)
34. C. 3
35. B. *Ladies Last* (1930)
36. B. *Ordinary People* (1980)
37. A. Cinematograph Films Act of 1927
38. B. *Mississippi Masala* (1991)
39. C. *Of Mice and Men* (1939)
40. D. *This Land Is Mine* (1943)
41. C. *Gentleman's Agreement* (1947)
42. A. *Lust for Life* (1956)
43. B. *I'll Cry Tomorrow* (1955)
44. C. Editor
45. A. Maria Ouspenskaya
46. B. A party girl who falls for a
married man

47. A. *The Texan* (1930)
48. D. Sydney Pollack
49. C. *Playtime* (1967)
50. D. *Up Tight!* (1968)
51. A. 1
52. A. *Cyrano de Bergerac* (1950)
53. D. *The Little Foxes* (1941)
54. A. *Billy Bathgate* (1991)
55. D. Political science
56. D. *The Hidden Fortress* (1958)
57. C. *I Love Lucy*
58. A. *All the King's Men* (1949)

Spotlight on Vincente Minnelli

1. C. *Gigi* (1958)
2. B. *The Cobweb* (1955)
3. B. *Lust for Life* (1956)
4. C. *Tea and Sympathy* (1956)
5. B. *Meet Me in St. Louis* (1944)

59. B. *La Vie de Bohème* (1992)
60. D. *Up Tight!* (1968)
61. B. *Notorious* (1946)
62. A. *Brief Encounter* (1945)
63. A. *All the President's Men* (1976)
64. D. *Two Living, One Dead* (1961)
65. D. Yale
66. B. George Cukor
67. A. *Author! Author!* (1982)
68. B. *Sunset Blvd.* (1950)
69. C. "Road Hogs"
70. A. Clarence Brown
71. B. *The Party* (1968)
72. A. *Falstaff on the Moon* (1993)
73. A. Alfred Hitchcock
74. C. *Mister Buddwing* (1966)
75. A. *Dangerous Paradise* (1930)
76. C. Karl Malden
77. B. *Heritage of the Desert* (1932)
78. B. 1945
79. A. *Angelo, My Love* (1983)
80. A. *Barabba* (1961)
81. D. *Stolen Holiday* (1937)
82. D. *The Legend of Bagger Vance* (2000)
83. C. *Of Human Bondage* (1934)
84. D. *Young Winston* (1972)
85. B. *Alexander the Great* (1956)
86. C. *House of Games* (1987)
87. D. *You're a Big Boy Now* (1966)
88. D. *The Paradine Case* (1947)

89. B. *Love That Brute* (1950)
90. C. 3
91. D. *The Baron of Arizona* (1950)
92. B. Michelangelo Antonioni
93. C. *The Prisoner of Zenda* (1937)
94. A. *Elmer Gantry* (1960)
95. A. *Sky West and Crooked* (1966)
96. A. Buntel Eriksson
97. D. Stanley Kramer
98. B. 2
99. B. *In Name Only* (1939)
100. A. A bank
101. B. He was a pilot.
102. C. *The Prince of Tides* (1991)
103. A. *Arruza* (1972)
104. D. *Separate Tables* (1958)
105. A. *Hell's Angels* (1930)
106. A. Anthony Quinn
107. D. 4
108. B. 5
109. B. *Frankenstein Unbound* (1990)
110. C. Golden Turkey Award
111. B. *Kramer vs. Kramer* (1979)
112. C. *The Prize* (1963)
113. B. *Always* (1989)
114. D. *Wake Island* (1942)
115. B. 13
116. D. Warren Beatty
117. A. *American Graffiti* (1973)
118. A. Akira Kurosawa
119. D. *Pack Up Your Troubles* (1932)
120. D. *The Prodigal* (1955)
121. D. *This Could Be the Night* (1957)
122. A. *Five Guns West* (1955)
123. B. *Jailhouse Rock*
124. A. *13 Ghosts* (1960)
125. C. *Spitfire* (1934)
126. A. *Saratoga Trunk* (1945)
127. A. *Always* (1989)
128. B. *Mrs. Doubtfire* (1993)
129. C. *The Man Who Loved Women* (1977)
130. B. *That Uncertain Feeling* (1941)
131. B. *The Damned* (1969)
132. C. Martin Scorsese
133. B. *Iron Man* (1931)
134. C. *Quick Before It Melts* (1964)
135. C. *Get to Know Your Rabbit* (1972)
136. D. Williams College

137. B. *I Loved a Soldier* (1936)
138. C. Greece
139. B. Cashmere sweaters
140. B. John Ford
141. C. Roy Del Ruth
142. B. Roman Polanski
143. B. *The Prisoner of Zenda* (1952)
144. D. *Spitfire* (1934)
145. C. *The Squaw Man* (1914)
146. D. *The Wild Bunch* (1969)
147. D. *Pretty Baby* (1978)
148. A. 1
149. C. *Tobruk* (1967)
150. B. *The More the Merrier* (1943)
151. A. *Seconds* (1966)
152. D. *The Four Seasons* (1981)
153. D. *Short Cuts* (1993)
154. A. *JFK* (1991)
155. C. *Tin Men* (1987)
156. B. *The Lodger* (1927)
157. A. *Dirigible* (1931)
158. B. *Glamour Girl*
159. D. *The Man Who Dared* (1946)
160. D. *Separate Tables* (1958)
161. B. *Detective Story* (1951)
162. D. *See You in the Morning* (1989)
163. C. *The Buccaneer* (1958)
164. B. Cecil B. DeMille
165. D. 7
166. D. *Pierrot le Fou* (1965)
167. C. *Phaedra* (1962)
168. B. *Love's Lariat* (1916)
169. D. Richard Lester
170. C. *The Member of the Wedding* (1952)
171. D. *The Man Who Came Back* (1931)
172. D. *The Bishop's Wife* (1947)

Spotlight on John Ford

1. C. *Sergeant Rutledge* (1960)
2. D. *What Price Glory* (1952)
3. C. 7
4. B. *The Cheyenne Social Club* (1970)
5. A. *Cheyenne Autumn* (1964)

173. A. *A River Runs Through It* (1992)
174. A. 0
175. B. *Tarzan, the Ape Man* (1932)
176. C. Stanford
177. C. *It Came from Outer Space* (1953)

178. A. *Nobody's Fool* (1994)
179. A. 0
180. B. *Play Misty for Me* (1971)
181. B. He was blacklisted in Hollywood.
182. C. *The Babe* (1992)
183. B. *The Late George Apley* (1947)
184. C. *The Scarlet Pimpernel* (1934)
185. C. Steven Spielberg
186. B. Height of under six feet tall
187. A. Aviation
188. C. *The Great Lover* (1949)
189. B. *Men of Tomorrow* (1932)
190. A. *All Fall Down* (1962)
191. C. *Laura* (1944)
192. B. *The Buccaneer* (1958)
193. D. *Under the Yum Yum Tree* (1963)
194. B. 1953
195. B. *Cleopatra* (1963)
196. C. *THX 1138* (1971)
197. B. *The Bridge on the River Kwai* (1957)
198. A. *China Gate* (1957)
199. A. *Dr. Socrates* (1935)
200. A. *Cottage to Let* (1941)
201. C. Norman Z. McLeod
202. B. *Never Fear* (1949)
203. D. *Resident Evil 2*
204. A. *Athena* (1954)
205. B. 1971
206. B. 2
207. B. Frank Capra
208. D. Rex Ingram
209. D. *The Way to the Stars* (1945)
210. A. *Sabrina* (1954)
211. A. *Fallen* (1998)
212. A. *Avalanche Express* (1979)
213. C. 7
214. C. *The Affairs of Martha* (1942)
215. A. Orson Welles
216. D. *The Pelican Brief* (1993)
217. B. *Close Encounters of the Third Kind* (1977)
218. D. *Underground* (1928)
219. D. *The Grass Harp* (1995)
220. C. *Quiz Show* (1994)
221. C. *Ronin* (1998)
222. C. *The Horsemen* (1971)
223. A. Best Picture
224. B. *Peyton Place* (1957)

225. B. Costume design
226. C. 4
227. B. Paramount
228. A. *Bad Girl*
229. B. *Forget Me Not* (1936)
230. D. Michael Curtiz
231. C. *Love Affair* (1939)
232. A. 0
233. A. California State University Long Beach
234. B. David Lean
235. C. *Nevada Smith* (1966)
236. C. 2
237. C. *The Art of Love* (1965)
238. D. *The Shamrock Handicap* (1925)
239. A. *Into the Night* (1985)
240. D. *The Wheeler Dealers* (1963)
241. D. *The Sugarland Express* (1975)
242. B. *Ready to Wear* (1994)
243. C. 29
244. C. *The Trouble with Angels* (1966)
245. D. *Variety Girl* (1947)
246. C. *Spartacus* (1960)
247. B. *Period of Adjustment* (1962)
248. C. *The Lives of a Bengal Lancer* (1935)
249. B. 1
250. B. *Come Back, Little Sheba* (1952)
251. A. Act
252. A. *Broken Lullaby* (1932)
253. D. *The Woman I Love* (1937)
254. D. *The Kiss Before the Mirror* (1933)
255. B. *Love in the Afternoon* (1957)
256. A. 10
257. C. *The Bride Came C.O.D.* (1941)
258. A. *Interlude* (1957)
259. B. *God's Gift to Women* (1931)
260. A. *All Night Long* (1981)
261. C. *The Witching Hour* (1934)
262. B. *Guns of Darkness* (1962)

Spotlight on George Cukor
1. A. *Her Cardboard Lover* (1942)
2. A. *A Life of Her Own* (1950)
3. A. *A Star Is Born* (1954)
4. D. Tybalt
5. A. *Edward, My Son* (1949)

263. D. *Towed in the Hole* (1932)
264. A. *52 Pick-Up* (1986)

265. C. 2
266. C. *The Outrage* (1964)
267. A. Louis Malle
268. A. *All the King's Men* (1949)
269. C. *The Indian Runner* (1991)
270. A. 1
271. A. Stanley Donen
272. A. *A.I.: Artificial Intelligence* (2001)
273. A. *Mutiny on the Bounty* (1962)
274. C. *Kid Glove Killer* (1942)
275. C. *Ordinary People* (1980)
276. C. 2
277. C. *Merrily We Live* (1938)
278. C. *The Master of Ballantrae* (1953)
279. C. *Hamlet* (1948)
280. A. *Never on Sunday* (1960)
281. A. *Elephant Boy* (1937)
282. C. International Ladies Garment Workers Union
283. B. John Ford

CHAPTER 10

1. A. *Handy Andy* (1934)
2. B. *She Wouldn't Say Yes* (1945)
3. C. *The Out of Towners* (1970)
4. B. *Radio Days* (1987)
5. A. *Dream Girl* (1948)
6. B. Billy Wilder
7. B. *Teahouse of the August Moon* (1956)
8. C. *Manhattan* (1979)
9. C. *No More Orchids* (1932)
10. C. *Popi* (1969)
11. B. *The Pharmacist* (1933)
12. A. *Bedtime Story* (1964)
13. D. *The Great Race* (1965)
14. D. Elizabeth Taylor
15. C. *The Jackpot* (1950)
16. B. Dustin Hoffman
17. C. Jean Arthur
18. C. *Teachers* (1984)
19. A. *The Mating Season* (1951)
20. A. *Laugh-In*
21. A. Ann-Margret
22. C. *We Were Dancing* (1942)
23. A. *I Remember Mama* (1948)
24. C. *The Romance of Rosy Ridge* (1947)
25. D. *That Touch of Mink* (1962)
26. A. *Monkey Business* (1952)

27. D. "The Hoosier Tornado"
28. A. *No Time for Love* (1943)
29. B. *It's a Gift* (1934)
30. C. Greek mythology
31. B. *No Man of Her Own* (1932)
32. B. Glenda Jackson
33. A. Hazel Flagg
34. C. *To Be or Not to Be* (1942)
35. C. *No Time for Sergeants* (1958)
36. B. *Promise Her Anything* (1965)
37. B. A dentist's office
38. C. *Mr. and Mrs. Smith* (1941)
39. D. William A. Wellman
40. B. *The Great Lover* (1949)
41. B. *Manhattan* (1979)
42. C. *The Remarkable Mr. Pennypacker* (1959)
43. D. *The Half Naked Truth*
44. C. Minor Watson
45. B. *Forever, Darling* (1956)
46. A. *A Midsummer Night's Sex Comedy* (1982)
47. B. Olivia de Havilland
48. B. *Half a Hero* (1953)
49. B. *Candy* (1968)
50. B. *The Heavenly Body* (1944)
51. A. *Carpool* (1996)
52. B. *George Washington Slept Here* (1942)
53. D. *The Seven Year Itch* (1955)
54. C. *To Be or Not to Be* (1942)
55. C. *Onionhead* (1958)
56. A. *Remember?* (1939)
57. B. Leslie Howard
58. A. *George Washington Slept Here*
59. D. *The Freshman* (1925)
60. B. *The Caddy* (1953)
61. C. Ralph Bellamy
62. B. 1961
63. B. Robin Williams
64. C. *Made in Paris* (1966)
65. C. *The Adventures of Pluto Nash* (2002)
66. B. *Some Like It Hot* (1959)
67. D. Peanuts "Boffo" White
68. A. *Oh, Men! Oh, Women!* (1957)
69. D. *The Wistful Widow of Wagon Gap* (1947)
70. D. *The Music Box*
71. D. *The Little Hut* (1957)

72. C. Second City Chicago
73. D. Ralph Bellamy
74. A. *Advance to the Rear* (1964)
75. A. Billy Wilder
76. B. *No Minor Vices* (1948)
77. A. Dudley Moore
78. B. *Monkey Business* (1952)
79. C. *Princess O'Rourke* (1943)

Spotlight on the Marx Brothers
1. B. Freedonia
2. A. *A Night at the Opera* (1935)
3. A. Achi Vachi Vachi Voo
4. D. Woody Allen
5. D. Salvador Dalí

80. B. *My Six Loves* (1963)
81. C. San Francisco
82. A. *Pete 'n' Tillie* (1972)
83. D. Walter Matthau
84. A. *Man on the Flying Trapeze* (1935)
85. B. *No Sad Songs for Me* (1950)
86. B. Blake Edwards
87. A. *Champagne for Caesar* (1950)
88. C. *The Moon Is Blue* (1953)
89. A. *Dance, Girl, Dance* (1940)
90. A. *A Shot in the Dark* (1964)
91. B. *Professional Sweetheart* (1933)
92. B. Frank Capra
93. C. *The Lonely Guy* (1984)
94. A. *Fools for Scandal* (1938)
95. D. *I'm No Angel* (1933)
96. A. *Louisa* (1950)
97. A. *Dear Brat* (1951)
98. C. Jane Peters
99. C. *Staircase* (1969)
100. A. Coca-Cola
101. D. *Tillie and Gus* (1933)
102. D. *The Milky Way* (1936)
103. C. George Burns and Gracie Allen
104. A. *If I Had a Million* (1932)
105. D. *The Happy Family* (1952)
106. A. Albert
107. B. *Laughter on the 23rd Floor*
108. D. *The Shaggy Dog* (1959)
109. D. *Storm in a Teacup* (1937)
110. A. *Never a Dull Moment* (1950)
111. C. We hardly think so
112. B. *Living It Up* (1954)
113. A. "Bean"

114. A. *I Take This Woman* (1931)
115. D. *The Princess and the Pirate*
116. D. *The Mating Season* (1951)
117. D. *The Bride Came C.O.D.* (1941)
118. D. Joan Rivers
119. A. Dianne Wiest
120. D. William Powell
121. C. Snake oil
122. C. *They Knew What They Wanted* (1940)
123. B. Blake Edwards

Spotlight on William Powell
1. D. All of the above
2. A. *Double Wedding* (1937)
3. B. *Song of the Thin Man* (1947)
4. D. *Twentieth Century* (1934)
5. C. *Personal Property* (1937)

124. C. Mae West
125. C. *Staircase* (1969)
126. C. *The Bride Wore Boots* (1946)
127. A. Gregory Peck
128. B. *A Very Young Lady* (1941)
129. B. *Romantic Comedy* (1983)
130. A. *A Guide for the Married Man* (1967)
131. D. *Who's Got the Action?* (1962)
132. B. Dudley Moore
133. B. *Latin Lovers* (1953)
134. C. *Suddenly, It's Spring* (1947)
135. C. *The Women* (1939)
136. B. *It's the Old Army Game* (1926)
137. B. *Sidewalks of London* (1938)
138. C. Gloria Grahame
139. A. *My Brother Talks to Horses* (1947)
140. D. *The Pink Panther* (1963)
141. C. Jean Harlow
142. A. *A Ticklish Affair* (1963)
143. C. *Once Upon a Time* (1944)
144. C. Claire Bloom
145. C. *Kansas City Princess* (1934)
146. C. *Limelight* (1952)
147. A. Hillary
148. A. *It Happened One Night* (1934)
149. A. *Dear Ruth* (1947)
150. D. *Topper* (1937)
151. C. *Simon Simon* (1970)
152. D. *The Women* (1939)

153. C. *The Richest Girl in the World* (1934)
154. B. *The Brass Bottle* (1964)
155. C. Lily Garland
156. B. Detective Vera Cruz
157. C. *The Moon Is Blue* (1953)
158. A. *Belle of the Nineties*
159. A. *Hollywood Ending* (2002)
160. D. *Only the Lonely* (1991)
161. B. George Burns
162. C. *Phffft!* (1954)
163. B. *History of the World: Part I* (1981)
164. B. *Mr. Universe* (1951)
165. B. *Hook, Line and Sinker* (1969)
166. A. *A Guide for the Married Man* (1967)
167. D. Television
168. B. *Half a Hero* (1953)
169. B. Horns
170. C. *Up Pops the Devil* (1931)
171. B. *The Remarkable Andrew* (1942)
172. D. Symphony conductor
173. B. *See No Evil, Hear No Evil* (1989)
174. D. *The Yellow Rolls-Royce* (1964)
175. C. Howard Hawks
176. A. Alfred Hitchcock
177. B. Loretta Young
178. A. Alcohol
179. B. Leslie Nielsen
180. B. *Fluffy* (1965)
181. C. Gene Kelly
182. A. *Don't Bet on Love* (1933)
183. C. *Sabrina* (1954)
184. A. Howard Hawks
185. C. *New York Town* (1941)
186. B. *International House* (1933)
187. C. *Mr. and Mrs. Smith* (1941)
188. C. Liquor
189. A. *Personal Property* (1937)
190. A. *Affectionately Yours* (1941)
191. B. *Phffft!* (1954)

Spotlight on Doris Day
1. B. *Teacher's Pet* (1958)
2. B. *Please Don't Eat the Daisies* (1960)
3. A. *Lover Come Back* (1961)
4. D. *Young at Heart* (1954)
5. C. *The Glass Bottom Boat* (1966)

192. A. *Remains to Be Seen* (1953)

193. D. *That Lady in Ermine* (1948)
194. B. *Hi, Nellie!* (1934)
195. D. *To Be or Not to Be* (1983)
196. D. *Never Wave at a WAC* (1953)
197. C. Roland Young
198. A. *Outrageous Fortune* (1987)
199. D. *Tillie's Punctured Romance* (1928)
200. B. *My Sister Eileen* (1942)
201. C. Taylor Tech
202. A. Sugarpuss O'Shea in *Ball of Fire* (1941)
203. B. *No Time for Love* (1943)
204. C. *There's a Girl in My Soup* (1970)
205. C. Lewis and Clark
206. C. *The Lonely Guy* (1984)
207. B. *Pete 'n' Tillie* (1972)
208. A. *Bedtime Story* (1964)
209. B. *His Girl Friday* (1940)
210. C. Dentist
211. B. *Abbott and Costello Meet Captain Kidd* (1952)
212. C. *The Affairs of Dobie Gillis* (1953)
213. B. *Easy to Wed* (1946)
214. C. *Man on the Flying Trapeze* (1935)
215. D. "Say It Isn't So"
216. A. *Pete 'n' Tillie* (1972)
217. C. *The Happy Time* (1952)
218. D. *Tillie and Gus* (1933)
219. A. Irene Bullock
220. D. *She Done Him Wrong* (1933)
221. B. *The Ambassador's Daughter* (1956)
222. B. *Promise Her Anything* (1965)
223. D. *My Little Chickadee* (1940)
224. A. Bissonette's Bluebird Oranges
225. B. *See No Evil, Hear No Evil* (1989)
226. A. *No Time for Comedy* (1940)
227. C. *Scared Stiff* (1953)
228. A. *No Minor Vices* (1948)
229. B. Fred MacMurray
230. D. James Stewart
231. B. *Peeper* (1975)
232. D. Lucille Ball
233. D. Walter Bernstein
234. B. *Sailors Beware* (1927)

CHAPTER 11

1. A. *Friendly Persuasion* (1956)
2. D. Natalie Wood

3. C. *Lonely Are the Brave* (1962)
4. C. *Winchester '73* (1950)
5. D. Best Musical Score
6. C. *Gunfight at the O.K. Corral* (1957)
7. D. *The Big Valley*
8. D. Marion Morrison
9. C. James Garner
10. A. Barbara Hershey
11. D. Warren Oates
12. B. 3
13. D. *The Naked Spur* (1953)
14. A. Burl Ives
15. B. *Cat Ballou* (1965)
16. C. Wild Bill Hickok
17. A. Anthony Perkins
18. C. Wild Bill Hickok
19. A. Claudia Cardinale
20. A. *The Deerslayer* (1957)
21. B. Disney
22. A. Gary Cooper
23. D. Victor Young
24. A. Anthony Perkins
25. B. *The Hurricane* (1937)
26. B. "The Empty Shell"
27. C. *The Ox-Bow Incident* (1943)
28. C. *Top Gun* (1955)
29. C. John Wayne
30. C. *Lonely Are the Brave* (1962)
31. C. *Shane* (1953)
32. D. Ronald Reagan
33. D. *Whispering Smith* (1949)
34. D. Robert Mitchum
35. C. *My Darling Clementine* (1946)
36. A. Cecil B. DeMille
37. C. James Stewart
38. A. *Butch Cassidy and the Sundance Kid* (1969)
39. D. *Viva Villa!* (1934)
40. B. Cinematographer Conrad L. Hall
41. B. Producing
42. D. Randolph Scott
43. D. Warner Baxter
44. A. Gary Cooper
45. D. Wyatt Earp
46. C. "The Green Leaves of Summer"
47. C. *The Ox-Bow Incident* (1943)
48. D. Ulysses S. Grant
49. A. Craig Belden
50. D. Lee Marvin

51. B. *Shane* (1953)
52. B. *Little Big Man* (1970)
53. A. Burt Lancaster
54. C. *Cowboy* (1958)
55. C. John Wayne

Spotlight on James Stewart
1. C. Their father
2. B. *Destry Rides Again* (1939)
3. B. A parasol and a birdcage
4. D. *Two Rode Together* (1961)
5. B. Dodge City

56. A. *How the West Was Won* (1962)
57. C. *Maverick*
58. D. Randolph Scott
59. A. Ann-Margret
60. A. Charles Bronson
61. C. Matthew McAdam
62. A. *I Married a Woman* (1958)
63. B. Burt Lancaster
64. C. *The Bad Man* (1941)
65. A. Joe Lamont
66. C. Matt Morgan
67. A. He did several one-armed push-ups.
68. B. Ralph Meeker
69. D. *The Wrath of God*
70. B. *The Kentuckian* (1955)
71. D. *Unforgiven* (1992)
72. D. Texas
73. B. *The Electric Horseman* (1979)
74. C. Liquor
75. B. James Coburn
76. C. "The Railroad"
77. A. Arthur Miller
78. D. Louis L'Amour
79. C. *The Singer Not the Song* (1961)
80. A. *Cowboy* (1958)
81. C. *The Conqueror* (1956)
82. D. *The Sons of Katie Elder* (1965)
83. A. Best Actor
84. B. *Ride the High Country* (1962)
85. B. *Shalako* (1968)
86. A. Burt Lancaster
87. C. *Tribute to a Bad Man*
88. C. *North West Mounted Police* (1940)
89. D. *Tribute to a Bad Man* (1956)
90. D. *High Plains Drifter* (1973)
91. C. John Ford
92. D. Robert Mitchum

93. D. John Wayne
94. A. Glenn Ford
95. D. Walter Brennan
96. B. Lee Marvin
97. D. *The Devil Is a Woman*
98. C. *The Plainsman* (1936)
99. A. DeForest Kelley
100. D. *Rio Bravo* (1959)
101. D. *They Died with Their Boots On* (1941)
102. A. Edna Ferber
103. B. Boris Karloff
104. D. *The Last Hunt* (1956)
105. D. Timothy Bottoms
106. A. *Cimarron* (1931)
107. D. Tom Mix
108. D. *The Shepherd of the Hills* (1941)
109. C. Paul Henreid
110. D. Yul Brynner
111. D. James Stewart
112. D. Sheriff
113. D. *The Wild Bunch* (1969)
114. A. *A Fistful of Dollars* (1964)
115. D. *Vuelve Pancho Villa* (1950)
116. A. *Cowboy* (1958)
117. A. Deputy Marshal Harvey Pell
118. B. Anarene
119. A. *Butch Cassidy and the Sundance Kid* (1969)
120. B. *Once Upon a Time in the West* (1968)
121. D. *True Grit* (1969)

Spotlight on John Wayne
1. D. *Red River* (1948)
2. A. A baby
3. C. 3
4. C. *Raw Deal* (1948)
5. B. Golden Spur Award

122. C. Paul Newman
123. C. John Huston
124. D. Waldon O. Watson
125. A. *The Cowboy and the Lady* (1938)
126. B. John Waters
127. B. *Dark Command* (1940)
128. A. *Arena* (1953)
129. C. *To the Last Man* (1933)
130. D. Robert Wagner
131. A. *Cimarron*

132. C. Restful
133. C. *Old Surehand* (1965)
134. C. *The Outlaw* (1943)
135. A. Clint Eastwood
136. A. John Ford
137. C. Snifty
138. D. *Wyoming Mail* (1950)
139. B. *The Quiet Man* (1952)
140. A. *Garden of Evil* (1954)
141. C. Jeff Chandler
142. B. Barbara Stanwyck
143. C. Rita Hayworth
144. D. Jason Robards
145. A. *Destry Rides Again* (1939) and *Destry* (1954)
146. C. *Hud* (1963)
147. B. John Ford
148. A. "Duke"
149. B. *Jubal* (1956)
150. C. General William Tecumseh Sherman
151. D. Stanley Kramer
152. D. *Yojimbo* (1961)
153. A. *Bad Day at Black Rock* (1955)
154. B. Grace Kelly
155. D. Kirk Douglas
156. B. Gary Cooper
157. B. Robert Ryan
158. C. Jean Louis
159. C. *Valerie* (1957)
160. A. Carroll Baker
161. A. Elmer Bernstein
162. A. *Ambush* (1950)
163. B. John Archer
164. C. *The Misfits* (1961)
165. A. Abraham Lincoln
166. C. *The Electric Horseman* (1979)
167. B. *Garden of Evil* (1954)
168. D. Wallace Beery
169. A. *Johnny Guitar* (1954)
170. D. Shirley Temple
171. B. Hole-in-the-Wall Gang
172. A. *Cattle King* (1963)
173. C. *Siege at Red River* (1954)
174. B. *Major Dundee* (1965)
175. A. Bra
176. D. *The Kentuckian* (1955)
177. A. *Brigham Young* (1940)
178. B. *The Second Time Around* (1961)

179. B. *In Old Oklahoma* (1943)
180. C. They are brothers.
181. B. Robert Aldrich
182. C. Porter Hall
183. C. 0.4 seconds
184. A. *Drums Along the Mohawk* (1939)
185. D. *Vera Cruz* (1954)
186. A. *Comanche* (1956)
187. A. Chill Wills

Spotlight on Glenn Ford

1. C. *The Desperadoes* (1943)
2. B. *The Last Challenge* (1967)
3. B. *Teahouse of the August Moon* (1956)
4. D. *The Badlanders* (1958)

188. A. Dawson Hash House
189. B. Geraldine Page
190. D. Zeb Calloway
191. A. *Breakheart Pass*
192. D. "Wand'rin Star"
193. D. *Way Out West* (1930)
194. B. *Shane* (1953)
195. D. An eye patch
196. D. *Red River* (1948)
197. B. 1939
198. D. Wes Studi
199. C. *Northwest Passage* (1940)
200. B. Jerry Thorpe
201. D. *The World Changes* (1933)
202. C. Loretta Young
203. B. *Ride, Vaquero!* (1953)
204. C. John Ford
205. B. *The Sons of Katie Elder* (1965)
206. B. Barbara Stanwyck
207. D. . . . you was just born?"
208. C. 4

CHAPTER 12

1. C. *The Sky's the Limit* (1943)
2. B. *Star!* (1968)
3. B. "The Dance of the Grizzly Bear"
4. B. Betty Garrett
5. D. *Young at Heart* (1954)
6. C. *The Prisoner of Zenda* (1937)
7. B. Best Interior Decoration—Black-and-White Film
8. C. "On the Sunny Side of the Street"
9. B. Gwen Verdon

10. D. *Strike Up the Band*
11. D. *The Pajama Game* (1957)
12. A. *Hallelujah, I'm a Bum* (1933)
13. C. *The Happiest Millionaire* (1967)
14. C. Joan Leslie
15. C. Hermes Pan
16. C. *Let's Dance* (1950)
17. C. Gap
18. B. *Oklahoma!* (1955)
19. A. Peter O'Toole
20. D. *This Way Please* (1937)
21. C. *The Rose of Panama*
22. A. Alfred Newman
23. C. Judy Garland
24. B. *The Girl from Chicago*
25. A. "Guilty"
26. D. *You Were Never Lovelier* (1942)
27. B. *Rose Marie* (1954)
28. C. *Nuts* (1987)
29. D. *The Gay Divorcee* (1934)
30. B. *My Fair Lady* and *The Sound of Music*
31. D. *The Girl Most Likely* (1958)
32. D. *The Women* (1939)
33. B. Lloyd Bacon
34. C. *Oklahoma!* (1955)
35. B. "If I Were a Bell"
36. D. Leslie Caron
37. D. Tallahassee, Florida
38. C. *Music in the Air* (1934)
39. A. *Carousel* (1956)
40. C. "Sweet Dreams, Sweetheart"
41. B. Pelican Falls
42. B. *Oklahoma!* (1955)
43. C. *Les Girls* (1957)
44. B. "Pass the Peace Pipe"
45. A. "Ain't Misbehavin'"
46. A. *Funny Face* (1957)
47. A. Busby Berkeley
48. B. *The Music Man* (1962)
49. A. Celine Dion
50. A. *Idiot's Delight*
51. D. Judy Garland and Mickey Rooney
52. B. Frank Sinatra
53. A. *A Star Is Born* (1954)
54. B. Jane Powell

Spotlight on Bing Crosby

1. A. "Accentuate the Positive"
2. C. "White Christmas"

3. C. "Sweet Leilani"
4. D. *The Emperor Waltz* (1948)
5. A. *Here Comes the Groom* (1951)

55. C. *White Christmas* (1954)
56. D. *Three Little Words* (1950)
57. C. Ethel Waters
58. D. *State Fair*
59. C. *The Great Ziegfeld* (1936)
60. C. Jane Powell
61. C. Lena Horne
62. D. *The Big Broadcast of 1938* (1938)
63. B. *Guys and Dolls* (1955)
64. A. *Easter Parade* (1948)
65. B. *Oklahoma!*
66. D. *The Duke Is Tops* (1938)
67. D. *Three Coins in the Fountain* (1954)
68. D. *The Belle of New York* (1952)
69. C. *Grounds for Marriage* (1951)
70. A. *Funny Face* (1957)
71. D. Yale
72. B. "Let's Face the Music and Dance"
73. A. *How to Succeed in Business Without Really Trying*
74. D. *West Side Story* (1961)
75. C. Jane Wyman
76. B. Ethel Merman
77. C. *Zorba*
78. C. *The Voyage of Suzette*
79. A. *Carousel*
80. B. *Some Like It Hot* (1959)
81. A. *Royal Wedding* (1951)
82. C. Max Steiner
83. A. James Caan
84. A. Jitterbug
85. C. *Up in Arms* (1944)
86. B. Gene Kelly
87. B. *Oklahoma!* (1955)
88. D. *Torch Singer* (1933)
89. B. *Sunset Blvd.* (1950)
90. A. Benny Goodman
91. D. *Yentl* (1983)
92. A. *Cabaret* (1972)
93. D. *The Sky's the Limit* (1943)
94. B. *The Happiest Millionaire* (1967)
95. C. *Oliver!*
96. C. *The Chocolate Soldier* (1941)
97. B. *Guys and Dolls*
98. D. *The Big Broadcast of 1938* (1938)

99. B. "Miss Marmelstein"
100. B. Pontipee
101. A. *Because You're Mine* (1952)
102. B. Donna Summer
103. C. *Summer Stock* (1950)
104. B. *Oklahoma!* (1955)
105. A. "Boss Lady"
106. C. "New York, New York"
107. D. *Wonderful Town*
108. B. 3
109. B. *Kiss Me Kate* (1953)
110. D. *The Big Broadcast of 1938* (1938)
111. C. *Pilot No. 5* (1943)
112. B. *The Dueling Cavalier*
113. D. *Xanadu* (1980)
114. D. *Sweeney Todd: The Demon Barber of Fleet Street*
115. D. *Tovarich*
116. B. *Star!* (1968)
117. C. . . . Remember"
118. A. *Funny Face* (1957)
119. D. Lunch-wagon proprietor
120. D. *Yankee Doodle Dandy* (1942)
121. C. *The Kissing Bandit* (1948)
122. A. *Destry Rides Again* (1939)
123. C. "The Continental"
124. C. Lena Horne
125. B. *Oh! What a Lovely War* (1969)
126. D. George Segal
127. B. Best Director
128. C. Fred Astaire
129. A. *Brigadoon* (1954)
130. D. "You Are Beautiful"
131. A. *Sunset Blvd.*
132. B. Monumental Pictures
133. D. *Three Daring Daughters* (1948)
134. A. *Romance on the High Seas* (1948)
135. C. *Oh, Boy*
136. B. Fred Astaire
137. B. *Second Chorus* (1940)

Spotlight on Judy Garland
1. B. . . . Happy"
2. D. "Over the Rainbow"
3. B. *In the Good Old Summertime* (1949)
4. B. *I Could Go on Singing* (1963)
5. B. Robert Donat

138. B. *Jamaica*
139. A. *April Love* (1957)

140. D. Marlon Brando
141. A. *Camelot*
142. D. *The King and I* (1956)
143. C. "How About You"
144. D. Shot on location
145. A. *Carmen Jones* (1954)
146. C. Julie Andrews
147. B. Johnny Green
148. C. *The Producers*
149. D. Paducah
150. A. *Brigadoon* (1954)
151. D. *The Great Ziegfeld* (1936)
152. C. George Cukor
153. A. *Carefree* (1938)
154. D. Walter Matthau
155. A. Betty Hutton
156. A. *Allure*
157. A. Buster Keaton

Spotlight on Gene Kelly
1. D. Vera-Ellen
2. A. *Brigadoon* (1954)
3. D. *Singin' in the Rain* (1952)
4. C. Don Lockwood
5. B. Madonna

158. A. *Candide*
159. A. *Cover Girl* (1944)
160. A. Busby Berkeley
161. B. Esther Williams
162. A. *Nancy Goes to Rio* (1950)
163. C. *Henry, Sweet Henry*
164. C. *The Philadelphia Story* (1940)
165. C. *Swing Time* (1936)
166. C. *Singin' in the Rain* (1952)
167. B. *Bye Bye Birdie* (1963)
168. A. *And the Angels Sing* (1944)
169. A. *Mr. Imperium* (1951)
170. D. *Moonlighting*
171. D. *Ziegfeld Girl* (1941)
172. C. *Irene*
173. C. *Sweet Adeline* (1934)
174. A. *Athena* (1954)
175. D. *South Pacific* (1958)
176. B. *On the Town*
177. B. *Lost Horizon* (1937)
178. D. *The Great Ziegfeld* (1936)
179. A. Coco Chanel
180. A. Cello
181. C. *Pal Joey*

182. A. *Mr. Imperium* (1951)
183. B. *Funny Girl* (1968)
184. C. "It's Magic"
185. D. *The Sky's the Limit* (1943)
186. D. Best Scoring of a Musical Picture
187. C. "One Last Kiss"
188. B. *My Fair Lady* (1964)
189. B. *Singin' in the Rain* (1952)
190. B. Ginger Rogers
191. B. *The Ritz*
192. C. *Going Hollywood* (1933)
193. D. *They're Playing Our Song*
194. D. *The Glass Slipper* (1955)
195. D. *The Pajama Game* (1957)
196. A. Howard Hawks
197. B. *Goodbye, Mr. Chips* (1969)
198. C. *Week-End at the Waldorf* (1945)
199. C. *Ten Thousand Bedrooms* (1957)
200. C. *South Pacific* (1958)
201. B. *Mississippi* (1935)
202. D. "Sing, Sing, Sing"
203. A. *Easter Parade*
204. D. *The Pied Piper of Hamelin* (1957)
205. A. Bing Crosby
206. D. *Ra-Ta-Plan*
207. C. Peter Bogdanovich
208. B. Moira Shearer
209. D. *On an Island with You* (1948)
210. C. "Pettin' in the Park"
211. B. *Cabin in the Sky* (1943)
212. B. *The Broadway Melody* (1929)
213. D. *The Great Waltz* (1938)
214. B. *John Murray Anderson's Almanac*
215. A. *Never Give a Sucker an Even Break* (1941)
216. C. "Too Late Now"
217. C. *The Full Monty*
218. C. . . . Wonderful"
219. A. *Porgy and Bess* (1959)
220. A. Chester Kent
221. D. Steve Martin
222. C. *Pagan Love Song* (1950)

CHAPTER 13

1. A. Charles Chaplin for *The Great Dictator* (1940)
2. D. *Watch on the Rhine* (1943)
3. B. *Hitler's Children* (1943)

4. C. *Subway in the Sky* (1959)

5. A. Alfred Hitchcock

6. D. *That Hagen Girl* (1947)

7. B. *The Best Years of Our Lives* (1946)

8. A. *Schindler's List* (1993)

9. C. Richard Harris

10. B. Joan Crawford

11. D. Robert Duvall

12. B. *Nazi Agent* (1942)

13. A. *A Bridge Too Far* (1977)

14. D. Wolfgang Petersen

15. D. *The White Cliffs of Dover* (1944)

16. A. *Action in the North Atlantic* (1943)

17. D. *Vigil in the Night* (1940)

18. B. *Battleground*

19. C. *The Diary of Anne Frank* (1959)

20. B. Golightly

21. D. Rex Harrison

22. D. John Garfield

23. D. *They Were Expendable* (1945)

24. D. *The Story of G.I. Joe* (1945)

25. D. Vincente Minnelli

26. D. Kirk Douglas

27. C. World War I

28. A. Frank Sinatra

29. D. Victor Fleming

30. D. Richard L. Breen

31. D. *Submarine* (1928)

32. A. *A Walk in the Sun* (1945)

33. B. Deborah Kerr

34. C. Franklin Delano Roosevelt

35. D. San Francisco

36. B. *Brother Rat* (1938)

37. C. Best Original Song

38. C. *In Harm's Way* (1965)

39. A. *Behold a Pale Horse* (1964)

40. D. *The Bridge on the River Kwai* (1957)

41. A. *A Bridge Too Far* (1977)

42. B. Ernest Hemingway

43. A. *Carolina* (1934)

44. D. Best Foreign Language Film

45. D. Best Scoring of a Dramatic or Comedy Picture

46. A. Cowardice

47. C. *The Night of the Generals* (1967)

48. C. Robert Mitchum

49. D. Best Special Effects

50. C. Mae West

51. A. Robert E. Lee

52. D. Best Sound, Recording

53. B. *Seven Days in May* (1964)

54. B. *Desperate Journey* (1942)

Spotlight on Dana Andrews

1. C. *The Best Years of Our Lives* (1946)

2. C. 8

3. C. *I Want You* (1951)

4. C. *The Best Years of Our Lives* (1946)

5. B. *Home of the Brave* (1949)

55. A. *John Paul Jones* (1959)

56. B. *Hell Below Zero* (1954)

57. B. Lloyd Bacon

58. B. John Huston

59. A. 1942

60. B. *Little Women* (1949)

61. B. Best Director

62. D. Steve McQueen

63. B. *Carbine Williams* (1952)

64. D. *The Young Lions* (1958)

65. D. *The Steel Helmet* (1951)

66. A. *Fail-Safe* (1964)

67. D. Wendy Hiller

68. A. Cary Grant

69. D. *The Outsider* (1961)

70. B. *Malta Story* (1953)

71. A. Glenn Ford

72. A. Best Cinematography

73. C. Steve McQueen

74. C. Army Motion Picture Unit

75. A. *The Deer Hunter* (1978)

76. C. Red Buttons

77. B. Claude Rains

78. C. *The Marines Are Coming* (1934)

79. A. British Foreign Legion

80. D. Marlene Dietrich

81. C. Lloyd Bridges

82. D. 7

83. D. Best Special Effects

84. B. *Since You Went Away* (1944)

85. A. U.S. Air Force

86. D. *The Secret of Santa Vittoria* (1969)

87. B. *Coming Home* (1978)

88. A. *Buck Privates* (1941)

89. C. James Wong Howe

90. A. Best Actor

91. B. Henry Fonda

92. C. "Thank you!"

93. C. Photographic model

94. B. Pink

95. B. *Commandos Strike at Dawn* (1942)

96. D. *Until They Sail* (1957)

97. B. World War II

98. C. *The Great Escape* (1963)

99. C. *The Honeymoon Machine* (1961)

100. D. *Tobruk* (1967)

101. A. Humphrey Bogart

102. C. *Pork Chop Hill* (1959)

103. D. *Sayonara* (1957)

104. B. Best Director

105. C. Walter Matthau

106. A. Arthur Penn

107. D. *Where Eagles Dare* (1968)

108. A. *Hellcats of the Navy* (1957)

109. D. *Two Arabian Nights* (1927)

110. A. Giuseppe

111. C. Helen

112. B. *The Valiant* (1962)

113. A. Denzel Washington

114. A. *49th Parallel* (1941)

115. C. Richard Burton

116. A. Beirne Lay Jr.

117. B. Elizabeth Taylor

118. A. *For Whom the Bell Tolls* (1943)

119. A. Best Actor in a Supporting Role

120. B. She wants sons with long mustaches.

121. B. General Lane

122. C. John Wayne

123. B. *Plenty* (1985)

124. B. U.S. Army

125. C. Best Film Editing

126. A. *Sahara* (1943)

127. D. *Schindler's List* (1993)

128. D. *Tobruk* (1967)

129. D. *Stalag 17* (1953)

130. B. The Hollywood Canteen

131. C. *Thirty Seconds Over Tokyo* (1944)

132. B. George Kennedy

133. A. *Au revoir les enfants* (1987)

134. A. *Strategic Air Command* (1955)

135. D. Van Johnson

136. C. Jean Simmons

137. B. *Never Wave at a WAC* (1953)

138. D. Matthew Broderick

139. D. Rossano Brazzi

140. A. *Miracle in the Rain* (1956)

141. C. Rear Admiral
142. B. Laurence Olivier
143. D. *Till the End of Time* (1946)
144. D. Best Picture
145. B. *Lacombe Lucien* (1974)
146. D. Wilkes
147. B. *The Best Years of Our Lives* (1946)
148. A. *Action of the Tiger* (1957)
149. B. *Tender Comrade* (1943)
150. A. *Bright Victory* (1951)
151. D. *Tell It to the Marines* (1927)
152. B. Dwight Eisenhower
153. C. *The Journey*
154. A. *Friendly Persuasion* (1956)
155. C. Miyoshi Umeki for *Sayonara* (1957)
156. A. *A Soldier's Story* (1984)
157. C. Humphrey Bogart
158. C. *Scaramouche* (1952)
159. A. Angela
160. C. Paramount
161. C. Joanne Woodward and Paul Newman

Spotlight on Greer Garson
1. D. 5 1/2 minutes
2. B. *Random Harvest* (1942)
3. C. On a mountain
4. C. 7
5. A. *Blossoms in the Dust* (1941)

162. B. *From Here to Eternity* (1953)
163. A. *All Quiet on the Western Front* (1930)
164. A. Jane Fonda
165. B. Claude Rains
166. A. *Casablanca*
167. A. Basil Rathbone
168. D. *Battle Zone*
169. B. *Miracle of the White Stallions* (1963)
170. D. Best Special Effects
171. B. Best Actress
172. B. *Enchantment* (1948)
173. D. June Mathis
174. D. Tony Curtis
175. A. Directed training films
176. C. *The House on 92nd Street* (1945)
177. C. Japan
178. D. James Stewart

179. A. Albert Finney
180. D. Ronald Reagan
181. A. *Miracle of the White Stallions* (1963)
182. D. Tim Conway

Spotlight on Errol Flynn
1. A. *Edge of Darkness* (1943)
2. A. *Istanbul* (1957)
3. A. *Dive Bomber* (1941)
4. D. *They Died with Their Boots On* (1941)
5. C. *Uncertain Glory* (1944)

183. D. *The Life and Death of Colonel Blimp* (1943)
184. B. Best Director
185. B. Philippines
186. B. *Kings Go Forth* (1958)
187. D. Joseph Ruttenberg
188. A. Caesar
189. B. Crazy Horse
190. B. *Gods and Generals* (2003)
191. B. *The Longest Day* (1962)
192. B. Deborah Kerr
193. D. *The Best Years of Our Lives* (1946)
194. B. *Sayonara* (1957)
195. C. Dachau
196. C. Winston Churchill
197. A. *1941* (1979)
198. C. John Wayne
199. B. *Sands of Iwo Jima* (1949)
200. A. *Battleground* (1949)
201. D. Best Screenplay
202. C. 5
203. C. *The Terror* (1963)
204. D. *Vigil in the Night* (1940)
205. C. Best Scoring of a Dramatic or Comedy Picture
206. D. *The Woman I Love* (1937)
207. D. *Rogues' Regiment* (1948)
208. D. *The Search* (1948)
209. A. Burt Lancaster
210. B. James Garner
211. D. *The Steel Helmet* (1951)
212. A. Air force
213. A. *Lord Jim* (1965)
214. C. *The Longest Day* (1962)
215. A. *Berkeley Square* (1933)
216. D. Italy

217. D. U.S. Navy
218. D. Best Special Effects
219. B. Best Cinematography
220. C. Lee J. Cobb
221. A. Howard Hawks
222. B. *In Which We Serve* (1942)

CHAPTER 14

1. A. Ann Darrow
2. C. Olympia Dukakis
3. B. Ida Lupino
4. B. *Sleepless in Seattle* (1993)
5. C. Best Musical Score
6. A. Bing Crosby
7. D. Lauren Bacall
8. B. A villa
9. A. Fire extinguishers
10. D. Scotland
11. A. Cary Grant
12. D. Ronald Colman
13. A. *Always* (1989)
14. B. *Heartburn* (1986)
15. D. . . . wipe my mouth."
16. A. Abbey Lincoln
17. A. Jane Fonda
18. B. "As Time Goes By"
19. D. Stanley Donen
20. D. "You Make It Easy to Be True"
21. B. Jessica Lange
22. C. James Stewart
23. B. *Love Is a Many-Splendored Thing* (1955)
24. A. A blond wig
25. D. *Night Song* (1947)
26. C. Ireland
27. C. *The Private Lives of Elizabeth and Essex*
28. A. *Night Into Morning* (1951)
29. A. C. S. Forester
30. A. Humphrey Bogart
31. A. *A Star for Two* (1991)
32. B. Katie
33. D. *Sabrina* (1954)
34. B. George Cukor
35. B. Jeff Bridges
36. C. Jerry
37. A. *Brown of Harvard* (1926)
38. A. Charles Boyer

39. B. . . . . stars."
40. C. Italy
41. B. Chauffeur
42. B. Eben
43. B. Best Director
44. C. Lise
45. B. Blond
46. C. Frank Sinatra
47. C. Shirley Jones
48. A. Deborah Kerr
49. C. Richard Denning
50. C. Janet Leigh
51. C. *The Great Lover* (1949)
52. B. Belle Massey
53. B. Fyodor Dostoyevsky

Spotlight on Ingrid Bergman
1. A. *Saratoga Trunk* (1945)
2. A. Anthony Perkins
3. A. Goldie Hawn
4. B. Ilsa
5. A. Actress

54. C. At college
55. C. King Mark of Cornwall
56. B. Katharine Hepburn
57. B. *Splendor in the Grass* (1961)
58. C. Gene Tierney
59. B. *Inside Daisy Clover* (1965)
60. A. Barbara Stanwyck
61. B. Debbie Reynolds
62. C. Janet Leigh
63. A. *Fast and Loose* (1930)
64. C. Rex Harrison
65. C. Walk
66. B. *Marie Antoinette* (1938)
67. B. Alla Nazimova
68. B. Olivia de Havilland
69. A. Cathy
70. B. Greece
71. D. Best Supporting Actor
72. D. *The White Cliffs of Dover* (1944)
73. A. *A Guy Named Joe* (1943)
74. D. Walter
75. D. Maggie Smith
76. B. Linda Hunt
77. D. *The Young Lovers* (1954)
78. C. Rock Hudson
79. C. Natalie Wood
80. C. Best Original Score

81. A. 0
82. B. *The Most Dangerous Game* (1932)
83. C. "Moon River"
84. A. *How to Steal a Million* (1966)
85. A. *Interlude* (1957)
86. C. Gregory Peck
87. D. Tom Courtenay
88. A. Manderley
89. C. Ricardo Montalban
90. D. July 1 at 5 PM
91. A. "Bing! Bang! Bong!"
92. D. Rex Harrison
93. D. Vivien Leigh
94. D. Mary
95. C. Best Musical Score

Spotlight on Deborah Kerr
1. C. *The End of the Affair* (1955)
2. B. French
3. B. Pink champagne
4. D. She whistles
5. D. Sheilah Graham

96. D. William Wyler
97. B. Best Art Direction
98. C. Jennifer Jones
99. D. "The Kiss in Your Eyes"
100. B. Gary Cooper
101. C. *Pride and Prejudice* (1940)
102. A. George Brent
103. C. *The Hunchback of Notre Dame* (1957)
104. D. *The House of the Spirits* (1993)
105. B. *In the Good Old Summertime* (1949)
106. C. Kim Hunter
107. A. *Dance Pretty Lady* (1932)
108. A. Bob Hope
109. A. Donna Reed
110. B. 11
111. B. Lighter
112. D. Peter Falk
113. C. James Stewart
114. B. *The Children's Hour*
115. A. Anthony Perkins
116. C. Paulette Goddard
117. C. June Allyson
118. A. A Jet
119. D. *The French Line* (1954)
120. A. Best Actor

121. C. *Tammy Tell Me True* (1961) and *Romanoff and Juliet* (1961)
122. B. France
123. B. Eleanor Roosevelt
124. A. *Dirty Mary Crazy Larry* (1974)
125. A. Bette Midler
126. D. Tony
127. A. Bethel Independent Mission
128. A. Champagne
129. B. C. C. Baxter
130. C. Pearls
131. C. Ralph Bellamy
132. C. Kathryn Grayson
133. A. Burt Lancaster
134. B. Milk and crackers
135. C. Paris
136. D. 5
137. A. Isak Dinesen
138. D. Robert Taylor
139. B. Vantine
140. A. Claudette Colbert
141. B. *It's a Wonderful Life* (1946)
142. D. Best Writing, Original Story
143. B. *The Midnight Lady* (1932)
144. B. Elaine
145. C. Ingrid Bergman
146. D. *Sense and Sensibility* (1995)
147. A. Carole Lombard
148. A. Best Original Screenplay
149. A. Charles Boyer
150. B. Macy's
151. B. *The Barretts of Wimpole Street* (1957)
152. D. Best Writing, Screenplay Based on Material from Another Medium
153. D. W. Somerset Maugham
154. C. *Teacher's Pet* (1958)
155. A. 16
156. B. Bette Davis
157. A. *Swiss Tour* (1950)
158. C. Katharine Hepburn
159. D. Marilyn Monroe
160. C. *Promises, Promises*
161. D. Robert Young

Spotlight on Clark Gable
1. A. Carroll Baker
2. D. Mary Astor
3. D. 1
4. B. *Idiot's Delight* (1939)

5. B. *Teacher's Pet* (1958)

162. D. Italy's *Nights of Cabiria*
163. A. *Quality Street* (1937)
164. B. Greer Garson
165. D. Merle Oberon
166. A. *Blood and Sand*
167. D. *What a Girl Wants*
168. D. Ralph Fiennes and
     Julianne Moore
169. B. John Amos
170. C. Prostitute
171. C. Scarlett O'Hara in *Gone With the Wind* (1939)
172. D. Leo Tolstoy
173. C. Photographer
174. C. *Sunnyside Up* (1929)
175. C. James Mason
176. A. A railroad line
177. A. Best Actress
178. A. *The Children's Hour*
179. A. Classics
180. D. Vic Damone
181. B. Cooking
182. A. *Latin Lovers* (1953)
183. D. Victor Laszlo
184. D. Shirley MacLaine
185. C. *Niagara* (1953)
186. B. 1
187. D. William Holden
188. C. *The Fox* (1968)
189. B. Henry Fonda
190. C. R
191. C. Paris
192. D. *The Purple Rose of Cairo* (1985)
193. C. *The Barefoot Contessa* (1954)
194. B. Hans Christian Andersen
195. D. *The Story of Vernon and Irene Castle* (1939)
196. C. *The Twilight Saga: New Moon* (2009)
197. B. Katharine Ross
198. A. *Alice Adams* (1935)
199. C. Dentist
200. D. *Sabrina* (1954)
201. C. Rome, Italy
202. D. Vivien Leigh
203. C. Venice
204. B. Robert Donat

205. D. Paris
206. B. Ernest Hemingway
207. C. Psychiatrist
208. A. *'Til We Meet Again* (1940)
209. A. Clifford Odets
210. C. *The Royal Romance of Charles and Diana* (1982)
211. C. Olive Higgins Prouty
212. D. Natalie Wood
213. B. Julie Mardsen
214. C. Norma Shearer
215. A. Budapest
216. B. Best Cinematography
217. A. Best Actress
218. D. Rita Hayworth
219. C. Shelley Fabares
220. C. Best Original Score
221. B. Gérard Depardieu
222. C. Ricardo Montalban
223. D. Sea
224. A. Alfred Newman
225. D. Best Scoring of a Dramatic or Comedy Picture
226. C. Spencer Tracy

CHAPTER 15

1. D. *The Big Knife* (1955)
2. B. *Out of the Fog* (1941)
3. C. Jean Louis
4. C. Fritz Lang
5. D. *Murder on the Orient Express* (1974)
6. D. *Rififi* (1955)
7. A. Doctor
8. B. *Rope*
9. A. Bette Davis
10. B. James Cagney
11. B. Gene Tierney
12. C. *Never a Dull Moment* (1968)
13. C. Robert De Niro
14. B. *The Glass Key* (1935)
15. D. Stella
16. C. Michael Curtiz
17. B. Jessica Lange
18. B. Dashiell Hammett
19. C. 5
20. B. *Man Hunt* (1941)
21. D. *Gilda* (1946)
22. C. 81

23. D. *Farewell, My Lovely*
24. D. *Strangers on a Train* (1951)
25. C. *The Freshman* (1990)
26. C. *No Way Out* (1950)
27. C. B. J. Harrison
28. B. *Scarface* (1932)
29. D. *Undercurrent* (1946)
30. B. *Shadow of a Doubt* (1943)
31. B. *Strangers on a Train* (1951)
32. A. Arthur "Cody" Jarrett
33. B. *Mildred Pierce* (1945)
34. D. Marilyn Monroe
35. D. William Wyler
36. C. *The Killers*
37. C. *Night and the City* (1950)
38. B. *The Public Enemy* (1931)
39. C. Phyllis Dietrichson
40. C. An ankle bracelet
41. C. *The Trouble with Harry* (1955)
42. A. *Something Wicked This Way Comes* (1983)
43. B. *Some Like It Hot* (1959)
44. B. *Jigsaw* (1949)
45. A. Barbara Graham
46. B. *Rififi* (1955)
47. C. Robert Taylor
48. C. *Dead End* (1937)
49. C. *The Maltese Falcon* (1941)
50. D. Sherlock Holmes
51. B. *Eyes in the Night* (1942)
52. C. *The George Sanders Mystery Theater*
53. C. *The Public Enemy* (1931)
54. D. *On the Waterfront* (1954)

Spotlight on Paul Muni

1. A. *Angel on My Shoulder* (1946)
2. B. *High Sierra* (1941)
3. A. *Bordertown* (1935)
4. B. *Bordertown* (1935)
5. D. *Scarface* (1932)

55. A. *Accidents Will Happen* (1938)
56. A. Barbara Stanwyck
57. C. Raoul Walsh
58. D. Virginia Mayo
59. D. Terry Malloy
60. A. Edward G. Robinson
61. B. 1
62. A. *Angel on My Shoulder* (1946)
63. B. *Outrage* (1950)

64. B. *Double Indemnity* (1944)
65. D. *Touch of Evil* (1958)
66. C. *Murder in the Family* (1938)
67. C. *Party Girl* (1958)
68. C. Raoul Walsh
69. B. *Short Cut to Hell* (1957)
70. D. Humphrey Bogart
71. D. *Vertigo* (1958)
72. B. Howard Hughes
73. B. Her glove
74. C. *Rear Window* (1954)
75. A. *Gaslight* (1944)
76. A. Fred MacMurray
77. A. *I Am a Fugitive from a Chain Gang* (1932)
78. D. *Undercurrent* (1946)
79. C. *Peyton Place* (1957)
80. C. *Madame X* by John Singer Sargent
81. B. Gwen Allen
82. B. *Sinners' Holiday* (1930)
83. C. *Strangers on a Train* (1951)
84. D. A wedding ring
85. D. *White Heat* (1949) and *Caged* (1950)
86. D. *The Killers* (1964)
87. B. "The Queen of Film Noir"
88. A. Charles Dickens
89. C. Norman Jewison
90. D. *They Won't Forget* (1937)
91. D. *While the City Sleeps* (1956)
92. D. *The Postman Always Rings Twice* (1946)
93. A. *Murder at the Gallop* (1963)
94. D. Otto Preminger
95. D. *The Midnight Story* (1957)
96. B. Billy Wilder
97. D. 1935
98. B. *Key Largo* (1948)
99. C. *The Big Knife* (1955)
100. D. *Ragtime* (1981)
101. B. 1
102. B. *Johnny Allegro* (1949)
103. C. Universal
104. A. *Crossfire* (1947)
105. D. *Laura* (1944)
106. A. Jack Nicholson
107. A. *Bonnie and Clyde* (1967)
108. B. Glenn Ford
109. A. *Double Indemnity* (1944)

110. C. Margaret Wycherly
111. C. *Leave Her to Heaven*
112. D. Sydney Greenstreet
113. B. Ridley Scott
114. D. *Women's Prison* (1955)
115. D. The Hardy Boys
116. D. Best Writing, Original Story
117. A. Archie Mayo
118. C. Robert Aldrich
119. A. Barbara Stanwyck

Spotlight on Ida Lupino

1. C. *Road House* (1948)
2. C. *On Dangerous Ground* (1952)
3. B. *On Dangerous Ground* (1952)
4. D. *While the City Sleeps* (1956)
5. C. *They Drive by Night* (1940)

120. A. *Colors* (1988)
121. C. Kim Novak
122. A. Argentina
123. C. Diana Rigg
124. C. *The Asphalt Jungle*
125. A. Edward Arnold
126. B. *The Men*
127. A. *Marlowe* (1969)
128. B. 4
129. D. *The Postman Always Rings Twice* (1946)
130. C. Robert De Niro
131. C. *Shadow of a Doubt* (1943)
132. D. *The Public Enemy* (1931)
133. D. Monkey
134. D. *Kid Galahad* (1937)
135. B. John G. Adolfi
136. A. Mike Hammer
137. D. *The Hitch-Hiker* (1953)
138. C. James Stewart
139. B. Pat O'Brien
140. B. *Spellbound* (1945)
141. C. John Patrick
142. B. Busby Berkeley
143. A. *Crimes and Misdemeanors* (1989)
144. C. *Paths of Glory* (1957)
145. B. *The Drowning Pool* (1975)
146. A. Best Actor
147. A. *Dead End* (1937)
148. A. Chester Gillette
149. A. *Madame X*
150. B. *Scarface* (1932)

151. D. "The Moon Killer"
152. C. *Suspicion* (1941)
153. C. Milos Forman
154. A. *Baby Face Nelson* (1957)
155. B. Janet Leigh
156. A. George C. Scott
157. C. Marilyn Monroe
158. B. *Odds Against Tomorrow* (1959)
159. C. Sam Spade
160. D. *The Amazing Dr. Clitterhouse* (1938)
161. A. Al Pacino
162. B. Best Adaptation
163. A. *Each Dawn I Die* (1939)

Spotlight on James Cagney

1. D. Mae Clark
2. A. 0
3. C. O'Caigne
4. D. *White Heat* (1949)
5. C. 3

164. D. William Wellman
165. C. *Gangster Story* (1959)
166. B. Best Black-and-White Cinematography
167. B. John Huston
168. D. Ted Tetzlaff
169. B. *Rope* (1948)
170. A. *Murder on the Orient Express* (1974)
171. A. *Klute* (1971)
172. C. Humphrey Bogart
173. D. William "Rocky" Sullivan in *Angels with Dirty Faces* (1938)
174. A. Burt Lancaster
175. A. Dashiell Hammett
176. D. Sidney Lumet
177. A. Barbara Stanwyck
178. C. *On the Waterfront* (1954)
179. A. *Double Indemnity* (1944)
180. D. *The Racket* (1951)
181. C. *The Killers* (1964)
182. B. Ralph Bellamy
183. B. *Manhattan Melodrama* (1934)
184. A. *Blonde Ice* (1948)
185. C. *Rififi* (1955)
186. B. Humphrey Bogart
187. C. *Smart Money* (1931)
188. B. *Gangster Story* (1959)

189. D. John Huston
190. C. Claire Trevor
191. B. Jean Harlow
192. B. Bugsy Siegel
193. D. Yorkville Nut Club
194. C. *The Chinese Parrot* (1927)
195. A. Miss Jane Marple
196. A. *Act of Violence* (1948)
197. B. *Crime of Passion* (1957)
198. A. *Anatomy of a Murder* (1959)
199. C. *The Green Glove* (1952)
200. B. *Angel on My Shoulder* (1946)
201. C. *Rebecca* (1940)
202. B. Dashiell Hammett
203. D. *Nora Prentiss* (1947)
204. C. *Johnny Eager* (1941)
205. C. Paul Muni
206. B. *Night and the City* (1950)

CHAPTER 16

1. C. Orson Welles
2. B. Ray Bradbury
3. B. *I Saw What You Did* (1965)
4. C. James Dean
5. A. Esther Williams
6. D. Raquel Welch
7. B. Clara Bow
8. B. Harry James
9. D. Lucien Ballard
10. A. *Bordertown* (1935)
11. A. *Father Goose* (1964)
12. A. Daffy Duck
13. A. Jean Harlow
14. D. Norma Shearer
15. A. Dies
16. C. Stephen McNally
17. D. Myrna Loy
18. B. Clint Eastwood
19. A. Greta Garbo
20. B. Gregory Peck
21. D. Neil Simon
22. A. *Basic Instinct* (1992)
23. A. Bob Hope
24. B. Cyd Charisse
25. B. Jack Warner
26. B. Greta Garbo
27. B. *From Here to Eternity* (1953)
28. A. Bach

29. C. Timing
30. D. *The Ghost Breakers* (1940)
31. A. Gary Cooper
32. C. *The Dover Boys* (1942)
33. B. Cloris Leachman for *The Last Picture Show* (1971)
34. D. W. C. Fields
35. C. *My Man Godfrey* (1936)
36. A. Hedy Lamarr
37. D. Robert Altman
38. A. Clark Gable
39. D. Stan Laurel
40. A. Clint Eastwood
41. A. Norman Z. McLeod
42. B. "Hello, Young Lovers"
43. C. Gary Cooper
44. A. Carroll Baker
45. C. *Places in the Heart* (1984)
46. A. Cary Grant
47. C. Humphrey Bogart
48. D. Natalie Wood
49. C. Loretta Young
50. C. Eva Marie Saint for *On the Waterfront*
51. A. *An Affair to Remember* (1957)
52. B. Judy Garland
53. C. "Under Corny Crap"
54. D. Harpo Marx
55. C. Louis Armstrong
56. B. *Lonesome Dove* (1989)
57. A. *Earthquake* (1974)
58. A. Bette Davis
59. C. Rudolph Valentino
60. A. Edward G. Robinson
61. A. Groucho Marx
62. C. Mickey Rooney
63. D. Lucille Ball
64. C. Lana Turner
65. D. *Wuthering Heights* (1939)
66. B. Chrysler
67. C. *Knute Rockne, All-American* (1940)
68. A. Frank Capra
69. A. Ava Gardner
70. D. Vietnam
71. D. Rod Steiger
72. C. Peter Lawford
73. D. *The Tales of Hoffman* (1951)
74. C. Groucho Marx
75. B. Katharine Hepburn

76. C. Tony Curtis
77. A. *Hell's Angels* (1930)
78. A. Jeff Corey
79. B. Marie Dressler
80. B. Myra Breckinridge
81. C. John Gielgud
82. D. 4
83. A. Alfred Hitchcock
84. C. *The Taming of the Shrew* (1967)
85. B. *Mommie Dearest* (1981)
86. D. Wives
87. D. Troy Donahue
88. A. Ann Sheridan
89. C. Fred Astaire
90. D. Spencer Tracy
91. D. Orson Welles
92. C. Marilyn Monroe
93. C. James Stewart
94. A. Bette Davis
95. B. Deborah Kerr
96. C. Marilyn Monroe
97. B. Clint Eastwood
98. A. Cary Grant
99. B. Elizabeth Taylor
100. B. Bernard Herrmann
101. A. Melanie Griffith
102. A. *Funny Girl* (1968)
103. C. Douglas Fairbanks
104. D. Spencer Tracy
105. A. Errol Flynn
106. A. Ginger Rogers
107. A. Barbara Stanwyck
108. B. John F. Kennedy
109. C. Montgomery Clift
110. B. King Vidor
111. A. *All About Eve* (1950)
112. D. Richard Burton
113. D. Shirley MacLaine
114. C. Katharine Hepburn
115. A. *East of Eden* (1955)
116. C. Roger Corman
117. B. Fred Astaire
118. A. *Brown of Harvard* (1926)
119. C. Richard Burton
120. A. Bette Davis
121. D. Humphrey Bogart
122. A. Charles Laughton
123. B. Greg Kinnear
124. C. Humphrey Bogart

125. D. Lucille Ball
126. D. Sugar Ray Leonard
127. A. Bette Davis
128. B. "With all my heart, I still love the man I killed."
129. A. Michael Curtiz
130. B. Frank Capra
131. B. Irving Berlin
132. D. 500 taps per minute
133. D. Tony Curtis
134. D. Woody Allen
135. A. A set of dishes
136. A. Quentin Tarantino
137. D. Sing
138. B. Ingrid Bergman
139. D. Rosalind Russell
140. B. Alfred Hitchcock
141. C. Katharine Hepburn
142. B. *Brigadoon* (1954)
143. B. Mother
144. C. Robin Williams
145. A. David O. Selznick
146. A. Groucho Marx
147. D. Tyrone Power
148. A. *Apocalypse Now* (1979)
149. A. . . . backward and in high heels"
150. A. *Tea and Sympathy* (1956)
151. C. Frank Sinatra
152. B. A grape
153. A. Farley Granger
154. B. Merian C. Cooper
155. C. Richard Burton
156. C. *Monkey Business* (1931)
157. A. Dick Powell
158. A. "Bette Davis Eyes"
159. C. Groucho Marx
160. D. Wallace Beery
161. C. The town doctor
162. A. *Bug* (1975)
163. D. *The Fatal Glass of Beer* (1933)
164. A. Cary Grant
165. A. Carl Laemmle
166. A. Australia
167. D. Rex Harrison
168. A. Burt Lancaster for *From Here to Eternity* (1953)
169. B. Claire Bloom
170. C. Empire State Building
171. A. *Bombshell* (1933)

172. B. Clint Eastwood
173. D. Mickey Rooney
174. A. David Niven
175. B. *Kings Row* (1942)
176. C. Ireland
177. D. Greta Garbo
178. C. Irving Berlin
179. D. William Powell
180. A. Cary Grant
181. A. Gene Tierney
182. D. Wallace Beery
183. C. *The Rabbit of Seville* (1950)
184. C. *The Bride Came C.O.D.* (1941)
185. D. *Yankee Doodle Dandy* (1942)
186. D. Lauren Bacall
187. A. *As Good as It Gets* (1997)
188. A. *All About Eve* (1950)
189. B. *From Russia with Love* (1963)
190. A. Hayley Mills
191. C. Greg Kinnear
192. B. *Charade* (1963)
193. A. Billy Wilder
194. C. Groucho Marx
195. A. Cyd Charisse
196. B. Fred Astaire
197. B. "Our Baby"
198. C. *My Favorite Spy* (1951)
199. D. W. C. Fields
200. D. *Scudda Hoo! Scudda Hay!* (1948)
201. D. *The Grapes of Wrath* (1940)
202. A. Ronald Reagan
203. A. Fred Astaire
204. A. A man who has been transformed into a wolf
205. A. Bing Crosby
206. C. Mae West
207. B. "Me Tarzan, you Jane"
208. A. *Tender Is the Night*
209. C. Rita Hayworth
210. A. Frank Capra
211. A. Bette Davis
212. C. Owen Wilson
213. A. Ann Sheridan
214. A. Bette Davis
215. B. *Stage Door* (1937)
216. C. Charles Chaplin
217. B. Elvis Presley
218. C. Greta Garbo
219. C. Robert Mitchum

220. A. Cedric Hardwicke
221. C. Hedy Lamarr
222. D. Sean Connery
223. B. *Bitter Victory* (1957)

CHAPTER 17

1. C. Jean Louis
2. D. Edith Head
3. B. *Quo Vadis, Ivanhoe,* and *Julius Caesar*
4. C. *Monster from the Ocean Floor* (1954)
5. A. *Saboteur* (1942)
6. A. *Betrayed* (1954)
7. B. *Other People's Money* (1991)
8. C. Harold Arlen and Johnny Mercer
9. B. 26
10. B. Best Editing
11. B. *Hawaii* (1966)
12. A. Alexander Korda
13. C. *The Old Man and the Sea* (1958)
14. D. *Wife, Husband and Friend* (1939)
15. B. *The Citadel* (1938)
16. D. *West of the Pecos* (1934)
17. D. 9
18. C. *Naughty but Nice* (1939)
19. A. *Fahrenheit 451* (1966)
20. D. 5
21. D. *Sweet Smell of Success* (1957)
22. C. *They Made Me a Criminal* (1939)
23. D. Sam Goldwyn
24. D. Venice
25. D. *Who Was That Lady* (1960)
26. B. Leipzig
27. B. Jean Louis
28. D. *The 7th Voyage of Sinbad* (1958)
29. C. 3
30. C. *Doctor Faustus* (1967)
31. B. *The Prisoner of Zenda*
32. C. Orry-Kelly
33. C. Irene Sharaff
34. D. Thorne Smith
35. B. Edith Head
36. C. Jean Louis
37. A. *Blaze* (1989)
38. A. Gene Kelly
39. D. 5
40. D. Donald Ogden Stewart
41. A. *Creepshow* (1982)
42. B. *The Last Time I Saw Paris* (1954)

43. C. Herschel McCoy
44. D. Violin
45. C. D. W. Griffith
46. A. Betty Smith
47. D. *The Finger Points* (1931)
48. B. *Beloved Infidel* (1959)
49. C. Irving Berlin
50. A. *21 Days Together* (1940)
51. A. *Becky Sharp* (1935)
52. B. *Lawrence of Arabia* (1962)
53. A. *Kitty Foyle: The Natural History of a Woman* (1940)
54. D. As an actor
55. A. *Babbitt* (1934)
56. C. Best Art Decoration, Black-and-White
57. B. Rex Ingram
58. D. Marlene Dietrich
59. A. *Fantastic Voyage* (1966)
60. A. Charles Lang
61. D. *What's New, Pussycat?* (1965)
62. C. *Vivacious Lady* (1938)
63. B. *Red, Hot and Blue* (1949)
64. D. Winton C. Hoch for *Joan of Arc* and *She Wore a Yellow Ribbon*
65. D. Stephen Sondheim
66. D. William Rose
67. B. *It Came from Beneath the Sea* (1955)
68. B. *Sophie's Choice* (1982)
69. A. Gregg Toland
70. B. *Imitation of Life* (1959)
71. C. *The Good Earth* (1937)
72. B. *The African Queen* (1951)
73. A. Adrian
74. D. *The Power and the Prize* (1956)
75. D. *The Women* (1939)
76. B. *Looney Tunes: Back in Action* (2003)
77. C. Chicago
78. A. Pearl S. Buck
79. A. Columbia
80. C. 5
81. A. *Boom!* (1968)
82. C. *The Avengers* (1998)
83. D. Samuel Goldwyn
84. D. 60
85. A. *Bound for Glory* (1976)
86. D. Sheilah Graham
87. C. Universal
88. B. Johnny Mercer and Henry Mancini

89. A. *Bonnie and Clyde* (1967)
90. B. David Lean
91. D. *The Great Impersonation* (1942)
92. B. Carolco Pictures
93. A. *David Copperfield* (1935)
94. D. Lab assistant
95. A. Best Cinematography
96. C. Nolan Miller
97. A. Edith Wharton
98. B. Lee Garmes
99. D. *The Story of Esther Costello*
100. D. *You Only Live Twice* (1967)
101. A. Edward Stevenson
102. C. *Tomorrow Is Forever* (1946)
103. B. 1908
104. B. *In the Heat of the Night* (1967)
105. C. 2
106. D. *The Thief of Bagdad* (1940)
107. A. *Love in the Afternoon* (1957)
108. B. *The Fourth Protocol* (1987)
109. A. *Brigadoon* (1954)
110. B. Jean Louis
111. B. *Despair* (1978)
112. A. *Algiers* (1938)
113. C. *Picnic* (1955)
114. C. 5
115. D. He was the first film director ever to be knighted by the Queen.
116. D. Lucien Ballard
117. C. RKO
118. D. *There Was a Crooked Man . . .* (1970)
119. C. Jonathan Newman
120. B. George E. Stoll
121. D. Travis Banton
122. A. *Moby Dick* (1956)
123. D. 8
124. A. Boris Leven
125. D. *The Deadly Affair* (1966)
126. B. Ernest Laszlo
127. C. *The Omen* (1976)
128. C. *Fatso* (1980)
129. B. *Our Man in Havana* (1959)
130. B. *Pocketful of Miracles* (1961)
131. B. *Born Yesterday* (1950)
132. D. *Two for the Seesaw* (1962)
133. C. Best Editing
134. C. Best Interior Decoration, Black-and-White

135. D. Victor Young
136. D. *Shampoo* (1975)
137. A. Best Cinematography
138. C. Natacha Rambova
139. A. Aaron Copland for *The Heiress*
140. C. *The Little Foxes* (1941)
141. D. *No Name on the Bullet* (1959)
142. B. Los Angeles
143. A. *Romola* (1924)
144. B. *The Millionairess* (1960)
145. B. *Legend* (1985)
146. C. *The Member of the Wedding* (1952)
147. C. *The Judge* (1948)
148. B. *Kiss Me Kate* (1953)
149. C. Deborah Kerr
150. C. *The Odd Couple* (1968)
151. D. 5
152. B. John Mills
153. B. *It's a Wonderful Life* (1946)
154. B. *Robin and Marian* (1976)
155. B. *The Damned* (1969)
156. A. Alfred Newman
157. B. *Soldiers Three* (1951)
158. D. Niven Busch
159. D. *Hats Off* (1936)
160. B. Sidney Sheldon
161. B. *The Goodbye Girl* (1978)
162. D. *The Last Tycoon* (1976)
163. D. Raymond Queneau
164. A. *BUtterfield 8* (1960)
165. A. Laurence Olivier
166. A. *Air Force One* (1997)
167. B. *Macabre* (1977)
168. D. Joseph L. Mankiewicz and William Cameron Menzies
169. B. *Tender Is the Night* (1962)
170. B. *The Gambler* (1997)
171. D. *You Only Live Twice* (1967)
172. B. F. Scott Fitzgerald
173. C. *Queen Bee*
174. A. Billy Bob Thornton
175. B. Lillian Gish
176. D. John Williams
177. C. 1943
178. D. Best Original Screenplay
179. A. *The Postman Always Rings Twice* (1981)
180. C. *The Prince and the Pauper* (1937)

181. C. Ernest Hemingway
182. A. 100
183. C. *Show Boat* (1951)
184. B. Best Cinematography
185. C. Marvin Hatley
186. C. James Wong Howe
187. C. *The Human Stain* (2003)
188. A. *Executive Action* (1973)
189. B. *In the Street* (1948)
190. D. 1992
191. B. *Mr. Blandings Builds His Dream House* (1948)
192. D. *The Red Shoes* (1948)
193. D. Loretta Young
194. D. Judy Garland's ruby slippers from *The Wizard of Oz* (1939)
195. D. Joseph Ruttenberg
196. A. *Body and Soul* (1947)
197. B. Best Cinematography
198. A. *In the Heat of the Night* (1967)
199. B. *The Fixer* (1968)
200. B. 17
201. B. *One, Two, Three* (1961)
202. A. Los Angeles
203. C. James Wong Howe
204. A. Kate Douglas Wiggin
205. A. Best Actress
206. D. Best Scoring of a Musical Picture
207. D. William Cameron Menzies
208. A. *A Thousand Clowns* (1965)
209. B. *Houdini* (1953)
210. B. Jean Louis
211. A. *Escape* (1948)
212. C. 5
213. A. Connecticut
214. D. *The Right to Live* (1935)
215. B. 1961
216. B. *Ivanhoe* (1952)
217. C. *Splendor in the Grass* (1961)
218. C. *Medium Cool* (1969)
219. C. *The House of the Seven Hawks* (1959)
220. D. *The Miracle of Morgan's Creek*
221. D. 6
222. A. "Fools Rush In"
223. A. *A Foreign Affair* (1948)
224. C. *Runaway Romany* (1917)
225. B. *The Bridge on the River Kwai* (1957)

226. C. *One of Our Aircraft Is Missing* (1942)
227. B. Henry James
228. A. *Dodsworth* (1936)
229. C. *The African Queen* (1951)
230. A. *Funny Lady* (1975)
231. B. Ellen Burstyn
232. D. Sammy Cahn
233. B. Ernest Laszlo
234. B. Russell Metty
235. B. *Affair in Trinidad*
236. D. 2003
237. D. Maurice Jarre
238. C. James Wong Howe for *Hud*
239. D. *The Light That Failed* (1939)
240. D. Santo Loquasto
241. B. Best Color Cinematography

CHAPTER 18

1. C. Teacher
2. D. 7 minutes
3. A. *Life*
4. C. Santana
5. C. Junior Johnson
6. A. Ermes Borgnino
7. A. Erich Pommer
8. D. Gap
9. B. Mary Louise Streep
10. B. Daphne
11. D. 6'5"
12. A. Grace Kelly
13. A. 1941
14. A. Car accident
15. C. *Marty* (1955)
16. D. Glenford
17. B. Editor
18. D. Shocking
19. A. *Esquire*
20. D. 9
21. C. "Sexy Rexy"
22. C. Edward
23. B. Gin rummy
24. A. Baltimore Colts
25. D. "Road Hog"
26. A. "Doc"
27. D. *Posse* (1993)
28. B. *Plenty* (1985)
29. D. Miles and Flora

30. D. *The Story of Mankind* (1957)
31. B. Hat making
32. D. "The Shvontz"
33. B. 1950
34. B. 2
35. A. *An Affair to Remember* (1957)
36. C. Orson Welles
37. C. The Grand National
38. A. *Indiscretion of an American Wife* (1953)
39. D. Wilkins
40. D. *Wake of the Red Witch* (1948)
41. C. Spokane, Washington
42. B. Lex Barker
43. D. Maximillian
44. A. "Jake"
45. A. Dickie Moore
46. A. Libby Holman
47. D. Saks Fifth Avenue
48. B. Doris Day
49. B. *Hi, Nellie!* (1934)
50. C. Frank Sinatra
51. D. With his feet
52. C. Lawyer
53. C. "The Right Profile"
54. B. France
55. B. *Motion Picture*
56. A. "Babe"
57. B. He occasionally appeared in Mack Sennett film comedies when he was a child.
58. A. "Man in the Cellar"
59. C. A wedding dress
60. B. Leipzig Conservatory
61. D. "Obie"
62. B. *Seventy Light Years*
63. B. John F. Kennedy
64. C. UCLA
65. A. Cary Grant
66. A. *Adam's Rib* (1949)
67. A. *Chinese Gung-Fu: The Philosophical Art of Self-Defense*
68. C. $25
69. A. *Harvard Advocate*
70. B. *It's a Big Country* (1951)
71. A. $100,000
72. D. *Tammy Tell Me True* (1961)
73. A. Accounting
74. C. *Ordinary People* (1980)

75. C. Motion Picture Country Home and Hospital
76. B. Playing tennis in a tennis skirt
77. B. *House on Haunted Hill* (1959)
78. B. He was killed when a plane he was flying in was shot down during World War II.
79. D. Sophia
80. C. Philip of Macedonia
81. C. Jimmy Carter
82. C. 2
83. D. The Revuers
84. D. Railroad
85. B. 2
86. D. Rita Hayworth
87. B. Clark Gable
88. A. *Our Town*
89. B. Greer Garson
90. B. *Methods to Acting*
91. B. 1955
92. A. 11
93. C. "Puffin"
94. C. Larkspur
95. B. *Down to Earth* (1947)
96. B. Kent
97. C. Scotland
98. C. Morning glory
99. C. Selling Hershey's Kisses
100. D. Professional boxer
101. C. Joan Crawford
102. B. Lifeguard
103. D. Louis
104. C. University of Chicago
105. B. Elvis Presley
106. C. Elizabeth Barrett
107. B. Samuel
108. C. *The Private Life of Sherlock Holmes* (1970)
109. D. Martin Van Buren
110. D. Nora Bayes
111. C. Perfume
112. C. Optometrist
113. B. *My Favorite Spy* (1951)
114. D. *White Album*
115. D. *The Cocoanuts* (1929)
116. C. *The Natural* (1984)
117. B. *Let's Dance*
118. C. 6
119. B. Queen

120. B. Neauphle-le-Château
121. D. USC
122. C. *West Side Story* (1961)
123. C. Vanderbilt
124. B. Mime
125. D. Roald Dahl
126. A. Gloria Grahame
127. D. *Sam Whiskey* (1959)
128. D. *Yesterday, Today and Tomorrow* (1963)
129. D. Williams
130. D. *With Ossie and Ruby: In This Life Together*
131. C. *The Wild Geese* (1978)
132. B. Receptionist
133. D. Jonathan Swift
134. A. Baby food
135. C. Katharine Hepburn
136. B. Delivery man
137. D. *Sgt. Pepper's Lonely Hearts Club Band*
138. B. *Green Mansions* (1959)
139. B. Harry Truman
140. B. *The Fall of the Roman Empire* (1964)
141. A. Hoagy Carmichael
142. B. "In the Mood"
143. B. *The Cassandra Crossing* (1976)
144. B. Dracula
145. A. 1949
146. B. It was a photograph.
147. C. Pippo Popolino
148. B. $10,000
149. B. Bouncer
150. B. "Dancing on the Ceiling"
151. C. Vernet
152. B. "Celluloid Heroes"
153. A. Ballerina
154. C. Richard Burton
155. D. Psychosurgery
156. C. Light Egyptian
157. B. Influenza
158. A. *All the Cats Join In*
159. C. 1970
160. D. *The Gay Falcon* (1941)
161. D. *The Trip to Bountiful* (1985)
162. D. *Two for the Road* (1967)
163. C. Cleveland Rams
164. D. Dodd

165. C. *Girls! Girls! Girls!* (1962)
166. B. Eliot
167. A. Byron
168. C. Red Emeralds
169. B. His footprints
170. B. Maurice
171. A. Bank teller
172. C. Martin Goldsmith
173. D. Robert Taylor
174. A. Dalton Trumbo
175. B. James
176. B. 1980
177. D. The use of sealed envelopes to keep the identities of the winners secret
178. C. $250,000 a year
179. B. *FTA* (1972)
180. B. Coca-Cola
181. D. *The Odd Couple* (1968)
182. B. *The Green Sash*
183. A. 13
184. A. Miss Ellie
185. A. The Archers
186. C. 1959
187. D. Yale
188. D. She wrote two children's books.
189. D. *The Bird of Paradise*
190. C. *Lassie Come Home* (1943)
191. D. *William, the Backwards Skunk*
192. D. Sons
193. C. A soccer team
194. D. He was the original center square when the game show *Hollywood Squares* first premiered in 1966.
195. D. Smashing Pumpkins
196. C. Sulfa drugs
197. A. *Barton Fink* (1991)
198. C. Photography
199. B. Nita Talbot
200. C. Major Boothroyd
201. B. Helen Parrish
202. D. The Vanderbilts
203. C. John Wayne
204. B. Howard Hughes
205. A. Anna Maria Louisa Italiano
206. D. Steve in *To Have and Have Not* (1944)
207. C. *Loving* (1970)
208. A. *Hide and Shriek* (1938)

209. C. Rudolph Valentino and Pola Negri
210. D. The Wolves
211. A. Grace Kelly
212. B. Jennifer Love Hewitt
213. C. NYU
214. C. *The Years Between* (1946)
215. D. *Quo Vadis*
216. B. Chicago Cubs
217. B. 1954
218. D. On the Western Front of World War I
219. A. *It Happened in Brooklyn* (1947)
220. B. *Portrait of Jennie* (1948)
221. B. 63 years
222. B. *Scudda Hoo! Scudda Hay!* (1948)
223. B. Mayfield Productions
224. D. Columbia, South Carolina
225. A. Form Fit Rogers
226. D. *Where Love Has Gone*
227. D. *Topper Takes a Trip* (1938)
228. A. Ava Gardner
229. B. *Three Dumb Clucks* (1937)
230. A. *Bright Eyes* (1934)
231. A. Baby blue
232. D. Yale
233. C. Paris
234. B. *Breakfast at Tiffany's* (1961)
235. D. Swimming
236. C. Her brother's
237. C. Playing the piano
238. D. *Tobruk* (1967)
239. A. Burt Reynolds
240. B. Henry
241. C. Memphis, Tennessee
242. C. Chicago, Illinois
243. C. "Low Key Hoe"
244. D. *The Mirror Crack'd from Side to Side*
245. B. Clergy
246. A. Helena Bonham Carter
247. A. Calgary Stampeders
248. C. The sex of the character was changed for Shirley Temple.
249. B. Katharine Hepburn
250. A. Adolf Hitler

ACKNOWLEDGMENTS

As with all great film productions, this book reflects the collaborative efforts of many: from the web editorial staff, Christina Chyn, Justine Lee, and Jeff Stafford; from Turner Image Management, Christopher Grakal, Cynthia Martinez, Christian Pierce, Sara VanderRoest, Jason Williams, and Brandy Ivins Wright.

TCM contributors to project development and management and to editorial and research include Dennis Adamovich, Shannon Clute, Alexa Foreman, Lindsey Griffin, Genevieve McGillicuddy, Heather Margolis, Robert Osborne, John Renaud, John Robert Smith, and Kristen Welch.

Thanks to Frank Miller, Andrea Passafiume, Anna Millman, and Michon Wise for their commitment and contributions to TCM.

ABOUT THE AUTHORS

ROBERT OSBORNE is the prime time host and anchor of Turner Classic Movies and a columnist-critic for *The Hollywood Reporter*. He is known as the official biographer of Oscar, and his latest book, *80 Years of the Oscar*, was written at the special request of the Academy of Motion Picture Arts and Sciences.

TURNER CLASSIC MOVIES is widely considered by film and television critics to be the definitive resource for classic films. Featuring movies from all the major studios, unedited and commercial free, TCM is available on most cable and satellite systems. Please visit www.tcm.com.

TEXT

Editorial

Frank Miller is head of the theater program at Georgia State University, where he also lectures. He is the author of *Casablanca: As Time Goes By* and *Censored Hollywood: Sin, Sex & Violence on the Screen*. He also wrote the TCM titles *Leading Ladies: The 50 Most Unforgettable Actresses of the Studio Era*, *Leading Men: The 50 Most Unforgettable Actors of the Studio Era*, and *Leading Couples: The Most Unforgettable Screen Romances of the Studio Era*.

Questions

Numerous TCM staff members and free-lancers contributed to the creation of trivia questions for this book, most notably Christina Chyn, Anna Davis, Lacey Rice, and Andrea Passafiume.

EDITOR

Shannon Clute is a brand manager for Turner Classic Movies. He holds a Ph.D. in Romance Studies from Cornell University. He is the co-creator of the popular *Out of the Past: Investigating Film Noir* podcast series and co-author, with Richard L. Edwards, of *The Maltese Touch of Evil: Film Noir and Potential Criticism*.

Editorial support
Several TCM employees were involved in the substantial editorial support required to bring this project to press, most notably Lindsey Griffin, John Robert Smith, and Kristen Welch.

RESEARCHER

Alexa L. Foreman is the senior researcher/producer at Turner Classic Movies. She is the author of *Women in Motion*, coauthor of *In the Picture: Production Stills from the TCM Archives* and a contributor to *The St. James Women Filmmaker's Encyclopedia* and *International Dictionary of Films and Filmmakers*.

ALSO AVAILABLE FROM
CHRONICLE BOOKS AND TURNER CLASSIC MOVIES

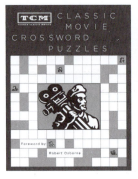

TCM Classic Movie Crossword Puzzles

Leading Couples: The Most Unforgettable Screen Romances of the Studio Era

Leading Ladies: The 50 Most Unforgettable Actresses of the Studio Era

Leading Men: The 50 Most Unforgettable Actors of the Studio Era